Thank you for considering *The American People, Creating a Nation and a Society, Brief Third Edition* for use in your American History course. As you consider this text for adoption, Longman Publishers is pleased to offer you six months of access to *The History Place*, a unique Web resource for history educators and students.

To explore this valuable teaching and learning resource:

1. Go to **www.awlonline.com/nash**
2. Click "*The History Place* Login" to enter *The History Place*.
3. Choose the Register Here Button
3. Enter your pre-assigned activation ID and password exactly as they appear below:

Activation ID **HPPPEA06001154**

Password **mimeograph**

4. Complete the online form to establish your personal user ID and password.
5. Once your personal user ID and password are confirmed, go back to **www.ushistoryplace.com** to enter the site with your new user ID and password.

Your pre-assigned activation ID and password can be used only once to establish your subscription, which is not transferable.

If you choose to adopt this text, you will receive complimentary access to *The History Place* for the duration of the adoption. Additionally, all new student copies of the book will include a 6-month subscription to *The History Place*. If you would like to make subscriptions available to students who do not buy a new copy of this book, you can direct students to purchase subscriptions directly online at **www.ushistoryplace.com**

THE AMERICAN PEOPLE

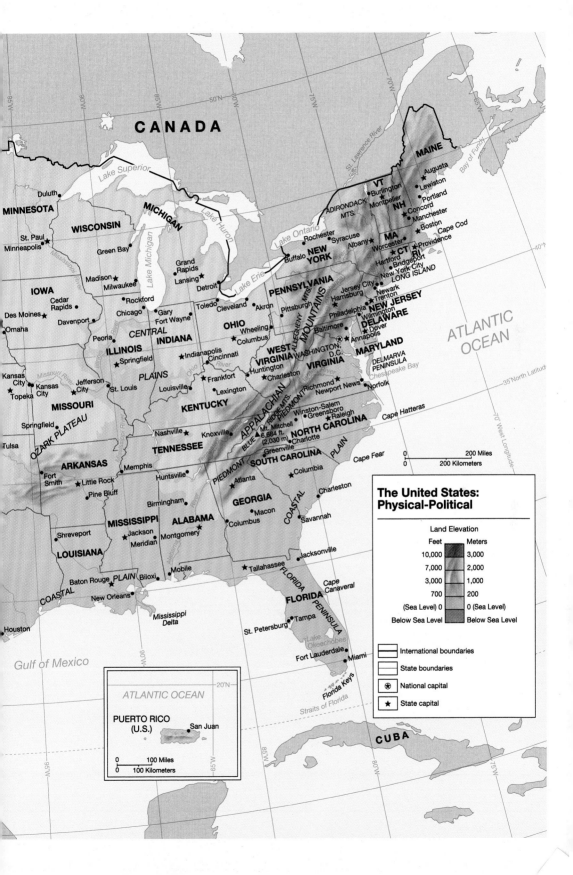

THE AMERICAN PEOPLE

Creating a Nation and a Society

Brief Third Edition

Volume I: To 1877

Gary B. Nash
University of California, Los Angeles
General Editor

Julie Roy Jeffrey
Goucher College
General Editor

John R. Howe
University of Minnesota

Peter J. Frederick
Wabash College

Allen F. Davis
Temple University

Allan M. Winkler
Miami University

An imprint of Addison Wesley Longman, Inc.

New York • Menlo Park, California • Reading, Massachusetts • Harlow, England
Don Mills, Ontario • Sydney • Mexico City • Madrid • Amsterdam

Editor-in-Chief: Priscilla McGeehon
Acquisitions Editor: Jay O'Callaghan
Development Manager: Betty Slack
Development Editor: Karen Helfrich
Executive Marketing Manager: Sue Westmoreland
Supplements Editor: Joy Hilgendorf
Full Service Production Manager: Valerie Zaborski
Project Coordination, Text Design, and Electronic Page Makeup: Elm Street Publishing
    Services, Inc.
Cover Design Manager: Nancy Danahy
Cover Designer: Kay Petronio
Cover Illustration: Newell, James Michael. "The Underground Railroad" (Mural study,
    Dolgeville, NY, Post Office, WPA project). 1940. Oil on paperboard, 17" x 27–5/8".
    National Museum of American Art, Washington, DC, U.S.A.
Photo Researcher: Photosearch, Inc.
Senior Print Buyer: Hugh Crawford
Printer and Binder: R. R. Donnelley & Sons Company
Cover Printer: The Lehigh Press, Inc.

For permission to use copyrighted material, grateful acknowledgment is made to the
copyright holders on p. 442, which is hereby made part of this copyright page.

Please visit our website at http://awlonline.com/nash

ISBN 0-321-00564-3 (Single Volume Edition)
ISBN 0-321-00566-X (Volume I)
ISBN 0-321-00568-6 (Volume II)

12345678910—DOC—02010099

BRIEF CONTENTS

DETAILED CONTENTS

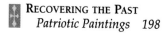

RECOVERING THE PAST

MAPS

PREFACE

The Yoruba people of West Africa have an old saying: "However far the stream flows, it never forgets its source." Why, we wonder, do such ancient societies as the Yoruba find history so important, while modern American students question its relevance? This book aims to end such skepticism about the usefulness of history.

As we begin the twenty-first century, in an ethnically and racially diverse society caught up in an interdependent global society, history is of central importance in preparing us to exercise our rights and responsibilities as free people. History cannot make good citizens, but without history we cannot understand the choices before us and think wisely about them. Lacking a collective memory of the past, we lapse into a kind of amnesia, unaware of the human condition and the long struggles of men and women everywhere to deal with the problems of their day and to create a better society. Unfurnished with historical knowledge, we deprive ourselves of knowing about the huge range of approaches people have taken to political, economic, and social life; to solving problems; and to conquering the obstacles in their way.

History has a deeper, even more fundamental importance: the cultivation of the private person whose self-knowledge and self-respect provide the foundation for a life of dignity and fulfillment. Historical memory is the key to self-identity; to seeing one's place in the long stream of time, in the story of humankind.

When we study our own history, we see a rich and extraordinarily complex human story. This country, whose written history began with a convergence of Native Americans, Europeans, and Africans, has always been a nation of diverse peoples—a magnificent mosaic of cultures, religions, and skin shades. This book explores how American society assumed its present shape and developed its present forms of government; how as a nation we have conducted our foreign affairs and managed our economy; how as individuals and in groups we have lived, worked, loved, married, raised families, voted, argued, protested, and struggled to fulfill our dreams and the noble ideals of the American experiment.

Several ways of making the past understandable distinguish this book from most textbooks written in the last 20 years. The coverage of public events like presidential elections, diplomatic treaties, and economic legislation is integrated with the private human stories that pervade them. Within a chronological framework, we have woven together our history as a nation, as a people, and as a society. When, for example, national political events are discussed, we analyze their impact on social and economic life at the state and local levels. Wars are described not only as they unfolded on the battlefield and in the salons of diplomats but also on the home front, where they are history's greatest motor of social change. The interaction of ordinary Americans with extraordinary events runs as a theme throughout this book.

Above all, we have tried to show the "humanness" of our history as it is revealed in people's everyday lives. The authors have often used the words of ordinary Americans to capture the authentic human voices of those who participated in and responded to epic events such as war, slavery, industrialization, and reform movements.

GOALS AND THEMES OF THE BOOK

Our primary goal is to provide students with a rich, balanced, and thought-provoking treatment of the American past. By this we mean a history that treats the lives and experiences of Americans of all national origins and cultural backgrounds, at all levels of society, and in all regions of the country. It also means a history that seeks connections between the many factors—political, economic, technological, social, religious, intellectual, and biological—that have molded and remolded American society over four centuries. And, finally, it means a history that encourages students to think about how we have all inherited a complex past filled with both notable achievements and thorny problems. The only history befitting a democratic nation is one that inspires students to initiate a frank and searching dialogue with their past.

To speak of a dialogue about the past presumes that history is interpretive. Students should understand that historians are continually reinterpreting the past. New interpretations may result from the discovery of new evidence, but more often they emerge because historians reevaluate old evidence in the light of new ideas that spring from the times in which they write and from their personal views of the world.

Through this book, we also hope to promote class discussions, which can be organized around six questions that we see as basic to the American historical experience:

1. How has this nation been peopled, from the first inhabitants to the many groups that arrived in slavery or servitude during the colonial period to the voluntary immigrants of today? How have these waves of newcomers contributed to the American cultural mosaic? To what extent have different immigrant groups preserved elements of their ethnic, racial, and religious heritages?

2. To what extent have Americans developed a stable, democratic political system flexible enough to address the wholesale changes occurring in the last two centuries and to what degree has this political system been consistent with the principles of our nation's founding?

3. How have economic and technological changes affected daily life, work, family organization, leisure, sexual behavior, the division of wealth, and community relations in the United States?

4. Has American religion served more to promote or retard social reform in our history? Whatever their varied sources, how have the recurring reform movements in our history dealt with economic, political, and social problems in attempting to square the ideals of American life with the reality?

5. What has been the role of our nation in the world? To what extent has the United States served as a model for other peoples, as an interventionist savior of other nations around the globe, and as an interfering expansionist in the affairs of other nations?

6. How have American beliefs and values changed over time, and how have they varied between different groups—women and men; Americans of many colors and cultures; people of different regions, religions, sexual orientations, ages, and classes?

In writing a history that revolves around these themes, we have tried to convey two dynamics that operate in all societies. First, we observe people continuously adjusting to new developments, such as industrialization and urbanization, over which they seemingly have little control; yet we realize that people are not paralyzed by history but are the fundamental creators of it. They retain the ability, individually and collectively, to shape the world in which they live and thus in considerable degree to control their own lives. Second, we emphasize the connections that always exist among social, political, economic, and cultural events.

STRUCTURE OF THE BOOK

The chapters of this book are grouped into six parts that relate to major periods in American history. The titles for each part suggest the large themes uniting the chapters.

Individual chapters have a clear structure, beginning with a personal story recalling the experience of an ordinary or lesser-known American. Chapter 1, for example, is introduced with the tragic account of Opechancanough, a Powhatan tribesman whose entire life of nearly 90 years was consumed by a struggle against the land, hunger, and alien values brought by Spanish and English newcomers. This brief anecdote serves several purposes. First, it introduces the overarching themes and major concepts of the chapter, in this case the meeting of three societies—Native American, European, and African—each with different cultural values, lifestyles, and aspirations. Second, the personal story suggests that ordinary as well as extraordinary people shaped our history. At the end of the personal story, a *brief overview* links the biographical sketch to the text by elaborating the major themes of the chapter.

We aim to facilitate the learning process for students in other ways as well. Every chapter ends with pedagogical features to reinforce and expand the presentation. A *conclusion* briefly summarizes the chapter's main concepts and developments and serves as a bridge to the following chapter. A list of *recommended readings* provides supplementary sources for further study; novels contemporary to the period are often included. Finally, a *time line* reviews the major events covered in the chapter. Each map, figure, and table has been chosen to relate clearly to the narrative. *Captions* are specially written to help students understand and interpret these visual materials.

THE BRIEF THIRD EDITION

This Brief Third Edition is condensed from the very successful full Fourth Edition of *The American People,* with its balance of political, social, and economic history. While we have eliminated detail and extra examples, and compressed the text, we have retained the interpretive connections and the "humanness" of history, the focus on history as it is revealed through the lives of ordinary Americans, and the interplay of social and political factors.

New Format and Features

The Brief Third Edition offers a new format and a more compact size than the previous brief edition. The new four-color design enhances the value of the maps and graphs and gives the book a vibrant appearance. We believe these changes make the book extremely accessible, easy to read, and convenient for students to carry to and from class.

An important new addition is the inclusion of one of the most popular features of *The American People*, the two-page sections entitled *Recovering the Past*. Twelve RTPs, as the authors affectionately call them, introduce students to the fascinating variety of evidence—ranging from novels, political cartoons, and diaries to houses, clothing, and popular music—that historians have learned to employ in reconstructing the past. Each RTP gives basic information about the source and its use by historians and then raises questions for students to consider as they study the example reproduced for their inspection. The RTPs included in this edition are Archaeological Artifacts (Chapter 1), Houses (Chapter 2), Military Muster Rolls (Chapter 6), Patriotic Paintings (Chapter 8), Personal Diaries (Chapter 13), Photography (Chapter 15), and Novels (Chapter 16).

Major Changes

Throughout the Brief Third Edition there are new materials on the role of religion, the environment, and the West. The structure and organization of the text—parts, chapters, sections, and subsections—reflect the full Fourth Edition where the authors significantly reorganized chapters focusing on the period following World War II and the contemporary period (Chapters 26–30). Chapter-by-chapter changes include the following:

- **Chapter 1:** new material on the environment
- **Chapter 2:** new section on New Spain's Northern Frontier
- **Chapter 4:** added material on French settlement and the French inland empire
- **Chapter 6:** added material on Indian allies of the Americans in the Revolutionary War
- **Chapter 9:** reorganized with new subsections on The Urban Northeast, The Evangelical Impulse, and A New Style of Politics
- **Chapter 11:** expanded discussion of African-American churches
- **Chapter 12:** reorganized with new subsections on Jackson's Indian Policy and The Dilemmas of Reform
- **Chapter 13:** new material on religious idealism as a motive for westward expansion
- **Chapter 14:** added material on growth of the Catholic Church in the United States

In this Brief Third Edition we have tried to present American history in its rich complexity but in a form that students will find comprehensible and interesting. Additionally, we have tried to provide the support materials necessary to make teaching and learning enjoyable and rewarding. The reader will be the judge of our success. The authors and Addison Wesley Longman welcome your comments.

ACKNOWLEDGMENTS

The authors wish to thank the following reviewers who gave generously of their time and expertise and whose thoughtful and constructive work have contributed greatly to this edition:

Linda J. Borish, Western Michigan University
Thomas A. Britten, Briar Cliff College
Steven J. Bucklin, University of South Dakota
Stacy A. Cordery, Monmouth College
Stephen A. Harmon, Pittsburg State University
Jeff Livingston, California State University, Chico
Elizabeth Neumeyer, Kellogg Community College
A.J. Scopino, Jr., Central Connecticut State University
Michael Welsh, University of Northern Colorado

Over the years, as previous editions of this text were being developed, many of our colleagues read and criticized the various drafts of the manuscript. For their thoughtful evaluations and constructive suggestions, the authors wish to express their gratitude to the following reviewers:

Richard H. Abbott, Eastern Michigan University; John Alexander, University of Cincinnati; Kenneth G. Alfers, Mountain View College; Terry Alford, Northern Virginia Community College; Gregg Andrews, Southwest Texas State University; Robert Asher, University of Connecticut at Storrs; Harry Baker, University of Arkansas at Little Rock; Michael Batinski, Southern Illinois University; Gary Bell, Sam Houston State University; Virginia Bellows, Tulsa Junior College; Spencer Bennett, Siena Heights College; Jackie R. Booker, Western Connecticut State University; James Bradford, Texas A&M University; Neal Brooks, Essex Community College; Jeffrey P. Brown, New Mexico State University; Dickson D. Bruce, Jr., University of California at Irvine; David Brundage, University of California at Santa Cruz; Colin Calloway, Dartmouth University; D'Ann Campbell, Indiana University; Jane Censer, George Mason University; Vincent A. Clark, Johnson County Community College; Neil Clough, North Seattle Community College; Matthew Ware Coulter, Collin County Community College; David Culbert, Louisiana State University; Mark T. Dalhouse, Northeast Missouri State University; Bruce Dierenfield, Canisius College; John Dittmer, DePauw University; Gordon Dodds, Portland State University; Richard Donley, Eastern Washington University; Dennis B. Downey, Millersville University; Robert Downtain, Tarrant County Community College; Robert Farrar, Spokane Falls Community College; Bernard Friedman, Indiana University–Purdue University at Indianapolis; Bruce Glasrud, California State University at Hayward; Brian Gordon, St. Louis Community College; Richard Griswold del Castillo, San Diego State University; Carol Gruber, William Paterson College; Colonel William L. Harris, The Citadel Military College; Robert Haws, University of Mississippi; Jerrold Hirsch, Northeast Missouri State University; Frederick Hoxie, University of Illinois; John S. Hughes, University of Texas; Link Hullar, Kingwood College; Donald M. Jacobs,

Northeastern University; Delores Janiewski, University of Idaho; David Johnson, Portland State University; Richard Kern, University of Findlay; Robert J. Kolesar, John Carroll University; Monte Lewis, Cisco Junior College; William Link, University of North Carolina at Greensboro; Patricia M. Lisella, Iona College; Ronald Lora, University of Toledo; Paul K. Longmore, San Francisco State University; Rita Loos, Framingham State College; George M. Lubick, Northern Arizona University; Suzanne Marshall, Jacksonville State University; John C. Massman, St. Cloud State University; Vernon Mattson, University of Nevada at Las Vegas; Arthur McCoole, Cuyamaca College; John McCormick, Delaware County Community College; Sylvia McGrath, Stephen F. Austin University; James E. McMillan, Denison University; Otis L. Miller, Belleville Area College; Walter Miszczenko, Boise State University; Norma Mitchell, Troy State University; Gerald F. Moran, University of Michigan at Dearborn; William G. Morris, Midland College; Marian Morton, John Carroll University; Roger Nichols, University of Arizona; Paul Palmer, Texas A&I University; Albert Parker, Riverside City College; Judith Parsons, Sul Ross State University; Carla Pestana, Ohio State University; Neva Peters, Tarrant County Community College; James Prickett, Santa Monica Community College; Noel Pugash, University of New Mexico; Juan Gomez-Quiñones, University of California at Los Angeles; George Rable, Anderson College; Joseph P. Reidy, Howard University; Leonard Riforgiato, Pennsylvania State University; Randy Roberts, Purdue University; Mary Robertson, Armstrong State University; David Robson, John Carroll University; Judd Sage, Northern Virginia Community College; Sylvia Sebesta, San Antonio College; Phil Schaeffer, Olympic College; Herbert Shapiro, University of Cincinnati; David R. Shibley, Santa Monica Community College; Ellen Shockro, Pasadena City College; Nancy Shoemaker, University of Connecticut; Bradley Skelcher, Delaware State University; Kathryn Kish Sklar, State University of New York at Binghamton; James Smith, Virginia State University; John Snetsinger, California Polytechnic State University at San Luis Obispo; Jo Snider, Southwest Texas State University; Stephen Strausberg, University of Arkansas; Katherine Scott Sturdevant, Pikes Peak Community College; Nan M. Sumner-Mack, Hawaii Community College; Cynthia Taylor, Santa Rosa Junior College; Thomas Tefft, Citrus College; John A. Trickel, Richland College; Donna Van Raaphorst, Cuyahoga Community College; Morris Vogel, Temple University; Michael Wade, Appalachian State University; Jackie Walker, James Madison University; Paul B. Weinstein, University of Akron-Wayne College; Joan Welker, Prince George's Community College; Kenneth H. Williams, Alcorn State University; Mitch Yamasaki, Chaminade University; and Charles Zappia, San Diego Mesa College.

GARY B. NASH

JULIE ROY JEFFREY

SUPPLEMENTS

For Qualified College Adopters

Teaching the American People. Julie Roy Jeffrey and Peter J. Frederick with Frances Jones-Sneed of Massachusetts College of Liberal Arts. This guide was written based on ideas generated in "active learning" workshops and is tied closely to the text. In addition to suggestions on how to generate lively class discussion and involve students in active learning, this supplement also offers a file of exam questions and lists of resources, including films, slides, photo collections, records, and audiocassettes.

Test Bank. This test bank, prepared by Diane Beers of Dickinson College, contains more than 3500 objective, conceptual, and essay questions. All questions are keyed to specific pages in the text.

Test Gen 3.0 Computerized Testing System. This flexible, easy-to-master computer test bank includes all the test items in the printed test bank. The software allows you to edit existing questions and add your own items. Tests can be printed in several different formats and can include figures such as graphs and tables. It comes with *QuizMaster,* a program that enables you to design Test Gen generated tests your students can take on a computer rather than in printed form. Available on CD-Rom for Windows and Macintosh, and on floppies.

The History Place Website (www.ushistoryplace.com). Available free to adopters of the text, this new website combines quality educational publishing with the immediacy and interactivity of the Internet. At *The History Place,* you'll find a continually updated source of maps, time lines, and other interactive learning activities, as well as a rich collection of primary documents, news, and online quizzes. A free subscription to *The History Place* is included with every new copy of the student text.

The American People, *Brief Third Edition Website* (www.awlonline.com/nash). This website, designed specifically for this book by Patrick McCarthy of the University of Georgia, is an invaluable tool for both students and instructors. It contains student resources such as self-testing, chapter outlines, web activities, and links to outside sources; instructor resources such as the instructor's manual and testing ideas; and our unique syllabus manager that gives instructors and students access to the up-to-date syllabus at any time from any computer.

American Impressions: A CD-ROM for U.S. History. This unique CD-ROM for the U.S. history course is organized in a topical and thematic framework which allows in-depth coverage with a media-centered focus. Hundreds of photos, maps, works of art, graphics, and historical film clips are organized into narrated vignettes and interactive activities to create a tool for both professors and students. Topics include "The Encounter Period," "Revolution to Republic," "A Century of Labor and Reform," and "The Struggle for Equality." A guide for instructors provides teaching tips and suggestions for using advanced media in the classroom. The CD-ROM is available in both Macintosh and Windows formats.

Visual Archives of American History, *Second Edition*. This two-sided video laserdisc explores history from the meeting of three cultures to the present. It is an encyclopedic chronology of U.S. history offering hundreds of photographs and illustrations, a variety of source and reference maps—several of which are animated—plus 50 minutes of video. For ease in planning lectures, a manual listing barcodes for scanning and frame numbers for all the material is available.

Video Lecture Launchers. Prepared by Mark Newman, University of Illinois at Chicago, these video lecture launchers (each two to five minutes in duration) cover key issues in American history from 1877 to the present. The launchers are accompanied by an instructor's manual.

"This Is America" Immigration Video. Produced by the American Museum of Immigration, this video tells the story of American immigrants, relating their personal stories and accomplishments. By showing how the richness of our culture is due to the contributions of millions of immigrant Americans, the videos make the point that America's strength lies in the ethnically and culturally diverse backgrounds of its citizens.

Discovering American History Through Maps and Views. Created by Gerald Danzer of the University of Illinois at Chicago, the recipient of the AHA's 1990 James Harvey Robinson Prize for his work in the development of map transparencies, this set of 140 four-color acetates is a unique instructional tool. It contains an introduction on teaching history through maps and a detailed commentary on each transparency. The collection includes cartographic and pictorial maps, views and photos, urban plans, building diagrams, and works of art.

Comprehensive American History Transparency Set. This vast collection of American history map transparencies includes more than 200 map transparencies ranging from the first Native Americans to the end of the Cold War, covering wars, social trends, elections, immigration, and demographics. Also included are a reproducible set of student map exercises, teaching tips, and correlation charts.

Text-Specific Map Transparencies. A set of 30 transparencies drawn from *The American People*, Fourth Edition, is available.

Longman American History Atlas Overhead Transparencies. These 69 acetates from our four-color historical atlas were especially designed for this volume.

A Guide to Teaching American History Through Film. Written by Randy Roberts of Purdue University, this guide provides instructors with a creative and practical tool for stimulating classroom discussion. The sections include "American Films: A Historian's Perspective," a list of films, practical suggestions, and bibliography. The film listing is presented in narrative form, developing connections between each film and the topics being discussed.

For Students

The History Place Website (www.ushistoryplace.com). Available free to adopters of the text, this new website combines quality educational publishing with the immediacy and interactivity of the Internet. At *The History Place,* you'll find a continually updated source of maps, time lines, and other interactive learning activities, as well as a rich collection of primary documents, news, and online quizzes. A free subscription to *The History Place* is included with every new copy of the student text.

The American People, *Brief Third Edition Website* (www.awlonline.com/nash). This website, designed specifically for this book by Patrick McCarthy of the University of Georgia, is an invaluable tool for both students and instructors. It contains student resources such as self-testing, chapter outlines, web activities, and links to outside sources; instructor resources such as the instructor's manual and testing ideas; and our unique syllabus manager that gives instructors and students access to the up-to-date syllabus at any time from any computer.

StudyWizard Computerized Tutorial. This interactive study guide by Ken Weatherbie of Del Mar College helps students learn major facts and concepts through drill and practice exercises and diagnostic feedback. StudyWizard provides correct answers, answer explanations, and the text page number on which the material is discussed. The easy-to-use CD-ROM for Windows and Macintosh is available to instructors through their sales representative. Also available on floppies.

Study Guides and Practice Tests. This two-volume study guide, created by Julie Roy Jeffrey and Peter J. Frederick, has been revised by Ken Weatherbie of Del Mar College. It includes chapter outlines, significant themes and highlights, a glossary, learning enrichment ideas, sample test questions, exercises for identification and interpretation, and geography exercises based on maps in the text.

Time Line to accompany The American People, *Brief Third Edition.* Created especially for this edition of the text, this five-page, fold-out, full-color, illustrated time line is designed to be hung on a wall and referred to throughout the semester. Arranged in an easy-to-read format around important political and diplomatic, social and economic, and cultural and technological events in United States history, it gives students a chronological context in which to place their knowledge.

Everything You Need to Know About Your History Course. Authored by Sandra Mathews-Lamb of Nebraska Wesleyan University and written for first-year university students, this guide provides invaluable tips on how to study, how to use a textbook, how to write a good paper, how to take notes, how to read a map, graph, or bar chart, and how to read primary and secondary sources.

Everything You Need To Know About The American People, *Brief Third Edition.* This guide to the text explains the text's organization, pedagogy, and special features.

Revised! Guide to the Internet for History, *Second Edition.* Written by Richard Rothaus of St. Cloud State University, this guide details all the World Wide Web has to offer and advises students on how to make the most of it.

Longman American History Atlas. This full-color historical atlas includes 69 maps, all designed especially for this course. This valuable reference tool is available shrinkwrapped with *The American People* at low cost.

Mapping America: A Guide to Historical Geography. Each volume of this workbook by Ken Weatherbie of Del Mar College contains 18 exercises corresponding to the map program in the text, each concluding with interpretive questions about the role of geography in American history. This free item is designed to be packaged with *The American People*.

Mapping American History: Student Activities. Written by Gerald Danzer of the University of Illinois at Chicago, this free map workbook for students features exercises designed to teach students to interpret and analyze cartographic materials as historical documents. This free item is designed to be packaged with *The American People*.

Retracing the Past, *Fourth Edition.* This two-volume reader is edited by Ronald Schultz of the University of Wyoming and Gary B. Nash of the University of California, Los Angeles. These secondary source readings cover economic, political, and social history with special emphasis on women, racial and ethnic groups, and working-class people.

America Through the Eyes of Its People: Primary Sources in American History, *Second Edition.* This one-volume collection of primary documents portrays the rich and varied tapestry of American life. It contains documents by women, Native Americans, African-Americans, Hispanics, and others who helped to shape the course of U.S. history along with student study questions and contextual headnotes. Available free when bundled with the text.

Sources of the African American Past. Edited by Roy Finkenbine of University of Detroit at Mercy, this collection of primary sources covers key themes in the African-American experience from the West African background to the present. Balanced between political and social history, it offers a vivid snapshot of the lives of African Americans in different historical periods and includes documents representing women and different regions of the United States. Available at a minimum cost when bundled with the text.

Women and the National Experience. Edited by Ellen Skinner of Pace University, this primary source reader contains both classic and unusual documents describing the history of women in the United States. The documents provide dramatic evidence that outspoken women attained a public voice and participated in the development of national events and policies long before they could vote. Chronologically organized and balanced between social and political history, this reader offers a striking picture of the lives of women across American history. Available at a minimum cost when bundled with the text.

Reading the American West. Edited by Mitchell Roth of Sam Houston State University, this primary source reader uses letters, diary excerpts, speeches, interviews, and newspaper articles to let students experience what historians really do and how history is written. Every document is accompanied by a contextual headnote and study questions. The book is divided into chapters with extensive introductions. Available at a minimum cost when bundled with the text.

A Short Guide to Writing About History. Written by Richard Marius of Harvard University, this short guide introduces students to the pleasures of historical research and discovery while teaching them how to write cogent history papers. Focusing on more than just the conventions of good writing, this supplement shows students first how to think about history, and then how to organize their thoughts into coherent essays.

New! Longman-Penguin Putnam Inc. Value Bundles. A variety of classic texts are available at a significant discount when packaged with *The American People,* Brief Third Edition. Ask your local sales representative for details or visit our website at http://longman.awl.com/penguin.

Library of American Biography Series. Edited by Oscar Handlin of Harvard University, each of these interpretive biographies focuses on a figure whose actions and ideas significantly influenced the course of American history and national life. At the same time, each biography relates the life of its subject to the broader theme and developments of the times. Brief and inexpensive, they are ideal for any U. S. history course. New editions include *Abigail Adams: An American Woman,* Second Edition, by Charles W. Akers; *Andrew Carnegie and the Rise of Big Business,* Second Edition, by Harold C. Livesay; and *Eleanor Roosevelt: A Personal and Public Life,* Second Edition, by J. William T. Youngs.

Learning to Think Critically: Films and Myths About American History. Randy Roberts and Robert May of Purdue University use well-known films such as *Gone with the Wind* and *Casablanca* to explore some common myths about America and its past. This short handbook subjects some popular beliefs to historical scrutiny in order to help students develop a method of inquiry for approaching the subject of history in general.

ABOUT THE AUTHORS

Gary B. Nash received his Ph.D. from Princeton University. He is currently Director of the National Center for History in the Schools at the University of California, Los Angeles, where he teaches colonial and revolutionary American history. Among the books Nash has authored are *Quakers and Politics: Pennsylvania, 1681–1726* (1968); *Red, White, and Black: The Peoples of Early America* (1974, 1982, 1992, 1999); *The Urban Crucible: Social Change, Political Consciousness, and the Origins of the American Revolution* (1979); and *Forging Freedom: The Black Urban Experience in Philadelphia, 1720–1840* (1988). A former president of the Organization of American Historians, his scholarship is especially concerned with the role of common people in the making of history. He wrote Part I and served as a general editor of this book.

Julie Roy Jeffrey earned her Ph.D. in history from Rice University. Since then she has taught at Goucher College. Honored as an outstanding teacher, Jeffrey has been involved in faculty development activities and curriculum evaluation. Jeffrey's major publications include *Education for Children of the Poor* (1978); *Frontier Women: The Trans-Mississippi West, 1840–1880* (1979, 1997); *Converting the West: A Biography of Narcissa Whitman* (1991); and *The Great Silent Army of Abolitionism: Ordinary Women in the Antislavery Movement* (1998). She is the author of many articles on the lives and perceptions of nineteenth-century women. She wrote Parts III and IV in collaboration with Peter Frederick and acted as a general editor of this book.

John R. Howe received his Ph.D. from Yale University. At the University of Minnesota, his teaching interests include early American politics and relations between Native Americans and whites. His major publications include *The Changing Political Thought of John Adams* (1966) and *From the Revolution Through the Age of Jackson* (1973). His major research currently involves a manuscript entitled "The Transformation of Public Life in Revolutionary America." Howe wrote Part II of this book.

Peter J. Frederick received his Ph.D. in history from the University of California, Berkeley. Innovative student-centered teaching in American history has been the focus of his career at California State University, Hayward, and since 1970 at Wabash College (1992–1994 at Carleton College). Recognized nationally as a distinguished teacher and for his many articles and workshops for faculty on teaching and learning, Frederick has also written several articles on life-writing and a book, *Knights of the Golden Rule: The Intellectual as Christian Social Reformer in the 1890s*. He coordinated and edited all the "Recovering the Past" sections and coauthored Parts III and IV.

Allen F. Davis earned his Ph.D. from the University of Wisconsin. A former president of the American Studies Association, he is a professor of history at

Temple University and Director of the Center for Public History. He is the author of *Spearheads for Reform: The Social Settlements and the Progressive Movement* (1967) and *American Heroine: The Life and Legend of Jane Addams* (1973). He is coauthor of *Still Philadelphia* (1983), *Philadelphia Stories* (1987), and *One Hundred Years at Hull House* (1990). He is currently working on a book on masculine culture in America. Davis wrote Part V of this book.

Allan M. Winkler received his Ph.D. from Yale. He is presently teaching at Miami University. An award-winning historian, his books include *The Politics of Propaganda: The Office of War Information, 1942–1945* (1978); *Modern America: The United States from the Second World War to the Present* (1985); *Home Front U.S.A.: America During World War II* (1986); and *Life Under a Cloud: American Anxiety About the Atom* (1993). His research centers on the connections between public policy and popular mood in modern American history. Winkler wrote Part VI of this book.

THE AMERICAN PEOPLE

CHAPTER 1

Three Worlds Meet

In the late 1550s, a few years after Catholic King Philip II and Protestant Queen Elizabeth assumed the throne in Spain and England, respectively, Opechancanough was born in Tsenacommacah. In the Algonquian language, the word *tsenacommacah* meant "densely inhabited land." Later, English colonizers would rename this place Virginia after their monarch, the virgin queen Elizabeth. Before he died in the 1640s, in the ninth decade of his life, Opechancanough had seen light-skinned, swarthy, and black-skinned newcomers from a half-dozen European and African kingdoms swarm into his land. Like thousands of other Native Americans, he was witnessing the early moments of European expansion across the Atlantic Ocean.

Opechancanough was only an infant when Europeans first reached the Chesapeake Bay region. A small party of Spanish had explored the area in 1561, but they found neither gold nor silver nor anything else of value. Upon departing, they took with them the brother of one of the local chieftains, who was a member of Opechancanough's clan. They left behind something of unparalleled importance in the history of contact between the peoples of Europe and the Americas: a viral infection that spread like wildfire through a population that had no immunity against it. Many members of Opechancanough's tribe died, although their casualties were light compared with those of other tribes that caught the deadly European diseases.

In 1570, when Opechancanough was young, the Spanish returned and established a Jesuit mission near the York River. Violence occurred, and before the Spanish abandoned the Chesapeake in 1572, they put to death a number of captured Indians, including a chief who was Opechancanough's relative. The Native Americans learned that Europeans, even when they came bearing the crosses of their religion, were a volatile and dangerous people.

Opechancanough was in his forties when three ships of fair-skinned settlers disembarked in 1607 to begin the first permanent English settlement in the New World. For several months he watched his half brother Powhatan, high chief of several dozen loosely confederated tribes in the region, parry and fence with the newcomers. Then Powhatan sent him to capture the English leader John Smith and escort him to the Indians' main village. Smith was put through a mock execution but then released. He later got the best of Opechancanough, threatening him with a pistol, humiliating him in front of his warriors, and assaulting one of his sons, whom Smith "spurned like a dog."

Opechancanough nursed his wounds for years while Powhatan grew old and the English settlements slowly spread in the Chesapeake region. Then, in 1617, he became leader of the Powhatan Confederacy. Two years later, a Dutch trader sold 20 Africans to the settlers after docking at Jamestown. Three years after that, Opechancanough led a determined assault on the English plantations that lay along the rivers and streams emptying into the bay. The

Indians killed nearly one-third of the intruders. But they paid dearly in the retaliatory raids that the colonists mounted in succeeding years.

As he watched the land-hungry settlers swarm in during the next two decades, Opechancanough's patience failed him. Finally, in 1644, now in his eighties, he galvanized a new generation of warriors and led a final desperate assault on the English. It was a suicidal attempt, but the "great general" of the Powhatan Confederacy, faithful to the tradition of his people, counseled death over enslavement and humiliation. Though the warriors inflicted heavy casualties, they could not overwhelm the colonizers, who vastly outnumbered them. For two years, Opechancanough was kept prisoner by the Virginians. Nearly blind and "so decrepit that he was not able to walk alone," he was fatally shot in the back by an English guard in 1646.

◆◆◆◆◆◆

Over a long lifetime, Opechancanough painfully experienced the meeting of people from three continents. His land was one of many that would be penetrated by Europeans over the next three centuries, as Christian civilization girdled the globe. On the Chesapeake Bay, this clash of cultures formed the opening chapter of what we know as American history. That history, in turn, was one scene in a much broader drama of European colonization and exploitation of many indigenous cultures thousands of miles from the Old World. The nature of this violent intermingling of Europeans, Africans, and Native Americans is an essential part of early American history. But to understand how the destinies of red, white, and black people became intertwined in Opechancanough's land, we must look at the precontact history and cultural foundations of life in the homelands of each of them.

THE PEOPLE OF AMERICA BEFORE COLUMBUS

Thousands of years before the European voyages of discovery, the history of humankind in North America began. Nomadic bands from Siberia hunting big game animals began to migrate across a land bridge connecting northeastern Asia with Alaska. The main migration apparently occurred between 12,000 and 14,000 years ago, although possibly much earlier.

Hunters and Farmers

For thousands of years the early hunters trekked on, following vegetation and game. In time, they reached the tip of South America and the eastern edge of North America. Thus did people from the "Old World" discover the "New World" thousands of years before Columbus.

Archaeologists have excavated and dated sites of early life in the Americas, tentatively reconstructing the dispersion of these first Americans over an immense land mass. Although much remains unknown, archaeological evidence suggests that as centuries passed and population increased, the earliest inhabitants evolved into separate cultures, adjusting to various environments in distinct ways. Europeans who rediscovered the New World thousands of years later would lump together the myriad societies they found. But by the 1500s, the "Indians" of the Americas were enormously diverse in the size and complexity of their societies, languages, and forms of social organization.

Archaeologists and anthropologists have charted several phases of "Native American" history. The Beringian period of initial migration ended about 14,000 years ago. During the Paleo-Indian era, 14,000 to 10,000 years ago, big-game hunters flaked hard stones into spear points and chose "kill sites" where they slew herds of Pleistocene mammals. Population growth accelerated, and nomadism began to give way to settled habitations or local migration within limited territories.

Then, during the Archaic era, from about 10,000 to 2,500 years ago, great geological changes brought further adaptations to the land. As the massive Ice Age glaciers slowly retreated, a warming trend turned vast areas from grasslands into desert. Mammals were weakened by more arid conditions, but human populations ably adapted. They learned to exploit new sources of food, especially plants. In time, a second technological breakthrough, the "agricultural revolution," occurred.

Recent archaeological evidence points to examples of environmental devastation that severely damaged the biodiversity of the Americas. The first wave of intruders found a wilderness teeming with so-called megafauna, including saber-toothed tigers and woolly mammoths. But by about 10,000 years ago, these animals were almost extinct. Both overhunting and a massive shift of climate that deprived the huge beasts of their accustomed environment were to blame. The extinction of the huge beasts forced people to kill new sources of food such as turkeys, ducks, and guinea pigs, and may have gradually reduced human numbers.

Over many centuries, salinization and deforestation put the environment under additional stress. In what is today central Arizona, the Hohokam civilization collapsed hundreds of years ago when the irrigation system became too salty to support agriculture. At Arizona's Chaco Canyon, the fast-growing Anasazi denuded a magnificently forested region for firewood and building materials, and soil erosion then impoverished the region for the Anasazi.

When Native Americans learned to domesticate plants, they began the long process of transforming their relationship to the physical world. Discovering agriculture created a new relationship to once-ungovernable natural forces. Anthropologists believe that this process began independently in widely separated parts of the world about 9,000 to 7,000 years ago.

Over the millennia, humans began a systematic clearing and planting of bean and maize fields, and settled village life began to replace nomadic existence. Increases in food supply brought about by agriculture triggered other major changes. As more ample food fueled population growth, large groups split off to form separate societies. Greater social and political complexity arose. Men cleared the land and hunted; women cared for crops. Many societies empowered religious figures, trusting them to ward off unseen but hostile forces.

Everywhere in the Americas, regional trading networks formed. Along trade routes carrying commodities such as salt, obsidian rock for projectile points, and copper for jewelry also traveled technology, religious ideas, and agricultural practices. By the end of the Archaic period, about 500 B.C., hundreds of independent kin-based groups had learned to exploit the resources of their particular area and to trade with other groups in their region.

Archaeological Artifacts

The recovery of the past before there were written records is the domain of archaeology. Virtually our entire knowledge of Indian societies in North America before the arrival of European colonizers is drawn from the work of archaeologists who have excavated the ancient living sites of the first Americans. Many Native Americans today strongly oppose this rummaging in the ancient ancestral places; they particularly oppose the unearthing of burial sites. But the modern search for knowledge about early people in the Americas goes on.

Archaeological data have allowed us to overcome the stereotypic view of Native Americans as a primitive people whose culture was static for thousands of years before Europeans arrived in North America. This earlier view allowed historians to argue that the tremendous loss of Native American population and land accompanying the initial settlement and westward migration of white Americans was more or less inevitable. When two cultures, one dynamic and forward-looking and the other static and backward, confronted each other, historians have frequently maintained, the more advanced or "civilized" culture almost always prevailed.

Much of the elaborate early history of people in the Americas is unrecoverable. But many fragments of this long human history are being recaptured through archaeological research. Particularly important are studies that reveal how Indian societies were changing during the few centuries immediately preceding the European arrival in the New World. These studies give us a much better chance to interpret the seventeenth-century interaction of Native Americans and Europeans because they provide an understanding of Indian values, social and political organization, material culture, and religion as they existed when the two peoples first met. To understand only one of the two interacting societies is a recipe for biased interpretation.

One highly important archaeological investigation has been carried out over the last century at the confluence of the Mississippi and Missouri rivers near modern-day East St. Louis, Illinois. Here archaeologists have found the center of a vast Mississippi culture that began about A.D. 600, reached its peak about 300 years before Columbus's voyages, and then declined through a combination of drought, dwindling food supplies, and internal tensions. Cahokia is the name given to the urban center of a civilization that at its height dominated an area as large as New York State. At its center stood one of the largest earth constructions built by ancient man anywhere on the planet. Its base covering 15 acres, this gigantic earthen temple rises in four terraces to a height of 100 feet. The imaginary drawing shown here indicates some of the dozens of smaller geometric mounds discovered near this major temple. Notice the outlying farms, a sure sign of the settled (as opposed to nomadic) existence of the people who flourished ten centuries ago in this region. How does this depiction of ancient Cahokia change your image of Native American life before the arrival of Europeans?

By recovering artifacts from Cahokia burial mounds, archaeologists have pieced together a picture of a highly elaborate civilization along the Mississippi bottomlands, where indigenous people mined salt and produced knives and stone hoe blades for local consumption and export. Cahokian artisans made sophisticated pottery, ornamental jewelry, metalwork, and tools. They used copper and furs from the Lake Superior region, black obsidian stone from the Rocky Mountains, and seashells from the Gulf of Mexico—demonstrating that Cahokia people conducted long-distance trade. Understanding this, we can more readily see that when Europeans arrived in North America, they found it easy to strike up trade with peoples who for centuries had bartered with other peoples within vast trading networks.

A reconstructed view of Cahokia, the largest town in North America before European arrival, painted by William R. Iseminger. An estimated 50 million cubic feet of earth was used to construct the ceremonial and burial mounds. (Cahokia Mounds State Historic Site)

The fact that some graves uncovered at Cahokia contain large caches of finely tooled objects and other burial mounds contain many skeletons unaccompanied by any artifacts leads archaeologists to conclude that this was a stratified society much like those of the European intruders. Knowing about this socially differentiated, urban society undermines stereotypical notions of a primitive, sparsely settled, nomadic, hunter-and-gatherer people who met Europeans at the water's edge.

Native Americans in 1600

The pre-Columbian (or post-Archaic) era spanned the 2,000 years before contact with Europeans. It involved a complex process of growth and environmental adaptation among many distinct societies—and crisis in some of them. In the Southwest, the ancestors of the Hopi and Zuni developed large terraced multistoried and multiroom buildings. By the time the Spanish arrived in the 1540s, the indigenous Pueblo people were using irrigation canals, dams, and hillside terracing to water their arid maize fields. In their agricultural techniques, their skill in ceramics, their use of woven textiles for clothing, and their village life, Pueblo society resembled that of peasant communities in many parts of Europe and Asia.

Far to the east were the mound-building societies of the Mississippi and Ohio valleys. When European settlers first crossed the Appalachian Mountains a century and a half after arriving on the continent, they were amazed to find hundreds of ceremonial mounds and gigantic sculptured earthworks. Believing all "Indians" to be forest primitives, they reasoned that these were the remains of an ancient civilization that had found its way to North America.

The mound-building societies of the Ohio valley declined many centuries before Europeans reached the continent, perhaps attacked by other tribes or damaged by severe climatic changes. But about A.D. 600, another mound-building, agricultural society arose in the Mississippi valley. Its center, the city of Cahokia with perhaps 40,000 inhabitants, stood near present-day St. Louis. Great ceremonial plazas, flanked by a temple 100 feet high, marked this first metropolis in America. This was the urban center of a far-flung Mississippi culture that encompassed hundreds of villages from Wisconsin to Louisiana.

Before the mound-building cultures declined, their influence was already transforming the woodlands societies along the Atlantic. The numerous small tribes there were far from the "savages" that the first European explorers described. They had added limited agriculture to their skill in using natural plants and had developed food procurement strategies that exploited all the resources around them.

Most eastern woodlands tribes lived in waterside villages, and they often migrated seasonally between inland and coastal village sites. In the Northeast, their light birchbark canoes helped them trade and communicate over immense territories. In the Southeast, population was denser and social and political organization more elaborate.

On the eve of European exploration of the Americas, the continent north of the Rio Grande contained at least 3 to 4 million people, of whom perhaps 500,000 lived along the eastern coastal plain and in the piedmont region accessible to the early European settlers. Though estimates vary widely, perhaps 40 to 60 million people lived in the entire hemisphere about 1500, when the Europeans arrived. (At the same time there were some 70 to 90 million people in Europe and about 50 to 70 million in Africa.) The colonizers were coming to a land inhabited for thousands of years by people whose village existence in many ways resembled that of the arriving Europeans.

In some important ways, however, Indian culture differed from that of Europeans. Horses and oxen, for example, did not exist in the New World. Without large draft animals, Indians had no incentive to develop wheels. Many inventions—such as the technology for smelting iron, which had diffused widely in the

The French, under Jean Ribault, discovering the River of May in Florida on May 1, 1564. Engraving by Theodore De Bry, 1591, after a painting by Jacques Le Moyne, who accompanied the expedition in 1564. As the illustration shows, many initial encounters between Native Americans and Europeans were friendly. Here, a party of the local indigenous people swims out to meet the French with gifts, and another Native American leads a small group of French inland to a village. (The Granger Collection, New York)

Old World—had not crossed the ocean barrier. But valuable New World crops, such as corn and potatoes, which Indians raised, were unknown in the Old World before Columbus.

Contrasting World Views

Colonizing Europeans called themselves "civilized" and typically described the people they met in the Americas as "savage." The gulf separating people in Europe and North America was defined not only by their material cultures, but also by how they viewed their relationship to the environment and how they defined social relations in their communities.

Regarding land as a resource to be exploited for human benefit, Europeans believed that it should be privately possessed. From this belief developed much that Europeans took for granted: for example, property lines, inheritance customs for passing land on, and courts to settle the resulting disputes. Property was the basis not only of sustenance, but also of independence, wealth, status, and identity. The social structure directly mirrored patterns of land ownership, with a land-wealthy elite at the top and a propertyless mass at the bottom.

Indians also had concepts of property and boundaries. But they believed that land had sacred qualities and should be held in common. As one missionary explained the Indian view in the eighteenth century, the Creator "made the Earth and all that it contains for the common good of mankind."

Communal ownership sharply limited social stratification and increased a sense of sharing in most Native American communities, much to the amazement of Europeans accustomed to wide disparities of wealth. The majority of Europeans were peasants scratching a subsistence living from the soil, living in kin-centered villages with little contact with the outside world, and exchanging goods and labor through barter. But in Europe's cities, a wealth-conscious, ambitious individual who valued and sought wider choices and greater opportunities to enhance personal status was coming to the fore. In contrast, Native American traditions stressed the group over the individual, and valor more than wealth.

There were exceptions. The Aztec and Inca empires were highly developed, populous, and stratified. So, in North America, were a few tribes such as the Natchez. But on the eastern and western coasts of the continent and in the Southwest—the regions of contact in the sixteenth and seventeenth centuries—the Europeans encountered a people whose values differed strikingly from theirs.

European colonizers in North America also found disturbing the matrilineal organization of many tribal societies. Contrary to European practice, family membership among the Iroquois, for example, was determined through the female line. When a son or grandson married, he moved from his female-headed household to one headed by the matriarch of his wife's family. Divorce was also the woman's prerogative. Clans were composed of several matrilineal kin groups related by a blood connection on the mother's side. To Europeans, this was a peculiar and dangerous reversal of their male-dominated sexual hierarchy.

Native American women were subordinate, but not nearly to the extent found among European women. For example, European women were almost entirely excluded from politics. But in Native American villages, again to take the Iroquois example, designated men sat in a circle to deliberate and make decisions, but the senior women of the village stood behind them, lobbying and instructing. Village chiefs were male, but they were chosen by the elder women of their clans. If they moved too far from the will of the women who appointed them, these chiefs were removed.

The role of women in the tribal economy reinforced male-female power-sharing. Men hunted, fished, and cleared land, but women controlled the raising and distribution of crops, supplying probably three-quarters of their family's nutritional needs. When the men were away hunting, women directed village life. Europeans perceived such sexual equality as another mark of "savagery."

In economic relations, Europeans and Indians differed in ways that sometimes led to misunderstanding and conflict. Over vast stretches of the continent, Indians had built trading networks for centuries before Europeans arrived, making it easy for them to trade with whites and incorporate their goods into their culture. But trade for Indian peoples was also a way of preserving reciprocity between individuals and communities. Europeans saw trade largely as economic exchange.

In the religious beliefs of Native Americans, the English saw a final damning defect. Europeans built their religious life around the belief in a single divinity, written scriptures, a trained and highly literate clergy, and churches with structured ceremonies. Native American societies, sharing no literary tradition, had less structured religious beliefs. Believing that human life could be affected—pos-

INDIAN SOCIETIES DURING THE PERIOD OF EARLY EUROPEAN SETTLEMENT   The great number of Indian societies within the present-day boundaries of the United States—each with its own language—indicates the cultural diversity of the first peoples of North America at the time Europeans arrived.

itively or negatively—by the mysterious power pervading everything in nature, Indian people sought to conciliate these spirits, even in the animals they hunted.

For Europeans, the Indians' polytheism was pagan and devilish. Indian religious leaders, called *shamans,* used medicinal plants and magical chants to heal and facilitated people's quests to communicate with the spiritual world. But Europeans regarded the *shamans* as especially dangerous because they occupied powerful positions among a spiritually misled people. Their fear and hatred of infidels intensified by the Protestant Reformation, Europeans saw a holy necessity to convert—or destroy—these enemies of God.

AFRICA ON THE EVE OF CONTACT

Half a century before 1492, a Portuguese sea captain made the first known European landing on the west coast of sub-Saharan Africa. If he had been able to travel the length and breadth of the immense continent, he would have encountered a rich variety of African states, peoples, and cultures. African "backwardness" was a myth perpetuated after the slave trade had begun transporting millions of Africans to the New World. During the period of early contact with Europeans, Africa, like pre-Columbian America, was recognized as a diverse continent with a long history of cultural evolution.

The Kingdoms of Africa

The estimated 50 million peoples of fifteenth-century Africa lived in vast deserts, grasslands, and tropical forests. Most tilled the soil. Part of their skill in farming derived from iron metallurgy, which may have been known in West Africa long before it reached northwestern Europe. More efficient iron implements increased agricultural productivity, in turn spurring population growth.

Before fifteenth-century Europeans reached the west coast of Africa, a number of large empires had risen there. The first was the kingdom of Ghana, which from the sixth to the eleventh centuries embraced most of West Africa. Large towns, elaborate sculpture and metalwork, long-distance commerce, and a complex political structure marked the Ghanaian kingdom. A thriving caravan trade across the Sahara brought extensive Muslim influence by the eleventh century, when the king of Ghana boasted an army of 200,000, maintained trading contacts as far east as Cairo and Baghdad, and was furnishing, through Muslim middlemen in North Africa, much of the gold supply for the Christian Mediterranean region.

After Ghana fell to invading North African Muslims, there arose a new Islamic kingdom, Mali. Prospering through its control of the gold trade, Mali flourished until the early sixteenth century. Its city of Timbuktu contained a distinguished faculty of scholars to whom North Africans and even southern Europeans came to study. Elsewhere along the Atlantic coast, other kingdoms such as Kongo, Songhay, and Benin grew in the centuries before seaborne Europeans reached Africa. In

The art of sixteenth-century West Africa, much of it ceremonial, shows a high degree of aesthetic development. On the left is Gou, god of war, a metal sculpture from the Fon culture in Dahomey; above is a pair of antelope headdresses (worn by running a cord through holes in the base and tying them atop the head) carved of wood by the Bambara people of Senegambia. (Musée de l'Homme, Paris)

their towns, rivaling those of Europe in size, lived people skilled in metalworking, weaving, ceramics, architecture, and aesthetic expression. Law codes, regional trade, and effective political organization all developed by the fifteenth century.

Population growth and cultural development in Africa, as elsewhere in the world, proceeded at different rates in different regions. Where soil was rich, rainfall adequate, and minerals abundant—as in western Sudan—population grew and cultures changed rapidly. Where inhospitable desert or impenetrable jungle ruled, societies remained small and changed very slowly. Cultural innovation accelerated in East African Swahili-speaking societies facing the Indian Ocean after trading contacts began with the Eastern world in the ninth century. Around the same time, traders from the Arab world began to spread Muslim influence in West Africa.

The African Ethos

The many peoples of Africa, who were to supply at least two-thirds of all the "Old World" immigrants crossing the Atlantic in the sixteenth through eighteenth centuries, shared certain ways of life that differentiated them from Europeans.

As in Europe, the family was the basic unit of social organization. Unlike European societies, however, African societies were organized in a variety of kinship and political systems. In many African (like Native American) societies, descent was through the mother: The son of a chief's sister inherited his position, and a married man joined his bride's people.

West Africans believed in a supreme Creator and in lesser deities associated with natural forces. Because these deities could intervene in human affairs, they were elaborately honored. Like most North American Indians, West Africans treated with respect those natural objects that they believed spirits inhabited.

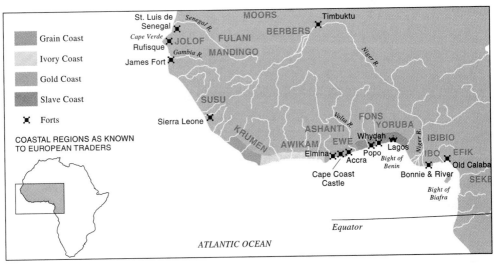

WEST AFRICAN CULTURES AND SLAVING FORTS Europeans fought lustily for control of slaving forts on the West African coast, and many forts changed hands several times during the long period of the Atlantic slave trade.

Africans also worshipped ancestors, who were believed to mediate between the Creator and the living. The more ancient an ancestor, the greater was this deceased person's power to affect the living. Deep family loyalty flowed naturally from ancestor worship.

Social organization in much of West Africa by the time Europeans arrived was as elaborate as in fifteenth-century Europe. At the top stood nobles and priests, usually elderly men. Beneath them were the great masses of people—mostly farmers, but also some craftsmen, traders, teachers, and artists. Slaves occupied the bottom social rung. As in ancient Greece and Rome, they were "outsiders"-war captives, criminals, or sometimes people who sold themselves because of debt. Slaves had restricted rights and narrow opportunities. Nevertheless, they were entitled to protection under the law and allowed the privileges of education, marriage, and parenthood. Their servile condition was not permanent, nor was it automatically inherited by their children, as would be the fate of Africans enslaved in the Americas.

EUROPE IN THE AGE OF EXPLORATION

In the ninth century, western Europe was an economic and cultural backwater. The center of political power and economic vitality in the Old World had shifted eastward to Christian Byzantium, which controlled Asia Minor, the Balkans, and parts of Italy. The other dynamic culture of this age, Islam, had spread through the Middle East, North Africa, and Spain, and was reaching Africa south of the Sahara.

Over the next six centuries, an epic revitalization of western Europe occurred, creating the conditions that enabled its leading maritime nations to vastly extend their oceanic frontiers. By the fifteenth century, a 400-year epoch of European expansion into other continents was under way. Only in the twentieth century was this process of Europeanization reversed.

The Rise of Europe

The rebirth of western Europe, which began around A.D. 1000, owed much to a revival of long-distance trading from Italian ports on the Mediterranean and the rediscovery of ancient knowledge. These new contacts brought wealth and power to the Italian commercial cities, which gradually evolved into merchant-dominated city-states that freed themselves from the rule of feudal lords in control of the surrounding countryside. In the thirteenth and fourteenth centuries, kings began to reassert their authority, unify their realms, and curb the power of the great lords.

The Black Death (bubonic plague), which devastated western Europe and Africa in 1348 and 1349, promoted the unification of old realms into early modern states. The plague killed one-third of the population. The nobilities with which monarchs had to contend were reduced in size, for the plague defied class distinction. Lords treated their peasants better for a time because their labor, tremendously reduced by the plague, became more valuable.

England acquired a distinctive political system. In 1215, the aristocracy curbed the powers of the king when they forced him to accept Magna Carta. Later, a parliament composed of elective and hereditary members gained the right to meet regularly to pass money bills and to act as a check on the crown, an arrangement unknown on the Continent. During the sixteenth century, the crown and Parliament worked together toward a more unified state.

Economic changes of great significance also occurred in England during the sixteenth century. To practice more profitable agriculture, great landowners began to "enclose" (consolidate) their estates, throwing peasants off their plots and turning many into wage laborers.

Continental Europe lagged behind England in two respects. First, it was far less affected by the move to "enclose" agricultural land, for continental aristocrats regarded the maximization of profit as unworthy of gentlemen. Second, continental rulers were less successful in engaging the interests of their nobilities, and these nobles never shared governance with their king, as did English aristocrats. In France, a noble faction assassinated Henry III in 1589, and the nobles remained disruptive for nearly a century more. In Spain, the final conquest of the Muslims and expulsion of the Jews (both in 1492) strengthened the monarchy's hold, but regional cultures and leaders remained strong.

The New Monarchies and the Expansionist Impulse

In the second half of the fifteenth century, ambitious monarchs coming to power in France, England, and Spain sought social and political stability in their kingdoms by creating armies and bureaucracies to quell internal conflict and raise taxes. In these countries, and in Portugal as well, economic revival and the reversal of more than a century of population decline and civil disorder nourished the impulse to expand. This impulse was also fed by Renaissance culture. The Renaissance (Rebirth) encouraged an emphasis on human abilities. Beginning in Italy and spreading through Europe, the Renaissance peaked in the late fifteenth century.

The exploratory urge had two initial objectives: first, to circumvent Muslim traders by finding an eastward oceanic route to Asia; and second, to tap the African gold trade at its source, avoiding North African middlemen in North Africa. Since 1291, when Marco Polo returned to Venice with tales of Eastern treasures, Europeans had traded with the Orient, through the Near East. But not until almost 1500 could Europe's mariners voyage to Cathay by both eastward and westward water routes.

Portugal, a poor country of only one million inhabitants, led the effort to blaze new routes to the East. Led by Prince Henry the Navigator, for whom trade was secondary to the conquest of the Muslim world, Portugal breached the unknown. In the 1420s, Henry began dispatching Portuguese mariners to probe the Atlantic "sea of darkness." His intrepid sailors were aided by important improvements in navigation, mapmaking, and ship design.

Portuguese captains operated at sea on three ancient principles: that the earth was round, that distances on its surface could be measured by degrees, and that navigators could "fix" their position on a map by measuring the position of the stars. The invention in the 1450s of the quadrant, which allowed the precise observation of stars necessary for determining latitude, represented a leap forward in navigation. Equally important was the design of a lateen-rigged caravel, adapted from Moorish ship models. Its triangular sails permitted ships to sail into the wind, allowing them to go south along the African coast and—a feat the old square-rigged European vessels could never perform—return northward against prevailing winds.

By the 1430s, the ability of Prince Henry's captains to break through the limits of the world known to Europeans had carried them to Madeira, the Canaries, and the Azores. These were soon developed as the first European agricultural plantations. From there, the Portuguese sea captains pushed farther south.

By the time of Prince Henry's death in 1460, Portuguese mariners had reached the west coast of Africa, where they began a profitable trade in ivory, slaves, and especially gold. By 1500, they had captured control of the African gold trade. In 1497, Vasco da Gama became the first European to sail around the Cape of Africa, allowing the Portuguese to colonize the Indian Ocean and to reach modern Indonesia and south China by 1513. By forcing trade concessions in the islands and coastal states of the East Indies, the Portuguese unlocked the fabulous Asian treasure houses that since Marco Polo's time had whetted European appetites.

Reaching the Americas

The independent Spanish kingdoms of Aragon and Castile were united in 1469 by the marriage of their rulers, King Ferdinand and Queen Isabella. At their court an Italian sailor, Christopher Columbus, the son of a poor weaver, had important contacts.

Once hailed as a heroic discoverer and now often damned as a racist villain, Columbus is best understood in the context of his own times—an age of great brutality and violence. Columbus's urge to explore was nourished by ideas and questions about the geographical limits of his world, and he was inspired by hopes of contributing to the reconquest of Moorish Spain.

Like many sailors, Columbus had listened to sea tales about lands to the west. He may have heard Icelandic sagas about the Norse voyages to Newfoundland five centuries before. Other ideas circulated that the Atlantic Ocean stretched to India and eastern Asia. Could one reach the Indies by sailing west rather than by sailing east around Africa, as the Portuguese were attempting? Columbus hungered to know.

For nearly ten years, Columbus tried unsuccessfully to secure financial backing and royal sanction in Portugal for exploratory voyages. Many mocked his modest estimates of the distance westward from Europe to Japan. Finally, in 1492, Queen Isabella commissioned him, and he sailed west with three tiny ships and a crew of about 90 men. In the fifth week at sea—longer than any European sailors had been out of the sight of land—mutinous rumblings swept through the crews. But on the seventieth day, long after Columbus had calculated he would reach Japan, a lookout sighted land. On October 12, 1492, the sailors clambered ashore on a tiny island in the Bahamas, which Columbus named San Salvador (Holy Savior).

Believing he had reached Asia, Columbus explored the island-speckled Caribbean for ten weeks. After landing on a heavily populated island that he named Hispaniola (today, Haiti and the Dominican Republic) and on Cuba, he set sail for Spain with cinnamon, coconuts, a bit of gold, and several kidnapped natives. Homeward bound, he penned a report of what he believed were his Asian discoveries: hospitable people, fertile soils, magnificent harbors, and gold-filled rivers. When he landed, his report was quickly distributed throughout Europe.

Columbus's report brought him financing between 1494 and 1504 for three much larger expeditions to explore the newfound lands. The second voyage, car-

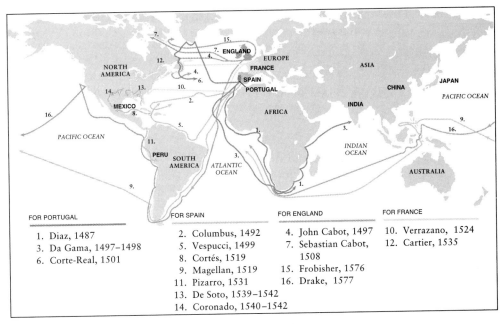

OCEANIC EXPLORATIONS IN THE FIFTEENTH AND SIXTEENTH CENTURIES

rying over 1,200 Spanish in 17 ships, initiated the first extended contact between Europeans and Native Americans. In an ominous display of what was to come, Columbus's men captured some 1,600 Tainos on Hispaniola and carried 550 of them back to Spain as slaves in 1495. Here began the Atlantic slave trade that would alter the history of the world. Although his discoveries seemed less significant than the Portuguese exploits, Columbus had led Spain to the threshold of a mighty empire. He, however, died penniless in 1506, to the end believing that he had found the water route to Asia.

The expansion of Spain and Portugal into new areas of the world profoundly affected patterns of economic activity in Europe. Its commercial center began to shift away from the Mediterranean to the Atlantic ports.

The New World also beckoned as a field of religious contest. The heavily populated Americas offered millions of potential Christian converts. But the Catholic-Protestant division within Christianity complicated Christian dreams of converting a "heathen" continent. The people of western Europe, just as they were unlocking the secrets of the new worlds in the sixteenth century, were torn by religious schisms that magnified national rivalries.

Religious Conflict During the Reformation

At the heart of Europe's religious strife was a continental movement to return the Christian Church to the purity of early Christianity. Criticism of the worldliness of the church mounted during the Renaissance. Then a German friar, Martin Luther, broke successfully with Rome, initiating the Protestant Reformation. As Protestant sects multiplied, a Catholic Reformation grew up within the church.

Attempting to be a good friar, Luther had lost faith in the power of the age-old rituals of the Church—the Mass, confession, pilgrimages to holy places. He believed that salvation came through an inward faith, or "grace," that God conferred on those he chose. Good works, Luther believed, did not earn grace but were only the external evidence of faith. Insisting on "justification by faith," Luther had taken the revolutionary step of rejecting the church's elaborate hierarchy of officials, who presided over the rituals that guided individuals toward salvation.

In 1517, Luther openly attacked the sale of "indulgences" for sins, by which the pope raised money for the building of St. Peter's in Rome. By purchasing indulgences, individuals had been told, they could reduce their time (or that of a deceased relative) in purgatory. Printing, invented less than 70 years before, allowed the rapid circulation of Luther's protest. The printed word and the ability to read it were to become revolutionary weapons.

Luther's cry for reform soon inspired Germans of all classes. He denounced five of the seven sacraments of the church, calling for a return to baptism and communion alone. He attacked the upper clergy for luxurious living and urged priests—who were nominally celibate but often involved in irregular sexual relationships—to marry respectably. He railed against the "detestable tyranny of the clergy over the laity" and called for a priesthood of all believers. He urged people to seek faith individually by reading the Bible, which he translated into German and made widely available for the first time in printed form. Most dangerously, he called on the German princes to assume control over religion in their states, directly challenging the authority of Rome.

The basic issue dividing Catholics and Protestants thus centered on the source of religious authority. To Catholics, religious authority resided in the organized Church, headed by the pope. To Protestants, the Bible was the sole authority, and access to God's word or God's grace did not require the mediation of the Church.

Building on Luther's redefinition of Christianity, John Calvin, a Frenchman, brought new intensity and meaning to the Protestant Reformation. By Calvin's doctrine, God had saved a few souls before Creation and damned the rest. Human beings could not alter this predestination, but those who were good Christians must struggle to understand and accept God's saving grace if he chose to impart it. Without mediation of ritual or priest but by "straight-walking," one was to behave as one of God's elect, the "saints."

Calvin proposed reformed Christian communities structured around the elect few. To remake the corrupt world and follow God's will, communities of "saints" must control the state. Elected bodies of ministers and dedicated laymen, called presbyteries, were to govern the church, directing the affairs of society so that all, whether saved or damned, would work for God's ends.

Calvinism, a fine-tuned system of self-discipline and social control, was first put into practice in the 1550s in the city-state of Geneva, between France and Switzerland. Here Calvin established his model Christian community. A council of 12 elders drove nonbelievers from the city, rigidly disciplined daily life, and stripped the churches of every appeal to the senses—images, music, incense, and colorful clerical gowns. Religious reformers from all over Europe flocked to the new holy community, and Geneva soon became the continental center of the reformist Christian movement.

Calvin's radical program converted large numbers of people to Protestantism throughout Europe. Like Lutheranism, it recruited most successfully among merchants, landowners, lawyers, nobles, master artisans, and shopkeepers.

The most important monarch to break with Catholicism was Henry VIII of England. When the pope refused him permission to divorce and remarry, Henry declared himself head of the Church of England, or Anglican church. Although it retained many Catholic features, the Church of England moved further in a Protestant direction under Henry's son Edward VI. But when Mary, Henry's older Catholic daughter, became queen, she vowed to reinstate her mother's religion by force if necessary. Protestant clergy were burned. Many were relieved when she died in 1558, bringing Henry's younger Protestant daughter, Elizabeth, to the throne. During her long rule, the flinty Elizabeth I steered Anglicanism along a middle course between the radicalism of Geneva and the Catholicism of Rome.

Some of the countries most affected by the Reformation—England, Holland, and France—were slow in trying to colonize the New World. So Protestantism did not gain an early foothold in the Americas. Catholicism in Spain and Portugal remained almost immune from the Protestant Reformation. Thus, even while under attack, Catholicism swept across the Atlantic almost unchallenged during the century after Columbus's voyages.

THE IBERIAN CONQUEST OF AMERICA

From 1492 to 1518, Spanish and Portuguese explorers opened up vast parts of Asia and the Americas to European knowledge. Only modest attempts at settlement were made, mostly by the Spanish on Caribbean islands. The three decades after 1518, however, became an age of conquest. In some of the bloodiest chapters in recorded history, the Spanish nearly exterminated the native Caribbean peoples, toppled and plundered great Indian empires in Mexico and Peru, discovered fabulous silver mines, and built an oceanic trade. This short era of conquest had immense consequences for global history.

Portugal concentrated mostly on building an eastward oceanic trade to Asia. In 1493, the pope had demarcated Spanish and Portuguese spheres of exploration in the Atlantic. Drawing a north-south line 100 leagues (about 300 miles) west of the Azores, the pope confined Portugal to the eastern side. One year later, Portugal obtained Spanish agreement to move the line 270 leagues farther west. These were some of the most significant lines ever drawn on a map. Nobody knew at the time that a large part of South America, as yet undiscovered by Europeans, bulged east of the new demarcation line and therefore fell within the Portuguese sphere. In time, Portugal would develop this region, Brazil, into one of the most profitable areas of the New World.

The Spanish Onslaught

Within a single generation of Columbus's death in 1506, Spanish *conquistadores* explored, claimed, and conquered all of South America except Brazil, and the southern ports of North America from present-day Florida to California. Led by audacious explorers and soldiers, and usually accompanied by enslaved Africans, they established Spanish authority and Catholicism over an immense area and huge populations. "We came here," explained one Spanish foot soldier, "to serve God and the king, and also to get rich."

In two bold and bloody strokes, the Spanish overwhelmed the ancient civilizations of the Aztecs and Incas. In 1519, Hernando Cortés with 600 soldiers marched over rugged mountains to attack Tenochtitlán (now Mexico City), the Aztec capital. At its height, centuries before, the ancient city in the Valley of Mexico had contained perhaps 200,000 people. But in 1521, following two years of tense relations between the Spanish and Aztecs, it fell before Cortés's assault. The Spanish use of horses and firearms provided an important advantage; so did a murderous smallpox epidemic in 1520 that felled thousands of Aztecs. Support from local peoples oppressed by Aztec tyranny was also indispensable. From the Valley of Mexico, the Spanish extended their dominion over the Mayan Indians of the Yucatán and Guatemala in the next few decades.

In the second conquest, Francisco Pizarro, marching from Panama through the jungles of Ecuador and into the towering mountains of Peru with a mere 168 men, most of them not even soldiers, felled the Inca empire. Like the Aztecs, the populous Incas lived in a highly organized social system. But also like the Aztecs, they were riddled by smallpox and weakened by internal violence. This ensured Pizarro's success in capturing their capital at Cuzco in 1533, and soon other gold- and silver-rich cities. Further expeditions into Chile, New Granada (Colombia), Argentina, and Bolivia in the 1530s and 1540s brought under Spanish control an empire larger than any in the Western world since the fall of Rome.

By 1550, Spain had overwhelmed the major centers of native population in the Americas. Spanish ships carried gold, silver, dyewoods, and sugar east across the Atlantic and transported African slaves, colonizers, and finished goods west. In a brief half century, Spain had exploited the advances in geographical knowledge and maritime technology of its Portuguese rivals and brought into harsh but profitable contact with each other the people of three continents. The triracial character of the Americas was firmly established by 1600.

For nearly a century after Columbus's voyages, Spain enjoyed almost unchallenged dominion over the fabulous hemisphere newly revealed to Europeans. Greedy buccaneers snapped at the heels of homeward-bound Spanish treasure fleets, but this was only a nuisance. France tried to contest Spanish or Portuguese control by planting small settlements in Brazil and Florida in the mid-sixteenth century, but they were quickly wiped out. England remained island-bound until the 1580s. Until the seventeenth century, only Portugal, which staked out important claims in Brazil in the 1520s, challenged Spanish rule in the New World.

The Great Dying

Spain's conquest in the Americas set in motion two of the most far-reaching processes in modern history. One involved microbes; the other, silver.

The sixteenth century saw the most dramatic and disastrous population decline in recorded history. The Americas' population on the eve of European arrival may have been 50 to 60 million, or more. In central Mexico, the highlands of Peru, and certain Caribbean islands, population density exceeded that of most of Europe. But though they were less populous than the people of the Americas,

European colonizers had one extraordinary biological advantage: For centuries, Old World peoples had been exposed to nearly every lethal microbe that infects humans on an epidemic scale in the temperate zone. Over the centuries, Europeans had built up immunities to these diseases. Such defenses did not eliminate afflictions like smallpox, measles, and diphtheria, but they reduced their deadliness. Geographical isolation, however, had kept these diseases from the peoples of the Americas. So, too, did the Native Americans' lack of large domesticated animals, which were major disease carriers. Arriving Europeans therefore unknowingly encountered a huge component of the human race that was utterly defenseless against the "domesticated" infections the Europeans and their animals carried.

The results were catastrophic. On Hispaniola, a population of about one million that had existed when Columbus arrived had only a few thousand survivors by 1530. Of some 15 million inhabitants in central Mexico before Cortés's arrival, nearly half perished within 15 years. Demographic disaster also struck the populous Inca peoples of the Peruvian Andes, speeding ahead of Pizarro's *conquistadores*. Smallpox "spread over the people as great destruction," an old Indian told a Spanish priest in the 1520s. "There was great havoc. Very many died of it. They could not stir, they could not change position, nor lie on one side, nor face down, nor on their backs. And if they stirred, much did they cry out . . . . And very many starved; there was death from hunger, [for] none could take care of [the sick]." Such terrifying sickness convinced many Indians that their gods had failed and left them ready to acknowledge the greater power of the Spaniards' God.

In most areas where Europeans intruded in the hemisphere for the next three centuries, the catastrophe repeated itself. Every European and African participated accidentally in the spread of disease that typically eliminated, within a few generations, at least two-thirds of the native population.

The enslavement and brutal treatment of the native people intensified the lethal effects of European diseases. Having conquered the Incas and Aztecs, the Spanish enslaved thousands of native people and assigned them work regimens that severely weakened their resistance to disease. Some priests waged lifelong campaigns to reduce the exploitation of the Indians, but they had only limited power to control their colonizing compatriots.

Silver, Sugar, and Their Consequences

The small amount of gold that Columbus brought home raised hopes that this metal, which along with silver formed the standard of wealth in Europe, might be found in the transatlantic paradise. Some gold was gleaned from the Caribbean islands and later from Colombia, Brazil, and Peru. But though men pursued it fanatically, not for three centuries would they find gold in windfall quantities in North America. But silver proved abundant—so plenteous, in fact, that when bonanza strikes were made in Bolivia in 1545 and in Mexico in the 1550s, much of Spain's New World enterprise focused on its extraction.

Native people, along with some African slaves, provided the first labor supply for the mines. The Spaniards permitted the highly organized Indian societies to maintain control of their own communities but exacted from them huge labor drafts for mining. At Potosí, in Bolivia, 58,000 workers labored at elevations of up

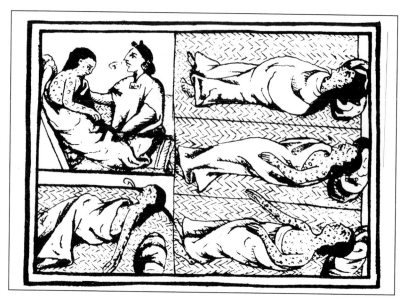

Aztec victims of smallpox, contracted during Cortés's invasion of Tenochtitlan in the 1520s. The woodcut is from the sixteenth-century work *Historia de las Casas de Nueva Espana* by Fray Bernardo de Sahagun. According to the account of the disease, "The sores were so terrible that the victims could not lie face down,. . . nor move from one side to the other. And when they tried to move even a little, they cried out in agony." (Biblioteca Medicea Laurenziana)

to 13,000 feet to dig the precious metal from a fabulous "mountain of silver." The town's population reached 120,000 by 1570, making it larger than any in Spain at the time. Thousands of other workers toiled in Mexican mines. By 1660, they had scooped up more than seven million pounds of silver from the Americas, tripling the entire European supply.

The flood of American bullion into Europe triggered profound changes. It financed further conquests and settlement in Spain's American empire, spurred long-distance trading in East Asian silks and spices, and capitalized agricultural development in the New World of sugar, coffee, cacao, and indigo. The bland diet of Europeans gradually changed as sugar and spices, previously luxury articles, became accessible to ordinary people.

The enormous increase of silver circulating in Europe after the mid-sixteenth century caused a "price revolution." The supply of silver increased faster than the demand for goods and services that Europeans could produce, so the value of silver coins declined. Put differently, prices rose. Between 1550 and 1600, they doubled in many parts of Europe and rose another 50 percent in the next half century. Farmers got more for their produce, and merchants thrived on the increased circulation of goods. But artisans, laborers, and landless agricultural workers (the vast majority of the people) suffered when wages did not keep up with rising prices.

Overall, the price revolution brought a major redistribution of wealth and increased the number of people in western Europe living at the margins of society. It thus built up the pressure to emigrate to the Americas. At the same time, rising prices stimulated commercial development. Expansion overseas fed expansion at home and intensified changes toward capitalist modes of production already under way in the sixteenth century.

While the Spaniards organized their overseas empire around the extraction of silver from the highlands of Mexico, Bolivia, and Peru, the Portuguese staked their future on sugar production in Brazil. Spanish colonial agriculture supplied the huge mining centers, but the Portuguese, using cultivation techniques developed earlier on their Atlantic islands, produced sugar for export markets.

Whereas Spanish mining operations rested primarily on the backs of the native labor force, Portuguese sugar planters scattered the indigenous people and replaced them with platoons of African slaves. In 1570, this regimented work force produced nearly 6 million pounds of sugar annually; by the 1630s, output reached 32 million pounds per year. The sweet "drug food" revolutionized the tastes of millions of Europeans and stimulated the transporting of millions of African slaves across the Atlantic.

From Brazil, sugar production jumped to the Caribbean. Here, in the early seventeenth century, England, Holland, and France challenged Spain and Portugal. Once into the West Indies, Spain's enemies stood at the gates of the Hispanic New World empire. Through contraband trading with Spanish settlements, piratical attacks on Spanish treasure fleets, and outright seizure of Spanish-controlled islands, the Dutch, French, and English in the seventeenth century gradually sapped imperial Spain's strength.

Spain's Northern Frontier

Distinctly third in importance to Spain after Mexico, Peru, and the Caribbean islands, were the northern borderlands of New Spain—the present-day Sun Belt of the United States. Yet the early Spanish influence in Florida, the Gulf region, Texas, New Mexico, Arizona, and California indelibly marked the history of the United States. Spanish control of the southern fringes of North America began in the early 1500s and did not end for three centuries. Far outlasting the Spaniards' rule were the plants and animals they introduced to North America, ranging from sheep, cattle, and horses to weeds that crowded out native plants.

Spanish explorers began charting southeastern North America in the early sixteenth century. First came Juan Ponce de León's expeditions to Florida in 1515 and 1521 and a short-lived settlement in South Carolina in 1526. For the next half century, Spaniards planted small settlements as far north as Chesapeake Bay. The Spanish traded some with the natives, but the North American coast, especially Florida, was chiefly important to the Franciscan friars, who attempted to gather the local tribes into mission villages and convert them to Catholicism.

The Spanish made several attempts to bring the entire Gulf of Mexico region under their control. From 1539 to 1542, Hernando de Soto, a veteran of Pizarro's army, led a military expedition deep into the homelands of the Creeks and Choctaws and explored from Tampa Bay to Arkansas.

De Soto's expedition could not provide what the Spanish most wanted—gold. Pillaging Indian villages and seizing food supplies, de Soto's men cut a brutal swath, and disease followed everywhere they went. The Spanish were paving the way for later English-speaking conquerors by spreading lethal microbes that devastated Indian societies and broke up the great chiefdoms of the Southeast.

In 1559, Spaniards again marched northward from Mexico in an attempt to establish their authority in the lower Gulf region. Everywhere they went, they enslaved Indians to carry provisions. In 1565, they sought to secure Florida. Building a fort at St. Augustine, they evicted their French rivals 40 miles to the north. St. Augustine became the center of Spain's northeastern frontier, and Florida remained Spanish for more than two centuries.

The Southwest became a more important region of early Spanish activity in North America. Francisco Vásquez de Coronado explored the region from 1540 to 1542. He never found the fabulous Seven Cities of Cíbola, reported by earlier Spanish explorers. But he opened much of Arizona, New Mexico, and Colorado to eventual Spanish control, happened upon the Grand Canyon, and probed as far north as the Great Plains.

The Southwest, like Florida and the Gulf region, had no golden cities. In New Mexico, however, Franciscans tried to harvest souls. A half century after Coronado's exploratory intrusions, Juan de Oñate led 400 Spanish soldiers and ten Franciscan friars up the Rio Grande in 1598 to find some 60,000 Pueblos gathered in scores of settled towns where for centuries they had been practicing agriculture. For the next 80 years, the Franciscans tried to graft Catholicism onto Pueblo culture by building churches on the edges of ancient native villages. As long as the priests were content to overlay Indian culture with a Catholic veneer, they encountered little resistance. The Pueblos wanted Spanish military protection from their Apache enemies and valued access to mission livestock and grain during years of drought. So, outwardly, they professed the Christian faith. But secretly the Pueblo still adhered to their traditional religion.

ENGLAND LOOKS WEST

By the time England awoke to the promise of the New World, Spain and Portugal were firmly entrenched there. But by the late sixteenth century, conditions that would propel England overseas had ripened. During the seventeenth century, the English, as well as the Dutch and French, began overtaking their southern European rivals. The first challenge came in the Caribbean, where between 1604 and 1640 the English planted several small colonies producing tobacco and later sugar. Few guessed that some relatively unproductive settlements then being planted on the North American mainland would become some of England's most prized possessions.

England Challenges Spain

England was the slowest of the Atlantic powers to begin exploring and colonizing the New World. Although far more numerous than the Portuguese, the English in the fifteenth century had little experience with long-distance trade and relatively few contacts with cultures beyond their island. Only the voyages of John Cabot (the Genoa-born Giovanni Caboto) gave England any claim in the New World sweepstakes. But Cabot's voyages to Newfoundland and Nova Scotia a few years after Columbus's first voyage—the first northern crossing of the Atlantic since the Vikings—were never followed up.

At first, England's interest in the far side of the Atlantic centered primarily on fish. This high-protein food, basic to the European diet, was the gold of the North Atlantic. Early North Atlantic explorers found the waters off Newfoundland and Nova Scotia teeming with fish, not only the ordinary cod but also the delectable salmon. But the fishermen of Portugal, Spain, and France, more than those of England, began making annual spring trips to the offshore fisheries in the 1520s. Not until the end of the century would the French and English drive Spanish and Portuguese fishermen from the Newfoundland banks.

Exploratory voyages along the eastern coast of North America were launched not by the English but by the French. Between 1524 and 1535, the king of France sent Jacques Cartier and Giovanni da Verrazano across the Atlantic to find straits so that India-bound ships could sail around the northern land mass (still thought to be an island). The two navigators encountered many Indian tribes, charted the coastline from the St. Lawrence River to the Carolinas, and realized that the northern latitudes of North America were suitable for settlement. But they found nothing of immediate value. The time had not yet arrived when Europeans would want to settle in America, rather than merely extract its riches.

Changes in the late sixteenth century, however, propelled the English overseas. The rising production of woolen cloth, a mainstay of the English economy, had sent merchants scurrying for new markets after 1550. Their success in establishing trading companies in Russia, Scandinavia, the Middle East, and India vastly widened England's commercial orbit and raised hopes for developing still other spheres. Meanwhile, population growth and rising prices depressed the economic conditions of ordinary people and made them look across the ocean for new opportunities.

The cautious policy of Queen Elizabeth I, who ruled from 1558 to 1603, did not include promoting overseas colonies. She favored Protestantism, partly as a vehicle of national independence. Ambitious and talented, she had to contend with Philip II, the fervently Catholic king of Spain. Regarding Elizabeth as a Protestant heretic, Philip plotted incessantly against her. The pope added to Catholic-Protestant tensions in England by excommunicating Elizabeth in 1571 and absolving her subjects from paying her allegiance—in effect, inciting them to overthrow her.

The smoldering conflict between Catholic Spain and Protestant England broke into open flames in 1587. Two decades before, Philip II had sent 20,000 Spanish soldiers into his Netherlands provinces to suppress Protestantism. Then, in 1572, he had helped arrange the massacre of thousands of French Protestants. By the 1580s, Elizabeth was providing covert aid to the Protestant Dutch revolt against Catholic rule. Philip vowed to crush the rebellion and decided as well to attack England in order to wipe out this growing center of Protestant power.

Elizabeth fed the flames of the international Catholic-Protestant conflict in 1585 by sending 6,000 English troops to aid the Dutch Protestants. Three years later, Philip dispatched a Spanish Armada of 130 ships carrying 30,000 men and 2,400 artillery pieces to conquer Elizabeth's England. For two weeks in the summer of 1588 a sea battle raged off the English coast. A motley collection of smaller English ships, with the colorful sea dog Francis Drake in the lead, defeated the Armada, sinking many of the lumbering Spanish galleons and then retiring as the legendary "Protestant wind" blew the crippled Armada into the North Sea.

The Spanish defeat prevented a crushing Catholic victory in Europe and brought a temporary stalemate to the religious wars. It also solidified Protestantism in England and brewed a fierce nationalistic spirit there. Shakespeare's love of "this other Eden, this demi-paradise" summed up popular sentiments; and with Spanish naval power checked, both the English and the Dutch found the seas more open to their rising maritime and commercial interests.

The Westward Fever

In the last decades of the sixteenth century, the idea of overseas expansion captured the imagination of important elements of English society. Urging them on were two men both named Richard Hakluyt, uncle and nephew. In the 1580s and 1590s, they advertised the advantages of colonizing across the Atlantic. For nobles at court, colonies offered new baronies, fiefdoms, and estates. For merchants, the New World promised exotic produce to sell at home and a new outlet for English cloth. For militant Protestant clergy, there awaited a continent of heathen to be saved from devilish savagery and Spanish Catholicism. For the commoner, opportunity meant bounteous land, almost for the taking. The Hakluyts' pamphlets trumpeted that the time was ripe for England to break the Iberian monopoly on the New World riches.

England first attempted colonizing, however, in Ireland. In the 1560s and 1570s, the English gradually extended control over the island through brutal military conquest. Ireland became a turbulent frontier for thousands of career-hungry younger sons of gentry families, as well as landless commoners. Many of the leaders of England's initial New World colonization got their training in subjugating "savages" in Ireland.

The first English attempts at transatlantic settlement were small, feeble, and ill-fated. Whereas the Spanish encountered unheard-of wealth and scored epic victories over ancient and populous civilizations, the English at first met only failure in relatively thinly settled lands. Beginning in 1583, they mounted several unsuccessful attempts to settle Newfoundland. Other settlers, organized by Walter Raleigh, planted a settlement from 1585 to 1588 at Roanoke Island, off the North Carolina coast. They apparently perished in attacks by a local tribe after killing a tribal leader and displaying his head on a pike. Small groups of men sent out to establish a tiny colony in Guiana, off the South American coast, failed in 1604 and 1609, and another group that set down in Maine in 1607 lasted only a year. Even the colonies founded in Virginia in 1607 and Bermuda in 1612, although they would flourish in time, floundered badly for several decades.

English merchants, sometimes supported by gentry investors, undertook these first tentative efforts. They risked their capital in hopes that small-scale ventures in North America might produce the profits of their other overseas commercial ventures. They had their queen's blessing, though little royal backing in forms like subsidies or naval protection. The Spanish and Portuguese colonizing efforts were national enterprises, sanctioned, capitalized, and coordinated by the crown. By contrast, English colonies were private ventures, organized and financed by small partnerships of merchants who pooled their slender resources.

English colonization could not succeed until these first merchant adventurers solicited the wealth and support of the prospering middle class. This support grew steadily in the first half of the seventeenth century, but even then investors were drawn far more to the quick profits promised in West Indian tobacco production than to the uncertainties of mixed farming, lumbering, and fishing on the North American mainland. In the 1620s and 1630s, most of the English capital invested overseas went into establishing tobacco colonies in tiny Caribbean islands.

Apart from the considerable financing required, the vital element in launching a colony was a suitable body of colonists. About 80,000 streamed out of England between 1600 and 1640, as economic, political, and religious developments pushed them from their homeland at the same time that dreams of opportunity and adventure pulled them westward. In the next 20 years, another 80,000 departed.

Economic difficulties in England prompted many to try their luck in the New World. The changing agricultural system, combined with population growth and the unrelenting increase in prices caused by the influx of New World silver, produced a surplus of unskilled labor, squeezed many small producers, and spread poverty and crime. By the late 1500s, the roads, wrote one of the Hakluyts, were swarming with "valiant youths rusting and hurtful for lack of employment."

A generation later, beginning in 1618, the renewed European religious wars between Protestants and Catholics devastated the continental market for English woolen cloth. Unemployment stalked the textile regions. Probably half the households in England lived on the edge of poverty.

Religious persecution and political considerations intensified the pressure to emigrate from England in the early seventeenth century. How this operated in specific situations will be considered in the next chapter. The largest number of emigrants went to the West Indies. The North American mainland colonies attracted perhaps half as many, and the plantations in northern Ireland fewer still. For the first time in their history, large numbers of English people were abandoning their island homeland to carry their destinies to new frontiers.

Anticipating North America

The early English settlers in North America were far from uninformed about the indigenous people of the New World. Beginning with Columbus's first description of the New World, published in several European cities in 1493 and 1494, reports and promotional accounts circulated among the participants in early voyages of discovery, trade, and settlement. This literature became the basis for anticipating the world that had been discovered beyond the setting sun.

Colonists who read or listened to these accounts got a dual image of the native people. On the one hand, the Indians were depicted as a gentle people who eagerly received Europeans. Columbus had written of the "great amity toward us" that he encountered in San Salvador in 1492 and had described the Arawaks there as "a loving people" who "were greatly pleased and became so entirely our friends that it was a wonder to see." Verrazano, the first European to touch the eastern edge of North America, wrote optimistically about the native people in 1524. The natives, he related, "came toward us joyfully uttering loud cries of wonderment, and showing us the safest place to beach the boat."

This positive image of the Native Americans reflected both the friendly reception that Europeans often actually received and the European vision of the New World as an earthly paradise where war-torn, impoverished, or persecuted people could build a new life. The strong desire to trade with the native people also encouraged a favorable view because only a friendly Indian could become a suitable partner in commercial exchange.

A counterimage of a savage, hostile Indian, however, also entered the minds of settlers coming to North America. Like the positive image, it originated in the early travel literature. As early as 1502, Sebastian Cabot had paraded in England three Eskimos he had kidnapped on an Arctic voyage. They were described as flesh-eating savages and "brute beasts." Many other accounts portrayed the New World natives as halfmen, who lived, as Amerigo Vespucci put it, without "law, religion, rulers, immortality of the soul, and private property."

The English had another reason for believing that all would not be peace and friendship when they came ashore. For years they had read accounts of the Spanish experience in the Caribbean, Mexico, and Peru—and the story was not pretty. Many books described in gory detail the wholesale violence that occurred when

TIMELINE *Pre-Columbian epochs*

12,000 B.C. Beringian epoch ends	**6000 B.C.** Paleo-Indian phase ends	**500 B.C.** Archaic era ends	**500 B.C. –500 A.D.** Post-Archaic era in North America	**c. 1000** Norse seafarers establish settlements in Newfoundland
A.D. 1500 Kingdoms of Ghana, Mali, Songhay in Africa	**1420s** Portuguese sailors explore west coast of Africa	**1492** Christopher Columbus lands on Caribbean islands; Spanish expel Moors (Muslims) and Jews	**1494** Treaty of Tordesillas	**1497–1585** French and English explore northern part of the Americas
1498 Vasco da Gama reaches India after sailing around Africa	**1513** Portuguese explorers reach China	**1515–1565** Spanish explore Florida and southern part of North America	**1520s** Luther attacks Catholicism	**1521** Cortés conquers the Aztecs
1530s Calvin calls for religious reform	**1533** Pizarro conquers the Incas	**1540–1542** Coronado explores the Southwest	**1558** Elizabeth I crowned queen of England	**1585** Roanoke Island settlement
1588 English defeat the Spanish Armada	**1603** James I succeeds Elizabeth I	**1607** English begin settlement at Jamestown, Virginia		

Spaniard met Mayan, Aztec, or Inca. Accounts of Spanish cruelty, even genocide, were useful to Protestant pamphleteers, who labeled the Catholic Spaniards "hellhounds and wolves." Immigrants embarking for North America wondered whether similar violent confrontations awaited them.

Another factor nourishing negative images of the Indian stemmed from the Indians' possession of the land necessary for settlement. For Englishmen, rooted in a tradition of private property ownership, this presented moral, legal, and practical problems. As early as the 1580s, George Peckham, an early promoter of colonization, had admitted that the English doubted their right to take the land of others.

The problem could be partially solved by arguing that English settlers did not intend to take the Indians' land but only wanted to share it. In return, they would offer the natives the advantages of a more advanced culture and, most important, the Christian religion. This argument would be repeated for generations.

But a more ominous argument also justified English rights to native soil. By denying the humanity of the Indians, the English, like other Europeans, claimed that the native possessors of the land disqualified themselves from rightful ownership of it. "Although the Lord hath given the earth to children of men," one Englishman reasoned, "the greater part of it [is] possessed and wrongfully usurped by wild beasts and unreasonable creatures, or by brutish savages, which by reason of their godless ignorance and blasphemous idolatry, are worse than those beasts which are of the most wild and savage nature."

Defining the Native Americans as "savage" and "brutish" did not give the English arriving in Opechancanough's land the power to dispossess his people of their soil, but it armed them with a moral justification for doing so when their numbers became sufficient. Few settlers arriving in North America doubted that their technological superiority would allow them to overwhelm the indigenous people. For their part, people like Opechancanough probably perceived the arriving Europeans as impractical, irreligious, aggressive, and strangely intent on accumulating things.

✦✦✦✦✦✦

CONCLUSION

Converging Worlds

The English immigrants who began arriving on the eastern edge of North America in the early seventeenth century came late to a New World that other Europeans had been colonizing for more than a century. The first English arrivals, the immigrants to Virginia, were but a small advance wave of the large, varied, and determined fragment of English society that would flock to the western Atlantic frontier during the next few generations. Like Spanish, Portuguese, and French colonizers before them, they would establish new societies in the newfound lands in contact with the people of two other cultures—one made up of ancient inhabitants of the lands they were settling and the other composed of those brought across the Atlantic against their will. We turn now to the richly diverse founding experience of the English latecomers in the seventeenth century.

Recommended Reading

The People of America Before Columbus

Brian M. Fagan, *The Great Journey: The Peopling of Ancient America* (1987) and *Ancient North America: The Archaeology of a Continent* (1991); Nigel Davis, *The Aztecs* (1973); Marshall Sahlins, *Stone Age Economics* (1972); Philip Kopper, *The Smithsonian Book of North American Indians: Before the Coming of Europeans* (1986); Alvin M. Josephy, Jr., *America in 1492: The World of the Indian Peoples Before the Arrival of Columbus* (1992); Lynne Sebastian, *The Chaco Anasazi: Sociopolitical Evolution in the Prehistoric Southwest* (1994).

Africa on the Eve of Contact

Basil Davidson, *The African Genius* (1969); Richard Olaniyan, *African History and Culture* (1982); George E. Brooks, *Landlords and Strangers: Ecology, Society, and Trade in Western Africa, 1000–1630* (1993); Paul E. Lovejoy, *Transformations in Slavery: A History of Slavery in Africa* (1983); Roland Oliver and Anthony Atmore, *The African Middle Ages, 1400–1800* (1981); John Thornton, *Africa and Africans in the Making of the Atlantic World, 1400–1600* (1992).

Europe in the Age of Exploration

W. H. McNeill, *The Rise of the West* (1963); Ralph Davis, *The Rise of the Atlantic Economies* (1973); Carlo M. Cipolla, *Guns, Sails, and Empires: Technological Innovations and the Early Phases of European Expansion, 1400–1700* (1966); Eric Wolf, *Europe and the People Without History* (1982); J. H. Elliot, *The Old World and the New, 1492–1650* (1970); William D. Phillips, Jr., and Carla Rahn Phillips, *The Worlds of Christopher Columbus* (1992).

The Iberian Conquest of America

James Lockhart and Stuart B. Schwartz, *Early Latin America* (1983); Alfred Crosby, Jr., *The Columbian Exchange: Biological and Cultural Consequences of 1492* (1972) and *Ecological Imperialism: The Biological Expansion of Europe, 900–1900* (1986); David E. Stannard, *American Holocaust: Columbus and the Conquest of the New World* (1992); R. C. Padden, *The Hummingbird and the Hawk: Conquest and Sovereignty in the Valley of Mexico, 1503–1541* (1962); J. H. Parry, *The Spanish Seaborne Empire* (1966); C. R. Boxer, *The Portuguese Seaborne Empire, 1415–1825* (1972); M. Leon Portilla, *The Broken Spears: The Aztec Account of the Conquest of Mexico* (1962); Charles Hudson, *Knights of Spain, Warriors of the Sun: Hernando de Soto and the South's Ancient Chiefdoms* (1997).

England Looks West

Kenneth R. Andrews, *Trade, Plunder, and Settlement: Maritime Enterprise and the Genesis of the British Empire, 1480–1630* (1985); De Lamar Jensen, *Reformation Europe, Age of Reform and Revolution* (1981); Peter Laslett, *The World We Have Lost* (1971); Keith Wrightson, *English Society, 1580–1680* (1982); A. L. Rowse, *The Expansion of Elizabethan England* (1955); Nicholas P. Canny, *The Elizabethan Conquest of Ireland* (1976); David B. Quinn, *England and the Discovery of America, 1481–1620* (1974), and *Set Fair for Roanoke: Voyages and Colonies, 1584–1606* (1985); Karen Kupperman, *Roanoke: the Abandoned Colony* (1984).

CHAPTER 2

Colonizing a Continent

By 1637, after five years in New England, John Mason knew both the prospects and perils of England's new overseas frontier. In his early thirties, Mason had emigrated from southeastern England, part of the flock of a Puritan minister from the village of Dorchester. In Massachusetts, the group commemorated their origins by giving the name Dorchester to the area assigned to them. Here, six miles south of Boston, they built a simple house of worship, assigned town lots and outlying farms, and began serving their God in the wilderness of North America.

Like many Puritans, Mason had been thrilled by southern New England's game-filled forests and fish-filled streams, by the fields cleared and tilled by Algonquian agriculturists, and by the lush meadows available for grazing stock. Despite harsh winters, it seemed this might be the Promised Land where Puritan refugees could plant their New World Zion. But Mason also recognized that these lands were not vacant. From the earliest days of the Pilgrim settlers at Plymouth in 1620, it was evident that the native occupiers of the region, whose claim went back a hundred generations, stood in the way of the Puritan "errand into the wilderness."

In the fall of 1636, Mason followed many of his Dorchester friends out of Massachusetts. Wanting better land and restless with the political squabbling in the Massachusetts Bay Colony, the Dorchester settlers set out for the Connecticut River, 100 miles to the west. For 14 days, nipped by the frost, they trekked wearily along Indian paths, carrying their meager possessions. At their journey's end, they founded the town of Windsor, on the west bank of the Connecticut River.

Six months later, when his new village was no more than a collection of crude lean-tos, militia captain John Mason marched south against the Pequots. He owed his officership to military experience in the Netherlands, where thousands of English soldiers had gone in the 1620s to help the Protestant Dutch break the yoke of Catholic Spain. Now he commanded several hundred men whom the fledgling Connecticut River towns had dispatched to drive away the Pequots. In the years before the English arrival, the powerful Pequots had formed a network of tributary tribes. Finding it impossible to placate the English as they swarmed into the Connecticut River valley, the Pequots chose resistance.

At dawn on May 26, 1637, Mason and his men approached a Pequot village on the Mystic River. Supported by Narragansett allies, the English slipped into the town. After a few scuffles, Mason cried, "We must burn them," and his men began torching the Pequot wigwams. Then they rushed from the fortified village. As flames engulfed the huts, the Pequots fled, only to be cut down by English soldiers. Most of the terrified victims were noncombatants—old men, women, and children—for the Pequot warriors were preparing for war at another village about five miles away.

Before the sun rose, a major portion of the Pequot tribe had been exterminated. The resistance of the others crumbled when they heard. "It was a fearful sight to see them thus frying in the fire," wrote one Puritan, "and horrible was the stink and scent thereof; but the victory seemed a sweet sacrifice, and they gave the praise thereof to God, who had wrought so wonderfully for them." Mason himself wrote that God had "laughed at his enemies and the enemies of his people, . . . making them as a fiery oven."

✦✦✦✦✦✦

John Mason was a God-fearing Puritan, highly esteemed by his fellow colonists. His actions at the Mystic River, seven years after the great Puritan migration to New England had begun in 1630, testify that European colonization of America involved a violent clash of two cultures. We often speak of the "discovery" and "settlement" of North America by English and other European colonists. But the penetration of the eastern edge of what today is the United States might more accurately be called the "invasion of America."

Yet mixed with violence was utopian idealism. In the New World, Puritans—and countless waves of immigrants who followed them—sought both spiritual and economic renewal. Settlement in America represented a chance to escape European war, despotism, privation, and religious corruption. The New World was a place to rescue humankind from the ruins of the Old World. This chapter reconstructs the manner of settlement and the character of immigrant life in six areas of early colonization: Chesapeake Bay, southern New England, the French and Dutch area from the St. Lawrence River to the Hudson River, the Carolinas, Pennsylvania, and the Spanish toeholds on the southern fringe of the continent. The colonizers' backgrounds, ideologies, goals, and modes of settlement produced distinctly different societies in North America in the seventeenth century.

THE CHESAPEAKE TOBACCO COAST

In 1585, England gained a first foothold in a hemisphere dominated by Spanish and Portuguese colonizers. An expedition organized by the courtier Walter Raleigh scouted the Carolina coast and brought back two natives and tales of rich soil, friendly Indians, and mineral wealth. Two more voyages in 1585–1587 planted a small colony on Roanoke Island. But the enterprise failed. The voyages to Roanoke were too small and poorly financed to establish successful settlements.

The Roanoke colony also failed resoundingly as the first sustained contact between English and Native American peoples. Relations soon turned violent. In 1591, when a relief expedition reached Roanoke, no settlers could be found. Mostly likely, they had succumbed to Indian attacks. It was an ominous beginning for England's overseas ambitions.

Jamestown

In 1607, a generation after the first Roanoke expedition, a group of merchants established England's first permanent colony in North America at Jamestown, Virginia. Under a charter from King James I, they operated as a joint-stock company, selling shares of stock and using the pooled capital to finance overseas expeditions. They expected to find gold, a rewarding trade with Indians, and a water

As seen in this sixteenth-century watercolor by John White, a member of the expedition to Roanoke Island, the natives who inhabited the village of Secotan lived much like English or Irish peasants. (The British Museum)

route to China. But investors and settlers got a rude shock. Dysentery, malaria, and malnutrition carried off most of the first colonists. More than 900 settlers arrived between 1607 and 1609; only 60 survived. There were no profits.

One-third of the first immigrants were gentlemen—gold-seeking adventurers who constituted a proportion of the colony's population six times as great as did the gentry in England. Many others were unskilled servants, some with criminal backgrounds, who (said John Smith) "never did know what a day's work was." Both types adapted poorly.

The Jamestown colony was also hampered by the common assumption that Englishmen could exploit the Indians, as Cortés and Pizarro had done. But the English found that the 20,000 local Powhatan Indians were not densely settled and so could not be easily subjugated. Unlike Spain, England had sent neither an army of *conquistadores* nor an army of priests to subdue the natives. Instead, relations with some 40 small groups that the able Powhatan had united in a confederacy were bitter almost from the beginning. Powhatan brought supplies of corn to the sick and starving Jamestown colony during the first autumn. However, John Smith, whose military experience in eastern Europe had schooled him in dealing with "barbarians," raided Indian corn supplies and tried to cow the local tribes. In response, Powhatan withdrew from trade with the English. Many settlers died in the "starving times" of the first years.

Still, the Virginia Company of London poured in more money and settlers, many enticed with promises of free land after seven years' labor. In 1618, the company even offered 50 acres of land outright to anyone journeying to Virginia.

Sot Weed and Indentured Servants

To people on the margins of English society, the promise of land in America seemed irresistible. More than 9,000 crossed the Atlantic between 1610 and 1622. Yet only 2,000 remained alive at the end of that period.

Besides the offer of free land, a crucial factor in the migration was a discovery that tobacco grew splendidly in Chesapeake soil. Francis Drake's boatload of the "jovial weed," procured in the West Indies in 1586, popularized it among the upper class and launched an addiction that still ravages the world.

James I's prophetic denunciation of smoking as "loathsome to the eye, hateful to the nose, harmful to the brain, and dangerous to the lungs" failed to halt the smoking craze. The "sot weed" became Virginia's salvation. Planters shipped the first crop in 1617, and cultivation spread rapidly. Tobacco yielded enough profit for settlers to plant it in the streets and marketplace of Jamestown. By 1624, Virginia exported 200,000 pounds of the "stinking weed;" by 1638, though, the price had plummeted and the crop exceeded three million pounds. Tobacco became to Virginia in the 1620s what sugar was to the West Indies and silver to Mexico and Peru.

Tobacco required intensive care, obliging Virginia's planters to find a reliable supply of cheap labor. They found it by recruiting mostly English and Irish indentured servants, who willingly sold years of their working lives for free passage to America. About four of every five seventeenth-century immigrants to Virginia—and later, Maryland—were indentured. Nearly three-quarters of them were male, mostly 15 to 24 years old. Many had been unemployed. Others were orphans, political prisoners, or convicts who escaped the gallows by going abroad. Some were younger sons unlikely to inherit a father's farm or shop, or young men fleeing an unfortunate marriage. Others were drawn simply by the prospect of adventure. Overwhelmingly, though, indentured servants came from the lower rungs of the social ladder at home.

Perhaps one servant in 20 realized the dream of freedom and land. If malarial fevers or dysentery did not quickly kill them, they often succumbed to brutal work. Even by the middle of the seventeenth century, about half died during the first few years of "seasoning." Masters bought and sold servants as property, gambled for them, and worked them to death, for there was little motive for keeping them alive beyond their term. When servants neared the end of their contract, masters found ways to add time and were backed by courts that they controlled.

Contrary to English custom, masters often put women servants to work at the hoe. Sexual abuse was common, and servant women paid dearly for illegitimate pregnancies. The courts fined them heavily and ordered them to serve an extra year or two to repay the time lost during pregnancy and childbirth. They also deprived mothers of their illegitimate children, indenturing them out at an early age. For many servant women, marriage was the best release; many accepted the purchase of their indenture by any man who suggested marriage.

Expansion and Indian War

As tobacco production caused Virginia's population to increase, violence mounted between white colonizers and the Powhatan tribes. In 1614, the sporadic hostility of the early years ended temporarily with the arranged marriage of Powhatan's daughter, Pocahontas, to planter John Rolfe. However, the profitable cultivation of tobacco created an intense demand for land.

In 1617, when Powhatan retired, leadership of the Chesapeake tribes fell to Opechancanough. This proud and talented leader began preparing an all-out attack on his English enemies. The English murder of a Powhatan war captain and religious prophet triggered a fierce Indian assault in 1622 in which the Indians wiped out more than one-quarter of the white population and much of the colony's physical infrastructure.

The devastating attack bankrupted the Virginia Company. The king annulled its charter in 1624 and established a royal government, which allowed the elected legislative body established in 1619, the House of Burgesses, to continue lawmaking in concert with the royal governor and his council.

The Indian assault of 1622 fortified the determination of the surviving planters to pursue a ruthless new Indian policy. John Smith, writing from England two years later, noted the grim satisfaction that had followed the Indian attack. Many, he reported, believed that "now we have just cause to destroy them by all means possible." Virginians mounted annual military expeditions against native villages.

Population growth after 1630 and settlers' perpetual need for fresh acreage (tobacco quickly exhausted the soil) intensified pressure on Indian land. The tough, ambitious planters soon encroached on Indian territories, provoking war in 1644 and 1675. Greatly outnumbering their opponents, the colonists reduced the native population of Virginia to less than 1,000 by 1680. The Chesapeake tribes, Virginians came to believe, were merely obstacles in the way.

Proprietary Maryland

By the time Virginia had achieved commercial success in the 1630s, another colony on the Chesapeake took root. The founder's main aim was not profit but a refuge for Catholics and a New World version of the English manorial countryside.

George Calvert, an English nobleman, designed and promoted the new colony. Closely connected to the royal family, he had received a huge grant of land in Newfoundland in 1628, just three years after James I had made him Lord Baltimore. In 1632, Charles I, James's son, prepared to grant him a more hospitable domain of ten million acres. In honor of the king's Catholic queen Henrietta Maria, it was named Maryland.

Catholics were an oppressed minority in England, and Calvert planned his colony as a haven for them. But knowing that he needed more than a small band of Catholic settlers, the proprietor invited others, too. Catholics, never a majority in Maryland, were quickly overwhelmed by Protestants who jumped at the offer of free land with only a modest yearly fee to the Calverts.

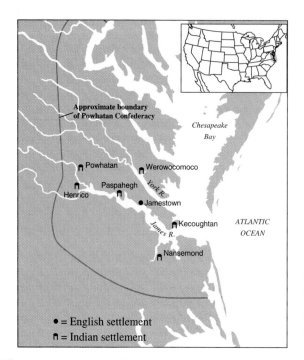

EARLY CHESAPEAKE SETTLEMENT
Only the major Indian villages in the
early 1600s are indicated on this map.
Note that the town sites are all
oriented to the rivers—the source of
both food and transportation.

Lord Baltimore died in 1632, leaving his son, Cecilius Calvert, to carry out his plans. The charter guaranteed the proprietor control over all branches of government, but young Calvert learned that his colonists would not be satisfied with fewer liberties than they enjoyed at home or could find in other colonies. Arriving in 1634, immigrants ignored plans for 6,000-acre manors for Calvert relatives and 3,000-acre manors for lesser aristocrats, each worked by serflike tenants. The settlers took up their free land, imported as many indentured servants as they could afford, maintained generally peaceful relations with Indians, grew tobacco on scattered riverfront plantations like their Virginia neighbors, and governed themselves locally as much as possible. Although Maryland grew slowly at first—in 1650, it had a population of only 600—it developed rapidly in the second half of the seventeenth century. By 1700, its population of 33,000 was half that of Virginia.

Daily Life on the Chesapeake

Most immigrants found Chesapeake life dismal. Only a minority could marry and rear a family, because marriage had to be deferred until the indenture was completed. And there were three times more men than women. Marriages were fragile. Either husband or wife was likely to die of disease within about seven years. The vulnerability of pregnant women to malaria frequently terminated marriages, and death claimed half the children born before they reached adulthood. Few children had both parents alive while growing up. Grandparents were almost unknown.

In a society so numerically dominated by men, widows were prized and remarried quickly. Such conditions produced complex families, full of stepchildren and stepparents, half-sisters and half-brothers. Cases existed of families of half-siblings, headed by parents to whom some of the children were not biologically related.

Plagued by horrendous mortality, the Chesapeake remained, for most of the seventeenth century, a land of immigrants rather than of settled families. Churches and schools took root very slowly. The large number of indentured servants further destabilized community life. Strangers in a household, they served their time and moved on, or died, replaced by other strangers fresh from England.

The region's architecture reflected the difficult conditions. Life was too uncertain, the tobacco economy too volatile, and the desire to invest every spare shilling in field labor too great for men to build grandly. Even by the early eighteenth century, most Chesapeake families lived in a crude house without interior partitions. Eating, dressing, working, and loving all took place with hardly a semblance of privacy. For nearly two centuries, most ordinary Virginians and Marylanders were "pigg'd lovingly together," as one planter put it. Even prosperous planters did not begin constructing fully framed, substantial homesteads until a century after the colony was founded.

The crudity of life also showed in the household possessions of the Chesapeake colonists. Struggling farmers and tenants were likely to own only a straw mattress, a simple chest, and the tools for food preparation and eating. Most ordinary settlers owned no chairs, dressers, plates, or silverware. To be near the top of Chesapeake society meant having three or four rooms, sleeping more comfortably, sitting on chairs rather than squatting on the floor, and owning chamber pots, candlesticks, bed linen, a chest of drawers, and a desk. Only a few boasted such luxuries as clocks, books, punch bowls, wine glasses, and imported furniture. Four generations elapsed in the Chesapeake settlements before the frontier quality of life slowly gave way to more refined living.

MASSACHUSETTS AND ITS OFFSPRING

While some English settlers in the reign of James I (1603-1625) scrambled for wealth on the Chesapeake, others in England looked to the wilds of North America as a place to build a tabernacle to God. The society they fashioned aimed at unity of purpose and utter dedication to reforming the corrupt world. American Puritanism would powerfully affect the nation's history, especially by nurturing a belief in America's special mission in the world. But it also represented a visionary attempt to banish diversity on a continent where the arrival of streams of immigrants from around the globe was destined to become the primary phenomenon.

Puritanism in England

England had been officially Protestant since 1558. Many English in the late sixteenth century, however, thought the Church of England was still riddled with Catholic vestiges. Because they wished to purify the Church of England, they were dubbed Puritans.

People attracted to the Puritan movement were not only religious reformers, but also men and women who hoped to find in religion an antidote to the changes

Houses

Homesteading is central to our national experience. For 300 years after the founding of the first colonies, most Americans were involved in taming and settling the land. On every frontier, families faced the tasks of clearing the fields, beginning farming operations, and building shelter for themselves and their livestock. The kinds of structures they built depended on available materials, their resources and aspirations, and their notions of a "fair" dwelling. The plan of a house and the materials used in its construction reveal much about the needs, resources, priorities, and values of the people who built it.

By examining the remains of early houses built by European settlers, historians are reaching new understandings of the social life of pioneering societies. Studies of early housing in the Chesapeake Bay and New England regions show a familiar sequence of house types—from temporary shanties and lean-tos to rough cabins and simple frame houses to larger and more substantial dwellings of brick and finished timber. This hovel-to-house-to-home pattern has existed on every frontier as sodbusters, gold miners, planters, and cattle raisers secured their hold on the land and then struggled to move from subsistence to success.

What is striking in the findings of the Chesapeake researchers is the discovery that the second phase in the sequence—the use of temporary, rough-built structures—lasted for more than a century. Whereas many New Englanders had rebuilt and extended their temporary clapboard houses into timber-framed, substantial dwellings by the 1680s, Chesapeake planters continued to construct small, rickety buildings that had to be repaired or replaced every 10 to 15 years.

Historians have puzzled over this contrast between the architecture of the two regions. Part of the explanation may lie in the different climatic conditions and different immigration patterns of New England and the Chesapeake. In the southern region, disease carried off thousands of settlers in the early decades. The imbalance of men and women produced a stunted and unstable family life, hardly conducive to an emphasis on constructing fine homes. In New England, good health prevailed almost from the beginning, and the family was at the core of the Puritan value system. It made more sense in this climatic and religious environment to make a substantial investment in larger and more permanent houses. Some historians argue, moreover, that the Puritan work ethic impelled New Englanders to build solid homes—a compulsion unknown in the culturally backward, "lazy" South.

Archaeological evidence combined with data recovered from land, tax, and court records, however, suggests another reason for the impermanence of housing in the Chesapeake region. Living in a labor-intensive tobacco world, planters large and small economized on everything possible in order to buy as many indentured servants and slaves as they could. Better to live in a shanty and have ten slaves than to have a mansion and nobody to cultivate the fields. As late as 1775, the author of American Husbandry calculated that in setting up a tobacco plantation, five times as much ought to be spent on purchasing 20 black fieldhands as on the "house, offices, and tobacco-house."

Reconstructed Chesapeake planter's house, typical of such simply built and unpainted structures in the seventeenth century. (Photograph by Julie Roy Jeffrey)

Only after the Chesapeake region had emerged from its prolonged era of mortality and gender imbalance and a mixed economy of tobacco, grain, and cattle had replaced the tobacco monoculture did the rebuilding of the region begin. Excavated house sites indicate that this occurred only after about 1720 when substantial mansions of the sort we have always associated with the planter aristocracy began to rise. New research is revealing that the phases of home building and the social and economic history of a society were closely interwoven. What do houses today reveal about the resources, economic livelihood, priorities, and values of contemporary Americans? Do class and regional differences in house design continue?

sweeping over English society. The growth of turbulent cities, the increase of wan-
dering poor, rising prices, and accelerating commercial activity made them fear for
the future and long for restraining institutions and values.

The concept of the individual operating as freely as possible, maximizing both
opportunities and personal potential, is at the core of our modern beliefs and
behavior. But many in Elizabethan England dreaded the crumbling of traditional
restraints. They wanted to preserve the notion of community—the belief that
people were bound together by reciprocal rights and responsibilities. Symptoms of
the "degeneracy of the times" included the defiling of the Sabbath by maypole
dancing, card playing, fiddling, and bowling. Puritans vowed to reverse the march
of disorder by imposing a new discipline.

One part of the Puritan plan was a social ethic stressing work as a primary way
of serving God. This emphasis on work made the religious quest of every member
of society equally worthy. The "work ethic" would banish idleness and impart
discipline throughout the community. Second, Puritans organized themselves into
congregations where each member hoped for personal salvation but also supported all others in their quest. Third, Puritans assumed responsibility for coercing and
controlling "unconverted" people around them.

In 1603, James VI of Scotland succeeded his cousin Elizabeth, becoming James
I of England. As king and head of the Church of England, he claimed to be responsible only to God, and he clashed with the Puritans. They occupied the pulpits in
hundreds of churches, gained control of several colleges at Oxford and Cambridge,
and recruited many followers. Puritans obtained many seats in Parliament and
aggressively challenged royal power. James responded by harassing them, firing
dozens of Puritan ministers, and threatening many others.

When Charles I succeeded to the throne in 1625, the situation worsened for
Puritans. Determined to strengthen the monarchy and stifle dissent, the king sum-
moned a new Parliament in 1628 and one year later adjourned this venerable body
(which was the Puritans' main instrument of reform) when it would not accede to
royal demands.

By 1629, as the king began ruling without Parliament, many Puritans were
turning their eyes to northern Ireland, Holland, the Caribbean, and, especially,
North America. They were convinced that God intended them to carry their religious and social reforms beyond the reach of persecuting authorities. A declining
economy added to their discouragement about England, for the depression in the
cloth trades was most severe in Puritan strongholds. To some distant shore, many
Puritans decided, they should transport a fragment of English society and complete the Protestant Reformation.

Puritan Predecessors in New England

Puritans were not the first Europeans to reach northeastern North America.
Fishermen of various European nations had been fishing off Newfoundland and
drying the cod they caught on the coast of Cape Cod and Maine since the early
1500s. They frequently made contact with the Algonquian-speaking tribes of the
area. A short-lived attempt at settlement in Maine had also been made in 1607.
Seven years later, the aging Chesapeake war dog John Smith coined the name
"New England."

No permanent settlement took root, however, until the Pilgrims—actually outnumbered by non-Pilgrims—arrived in Plymouth in 1620. Unlike the Puritans who followed, these humble Protestant farmers did not expect to convert a sinful world. Rather, they wanted to be left alone to realize their radical vision of a pure and primitive life. Instead of reforming the Church of England, they left it. They had first fled from England to Amsterdam in 1608, then to Leyden when they found the commercial capital of Holland too corrupt, and, finally, in 1620, to North America.

Arriving at Cape Cod in November 1620, the Pilgrims were weakened by a stormy nine-week voyage and ill-prepared for the harsh winter ahead. By the following spring, half the *Mayflower* passengers were dead, including 13 of the 18 married women.

The survivors, led by staunch William Bradford, settled at Plymouth. Squabbles soon erupted with local Indians, whom Bradford considered "savage and brutish men." For two generations, the Pilgrims tilled the soil, fished, and tried to keep intact their religious vision. But with the much larger Puritan migration that began in 1630, the Pilgrim villages around Cape Cod Bay became a backwater of the thriving, populous Massachusetts Bay Colony, which absorbed them in 1691.

Errand into the Wilderness

In 11 ships, 1,000 Puritans set out from England in 1630 for the Promised Land, the vanguard of a movement that by 1642 brought about 18,000 colonizers to New England. Led by John Winthrop, a talented English gentleman, they operated under a royal charter to the Puritan-controlled Massachusetts Bay Company. The Puritans set about building their utopia convinced they were carrying out a divine task. "God hath sifted a nation," wrote one Puritan, "that he might send choice grain into this wilderness."

Their intention was to establish communities of pure Christians who collectively swore a covenant with God. Puritan leaders agreed to employ severe means. Civil and religious transgressors must be severely punished. They emphasized forging homogeneous communities where the good of the group outweighed individual interests.

Puritans willingly gave up freedoms that their compatriots sought. An ideology of rebellion in England, Puritanism in North America became an ideology of control—and of a powerful mission that is still part of the distinctive American self-image. As Winthrop reminded the first settlers, "we shall be as a city upon a hill [and] the eyes of all people are upon us."

As in Plymouth and Virginia, the first winter tested the strongest souls. More than 200 of the first 700 settlers perished, and 100 others, disillusioned and sickened by the forbidding climate, soon returned to England. But Puritans kept coming, settling along the rivers that emptied into Massachusetts Bay. A few years later they pushed south into what became Connecticut and Rhode Island, as well as north along the rocky coast.

Motivated by their militant work ethic and sense of mission, and led by men experienced in local government, law, and exhortation, the Puritans thrived. The early leaders of Virginia were soldiers of fortune or roughneck adventurers with predatory instincts, men who had no families or had left them at home; ordinary

John Winthrop was one of the lesser English gentry who joined the Puritan movement and in the 1620s looked westward for a new life. Always searching himself as well as others for signs of weakness, Winthrop was one of the Massachusetts Bay Colony's main leaders for many years. (American Antiquarian Society)

Chesapeake settlers were mostly young men with little stake in English society who sold their labor to cross the Atlantic. But the early leaders in Massachusetts were university-trained ministers, members of the lesser gentry, and men with a compulsion to fulfill God's prophecy for New England. Most ordinary settlers came as freemen in families. Artisans and farmers from the middle ranks of English society, they established tight-knit communities in which, from the outset, the brutal exploitation of labor rampant in the Chesapeake had no place.

An Elusive Utopia

The Puritans built a sound economy based on agriculture, fishing, timbering, and trading for beaver furs with local Indians. Even before leaving England, the directors of the Massachusetts Bay Company transformed their commercial charter into a rudimentary government. In America, they laid the foundations of self-government. Free male church members annually elected a governor and deputies from each town, who formed one house of a colonial legislature, the General Court. The other house was composed of the governor's assistants, later to be called councillors. Consent of both houses was required to pass laws.

The Puritans also established the first printing press in the English colonies and established Harvard College, which opened its doors in 1636 to train clergymen. The Puritan leaders also launched a brave attempt in 1642 to create a tax-supported school system, open to all who wanted an education.

The Puritan colony, however, suffered many of the tensions besetting people bent on human perfection. Nor did Puritans prove any better at reaching an accommodation with the Native Americans than their less pious countrymen on the

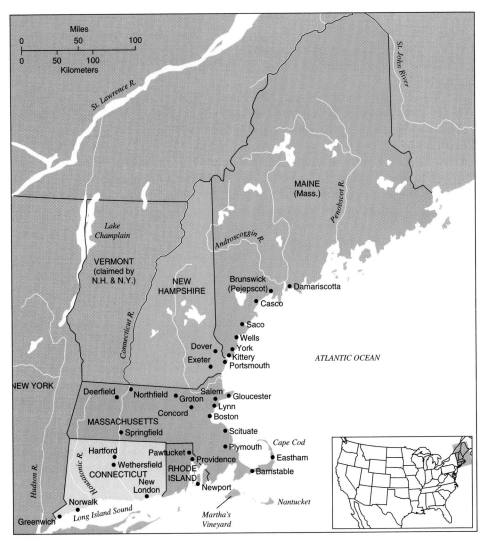

EARLY NEW ENGLAND Maine and New Hampshire became the frontier to which New England settlers migrated when their towns and farmlands became too crowded.

Chesapeake. Surrounded by seemingly boundless land, Puritans found it difficult to stifle acquisitive instincts and to keep families confined in compact communities. Those in Boston agitated for broader political rights. Winthrop wondered if the Puritans had not gone "from the snare to the pit."

Winthrop's troubles multiplied in 1633 when Salem's Puritan minister, Roger Williams, began to voice disturbing opinions. The contentious and visionary young man argued that the Massachusetts Puritans were not truly pure because they would not completely separate from the polluted Church of England (which most Puritans still hoped to reform). Williams also denounced mandatory worship and argued that government officials should not interfere with religious matters. "Coerced religion," he warned, "on good days produces hypocrites, on bad days rivers of blood." Today honored as the earliest American spokesman for the separation of church and state, Williams in 1633 seemed to strike at the heart of the Bible commonwealth, whose leaders regarded civil and religious affairs as inseparable. And Williams also charged the Puritans with illegally intruding on Indian land.

For two years, the Puritans could not quiet Williams. Finally, warned by Winthrop that he would be deported to England, Williams fled through snow with a small band of followers to found Providence, a settlement in what would become Rhode Island.

Even as they were driving Williams out, the Puritan authorities confronted another threat: a magnetic woman of extraordinary talent and intellect. Anne Hutchinson was a devout Puritan. Arriving in 1634 with her husband and seven children, she gained great respect among Boston's women as a midwife, healer, and spiritual counselor. She soon began to discuss religion, suggesting that the "holy spirit" was absent in the preaching of some ministers. Before long Hutchinson was leading a movement labeled *antinomianism,* which stressed the mystical nature of God's free gift of grace while discounting the efforts the individual could make to gain salvation.

By 1636, Boston was dividing into two camps, those who followed the male clergy and those who cleaved to the theological views of a gifted, untrained woman with no official standing. Her followers included most of the community's malcontents—merchants who chafed under the price controls the magistrates imposed in 1635, young people resisting the rigid rule of their elders, women disgruntled by male authority, and artisans who resented wage controls designed to arrest inflation. Hutchinson doubly offended the male leaders of the colony because she boldly stepped outside the subordinate position expected of women.

Determined to remove this thorn from their sides, the clergy and magistrates put Hutchinson on trial in 1637, convicting her of sedition and contempt in a civil trial. They banished her "as a woman not fit for our society." Six months later, the Boston church excommunicated her for preaching 82 erroneous theological opinions. In the last month of her eighth pregnancy, Hutchinson, with a band of supporters, followed Roger Williams's route to Rhode Island.

Ideas proved harder to banish. The magistrates could never enforce uniformity of belief, nor curb the appetite for land. Growth, geographic expansion, and commerce with the outside world all eroded the ideal of integrated, self-contained communities vibrant with piety. Leaders never wearied of reminding Puritan settlers that the "care of the public must oversway all private respects." But they faced the nearly impossible task of containing land-hungry immigrants in an expansive region. By 1636, groups of Puritans had swarmed not only to Rhode Island, but also to Hartford and New Haven, in what later became Connecticut.

New Englanders and Indians

The charter of the Massachusetts Bay Company spoke of converting the Indians to Christianity. But the instructions that Governor Winthrop carried from England reveal other Puritan thoughts about the native inhabitants. According to Winthrop's orders, all men were to receive training in the use of firearms, a reversal of the sixteenth-century English policy of disarming citizens so as to quell public disorders. New England magistrates prohibited Indians from entering Puritan towns and threatened to deport any colonist selling arms to an Indian or instructing one in their use.

Only sporadic conflict with local tribes occurred at first because disease had left much of New England vacant. Visiting English fishermen in 1616 had triggered a ferocious outbreak of respiratory viruses and smallpox that wiped out three-quarters of the population. Five years later, an Englishman exploring the area described walking through a forest where human skeletons covered the ground.

The Puritans believed that God had intervened on their side, especially when smallpox returned in 1633, killing thousands more natives and allowing new settlers to find land. Many surviving Indians welcomed the Puritans because they now had surplus land and through trade hoped to gain English protection against enemies to the north. The settler pressure for new land, however, soon reached areas untouched by disease. Land hunger mingled with the Puritan sense of mission made an explosive mix. To a people brimming with messianic zeal, the heathen Indians were a mocking challenge to the building of a religious commonwealth that would "shine as a beacon" back to decadent England. Puritans believed that God would blame them for not civilizing and Christianizing the natives, and would punish them with his wrath.

Making the "savages" of New England strictly accountable to the ordinances that governed white behavior was part of this quest for fulfilling the Puritan mission. They succeeded with the smaller, disease-ravaged tribes of eastern Massachusetts. But their attempts to control the stronger Pequots led to the bloody war in 1637 in which John Mason was a leader. The Puritan victory assured English domination over all the tribes of southern New England except the powerful Wampanoags and Narragansetts of Rhode Island, and removed the last obstacle to expansion into the Connecticut River valley. Missionary work, led by John Eliot, began among the remnant tribes in the 1640s. After a decade, about 1,000 Indians had been settled in four "praying villages," learning to live according to white ways.

The Web of Village Life

The village was the vital center of Puritan life. Unlike the spread-out Chesapeake tobacco planters, the Puritans established small, tightly settled villages. Most pursued "open field" agriculture, trudging out from the village each morning to farm narrow strips. They grazed their cattle on common meadow and cut firewood on common woodland. In other towns, Puritans used the "closed field" system of self-contained farms. Both systems recreated agricultural life in different parts of England.

In either system, families lived close together in compact towns built around a common, with its meetinghouse and tavern. These small, communal villages kept families in close touch so that each could be alert not only to its own transgressions, but also to those of its neighbors. To achieve godliness and communal unity, Puritans prohibited single men and women from living by themselves, beyond patriarchal authority and group observation. As one leader put it, "every natural man and woman is born full of sin, as full as a toad of poison." Virginia planters saw absence of restraint as a blessing. New Englanders feared it as the Devil.

In the middle of every Puritan village stood the meetinghouse. These plain wooden structures, sometimes called "Lord's barns," gathered in every soul in the village, twice a week. No man stood higher in the community than the minister. He was the spiritual leader in these small, family-based, community-oriented settlements.

The unique Puritan mixture of strict authority and incipient democracy, of hierarchy and equality, can be seen in the way the Massachusetts town distributed land and devised local government. Each town was founded by a grant of the General Court. Only groups of Puritans who had signed a compact signifying their unity of purpose received settlement grants.

After receiving a grant, townsmen met to parcel out land. They awarded individual grants according to the size of a man's household, his wealth, and his usefulness to the church and town. Such a system perpetuated existing differences in wealth and status. But Puritans believed that the community's welfare transcended individual ambitions or accomplishments and that unity demanded limits on the accumulation of wealth. Every family should have enough land to sustain it, and prospering men were expected to use their wealth for the community's benefit. Repairing the meetinghouse, building a school, aiding a widowed neighbor—such were the proper uses of wealth.

Having felt the sting of centralized power in church and state, Puritans emphasized local exercise of authority. Until 1684, only male church members could vote. These voters elected selectmen, who allocated land, passed local taxes, and settled disputes. Once a year, all townsmen gathered for the town meeting, at which citizens selected town officers for the next year and decided matters large and small.

The predominance of families lent cohesiveness to Puritan village life. Strengthening this family orientation was the remarkably healthy environment of the Puritans' "New Israel." Whereas the germs carried by English colonizers devastated neighboring Indian societies, the effect on the newcomers of entering a new environment was the opposite. The low density of settlement prevented infectious diseases from spreading, and the isolation of inland New England villages from the Atlantic commerce, along which diseases as well as cargo flowed, minimized biological hazards.

The result was a spectacular natural increase in the population and a life span unknown in Europe. At a time when the population of western Europe was barely growing—deaths almost equaled births—the population of New England, discounting new immigrants, doubled every 27 years. The difference was not a higher birthrate. New England women typically bore about seven children during the course of a marriage, but this barely exceeded the European norm. The crucial factor was that chances for survival after birth were far greater than in England because of the healthier climate and better diet. In most of Europe, only half the babies born lived long enough to produce children themselves. Life expectancy for the population at large was less than 40 years. In New England, nearly 90 percent of the infants born in the seventeenth century survived to marriageable age, and life expectancy exceeded 60 years—longer than for the American population as a whole at any time until the early twentieth century. About 25,000 people immigrated to New England in the seventeenth century, but by 1700 they had produced a population of 100,000. By contrast, some 75,000 immigrants to the Chesapeake colonies had yielded a population of about 70,000 by the end of the century.

Women played a vital role in this family-centered society. The Puritan woman was not only a wife, mother, and housekeeper; she also kept a vegetable garden, salted and smoked meats, preserved vegetables and dairy products, spun yarn, wove cloth, and made clothes.

The presence of women and a stable family life strongly affected New England's regional architecture. As communities formed, the Puritans converted early economic gains into more substantial housing rather than investing in bound labor as Chesapeake colonists did, retarding family formation and rendering the economy unstable. In New England, well-constructed one-room houses with sleeping lofts quickly replaced early "wigwams, huts, and hovels." Families added parlors and lean-to kitchens as soon as they could. Within a half century, New England immigrants accomplished a general rebuilding of their living structures. The Chesapeake lagged far behind.

A final binding element in Puritan communities was the stress on literacy and education, eventually to become a hallmark of American society. Placing religion at the center of their lives, Puritans emphasized the ability to read catechisms, psalmbooks, and especially the Bible. In literacy, Puritans saw guarantees that they would not succumb to the savagery they perceived all around them in the new land. Through education, they could preserve their central values.

In 1642, King Charles I pushed England into revolution by violating the country's customary constitution and continuing earlier attacks against Puritans. By 1649, the ensuing civil war climaxed with the trial and beheading of the king. Thereafter, during the so-called Commonwealth period (1649–1660), Puritans in England could complete the reform of religion and society at home. Meanwhile, migration to New England abruptly ceased.

The 20,000 English immigrants who had come to New England by 1649 were scattered from Maine to Long Island. Governor Winthrop of Massachusetts and Roger Williams deplored the dispersal. Yet in this rock-strewn terrain it was natural that farmers should seek better plow land.

Although the Puritans fashioned stable communities, developed the economy, and constructed effective government, their leaders, as early as the 1640s, complained that the founding vision of Massachusetts Bay was faltering. Material concerns seemed to transcend religious commitment; the individual prevailed over the community. In 1638, the General Court declared a day of humiliation and prayer to atone for the colony's "excess idleness and contempt of authority." A generation later, the synod of 1679—a convention of Puritan churches—cried out that the "church, the commonwealth and the family are being destroyed by self-assertion."

But despite such complaints about moral laxness, New England had achieved economic success and political stability by the end of the seventeenth century. Towns functioned efficiently, poverty was uncommon, public education had been mandated, and family life was stable. If social diversity increased and the religious zeal of the founding generation waned, that was only to be expected. One second-generation Bay colonist put the matter bluntly. His minister had noticed his absence in church and found him late that day at the docks, unloading a boatload of cod. "Why were you not in church this morning?" asked the clergyman. Back came the reply: "My father came here for religion, but I came for fish."

Noah did view
The old World & new

Young Obadias,
David, Jehas,
All were pious.

Peter deny'd
His Lord, and cry'd.

Queen Esther sues,
And saves the Jews.

Young pious Ruth,
Left all for Truth.

Young Samuel dear
The Lord did fear.

Primers such as this with biblical themes
served to instill religious values as well
as literacy in the Puritan colonies.
(American Antiquarian Society)

FROM THE ST. LAWRENCE TO THE HUDSON

The New Englanders were not the only European settlers in the northern region, for both France and Holland created colonies there. While English settlers founded Jamestown, the French were resettling Canada, where they had failed in the 1540s.

France's America

Henry IV, the first strong French king in half a century, sent Samuel de Champlain to explore deep into the territory even before the English had obtained a foothold on the Chesapeake. Champlain established a small settlement in Acadia (later Nova Scotia) in 1604 and another at Quebec in 1608. French trading with Indians for furs had already begun in Newfoundland, and Champlain's settlers hoped to keep making these easy profits. But the holders of the fur monopoly in France did not encourage immigration to the colony, fearing to reduce the forests from which the furs were harvested. New France remained lightly populated.

In 1609–1610, Champlain allied with the Algonquian Indians of the St. Lawrence region in attacking their Iroquois enemies to the south, earning their eternal enmity. This drove the Iroquois to trade furs for European goods with the Dutch on the Hudson River, and when the Iroquois exhausted the furs of their own territory, they turned north and west, determined to seize forest-rich resources from the Hurons, French allies in the Great Lakes region.

As the fury of the Iroquois descended on them in the 1640s, the Hurons were decimated by epidemics that spread among them as Jesuit priests entered their villages. In the "beaver wars" of the 1640s and 1650s, the Iroquois used Dutch guns to attack Huron parties carrying beaver pelts to the French. By mid-century, Iroquois attacks had scattered the Hurons, all but ending the French fur trade and reducing the Jesuit influence to a few villages of Christianized Hurons.

The bitterness bred in these years colored future colonial warfare, driving the Iroquois to ally with the English against the French. By the mid-seventeenth century the English remained unhindered by the beleaguered French colonists, who numbered only about 400.

England Challenges the Mighty Dutch

By 1650, the Chesapeake and New England regions each had about 50,000 settlers. Between them lay the mid-Atlantic area controlled by the Dutch, who planted a small colony named New Netherland at the mouth of the Hudson River in 1624 and in the next four decades extended their control to the Connecticut and Delaware river valleys. South of the Chesapeake lay a vast territory where only the Spanish, from their mission frontier in Florida, challenged the power of Native American tribes.

Although for generations they had been the Protestant bulwarks in a mostly Catholic Europe, England and Holland became bitter commercial rivals in the mid-seventeenth century. By the time the Puritans arrived in New England, the Dutch had become the mightiest carriers of seaborne commerce in western Europe. The Dutch had also muscled in on Spanish and Portuguese transatlantic commerce, trading illegally with Iberian colonists who gladly violated their government's commercial policies in order to obtain cloth and slaves more cheaply. By 1650, the Dutch had temporarily overwhelmed the Portuguese in Brazil, and soon their vast trading empire reached southeast and east Asia.

In the western hemisphere, the Dutch West India Company's New Netherland colony was small, profitable, and multicultural. Dutch, people from all over Europe, and Africans commingled in a babel of languages and religions. Company agents fanned out from Fort Orange (Albany) and New Amsterdam (New York City), establishing a lucrative fur trade with local tribes by hooking into the sophisticated trading network of the Iroquois Confederacy as far as the Great Lakes. The Iroquois welcomed the Dutch, who were few in number, did not have voracious appetites for land, and were willing to exchange desirable goods for the pelts of animals that abounded in the vast Iroquois territory. At Albany, the center of the Dutch-Iroquois trade, relations remained peaceful and profitable for several generations because both peoples admirably served each other's needs.

Although the Dutch never settled more than 10,000 people in their mid-Atlantic colonies, their commercial and naval powers were impressive. The Virginians learned that in 1667 when brazen Dutch raiders captured 20 tobacco ships on the James River and confiscated virtually the entire tobacco crop for that year.

By 1650, England was ready to challenge Dutch maritime supremacy. Three times between 1652 and 1675, war broke out between the two Protestant competitors for control of the emerging worldwide capitalist economy. In the second and

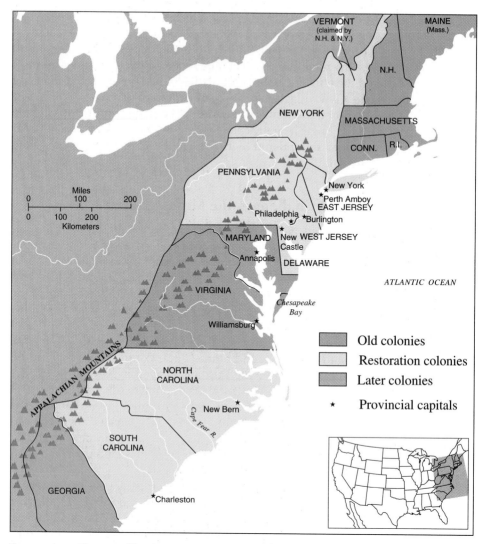

RESTORATION COLONIES: NEW YORK, THE JERSEYS, PENNSYLVANIA, AND THE CAROLINAS   After founding the Restoration colonies from the 1660s to the 1680s, England's colonists claimed the entire seaboard between Spanish Florida and French Canada.

third wars, New Netherland became an easy target for the English. They captured it in 1664. By 1675, the Dutch had been permanently dislodged from the North American mainland. But they remained powerful commercial competitors of the English around the world.

New Netherland now became New York—so named because Charles II gave it (along with the former Dutch colonies on the Delaware River) to the duke of York, his brother, later King James II. Under English rule, the Dutch settlers remained ethnically distinctive for several generations, clinging to their language, their Dutch Reformed Calvinist churches, and their architecture. In time, however, English immigrants overwhelmed the Dutch, and gradual intermarriage between Dutch, French Huguenots (Protestants), and English—the three main groups—

diluted ethnic loyalties. But New York retained its polyglot, religiously tolerant character, and its people never allowed religious concerns or utopian plans to interfere with the pragmatic conduct of business.

PROPRIETARY CAROLINA: A RESTORATION REWARD

In 1663, three years after he was restored to his father's throne, England's Charles II granted a vast territory named Carolina to a group of supporters during his years of exile. Its boundaries extended from Virginia south to central Florida and westward to the Pacific. Within this potential empire, eight London-based proprietors, including several involved in Barbados sugar plantations, gained large powers of government and semifeudal rights to the land. The system of government planned for Carolina had both feudal and modern features. To lure settlers, they promised religious freedom and land free for the asking. But onto this generous land offer, they grafted a scheme for a semimedieval government in which they, their deputies, and a few noblemen would monopolize political power. Reacting to a generation of revolutionary turbulence in England, they designed Carolina as a model of social and political stability in which a hereditary aristocracy would check boisterous small landholders.

Carolina realities bore faint resemblance to these hopes. The rugged sugar and tobacco planters who streamed in from Barbados and Virginia, where depressed economic conditions made a new beginning seem attractive, claimed their 150 acres of free land, as well as additional acreage for each family member or servant they brought. But they ignored proprietary regulations about settling in compact rectangular patterns and reserving two-fifths of every county for an appointed nobility. In government, they also did as they pleased. Meeting in assembly for the first time in 1670, they refused to accept the proprietors' "Fundamental Constitutions" and ignored orders from the proprietors' governor. Most of the settlers already knew how to run a slave society from having lived in Barbados, and from that experience they shaped local government.

The Indian Debacle

Carolina was the most elaborately planned colony in English history but the least successful in achieving harmony with the natives. The proprietors had intended otherwise. Mindful of the violence that had plagued other settlements, they projected a well-regulated Indian trade, run exclusively by their appointed agents. But the aggressive settlers from the West Indies and the Chesapeake flouted all this. Those from Barbados, accustomed to exploiting African slave labor, saw that if the major tribes of the Southeast—the Cherokees, Creeks, and Choctaws—could be drawn into trade, the planters might reap vast wealth, which the Spanish based in Florida had failed to tap.

The southern colonies' great commercial fur was the deerskin, which the farming and hunting southeastern tribes were eager to swap for European trade goods, but the business soon turned into a trade in Indian slaves. Capturing Indians for sale as slaves in New England and the West Indies became the cornerstone of commerce in Carolina in the early years, plunging the colony into a series of wars. Planters and merchants selected a tribe, armed it, and rewarded it handsomely for bringing in enemy captives. But even strong tribes found that after they had used English guns to enslave their weaker neighbors, they themselves were scheduled for elimination. The colonists claimed that "thinning the barbarous Indian natives" was needed to make room for white settlement, and by the early eighteenth century the two main tribes of the coastal plain were nearly extinct.

Early Carolina Society

Carolina's fertile land and warm climate convinced many that it was a "country so delicious, pleasant, and fruitful that were it cultivated doubtless it would prove a second Paradize." In came Barbadians, Swiss, Scots, Irish, French Huguenots, English, and migrants from northern colonies. But far from creating paradise, these people clashed abrasively in an atmosphere of fierce competition, ecological exploitation, brutal race relations, and stunted social institutions. Decimating the coastal Indians made it easier to expand the initial settlements around Charleston. And after much experimentation, the planters found a profitable staple crop that would flourish in this forbidding environment: rice.

Rice cultivation required backbreaking labor to drain swamps, build dams and levees, and hoe, weed, cut, thresh, and husk the crop. Many early settlers had owned African slaves in Barbados, so their early reliance on slave labor came naturally. On widely dispersed plantations, black labor came to predominate. In 1680, four-fifths of South Carolina's population was white, but by 1720, in a colony grown to 18,000, black slaves outnumbered whites two to one.

As in Virginia and Maryland, the low-lying areas of coastal Carolina were so disease-ridden that population grew slowly in the early years. "In the spring a paradise, in the summer a hell, and in the autumn a hospital," remarked one traveler.

This painting of Mulberry Plantation in South Carolina shows the mansion house, built in 1708, and rows of slave huts constructed in an African style. Most enslaved Africans lived in far more primitive structures in the eighteenth century. (Gibbes Museum)

Malaria and yellow fever, especially dangerous to pregnant women, were the main killers that retarded population growth, and the scarcity of women further limited natural increase. Like the West Indies, the rice-growing region of Carolina was at first more a place to accumulate a fortune than to rear a family.

In healthier northern Carolina, a different kind of society emerged amid the pine barrens along a sandy coast. Settled largely by small tobacco farmers from Virginia, the Albemarle region developed a mixed economy of livestock grazing, tobacco and food production, and the extraction of naval stores—lumber, turpentine, resin, pitch, and tar. In 1701, North and South Carolina became separate colonies, but their distinctiveness had already emerged. Slavery took root slowly in North Carolina, which was still 85 percent white in 1720. North Carolina had the potential for sustained growth: a healthier climate and settlement by families rather than slave-owning single men. But in North as well as South Carolina, settlement patterns, ethnic and religious diversity, and a lack of shared assumptions about social and religious goals inhibited the growth of a strong corporate identity.

THE QUAKERS' PEACEABLE KINGDOM

Of all the utopian dreams imposed on the North American landscape in the seventeenth century, the most remarkable was the Quakers'. During the English civil war, the Society of Friends, as Quakers called themselves, had sprung up as one of the many radical sects searching for a juster society and a purer religion. Their visionary ideas and defiance of civil authority cost them dearly in fines, brutal punishment, and imprisonment. After Charles II and Parliament stifled radical dissent in the 1660s, they, too, sent many converts across the Atlantic. The society they founded in Pennsylvania foreshadowed more than any other colony the religious and ethnic pluralism of the future United States.

The Early Friends

Like Puritans, Quakers regarded the Church of England as corrupt. But Quakers went much further, rejecting all Church institutions and holding that every believer could find grace through the "inward light," a redemptive spark in every human soul. Rejecting original sin and predestination, Quakers offered a radical alternative to Calvinism. Other Protestants regarded them as dangerous fanatics, for the Quakers' doctrine of the "light within" took precedence even over Scripture and elevated all lay people to the position of the clergy.

Garbing themselves in plain black cloth and practicing civil disobedience, the Quakers also threatened social hierarchy and order. They refused to observe the customary marks of deference, such as doffing one's hat to a superior, believing that God made no social distinctions. They used the familiar *thee* and *thou* instead of the deferential *you*, they resisted taxes supporting the Church of England, and they refused to sign witnesses' oaths on the Bible. Most shocking, they renounced the use of force in human affairs and refused to perform militia service.

Quakers also affronted traditional views when they insisted on the spiritual equality of the sexes and the right of women to participate in church matters on an equal, if usually separate, footing with men. Quaker leaders urged women to preach and to establish separate women's meetings. Among Quakers who went out from England to proclaim the inward light, 26 of the first 59 to cross the Atlantic were women. All but four of them were unmarried or without their husbands and therefore living, traveling, and ministering outside male authority.

Intensely committed to converting the world, Quakers ranged westward to North America and the Caribbean in the 1650s and 1660s. Nearly everywhere, they faced jeers, prison, mutilation, deportation, and death. The Puritan magistrates of Massachusetts in 1659 hanged two Quaker men on the Boston Common, threatening to do the same to Mary Dyer, an old woman who had followed Anne Hutchinson a quarter century before. Led from the colony, she returned the next year, undaunted, to meet her death at the end of a rope.

Early Quaker Designs

By the 1670s, the English Quakers were looking for a place in the New World to realize their millennial dreams and escape severe repression. They found a leader in William Penn. His decision to identify with this radical and persecuted sect was surprising, for he was son of Sir William Penn, the admiral who had captured Jamaica from Spain in 1654. But in 1666, the 23-year-old Penn was converted to Quakerism and thereafter devoted himself to the Friends' cause.

In 1674, Penn joined other Friends in establishing an American colony, West Jersey. They had bought the land from one of the proprietors of New Jersey, itself a new English colony recently carved out of the former New Netherland. For West Jersey, Penn helped fashion a constitution—extraordinarily liberal for its time—that allowed virtually all free males to vote for legislators and local officials. Settlers were guaranteed freedom of religion and trial by jury. As Penn and the other trustees of the colony explained, "We lay a foundation for [later] ages to understand their liberty as men and Christians, that they may not be brought in bondage, but by their own consent; for we put the power in the people."

The last phrase, summing up the document, would have shocked anyone of property and power in England or America at the time. Most regarded "the people" as ignorant, dangerous, certain to bring society to a state of anarchy if allowed to rule themselves. Nowhere in the English world had ordinary citizens, especially those who owned no land, enjoyed such extensive privileges. Nowhere had a popularly elected legislature received such broad authority.

West Jersey sputtered at first. Only 1,500 immigrants arrived in the first five years, and for several decades the colony was preoccupied with legal tangles. The center of Quaker hopes lay across the Delaware River, where in 1681 Charles II granted Penn a territory almost as large as England, paying off a large royal debt to Penn's father. Charles also benefited by getting the pesky Quakers out of England. Thus Penn and the Quakers came into possession of the last unassigned segment of the eastern coast of North America, and one of the most fertile.

Pacifism in a Militant World: Quakers and Indians

On the day Penn received his royal charter for Pennsylvania, he wrote a friend, "My God that has given it to me will, I believe, bless and make it the seed of a nation." The nation that Penn envisioned was unique among colonizing schemes. Penn intended to make his colony an asylum for the persecuted, a refuge from arbitrary state power. Puritans had striven for social homogeneity and religious uniformity. In the Chesapeake and Carolina colonies, aggressive, unidealistic men had sought to exploit their lands and bondspeople. But Penn dreamed of inviting to his forested colony people of all religions and ethnicities, offering them peaceful coexistence. His state would neither claim authority over citizens' consciences nor demand military service of them.

The Quakers who began streaming into Pennsylvania in 1682 quickly absorbed earlier Dutch, Finnish, and Swedish settlers. They participated in the government by electing representatives who initiated laws. They were primarily farmers, and like colonists elsewhere they avidly acquired land, which Penn sold at reasonable rates. But unlike other colonizers, the Quakers practiced pacifism.

Even before arriving, Penn laid the foundation for peaceful relations with the Delaware tribe inhabiting his colony. "The king of the Country where I live, hath given me a great Province," he wrote to the Delaware chiefs, "but I desire to enjoy it with your Love and Consent, that we may always live together as Neighbors and friends." In this single statement Penn dissociated himself from the entire history of European colonization in the New World and from the widely held negative view of Indians. Recognizing the Indians as the rightful owners of the land included in his grant, Penn pledged not to sell one acre until he had first purchased it from local chiefs. He also promised to strictly regulate the Indian trade and to ban alcohol sales.

The Quaker accomplishment is sometimes disparaged with the claim that there was little competition for land in eastern Pennsylvania between natives and newcomers. However, a comparison between Pennsylvania and South Carolina, both established after the restoration of Charles II to the English throne in 1660, shows the power of pacifism. A quarter century after initial settlement, Pennsylvania had a population of about 20,000 whites. Penn's peaceful policy had so impressed Native American tribes that Indian refugees began migrating into Pennsylvania from all sides. During the same 25 years, South Carolina had grown to only about 4,000 whites, while becoming a cauldron of violence.

As long as the Quaker philosophy of pacifism and friendly relations with the local Indians held sway, interracial relations in the Delaware River valley contrasted sharply with those in other parts of North America. But ironically, the Quaker policy of toleration, liberal government, and exemption from military service attracted to the colony, especially in the eighteenth century, thousands of immigrants whose land hunger and disdain for Indians undermined Quaker trust and friendship. Germans and Scots-Irish flooded in, swelling the population to 31,000 by 1720. Neither shared Quaker idealism about racial harmony. Driven from their homelands by hunger and war, they pressed inland and, sometimes encouraged by the land agents of Penn's heirs, encroached on the lands of the local tribes. This created conflict with the natives who had sought sanctuary in Pennsylvania. By the mid-eighteenth century, a confrontation of displaced people, some red and some white, was occurring in Pennsylvania.

Building the Peaceable Kingdom

Although Pennsylvania came closer to matching its founder's goals than any other European colony, Penn's dreams never completely materialized. Nor could he convince people to settle in compact villages, which he believed necessary for his "holy experiment." Instead, they created open country networks without any particular centers or boundaries. Yet a sense of common endeavor persisted.

Quaker farmers prized family life and emigrated almost entirely in kinship groups. This helped them maintain their distinctive identity. So did other practices such as allowing marriage only within their society, carefully providing land for their offspring, and guarding against too great a population increase (which would cause too rapid a division of farms) by limiting the size of their families.

Pennsylvania boomed. Its countryside became a rich grainland. By 1700, Philadelphia overtook New York City in population, and a half century later it was the largest city in the colonies, bustling with artisans, mariners, merchants, and professionals.

The Limits of Perfectionism

Despite commercial success and peace with Native Americans, not all was harmonious in early Pennsylvania. Politics were often turbulent, in part because of Pennsylvania's weak leadership. Penn, a much-loved proprietor, did not tarry long to guide the colony, leaving a leadership vacuum.

A more important cause of disunity resided in the Quaker attitude toward authority. In England, balking at authority was almost a daily part of Quaker life. But in Pennsylvania, the absence of persecution eliminated a crucial binding element from Quaker society. Quakers developed an intense factionalism, demonstrating that people never unify so well as when under attack. Rather than looking inward and banding together, they looked outward in an environment filled with opportunity. Their squabbling filled Penn with dismay.

At the same time, Quaker industriousness and frugality helped produce great material success. After a generation, social radicalism and religious evangelicalism began to fade. As in other colonies, settlers discovered the door to prosperity wide open, and in they surged.

Pennsylvania, it is said, was the first community since the Roman Empire to allow people of different national origins and religious persuasions to live together under the same government on terms of near equality. Their relations may not always have been friendly, but few attempts were made to discriminate against dissenting groups. Pennsylvanians thereby laid the foundations for the pluralism that was to become the hallmark of American society.

NEW SPAIN'S NORTHERN FRONTIER

Spain's outposts in Florida and New Mexico, preceding all English settlements on the eastern seaboard, fell into disarray between 1680 and the early eighteenth century, just as England's colonies were sinking deep roots. Trying to secure a vast northern frontier with only small numbers of settlers, the Spanish relied on forced Indian labor. This reliance proved to be their undoing in Florida and New Mexico.

Popé's Revolt

During the 1670s, when the Franciscans developed a new zeal to root out traditional Indian religious ceremonies, the Pueblo people turned on the Spanish

TIMELINE

1590	1607	1616–1621	1617	1619
Roanoke Island colony fails	Jamestown settled	Native American population in New England decimated by European diseases	First tobacco crop shipped from Virginia	First Africans arrive in Jamestown
1620	**1622**	**1624**	**1630**	**1632**
Pilgrims land at Plymouth	Powhatan tribes attack Virginia settlements	Dutch colonize mouth of Hudson River	Puritan immigration to Massachusetts Bay	Maryland grant to Lord Baltimore (George Calvert)
1633–1634	**1635**	**1636**	**1637**	**1642–1649**
Native Americans in New England again struck by European diseases	Roger Williams banished to Rhode Island	Anne Hutchinson exiled to Rhode Island	New England wages war against the Pequot people	English civil war ends great migration to New England
1643	**1659–1661**	**1660**	**1663**	**1664**
Confederation of New England	Massachusetts Puritans hang three Quaker men and one Quaker woman	Restoration of King Charles II in England	Carolina charter granted to eight proprietors	English capture New Netherland and rename it New York; Royal grant of the Jersey lands to proprietors
1680	**1681**			
Popé's revolt in New Mexico	William Penn receives Pennsylvania grant			

intruders. In years of harsh rule, the Spanish had extracted tribute labor from the Pueblo people, who at the same time suffered the ravaging effects of European diseases. Both of these punishing long-term effects contributed to Pueblo alienation. But pushing the Pueblos to the edge was an assault on their religion. Launching a campaign to restrict native religious ceremonies in the 1670s, the Spanish friars began to seize the Pueblo *kivas* (underground ceremonial religious chambers), to forbid native dances, and to destroy priestly Indian masks and prayer sticks. In August 1680, led by the medicine man Popé, about two dozen Pueblo villages scattered over several hundred miles rose up in fury. They burned Spanish ranches and government buildings, systematically desecrated and destroyed churches, lay waste to Spanish fields, and killed half the friars.

The Spaniards abandoned the Southwestern frontier for more than a decade. Only in 1694 did a new Spanish governor regain Santa Fe and gradually subdue most of the Pueblo. Learning from the rebellion, the Spanish declared a kind of cultural truce, easing demands for Pueblo labor service and tolerating certain Pueblo rituals in return for nominal Christianization. There was still tension, but the Pueblo had to come to terms with the Spanish because of their need for defense against their old enemies-the Navajos, Utes, and Apaches.

Decline of Florida's Missions

The Franciscan missions in Florida were as severely pummeled as those in New Mexico in the late seventeenth and early eighteenth centuries. Rapidly settling in South Carolina, the English were eager to use Indian allies to attack the Spanish Indian villages and sell the captives into slavery. The resentment of missionized Indians, wearying under demands on their labor, further weakened the tenuous Spanish hold on them. The attacks of Carolinians in the early 1680s destroyed a number of Spanish missions. When England and Spain went to war in 1701— called Queen Anne's War in the colonies—the Carolinians attacked Florida. Burning mission villages to the ground, they slaughtered the Spanish friars and captured some 4,000 women and children to be sold as slaves. The Spanish mission frontier was thoroughly devastated, and only St. Augustine remained as a Spanish stronghold. Unlike New Mexico, there was no Spanish reconquest. From this time onward, English and French traders, offering more attractive trade goods, would have the main influence over Florida Indians.

✦✦✦✦✦✦

CONCLUSION

The Achievement of New Societies

Nearly 200,000 immigrants who had left their European homelands reached the coast of North America in the seventeenth century. Coming from a variety of social backgrounds and spurred by different motives, they represented the rootstock of distinctive societies that would mature in the North American colonies of England, France, Holland, and Spain. For three generations, North America served as a social laboratory for religious and social visionaries, political theorists, fortune seekers, social outcasts, and, most of all, ordinary men and women seeking a better life than they had known in their European homelands.

Nearly three-quarters of them came to the Chesapeake and Carolina colonies. Most of them found this region a burial ground rather than an arena of opportunity. Disease, stunted family life, and the harsh work regimen imposed by the planters who commanded the labor of the vast majority ended the dreams of most who came. Yet population inched upward, and the bone and sinew of a workable economy formed. In the northern colonies, to which the fewest immigrants came, life was more secure. Organized around family and community, favored by a healthier climate, and motivated by religion and social vision, the Puritan and Quaker societies thrived. Utopian expectations were never completely fulfilled. But nowhere else in the Western world at that time could they even have been attempted. What did succeed was the rooting of agricultural life based on family farms and the establishment of locally oriented political institutions marked by widespread participation. Thus, as the seventeenth century progressed, the scattered settlements along the North American coast, largely isolated from one another, as well as a few inland French and Spanish settlements, pursued their separate paths of development.

Recommended Reading

The Chesapeake Tobacco Coast

Philip D. Morgan and Jean Russo, eds., *Colonial Chesapeake Society* (1989); Edmund S. Morgan, *American Slavery, American Freedom: The Ordeal of Colonial Virginia* (1975); David B. Quinn, ed., *Early Maryland in a Wider World* (1982); Darrett B. Rutman and Anita H. Rutman, *A Place in Time: Middlesex County, Virginia, 1650–1750* (1984); James Horn, *Adapting to a New World: English Society in the Seventeenth-Century Chesapeake* (1994); Alden Vaughan, *American Genesis: Captain John Smith and the Founding of Virginia* (1975); Kathleen M. Brown, *Good Wives, Nasty Wenches, and Anxious Patriarchs: Gender, Race, and Power in Colonial Virginia* (1996).

Massachusetts and Its Offspring

Perry Miller, *Errand into the Wilderness* (1956); David Cressy, *Coming Over: Migration and Communication Between England and New England in the Seventeenth Century* (1987); David D. Hall, *Worlds of Wonder, Days of Judgment: Popular Religious Belief in Early New England* (1989); John Demos, *A Little Commonwealth: Family Life in Plymouth Colony* (1970); Kenneth Lockridge, *A New England Town* (1970); Stephen Innes, *Labor in a New Land* (1983); Darrett B. Rutman, *Winthrop's Boston* (1965); Edmund S. Morgan, *The Puritan Dilemma: The Story of John Winthrop* (1958); Robert Middlekauff, *The Mathers* (1971); Roger Thompson, *Sex in Middlesex: Popular Mores in a Massachusetts County, 1649–1699* (1986); Stephen Innes, *Creating the Commonwealth: The Economic Culture of Puritan New England* (1995); Virginia D. Anderson, *New England's Generation: The Great Migration and the Formation of Society and Culture in the Seventeenth Century* (1991).

From the St. Lawrence to the Hudson

Robert C. Ritchie, *The Duke's Province: A Study of Politics and Society in Colonial New York, 1660–1691* (1977); Joyce Goodfriend, *Before the Melting Pot: Society and Culture in Colonial New York City, 1664–1730* (1992); Michael Kammen, *Colonial New York* (1975); Daniel K. Richter, *The Ordeal of the Longhouse: The Peoples of the Iroquois League in the Era of European Colonization* (1992); Bruce G. Trigger, *Children of the Aataentsic: A History of the Huron People, 1600–1664* (1976); James Axtell, *The Invasion Within: The Contest of Cultures in Colonial North America* (1985).

Proprietary Carolina

M. Eugene Sirmans, *Colonial South Carolina* (1966); Robert M. Weir, *Colonial South Carolina* (1983); Richard Waterhouse, *A New World Gentry: The Making of a Merchant and Planter Class in South Carolina, 1670–1770* (1989); Daniel C. Littlefield, *Rice and Slaves: Ethnicity and the Slave Trade in Colonial South Carolina* (1981).

The Quakers' Peaceable Kingdom

Frederick B. Tolles, *Meeting House and Counting House: The Quaker Merchants of Colonial Philadelphia* (1948); Gary B. Nash, *Quakers and Politics: Pennsylvania, 1681–1726* (1968); J. William Frost, *The Quaker Family in Colonial America* (1972); Sharon V. Salinger, *"To Serve Well and Faithfully:" Labor and Indentured Servitude in Pennsylvania* (1987); Sally Schwartz, *A Mixed*

Multitude: The Struggle for Toleration in Colonial Pennsylvania (1987); Barry J. Levy, *Quakers and the American Family* (1988).

New Spain's Northern Frontier

David J. Weber, *The Spanish Frontier in North America* (1992); Ramon A. Gutiérrez, *When Jesus Came, the Corn Mothers Went Away: Marriage, Sexuality, and Power in New Mexico, 1500–1846* (1991); Marvin T. Smith, *Archaeology of Aboriginal Culture Change in the Interior Southeast: Depopulation During the Early Historical Period* (1987); Andrew L. Knaut, *The Pueblo Revolt of 1680* (1995); Jerald T. Milanich, *Florida Indians and the Invasion from Europe* (1995).

CHAPTER 3

Mastering the New World

Anthony Johnson, an African, arrived in Virginia in 1621 with only the name Antonio. Caught as a young man by Portuguese slavers, he eventually reached Virginia. There he was purchased by Richard Bennett and sent to work at Bennett's tobacco plantation on the James River. In the next year, Antonio came face-to-face with the world of triracial contact and conflict that would shape the remainder of his life. On March 22, 1622, the Powhatan tribes of tidewater Virginia fell on the white colonizers in a determined attempt to drive them from the land. Of the 57 people on the Bennett plantation, only Antonio and four others survived.

Antonio—anglicized to Anthony—labored on the Bennett plantation for some 20 years, slave in fact if not in law, for legally defined bondage was still in the formative stage. During this time, he married Mary, another African trapped in the labyrinth of servitude, and fathered four children. In the 1640s, Anthony and Mary Johnson gained their freedom after half a life-time of servitude. Probably then they chose a surname, Johnson, to signify their new status. Already past middle age, the Johnsons began carving out a niche for themselves on Virginia's eastern shore. By 1650, they owned 250 acres, a small herd of cattle, and two black servants. In a world in which racial boundaries were not yet firmly marked, the Johnsons had entered the scramble of small planters for economic security.

By learning the workings of the English legal process, carefully cultivating white patronage, and laboring industriously on the land, the Johnsons gained their freedom and property, established a family, warded off contentious neighbors, and hammered out a decent existence. But by the late 1650s as the lines of racial slavery tightened, the "customs of the country" began closing in on Virginia's free blacks.

In 1664, convinced that ill winds were blowing away the chances for their children and grandchildren in Virginia, the Johnsons began selling their land to white neighbors. The following spring, most of the clan moved north to Maryland, where they rented land to farm and raise cattle. Five years later, Anthony Johnson died, leaving his four children and his wife. Virginia's growing racial prejudice followed Johnson beyond the grave. A jury of white men declared that because Johnson "was a Negroe and by consequence an alien," the 50 acres he had deeded to his son Richard before moving to Maryland should go to a local white planter.

Johnson's children and grandchildren, born in America, could not duplicate the modest success of the African-born patriarch. By the late seventeenth century, people of color faced much greater difficulties in escaping slavery. When they did, they found themselves forced to the margins of society. Anthony's sons never rose higher than tenant farmer or small freeholder. John Johnson moved farther north into Delaware in the 1680s, following a period of great conflict with Native Americans in the Chesapeake region. Members of his family married local Indians, joining a triracial community that still survives. Richard Johnson stayed in Virginia.

When he died in 1689, just after a series of colonial insurrections connected with the overthrow of James II in England, he had little to leave his four sons. They became tenant farmers and hired servants on plantations owned by whites. By now, in the early eighteenth century, slave ships were pouring Africans into Virginia and Maryland to replace white indentured servants, the backbone of the labor force for four generations. To be black had at first been a handicap. Now it became a fatal disability, an indelible mark of bondage.

❖❖❖❖❖❖

Mastering the North American environment involved several processes that would echo down the corridors of American history. Prominent among them were the molding of an African labor force and the gradual subjection of Native American tribes who contested white expansion. Both developments occurred in the lifetimes of Anthony and Mary Johnson and their children. Both involved a level of violence that made this frontier of European expansion a place of growing inequality and servitude.

This chapter surveys the fluid, conflict-filled era from 1675 to 1715, a time when five overlapping struggles for mastery occurred. First, in determining to build a slave labor force, the colonists struggled to establish their mastery over resistant African captives. Second, the settlers sought mastery over Native American tribes, both those that stood in the way of white expansion and those that were their trading and military partners. Third, the colonists resisted the attempts of English imperial administrators to bring them into a more dependent relationship. Fourth, within colonial societies, emerging elites struggled to establish their claims to political and social authority. Finally, the colonizers, aided by England, strove for mastery over French, Dutch, and Spanish contenders in North America.

AFRICAN BONDAGE

For almost four centuries after Columbus's voyages, European colonizers forcibly transported Africans from their homelands and used their labor to produce wealth. At least 12 million Africans were brought to the New World, and millions more perished on the long, terrible journey. Of all the immigrants who peopled the New World between the fifteenth and eighteenth centuries, the Africans were by far the most numerous, probably outnumbering Europeans two or three to one.

Slave traders carried most blacks to the West Indies, Brazil, and Spanish America. Fewer than one out of every 20 reached North America, a fringe area for slave traders until the eighteenth century. Yet those who came to the American colonies, about 10,000 in the seventeenth century and 350,000 in the eighteenth, profoundly affected American society. In a prolonged period of labor scarcity, their labor and skills were indispensable. Their culture mixed continuously with that of their European masters. And the race relations shaped by slavery so deeply marked American society that race has ever since been one of this nation's most difficult problems.

The Slave Trade

The African slave trade began as an attempt to fill a labor shortage in the Mediterranean world. As early as the eighth century, Arab and Moorish traders had driven slaves across Saharan caravan trails to Mediterranean ports. Seven centuries later, Portuguese merchants became the first European slave traders.

Portuguese ship captains exploring the west coast of Africa tapped into a slave-trading network that had operated for many generations. Slaveholding was deeply rooted in African societies. Slaves were employed as soldiers, administrators, and even occasionally as royal advisors. Many Africans became slaves as punishment for crimes, but far more were war captives. For several centuries, the economy of the African kingdom of Dahomey leaned heavily on commerce in slaves. One former slave came to own a fleet of slave ships. But mainly the carrying trade was in the hands of Europeans.

More than anything else, sugar transformed the African slave trade. By the sixteenth century the center of production was Portugal's Atlantic island of Madeira, the first European colony organized around slave labor. From it, sugar cultivation spread to Portuguese Brazil and Spanish Santo Domingo. By the seventeenth century, with Europeans developing a taste for sugar almost as insatiable as their craving for tobacco, they vied fiercely for Caribbean islands and West African coastal trading forts. African kingdoms, eager for European trade goods, fought each other to supply the "black gold" to white ship captains.

European nations competed for West African trading rights. In the seventeenth century, when about one million Africans were brought to the New World, the Dutch replaced the Portuguese as the major supplier. In the 1690s, when they began their century-long rise to maritime greatness, the English challenged the Dutch. By the 1790s, the English were the foremost European slave traders.

Eighteenth-century European traders carried at least six million Africans to the Americas, probably the greatest forced migration in history. By then an Englishman called slavery the "strength and the sinews of this western world."

The slave trade's horrors were almost unimaginable. Olaudah Equiano, an eighteenth-century Ibo from what is now Nigeria, described how raiders from another tribe kidnapped him and his younger sister when he was only 11 years old. He passed from one trader to another while being marched to the coast. Many slaves attempted suicide or died from exhaustion or hunger. But Equiano survived. Reaching the coast, he encountered the next humiliation, confinement in barracoons, fortified enclosures on the beach where a surgeon from an English slave ship inspected him. Equiano was terrified by the light skins, strange language, and long hair of the English and was convinced that he "had got into a world of bad spirits and that they were going to kill me."

More cruelties followed. European traders often branded the African slaves. The next trauma came with the ferrying of slaves in large canoes to the ships anchored in the harbor. "The Negroes are so loath to leave their own country," wrote one Englishman, "that they have often leaped out of the canoes, boat and ship, into the sea, and kept under the water till they were drowned."

Conditions aboard the slave ships were miserable, even though the traders hoped to bring as many slaves as possible across the Atlantic alive. Manacled slaves below decks were crowded together like corpses in coffins. "With the loathsomeness of the stench, and crying together," said Equiano, "I became so sick and low that I was not able to eat, nor had I the least desire to taste anything." Slavers brutally flogged the many people who tried to kill themselves by starvation and applied hot coals to their lips. If this did not suffice, they force-fed with a mouth wrench.

The Atlantic passage usually took four to eight weeks, and one of every seven captives died en route. Many others arrived deranged or dying. In all, the relocation of any African may have averaged about six months from the time of capture to the time of arrival at the plantation of a colonial buyer, throughout which the slave was completely cut off from the moorings of a previous life. Ahead lay endless bondage.

The Southern Transition to Black Labor

English colonists on the mainland of North America at first had regarded Native Americans as the obvious source of labor. But European diseases ravaged native societies, and Indians, more at home in the environment than the white colonizers, were difficult to subjugate. Indentured white labor proved the best way to meet the demand for labor during most of the seventeenth century.

Beginning in 1619, a few Africans entered the Chesapeake colonies to labor in the tobacco fields alongside white servants. But as late as 1671, when some 30,000 slaves toiled in English Barbados, fewer than 3,000 served in Virginia. They were still outnumbered there at least three to one by white indentured servants.

Only in the last quarter of the seventeenth century did the southern labor force begin to change into one in which black slaves performed most of the field labor. Three reasons explain this shift. First, the rising commercial power of England, at the expense of the Spanish and Dutch, swelled English participation in the African slave trade. Beginning in the 1680s, southern planters could purchase slaves more readily and cheaply than before. Second, the supply of white servants from England began drying up. Third, white servant unrest and a growing population of disgruntled, landless, and potentially rebellious ex-servants led white planters to seek a more pliable labor force. By the 1730s, the number of white indentured servants had dwindled to insignificance. Black hands tilled and harvested Chesapeake tobacco and Carolina rice. Nothing had greater priority in starting a plantation than procuring slave labor.

In enslaving Africans, English colonists in North America merely copied their European rivals in the New World and emulated their countrymen on Barbados and Jamaica. There, from the 1630s on, Englishmen had used brutal repression to mold Africans into a sugar-producing, slave labor force. Virtually no seventeenth-century whites questioned the morality of slavery.

Slavery in the Northern Colonies

Slavery never became the foundation of the northern colonial work force, for labor-intensive crops such as sugar and rice would not grow in colder climates. Slavery took substantial root mainly in the cities, where slaves worked as artisans and domestic servants.

But northern colonists' economies became enmeshed in the Atlantic commercial network, which depended on slavery and the slave trade. New England's merchants eagerly pursued profits in the slave trade as early as the 1640s. By 1750 half the merchant fleet of Newport, Rhode Island, reaped profits from human cargo. In New York and Philadelphia, building and outfitting slave vessels proved

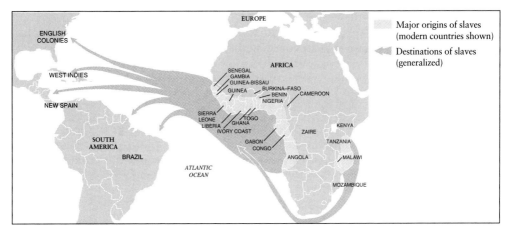

THE ORIGIN AND DESTINATION OF ENSLAVED AFRICANS, 1526–1810

profitable. New England seaports became centers for distilling that "hot, hellish and terrible liquor," rum, made from West Indian sugar and one of the principal commodities traded for slaves on the African coast. As the number of slaves in the Caribbean multiplied—from about 50,000 in 1650 to 500,000 in 1750—New England's large fishing fleet found important markets for their cod. Wheat from the middle colonies and barrel staves and hoops from North Carolina also serviced the slave-based West Indies economy. In short, every North American colony participated in the slave business.

The System of Bondage

The first Africans in the American colonies came as bound servants. They served their term, and if (like Anthony and Mary Johnson) they survived, they gained freedom. Then they could own land, hire out their labor, and move as they pleased. Their children, like those of white indentured servants, were born free.

But gradually, seventeenth-century Chesapeake planters began to draw tighter lines around the activities of black servants. By the 1640s, Virginia forbade blacks, free or bound, to carry firearms. In the 1660s, marriages between white women and black servants were banned as "shameful matches." By the end of the century, when incoming Africans increased from a trickle to a torrent, even the few free blacks found themselves pushed to the margins of society. Slavery, which had existed for centuries in many societies as the lowest social status, was in the Americas becoming a caste reserved for those with black skin. White society was turning the black servant from a human being into a chattel.

In this dehumanization of Africans, which the English largely copied from their colonial rivals, the key step was instituting hereditary lifetime service. Once servitude ended only with death, all other privileges quickly vanished. When a mother's slave condition legally passed to her newborn black infant (not the case in slavery in Africa), slavery became self-perpetuating.

Slavery was not only a system of forced labor, but also a pattern of human relationships legitimated by law. By the early eighteenth century, most provincial legislatures limited black rights. Borrowed largely from England's Caribbean colonies, "black codes" forced Africans into an ever narrower world. Slaves could not testify in court, engage in commercial activity, hold property, participate in politics, congregate, travel without permission, or legally marry or be parents. Nearly stripped of human status, they became defined as property, and gradually all legal restraints on masters' treatment of them disappeared.

Eliminating slave rights had both pragmatic and psychological dimensions. With every African in chains a potential rebel, the rapid increase in the slave population brought demands for strict control and justifications for brutality. "The planters," wrote one Englishman in Jamaica, "do not want to be told that their Negroes are human creatures. If they believe them to be of human kind, they cannot regard them as no better than dogs or horses."

Dehumanizing slaves involved one of the great paradoxes of modern history. Many Old World immigrants saw the Americas as a liberating and regenerating arena. Yet the opportunity to exploit its resources led to a historic process by which masses of people were wrenched from their homelands and forced into a system of slavery that could be maintained only by increasing intimidation and brutality.

SLAVE CULTURE

The basic struggle for Africans toiling on plantations 5,000 miles from their homes was to create strategies for living as satisfactorily as possible despite horrifying treatment. The master hoped to convert the slave into a mindless drudge who obeyed every command and worked efficiently for his profit. But attempts to cow slaves rarely succeeded completely. Masters could set the external boundaries of existence for their slaves, controlling physical location, work roles, diet, and shelter. But the authority of the master class impinged far less on slaves' private lives, in which slaves drew on their African heritage, laying foundations for an African-American culture. At first, this culture had many variations because slaves came from many areas in Africa and lived under different conditions in the colonies. But common elements emerged, led by developments in the South, where about 90 percent of American slaves labored in colonial times.

The Growth of Slavery

Arriving in North America, Africans entered a relatively healthy environment compared to other slave-labor areas in the Western Hemisphere. In the southern colonies, where the ghastly mortality of the early decades had subsided by the time Africans were arriving in large numbers, blacks' chances for survival were much better than in the West Indies or Brazil. This, as well as a more even sex ratio, led to a natural increase in the North American slave population unparalleled elsewhere. In 1675, about 4,000 slaves were scattered across Virginia and Maryland. Most were men. Together with their masters and a larger number of white indentured servants, they cleared the land, planted, hoed, and harvested tobacco. A half century later, with the decline of white servitude, 45,000 slaves labored on Chesapeake plantations. By 1760, when the number of slaves exceeded 185,000, the Chesapeake plantations relied almost entirely on black labor.

Although slave codes severely restricted the lives of slaves, the possibility for family life increased as the southern colonies matured. Larger plantations employed dozens and even hundreds of slaves, and the growth of roads and market towns permitted them greater opportunities to forge relationships beyond their own plantation. By the 1740s, a growing proportion of Chesapeake slaves were American-born, established families, and lived in plantation outbuildings where after sundown they could fashion personal lives.

In South Carolina, slaves drew on agricultural skills they had practiced in Africa and made rice the keystone of the coastal economy by the early eighteenth century. Their numbers increased rapidly, from about 4,000 in 1708 to 90,000 by 1760. Working mostly on large plantations in swampy lowlands, they endured the worst conditions on the continent. But there they also outnumbered whites three to one by 1760 and hence could maintain more of their African culture than slaves in the Chesapeake. Many spoke Gullah, a "pidgin" mixing several African languages. They often gave African names to their children and kept alive African religious customs.

In the northern colonies, slaves made up less than 10 percent of the population. They, along with occasional Indian slaves, typically worked as artisans, farmhands, or personal servants. Whereas about two-thirds of all southern slaves worked on plantations with at least ten of their fellows by the 1720s, in the North the typical slave labored alone or with only a few others. Living in the same house as the master, slaves adapted to European ways much faster than in the South. Slavery was less repressive in the North. Slaves were more widely dispersed among the white population, and black-white contact was so extensive that African culture faded more quickly.

The physical appearance of Africans captured the imaginations of some American artists. John Singleton Copley's *Head of a Negro* depicted a slave in the eighteenth century. (1777–78, Detroit Institute of Arts, Founders Society Purchase, Gibbs-Williams Fund)

Northern slavery grew fastest in the ports. Artisans invested profitably in slaves; ship captains bought them for maritime labor; an emerging elite of merchants, lawyers, and landlords displayed its wealth with slave coachmen and personal servants. By the beginning of the eighteenth century, more than 40 percent of New York City's households owned slaves. In Quaker Philadelphia, slaveholding increased sharply in the eighteenth century. Struggling white artisans resented slave workers for undercutting wages, and white citizens feared black arsonists and rebels. Yet such reservations were outweighed by high labor demand and by the advantage of purchasing lifelong servants for just two years' worth of a free white laborer's wages.

Resistance and Rebellion

Slaves not only adapted to bondage but also resisted and rebelled in ways that constantly reminded their masters that slavery's price was eternal vigilance. Slaveowners interpreted rebelliousness as evidence of the "barbarous, wild savage natures" of Africans, as a South Carolina law of 1712 phrased it. But from the African point of view, resistance was essential to maintaining meaning and dignity in a life of degrading toil.

"Saltwater" Africans, fresh from their homelands, often fought slavery fiercely. "They often die before they can be conquered," said one white. Commonly, initial resistance took the form of fleeing—to renegade frontier settlements, to interior Indian tribes (which sometimes offered refuge), or to Spanish Florida. Rebellions, such as those in New York City in 1712 and at Stono, South Carolina, in 1739, mostly involved newly arrived slaves. There was no North American parallel, however, for the massive slave uprisings of the West Indies and Brazil.

The relatively small rebellions that did occur (or were feared) led to atrocious repression. Near Charleston in 1739, officials tortured and hanged 50 black rebels; their decapitated heads, impaled on posts, warned other potential insurrectionists. In New York City a year later, rumors of a planned insurrection caused the hanging of 18 slaves and 4 white allies and the burning of 13 other slaves.

Open rebelliousness often gave way to more subtle forms of resistance as slaves learned English, adjusted to work routines, and began forming families. Dragging out jobs, pretending illness or ignorance, and breaking tools were ways of avoiding physical exhaustion and indirect forms of opposing slavery itself. More direct resistance included truancy, arson, crop destruction, pilfering, and direct assault. Overall, slave masters did extract labor and obedience from their slaves; if they had not, the system would have collapsed. But they did so only with difficulty. To push slaves too hard could be costly.

Black Religion and Family

The balance of power was always massively stacked against slaves. Only the most desperate challenged the system directly. But most slaves struggled to find meaning and worth in their existence. Religion and family played a central role—one destined to continue far into the post-slavery period.

Africans brought to the New World a complex religious heritage that no desolation or abuse could crush. Coming from cultures where the division between sacred and secular activities was less clear than in Europe, slaves made religion central to their existence. The black Christianity that emerged in the eighteenth century blended African religious practices with the religion of the master class. It laid the foundations for the black Church that later became the central institution in African-American life.

Masters were not eager to see their slaves exposed to Christianity, whose teachings might undermine bondage. Yet Christianity's emphasis on meekness and obedience might restrain black rebelliousness, and gradually eighteenth-century slaves did learn about Christianity. They used it both to light the spark of resistance and to find comfort. A religious revival that began in the 1720s among whites in the northern colonies and spread southward made important contributions to African-American religion. Evangelicalism stressed personal rebirth, used music and body motion, and produced an intense emotional experience. The dancing, shouting, rhythmic clapping, and singing that came to characterize slaves' religious expression represented a creative mingling of West African and Christian religions.

Besides religion, the slaves' greatest refuge from their dreadful fate lay in their families. In West Africa, all social relations centered in kinship lines, which included dead ancestors. Torn from their native societies, slaves placed great importance on rebuilding extended kin groups.

Most English colonies prohibited slave marriages. But in practice, slaves and masters struck a bargain. Slaves desperately wanted families, and masters found that slaves with families would work harder and be less inclined to escape or rebel.

Slaves fashioned a family life only with difficulty, however. The general practice of importing three male slaves for every two females stunted family formation. Female slaves, much in demand, married in their late teens, but males usually had to wait until their mid- to late twenties. But as natural increase swelled the slave population in the eighteenth century, the sex ratio became more even.

The sale of either husband or wife could abruptly sever their fragile union. Broken marriages were frequent, especially when a deceased planter's estate was divided among heirs or his slaves were sold to creditors. Children usually stayed with their mothers until about age eight; then they were frequently torn from their families through sale, often to small planters needing only a hand or two. Few slaves escaped separation from family members at some time during their lives.

White male exploitation of black women represented another assault on family life. How many black women were coerced or lured into sex with white masters or overseers cannot be known, but the sizable mulatto (mixed-race) population by the end of the eighteenth century suggests that many were.

In some interracial relationships, the coercion was subtle. In some cases, black women sought the liaison to gain advantages for themselves or their children. These unions nonetheless threatened both the slave community and the white plantation ideal. They bridged the supposedly unbridgeable gap between slave and free society and produced children who did not fit into the plantation ideal of separate racial categories.

Despite such obstacles, slaves fashioned intimate ties as husband and wife, parent and child. If monogamous relationships did not last as long as in white society, much of the explanation lies in slave life: the shorter life span of African-Americans, the shattering of marriage through sale, and the call of freedom that impelled some slaves to run away.

Whereas slave men struggled to preserve their family role, many black women assumed a position in the family that differed from that of white women. Plantation mistresses usually worked hard in helping manage estates, but nonetheless the ideal grew that they should remain in the house, guarding white virtue and setting standards for white culture. In contrast, the black woman remained indispensable to both the work of the plantation and the functioning of the slave quarters. She toiled in fields and slave cabins alike. Paradoxically, black women's constant labor made them more equal to men than was the case of women in white society.

Above all, slavery was a set of power relationships designed to extract the maximum labor from its victims. Hence it regularly involved cruelties that filled family life with tribulation. Still, slaves made family the greatest monument to their will to endure to endure captivity and eventually gain freedom.

THE STRUGGLE FOR LAND

As slavery became entrenched in North America, New England, Virginia, and later South Carolina fought major wars against Native Americans. All resulted from white desire for land, and all left legacies of widespread destruction, heavy casualties, and bitterness. The coastal tribes suffered disastrous defeat and decline; for the colonists, the wars added to the turbulence of the times. Sometimes, as in Virginia, Indian war overlapped with a power struggle within white society.

King Philip's War in New England

Following the Pequot War of 1637 in New England, the Wampanoags and Narragansetts tried to keep their distance from the New England colonists. But the New Englanders coveted Indian territories. As they quarreled over provincial boundaries, they gradually reduced the Indians' land base.

By the 1670s, when New England's population had grown to about 50,000, younger Indians brooded over their situation. Their leader, Metacomet (called King Philip by the English), was the son of the Wampanoag chief who had allied with the first Plymouth settlers in 1620. Metacomet had watched his older brother preside over the deteriorating position of his people after their father's death in 1661. Becoming chief in his turn, Metacomet faced one humiliating challenge after another, climaxing in 1671 when Plymouth forced him to surrender a large stock of guns and accept his people's subjection to English law. Metacomet began organizing a resistance movement. Insurrection was triggered in 1675 by the execution of three Wampanoags for murdering a Christianized Indian who had allegedly warned Plymouth of an impending Indian attack.

But a deeper cause of the war was the anger of the young Wampanoag males. As would happen repeatedly in the next two centuries, younger Native Americans refused to imitate their fathers, who had permitted the colonizers' encroachments. Rather than submit further, they attempted a pan-Indian offensive against the ever-stronger intruder. For the young tribesmen, revitalization of their ancient culture through war became as important a goal as defeating the enemy.

In the summer of 1675, the Wampanoags unleashed daring hit-and-run attacks on villages in the Plymouth colony. By autumn, many New England tribes, including the powerful Narragansetts, had joined Metacomet. White towns all along the frontier reeled under Indian attacks. By November, Indian warriors had devastated the upper Connecticut River valley, and by March 1676 they were less than 20 miles from Boston and Providence. As assumptions about English military superiority faded, New England officials passed America's first draft laws. Evasion was widespread, and friction among the colonies slowed a counteroffensive.

Metacomet's offensive faltered in the spring of 1676, sapped by food shortages, disease, and the Mohawks' refusal to join the New England tribes. Then Metacomet fell in battle. The head of this "hell-hound, fiend, serpent, caitiff and dog" was displayed in Plymouth for 25 years.

Several thousand colonists and perhaps twice as many Indians died. Of some 90 Puritan towns, 52 had been attacked and 13 completely destroyed; 1,200 homes lay in ruins and 8,000 cattle were dead. The estimated cost of the war exceeded the value of all personal property in New England. Indian towns were devastated even more completely, including several of the "praying Indians" who had converted to Christianity and allied with the whites. An entire generation of young men had been nearly annihilated. Many survivors, including Metacomet's wife and son, were sold into West Indian slavery.

Bacon's Rebellion Engulfs Virginia

While New Englanders fought local tribes in 1675 and 1676, the Chesapeake colonies became locked in a struggle involving both an external war between the red and white populations and a civil war among the colonizers. This deeply tangled conflict was called Bacon's Rebellion, after the headstrong Cambridge-educated planter Nathaniel Bacon, who arrived in Virginia at age 28.

Bacon and many other ambitious young planters detested the Indian policy of Virginia's royal governor, Sir William Berkeley. In 1646, after the second Indian uprising against the Virginians, the Powhatan tribes had been granted exclusive rights to territory beyond the limits of white settlement. Stable Indian relations suited the established planters, some of whom traded profitably with the Indians, but became obnoxious to new settlers. Nor did the harmonious conditions please the white ex-indentured servants who hoped for cheap frontier land.

Land hunger and dissatisfaction with declining tobacco prices, rising taxes, and lack of opportunity erupted into violence in the summer of 1675. A group of frontiersmen used an incident with a local tribe as an excuse to attack the Susquehannocks, whose rich land they coveted. Governor Berkeley denounced the attack, but few supported his position. The badly outnumbered Susquehannocks prepared for war. Rumors swept the colony that the Susquehannocks were offering large sums to gain western Indian allies, or that King Philip would support them.

Thirsting for revenge, the Susquehannocks attacked during the winter of 1675–1676. In the spring, hot-blooded Bacon became the frontiersmen's leader. Joined by hundreds of runaway servants and some slaves, he attacked friendly and hostile Indians alike. Governor Berkeley refused to sanction these attacks and declared Bacon a rebel, sending 300 militiamen to drag him to Jamestown for trial. Bacon recruited more followers, including many substantial planters. Frontier skirmishes with Indians had turned into civil war. During the summer of 1676, Bacon's and Berkeley's troops maneuvered, while Bacon's men continued their forays against the Indian tribes. Then Bacon boldly captured and razed Jamestown. Berkeley fled across Chesapeake Bay.

Virginians at all levels had chafed under Berkeley's rule. High taxes, an increase in the governor's powers at the expense of local officials, and the monopoly that Berkeley and his friends held on the Indian trade were especially unpopular. This opposition surfaced in the summer of 1676 as Berkeley's and Bacon's troops pursued each other through the wilderness. Berkeley tried to rally public support by holding new assembly elections and extending the vote to all freemen. But the new assembly turned on the governor, passing laws to make government more responsive to ordinary people and to end rapacious officeholding. It also legalized enslaving Native Americans.

Time was on the governor's side, however. Having crushed the Indians, Bacon's followers drifted home to tend their crops. Meanwhile, 1,100 royal troops were dispatched from England. By the time they arrived, in January 1677, Bacon died of swamp fever and most of his followers had melted away. Berkeley hanged 23 rebel leaders.

As royal investigators who arrived in 1677 reported, Bacon's followers "seem[ed] to wish and aim at an utter extirpation of the Indians." Even a royal governor could not restrain such men, with their hopes of land ownership and independence. Hatred of Indians, bred into white society during the war, became a permanent feature of Virginia life. A generation later, in 1711, the legislature spurned a governor's plea for quieting the Indians with educational missions and regulated trade, instead voting £20,000 "for extirpating all Indians without distinction of Friends or Enemys" by military force. The remnants of Powhatan Confederacy had lost their last struggle for the world they had known. They moved west or submitted to a life on the margins of white society.

After Bacon's Rebellion, an emerging planter aristocracy annulled most of the reform laws of 1676. But the war relieved much of the social tension among white Virginians. Newly available Indian land created fresh opportunities for small planters and former servants. Equally important, Virginians with capital to invest were turning from the impoverished rural villages of England and Ireland to the villages of West Africa for their labor. This halted the influx of poor white servants who, once free, had formed a discontented mass at the bottom of Chesapeake society. A racial consensus, uniting whites of different ranks in the common pursuit of a prosperous, slave-based economy, began to take shape.

Bacon's Rebellion caused rumblings outside Virginia. Many of his followers fled to North Carolina, joining disgruntled farmers there in briefly seizing power. In Maryland, Protestant settlers chafed under high taxes, quitrents, and venal or Catholic officeholders. Declining tobacco prices and a fear of Indian attacks increased their touchiness. A month after Bacon razed Jamestown, insurgent small planters tried to seize the Maryland government. Two leaders were hanged for the attempt.

In all three southern colonies, the volatility of late-seventeenth-century life owed much to the region's peculiar social development. Where family formation was retarded by imbalanced sex ratios and fearsome mortality, and where geographic mobility was high, little social cohesion or attachment to community could grow. Missing in the southern colonies were the stabilizing power of mature local institutions, a vision of a larger purpose, and the presence of experienced and responsive political leaders.

AN ERA OF INSTABILITY

A dozen years after the major Indian wars in New England and Virginia, a series of insurrections and a major witchcraft incident convulsed colonial society. The rebellions were triggered by the Revolution of 1688, known thereafter to English Protestants as the Glorious Revolution because it ended forever the notion that kings ruled by "divine right" and marked the last serious Catholic challenge to Protestant supremacy. But these colonial disruptions also signified a struggle for social and political dominance in the expanding colonies. So did the witchcraft trials in Salem, Massachusetts.

Organizing the Empire

From the beginning of colonization, the English assumed that overseas settlements existed to promote the national interest. Mercantilist theory held that colonies served as outlets for English manufactured goods, provided foodstuffs and raw materials, stimulated trade (and hence promoted a larger merchant fleet), and filled royal coffers with duties on sugar and tobacco. In return, colonists benefited from English military protection and markets.

Beginning with small steps in 1621, England slowly began to intervene in the colonies. However, not until 1651, when the colonists were trading freely with the commercially aggressive Dutch, did Parliament consider regulating colonial affairs. It passed a navigation act requiring that English or colonial ships and crews carry all goods entering England, Ireland, and the colonies, no matter where those goods originated. These first steps toward a regulated empire were also the first steps to place England's power behind national economic development.

In 1660, after the monarchy was restored, Parliament passed a more comprehensive navigation act that listed colonial products that could be shipped only to England or other English colonies. Like its predecessor, the act took dead aim at Holland's domination of Atlantic commerce, while increasing England's revenues by imposing duties on the enumerated articles. Later navigation acts closed loopholes in the 1660 law and added other enumerated articles. Regulation bore lightly on the colonists, for the laws lacked enforcement mechanisms.

After 1675, international competition and war led England to impose greater imperial control. That year marked the establishment of the Lords of Trade, a committee of the king's privy council empowered to make and enforce decisions regulating the colonies. Their chief goal was to create more uniform colonial governments that would do the crown's will. Although movement toward imperial centralization often sputtered, the trend was unmistakable, especially to colonists who faced royal customs agents enforcing the navigation acts. England was becoming the shipper of the world, and its state-regulated policy of economic nationalism was essential to this rise to commercial greatness.

The Glorious Revolution in New England

When Charles II died in 1685, his brother, the duke of York, became King James II. Like Charles, James II professed Catholicism. But unlike Charles, who had disclosed this only on his deathbed, the new king announced his faith immediately on assuming the throne. James, Protestants feared, dangerously empowered Catholics. When his wife, supposedly too old for childbearing, bore a son in 1688, a Catholic succession loomed. Convinced that James aimed at absolute power, Protestant leaders in 1688 invited a Dutch prince, William of Orange, to seize the throne with his wife, Mary, James's Protestant daughter. James abdicated rather than fight. It was a bloodless victory for Protestantism, for parliamentary power and the limitation of royal prerogatives, and for the merchants and gentry of England.

The response of New Englanders to these events stemmed from their previous experience with royal authority and their fear of "papists." In 1676, New England had become a prime target for efforts to reorganize the empire and crack down on smuggling. Charles II annulled the Massachusetts charter in 1684, and two years later James II appointed Sir Edmund Andros, a crusty professional soldier and former governor of New York, to rule over the newly created Dominion of New England. Soon the Dominion gathered under one government all the English colonies from Maine to New Jersey. Puritans now had to swallow the bitter fact that they were subjects of London bureaucrats who cared more about shaping a disciplined empire than about New England's special religious vision.

At first, New Englanders accepted Andros, coolly. But he soon earned their hatred. He imposed taxes without legislative consent, ended trial by jury, abolished the General Court of Massachusetts (which had met annually since 1630), muzzled Boston's town meeting, and questioned land titles. He also converted a Boston Puritan meetinghouse into an Anglican chapel, held services there on Christmas Day—a gesture that to Puritans stank of popery—and tolerated religious dissent.

When news reached Boston in April 1689 that William of Orange had landed in England, Bostonians streamed into the streets. They imprisoned Andros, a suspected papist, and overwhelmed the fort in Boston harbor, which held most of the governor's small contingent of red-coated royal troops. Boston's ministers, along with merchants and former magistrates, led the rebellion.

Although Bostonians had dramatically rejected royal authority and the "bloody Devotees of Rome," no internal revolution occurred. However, growing social stratification and the emergence of a political elite caused some citizens to argue that men of modest means but common sense might better be trusted with power. "Anarchy" was the word chosen by Samuel Willard, a Boston minister, to tar the popular spirit unloosed in Boston in the aftermath of Andros's ouster.

Leisler's Rebellion in New York

In New York, the Glorious Revolution was similarly bloodless at first but far more disruptive. Royal government melted away on news of James's abdication. Displacing the governor's "popishly affected dogs and rogues," German-born militia captain Jacob Leisler established an interim government and ruled with an elected Committee of Safety for 13 months until a governor appointed by King William arrived.

Leisler's government enjoyed popularity among small landowners and urban laboring people. Most of the upper echelon, however, detested him as an upstart— "hott brain'd Capt. Leisler," who had married a wealthy widow. Such antipathy was returned in kind by lower- and middle-class Dutch inhabitants. Many Dutch merchants had readily adjusted to the English conquest of New Netherland in 1664, and many incoming English merchants had married into Dutch families. But beneath the upper class, where economic success softened ethnic friction, Anglo-Dutch hostility was common. Ordinary Dutch families felt that the English were crowding them out of the society they had built.

The Glorious Revolution was the spark igniting this smoldering social conflict. Leisler shared Dutch hostility toward New York's English elite, and his sympathy for ordinary people, mostly Dutch, earned him the hatred of the city's oligarchy. Leisler freed imprisoned debtors, planned a town-meeting system of government, and replaced merchants with artisans in important posts. By the autumn of 1689, Leislerian mobs were attacking the property of some of New York's wealthiest merchants. Two merchants, rejecting Leisler's authority, were jailed.

Leisler's opponents were horrified at the power of the "rabble." They believed that ordinary people had no right to rebel against authority or to exercise political power. When a new English governor arrived in 1691, the anti-Leislerians embraced him and charged Leisler and seven of his assistants with treason for assuming the government without royal instructions.

In the ensuing trial, Leisler and his son-in-law were convicted by an all-English jury and hanged. Leisler's popularity among the artisans of the city was evident when his wealthy opponents could find no carpenter in the city who would make a ladder for the scaffold. After his execution, peace gradually returned to New York, but for years provincial and city politics reflected the deep rift between Leislerians and anti-Leislerians.

Southern Rumblings

The Glorious Revolution also focused dissatisfactions in several southern colonies. Because Maryland was ruled by a Catholic proprietor, the Protestant majority seized power on word of the Glorious Revolution and used it for their own purposes. They vowed to cleanse Maryland of popery and to reform a corrupt customs service, cut taxes and fees, and extend the rights of the representative assembly. Militant Protestants held power until the arrival of Maryland's first royal governor in 1692.

In neighboring Virginia, the wounds of Bacon's Rebellion were still healing when word of the Glorious Revolution arrived. Virginia lived under a Catholic governor and a number of Catholic officials, fostering rumors of a Catholic plot. News of the revolution in England led a group of planters, suffering a prolonged drop in tobacco prices, to try to overthrow the governor, but the governor's council defended itself, partly by removing Catholics from positions of authority.

The Glorious Revolution brought lasting political changes to several colonies. The Dominion of New England collapsed. Connecticut and Rhode Island regained the right to elect their governors, but Massachusetts (now including Plymouth) and New Hampshire became royal colonies with governors appointed by the king. In Massachusetts, a new royal charter in 1691 eliminated Church membership as a voting requirement. The Maryland proprietorship was abolished (to be restored in 1715 when the Calverts became Protestant), and Catholics were barred from office. Everywhere Protestant Englishmen celebrated their liberties.

The Social Basis of Politics

The colonial insurrections associated with the Glorious Revolution revealed social and political tensions that accompanied the transplanting of English society to frontier societies. Colonial life was fluid, unruly, and competitive, lacking the stable political systems and leadership class that contemporaries thought necessary for social order.

The emerging colonial elite tried to foster stability by upholding a stratified, Old-World-style society where children were subordinate to parents, women to men, servants to masters, and poor to rich. Hence leaders everywhere tried to maintain gradations and subordination. Puritans did not stroll into the meetinghouse and occupy pews randomly; seats were assigned according to customary yardsticks of respectability—age, parentage, social position, wealth, and occupation. In Virginia, lower-class people were hauled before courts for horse racing, a sport legally reserved for men of social distinction.

But this social ideal proved difficult to maintain. Regardless of previous rank, settlers rubbed elbows so frequently and faced such raw conditions together that those without pedigrees often saw little reason to defer. "In Virginia," Captain John Smith had explained, "a plain soldier that can use a pickaxe and spade is better than five knights." Colonists everywhere gave respect not to those who claimed it by birth, but to those who earned it by deed. The colonial elite that was emerging by the late seventeenth century had no basis in legally defined and hereditary social rank. Planters and merchants, accumulating large estates, aped the English gentry. Yet their place was rarely secure. New competitors nipped constantly at their heels.

Amid such social flux, elites never commanded general allegiance to the ideal of a fixed social structure. Ambitious men on the rise such as Nathaniel Bacon and Jacob Leisler, and thwarted men below them who followed their lead, rose up against the constituted authorities, which they almost certainly would not have dared do in their homelands. When they gained power during the Glorious Revolution, in every case only briefly, the leaders of these uprisings linked themselves with a tradition of English struggle against tyranny and oligarchical power. They vowed to make government more responsive to the ordinary people who composed most of their societies.

Witchcraft in Salem

The ordinary people in the colonies, for whom Bacon and Leisler tried to speak, could sometimes be misled, as the tragic Salem witch hunts demonstrated. In Massachusetts, the deposing of Governor Andros left the colony in political limbo for three years, and this allowed what might have been a brief outbreak of witchcraft in the little community of Salem to escalate into a bloody battle. The provincial government, caught in transition, reacted only belatedly.

On a winter's day in 1692, 9-year-old Betty Parris and her 11-year-old cousin Abigail Williams began to play at magic in the kitchen of a small house in Salem, Massachusetts. They enlisted the aid of Tituba, the slave of Betty's father, Samuel Parris, the minister of the small community. Tituba told voodoo tales from her African past and baked "witch cakes." The girls soon became seized with fits and began making wild gestures and speeches. Soon other village girls were behaving strangely. Village elders extracted confessions that they were being tormented by Tituba and two other women, both social outcasts.

What began as the play of young girls turned into a ghastly rending of a farm community, capped by the execution of 20 people accused of witchcraft. In the seventeenth century, people still took literally the biblical injunction "Thou shalt not suffer a witch to live." For centuries throughout western Europe, people had believed that witches followed Satan's bidding and did evil to anyone he designated. Communities had accused and sentenced women to death for witchcraft far more often than men. In Massachusetts, more than 100 people, mostly older women, had been accused of witchcraft before 1692, and more than a dozen had been hanged.

In Salem, the initial accusations against three older women quickly multiplied. Within weeks, dozens had been charged with witchcraft, including several prominent figures. But formal prosecution of the accused witches could not proceed because neither the new royal charter of 1691 nor the royal governor to rule the colony had yet arrived. For three months, while charges spread, local authorities could only jail the accused without trial. When Governor William Phips arrived from England in May 1692, he ordered a special court to try the accused. By then, events had careened out of control.

All through the summer, the court listened to testimony. By September it had condemned about two dozen villagers. The authorities hanged 19 of them on barren "Witches Hill" outside the town and crushed 80-year-old Giles Corey to death under heavy stones. The trials rolled on into 1693, but by then, colonial leaders, including many of the clergy, recognized that a feverish fear of neighbors, rather than witchcraft itself, had possessed the little village of Salem.

Many factors contributed to the hysteria. Among them were generational differences between older Puritan colonists and the sometimes less religiously motivated younger generation, old family animosities, population growth and pressures on available farmland, and tensions between agricultural Salem Village and the nearby commercial center called Salem Town. An outbreak of food poisoning may also have caused hallucinogenic behavior. Probably nobody will ever fully understand the exact mingling of causes, but the fact that most of the individuals charged with witchcraft were women underscores the relatively weak position of women in Puritan society. The relentless spread of accusations of witchcraft suggests the anxiety of this tumultuous era of war, economic disruption, and political tension, and the erosion of the early generation's utopian vision.

CONTENDING FOR A CONTINENT

At the end of the seventeenth century, Indian wars and internal upheaval gave way to protracted international war. The smoldering struggle for mastery of the New World among four contending European powers—Holland, Spain, France, and England—became overt. North America was less an arena of armed rivalry among the European powers than were the Caribbean sugar islands. Nonetheless, the global struggle for power that erupted late in the seventeenth century—beginning nearly 100 years of conflict—reached the doorsteps of those who thought that in immigrating to North America they had left war behind.

Anglo-French Rivalry

In 1661, France's Louis XIV ushered in a new era for New France. Determined to make his country the most powerful in Europe, the king regarded North America and the Caribbean with renewed interest. New France's timber would build the royal navy, its fish would feed the growing mass of slaves in the French West Indies, and its fur trade, if greatly expanded, would fill royal coffers.

Under able governors, New France grew in population, economic strength, and ambition in the late seventeenth century. In the 1670s, Louis Jolliet and Father Jacques Marquette, a Jesuit priest, explored an immense territory watered by the Mississippi and Missouri rivers, previously unknown to Europeans. A decade later, military engineers and priests began building forts and missions in the Great Lakes region and the Mississippi valley. In the 1680s, René Robert de La Salle canoed down the Mississippi to the Gulf of Mexico and planted a settlement in Texas. Friendly Indian tribes allowed the French to establish trading posts far and wide in the North American interior. French traders and missionaries seemed very different in Indian villages than expansionist English settlers.

The growth of French strength and ambitions brought New England and New France into deadly conflict for a generation, beginning in the late seventeenth century. Religious hostility overlaid commercial rivalry. Protestant New Englanders regarded Catholic New France as a satanic challenge to their divinely sanctioned mission. When the European wars began in 1689, precipitated by Louis XIV, conflict between England and France quickly extended into every overseas theater where the two powers had colonies, including New York, New England, and eastern Canada.

In two wars, from 1689 to 1697 and 1701 to 1713, the English and French, while fighting in Europe, also sought to oust each other from the New World. The zone of greatest importance was the Caribbean, where slaves produced huge sugar fortunes. Both home governments understood that the North American settlements were important chiefly as a source of the timber and fish that sustained the West Indian colonies. On the North American mainland, weather, disease, transport, and supply problems made possible only irregular warfare.

The English struck three times at the centers of French power—Port Royal, which commanded the access to the St. Lawrence River, and Quebec, the capital of New France. In 1690, during King William's War (1689–1697), their small flotilla captured Port Royal, the hub of Acadia (which was returned to France at the end of the war). The English assault on Quebec, however, failed disastrously. In Queen Anne's War (1701–1713), New England attacked Port Royal three times before finally capturing it in 1710. A year later, when England sent a flotilla of 60 ships and 5,000 men to conquer Canada, the land and sea operations foundered before reaching their destinations.

With European-style warfare miserably unsuccessful in America, both England and France attempted to subcontract military tasks to their Indian allies. This policy occasionally succeeded, especially with the French, who gladly sent their own troops into the fray alongside Indian partners. In both wars, French and Indian allies wiped out frontier posts in New York and Maine and battered other towns along New England's fringes. Retaliating, the English-supplied Iroquois left New France "bewildered and benumbed" after a massacre near Montreal in 1689. Assessing their own interests, and too powerful to be bullied by either France or England, the Iroquois sat out the second war in the early eighteenth century. Convinced that neutrality served their purposes better than acting as mercenaries for the English, they held to the principle that "we are a free people uniting ourselves to whatever sachem [chief] we wish."

The Results of War

The Peace of Utrecht in 1713, which ended the war, capped the century-long rise of England and the decline of Spain in the rivalry for the sources of wealth outside

Visiting French Louisiana in 1735, Alexander de Batz painted members of the Illinois tribe who traded at New Orleans. Note the hatted African who apparently has been adopted by the Illinois. (Alexander De Batz, *Desseins de Sauvages de Plusieurs Natims*, 1735/ Peabody Museum, Harvard University)

Europe. England, the big winner, received Newfoundland and Acadia (renamed Nova Scotia), and France recognized English sovereignty over the fur-rich Hudson Bay territory. France retained Cape Breton Island, controlling the entrance to the St. Lawrence River. In the Caribbean, France yielded a few small islands to England. Spain, besides giving up important European provinces, surrendered Gibraltar to the English and awarded them the lucrative privilege of supplying the Spanish empire in America with African slaves.

The French were the big losers in these wars, but they did not abandon their New World ambitions. Soon after Louis XIV died in 1715, his successors tried to regain lost time in America by mounting a huge expedition to settle Louisiana. Because France deported many undesirables to the colony and because the French aristocracy destroyed by a wild speculation the joint-stock company that financed the project, few French immigrants joined the settlement of New Orleans. French colonies grew only in the Caribbean. Although these sugar colonies enriched a few, they strengthened the empire little, because slaves could not be armed and the islands were expensive to defend.

After the Peace of Utrecht in 1713, Spain still retained a vast empire in North America. However, its hold on the southern tier of the continent was very tenuous, and it had learned how easily its thinly-peopled missions and frontier outposts could be crippled or destroyed by chafing Native Americans and invading English. In the first half of the eighteenth century, the Spanish settlements stagnated, suffering from Spain's colonial policy that regarded them as marginal, money-losing affairs, useful only as defensive outposts.

Spain's priority was not to expand in North America, but to preserve what it had by keeping others away. That in itself would prove to be difficult, for this garrison mentality had to compete with the commercially-minded English and French, whose colonial population, especially the former's, was growing rapidly.

Though England had rebuffed France after a generation of war, New England suffered grievous economic and human losses. Massachusetts bore the heaviest burden. Probably one-fifth of all able-bodied males in the colony participated in the Canadian campaigns, and of these about one-quarter never lived to tell of the terrors of New England's first major experience with international warfare. The war debt was £50,000 sterling in Massachusetts alone, a greater per capita burden than the U.S. national debt today. At the end of the second conflict in 1713, war widows were so numerous that the Bay Colony faced its first serious poverty problem.

War at sea between European rivals affected even those colonies that sat out the land war. New York lost one of its best grain markets when Spain, allied with France, banned American foodstuffs in its West Indian colonies. The French navy seized about one-quarter of New York's fleet, and disrupted Philadelphia grain merchants' access to the Caribbean.

The burdens and rewards fell unevenly on the participants, as usually happens in wartime. Some lowborn men could rise spectacularly. William Phips, the twenty-sixth child in his family, had been a poor sheep farmer and ship's carpenter in Maine, seemingly destined for oblivion. Then he won a fortune by recovering a sunken Spanish treasure ship in the West Indies in 1687. For that feat, he was given command of the expedition against Port Royal in 1690. Victory there catapulted him to the governorship of Massachusetts in 1691. His status was secure.

Other men, already rich, got richer. Andrew Belcher of Boston, who had grown wealthy on provisioning contracts during King Philip's War, supplied warships and

TIMELINE

1600–1700	**1619**	**1637**	**1640s**	**1650–1670**
Dutch monopolize slave trade	First Africans imported to Virginia	Pequot War in New England	New England merchants enter slave trade; Virginia forbids blacks to carry firearms	Judicial and legislative decisions in Chesapeake colonies solidify racial lines

1651	**1664**	**1673–1685**	**1675–1677**	**1676**
Parliament passes first navigation act	English conquer New Netherland	French expand into Mississippi valley	King Philip's War in New England	Bacon's Rebellion in Virginia

1682	**1684**	**1688**	**1689**	**1689–1697**
La Salle canoes down Mississippi River and claims Louisiana for France	Massachusetts charter recalled	Glorious Revolution in England, followed by accession of William and Mary	Overthrow of Governor Andros in New England; Leisler's Rebellion in New York	King William's War

1690s	**1692**	**1700**	**1702–1713**	**1713**
Transition from white indentured servant to black slave labor begins in Chesapeake	Witchcraft hysteria in Salem	Spanish establish first mission in Arizona	Queen Anne's War	Peace of Utrecht

outfitted the New England expeditions to Canada. He became a Boston titan, riding in London-built coaches, erecting a handsome mansion, and purchasing slaves.

Most men, especially those who did the fighting, gained little, and many lost all. The least securely placed New Englanders supplied most of the voluntary or involuntary recruits, and they died in numbers that seem staggering today. Antipopery, dreams of glory, and promises of plunder in French Canada lured most of them into uniform. Having achieved no place on the paths leading upward, they grasped at straws, and usually failed again.

←←←←←←

CONCLUSION

Controlling the New Environment

By the second decade of the eighteenth century, the 12 English colonies on the eastern edge of North America had secured footholds in the hemisphere and erected the basic scaffolding of colonial life. With the aid of England, they had ousted the Dutch from their mid-Atlantic perch. They had fought the French to a draw and held their own against the Spanish. The coastal Indian tribes were reeling from disease and a series of wars that secured the colonists' land base along 1,000 miles of coastal plain. Though never controlling the powerful Indian tribes of the interior, the colonists had established a profitable trade with them. The settlers had overcome a scarcity of labor by copying the other European colonists in the hemisphere, who had linked the west coast of Africa to the New World through the ghastly trade in human flesh. Finally, the colonists had engaged in insurrections against what they viewed as arbitrary and tainted governments imposed by England.

The embryo of British America carried into the eighteenth century contained peculiarly mixed features. Still physically isolated from Europe, the colonists developed of necessity a large measure of self-reliance. Slowly, they began to identify themselves as the permanent inhabitants of a new land rather than as transplanted English, Dutch, or Scots-Irish. Viewing land and labor as the indispensable elements of a fruitful economy, they learned to exploit without apologies the land of one dark-skinned people and the labor of another. Yet even as they attained a precarious mastery in a triracial society, they were being culturally affected by the very people to which whose land and labor they laid claimed. Although utopian visions of life in America still reverberated in the heads of some, most colonists had awakened to the reality that life in the New World was a puzzling mixture of unpredictable opportunity and sudden turbulence, unprecedented freedom and debilitating wars, racial intermingling and racial separation. It was a New World in much more than geographic sense, for the people of three cultures who now inhabited it had remade it; and, while doing so, they were remaking themselves.

Recommended Reading

The Atlantic Slave Trade and the Beginnings of Slavery

Philip Curtin, *The Atlantic Slave Trade: A Census* (1969) and *The Rise and Fall of the Plantation Complex* (1990); Walter Rodney, *West Africa and the Atlantic Slave Trade* (1969); Patrick Manning, *Slavery and African Life: Occidental, Oriental, and African Slave Trades* (1990); Basil Davidson, *The African Slave Trade* (1961); James A. Rawley, *The Transatlantic Slave Trade* (1981); John Thornton, *Africa and Africans in the Making of the Atlantic World, 1440–1680* (1992); Carl N. Degler, *Neither Black nor White: Slavery and Race Relations in Brazil and the United States* (1971); H. Hoetink, *Slavery and Race Relations in the Americas* (1973); Richard S. Dunn, *Sugar and Slaves: The Rise of the Planter Class in the English West Indies, 1624–1713* (1972).

African Bondage and Slave Culture

T. H. Breen and Stephen Innes, *"Myne Owne Ground:" Race and Freedom on Virginia's Eastern Shore, 1640–1676* (1980); Peter H. Wood, *Black Majority: Negroes in South Carolina from 1670 Through the Stono Rebellion* (1974); Gerald Mullins, *Flight and Rebellion: Slave Resistance in Eighteenth-Century Virginia* (1972); Allan Kulikoff, *Tobacco and Slaves: The Development of Southern Cultures in the Chesapeake, 1680–1800* (1986); Winthrop D. Jordan, *White over Black: American Attitudes Toward the Negro, 1550–1812* (1968); Gwendolyn Midlo Hall, *Africans in Colonial Louisiana* (1992); Michael Mullin, *Africa in America: Slave Acculturation and Resistance in the American South* (1992); Mechal Sobel, *The World They Made Together: Black and White Relations in Eighteenth-Century Virginia* (1987); William Pierson, *Black Yankees: The Development of an African-American Subculture in Eighteenth-Century New England* (1988); Thomas J. Davis, *A Rumor of Revolt: The "Great Negro Plot" in Colonial New York* (1985); Ira Berlin, *Many Thousands Gone: The First Two Centuries of Slavery in North America* (1998); Philip

D. Morgan, *Slave Counterpoint: Black Culture in the Eighteenth-Century Chesapeake and Lowcountry* (1998).

Indian-White Relations

James Axtell, *The European and the Indian* (1981); David H. Corkran, *The Creek Frontier, 1540–1783* (1967); Wilcomb Washburn, *The Governor and the Rebel* (1957); Francis Jennings, *The Ambiguous Iroquois Empire* (1984); Calvin Martin, *Keepers of the Game: Indian-Animal Relationships and the Fur Trade* (1978); J. Leitch Wright, *The Only Land They Knew: The Tragic Story of the American Indians in the Old South* (1981); James H. Merrell, *The Indians' New World: Catawbas and Their Neighbors from European Contact through the Great Removal* (1989); Daniel Usner, Jr., *Indians, Settlers, and Slaves in a Frontier Exchange Economy: The Lower Mississippi Valley Before 1783* (1992); Gary B. Nash, *Red, White, and Black*, 4th ed. (1999); Colin G. Calloway, *New Worlds for All: Indians, Europeans, and the Remaking of Early America* (1997).

The Glorious Revolution and the Era of Instability

David Lovejoy, *The Glorious Revolution in America* (1972); Paul Boyer and Steven Nissenbaum, *Salem Possessed: The Social Origins of Witchcraft* (1974); John P. Demos, *Entertaining Satan: Witchcraft and the Culture of Early New England* (1982); Carol F. Karlsen, *The Devil in the Shape of a Woman* (1987).

Contending for a Continent

W. J. Eccles, *France in America* (1972); Richard White, *The Middle Ground: Indians, Empires, and Republics in the Great Lakes Region, 1650–1815* (1991); Charles Gibson, *Spain in America* (1966); Edward Spicer, *Cycles of Conquest: The Impact of Spain, Mexico, and the United States on the Indians of the Southwest, 1533–1960* (1962); D. W. Meinig, *The Shaping of America: Atlantic America, 1492–1800* (1986); David J. Weber, *The Spanish Frontier in North America* (1992); Ramon A. Gutiérrez, *When Jesus Came, the Corn Mothers Went Away: Marriage, Sexuality, and Power in New Mexico, 1500–1846* (1992); Robert H. Jackson and Edward Castillo, *Indians, Franciscans, and Spanish Colonization: The Impact of the Mission System on California Indians* (Albuquerque, 1995); Oakah L. Jones, Jr., *Los Paisanos: Spanish Settlers on the Northern Frontier of New Spain* (1979); Ian K. Steele, *Warpaths: Invasions of North America* (1994).

CHAPTER 4

The Maturing of Colonial Society

As a youth, Devereaux Jarratt knew only the isolated life of the small southern planter. Born in 1733 on the Virginia frontier, he was the third son of an immigrant yeoman farmer. In New Kent County, where Jarratt grew up, class status showed in a man's dress, his leisure habits, his house, even in his religion. A farmer's "whole dress and apparel," Jarratt recalled later, "consisted in a pair of coarse breeches, one or two shirts, a pair of shoes and stockings, an old felt hat, and a bear skin coat." In a maturing colonial society that was six generations old by the mid-eighteenth century, such simple folk stepped aside and tipped their hats when prosperous neighbors went by. "A periwig, in those days," recalled Jarratt, "was a distinguishing badge of gentle folk, and when I saw a man riding the road, near our house, with a wig on, it would so alarm my fears . . . that, I dare say, I would run off, as for my life."

As the colonies grew rapidly after 1700, economic development brought handsome gains for some, opened modest opportunities for many, but produced disappointment and privation for others. Jarratt remembered that his parents "neither sought nor expected any title, honors, or great things, either for themselves or their children. They wished us all brought up in some honest calling that we might earn our bread, by the sweat of our brow, as they did." But Jarratt was among those who advanced. His huge appetite for learning was apparent to his parents when as a small child he proved able to repeat entire chapters of the Bible before he had learned to read. That earned him some schooling. But at age 8, when his parents died, he had to take his place behind the plow alongside his brothers. Then, at 19, Jarratt was "called from the ax to the quill" by a neighboring planter's timely offer of a job tutoring his children.

Tutoring put Jarratt in touch with the world of wealth and status. Gradually, he advanced to positions in the households of wealthy Virginia planters. His modest success also introduced him to evangelical religion. In the eighteenth century, an explosion of religious fervor dramatically reversed the growing secularism of the settlers. Jarratt first encountered evangelicalism in the published sermons of George Whitefield, an English clergyman.

But it was later, at the plantation of John Cannon, "a man of great possessions in lands and slaves," that he personally experienced conversion under the influence of Cannon's wife. Jarratt later became a clergyman in the Anglican Church, which was dominated in the South by wealthy and dignified planters. But he never lost his religious zeal and desire to carry religion to ordinary people. In this commitment to spiritual renewal, he participated in the first mass religious movement to occur in colonial society.

❦❦❦❦❦

Colonial North America in the first half of the eighteenth century was a thriving, changing set of regional societies that had developed from turbulent seventeenth-century beginnings. New

England, the mid-Atlantic colonies, the Upper and Lower South, New France, and the northern frontier of New Spain were all distinct regions. Even within regions, diversity increased in the eighteenth century as incoming streams of immigrants, mostly from Africa, Germany, Ireland, and France, added new pieces to the emerging American mosaic.

Despite their bewildering diversity and lack of cohesion, the colonies along the Atlantic seaboard were affected similarly by population growth and economic development. Everywhere except on the frontier, class differences grew. A commercial orientation spread from north to south, especially in the towns, as local economies matured and forged links with the network of trade in the Atlantic basin. The exercise of political power of elected legislative assemblies and local bodies produced seasoned leaders, a tradition of local autonomy, and a widespread belief in a political ideology stressing the liberties that freeborn Englishmen should enjoy. All regions experienced a deep-running religious awakening that was itself connected to secular changes. All these themes will be explored as we follow the way in which scattered frontier settlements developed into mature provincial societies.

AMERICA'S FIRST POPULATION EXPLOSION

In 1680, some 150,000 colonizers clung to the eastern edge of North America. By 1750, they had swelled sevenfold to top one million. Such growth, never experienced in Europe, staggered English policymakers. Perceptive observers saw that the population gap between England and its American colonies was closing rapidly. A high marriage rate, large families, and lower mortality than in Europe prevailed among whites by the 1720s, accounting for much of the population boom in all the colonies and nearly all of it in New England. The black population also began to increase naturally by the 1720s. American-born slaves, forming families and producing as many children as white families, soon began to outnumber slaves born in Africa. The 15,000 blacks in 1690 grew to 80,000 in 1730 and 325,000 in 1760. By then, when they composed one-fifth of the colonial population, their numbers were growing far more from natural increase than from importation.

The New Immigrants

Expanding through natural increase, the colonial population also absorbed waves of new immigrants. But the last sizable group of settlers from England had arrived at the end of the seventeenth century. The eighteenth-century newcomers, who far outnumbered those emigrating before 1700, came overwhelmingly from Germany, Switzerland, Ireland, and Africa, and they were mostly indentured servants and slaves. Of all the eighteenth-century arrivals, Africans were the most numerous.

About 90,000 Germans flocked in during the eighteenth century, many fleeing famine, war, and pestilence. They settled where promoters promised cheap and fertile land, low taxes, and freedom from military duty—mostly between New York and South Carolina, with Pennsylvania absorbing most. Much of the mid-Atlantic hinterland became German-speaking.

Even more Protestant Scots-Irish arrived. Mostly poor farmers, they streamed into the same backcountry areas where Germans were settling, and many went farther, into the mountain valleys of the Carolinas and Georgia. No major Indian

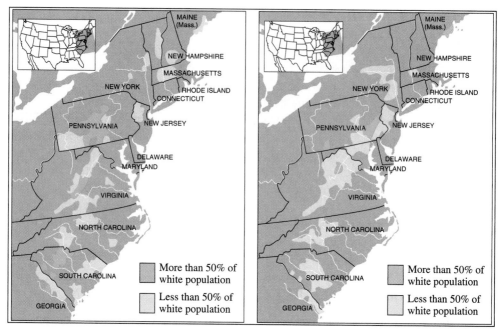

GERMAN SETTLEMENT AREAS, 1775 (left) SCOTS-IRISH SETTLEMENT AREAS, 1775 (right)   Most German and Scots-Irish immigrants in the 1700s were farmers, and they quickly moved into the interior where land was cheapest and most available.

wars occurred between 1715 and 1754, but the frontier bristled with tension as new settlers pushed westward.

The region southward from Pennsylvania increased most spectacularly. Pennsylvania, with its fertile lands and open door policy, grew fastest. Virginia, with a population of 340,000 by 1760, remained by far the largest colony.

The social background of these new European immigrants differed much from their seventeenth-century predecessors. Unlike Puritan settlers, few were from the upper or middle rungs of the social ladder. Such people came rarely in the eighteenth century. Instead, slaves and indentured servants made up most of the incoming human tide after 1713. The westward traffic in servants became a regular part of the commerce linking Europe and America.

Shipboard conditions for servants worsened in the eighteenth century and were hardly better than on slave ships. Official attempts to reduce the "tight packing" of immigrants were little help. Crammed between decks in stifling air, they suffered from smallpox and fevers, rotten food, bad water, cold, and lice. "Children between the ages of one and seven seldom survive the sea voyage," bemoaned one German immigrant, "and parents must often watch their offspring suffer miserably, die, and be thrown into the ocean." A shipboard mortality rate of about 15 percent made this the most unhealthy of all times to seek American shores.

Like indentured servants in the seventeenth century, servant immigrants after 1715 came mostly from the bottom of society—petty criminals, political prisoners, urban castoffs, and a few bold, ambitious souls. "Men who emigrate," an

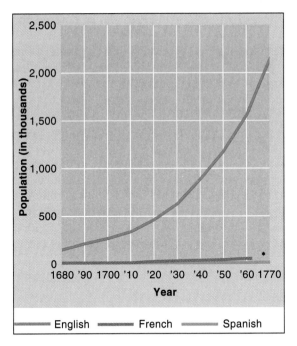

POPULATION OF EUROPEAN COLONIES IN NORTH AMERICA, 1680-1770 Whereas the French and Spanish populations in North America inched upward (the result of few arriving immigrants and a low birthrate in settlements dominated by males), the English and African American populations soared
*France's North American colonies in Canada and Louisiana ceded to England and Spain, respectively, in 1763.

Englishman commented, "are from the nature of their circumstances, the most active, hardy, daring, bold and resolute spirits, and probably the most mischievous also."

Most indentured servants, especially males, found the labor system harsh. Merchants sold them, a shocked Britisher reported in 1773, "as they do their horses, and advertise them as they do their beef and oatmeal." Colonial newspapers were filled with notices of runaways, servants and slaves alike, and penalties were harsh. Even joining the British army often seemed preferable to servitude.

"The hope of buying land in America," a New Yorker noted, "is what chiefly induces people into America." Many died before finishing their time; others won freedom only to toil for years as poor day laborers and tenant farmers. The relatively few seventeenth-century indentured servants who had survived the fearful Chesapeake death rates often rose in society. Eighteenth-century servants had much better chances to complete their labor contract but much less opportunity afterwards to enter the propertied ranks. The chief beneficiaries of the system of bound white labor were the masters.

Africans in Chains

The most numerous of the thousands of ships plying the Atlantic in the eighteenth century were those fitted out as seagoing dungeons for slaves. The slave trade to the southern colonies after the Peace of Utrecht expanded so sharply that within two generations what had been a society with many slaves became a society built on slavery. From 1690 to 1715, annual importations rarely exceeded 1,000, but in the next 15 years, the number probably doubled. The generation after 1730 witnessed the largest influx of African slaves in the colonial period, averaging about

5,000 a year. From 1700 to 1775, more than 350,000 African slaves entered the American colonies.

Most of these miserable captives were auctioned off to southern planters. But some landed in the northern cities, especially New York and Philadelphia, where merchants sold them to artisans, farmers, and upper-class householders.

Even as the slave traffic peaked, opposition to slavery arose. A few, mostly Quakers, had objected to slavery on moral grounds since the late seventeenth century. But the idea grew in the 1750s that slavery contradicted the Christian brotherhood and Enlightenment notions of natural human equality. Abolitionist sentiment was also fed by the growing belief that a master's power "depraved the mind," as the Quaker tailor John Woolman put it. Woolman dedicated his life in the 1750s to a crusade against slavery, traveling thousands of miles on foot to convince every Quaker slaveholder of his or her wrongdoing. Only a few hundred eighteenth-century masters freed their slaves, but men such as Woolman had planted the seeds of abolitionism.

BEYOND THE APPALACHIANS

Of about 1.2 million settlers and slaves in 1750, only a tiny fraction lived farther than 100 miles from the Atlantic. But between them and the Pacific Ocean lay rich soils in the river valleys of the Ohio and Mississippi and beyond that a vast domain that they had not even imagined. Beginning in the 1750s, westward-moving, land-hungry colonists would encounter four other groups: the populous interior Native American tribes and smaller groups of French Americans, Spanish Americans, and African-Americans. Changes already occurring among these groups would affect settlers breaching the Appalachian barrier and, in the third quarter of the eighteenth century, would even reach eastward to the original British settlements.

Cultural and Ecological Changes Among Interior Tribes

During the first half of the eighteenth century, the inland tribes proved their capacity to adapt to the contending European colonizers in their region while maintaining independence. Yet extensive contact with Europeans slowly brought ominous changes to Indian ways of life. Trade goods, especially iron implements, textiles, firearms and ammunition, and alcohol, altered lifeways. Subsistence hunting turned into commercial hunting, restricted only by the quantity of trade goods desired. Indian males, gradually wiping out deer and beaver east of the Mississippi River, spent far more time away from the villages trapping and hunting. Women were also drawn into the new economy, skinning animals and fashioning pelts into robes. Among some tribes, all this became so time-consuming that they had to procure food from other tribes.

The fur trade altered much in traditional Native American life. Spiritual beliefs that the destinies of humans and animals were closely linked eroded when trappers and hunters declared all-out war on fur-bearing animals to exchange pelts for attractive trade goods. Competition for furs sharpened intertribal tensions, often to the point of war. The introduction of European weaponry, which Indians quickly mastered, made these conflicts worse. Tribal political organization in the interior changed, too. Earlier, most tribes had been loose confederations of villages and

The communalistic Moravian immigrants who came to Pennsylvania in the 1740s dedicated themselves, like the Quakers, to peaceful relations with the Indians. The Prussian John Jacob Schmick and his Norwegian wife Johanna were missionaries to the Delawares. (Moravian Historical Society, Nazareth, PA)

clans. Creek, Cherokee, and Iroquois gave primary loyalty to the village. But trade, diplomatic contact, and war with Europeans required coordinated policies. So villagers gradually adopted more centralized leadership.

While incorporating trade goods into their material culture and adapting their economies and political structures to new situations, the interior tribes held fast to tradition in many ways. They saw little reason to replace what they valued in their own culture. What they saw of the colonists' law and justice, religion, education, family organization, and child rearing usually convinced Native Americans that their own ways were superior.

The Indians' refusal to accept the superiority of white culture frustrated English missionaries, eager to win Native Americans from "savage" ways. A Carolinian admitted that "they are really better to us than we are to them. We look upon them with scorn and disdain, and think them little better than beasts in human shape, though if well examined, we shall find that, for all our religion and education, we possess more moral deformities and evils than these savages do."

Overall, the interior tribes suffered from contact with the British colonizers. The fur trade spread epidemics, intensified warfare, depleted game animals, and drew Native Americans into a market economy where their trading partners gradually became trading masters.

France's Inland Empire

While the powerful Iroquois, Cherokee, Creek, and Choctaw tribes interacted with British colonists to their east, they also faced a growing French presence to their west. Between 1699 and 1754, the French developed a system of small forts, trading posts, and agricultural villages throughout the heart of the continent, threatening to pin the English to the seaboard. French success hinged partly on shrewd dealing with the Indian tribes, which kept sovereignty over the land but gradually succumbed to French diseases, French arms, and French-promoted intertribal wars.

Because France's interior empire was organized primarily as a military, trading, and missionizing operation, male French settlers arrived with few French women. For a long time, French men encountered Indians in a state of need—not only for trading partners, allies, and converts, but also for wives. These needs produced a mingling of French and Indian peoples in the vast interior.

Such interracial marriages were welcomed by the Indians as well as the French. Marital alliances cemented trade relations and military alliances. French traders entered Indian kinship circles, making trade flow smoothly, while Indians gained protection against their enemies and access to provisions at the French trading posts. Though the French sometimes descended into fierce warfare with Indian peoples, the North American heartland was a cultural melting pot as well as a marketplace and a battleground.

Thinly dotted with farming communities, the vast French presence in the continent's heartland created an effective shield against the expansive British. As the French population grew to about 70,000 by 1750, they demonstrated uniquely how Europeans and Indians could coexist. Almost all French settlements in North America's interior were mixed-race communities. French Louisiana had more mixed-race children, and more white and black men who lived with Native Americans, than any Anglo-American colony.

In 1718, the few hundred early French pioneers of the interior were suddenly inundated when France settled New Orleans at great cost by transporting almost 7,000 whites and 5,000 African slaves to the mouth of the Mississippi River. Disease rapidly whittled down these numbers, and an uprising of the powerful Natchez tribe in 1729 discouraged further French immigration. Most of the survivors settled around the little town of New Orleans in long, narrow plantations stretching back from the Mississippi and supplied from all parts of the French interior.

New Orleans resembled early Charleston socially and economically, but not politically. The colony was run—and financed—by the royal government, and knew nothing of representative political institutions. Its people had no elections or assembly, newspapers or taxes.

From its first introduction in Louisiana in 1719, French plantation slavery grew so rapidly that blacks outnumbered whites by 1765. Most slaves and a majority of whites lived in the New Orleans area. The conditions of life for slaves differed little from the southern English colonies. But French law gave slaves some protection in courts. When the Spanish took over the colony in 1769, they guaranteed slaves the right to buy freedom with money earned in their free time. Soon a large free black class emerged. When Americans acquired the colony in 1803, they suppressed freedom purchase and discouraged manumission.

Spain's America

In the first half of the eighteenth century, the Spanish still possessed by far the largest empire in the Americas. (But the Spanish had difficulty defending Florida against the British while trying to counter French expansion in the Mississippi

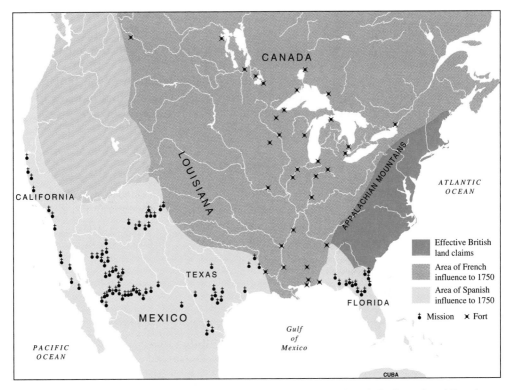

FRENCH AND SPANISH OCCUPATION OF NORTH AMERICA, TO 1776 Although the Spanish and French settled only puny numbers of colonists in comparison to the English, they established themselves through trade and missionary activities over vast regions of North America.

River watershed with only a few military posts in Texas and New Mexico.) The number of Hispanics, mestizos, and detribalized Indians began to increase modestly in Texas, New Mexico, and California in the first half of the eighteenth century, but not as fast as the English and French colonies were growing. The English in South Carolina were ten times as numerous as the Spanish in Florida by 1745. New Mexico's Hispanic population of about 10,000 at mid-century could defend the vast region only because no European challenger appeared.

As in New France, there was more racial intermixture and social fluidity in New Spain than in the English colonies. Precisely how much is uncertain because the Spanish never defined racial groups as distinctly as the English. Social mobility was considerable: The crown would raise even a commoner to the status of *hidalgo* (minor nobleman) as an inducement to settle and ranch in New Mexico.

Native Americans had mixed success resisting Christian domination in different colonies. In New Mexico, an early nineteenth-century Spanish investigator saw the key to Pueblos' cultural autonomy as the underground *kivas*, which were "like impenetrable temples, where they gather to discuss mysteriously their misfortunes or good fortunes, their happiness or grief." California tribes, though, had a hard time maintaining cultural cohesion. In the 1770s, the Spanish rapidly completed their western land and sea routes from San Diego to Yerba Buena (San Francisco) to block Russian encroachment. California's Spanish pioneers were

Franciscan missionaries, accompanied by royal soldiers. The priests would choose a good location and attract a few Indians to be baptized and resettle around the mission. Visiting relatives would then be induced to stay, and the Indians were eventually reduced to virtual slaves. The California mission, with its extensive and profitable herds and grain crops, theoretically belonged to the Indian converts, but they did not enjoy the profits. Ironically, the spiritual motives of the priests brought the same degradation of tribal Americans as elsewhere.

A LAND OF FAMILY FARMS

Population growth and economic development gradually transformed eighteenth-century British America. Three variations of colonial society emerged: the farming society of the North, the plantation society of the South, and the urban society of the seaboard commercial towns. Although they shared some important characteristics, each was distinct.

Northern Agricultural Society

In the mid-eighteenth-century northern colonies, especially New England, tightknit farming families, organized in communities of several thousand people, dotted the landscape. New Englanders staked their future on a mixed economy. They cleared forests for timber used in barrels, ships, houses, and barns. They plumbed the offshore waters for fish that fed both local populations and the ballooning slave population of the West Indies. And they cultivated and grazed as much of the thin-soiled, rocky hills and bottomlands as they could recover from the forest.

The farmers of the middle colonies—Pennsylvania, Delaware, New Jersey, and New York—drove their wooden plows through much richer soils than New Englanders. They enjoyed the additional advantage of settling an area cleared by Native Americans who had relied more on agriculture than New England tribes. Thus favored, mid-Atlantic farm families produced modest surpluses of corn, wheat, beef, and pork. By the mid-eighteenth century, New York and Philadelphia ships were carrying these foodstuffs not only to the West Indies, always a primary market, but also to England, Spain, Portugal, and even New England.

In the North, the broad ownership of land distinguished farming society from every other agricultural region of the Western world. Although differences in circumstances and ability led gradually toward greater social stratification, in most communities few were truly rich or abjectly poor. Except for indentured servants, most men had bought or inherited a farm of at least 50 acres. With their family's labor, they earned a decent existence and provided a small inheritance for each of their children. Settlers valued land highly, for freehold tenure ordinarily guaranteed both economic independence and political rights.

Amid widespread property ownership, a rising population pressed against a limited land supply by the eighteenth century, especially in New England. Family farms could not be divided and subdivided indefinitely, for it took at least 50 acres to support a family. In Concord, Massachusetts, for example, the founders had worked farms averaging about 250 acres. A century later, in the 1730s, the average farm had shrunk by two-thirds, as farm owners struggled to provide an inheritance for the three or four sons that the average marriage produced.

Decreasing fertility compounded the problem of dwindling farm size. When land had been plentiful, farmers planted crops in the same field for three years and then let it lie fallow seven years or more until it regained fertility. But on the smaller farms of the eighteenth century, farmers reduced fallowing to only a year or two. Such intense use of the soil reduced crop yields, forcing farmers to plow marginal land or shift to livestock production.

The diminishing size and productivity of family farms drove many eighteenth-century New Englanders to the frontier or out of the area. In Concord, one of every four adult males migrated from town every decade from the 1740s on, and in many towns out-migration was even greater. Some drifted to New York and Pennsylvania, sought opportunities as artisans in coastal towns, or took to the sea. More went to western Massachusetts, New Hampshire, Maine, or Nova Scotia.

Northern farming was far less intense than in the South. The growing season was much shorter, and cereal crops required incessant labor only during spring planting and autumn harvesting. This seasonal rhythm led many northern farmers to fill out their calendars with work as clockmakers, shoemakers, carpenters, and weavers.

Changing Values

Boston's weather on April 29, 1695, began warm and sunny, noted the devout merchant Samuel Sewall in his diary. But by afternoon, lightning and hailstones "as big as pistol and musket bullets" pummeled the town. Sewall dined that evening with Cotton Mather, New England's most prominent Puritan clergyman. Mather wondered why "more ministers' houses than others proportionately had been smitten with lightning"—and immediately hailstones began to shatter the windows. Sewall and Mather fell to their knees in prayer "after this awful Providence."

These two third-generation Massachusetts Puritans understood that God was angry with them as leaders of a people whose piety was giving way to worldliness. Massachusetts was becoming "sermon-proof," said one dejected minister.

In other parts of the North, the expansive environment and the Protestant emphasis on self-discipline and hard work were also breeding qualities that would become hallmarks of American culture: ambition, individualism, and materialism. "Every man," one colonist remarked, "expects one day or another to be upon a footing with his wealthiest neighbor."

Commitment to religion, family, and community did not disappear, but fewer people saw daily existence just as a preparation for the afterlife. They began to regard land not simply as a source of livelihood, but as a commodity to be bought and sold for profit. A slender almanac, written by the twelfth child of a poor Boston candlemaker, captured the new outlook with wit and charm. Born in 1706, Benjamin Franklin climbed the ladder of success spectacularly. Running away from a harsh apprenticeship to an older brother when he was 16, he abandoned a declining Boston for a rising Philadelphia. By 23, he had learned the printer's trade and was publishing the *Pennsylvania Gazette*. Three years later, he began *Poor Richard's Almanack*, next to the Bible the most widely read book in the colonies, filled with quips, adages, and homespun philosophy: "Lost time is never found again." "It costs more to maintain one vice than to raise two children." "Sloth makes all things difficult but industry all easy." Ever cocky, Franklin caught the spirit of the rising secularism of the eighteenth century. He embodied the growing utilitarian doctrine that the good is whatever is useful and the notion that the community is best served through individual self-improvement and accomplishment.

Women and the Family in Northern Colonial Society

In 1662, Elnathan Chauncy, a Massachusetts schoolboy, copied into his writing book that the soul "consists of two portions, inferior and superior; the superior is masculine and eternal; the feminine inferior and mortal." This lesson had been taught for generations on both sides of the Atlantic. It was part of a larger conception of God's design that assigned degrees of status and stations in life to all individuals. In that world, women were subordinate, taught from infancy to be modest, patient, compliant. Regarded by men as weak of mind and large of heart, they existed for and through men, subject first to their fathers and then to their husbands.

European women usually accepted these narrowly circumscribed roles. Few complained, at least openly, that their work was generally limited to housewifery and midwifery. They silently accepted exclusion from early public schools and laws that transferred to their husbands any property or income they brought into a marriage. Nor could women speak in their churches or participate in governing them (except in Quaker meetinghouses), and they had no legal voice in politics. Few women chose a husband for love; parental guidance prevailed in a society in which producing legal heirs was the means of transmitting property. Once wed, women expected to remain so until death, for they could rarely obtain a divorce.

On the colonial frontier, women's lives changed in modest ways. One European woman in ten did not marry; in the colonies, where men outnumbered women for the first century, a spinster was almost unheard of, and widows remarried with astounding speed. *Woman* and *wife* became nearly synonymous.

A second difference concerned property rights. Single women and widows in the colonies, as in England, could make contracts, hold and convey property, represent themselves in court, and conduct business. Under English common law, a woman forfeited these rights, as well as all property, when she married. In the colonies, however, legislatures and courts gave wives more control over property brought into marriage or left at their husbands' death. They also enjoyed broader rights to act for and with their husbands in business transactions. In addition, young colonial women slowly gained the right of consenting to a marriage partner—a right that came by default to the thousands of female indentured servants who completed their labor contracts and had no parents within 3,000 miles to dictate to them.

Although colonial society did not encourage female individuality, women worked alongside their husbands. Women had limited career choices and rights but broad responsibilities. The work spaces and routines of husband and wife overlapped far more than today. "Deputy husbands" and "yoke mates" were revealing terms used by New Englanders to describe eighteenth-century wives.

Despite conventional talk of inferiority, women within their families and localities nevertheless shaped the world around them. Older women shaped the behavior of young women, aided the needy, and subtly affected menfolk who held

Childbirth was an oft-repeated event in the lives of most colonial wives. In this portrait of the Cheney family, the older woman is a nanny or mother-in-law; the younger woman holding a baby is Mr. Cheney's second wife. (Anonymous, The Cheney Family, c. 1795, National Gallery of Art, Washington, D.C., Gift of Edgar William and Bernice Chrysler Garbisch)

formal authority. Women outnumbered men in church life and worked within their families to promote religion in outlying areas, oversee ministers, and influence morals. Periodically, they appeared as visionaries and mystics. Until the late eighteenth century, the "obstetrick art" was almost entirely in their hands. Midwives counseled pregnant women, delivered babies, supervised postpartum recovery, and participated in baptismal and burial ceremonies. Because colonial women were pregnant or nursing for about half their years between 20 and 40, and because childbirth was dangerous, the circle of female friends and relatives attending childbirth created strong networks of mutual assistance.

In her role as wife and mother, the eighteenth-century northern woman differed somewhat from her English counterpart. Whereas English women married in their mid-twenties, American women typically took husbands a few years earlier. This head start increased their childbearing years. Hence, the average colonial family included five children (two more typically died in infancy), whereas the English family had fewer than three.

Northern child-rearing patterns differed considerably. In the seventeenth century, stern fathers dominated Puritan family life, and few were reluctant to punish unruly children. "Better whip'd than damn'd," advised Cotton Mather, reinforcing many Puritan parents' belief that breaking the child's will created a pious and submissive personality. Quaker mothers, however, tended to use love rather than guilt to mold their children. Attitudes toward choosing a marriage partner also separated early Puritans and Quakers. Puritan parents usually arranged their children's marriages but allowed them the right to veto. Young Quaker men and women made their own matches, subject to parental veto.

The father-dominated family of New England gradually declined in the eighteenth century. In its place rose the mother-centered family, in which affectionate parents encouraged self-expression and independence in their children. This "modern" approach, on the rise in Europe as well, brought colonists closer to the methods of parenthood found among the coastal Native Americans, who initially had been widely disparaged for their permissiveness.

ECOLOGICAL TRANSFORMATION

Wherever Europeans settled in the Americas, they brought with them animals, plant life, diseases, and ways of viewing natural resources—all with enormous consequences. The introduction of grazing animals profoundly altered New Spain's landscape: Prolifically multiplying pigs and cattle devoured the tall grasses and most palatable plant species, and within a half century huge areas had little or no ground cover. Then new, unwelcome plant species took hold—stinging nettles, dandelions, and nightshade.

In England's North American colonies, the rapid increase of settlers after 1715 had different environmental effects. First, the demand for wood—for building and heating houses, for producing the charcoal necessary for ironmaking, for shipbuilding and barrelmaking—swiftly depleted coastal forests. Rapid and often wasteful harvesting of the forests had many effects. As the colonists chopped down the forest canopy that had previously moderated the weather, summers became hotter and winters colder. Snow melted sooner and watersheds emptied faster, in turn causing erosion and drought.

A second ecological transformation occurred when animals brought by Europeans began to replace animals already in North America. Pigs and cattle "swarm like vermin upon the earth," reported one Virginia account as early as 1700. Native grasses and shrubs disappeared so quickly that the European livestock began to die for lack of grazing land. Meanwhile native fur-bearing animals—beaver, deer, bear, wolf, raccoon, and marten—rapidly became extinct in the areas of settlement. Prized for their skins or hated as predators, these species were hunted relentlessly. One broken link in the ecological chain affected others. For example, the dams and ponds of the beaver, which had been breeding grounds for many species of wild ducks, soon were drained and converted to meadows for cattle.

Animals prized for dinner table fare also quickly reached extinction along the East Coast. Wild turkeys were a rarity in Massachusetts by the 1670s. Deer disappeared by the early 1700s in settled areas.

All these environmental changes were linked not only to the numbers of Europeans arriving in North America, but also to their ways of thinking about nature. Transplanted Europeans saw only the possibility of raising valuable crops. Land, lumber, fish, and fur-bearing animals could be converted into sources of cash that would buy imported commodities that improved one's material condition.

Coming from places where land was scarce, the settlers viewed their ability to reap nature's abundance in North America as proof of their success. From their perspective, they were correct because, in fact, colonial agriculture was abundantly successful in terms of what the settlers obliged the land to yield. Yet the "rage for commerce" and for an improved life produced wasteful practices on farms and in forests and fisheries. "The grain fields, the meadows, the forests, the cattle, etc.," wrote a Swedish visitor in the 1750s, "are treated with equal carelessness." Accustomed to the natural abundance once the native peoples had been driven from the land, and seeing no limits to the land that was available, the colonists embarked on ecologically destructive practices that over a period of many generations profoundly altered the natural world of North America.

THE PLANTATION SOUTH

Between 1680 and 1750, the southern white tidewater settlements changed from a frontier society with high immigration, a surplus of males, and an unstable social organization to a settled society composed mostly of native-born families. But while a mature southern culture took form from the ocean to the piedmont, after 1715 Scots-Irish and German immigrants flooded into the backcountry of Virginia, the Carolinas, and the new colony of Georgia.

The Tobacco Coast

Rapidly expanding tobacco production in seventeenth-century Virginia and Maryland sent exports to 25 million pounds annually during the 1680s. But then two decades of war drove up transportation costs, depressing the tobacco market until about 1715.

Yet in these years the Upper South underwent a profound social transformation. First, slaves replaced indentured servants so rapidly that by 1730 the unfree labor force was overwhelmingly black. Second, planters diversified: They shifted some tobacco fields to grain, hemp, and flax; they increased herds of cattle and swine; and they developed iron, leather, and textile production. By the 1720s, when a profitable tobacco trade with France created a new period of prosperity, the economy was much more diverse and resilient. Third, the population structure changed rapidly. Black slaves grew from about 7 percent to more than 40 percent of the region's population between 1690 and 1750, and the drastic imbalance between white men and women disappeared. Families, rather than single men, now predominated. The earlier frontier society of white immigrants, mostly living short lives as indentured servants, grew into an eighteenth-century plantation society of native-born freeholder families.

Slave owning was far from universal. As late as 1750, a majority of families owned no slaves at all. Not more than one-tenth of slaveholders owned more than 20 slaves. Nonetheless, the common goal was the large plantation where black slaves made the earth yield up profits to support an aristocratic life.

The Chesapeake planters who acquired the best land and accumulated enough capital to invest heavily in slaves created a gentry lifestyle that set them apart from ordinary farmers such as Devereaux Jarratt's father. By the eighteenth century, the development of the northern colonies had produced prosperous farmers worth several thousand pounds. But such wealth paled alongside that of the leading Chesapeake planters, who counted their slaves by the hundreds, their acres by the thousands, and their fortunes by the tens of thousands of pounds.

Ritual display of wealth marked southern gentry life. Racing thoroughbred horses and gambling on them recklessly became common sport for young gentlemen, who had often been educated in England. Planters built stately brick Georgian mansions filled with imported furniture. The emerging Chesapeake planter elite controlled the county courts, officered the militia, ruled the parish vestries of the Anglican Church, made law in their legislative assemblies, and passed to their sons the mantle of political and social leadership.

For all their airs, these squires were essentially agrarian businessmen. They spent their days haggling over credit, land, slaves, and leases, in scheduling planting and harvesting, in conferring with overseers, and in disciplining slaves. Tobacco cultivation (unlike that of wheat and corn) claimed the planter's year-round attention. His reputation rested on the quality of his crop.

Planters' wives also shouldered many responsibilities. They superintended cloth production and the processing and preparation of food while ruling over households crowded with children, slaves, and visitors. An aristocratic veneer gave the luster of gentility to plantations from Maryland to North Carolina, but in fact these were large working farms, often completely isolated.

The Rice Coast

The plantation economy of the Lower South in the eighteenth century rested on rice and indigo. Rice exports surpassed 1.5 million pounds per year by 1710 and reached 80 million pounds by the eve of the Revolution. Indigo, a blue dye obtained from plants for use in textiles, became a staple crop in the 1740s after Eliza Lucas Pinckney, a wealthy South Carolina planter's wife, experimented successfully with its cultivation. Within a generation, indigo production had spread into Georgia. It soon ranked among the leading colonial exports.

The expansion of rice production transformed the region around Charleston, where planters imported thousands of slaves after 1720. By 1740, slaves composed nearly 90 percent of the region's inhabitants. White population declined as wealthy planters entrusted their estates to resident overseers. At mid-century, a shocked New England visitor described it as a society "divided into opulent and lordly planters, poor and spiritless peasants, and vile slaves."

Throughout the plantation South, the courthouse became a central male gathering place. All classes came to settle debts, dispute over land, sue and be sued. When court was over, a multitude lingered on, drinking, gossiping, and staging horse races, cockfights, wrestling matches, footraces, and fiddling contests—all tests of male prowess.

The church, almost always Anglican in the South before 1750, also became a center of community gathering. A visiting northerner described the animated socializing before worship, men "giving and receiving letters of business, reading advertisements, consulting about the price of tobacco and grain, and settling either the lineage, age, or qualities of favourite horses." Then people filed into church, with the lesser planters entering first and standing attentively until the wealthy gentry "in a body" took their pews at the front. After church, socializing continued, with young people strolling together and older ones extending invitations to Sunday dinner. New England's pious Sabbath atmosphere was little in evidence.

The Backcountry

As late as 1730, only hunters and Indian fur traders had known the vast expanse of hilly red clay and fertile limestone soils from Pennsylvania to Georgia. Over the next four decades, it attracted some 250,000 inhabitants, nearly half the southern white population.

Thousands of land-hungry German and Scots-Irish filled the valleys along the eastern side of the Appalachians. Living tensely with Indians, they created a subsistence society. Gradually they acquired slaves and pursued mixed farming and cattle raising. Their enclaves remained isolated for several generations, which helped these pioneers cling fiercely to folkways they had brought across the Atlantic. Crude backcountry life appalled visitors from the more refined seaboard.

What such observers were really observing was the poverty of frontier life and the lack of schools, churches, and towns. Most families plunged into the backcountry with only a few crude household possessions, tools, animals, and the clothes on their backs. They lived in log cabins and planted their corn, beans, and wheat between tree stumps. Women toiled alongside men. For a generation, everyone endured a poor diet, endless work, and meager rewards.

By the 1760s, the southern backcountry had begun to emerge from the frontier stage. Small marketing towns became centers of craft activity, church life, and local government. Farms began producing surpluses for shipment east. Density of settlement increased, creating a social life known for harvest festivals, log-rolling contests, horse races, wedding celebrations, dances, and prodigious drinking bouts. Class distinctions remained narrow compared with the older seaboard settlements, as many backcountry settlements acquired the look of permanence.

Family Life in the South

As the South emerged from the early era of withering mortality and stunted families, male and female roles gradually became more physically and functionally separated. In most areas, the white gender ratio reached parity by the 1720s, depriving women of their leverage in the marriage market. The growth of slavery also changed white women's work role, with the wealthy planter's wife becoming a domestic manager.

The balanced sex ratio and the growth of slavery also brought changes for southern males. The planter's son had always been trained in horsemanship, the use of a gun, and the rhythms of agricultural life. Learning how to manage slaves was as important as lessons with tutors. Bred to command, southern planters' sons developed a self-confidence and authority that propelled many of them into leadership during the American Revolution.

On the small farms of the tidewater region and throughout the back settlements, women's roles closely resembled those of northern women. Women labored in the fields alongside their menfolk. "She is a very civil woman," noted an observer of a southern frontierswoman, "and shows nothing of ruggedness or immodesty in her carriage; yet she will carry a gun in the woods and kill deer and turkeys, shoot down wild cattle, catch and tie hogs, knock down beeves with an ax, and perform the most manful exercises as well as most men in those parts."

Marriage and family life were more informal in the backcountry. With vast areas unattended by ministers or courts, most couples married or "took up" with each other until an itinerant clergyman on horseback showed up to bless marriages and baptize children.

THE URBAN WORLD OF COMMERCE AND IDEAS

Only about 5 percent of eighteenth-century colonists lived in towns as large as 2,500; no cities had a population above 16,000 in 1750 or 30,000 in 1775. Yet urban societies were at the leading edge of the transition to "modern" life. There, a barter economy first gave way to a commercial economy, a social order based on assigned status turned into one based on achievement, rank-conscious and deferential politics faded into participatory and contentious politics, and small-scale craftsmanship was gradually replaced by factory production. From cities, intellectual life diffused and European ideas flowed into the colonies.

Sinews of Trade

In the half century after 1690, Boston, New York, Philadelphia, and Charleston blossomed into thriving commercial centers. Their growth accompanied the development of the agricultural interior. As the colonial population rose and spread out, minor seaports gathered 5,000 or more inhabitants.

Cities were trade centers. Through them flowed colonial exports (tobacco, rice, furs, wheat, timber products, and fish) and the imported goods that colonists needed: manufactured and luxury goods from England (glass, paper, iron implements, and cloth); wine, spices, coffee, tea, and sugar; and laborers. In these seaports, the pivotal figure was the merchant. Frequently engaged in both retail and wholesale trade, the merchant was also moneylender, shipbuilder, insurance agent, land developer, and often coordinator of artisan production.

By the eighteenth century, the American economy was integrated into an Atlantic trading system that connected Great Britain, western Europe, Africa, the West Indies, and Newfoundland. Britain, like other major trading nations of western Europe, pursued mercantilist trade policies. Mercantilism's core idea was that a country must gain wealth by increasing exports, taxing imports, regulating production and trade, and exploiting colonies. All these policies affected British treatment of North America.

Colonists could never produce enough exportable raw materials to pay for the imported goods they craved, so they had to earn credit in Britain by supplying the West Indies with foodstuffs and timber products. They also accumulated credit by providing shipping and distribution services, which Yankee merchant seamen and Yankee-built ships dominated.

The Artisan's World

Though merchants stood first in wealth and prestige in the colonial towns, artisans were far more numerous. About two-thirds of urban adult males (slaves excluded) labored at handicrafts. By the mid-eighteenth century, the colonial cities contained scores of specialized "leather apron men" besides the proverbial butcher, baker, and candlestick maker. Handicraft specialization increased as the cities matured, but every artisan worked with hand tools, usually in small shops.

Work patterns for artisans were irregular, dictated by weather, length of daylight, erratic delivery of raw materials, and shifting consumer demand. Ordinary laborers dreaded winter, when work was slow and firewood could cost several months' wages.

Urban artisans took fierce pride in their crafts. While deferring to those above them, they saw themselves as the backbone of the community, contributing essential products and services. "Our professions rendered us useful and necessary members of our community," Philadelphia shoemakers asserted; "proud of that rank, we aspired to no higher." This self-esteem and desire for community recognition sometimes jostled with the upper-class view of artisans as mere "mechanicks," part of the "vulgar herd."

Striving for respectability, artisans placed a premium on achieving economic independence. Every craftsman began as an apprentice, spending five or more teenage years in a master's shop; then, after fulfilling his contract, he became a "journeyman," selling his labor to a master and frequently living in his house, eating at his table, and sometimes marrying his daughter. He hoped to complete within a few years the three-step climb from servitude to self-employment. But in trades requiring greater organization and capital, the rise from journeyman to master often proved impossible.

In good times, artisans did well. But success was not automatic, even for those following Poor Richard's advice. Luck—an advantageous marriage, avoiding illness, an inheritance—was often critical. In Philadelphia, about half the artisans in the first half of the eighteenth century died leaving enough personal property to have ensured a comfortable standard of living. New England artisans did not fare so well.

The Urban Social Structure

Population growth, economic development, and wars altered the urban social structure between 1690 and 1765. Stately townhouses displayed fortunes from trade, shipbuilding, war contracting, and—probably most profitable of all—urban land development. A merchant's estate of £2,000 sterling was impressive in the early eighteenth century. Two generations later, North America's first millionaires were accumulating estates of £10,000 to £20,000 sterling.

Alongside urban wealth grew urban poverty. From the beginning, every city had its disabled, orphaned, and widowed who required aid. But after 1720, poverty marred the lives of many more city dwellers. Many were war widows with numerous children and no means of support. Others were rural migrants or recent immigrants who found fewer chances for employment than earlier. Boston was hit especially hard. Its economy stagnated in the 1740s, and taxpayers groaned under the burden of paying for heavy war expenditures. Cities devised new ways of helping the needy, such as large almshouses where the poor could be housed and fed more economically. But many of the indigent preferred "to starve in their homes" rather than endure the discipline and indignities of the poorhouse.

The spreading gap between wealthy and poor in the colonial cities was record-ed in the eighteenth-century tax lists. The top 5 percent of taxpayers increased their share of the cities' taxable assets from about 30 to 50 percent between 1690 and 1770. The bottom half of the taxable inhabitants saw their share of the wealth shrink from about 10 to 4 percent. Except in Boston, the urban middle class continued to gain ground. But the growth of princely fortunes amid increasing poverty made some urban dwellers reflect that Old World ills were reappearing in the New.

The Entrepreneurial Ethos

In the traditional view of society, economic life was supposed to operate according to what was fair, not what was profitable. Regulated prices and wages, quality con-trols, supervised public markets, and other such measures seemed natural because a community was defined as a single body of interrelated parts where individual rights and responsibilities formed a seamless web.

But as cities grew, new values took hold. Subordinating private interests to the commonweal came to seem unrealistic. Prosperity required the encouragement of acquisitive appetites rather than self-denial, for ambition would spur economic activity as more people sought more goods. The new view held that if people pur-sued their material desires competitively, they would collectively form a natural, impersonal market of producers and consumers, to everyone's advantage.

As the colonial port towns took their places in the Atlantic world of com-merce, merchants became accustomed to making decisions according to an emerg-ing commercial ethic that rejected traditional restraints on entrepreneurial activity. If wheat fetched eight shillings a bushel in the West Indies but only five in Boston, a grain merchant felt justified in sending all he could purchase from local farmers to the more distant buyer. The new transatlantic market responded only to the invisible laws of supply and demand. Tension between the new economic freedom and the older concern for the public good erupted only with food shortages or gal-loping inflation. Because the American colonies experienced none of the famines that ravaged Europe in this period, such crises were rare, usually during war. Nonetheless, two conceptions of the relationship between community and eco-nomic life rubbed against each other for many decades.

The American Enlightenment

Ideas about not only economic life but also the nature of the universe and the improvement of the human condition filtered across the Atlantic. In the eighteenth century a colonial version of the European intellectual movement called the Enlightenment came into focus.

In what is called the Age of Reason, European thinkers rejected the pessimistic Calvinist concept of innate human depravity, replacing it with the optimistic notion that a benevolent God had blessed humankind with the supreme gift of reason. Thinkers like John Locke, in his influential *Essay Concerning Human Understanding* (1689), argued that God had not predetermined the content of the human mind, but had instead given it the capacity to acquire knowledge. All Enlightenment thinkers prized this acquisition of knowledge, for it allowed humankind to improve its condition. As the great mathematician Isaac Newton demonstrated, systematic investigation could unlock the secrets of the physical universe. Moreover, scientific knowledge could be applied to improve society.

The scientific and intellectual advances of the seventeenth and eighteenth centuries encouraged a belief in "natural law" and debate about "natural" human rights. Eighteenth-century Americans began to make significant contributions to the advancement of science. Naturalists such as John Bartram of Philadelphia gathered and described plants from all over eastern North America as part of the transatlantic attempt to classify all plant life into one universal system. Professor John Winthrop III of Harvard made an unusually accurate measurement of the earth's distance from the sun. Foremost of all was Benjamin Franklin, whose spectacular (and dangerous) experiments with electricity, the properties of which were just becoming known, earned him an international reputation.

Franklin's true genius as a figure of the Enlightenment came in his practical application of scientific knowledge. Among his inventions were the lightning rod, which nearly ended the age-old danger of fires when lightning struck wooden buildings; bifocal spectacles; and a stove that heated rooms far more cost-effectively than the usual open fireplace. Franklin also made his adopted city of Philadelphia a center of the American Enlightenment. He led the founding of America's first circulating library in 1731, an artisans' debating club for "mutual improvement" through discussion of the latest ideas from Europe, and an intercolonial scientific association that in 1769 became the American Philosophical Society.

Most colonists were not educated enough to participate actively in the American Enlightenment, and only a handful read French Enlightenment authors like Voltaire. But the efforts of men such as Franklin exposed thousands, especially in the cities, to new currents of thought. Hopes were being kindled that Americans, blessed by an abundant environment, might achieve the Enlightenment ideal of a perfect society.

THE GREAT AWAKENING

Many of the changes occurring in eighteenth-century colonial society converged in the Great Awakening, the first of many religious revivals that would sweep America during the next two centuries. The timing and character of the Awakening varied from region to region. But everywhere, this quest for spiritual renewal challenged old sources of authority and produced patterns of thought and behavior that helped fuel a revolutionary movement in the next generation.

Fading Faith

Early eighteenth-century America remained an overwhelmingly Protestant culture. Puritanism—that is, the Congregational Church—dominated all of New England except Rhode Island. Anglicanism held sway in much of New York and throughout the South except the backcountry. In the mid-Atlantic and in the back settlements, English Quakers and Baptists, Scots-Irish Presbyterians, and German

Mennonites, Dunkers, Moravians, and Lutherans all mingled. Yet only about one-third of Americans belonged to one of these groups; those who went to no church at all remained the majority. In many areas, ministers and churches were simply unavailable. In Virginia, the most populous colony, in 1761 there were 60 par-sons—one for every 5,800 people.

Most colonial churches were voluntary ("congregated") groups, formed for reasons of conscience, not because of government compulsion. Catholics, Jews, and nonbelievers could not vote or hold office. But the persecution of Quakers and Catholics had largely passed, and some dissenting groups by 1720 had gained the right to use long-obligatory church taxes to support their own congregations.

Most efforts to tighten organization and discipline failed. For example, Anglican ministers had to be ordained in England and regularly report to the bishop of London. But in his Chesapeake parish, an Anglican priest faced wealthy planters who controlled the vestry (the local church's governing body), set his salary, and would drive him out if he challenged them too forcefully. In Connecticut, the Saybrook Platform of 1708 created a network of Congregational Churches, but individual churches still preserved much of their autonomy.

As early as the 1660s, the Congregational clergy of New England had adopted the Half-Way Covenant in order to combat religious indifference. It allowed chil-dren of church members, if they adhered to the "forms of godliness," to join the church even if they could not demonstrate that they had undergone a conversion experience. They could not, however, vote in church affairs or take communion.

Such compromises and innovations could not halt the creeping religious apathy that many ministers sensed. An educated clergy, its energies often drained by doctrinal disputes, appealed too much to the mind and not enough to the heart. As one Connecticut leader remembered, "The spirit of God appeared to be awful-ly withdrawn."

The Awakeners' Message

The Great Awakening was not a unified movement, but rather a series of revivals that swept different regions between 1720 and 1760 with varying degrees of inten-sity. The first stirrings came in the 1720s in New Jersey, where Dutch Reformed minister Theodore Frelinghuysen excited his congregation by emotional preaching about the need to be "saved" rather than offering the usual theological abstrac-tions. The Awakening spread to Pennsylvania in the 1730s and then to the Connecticut River valley. There its greatest preacher was Jonathan Edwards in Northampton, Massachusetts. Later a philosophical giant in the colonies, Edwards as a young man gained renown by frightening his parishioners with the fate of "sinners in the hands of an angry God." "How manifold have been the abomina-tions of your life!" he intoned. "Are there not some here that have debased them-selves below the dignity of human nature, by wallowing in sensual filthiness, as swine in the mire . . . ?" Edwards paraded one sin after another before his trem-bling congregants and then drew such graphic pictures of hell that they were soon preparing frantically for the conversion by which they would be "born again." His *Faithful Narrative of the Surprizing Work of God* (1736), which described his

George Whitefield, who first toured the American colonies in 1739 and 1740, sent thousands of souls "flying to Christ" with his emotional sermons. More Americans heard Whitefield on his many seaboard itineracies than any other figure in the eighteenth century. (National Portrait Gallery, London)

town's awakening, was the first published revival narrative. This literary form would be used many times in the future to fan the flames of evangelical religion.

In 1739, these regional brushfires of evangelicalism were drawn together by a 24-year-old Anglican priest from England, George Whitefield. Inspired by John Wesley, the founder of English Methodism, Whitefield used his magnificent speaking voice in dramatic, spontaneous open-air preaching before huge gatherings.

Whitefield barnstormed seven times along the American seaboard, beginning in 1739 and 1740. With each success his fame and influence grew. In Boston, he preached to 19,000 in three days and at a farewell sermon left 25,000 writhing in fear of damnation. In his wake came American preachers whom he had inspired, like Devereaux Jarratt.

The appeal of the Awakeners lay in both the medium and the message. They preached that the established, college-trained clergy was too intellectual and tradition-bound. Congregations were dead, Whitefield declared, "because dead men preach to them." The fires of Protestant belief could be reignited only if individuals assumed responsibility for their own conversion.

An important part of the Awakening was "lay exhorting," which horrified most established clergymen. "Exhorting" meant that anyone—young or old, female or male, black or white—spontaneously preached about his or her conversion. This shattered the trained clergy's monopoly and gave new importance to the oral culture of ordinary people, whose spontaneous outpourings contrasted sharply with the controlled literary culture of the gentry. Through lay exhorting, all manner of ordinary people, including children, servants, and slaves, defied assigned roles.

How religion, social change, and politics became interwoven in the Great Awakening can be seen by examining two regions swept by revivalism. Both Boston, the heartland of Puritanism, and interior Virginia, a land of struggling small planters and slave-rich aristocrats, experienced the Great Awakening, but in different ways and at different times.

The Urban North

In Boston, Whitefield-inspired revivalism blazed up amid political controversy about paper money and land banks, which pitted large merchants against local traders, artisans, and the laboring poor. At first, Boston's elite applauded Whitefield's ability to call the masses to worship. He might, it seemed, restore social harmony by redirecting people away from earthly matters and toward concern for their souls. But when he left Boston in 1740, others followed him who were more critical of the "unconverted" clergy and the self-indulgent accumulation of wealth. One was James Davenport, who to the elite appeared anything but respectable.

Finding every meetinghouse closed to him, even those whose clergy had embraced the Awakening, Davenport preached daily on the Boston Common, aroused religious ecstasy among thousands, and stirred up feeling against the city's leading figures. Respectable people decided that revivalism had got out of hand when ordinary people began verbally attacking opponents as "carnal wretches, hypocrites, fighters against God, children of the devil, cursed Pharisees." A revival that had begun as a return to religion among backsliding Christians had overlapped with political affairs. Hence, it threatened polite culture, which stressed order and discipline from ordinary people.

The Rural South

The Great Awakening was ebbing in New England and the middle colonies by 1744, although aftershocks continued for years. But in Virginia, where the initial religious earthquake was barely felt, tremors of enthusiasm rippled through society from the mid-1740s onward. As in Boston, the Awakeners challenged and disturbed the gentry-led social order.

Whitefield stirred some religious fervor during his early trips through Virginia. Traveling "New Light" preachers were soon gathering large crowds both in the backcountry and in the traditionally Anglican parishes of the older settled areas. By 1747, worried Anglican clergyman convinced the governor to issue a proclamation restraining "strolling preachers." As in other colonies, Virginia's leaders despised traveling evangelists, who, like lay exhorters, conjured up a world without properly constituted authority. When the Hanover County court gave fiery James Davenport a license to preach in 1750, the governor ordered the suppression of all circuit riders.

New Light Presbyterianism, challenging the gentry-dominated Anglican Church's spiritual monopoly, spread in the 1750s. Then, in the 1760s, came the Baptists. Renouncing all status distinctions, this movement reached out to thousands of un-churched people. Like northern revivalists, Baptists focused on the conversion experience. Many of their preachers were uneducated farmers and artisans who called themselves "Christ's poor" and insisted that heaven was populated more by the humble than by the rich. Among the poorest of all, Virginia's 140,000 slaves in 1760, the evangelical message penetrated deeply.

The insurgent Baptist movement in rural Virginia became both a quest for a personal, emotionally satisfying religion among ordinary folk and a rejection of gentry values. Established Anglican pulpits denounced it as furiously as had respectable urban New England divines. In both regions, social changes had weakened the cultural authority of the upper class and, in the context of religious revival, produced a vision of a society drawn along more equal lines.

Legacy of the Awakening

By the time Whitefield returned to America for his third tour in 1745, the revival had burned out in the North. Its effects, however, were long-lasting. Notably, it promoted the idea that all denominations were equally legitimate.

By legitimizing the dissenting Protestant groups that had sprung up in seventeenth-century England, the Great Awakening gave them all a basis for living together in relative harmony. From this framework of denominationalism came a second change—the separation of church and state. Once a variety of churches gained legitimacy, it was hard to justify one denomination claiming special privileges. In the seventeenth century, Roger Williams had tried to sever church and state because he believed that ties with civil bodies would corrupt the Church. But during the Awakening, groups such as the Baptists and the Presbyterians in Virginia constituted their own religious bodies and broke the Anglican monopoly as *the* Church in the colony. This undermining of the church-state tie would be completed during the revolutionary era.

A third effect of the revival was to legitimate community diversity. Almost from their beginnings, Rhode Island, the Carolinas, and the middle colonies had recognized this. But uniformity had been prized elsewhere, especially in Massachusetts and Connecticut. There, the Awakening split Congregational Churches into New Lights and Old Lights. Mid-Atlantic Presbyterian Churches faced similar schisms. In hundreds of rural communities by the 1750s, two or three churches existed where only one had stood before. People learned that the fabric of community could be woven from threads of many hues.

New eighteenth-century colleges reflected the Awakening's pluralism. Before 1740, there existed only Puritan Harvard (1636) and Yale (1701) and Anglican William and Mary (1693). To these were added six new colleges between 1746 and 1769—Dartmouth, Brown, Princeton, and what are now Columbia, Rutgers, and the University of Pennsylvania. None was controlled by an established church, all had governing bodies composed of men of different faiths, and all admitted students regardless of religion. Eager for students and funds, they made nonsectarian appeals, and their curricula combined traditional Latin and Greek with the new natural sciences and natural philosophy.

Last, the Awakening nurtured a subtle change in values that crossed over into politics and daily life. Especially for ordinary people, religious revival created a new feeling of self-worth. People assumed new responsibilities in religious affairs and became skeptical of dogma and authority. Many, especially Baptists, decried the growing materialism and deplored the new acceptance of self-interested behavior. By learning to oppose authority and create new churches, thousands of colonists unknowingly rehearsed for revolution.

POLITICAL LIFE

"Were it not for government, the world would soon run into all manner of disorders and confusions," wrote a Massachusetts clergyman early in the eighteenth century. Few colonists or Europeans would have disagreed. Government existed to protect life, liberty, and property.

But how should political power be divided—in England, between the English government and the American colonies, and within each colony? Colonists naturally drew heavily on inherited political ideas and institutions—almost entirely English ones, for it was English charters that sanctioned settlement, English governors who ruled, and English common law that governed the courts. But meeting unexpected circumstances in a new environment, colonists modified familiar political forms.

Structuring Colonial Governments

All societies consider it essential to determine the final source of political authority. In England, the notion of supreme, God-given monarchical authority was crumbling even before the planting of the colonies. In its place arose the belief that stable government depended on blending and balancing the three pure forms of government: monarchy, aristocracy, and democracy. Unalloyed, each would degenerate into oppression. Most colonists felt that England's Glorious Revolution of 1688 had vindicated and strengthened a carefully balanced political system.

In the colonies, political balance was achieved somewhat differently. The governor, as the king's agent (or, in proprietary colonies, the agent of the proprietor to whom the king delegated authority), represented monarchy. Bicameral legislatures arose in most of the colonies in the seventeenth century, and in most colonies they had upper houses of wealthy men appointed by the governor; as a pale equivalent of Britain's House of Lords, it formed a nascent aristocracy. The assembly, elected by white male freeholders, replicated the House of Commons and was the democratic element. Every statute required the governor's assent (except in Rhode Island and Connecticut), and all colonial laws required final approval from the king's privy council. This royal check operated imperfectly, however. It took many months for a law to be sent to England and for word of its fate to come back; but in the meantime it was in effect in the colony.

In England, landownership conferred political rights. Only men with property producing an annual rental income of 40 shillings could vote or hold office. (They also had to profess Christianity.) The colonists closely followed this principle, except in Massachusetts, where until 1691 Church membership was the basic requirement. As in England, the poor and propertyless were excluded, for they lacked the "stake in society" that supposedly produced responsible voters.

In England the 40-shilling freehold requirement was intended to keep the electorate small; but in most colonies, where land was cheap, it conferred the vote on 50 to 75 percent of the adult free males. As the proportion of landless colonists increased in the eighteenth century, however, the franchise contracted.

Americans generally agreed that the wealthy and socially prominent should hold political power. Balancing this elitism, however, was the notion that the entire electorate should periodically judge the performance of those entrusted

Table 4.1	*Colonial Foundations of the American Political System*
1606	Virginia companies of London and Plymouth grant patents to settle lands in North America.
1619	First elected colonial legislature meets in Virginia.
1634	Under a charter granted in 1632, Maryland's proprietor is given all the authority "as any bishop of Durham" ever held—more than the king possessed in England.
1635	The council in Virginia deports Governor John Harvey for exceeding his power, thus asserting the rights of local magistrates to contest authority of royally appointed governors.
1643	The colonies of Massachusetts, Plymouth, Connecticut, and New Haven draw up articles of confederation and form the first intercolonial union, the United Colonies of New England.
1647	Under a charter granted in 1644, elected freemen from the Providence Plantations draft a constitution establishing freedom of conscience, separating church and state, and authorizing referenda by the towns on laws passed by the assembly.
1677	The Laws, Concessions, and Agreements for West New Jersey provide for a legislature elected annually by virtually all free males, secret voting, liberty of conscience, election of justices of the peace and local officeholders, and trial by jury in public so that "justice may not be done in a corner."
1689	James II deposed in England in the Glorious Revolution and royal governors, accused of abusing their authority, ousted in Massachusetts, New York, and Maryland.
1701	First colonial unicameral legislature meets in Pennsylvania under the Frame of Government of 1701.
1735	John Peter Zenger, a New York printer, acquitted of seditious libel for printing attacks on the royal governor and his faction, thus widening the freedom of the press.
1754	First congress of all the colonies meets at Albany (with seven colonies sending delegates) and agrees on a Plan of Union (which is rejected by the colonies and the English government).
1765	The Stamp Act Congress, the first intercolonial convention called outside England's authority, meets in New York.

with political power and reject those who were found wanting. And, following the precedent of England's Glorious Revolution, in British America the people were assumed to have the right to badger their leaders, to protest openly, and, in extreme cases of abuse of power, to assume control and put things right. Crowd action, frequently effective, gradually achieved a kind of legitimacy.

The Crowd in Action

Popular protests seldom faced effective police power. In the countryside, where most colonists lived, only the county sheriff insulated civil leaders from angry farmers. In the towns, the sheriff had only the night watch to keep order. (In 1757, New York's night watch was described as a "parcell of idle, drinking vigilant snorers, who never quelled any nocturnal tumult in their lives.") In theory, the militia stood ready to suppress public disturbances, but crowds usually included many militiamen.

Boston's impressment riot of 1747 vividly illustrates the people's readiness to defend their inherited privileges and the weakness of law enforcement. It began when Commodore Charles Knowles brought his Royal Navy ships to Boston for provisioning—and to replenish the ranks of mariners thinned by desertion. Knowles sent press gangs out to fill vacancies from Boston's waterfront population.

But before the press gangs could hustle away their victims, a crowd of angry Bostonians seized several British officers, surrounded the governor's house, and demanded the release of their townsmen. When the sheriff and his deputies attempted to intervene, the mob mauled them. The militia refused to respond. An enraged Knowles threatened to bombard the town, but negotiations amid further tumult averted a showdown. Finally, Knowles released the impressed Bostonians. After the riot, a young politician named Samuel Adams defended Boston's defiance of royal authority. The people, he argued, had a "natural right" to band together against press gangs that deprived them of their liberty. Local magnates who had supported the governor were "tools to arbitrary power."

The Growing Power of the Assemblies

While the Impressment Riot of 1747 was dramatic, a more gradual and restrained change was underway—the growing ambition and power of the legislative assemblies—that was far more important. For most of the seventeenth century, royal and proprietary governors had exercised greater power in relation to the elected legislatures than did the king in relation to Parliament. Governors could dissolve the lower houses and delay their sitting, control the election of their speakers, and in most colonies initiate legislation with their appointed councils. They had authority to appoint and dismiss judges at all levels and to create chancery courts, which sat without juries. Governors also controlled the expenditure of public monies and had authority to grant land to individuals and groups, which they sometimes used to confer vast estates on their favorites.

Since the seventeenth century, Virginia, Massachusetts, and New York had been royal colonies, with crown-appointed governors. In the eighteenth century, royal government came to New Jersey (1702), South Carolina (1719), and North Carolina (1729), replacing proprietary regimes.

Many royal governors were competent military officers or bureaucrats, but some were corrupt recipients of patronage jobs. Some never even came over, instead hiring a lieutenant governor. One committed suicide a week after arriving. But most governors were not crazy, corrupt, or absent; they were merely mediocre. And they lacked the vast patronage power that enabled English government ministers to manipulate elections and buy off opponents.

Eighteenth-century American legislatures challenged the swollen powers of the colonial governors. Bit by bit, they won new rights—to initiate legislation, to elect their own speakers, to settle contested elections, to discipline members, and to nominate provincial treasurers who disbursed public funds. Most important, they won the "power of the purse"—the authority to initiate money bills, specifying how much money should be raised by taxes and how it should be spent. Thus the elected assemblies gradually transformed themselves into governing bodies reflecting the interests of the electorate.

Local Politics

Binding elected officeholders to their constituents became an important feature of the colonial political system. In England, the House of Commons was filled with representatives from "rotten boroughs" (ancient places left virtually or totally uninhabited by population shifts) and with men whose vote was controlled by the government because they had accepted offices or favors. Nevertheless, its members claimed to represent the entire nation rather than narrow local interests. American assemblies, by contrast, contained mostly representatives sent by voters who instructed them on particular issues and held them accountable.

Royal governors and colonial grandees who sat as councillors often deplored this localist, popular orientation. Sniffed one aristocratic New Yorker, the assemblies were crowded with "plain, illiterate husbandmen [small farmers], whose views seldom extended farther than the regulation of highways, the destruction of wolves, wildcats, and foxes, and the advancement of the other little interests of the particular counties which they were chosen to represent." In actuality, most lower-house members were merchants, lawyers, and substantial planters and farmers—by the mid-eighteenth century, the political elite in most colonies. But they took pride in upholding their constituents' interests, for they saw themselves as bulwarks against oppression and arbitrary rule, which history taught them were most frequently imposed by monarchs and their appointed agents.

Local government was usually more important to the colonists than provincial government. In the North, local political authority generally rested in the towns (which included surrounding rural areas). The New England town meeting decided a wide range of matters, arguing until it could express itself as a single unit. In the South, the county was the primary unit of government, and by the mid-eighteenth century, a landed squirearchy of third- and fourth-generation families had achieved dominance. They ruled the county courts and the legislature, and substantial farmers served in minor offices. At court sessions, usually four times a year, deeds were read aloud and then recorded, juries impaneled and justice dispensed, elections held, licenses issued, and proclamations read. On election days, voters were first treated by the gentry to copious glasses of "bumbo."

The Spread of Whig Ideology

Whether in local or provincial affairs, a political ideology called Whig or "republican" had spread widely by the mid-eighteenth century. This body of thought, inherited from England, rested on the belief that concentrated power was historically the enemy of liberty and that too much power lodged in any person or group usually produced corruption and tyranny. The best defenses against concentrated power were balanced government, elected legislatures adept at checking executive authority, prohibition of standing armies (almost always controlled by tyrannical monarchs), and vigilance by the people in watching their leaders for telltale signs of corruption.

Much of this Whig ideology reached the people through the newspapers that began appearing in the seaboard towns in the early eighteenth century. By 1763, some 23 papers circulated in the colonies. Many reprinted pieces by English Whig

TIMELINE

1662 Half-Way Covenant in New England	**1685–1715** Stagnation in tobacco market	**1704** *Boston News-Letter*, first regular colonial newspaper, published	**1713** Beginning of Scots-Irish and German immigration	**1715–1730** Volume of slave trade doubles
1718 French settle New Orleans	**1720s** Black population begins to increase naturally	**1734–1736** Great Awakening begins in Northampton, Massachusetts	**1735** Zenger acquitted of seditious libel in New York	**1739–1740** Whitefield's first American tour spreads Great Awakening; Slaves compose 90 percent of population on Carolina rice coast
1740s Indigo becomes staple crop in Lower South	**1747** Benjamin Franklin publishes first *Poor Richard's Almanack;* Impressment riot in Boston	**1760** Africans compose 20 percent of American population	**1760s–1770s** Spanish establish California mission system	**1769** American Philosophical Society founded at Philadelphia

writers railing against corruption and creeping despotism. Though limited to a few pages and published only once or twice a week, the papers passed from hand to hand and were read aloud in taverns and coffeehouses, so that their contents probably reached most urban households and a substantial minority of rural farms.

The new power of the press and its importance in guarding the people's liberties against would-be tyrants (such as abrasive royal governors) was vividly illustrated in the Zenger case in New York. Young John Peter Zenger, a printer's apprentice, had been hired in 1733 by the antigovernment faction of Lewis Morris to start a newspaper that would publicize the tyrannical actions of Governor William Cosby. In Zenger's *New-York Weekly Journal*, the Morris faction fired salvos at Cosby's interference with the courts and his alleged corruption.

Arrested for seditious libel, Zenger was brilliantly defended by Andrew Hamilton, a Philadelphia lawyer hired by the Morris faction to convince the jury that Zenger had been simply trying to inform the people of attacks on their liberties. Although the jury acquitted Zenger, the libel laws remained very restrictive. But the acquittal did reinforce the notion that the government was the people's servant, and it brought home the point that public criticism could keep people with political authority responsible to the people they ruled. Such ideas about liberty and corruption, raised in the context of local politics, would shortly achieve a much broader significance.

✦✦✦✦✦

CONCLUSION

America in 1750

The American colonies, robust and expanding, matured rapidly between 1700 and 1750. Transatlantic commerce linked them closely to Europe, Africa, and other parts of the New World. Churches, schools, and towns—the visible marks of the receding frontier—appeared everywhere. A balanced sex ratio and stable family life had been achieved throughout the colonies. Seasoned political leaders and familiar political institutions functioned from Maine to Georgia.

Yet the sinew, bone, and muscle of American society had not yet fully knit together. The polyglot population, one-fifth of it bound in chattel slavery and its Native American component still unassimilated and uneasily situated on the frontier, was a kaleidoscopic mixture of ethnic and religious groups. Its economy, while developing rapidly, showed weaknesses, particularly in New England, where land resources had been strained. The social structure reflected the colonizers' emergence from a frontier stage, but the consolidation of wealth by a landed and mercantile elite was matched by pockets of poverty appearing in the cities and some rural areas. Full of strength, yet marked by awkward incongruities, colonial America in 1750 approached an era of strife and momentous decisions.

Recommended Reading

Population Growth and Economic Development

John J. McCusker and Russell R. Menard, *The Economy of British America, 1607–1789* (1985); James A. Henretta and Gregory Nobles, *Evolution and Revolution: American Society: 1620–1820* (1987); Edwin J. Perkins, *The Economy of Colonial America*, 2d ed. (1988); Stephanie G. Wolf, *Urban Village: Population, Community, and Family Structure in Germantown, Pennsylvania* (1977); Aaron S. Fogleman, *Hopeful Journeys: German Immigration, Settlement, and Political Culture in Colonial America* (1996); R. J. Dickson, *Ulster Immigration to Colonial America, 1718–1775* (1966); Jon Butler, *The Huguenots in Colonial America* (1983); Ned Landsman, *Scotland and Its First American Colony* (1985); Bernard Bailyn, *Voyagers to the West: A Passage in the Peopling of America on the Eve of the American Revolution* (1986); Stephen Innes, *Creating the Commonwealth: The Economic Culture of Puritan New England* (1995).

The Eighteenth-Century North

Richard Bushman, *From Puritan to Yankee* (1967); Christopher M. Jedrey, *The World of John Cleaveland: Family and Community in Eighteenth-Century New England* (1979); Daniel Vickers, *Farmers and Fishermen: Two Centuries of Work in Essex County, Massachusetts, 1630–1850* (1994); David W. Conroy, *In Public Houses: Drink and the Revolution of Authority in Colonial Massachusetts* (1995); Laurel T. Ulrich, *Good Wives: Image and Reality in the Lives of Women in Northern New England, 1650–1750* (1982); Cornelia Hughes Dayton, *Women before the Bar: Gender, Law, and Society in Connecticut, 1639–1789* (1995); Mary Beth Norton, *Founding Mothers and Fathers: Gendered Power and the Forming of American Society* (1996); James Lemon, *The Best Poor Man's Country: A Geographical Study of Early Southeastern Pennsylvania* (1972).

The Eighteenth-Century South

Paul G. E. Clemens, *The Atlantic Economy and Colonial Maryland's Eastern Shore: From Tobacco to Grain* (1980); Rhys Isaac, *The Transformation of Virginia, 1740–1790* (1982); Allan Kulikoff, *Tobacco and Slaves: The Development of Southern Culture in the Chesapeake, 1680–1800* (1986); T. H. Breen, *Tobacco Culture: The Mentality of the Great Tidewater Planters on the Eve of the Revolution* (1985); Daniel Blake Smith, *Inside the Great House: Planter Family Life in Eighteenth-Century Chesapeake Society* (1980); Joyce E. Chaplin, *An Anxious Pursuit: Agricultural Innovation and Modernity in the Lower South, 1730–1815* (1993); Robert Olwell, *Maters, Slaves, and Subjects: The Culture of Power in the Carolina Low Country, 1740–1790* (1998).

The Developing Cities

Gary B. Nash, *The Urban Crucible: Social Change, Political Consciousness, and the Origins of the American Revolution* (1979); Billy G. Smith, *The "Lower Sort": Philadelphia's Laboring People, 1750–1800* (1990); J. E. Crowley, *This Sheba Self: The Conceptualization of Economic Life in Eighteenth-Century America* (1974); G. B. Warden, *Boston, 1687–1776* (1970); Esmond Wright, *Franklin of Philadelphia* (1986).

The Great Awakening and the American Enlightenment

Alan Heimert, *Religion and the American Mind: From the Great Awakening to the Revolution* (1966); Harry S. Stout, *The New England Soul: Preaching and Religious Life in Colonial New England* (1986); Patricia Tracy, *Jonathan Edwards, Pastor* (1979); Susan Juster, *Disorderly Women: Sexual Politics and Evangelicalism in Revolutionary New England* (1994); Frank J. Lambert, *"Pedlar in Divinity": George Whitefield and the Transatlantic Revivals* (1994); Patricia Bonomi, *Under the Cope of Heaven: Religion, Society, and Politics in Colonial America* (1986); Henry May, *The American Enlightenment* (1976).

Colonial Politics

Bernard Bailyn, *The Origins of American Politics* (1968); Charles Sydnor, *American Revolutionaries in the Making: Political Practices in Washington's Virginia* (1965); William Pencak, *War, Politics, and Revolution in Provincial Massachusetts* (1981); Patricia Bonomi, *A Factious People: Politics and Society in Colonial New York* (1977); Robert Zemsky, *Merchants, Farmers, and River Gods: An Essay on Eighteenth-Century American Politics* (1971); Alan Tully, *Forming American Politics: Ideas, Interests, and Institutions in Colonial New York and Pennsylvania* (1994).

CHAPTER 5

Bursting the Colonial Bonds

In 1758, when he was 21 years old, Ebenezer MacIntosh of Boston laid down his shoe-maker's awl and enlisted in the Massachusetts expedition against the French on Lake Champlain. The son of a poor Boston shoemaker who had fought against the French in a previous war, MacIntosh had known poverty all his life. Service against the French offered the hope of plunder or at least an enlistment bounty worth half a year's wages. One among thousands of colonists who fought against the "Gallic menace" in the Seven Years' War, MacIntosh did his bit in the climactic Anglo-American struggle that drove the French from North America.

But a greater role lay ahead for the poor Boston shoemaker. Two years after the Peace of Paris in 1763, England imposed a stamp tax on the American colonists. In the massive protests that followed, MacIntosh emerged as the street leader of the Boston crowd. In two nights of the most violent attacks on private property ever witnessed in America, a Boston crowd nearly destroyed the houses of two of the colony's most important officials. On August 14, they tore through the house of Andrew Oliver, a wealthy merchant and the appointed distributor of stamps for Massachusetts. Twelve days later, MacIntosh led the crowd in attacking the mansion of Thomas Hutchinson, a wealthy merchant who served as lieutenant governor and chief justice of Massachusetts. "The mob was so general," wrote the governor, "and so supported that all civil power ceased in an instant."

For the next several months, the power of the poor Boston shoemaker grew. Called "General" MacIntosh and "Captain-General of the Liberty Tree" by his townspeople, he soon sported a militia uniform of gold and blue and a hat laced with gold. Two thousand townsmen followed his commands on November 5, when they marched in orderly ranks through the crooked streets of Boston to demonstrate their solidarity in resisting the hated stamps.

Five weeks later, a crowd publicly humiliated stamp distributor Oliver. Demanding that he announce his resignation before the assembled citizenry, they marched him across town in a driving December rain. With MacIntosh at his elbow, he finally reached the "Liberty Tree," which had become a symbol of resistance to England's new colonial policies. There the aristocratic Oliver ate humble pie. He concluded his resignation remarks with bitter words, hissing sardonically that he would "always think myself very happy when it shall be in my power to serve the people."

"To serve the people" was an ancient idea embedded in English political culture, but it assumed new meaning in the American colonies during the epic third quarter of the eighteenth century. Few colonists in 1750 held even a faint desire to break the connection with England, and fewer still might have predicted the form of government that 13 independent states in an independent nation might fashion. Yet in a whirlwind of events, two million colonists moved haltingly toward a showdown with mighty England. Little-known men like Ebenezer MacIntosh as well as his well-known and historically celebrated townsmen Samuel Adams, John Hancock, and John Adams were part of the struggle. Collectively, ordinary people such as MacIntosh influenced—and in fact sometimes even dictated—the revolutionary movement in the colonies. Though we read and speak mostly of a small group of "founding fathers," the wellsprings of the American Revolution can be fully discovered only among a variety of people from different social groups, occupations, regions, and religions.

✦✦✦✦✦

This chapter addresses the tensions in late colonial society, the imperial crisis that followed the Seven Years' War (in the colonies often called the French and Indian War), and the tumultuous decade that led to the "shot heard round the world" fired at Concord Bridge in April 1775. It portrays the origins of a dual American Revolution. Ebenezer MacIntosh, in leading the Boston mob against crown officers and colonial collaborators who tried to implement a new colonial policy after 1763, helped set in motion a revolutionary movement to restore ancient liberties thought by the Americans to be under deliberate attack in England. This movement eventually escalated into the war for American independence.

But MacIntosh's Boston followers were also venting years of resentment at the accumulation of wealth and power by Boston's aristocratic elite. Behind every swing of the ax, every shattered crystal goblet and splintered mahogany chair, lay the fury of a Bostonian who had seen the city's conservative elite try to dismantle the town meeting, had suffered economic hardship, and had lost faith that opportunity and just relations still prevailed in his town. This sentiment, which called for the reform of a colonial society that had become corrupt, self-indulgent, and dominated by an elite, fed an idealistic commitment to reshape American society even while severing the colonial bond. As distinguished from the war for independence, this was the American Revolution.

THE CLIMACTIC SEVEN YEARS' WAR

After a brief period of peace following King George's War (1744–1748), France and England fought the fourth, largest, and by far most significant of the wars for empire that had begun in the late seventeenth century. Known variously as the Seven Years' War, the French and Indian War, and the Great War for Empire, this global conflict in part represented a showdown for control of North America between the Atlantic Ocean and the Mississippi River. In North America, the Anglo-American forces ultimately prevailed, and their victory dramatically affected the lives of all the diverse people of the vast continent.

War and the Management of Empire

England began constructing a more coherent imperial administration after the Glorious Revolution. In 1696, a professional Board of Trade replaced the old Lords of Trade; the Treasury strengthened the customs service; and Parliament created overseas vice-admiralty courts, which dispensed with juries in prosecuting smugglers who evaded the Navigation Acts. Parliament began playing a more active role after the reign of Queen Anne (1702–1714) and continued to do so when weak, German-speaking King George I came to the throne. Royal governors received greater powers and more detailed instructions and came under more insistent demands from the Board of Trade to enforce British policies. England was quietly installing the machinery of imperial management and a corps of colonial bureaucrats.

The best test of an effectively organized state is its ability to wage war. Four times between 1689 and 1763, England matched its strength against France, its archrival in North America and the Caribbean. These wars of empire had tremendous consequences for home governments, colonial subjects, and Indians.

We have already seen (in Chapter 3) how the Peace of Utrecht that ended Queen Anne's War (1702–1713) brought victor's spoils of great importance to Great Britain. The generation of peace that followed was really only a time-out, which both Britain and France used to strengthen their war-making capacity. Britain's productive and efficiently governed New World colonies made important contributions. During this period of "salutary neglect," king and Parliament actually increased their control over colonial affairs.

Concerned mainly with economic regulation, Parliament added new articles to the list of items produced in America that had to be shipped to England before being exported to another country. Parliament also curtailed colonial production of articles important to the British economy: woolen cloth (1699), beaver hats (1732), and finished iron products (1750). Most important, Parliament passed the Molasses Act in 1733. Attempting to stop the trade between New England and the French West Indies, where Yankee traders exchanged fish, beef, and pork for molasses to convert into rum, Parliament imposed a prohibitive duty of six pence per gallon on French molasses. This turned many of New England's largest merchants and distillers into smugglers, for a generation schooling them, their captains and crews, and waterfront artisans in defying royal authority.

The generation of peace ended abruptly in 1739 when Britain declared war on Spain. The immediate cause was the ear of an English sea captain, Robert Jenkins, cut off eight years before when Spanish authorities caught him smuggling. Encouraged by his government, Jenkins publicly displayed his pickled ear in 1738 to whip up war fever against Spain. The real cause, however, was Great Britain's determination to continue its drive toward commercial domination of the Atlantic.

In 1744–1748 the Anglo-Spanish war merged into a much larger Anglo-French conflict, called King George's War in America and the War of the Austrian Succession in Europe. Its scale far exceeded previous conflicts, highlighting the need for discipline within the empire. Unprecedented military expenditures led Britain to ask its West Indian and American colonies to share the costs of defending—and extending—the empire and to tailor their behavior to home-country needs.

Outbreak of Hostilities

The tension between British and French colonists in North America, which reached back to the early seventeenth century, was intensified by the spectacular population growth of the English colonies: from 250,000 in 1700 to 1.25 million in 1750, and to 1.75 million in the next decade. Three-quarters of the increase came in the colonies south of New York, propelling thousands of land-hungry settlers toward the western trading empire of the French and their Indian allies.

Promoting this westward rush were fur traders and land speculators. In the 1740s and 1750s, speculators (including many future revolutionary leaders) formed land companies to capitalize on the seaboard population explosion. Colonial penetration of the Ohio valley in the 1740s established the first British outposts in the continental heartland, challenging the French where their interest was vital.

The French resisted. They attempted to block further British expansion by constructing new forts in the Ohio valley and by prying some tribes loose from their new English connections. By 1755, the French had driven the English traders out of the Ohio valley and established forts as far east as the fork of the Ohio River, near present-day Pittsburgh. It was there, at Fort Duquesne, that the French smartly rebuffed an ambitious young Virginia militia colonel named George Washington, dispatched by his colony's government to expel them from the region.

Men in the capitals of Europe, not in the colonies, made the decision to force a showdown in the interior of North America. England's powerful merchants, supported by American clients, had been emboldened by success in the previous war against the French. Now they argued that the time was ripe to destroy the French overseas trade. Convinced, the British ministry ordered several thousand troops to America in 1754; in France, 3,000 regulars embarked to meet the challenge.

With war looming, the colonial governments attempted to coordinate efforts. Representatives of seven colonies met at Albany, New York, in June 1754 to woo the Iroquois out of neutrality and plan a colonial union. Both failed. The 150 Iroquois chiefs left with no firm commitment to fight the French. And the colonies rejected Benjamin Franklin's plan for an intercolonial government to manage Indian affairs, provide for defense, and have the power to pass laws and levy taxes. Even the clever woodcut in the *Pennsylvania Gazette* showing a chopped-up snake over the motto "Join or Die" failed to overcome old jealousies.

With his British army and hundreds of American recruits, General Edward Braddock slogged across Virginia in the summer of 1755, each day cutting a few miles of road through forests and across mountains. A headstrong professional soldier who regarded his European battlefield experience as sufficient for war in the American wilderness, Braddock had contempt for the woods-wise French regiments and their stealthy Indian allies.

As Braddock neared Fort Duquesne, the entire French force and the British surprised one another in the forest. The French had 218 soldiers and militiamen and 637 Indian allies; Braddock commanded twice that many redcoats but few Indians. Pouring murderous fire into Braddock's tidy lines, the French and Indians won. Braddock perished, and two-thirds of the British and Americans were killed or wounded. Washington, his uniform pierced by four bullets, had two horses shot from beneath him. Although they had 1,000 men in reserve down the road, the Anglo-American force beat a hasty retreat. Braddock's ignominious defeat brought almost every tribe north of the Ohio River to the French side. For the next two years, French-supplied Indian raiders torched the backcountry. Never was disunity within the English colonies so glaring.

The turning point came when energetic William Pitt became England's prime minister in 1757. "I believe that I can save this nation and that no one else can," he boasted, abandoning Europe as the main theater of action against the French and throwing British military might into the American campaign. The forces he dispatched to America in 1757–1758 dwarfed all preceding commitments: about 23,000 British troops and a huge fleet with 14,000 seamen. But even such forces were not necessarily sufficient to the task without Indian support, or at least neutrality, in a war that had to be fought in the North American interior.

Tribal Strategies

Anglo-American leaders knew that Iroquois support was crucial and could be secured in only two ways: through purchase, or by a demonstration of power that would convince the tribes that the English would prevail with or without their assistance. The Iroquois knew that their interest lay in playing off one European power against the other. But in 1758 the huge English military buildup began to produce victories. Troops under Sir Jeffrey Amherst captured Louisbourg, on Cape Breton Island, and Fort Duquesne fell to another army of 6,000. The Royal Navy bottled up French shipping in the St. Lawrence River, cutting the Iroquois off from French trade goods. These victories finally moved the Iroquois away from neutrality. By early 1759, foreseeing a French defeat in North America, the Iroquois pledged 800 warriors for an attack on Fort Niagara, the strategic French trading depot on Lake Ontario.

But even dramatic Anglo-American victories did not always guarantee Indian support. Skirmishes with the Cherokee from Virginia to South Carolina turned into a costly war from 1759 to 1761. In 1760, the Cherokee mauled a British army of 1,300 under Amherst. The following summer, a much larger Anglo-American force invaded Cherokee country, burning towns and food supplies. English control of the sea interrupted the Indians' supply of French arms. Beset by food shortages, lack of ammunition, and smallpox, the Cherokee finally sued for peace.

Other Anglo-American victories in 1759, the "year of miracles," decided the outcome of the bloodiest war yet known in the New World. The capture of Fort Niagara, the critical link in the system of French forts, was followed by the conquest of sugar-rich Martinique in the West Indies. The culminating stroke came at Quebec. Led by 32-year-old General James Wolfe, 5,000 men scaled a cliff and overcame the French. The capture of Montreal late in 1760 completed the shattering of French power in North America. Although war raged for three more years elsewhere, in the American colonies the old English dream of destroying the Gallic menace had finally come true.

Consequences of War

The Treaty of Paris, ending the Seven Years' War in 1762–1763, brought astounding changes to European and Indian peoples in North America. Spain acquired New Orleans and the vast Louisiana territory west of the Mississippi, in exchange giving Florida to the British. The interior tribes, which had adeptly forced Britain and France to compete for their support, suffered a severe setback when the French disappeared and the British became their sole source of trade goods.

After making peace, the British government launched a new policy designed to separate Native Americans and colonizers by creating a racial boundary roughly following the crestline of the Appalachian Mountains from Maine to Georgia. The Proclamation of 1763 reserved all land west of that line for Indian nations. White settlers already there were told to withdraw.

THE YEAR THAT RESHAPED NORTH AMERICA AFTER 1763 At the Paris Peace Treaty in 1763, France surrendered huge claims west of the Mississippi River to Spain and east of the river to England. England also acquired Florida from Spain.

This well-meaning attempt to legislate interracial accord failed completely. Even before the proclamation was issued, the Ottawa chief Pontiac, concerned that the elimination of the French threatened the old treaty and gift-giving system, had gathered together many of the northern tribes that had aided the French assaults on the English forts during the Seven Years' War. Although Pontiac's pan-Indian movement to drive the British out of the Ohio valley collapsed in 1764, it served notice that the interior tribes would fight for their lands.

London could not enforce the proclamation. Staggering under an immense wartime debt, Britain decided to maintain only small army garrisons in North America to regulate the interior. Nor could royal governors stop land speculators and settlers from privately purchasing land from trans-Appalachian tribes or from simply encroaching on their land. The western frontier seethed after 1763.

Although the epic Anglo-American victory redrew the continent's map, the war also had important social and economic effects on colonial society. It convinced the colonists of their growing strength, yet left them debt-ridden and weakened in manpower. Economic development had been spurred and British capital had poured in, yet the colonies were now more vulnerable to cyclic fluctuations in the British economy. And when the bulk of the British forces left North America in 1760, the economy slumped badly, especially in the coastal towns. When peace came, Boston had a deficit of almost 700 men in a town of about 2,000 families. The high rate of war widowhood feminized poverty and greatly expanded poor relief to maintain husbandless women and fatherless children.

Although even some wealthy merchants went bankrupt, the greatest hardships after 1760 fell on laboring people. Established craftsmen and shopkeepers were caught between rising prices and reduced demand for their goods and services. A New York artisan expressed a common lament in 1762. Thankfully, he still had employment, he wrote in the *New-York Gazette*. But despite every effort at unceasing labor and frugal living, he had fallen into poverty and found it "beyond my ability to support my family . . . [which] can scarcely appear with decency or have necessaries to subsist." His situation, he added, "is really the case with many of the inhabitants of this city."

The Seven Years' War paved the way for a far larger conflict in the next generation. The legislative assemblies, for example, which had been flexing their muscles in earlier decades, accelerated their bid for political power. The war also trained a new group of military and political leaders. In carrying out military operations on a scale unknown in the colonies and in shouldering heavier political responsibilities, men such as George Washington, Samuel Adams, Benjamin Franklin, Patrick Henry, and Christopher Gadsden acquired valuable experience.

The Seven Years' War, in spite of the severe costs, left many of the colonists buoyant. New Englanders rejoiced at the final victory over the "Papist enemy of the North." Frontiersmen, fur traders, and land speculators also celebrated the French withdrawal, for the West now appeared open for exploitation.

The outcome of the war also affected American and British attitudes towards each other. Colonists, surveying a world free of French and Spanish threats, began reassessing subordination to England and the advantages of standing alone. The British, however, came out of the war thinking the colonists unreliable and poor fighters. "He could take a thousand grenadiers to America," boasted one officer, "and geld all the males, partly by force and partly by a little coaxing."

THE CRISIS WITH ENGLAND

George Grenville became the chief minister of England's 25-year-old king, George III, at the end of the Seven Years' War. He inherited a national debt that had billowed from £75 million to £145 million and a nation of wearied taxpayers. So Grenville proposed new taxes in America, asking the colonists to bear their share of running the empire. His particular concern was financing the 10,000 British regulars left in North America after 1763 to police Canada and the Indians—and to remind unruly Americans that they were still subjects. He opened a rift between England and its colonies that in dozen years would become a revolution.

Sugar, Currency, and Stamps

In 1764, Grenville pushed through Parliament several bills that cumulatively pressed hard on colonial economies. First came the Revenue Act (or Sugar Act) of 1764. While reducing the tax on imported French molasses from six to three pence per gallon, it added various colonial products to the list of commodities that could be sent only to England. It also required American shippers to post bonds guaranteeing observance of the trade regulations before loading their cargoes, and strengthened the vice-admiralty courts, where violators of the trade acts were prosecuted.

Many colonial legislatures grumbled about the Sugar Act because a strictly enforced duty of three pence per gallon on molasses pinched more than the loosely enforced six-pence duty. But only New York objected that any tax by Parliament to raise revenue (rather than to control trade) violated the rights of overseas English subjects who were unrepresented in Parliament.

Next came the Currency Act. In 1751, Parliament had forbidden the New England colonies to issue paper money, and now it extended that prohibition to all the colonies. In a colonial economy chronically short of cash, this constricted trade.

The move to tighten up the machinery of empire confused the colonists because many of the new regulations came from Parliament. Before, Parliament had let the king, his ministers, and the Board of Trade run overseas affairs, while the colonists idealized Parliament as a bastion of English liberty. Now Parliament began to seem like a violator of colonial rights. Colonial leaders were uncertain about where Parliament's authority over the colonies began and ended.

After Parliament passed the Sugar Act in 1764, Grenville announced his intention to extend to America stamp duties—already imposed in England—on every newspaper, pamphlet, almanac, legal document, liquor license, college diploma, pack of playing cards, and pair of dice. Grenville gave the colonies a year to suggest alternative ways of raising revenue. The colonies objected strenuously, but none provided another plan. Knowing that colonial property taxes were low compared with those in England, Grenville drove the bill through Parliament. The Stamp Act became effective in November 1765.

Colonial reaction to the Stamp Act ranged from disgruntled submission to mass defiance. The breadth of the reaction shocked the British government—and many Americans as well. In many cases, resistance involved not only discontent over England's tightening of the screws on the American colonies but also internal resentments born out of local events. Especially in the cities, the defiance of authority and destruction of property by people from the middle and lower ranks redefined the dynamics of politics, setting the stage for a ten-year internal struggle for control among the various social elements alarmed by the new English policies.

Stamp Act Riots

In late 1764, Virginia's House of Burgesses had strenuously objected to the proposed stamp tax and argued that it was their "inherent" right to be taxed only by their own consent. It became the first legislature to react to the news of the Stamp Act. Virginians were already worried by a severe decline in tobacco prices and heavy war-related taxes, which mired most planters in debt. Led by newly elected, 29-year-old Patrick Henry, the House of Burgesses in May 1765 debated seven strongly worded resolutions. Old-guard burgesses regarded some of them as treasonable. The legislature finally adopted the four more moderate resolves, including one proclaiming Virginia's right to impose taxes.

Many burgesses had left for home before Henry introduced his resolutions, so less than a quarter of Virginia's legislators voted for the four moderate resolves. But within a month, newspapers of other colonies were publishing all seven resolves, which included a defiant assertion that Virginians did not have to pay externally imposed taxes and branded anyone who denied Virginia's sole right to tax itself "an enemy to this, his Majesty's colony."

From the time of his election to the Virginia House of Burgesses at the age of 29, Patrick Henry was an outspoken proponent of American rights. In this portrait, he pleads a case at a county courthouse crowded with local planters. (Virginia Historical Society, Richmond, VA)

Governor Francis Bernard of Massachusetts called the Virginia resolves an "alarm bell for the disaffected." Events in Boston in August 1765 amply confirmed his view. On August 14, Bostonians hung stamp distributor Andrew Oliver in effigy and leveled his new brick office and his mansion. Oliver got the message and promptly asked to be relieved of his commission. Twelve days later mobs destroyed the handsome homes of two British officials and of haughty vice-governor Thomas Hutchinson (a descendant of Anne Hutchinson). Shoemaker Ebenezer MacIntosh led the mobs.

In attacking the property of men associated with the stamp tax, the Boston crowd demonstrated not only its opposition to parliamentary policy but also its resentment of a local elite. For decades, ordinary Bostonians had aligned politically with the Boston "caucus," which led the colony's "popular party" against conservative aristocrats such as Hutchinson and Oliver. But the "rage-intoxicated rabble" had suddenly broken away from the leaders of the popular party and gone farther than they had intended. Hutchinson was one of their main targets. Characterized by young lawyer John Adams as "very ambitious and avaricious," Hutchinson was in the popular view chief among the "mean mercenary hirelings" of the British. Now, the more cautious political leaders knew that they would have to struggle to regain control of the protest movement.

Protest took a more dignified form at the Stamp Act Congress, attended by representatives of nine colonies, meeting in New York in October 1765—the first self-initiated intercolonial convention, and branded a "dangerous tendency" by

British officials. The delegates' 12 restrained resolutions accepted Parliament's right to legislate for the colonies but denied its right to tax them directly.

Violent protest also wracked New York and Newport, Rhode Island, the resistance led by groups calling themselves the Sons of Liberty and composed mostly of artisans, shopkeepers, and ordinary citizens. By late 1765, crowds all over America were convincing stamp distributors to resign. Colonists defied English authority even more directly by forcing most customs officers and court officials to open ports and courts for business after November 1 without using the hated stamps required after that date. This often took months of pressure and sometimes mob action, but the Sons of Liberty, often led by new faces in local politics, got their way by going outside the law.

In March 1766, Parliament debated the American reaction to the Stamp Act. Lobbied by many merchant friends of the Americans, Parliament voted to repeal it, bowing to expediency but also passing the Declaratory Act, which asserted Parliament's power to enact laws for the colonies in "all cases whatsoever."

The crisis had passed, yet nothing was solved. Americans had begun to recognize a grasping government trampling subjects' rights. The Stamp Act, one New England clergyman foresaw, "diffused a disgust through the colonies and laid the basis of an alienation which will never be healed." Stamp Act resisters had politicized their communities as never before. Generally cautious established leaders were often displaced by people lower down the social ladder.

An Uncertain Interlude

Ministerial instability in England hampered the quest for a coherent, workable American policy. Attempting to be a strong king, George III chose as ministers men with little respect in Parliament. This led to strife between Parliament and the king's chief ministers, and a generally chaotic political situation, just when the king was trying to overhaul the empire's administration. For example, the government installed in colonial cities three vice-admiralty courts (which did not use juries) to try accused smugglers. Still hard-pressed for revenue in the face of severe unemployment, tax protests, and riots over the high price of grain, a new British ministry pushed through Parliament the relatively small Townshend duties on paper, lead, painters' colors, and tea. A final law suspended New York's assembly until that body ceased defying the Quartering Act of 1765, which had required public funds for support of British troops garrisoned in the colony. New York knuckled under in order to save its legislature.

Colonial protests against the Townshend Acts were led by Massachusetts. Its House of Representatives sent a circular letter, written by Samuel Adams, to each colony objecting to the new Townshend duties. Under instructions from England, Governor Bernard dissolved the legislature after it refused to rescind the letter.

Showing more restraint than they had in resisting the Stamp Act, most colonists only grumbled and petitioned. But Bostonians protested stridently. In the summer of 1768, after customs officials seized a sloop owned by John Hancock for a violation of the trade regulations, an angry crowd mobbed them; for months, they took refuge on a British warship in Boston harbor. Newspapers warned of new measures designed to "suck the life blood" from the people and predicted that the English would send troops to "dragoon us into passive obedience." To many, beliefs grew that the English were plotting "designs for destroying our constitutional liberties."

Four regiments indeed came. The attack on the customs officials convinced the government that the Bostonians were insubordinate and selfish. It decided to bring them to a proper state of subordination and make them an example. On October 1, 1768, redcoats marched into Boston without resistance.

Thereafter the colonists' main tactic of protest against the Townshend Acts became economic boycott. In Boston, New York, and Philadelphia, merchants and consumers adopted nonimportation and nonconsumption agreements, pledging neither to import nor to use British articles. These measures promised to bring the politically influential English merchants to their aid, for half of British shipping was engaged in commerce with the colonies, and one-quarter of all English exports were consumed there. When the southern colonies also adopted nonimportation agreements in 1768, a new step toward intercolonial union had been taken.

Many colonial merchants, especially those with official connections, saw nonimportation agreements as lacking legal force, and refused to be bound by them. They had to be persuaded otherwise by street brigades, usually composed of artisans for whom nonimportation was a boon to home manufacturing. Crowd action welled up again in the seaports as patriot bands attacked the homes and warehouses of offending merchants and "rescued" contraband goods seized by customs officials.

England's attempts to discipline its colonies and oblige them to share the costs of governing an empire lay in shambles by the end of the 1760s. Using troops to restore order undermined the respect for the mother country on which colonial acceptance of its authority ultimately depended. The Townshend duties had failed miserably, yielding less than £21,000 by 1770 while costing British business £700,000 through the colonial nonimportation movement. On March 5, 1770, Parliament repealed all the Townshend duties except the one on tea.

On that same evening in Boston, British troops fired on an unruly crowd of heckling citizens. When the smoke cleared, five bloody bodies, including that of Ebenezer MacIntosh's brother-in-law, lay in the street. Bowing to furious popular reaction, Thomas Hutchinson, recently appointed governor, ordered the redcoats out of town and arrested the officer and soldiers involved. They were later acquitted, with two young patriot lawyers, John Adams and Josiah Quincy, Jr., providing a brilliant defense.

In spite of the potential of the "Boston massacre" for galvanizing the colonies into further resistance, opposition to English policies, including boycotts, subsided in 1770. Popular leaders such as Samuel Adams had few issues left, especially when the depression that had helped sow discontent ended. Yet the fires of revolution were not extinguished.

The Growing Rift

In June 1772, the crown created a new furor by announcing that it, rather than the provincial legislature, would henceforth pay the salaries of the royal governor and superior court judges in Massachusetts. Even though the measure saved the colony money, it looked like a scheme to impose despotic government. Judges paid from London presumably would obey London.

Boston's town meeting protested loudly and created a Committee of Correspondence to win other colonies' sympathy. By the end of 1772, another 80 towns in Massachusetts had created committees. In the next year, all but three colonies established Committees of Correspondence in their legislatures.

Samuel Adams was by now the leader of the Boston radicals, for the influence of laboring men like Ebenezer MacIntosh had been quietly reduced. Adams was an experienced caucus politicker, a skilled political journalist, and (despite his Harvard degree) had deep roots among the laboring people. He organized workers and secured the financial support of wealthy merchants such as John Hancock.

In 1772, Rhode Island gave Adams a new issue. The commander of the royal ship *Gaspee* was roundly hated by the fishermen and small traders of Narragansett Bay. When his ship ran aground while pursuing a suspected smuggler, Rhode Islanders burned it, and a local court convicted the captain of illegally seizing what he was convinced had been smuggled sugar and rum. London reacted with cries of high treason. Investigators found Rhode Islanders' lips sealed. The event was tailor-made for Samuel Adams, who used it to "awaken the American colonies, which have been too long dozing upon the brink of ruin."

The final plunge into revolution began when Parliament passed the Tea Act in early 1773, allowing the practically bankrupt East India Company to ship its tea directly to North America. Even with the small tax to be paid in the colonies, smuggled Dutch tea would be undersold. The Americans would get inexpensive tea, the crown a modest revenue, and the East India Company a new lease on life. But colonists reacted furiously. American merchants who competed with the East India Company denounced the monopoly in America, and colonists objected that the government's true object was to gain acceptance of Parliament's taxing power. As Americans drank the company's tea, they would be swallowing the English right to tax them. Showing that their principles were not entirely in their pocketbooks, Americans staged mass meetings that soon forced the resignation of East India Company agents, and citizens vowed to stop the obnoxious tea at the water's edge.

Governor Hutchinson vowed a showdown, convinced that to yield again to popular pressure would forever cripple English sovereignty in America. Samuel Adams's patriot party had been urging citizens to demonstrate that they were not yet prepared for the "yoke of slavery" by sending the tea back to England. When Hutchinson refused, a band of Bostonians, dressed as Indians, boarded the tea ships and flung £10,000 worth of the East India Company's property into Boston harbor.

The die was cast. Lord North, the king's chief minister, insisted that the dispute was now about whether England had any authority over the colonies. Parliament passed the Coercive Acts, stern laws that Bostonians promptly labeled the "Intolerable Acts." The acts closed the port of Boston to all shipping until the colony paid for the destroyed tea, and they barred local courts from trying British soldiers and officials for acts committed while suppressing civil disturbances. Moreover, Parliament amended the Massachusetts charter to transform the council from an upper legislative chamber, elected by the lower house, to a body appointed by the governor. The council lost its veto power over the governor's decisions, and authorized the governor to allow only one annual meeting in each town to elect local officials. Finally, General Thomas Gage, commander in chief of British forces in America, replaced Hutchinson as governor.

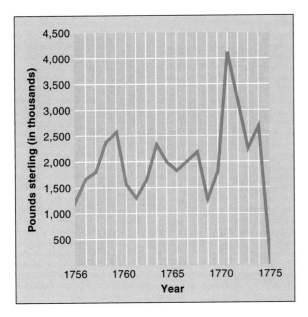

BRITISH EXPORTS TO NORTH AMERICA, 1756–1775
The on-again, off-again American boycotts of British imports can be seen in this chart. The first big dip, from 1760 to 1762, was caused by the departure of the free-spending British army and navy from the North American theater during the Seven Years' War. Source: U.S. Bureau of the Census.

"This is the day, then," declared Edmund Burke in the House of Commons, "that you wish to go to war with all America, in order to conciliate that country to this." Burke notwithstanding, Lord North's plan to strangle Massachusetts into submission and hope for acquiescence elsewhere in the colonies proved popular in England. Americans found their maneuvering room severely narrowed.

When the Intolerable Acts arrived in May 1774, Boston's town meeting urged all the colonies to ban trade with England. This met with faint support. But there was a better response to Boston's call for a delegates from all the colonies to meet in Philadelphia. The Continental Congress, as it was called, now began to transform a ten-year debate conducted by separate colonies into a unified American cause.

In September 1774, 55 delegates from all the colonies except Georgia converged on Carpenter's Hall in Philadelphia. The discussions centered not on how to prepare for a war that many sensed was inevitable, but on how to resolve the sectional differences that most delegates feared were irreconcilable.

The Continental Congress was by no means a unified body. Some delegates, led by cousins Samuel and John Adams from Massachusetts and Patrick Henry of Virginia, argued for outright resistance to Parliament's Coercive Acts. Moderate delegates from the middle colonies urged restraint and further attempts at reconciliation. After weeks of debate, the delegates agreed to a restrained Declaration of Rights and Resolves. It attempted to define American grievances and to justify the colonists' defiance of British policies and laws. More concrete was the Congress's agreement on a plan of resistance. If the government did not rescind the Intolerable Acts by December 1, 1774, a ban would take effect on all imports and exports between the colonies and Great Britain, Ireland, and the British West Indies. To keep reluctant southern colonies in the fold, some exceptions were made for the export of southern staple commodities.

By the time the Congress went home in late October, leaders from different colonies had transformed Boston's cause into a national movement. "Government

Liberty always had to struggle against power, as American colonists saw it; in this cartoon, England (power) forces Liberty (America in the form of a woman) to drink the "Bitter Draught" of tea. Uncompliant, America spits the tea into England's face while another corrupt Englishman peeks under her petticoat. (Massachusetts Historical Society)

is dissolved [and] we are in a state of nature," Patrick Henry argued dramatically. "I am not a Virginian, but an American." Many other delegates were a long way from that. Still, the Congress agreed to reconvene in May 1775.

By the time the Second Continental Congress met, the fabric of government became badly torn in most colonies. Illegal revolutionary committees, conventions, and congresses were replacing legal governing bodies. Assuming authority in defiance of royal governors, who suspended truculent legislatures in many colonies, they often operated on instructions from mass meetings where the legal franchise was ignored. These extralegal bodies created and armed militia units, bullied merchants and shopkeepers refusing to obey popularly authorized boycotts, levied taxes, operated the courts, and obstructed English customs officials. By the end of 1774, all but three colonies defied their own charters by appointing provincial assemblies without royal authority. In the next year, this independently created power became evident when trade with England practically ceased.

The Final Rupture

The last spark to hit the revolutionary powder keg was struck in early 1775. General Gage, the new governor, had already occupied Boston with 4,000 troops—one for every adult male in the town. In April 1775, London ordered Gage to arrest "the principal actors and abettors" of insurrection in Massachusetts. Under cover of night he sent 700 redcoats from Boston to seize arms and ammunition in nearby Concord. But Americans learned of the plan. When the troops reached Lexington at dawn, 70 "Minutemen" were waiting. In a skirmish, 18 Massachusetts farmers fell, eight of them mortally wounded. Marching six miles west to Concord, the British faced another firefight. Withdrawing, the redcoats made their way back to Boston, harassed all the way by militiamen. Before the bloody day ended, 273 British and 95 Americans lay dead or wounded.

The news swept through the colonies. Within weeks, thousands of men besieged the British troops in Boston. According to one colonist, everywhere "you see the inhabitants training, making firelocks, casting mortars, shells, and shot."

The outbreak of fighting vastly altered the debates of the Second Continental Congress, which assembled in Philadelphia in May 1775. The Congress had the same slim powers as its predecessor, but it acquired awesome new responsibilities, as well as fresh faces: Boston's wealthy merchant, John Hancock; a tall, young planter-lawyer from Virginia, Thomas Jefferson; and the much-applauded Benjamin Franklin, who had come home from London only four days before the Congress convened.

The Congress had no power to legislate or command; it could only request and recommend. And 14 months would elapse before the Congress issued a formal declaration of independence. But a war with England—and a civil war in America—had already begun. The Second Congress authorized a continental army of 20,000 and, partly to cement Virginia to the cause, chose as commander in chief George Washington. It issued a "Declaration of Causes of Taking-up Arms," sent the king an "Olive Branch Petition" begging him to remove the obstacles to reconciliation, made moves to secure the neutrality of the interior Indian tribes, issued paper money, erected a postal system, and approved plans for a military hospital.

While debate continued over whether the colonies ought to declare themselves independent, military action grew hotter. Hotheaded Ethan Allen and his Green Mountain Boys from eastern New York captured Fort Ticonderoga, controlling the Champlain valley, in May 1775. On New Year's Day in 1776, the British shelled Norfolk, Virginia. In March 1776, Washington's army forced the British to evacuate Boston. But many members of the Congress still hoped for reconciliation. Such hopes crumbled at the end of 1775 when news arrived that the king, rejecting the Olive Branch Petition, had dispatched 20,000 additional British troops to quell the insurrection and had proclaimed the colonies in "open and avowed rebellion." Those fateful words made all the Congress's actions treasonable and turned all who obeyed the Congress into traitors.

By the time Thomas Paine's hard-hitting pamphlet *Common Sense* appeared in Philadelphia on January 9, 1776, members of the Congress were talking less gingerly about independence. Paine's blunt words and compelling rhetoric smashed through the remaining reserve. "O ye that love mankind! Ye that dare oppose not only the tyranny, but also the tyrant, stand forth!" Within weeks, the pamphlet was in bookstalls all over the colonies.

The Continental Congress debated independence during the spring of 1776, even as the war became bloodier. An American assault on Quebec failed in May 1776. England embargoed all trade to the colonies and ordered the seizure of American ships, convincing the Congress to declare its ports open to all countries. Almost anticlimactically, Virginia's Richard Henry Lee introduced a resolution on June 7 calling for independence. After two days of debate, the Congress ordered a committee chaired by Jefferson to begin drafting such a document.

Soon to be revered as the nation's birth certificate, the declaration was not a highly original statement. It drew heavily on the Congress's earlier justifications of American resistance, and its theory of government had already been set forth in scores of patriot pamphlets over the previous decade. The ringing phrases that "all men are created equal, that they are endowed by their Creator with certain unalienable Rights, that among these are Life, Liberty and the pursuit of Happiness," were familiar in the writing of many pamphleteers.

Jefferson's committee presented the declaration to the Congress on June 28. On July 2, 12 delegations voted for independence, with New York's abstaining (rather than against, its earlier position). Thus the Congress could say that the vote for independence was unanimous. Two days more were spent cutting and polishing the document, most notably eliminating a long argument blaming the king for slavery in America. On July 4, Congress sent the document to the printer.

Four days later, Philadelphians thronged to the statehouse to hear the Declaration of Independence read aloud. They "huzzahed," tore the king's arms from above the statehouse door, and later that night, amid cheers, toasts, and clanging church bells, hurled this symbol of more than a century and a half of colonial dependency into a roaring bonfire.

THE IDEOLOGY OF REVOLUTIONARY REPUBLICANISM

Since 1763, colonists had been expressing many reactions to the crisis with Britain. Mostly these took the form of newspaper articles and pamphlets written by educated men. But the middling and lower ranks of society had also expressed themselves in printed broadsides and even ideologically-laden popular rituals, such as burning in effigy and tarring and feathering. Gradually, the colonists pieced together a political ideology, borrowed partly from English political thought, partly from the theories of the Enlightenment, and partly from their own experiences. Historians call this new ideology "revolutionary republicanism." But because colonists varied widely in interests and experiences, no single coherent ideology united them all.

A Plot Against Liberty

Many American colonists agreed with earlier English Whig writers who charged that corrupt and power-hungry men were slowly extinguishing the lamp of liberty in England. The so-called country party represented by these Whig pamphleteers proclaimed itself the guardian of the true principles of the English constitution and opposed the "court" party—the king and his appointees. From this perspective, every ministerial policy and parliamentary act from the Stamp Act on was a subversion of English liberties. Most Americans regarded resistance to such blows against liberty as wholly justified.

Among many Americans, especially merchants, the attack on constitutional rights blended closely with threats to their economic interests in the new trade policies. Merchants saw a coordinated attack on their "lives, liberties, and property." If a man was not secure in his property, he could not be secure in his citizenship, for it was property that gave a man the independence to shape his identity.

Revitalizing American Society

The continuing crisis over the imperial relationship by itself inspired many colonists to resist impending tyranny. But for others, the revolutionary mentality was also fed by a belief that an opportunity was at hand to revitalize American society. They believed that growing commercial connections with a corrupt mother country had injected poison into the American bloodstream. They worried about the luxury and vice around them and came to believe that resistance to England would return American society to civic virtue, spartan living, and godly purpose.

The colonial protest movement got much of its high-toned moralism from its fervent supporters, the colonial clergy. This was especially true in New England, where so secular a man as John Adams groaned at the "universal spirit of debauchery, dissipation, luxury, effeminacy and gaming." As in most revolutionary movements, talk of moral regeneration ennobled the cause, inspiring people in areas that had been stirred by the Great Awakening.

The growth of a revolutionary spirit among ordinary people also owed much to the plain style of polemical writers such as Thomas Paine and Patrick Henry. Paine's *Common Sense* transformed the terms of the imperial argument by attacking the king, "a royal brute." The pamphlet's astounding popularity stemmed not only from its argument, but also from its style. Paine wrote for ordinary people who knew nothing more than the Bible. He appealed to their Calvinist heritage and belief in a providential destiny: "We have it in our power to begin the world over again. The birthday of a new world is at hand," if only the Americans would stand up for Liberty, whom "Europe regards . . . like a stranger, and England hath given . . . warning to depart."

THE TURMOIL OF REVOLUTIONARY SOCIETY

The long struggle with England over colonial rights between 1764 and 1776 did not occur in a unified society. Social and economic change, which accelerated in the late colonial period, brought deep unrest and calls for reform from many quarters.

As agitation against English policy intensified, previously passive people took a more active interest in politics. The constitutional struggle with England spread quickly into uncharted territory. Groups emerged—slaves, urban laboring people, backcountry farmers, evangelicals, women—whose enunciated goals were sometimes only loosely connected to the struggle with England. The stridency and potential power of these groups frightened many upper-class leaders. Losing control of protests they had initially led, many would abandon the resistance movement.

Urban People

Although the cities had only about 5 percent of the colonial population, they were the core of revolutionary agitation. As centers of communications, government, and commerce, they led the way in protesting English policy, and they soon contained the most politicized citizens in America. Local politics could be rapidly transformed as the struggle against England meshed with calls for internal reform.

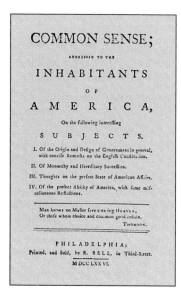

In *Common Sense*, Thomas Paine dared to articulate, in plain but muscular language, the thoughts of rebellion and independence that others had only alluded to. Note that Paine did not put his name on the title page of *Common Sense*, though he was quickly identified as the author. (Library of Congress (left)/National Portrait Gallery, London (right))

Philadelphia offers a good example of popular empowerment. Before the Seven Years' War, craftsmen had usually acquiesced in local leadership by merchant and lawyer politicos. But economic difficulties in the 1760s and 1770s led them to band together within their craft and community. Artisans played a central role in forging and—equally important—enforcing a nonimportation agreement in 1768. Cautious merchants complained that mere artisans had "no right to give their sentiments respecting an importation." But artisans, casting off their customary deference, forged ahead. By 1772, they were filling elected municipal positions and insisting on the right to participate equally with their social superiors in nominating assemblymen and other important officeholders. They also began lobbying for reform laws. The craftsmen called for elected representatives to be more accountable to constituents. Genteel Philadelphians muttered, "It is time the tradesmen were checked—they ought not to intermeddle in state affairs—they will become too powerful."

By 1774, the Philadelphia working class's meddling in state affairs reached a bold new stage—a de facto assumption of governmental powers by committees created by the people at large. Craftsmen had first assumed such extralegal authority in policing the nonimportation agreement in 1769. Now, responding to the Intolerable Acts, they proposed a radical slate of candidates for a committee to enforce a new economic boycott. Their ticket drubbed one nominated by conservative merchants. As the impasse with England climaxed in 1775, the political mobilization and heightened consciousness of laboring Philadelphians continued. By then, many pacifist Quaker leaders of the city had abandoned politics, and other conservative merchants had concluded that mob rule had triumphed. Into the leadership vacuum stepped a group of radicals from the middling ranks, including Thomas Paine.

The political support of the new radical leaders centered in the 31 companies of the Philadelphia militia, composed mostly of laboring men, and in the extralegal committees now controlling the city's economic life. Their leadership helped overcome the conservatism of the Pennsylvania legislature, which resisted the movement of the Continental Congress toward independence. The new radical leaders demanded internal reforms: opening up opportunity; curbing the accumulation of wealth by "our great merchants . . . at the expense of the people;" abolishing the property requirement for voting; allowing militiamen to elect their officers; and imposing stiff fines, to be used to support the families of poor militiamen, on men who refused militia service.

Philadelphia's radicals never controlled the city. They always jostled for position with prosperous artisans and shopkeepers of more moderate views and with cautious lawyers and merchants. But mobilization among artisans, laborers, and mariners, in other cities as well as Philadelphia, became part of the chain of events that led toward independence. Whereas most of the patriot elite fought only to change English colonial policy, the people of the cities also struggled for reforms and talked about how an independent American society might be reorganized.

Patriot Women

Colonial women also played a vital role in the relentless movement toward revolution, and they drew upon revolutionary arguments to define their own goals. They signed nonimportation agreements, harassed noncomplying merchants, and helped organize "fast days" on which communities prayed for deliverance from oppression. But the women's most important role was to facilitate the boycott of English goods. The success of the nonconsumption pacts depended on substituting homespun cloth for English textiles, on which colonists of all classes had always relied. From Georgia to Maine, women and children began spinning yarn and weaving cloth. Towns often vied in patriotically manufacturing cotton, linen, and woolen cloth, the women staging spinning contests to publicize their commitment.

After the Tea Act in 1773, the interjection of politics into the household economy increased as patriotic women boycotted their favorite drink. Newspapers carried recipes for tea substitutes. In Wilmington, North Carolina, women paraded solemnly through the town and then made a ritual display of their patriotism by burning their imported tea.

Women's perception of their role was also changed by colonial protests and petitions against England's arbitrary uses of power. The more male leaders talked about England's intentions to "enslave" the Americans and England's callous treatment of its colonial "subjects," the more American women began to rethink their own domestic situations. The language of protest against England reminded many American women that they, too, were badly treated "subjects" of their husbands, who often dealt with them cruelly and exercised arbitrary power over them. If there was to be independence, new laws must be passed, Abigail Adams reminded her husband John in March 1776. Male lawmakers should think about the rights of women and their enslavement by men. Choosing words and phrases that had

As marketgoers and consumers, urban women played a crucial role in applying economic pressure on England during the prerevolutionary decade. This British cartoon, published in 1775, derisively depicts a group of North Carolina women signing an anti-tea agreement. (Library of Congress)

been used over and over in the protests against England, she wrote: "Do not put such unlimited power into the hand of the husbands.... Put it out of the power of the vicious and the lawless to use us with cruelty and indignity," she insisted. "Remember, all men would be tyrants if they could." Borrowing directly from the republican ideology used to protest Parliament's attempts to tax the Americans, Abigail Adams warned that American women "will not hold ourselves bound by any laws in which we have no voice, or representation" and even promised that women would "foment a rebellion" if men did not heed their rightful claims.

Many American women were not ready to occupy such new territory. But the protests against England had prompted new thoughts about what seemed "arbitrary" or "despotic." What had been endured in the past was no longer acceptable. "We have it in our power," warned Abigail Adams to her husband, "not only to free ourselves but to subdue our masters, and without violence throw both your natural and legal authority at our feet."

Protesting Farmers

In most of the agricultural areas of the colonies, where many settlers made their livelihoods, passions over English policies awakened only slowly. After about 1740, farmers had benefited from a sharp rise in the demand for foodstuffs in England, southern Europe, and the West Indies. Rising prices and brisk markets brought a higher standard of living to thousands of rural colonists, especially south of New England. Living far from harping English customs officers, impressment gangs, and occupying armies, the colonists of the interior had to be drawn gradually into the resistance movement by their urban cousins. Even in Concord, Massachusetts, only a dozen miles from the center of colonial agitation, townspeople found little to protest in British policies until the port of Boston was closed in 1774.

Yet some parts of rural America seethed with social tension in the prewar era. The dynamics of conflict, shaped by the social development of particular regions, eventually became part of the momentum for revolution. In three western counties of North Carolina and in the Hudson River valley of New York, for example, widespread civil disorder marked the prerevolutionary decades.

For years, the small farmers of western North Carolina had suffered exploitation by corrupt county court officials appointed by the governor and a legislature dominated by eastern planter interests. Sheriffs and justices, allied with speculators and lawyers, seized property when farmers could not pay their taxes and sold it, often at a fraction of its worth, to their cronies. The legislature rejected western petitions for lower taxes, paper currency, and lower court fees. In the mid-1760s, frustrated at getting no satisfaction from legal forms of protest, the farmers formed associations—the so-called Regulators—that forcibly closed the courts, attacked the property of their enemies, and whipped judges and lawyers. When their leaders were arrested, the Regulators stormed the jails and released them.

In 1768 and again in 1771, Governor William Tryon led troops against the Regulators. Bloodshed was averted on the first occasion, but on the second, at the Battle of Alamance, two armies of more than 1,000 fired on each other. Nine men died on each side before the Regulators fled. Seven leaders were executed in the ensuing trials. Though the Regulators lost the battle, their protests became part of the larger revolutionary struggle. They railed against the self-interested behavior of a wealthy elite and asserted the necessity for people of humble rank to throw off deference and assume political responsibilities.

Rural insurgency in New York flared up in the 1750s, subsided, and then erupted again in 1766. The conditions under which land was held precipitated the violence. The Hudson River valley had long been controlled by a few wealthy families with enormous landholdings, which they leased to small tenant farmers. The Van Rensselaer manor, for example, totaled a million acres. Hundreds of tenants with their families paid substantial annual rents for the right to farm on these lands, which had been acquired as virtually free gifts from royal governors. When tenants resisted, the landlords began evicting them.

As the wealthiest men of the region, the landlords had the power of government, including control of the courts, on their side. Organizing themselves and going outside the law became the tenants' main strategy, as with the Carolina Regulators. By 1766, while New York City was absorbed in the Stamp Act furor, tenants led by William Prendergast began resisting sheriffs who tried to evict them from lands they claimed. The militant tenants threatened landlords with death and broke open jails to rescue friends. British troops from New York were used to break the tenant rebellion. Prendergast was tried and sentenced to be hanged, beheaded, and quartered. Although he was pardoned, the bitterness of the Hudson River tenants endured through the Revolution. Most of them, unlike the Carolina Regulators, fought for the British because their landlords were patriots.

TIMELINE

1696 Parliament establishes Board of Trade	**1701** Iroquois set policy of neutrality	**1702–1713** Queen Anne's War	**1713** Peace of Utrecht	**1733** Molasses Act
1744–1748 King George's War	**1754** Albany conference	**1755** Braddock defeated by French and Indian allies	**1756–1763** Seven Years' War	**1759** Wolfe defeats the French at Quebec
1759–1761 Cherokee War against the English	**1760s** Economic slump	**1763** Treaty of Paris ends Seven Years' War; Proclamation line limits westward expansion	**1764** Sugar and Currency acts; Pontiac's Rebellion in Ohio valley	**1765** Colonists resist Stamp Act; Virginia House of Burgesses issues Stamp Act resolutions
1766 Declaratory Act; Tenant rent war in New York; Slave insurrections in South Carolina	**1767** Townshend duties imposed	**1768** British troops occupy Boston	**1770** "Boston Massacre"; Townshend duties repealed (except on tea)	**1771** North Carolina Regulators defeated
1772 *Gaspee* incident in Rhode Island	**1773** Tea Act provokes Boston Tea Party	**1774** "Intolerable Acts"; First Continental Congress meets	**1775** Second Continental Congress meets; Battles of Lexington and Concord	**1776** Thomas Paine publishes *Common Sense;* Declaration of Independence

✦✦✦✦✦✦

CONCLUSION

Forging a Revolution

The colonial Americans who lived in the third quarter of the eighteenth century participated in an era of political tension and conflict that changed the lives of nearly all of them. The Seven Years' War removed French and Spanish challengers and nurtured the colonists' sense of separate identity. Yet it left them with difficult economic adjustments, heavy debts, and growing social divisions. The colonists heralded the Treaty of Paris in 1763 as the dawning of a new era, but it led to a reorganization of England's triumphant yet debt-torn empire that had profound repercussions in North America.

In the prerevolutionary decade, as England and the colonies moved from crisis to crisis, a dual disillusionment penetrated ever deeper into the colonial consciousness. Pervasive doubt arose concerning both the colonies' role, as assigned by England, in the economic life of the empire and the sensitivity of the government in London to the colonists' needs. At the same time, the colonists began to perceive British policies—instituted by Parliament, the king, and his advisors—as a systematic attack on the fundamental liberties and natural rights of British citizens in America.

The fluidity and diversity of colonial society and the differing experiences of Americans during and after the Seven Years' War evoked varying responses to the disruption that accompanied the English reorganization of the empire. In the course of resisting English policy, many previously inactive groups entered public life to challenge gentry control of political affairs. Often occupying the most radical ground in the opposition to England, they simultaneously challenged the growing concentration of economic and political power in their own communities.

When the Congress turned the 15-month undeclared war into a formally declared struggle for national liberation in July 1776, it steered its compatriots onto turbulent and unknown seas. Writing to his wife Abigail from his Philadelphia boardinghouse, the secularized Puritan John Adams caught some of the peculiar blend of excitement and dread that thousands shared. "You will think me transported with enthusiasm but I am not. I am well aware of the toil and blood and treasure that it will cost us to maintain this Declaration, and support and defend these States. Yet through all the gloom I can see the rays of ravishing light and glory. I can see that the end is more than worth all the means. And that posterity will triumph in that day's transactions, even though we should rue it, which I trust in God we shall not."

Recommended Reading

The Colonial Wars

Francis Jennings, *Empire of Fortune: Crowns, Colonies, and Tribes in the Seven Years' War in America* (1988); Howard H. Peckham, *Pontiac and the Indian Uprising* (1947); Fred Anderson, *A People's Army: Massachusetts Soldiers and Society in the Seven Years' War* (1984); Tom Hatley, *The Dividing Paths: Cherokees and South Carolinians through the Era of Revolution* (1993); Gregory Dowd, *A Spirited Resistance: The North American Indian Struggle for Unity, 1745–1815* (1992).

The Crisis with England

John Brewer, *Party Ideology and Popular Politics at the Accession of George III* (1976); Ian R. Christie, *Crisis of Empire: Great Britain and the American Colonies, 1754–1783* (1966); Edmund S. Morgan and Helen M. Morgan, *The Stamp Act Crisis* (1953); John Shy, *Toward Lexington: The Role of the British Army in the Coming of the American Revolution* (1965); Peter D. G. Thomas, *Tea Party to Independence: The Third Phase of the American Revolution, 1773–1776* (1991).

Revolutionary Republicanism

Nathan O. Hatch, *The Sacred Cause of Liberty: Republican Thought and the Millennium in Revolutionary New England* (1977); Edmund S. Morgan, *Inventing the People: The Rise of Popular Sovereignty in England and America* (1988); Bernard Bailyn, *The Ideological Origins of the American Revolution* (1967); Richard Bushman, *King and People in Provincial Massachusetts* (1985); Gary B. Nash, *The Urban Crucible: Social Change, Political Consuousness, and the Origins of the American Revolution* (1979); David Ammerman, *In the Common Cause: American Response to the Coercive Acts of 1774* (1974); Pauline Maier, *From Resistance to Revolution: Colonial Radicals and the Development of American Opposition to Britain, 1765–1776* (1972); Ruth Bloch, *Visionary Republic: Millennial Themes in American Thought, 1750–1800* (1985).

The Turmoil of Revolutionary Society

Robert Gross, *The Minutemen and Their World* (1976); Dirk Hoerder, *Crowd Action in Revolutionary Massachusetts, 1765–1780* (1977); David Hackett Fischer, *Paul Revere's Ride* (1994); Eric Foner, *Tom Paine and Revolutionary America* (1976); Edward Countryman, *A People in Revolution* (1981); Hiller Zobel, *The Boston Massacre* (1970); Steven Rosswurm, *Arms, Country, and Class: The Philadelphia Militia and the "Lower Sort" During the American Revolution* (1987); Richard Beeman, *Patrick Henry: A Biography* (1974); Linda K. Kerber, *Women of the Republic: Intellect and Ideology in Revolutionary America* (1980); Mary Beth Norton, *Liberty's Daughters: The Revolutionary Experience of American Women, 1750–1800* (1980); Alfred E. Young, ed., *The American Revolution: Essays in the History of American Radicalism* (1976).

CHAPTER 6

A People in Revolution

Among the Americans wounded and captured at the Battle of Bunker Hill in the spring of 1775 was Lieutenant William Scott of Peterborough, New Hampshire. Asked by his captors how he had come to be a rebel, "Long Bill" Scott replied:
"The case was this Sir! I lived in a Country Town; I was a Shoemaker, & got [my] living by my labor. When this rebellion came on, I saw some of my neighbors get into commission, who were no better than myself . . . . I was asked to enlist, as a private soldier. My ambition was too great for so low a rank. I offered to enlist upon having a lieutenant's commission, which was granted. I imagined my self now in a way of promotion. If I was killed in battle, there would be an end of me, but if my Captain was killed, I should rise in rank, & should still have a chance to rise higher. These Sir! were the only motives of my entering into the service. For as to the dispute between Great Britain & the colonies, I know nothing of it; neither am I capable of judging whether it is right or wrong."

Scott may have been trying to gain the sympathy of his captors, but people fought in America's Revolutionary War out of fear and ambition as well as on principle. We have no way of knowing whether Long Bill Scott's motives were typical. Certainly many Americans knew more than he about the colonies' struggle with England, but many did not.

In the spring of 1775, the Revolutionary War had just begun. So had Long Bill's adventures. When the British evacuated Boston a year later, Scott was transported to Halifax, Nova Scotia. After several months' captivity, he managed to escape and make his way home to fight once more. He was recaptured in November 1776 near New York City, when its garrison fell to a surprise British assault. Again Scott escaped, this time by swimming the Hudson River at night with his sword tied around his neck and his watch pinned to his hat.

During the winter of 1777, he returned to New Hampshire to recruit his own militia company. It included two of his eldest sons. In the fall, his unit helped defeat Burgoyne's army near Saratoga, New York, and later it took part in the fighting around Newport, Rhode Island. When his light infantry company was ordered to Virginia in early 1778, Scott's health broke, and he was permitted to resign from the army. After only a few months of recuperation, however, he was at it again. During the last year of the war, he served as a volunteer on a navy frigate.

For seven years, the war held Scott in its harsh grasp. Scott's oldest son died of camp fever after six years of service. In 1777, Long Bill sold his New Hampshire farm to meet family expenses. He lost a second farm in Massachusetts shortly afterward. After his wife died, he helplessly turned their youngest children over to his oldest son and set off to beg a pension or job from the government.

Long Bill's saga was still not complete. In 1792, he became famous by rescuing eight people when their boat capsized in New York harbor. Three years later, General Benjamin

Lincoln took Scott with him to the Ohio country, where they surveyed land that was opening for white settlement. At last he had a respectable job and even a small government pension as compensation for his nine wounds. But trouble would still not let him go. While surveying on the Black River near Sandusky, Scott and his colleagues contracted "lake fever." Though ill, he guided part of the group back to Fort Stanwix in New York, then returned for the others. It was his last heroic act. A few days after his second trip, on September 16, 1796, he died.

⬅⬅⬅⬅⬅⬅

American independence and the Revolutionary War that accompanied it were not as hard on everyone as they were on Long Bill Scott, yet together they transformed the lives of countless Americans. The war lasted for seven years, longer than any other of America's wars until Vietnam nearly two centuries later. And unlike the nation's twentieth-century contests, it was fought on American soil, among the American people. It called men by the thousands from shops and fields, disrupted families, destroyed communities, spread diseases, and made a shambles of the economy.

Amid this struggle for independence, the American people also mounted a political revolution of profound importance. Politics and government were transformed in keeping with republican principles and the rapidly changing circumstances of public life. What did republican liberty entail? How should governmental power be organized? Who should be considered republican citizens? How democratic could American society safely be? With such questions the American people wrestled at the nation's beginning.

As political activity quickened under the pressures of war and revolution, people clashed over such explosive issues as slavery, the separation of church and state, paper money and debt relief, the regulation of prices, and the toleration of political dissent. They argued over new state constitutions and the shape of a new national government. Seldom has America's political agenda been fuller, or more troubled.

The American Revolution dominated the lives of all who lived through it. But it had different consequences for men than for women, for black slaves than for their white masters, for Native Americans than for frontier settlers, for overseas merchants than for urban workers, for northern businessmen than for southern planters. Our understanding of the experience out of which the American nation emerged must begin with the Revolutionary War, for liberty came at a high cost.

THE WAR FOR AMERICAN INDEPENDENCE

The war began in Massachusetts in 1775, but within a year it shifted to the middle states. After 1779, the South became the primary theater. Why did this geographic pattern develop, what was its significance, and why did the Americans win?

The War in the North

For a brief time following Lexington and Concord, British officials thought of launching forays out from Boston into the surrounding countryside. They soon reconsidered, however, for the growing size of the continental army and the absence of significant Loyalist strength in the New England region urged caution. Even

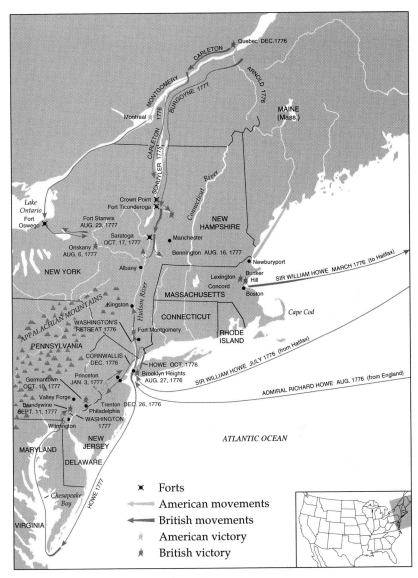

MILITARY OPERATIONS IN THE NORTH, 1776–1780 During the early years of the war, fighting was most intense in the mid-Atlantic states and upper New York. Note the importance of water routes to military strategies.

more important, Boston became untenable after the Americans placed artillery on the strategic Dorchester Heights. On March 7, 1776, the British commander, General William Howe, evacuated. Fearing retaliation against Loyalists and wishing not to destroy lingering hopes of reconciliation, Howe spared the city from the torch, but the departing British left it in shambles.

For a half dozen years after Boston's evacuation, British ships prowled the New England coast, confiscating supplies and attacking coastal towns. Yet away from the coast, there was little fighting. Most New Englanders had reason to be thankful.

Washington's victory at Princeton on January 3, 1777, following his rout of the British at Trenton a week earlier, cleared New Jersey of British forces and restored American confidence in the war. (William Mercer, *Battle of Princeton*, c. 1786–1790 (Historical Society of Pennsylvania).

The British established their new military headquarters in New York City, which offered important strategic advantages: a fine harbor, a water route to the interior, and access to the abundant grain and livestock of the Middle Atlantic states. Loyalist sentiment ran deep there, too. When in the summer of 1776 Washington challenged the British for control of New York City, he was badly outnumbered, outmaneuvered, and lost two battles. By late October, the city was firmly in British hands. It would remain so until the war's end.

In the fall of 1776, King George III instructed his two chief commanders in North America, the brothers General William Howe and Admiral Richard Howe, to make a final effort at reconciliation with the colonists. In early September, the Howes met with three delegates from the Congress on Staten Island. But when the Howes demanded revocation of the Declaration of Independence before negotiations could begin, all hope of reconciliation vanished.

For the next two years, the war swept back and forth across New Jersey and Pennsylvania. Reinforced by German mercenaries hired in Europe, the British moved virtually at will. Neither the state militias nor the weak, poorly supplied continental army offered serious opposition. At Trenton in December 1776 and at Princeton the following month, Washington surprised the British and scored victories that prevented the Americans' collapse. But survival remained the rebels' primary goal.

American efforts during the first year of the war to invade Canada and bring it into the rebellion also fared badly. In November 1775, American forces had taken Montreal. But the subsequent assault against Quebec ended with almost 100

Americans killed or wounded and more than 300 taken prisoner. The American cause could not survive many such losses.

Washington had learned the painful lesson at New York that his troops were no match for the British in frontal combat. He realized, moreover, that if the continental army was defeated, American independence would certainly be lost. He decided to harass the British and protect the civilian population as best he could but avoid major battles. This would be his strategy for the rest of the war.

So the war's middle years turned into a deadly chase that neither side could win. In September 1777, the British took Philadelphia, sending the Congress fleeing into the countryside, but then hesitated to press their advantage. On numerous occasions British commanders failed to act decisively, either reluctant to move through the hostile countryside or uncertain of their instructions. In October 1777 the Americans won an important victory at Saratoga, New York, where General John Burgoyne surrendered with 5,700 British soldiers.

Congress and the Articles of Confederation

As war erupted around them, the Continental Congress turned anxiously to the task of creating a more permanent and effective national government. It was a daunting assignment, for prior to independence the colonies had quarreled repeatedly. The crisis with England had forced them together, and the Congress was the initial embodiment of that union.

The Second Continental Congress, convening in May 1775 in the midst of the war crisis, began to exercise some of the most basic responsibilities of a sovereign government: raising an army and establishing diplomatic relations. Its powers, though, remained unclear and its legitimacy uncertain. As long as hopes of reconciliation with England lingered, these limitations posed no serious problems. But as independence and the prospects of an extended war loomed, pressure to establish a more durable central government increased. On June 20, 1776, shortly before independence was declared, Congress appointed a committee, chaired by John Dickinson of Pennsylvania, to draw up a plan of perpetual union. The plan was produced quickly, and debate soon began.

The delegates promptly clashed over whether to form a strong, consolidated government or a loose confederation of sovereign states, and as discussions went on, those differences sharpened. Determined opposition arose to Dickinson's draft, outlining a central government of considerable power. American experience with a "tyrannous" king and Parliament had revealed the dangers of central governments unmindful of the people's liberties.

As finally approved, the Articles of Confederation represented a compromise. Article 9 gave the Congress sole authority to regulate foreign affairs, declare war, mediate interstate boundary disputes, manage the post office, and administer relations with Indians living outside state boundaries. The Articles also stipulated that the inhabitants of each state were to enjoy the "privileges and immunities" of the citizens of every other state. Embedded in that clause was the basis for national, as distinguished from state, citizenship.

But the Articles sharply limited what the Congress could do and reserved broad governing powers to the states. For example, the Congress could neither

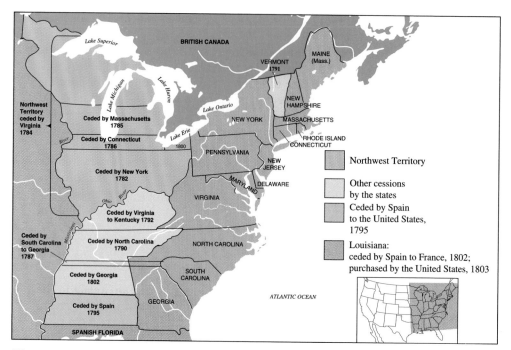

WESTERN LAND CLAIMS CEDED BY THE STATES, 1782–1802   Seven of the original states laid claim, based on their colonial charters, to lands west of the Appalachian Mountains. Eventually those states ceded their western claims to the Congress, thus making possible the creation of new states in the region.

raise troops nor levy taxes; it could only ask the states for such support. Article 2 stipulated that each state was to "retain its sovereignty, freedom and independence, and every power . . . which is not by this confederation expressly delegated to the United States in Congress assembled." And the Articles could be amended only by the unanimous agreement of the 13 states.

Though the Congress sent the Articles to the states for approval in November 1777, they were not ratified until March 1781. For one thing, ratification required approval by all 13 states, and that was hard to obtain. The biggest impediment, however, was a bitter dispute over the lands west of the Appalachian Mountains. Some states had western claims tracing back to their colonial charters, but other states, such as Maryland and New Jersey, had none. In December 1778, the Maryland assembly announced that it would not ratify until all the western lands had been ceded to the Congress. For several years, ratification hung in the balance while politicians and speculators jockeyed for advantage. Finally, in 1780 New York and Virginia agreed to transfer their western lands to the Congress. Those decisions paved the way for Maryland's ratification in early 1781, putting the Articles into effect.

The war, of course, did not wait during the struggle over ratification. The Congress managed the war effort as best it could, using the unratified Articles as a guide. Events, however, quickly proved its inadequacy, because it could do little more than pass resolutions and ask the states for support. If they refused, as they frequently did, the Congress could only protest and urge cooperation. Its ability to function was further limited by the stipulation that each state's delegation cast but one vote. Sometimes disagreements within state delegations prevented them from voting at all. That could paralyze the Congress, because most important decisions required a nine-state majority.

As the war dragged on, Washington repeatedly criticized the Congress for its failure to support the army. Acknowledging its own ineffectiveness, the Congress in 1778 temporarily granted Washington extraordinary powers and asked him to manage the war on his own. In the end, the Congress survived because enough of its members realized that disaster would follow its collapse.

The War Moves South

As the war in the North bogged down in a costly stalemate, British officials adopted an alternative strategy: invasion and pacification of the South. Royal officials in the South had heard that thousands of Loyalists would rally to the British standard. If the slaves could be lured to the British side, the balance might tip in Britain's favor, and even the threat of slave rebellion would weaken white southerners' will. With these thoughts, the British shifted the war to the South for its last three years.

Georgia—small, isolated, and largely defenseless—was the initial target. In December 1778, Savannah, the state's major port, fell to a seaborne attack. For nearly two years, the Revolution in the state virtually ceased. Encouraged, the British turned to the Carolinas, with equally impressive results. On May 12, 1780, Charleston surrendered after a month's siege. At a cost of only 225 casualties, the British captured the entire 5,400-man American garrison, the worst American defeat of the war.

After securing Charleston, the British quickly extended their control north and south along the coast. At Camden, South Carolina, the British commander Cornwallis killed nearly 1,000 Americans and captured 1,000 more, temporarily destroying the southern continental army. Scarcely pausing, the British pushed on into North Carolina. But there the British officers quickly learned the difficulty of stretching their lines into the interior: distances were too large, problems of supply too great, reliability of Loyalist troops too uncertain, and popular support for the Revolutionary cause too strong.

In October 1780, Washington sent Nathanael Greene south to lead the continental forces. It was a fortunate choice, for Greene knew the region and the kind of war that had to be fought. Determined, like Washington, to avoid large-scale encounters, Greene divided his army into small, mobile bands. Employing what today would be called guerrilla tactics, he harassed the British and their Loyalist allies at every opportunity, striking by surprise and then disappearing into the interior. Nowhere was the war more fiercely contested than through the Georgia and Carolina countryside. Neither British nor American authorities could restrain the violence. Bands of private marauders, roving the land and seizing advantage from the war's confusion, compounded the chaos.

In time, the tide began to turn. At Cowpens, South Carolina, in January 1781, American troops under General Daniel Morgan won a decisive victory, suffering fewer than 75 casualties to 329 British deaths and taking 600 prisoners. In March, at Guilford Court House in North Carolina, Cornwallis won, but at a cost that forced him to retreat to Wilmington, near the sea.

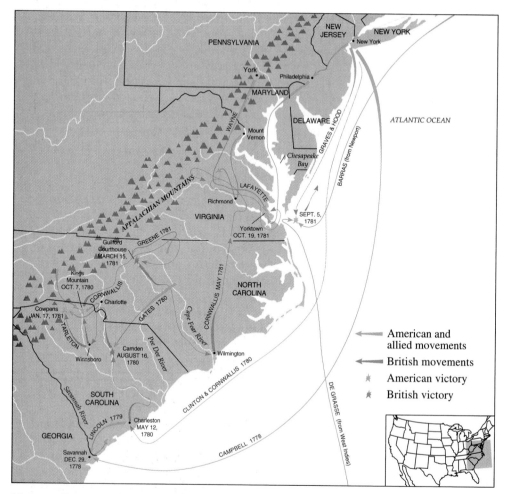

MILITARY OPERATIONS IN THE SOUTH, 1778–1781　The tide of battle in the South depended largely on British naval control of the coast and major riverways.

In April 1781, convinced that British authority could not be restored in the Carolinas while the rebels could still use Virginia as a supply and staging area, Cornwallis struck north. With a force of 7,500, he raided deep into Virginia, chasing Governor Jefferson and the state legislature from Charlottesville. But again Cornwallis found the costs of victory high, and turned back toward the coast. On August 1, he reached Yorktown.

Cornwallis's position was secure only as long as the British fleet controlled Chesapeake Bay, and that advantage did not last. In 1778, the French government, buoyed by the American victory at Saratoga in 1777, had signed an alliance with the Congress, promising to send its naval forces into the war. Initially, the French concentrated their fleet in the West Indies, hoping to seize some of the British sugar islands. But on August 30, 1781, the French admiral Comte de Grasse arrived in the Chesapeake and established naval superiority. At the same time, Washington's continentals and a French army marched south from Pennsylvania.

Cut off from the sea and pinned down on a peninsula between the York and James rivers by 17,000 French and American troops, Cornwallis's fate was sealed. On October 19, 1781, he surrendered to General Washington.

"Oh, God! It is all over." So said Lord North, the king's chief minister, when he heard the news of Yorktown in London a month later. He realized that French intervention had turned the tide. On February 27, 1782, the House of Commons cut off further support of the war, and North resigned the next month. In Philadelphia, citizens poured into the streets to celebrate while the Congress held a solemn ceremony of thanksgiving. It was not until November 1782 that the preliminary articles of peace were finally signed. But everyone knew after Yorktown that the war was over. Americans had won their independence.

Native Americans in the Revolution

The Revolutionary War drew in countless Native Americans as well as colonists and Englishmen. It could hardly have been otherwise, for the lives of all three peoples had been intimately connected since the first English settlements.

By the time of the Revolution the coastal tribes were mostly gone, displaced by white settlement and ravaged by European disease. Powerful tribes remained, however, between the Appalachians and the Mississippi. The Iroquois Six Nations, a confederation numbering 15,000 people, controlled a huge area stretching westward from Albany, New York, and dominated the "western tribes" of the Ohio Valley—the Shawnee, Delaware, Wyandotte, and Miami. Throughout the southeastern interior, five tribes prevailed: the Choctaw, Chickasaw, Seminole, Creek, and Cherokee; in all, 60,000 people.

When the Revolutionary War began, British and American officials urged neutrality on the Indians. Militarily, however, the Native Americans were too important for either side to ignore. By the spring of 1776, both sought Indian allies. Recognizing their immense stake, Native Americans up and down the interior debated their options.

Alarmed by encroaching white settlements, some Cherokee bands launched a series of raids in 1776, but in retaliation American militias laid waste the Cherokee towns. "I hope that the Cherokees will now be driven beyond the Mississippi," said Jefferson. The Cherokee never again mounted a sustained military effort against the rebels. Seeing what had become of their neighbors, the Creek kept aloof; their time for resistance would come in the early nineteenth century.

In the Ohio country, the struggle lasted longer. For several decades before the Revolution, explorers such as Daniel Boone had contested with the Shawnee and others for control of the region bordering the Ohio River. The Revolutionary War intensified these conflicts. In February 1778, George Rogers Clark led a ragtag body of Kentuckians through icy rivers and across 180 miles of forbidding terrain to attack an English outpost at Vincennes, in present-day Indiana. Clark fooled the British troops and their Indian allies into believing that his force was much larger, and the British surrendered without a shot. Clark's victory tipped the balance in the war's western theater.

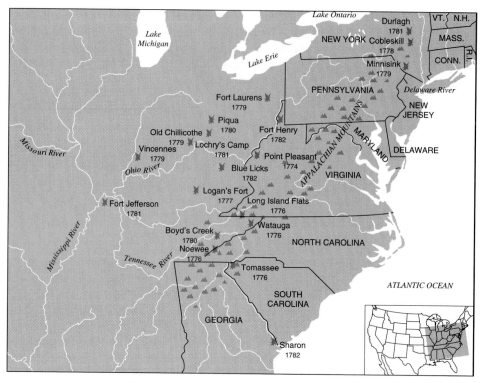

INDIAN BATTLES AND THE WAR IN THE WEST, 1775–1783   Though most battles were fought along the coastal plain, the British and their Indian allies opened a second front far to the west.

The Devastation of the Iroquois

The initial Iroquois neutrality did not last long. In 1776, after American troops raided deep into Mohawk territory west of Albany, the British persuaded the Iroquois to join them against the rebels. Most of them did so in the summer of 1777, at the urging of Joseph Brant, a Mohawk warrior who had visited England several years before and argued Britain's value as an ally against American expansion.

It was a fateful decision for Indians and whites alike. Over the next several years, the Iroquois and their English allies devastated large areas in central New York and Pennsylvania, destroying property and terrorizing the inhabitants. But the Americans' revenge came swiftly. During the summer of 1779, the Americans launched a series of punishing raids into the Iroquois country, burning the Iroquois villages, killing men, women, and children, and destroying fields of corn. Their motto was blunt: "Civilization or death to all American savages." By war's end, the Iroquois had lost as many as a third of their people as well as countless towns. Their domination of the northeastern interior was permanently shattered.

Not all the Eastern Woodland tribes sided with England in the Revolutionary War. The Oneida and the Tuscarora, members of the Iroquois confederation, fought with the Americans, their decision driven by intertribal politics and effective diplomacy by emissaries of the Continental Congress. Indians who fought for American

Mohawk chief Joseph Brant (Thayendanegea) played a major role in the Iroquois's decision to enter the war on the side of Britain. (The National Gallery of Canada, Ottawa)

independence, however, got little reward. The British and their Iroquois allies attacked them savagely, and later the Americans showed them no favors.

Negotiating Peace

In September 1781, formal peace negotiations began in Paris between the British commissioner and the American emissaries, Benjamin Franklin, John Adams, and John Jay. By now several European countries, seeking to weaken Great Britain, had become involved. As the Americans' main ally, France had entered the war in February 1778. Later, Spain declared war on England, though it declined to recognize American independence. Between 1780 and 1782, Russia, the Netherlands, and six other European countries joined in a League of Armed Neutrality aimed at protecting their maritime trade against British efforts to control it. America's Revolutionary War had become internationalized.

Dependent on French support, the Congress instructed the American commissioners to follow the advice of French foreign minister Vergennes. But the American commissioners soon learned that he was prepared to let the exhausting war continue in order to weaken England and tighten America's dependence on France. Even more alarming, Vergennes suggested that the new nation's western boundary follow the crest of the Appalachians and hinted that the British might keep whatever they controlled at the war's end, which would have meant New York City and other coastal enclaves.

In the end, the American commissioners ignored their instructions and, without a word to Vergennes, arranged a provisional peace agreement with the British

Military Muster Rolls

In almost all of America's wars, patriotism has run high and bombastic rhetoric has inspired citizens to arms. The American Revolutionary War was no exception. Though it is always difficult to assess human motivations in something as complex as war, if we knew which Americans did the fighting we could better understand why people fought and what the war meant to them.

The social composition of the revolutionary army changed markedly as the war went along. At the beginning, men from all walks of life and every class fought in defense of American liberty. As the war lengthened and its human costs increased, however, men who could afford to do so hired substitutes or arranged to go home, whereas poorer men increasingly carried the burden of fighting. Many did so out of choice, for the army promised an escape from the tedium of daily life, a way to make a living, and even, as for "Long Bill" Scott, the chance to rise in the world.

Enlistment lists of the continental army and the state militias offer one important source for studying the social history of the Revolutionary War. Although eighteenth-century records are imperfect by modern standards, recruiting officers kept track of the men they signed up so that bounties and wages could be paid and deserters accurately tracked. These lists usually give the recruits' names, ages, occupations, and places of birth and residence.

Revolutionary War muster rolls provide revealing glimpses of the social composition of the revolutionary army and how it changed over time. They also offers clues to social conditions in different regions during the war and how those conditions might have affected military recruitment.

The lists shown here of Captain Wendell's and Captain White's companies from New York and Virginia contain "social facts" on 81 men. What kind of group portrait can you draw from the data? Some occupations, such as tanner, cordwainer, and chandler, may be unfamiliar, but they are defined in standard dictionaries. How many of the recruits come from middling occupations, such as bookkeeper, tobacconist, shopkeeper, and the like? How many are skilled artisans and how many are unskilled laborers? What proportions are foreign-born, and why should such people have fought in the Revolutionary War? What do the ages of the recruits tell you about the fighting force that was assembled? How do the New York and Virginia companies differ in their makeup, and how would you explain these differences?

How would social historians describe and analyze the fighting force in a more recent American war? What would a social profile of Americans who fought in Vietnam, including their age, region, race, class, extent of education, and other differences, suggest to a social historian of this recent war?

New York Line—1st Regiment

Captain John H. Wendell's Company, 1776–1777

Men's Names	Age	Occupation	Place of Birth	Men's Names	Age	Occupation	Place of Birth
Abraham Defreest	22	Yeoman	N. York	Wm Miller	42	Yeoman	Scotland
Benjamin Goodales	20	"	Nobletown	Ephraim H. Blancherd	18	Yeoman	Ireland
Hendrick Carman	24	"	Rynbeck	Francis Acklin	40	Cardwainer	Ireland
Nathaniel Reed	32	Carpenter	Norwalk	William Orr	29	Cardwainer	Ireland
Jacob Crolrin	29	"	Germany	Thomas Welch	31	Labourer	N. York
James White	25	Weaver	Ireland	Peter Gasper	24	Labourer	N. Jersey
Joseph Battina	39	Coppersmith	Ireland	Martins Rees	19	Labourer	Fishkill
John Wyatt	38	Carpenter		Henck Able	24	"	Albany
Jacob Reyning	25	Yeoman	Amsterdam	Daniel Spinnie	21	"	Portsmouth
Patrick Kannely	36	Barber	Ireland	Patrick Kelly	23	Labourer	Ireland
John Russell	29	Penman	Ireland	Richd James Barker	12	"	America
Patrick McCue	19	Tanner	Ireland	John Patrick Cronkite	11		
James J. Atkson	21	Weaver	"	William Dougherty	17		Donyal, Ireland
William Burke	23	Chandler	Ireland				

Virginia Line—6th Regiment

Captain Tarpley White's Company, December 13th, 1780

Name	Age	Trade	Where Born State or Country	Town or Country
Win Balis, Serjt	25	Baker	England	Burningham
Arthur Harrup	24	Carpenter	Virg.	Southampton
Charles Caffatey	19	Planter	"	Caroline
Elisha Osborn	24	Planter	New Jersey	Trenton
Benj Allday	19	"	Virg.	Henrico
Wm Edwards Senr	25	"	"	Northamberland
James Hutcherson	17	Hatter	Jersey	Middlesex
Robert Low	31	Planter	"	Powhatan
Cannon Row	18	Planter	Virg.	Hanover
Wardon Pulley	18	"	"	Southampton
Richd Bond	29	Stone Mason	England	Cornwell
Tho Homont	17	Planter	Virg.	Loudon
Tho Pope	19	Planter	"	Southampton
Tho Morris	22	Planter	"	Orange
Littlebury Overby	24	Hatter	"	Dinwiddie
James [Pierce]	27	Planter	"	Nansemond
Joel Counsil	19	Planter	"	Southampton
Elisha Walden	18	Planter	"	P. Willliam
Wm Bush	19	S Carpenter	Virg.	Gloucester
Daniel Horton	22	Carpenter	"	Nansemond
John Soons	25	Weaver	England	Norfolk
Mara Lumkin	18	Planter	Virg.	Amelia
Wm Wetherford	27	Planter	"	Goochland
John Bird	16	Planter	"	Southampton
Tho Parsmore	22	Planter	England	London
Josiah Banks	27	Planter	Virg.	Gloucester
Richd Roach	28	Planter	England	London
Joseph Holburt	33	Tailor	"	Middlesex
Henry Willowby	19	Planter	Virg.	Spotsylvania
Thos Pearson	22	Planter		Pennsylvany
Jno Scarborough	19	Planter	Virg.	Brunswick
Chas Thacker	21	Planter	"	"
Nehemiah Grining	20	Planter	Virg.	Albemarle
Ewing David	19	Planter	"	King Wm
Isaiah Ballance	17	Shoemaker	"	Norfolk
Wm Alexander	20	Planter	Virg.	Northumbld
Wm Harden	26	Planter	"	Albemarle
John Ward	20	Sailor	England	Bristol
Daniel Cox	19	Planter	Virg.	Sussex
George Kirk	21	Planter	"	Brunswick
John Nash	19	Planter	"	Nothumld
Wm Edward, Jr.	19	Planter	"	Northlumld
John Fry	20	Turner	"	Albemarle
Jno Grinning	25	Hatter	"	"
Daniel Howell	30	Planter	"	Loudon
Milden Green	25	Planter	"	Sussex
Matthias Cane	32	Planter	"	Norfolk
Wm Mayo	21	Joiner	"	Dinwiddie
Jas Morgan	25	Shoemaker	England	Shropshire
Mathew Carson	19	Planter	Pennsylvania	York
Wm B[rown]	22	Planter		"
Richd Loyd	42	Planter	Virg.	Surry
Abram Foress	33	Planter	"	Gloster
Wm White	19	Planter	"	"

emissaries. The British were prepared to be generous. In the Treaty of Paris, signed in September 1783, England recognized American independence and set the western boundary of the United States at the Mississippi River. Moreover, Britain promised that U.S. fishermen would have the "right" to fish the waters off Newfoundland and that British forces would evacuate American territory "with all convenient speed." In return, the Congress would recommend that the states restore the rights and property of the Loyalists. Both sides agreed that prewar debts owed the citizens of one country by the citizens of the other would remain valid. Each of these issues would trouble Anglo-American relations in the years immediately ahead, but for the moment it seemed a splendid outcome.

It was not, however, a splendid outcome for Native Americans. For example, most of the Iroquois nations had good commercial and military reasons for siding with the British, but when the British lost, they lost too. The British negotiators ignored their Indian allies' interests, and the Iroquois received neither compensation for their losses nor guarantees of their land.

The Ingredients of Victory

How were the weak and disunited states of America able to defeat Great Britain, the most powerful nation in the Atlantic world? Certainly, Dutch and French loans and supplies, as well as French forces, were crucially important. More decisive, though, was the American people's determination not to submit. Often the Americans were disorganized and uncooperative. Repeatedly, it seemed that the war effort was about to collapse as continental troops drifted away, state militias refused to march, and supplies failed to materialize. Neither the Congress nor the states proved capable of providing consistent direction to the struggle. Yet as the war progressed, the people's estrangement from England deepened and their commitment to the "glorious cause" increased. To subdue the colonies, England would have had to occupy the entire eastern third of the continent, and that it could not do.

Even though state militias frequently refused to go beyond their own borders and after the first months of the war engaged in relatively few battles, they provided a vast reservoir of manpower capable of controlling the countryside, intimidating Loyalists, and harassing British forces. In doing so, they tied up British troops that would otherwise have been free to fight the continental army.

The American victory owed much, as well, to the administrative and organizational talents of George Washington. Against massive odds and often by the sheer force of his will, he held the continental army together and created a military force capable both of winning selected encounters and, more important, of surviving. Had he failed, the Americans could not possibly have won.

In the end, however, it is as accurate to say that Britain lost the war as that the United States won it. With vast economic and military resources, Britain enjoyed clear military superiority over the Americans. Its troops were more numerous, better armed and supplied, and more professional. Until the closing months of the contest, Britain enjoyed naval superiority as well, enabling its forces to move up and down the coast virtually at will.

Britain, however, could not capitalize on its advantages. It had difficulty extending its command structures and supply routes across several thousand miles of ocean. Because information flowed erratically across the water, strategic decisions made in London were often based on faulty or outdated intelligence. Given the difficulties of supply, British troops often had to live off the land, reducing their mobility and increasing the resentment of Americans whose crops and animals were commandeered.

Faced with these circumstances, British leaders were often overly cautious. Burgoyne's attempt in 1777 to isolate New England by invading from Canada failed because Sir William Howe decided to attack Philadelphia rather than move northward up the Hudson River to join him. Similarly, neither Howe nor Cornwallis pressed his advantage in the central states during the middle years of the war, when more aggressive action might have crushed the continentals.

Just as important, British commanders generally failed to adapt battlefield tactics to American realities. They continued to fight European style, emerging from winter quarters during certain times of the year and deploying set formations of troops in formal battlefield maneuvers. Much of the rough, wooded American terrain was better suited to the use of smaller units and irregular troops.

Washington and Greene were more flexible, often employing a patient strategy of raiding, harassment, and strategic retreat. Behind this strategy lay a willingness, grounded in necessity, to allow England control of considerable territory, especially along the coast. But it was based, as well, on the conviction that popular support for the Revolutionary cause would grow and that the costs of subduing the colonial rebellion would become greater than the British government could bear. As a much later American war in Vietnam would also show, a guerrilla force can win if it does not lose; a regular army loses if it does not consistently win.

The American strategy proved sound. As the war dragged on and its costs escalated, Britain's will wavered. After France and Spain entered the conflict, Britain had to worry about Europe, the Caribbean, and the Mediterranean as well as North America. Unrest in Ireland and massive food riots in London prevented England from sending more troops to North America. As the cost increased and prospects of victory dimmed, political support for the war eroded. With the defeat at Yorktown, it collapsed.

THE EXPERIENCE OF WAR

In terms of the loss of life and destruction of property, the Revolutionary War pales by comparison with America's more recent wars. Yet modern comparisons are misleading, for by eighteenth-century terms, the War for American Independence was terrifying and destructive to the people caught up in it.

Recruiting an Army

Estimates vary, but on the American side as many as 250,000 men may at one time or another have borne arms. That would amount to about one out of every two or three adult, white males.

Tens of thousands served in the state militias. In 1776, most state militias were not effective fighting forces. This was especially true in the South, where Nathanael Greene complained that the men came "from home with all the tender feelings of domestic life" and were not "sufficiently fortified . . . to stand the shocking scenes of war, to march over dead men, [or] to hear without concern the groans of the wounded." Greene knew that fighting was neither pleasant nor often heroic.

The militia did serve as a convenient recruiting system, for men were already enrolled, and arrangements were in place for calling them into the field on short notice. This was of special importance early in the war, before the continental army took shape. Given its grounding in local community life, the militia also legitimated the war among the people and secured their commitment to the Revolutionary cause. What better way to separate the Patriots from the Loyalists than by mustering the local company and seeing who turned out?

During the first year of the war, when enthusiasm ran high, men of all ranks—from the rich and middle classes as well as the poor—volunteered to fight the British. But as the war went on and casualties increased, the army soon had to be filled with conscripts. Eventually the war was transformed, as wars so often are, into a poor man's fight as wealthier men hired substitutes and communities filled their quotas with strangers lured by enlistment bonuses. This social transformation was most evident in the continental army, where terms were longer, discipline stiffer, and battlefields more distant from home.

For the poor and the jobless, whose ranks the war rapidly swelled, military bonus payments and the promise of board and keep proved attractive. But often the bonuses failed to materialize and pay got long overdue. Moreover, life in the camps was harsh, and soldiers frequently heard from their wives of their families' distress. Troops became disgruntled and insubordinate. As the war went on, Washington imposed harsher discipline on the continental troops to hold them in line.

Throughout the war, soldiers suffered from shortages of supplies. At Valley Forge during the terrible winter of 1777–1778, men went without shoes or coats. In the midst of that winter, Washington wrote, "There are now in this army 4,000 men wanting blankets, near 2,000 of which have never had one, altho' some of them have been 12 months in service." "I am sick, discontented, and out of humour," declared one despairing soul. "Poor food, hard lodging, cold weather, fatigue, nasty cloathes, nasty cookery, vomit half my time, smoaked out of my senses. The Devil's in't, I can't Endure it. Why are we sent here to starve and freeze?"

The states had food and clothing enough, but they were often reluctant to strip their own people of wagons and livestock, blankets and shoes for use elsewhere. Moreover, mismanagement and difficulties in transportation stood in the way. Neither the state governments nor the Congress could administer a war effort of such magnitude. Wagon transport was slow and costly, and the British fleet made coastal transport perilous. Though many individuals served honorably as supply officers, others exploited the army's distress. Washington commented bitterly on the "speculators, various tribes of money makers, and stock-jobbers of all denominations" whose "avarice and thirst for gain" threatened the country's ruin.

The Casualties of Combat

The death that soldiers dispensed to each other on the battlefield was intensely personal. The effective range of muskets was little more than 100 yards, so soldiers came virtually face-to-face with the men they killed. According to eighteenth-

The American rifleman, even as idealized in this engraving, lacked the pomp and formality—and often the discipline—of the British soldier. (Library of Congress)

century practice, armies formed in ranks on the battlefield and fired in unison. After massed volleys, the lines often closed for hand-to-hand combat with knives and bayonets. Partisan warfare in the South, with its emphasis on ambush, personalized combat even more. British officers were shocked at the "implacable ardor and revenge" with which the Americans fought.

The American ferocity is largely explained by the fact that this was a civil war. Not only did Englishmen fight Anglo-Americans, but American Loyalists and Patriots fought each other as well. As many as 50,000 Americans fought for the king in some of the war's most bitter encounters. Finally, American Patriots fervently believed that theirs was a struggle between irreconcilable principles of liberty and tyranny. Nothing was to be spared that might bring victory.

Medical treatment, whether for wounds or the diseases that raged through the camps, did little good. Casualties poured into hospitals, often overcrowding them beyond capacity. Dr. Jonathan Potts, the attending physician at Fort George in New York, reported that "we have at present upwards of one thousand sick crowded into sheds and labouring under the various and cruel disorders of dysentaries, bilious putrid fevers and the effects of a confluent smallpox; to attend to this large number we have four seniors and four mates, exclusive of myself."

Surgeons, operating without anesthetics and with the crudest of instruments, threatened life as often as they preserved it. Few knew anything about infection. Doctoring consisted mostly of bleeding, blistering, and induced vomiting. One doctor reported "that we lost no less than from 10 to 20 of camp diseases, for one by weapons of the enemy."

No one kept accurate records of how many soldiers died. But the most conservative estimate runs to over 25,000, a higher percentage of the total population than for any other American conflict except the Civil War. For the Revolutionary War soldier, death was an imminent reality.

Civilians and the War

Noncombatants also experienced the realities of war, especially in densely settled areas along the coast. The British concentrated most of their military efforts there, taking advantage of their naval power and striking at the political and economic centers of American life. At one time or another, British troops occupied every major port city.

Urban life suffered profound dislocations. About half of New York City's inhabitants fled when the British occupation began and were replaced by an almost equal number of Loyalists from the surrounding countryside, not to speak of 10,000 British and German troops.

In Philadelphia, the occupation was shorter and the disruptions less severe, but the shock of invasion was no less real. Elizabeth Drinker, living alone after local Patriots had exiled her Quaker husband, found herself the unwilling landlady of a British officer and his friends whose presence may, however, have protected her from the plundering that went on all around. She was constantly anxious, however, confiding to her journal that "I often feel afraid to go to Bed." British soldiers frequently tore down fences for their campfires and confiscated food. Even Loyalists complained about the "dreadful consequences" of British occupation.

Along the entire coastal plain, British landing parties descended without warning, seizing supplies and terrorizing inhabitants. In 1780 and 1781, the British mounted a punishing attack along the Connecticut coast. The southern coast was even more vulnerable. In December 1780, Benedict Arnold, the American traitor who by then was fighting for the British, ravaged Virginia's James River valley, uprooting tobacco, confiscating slaves, and terrorizing whites.

Such onslaughts sent civilians fleeing into the interior. During the first years of the war, the port cities lost nearly half their population. So many Bostonians crowded into Concord, Massachusetts, by July 1775 that they decided to hold a town meeting there. By March 1776, Concord's population had grown by 25 percent, creating major problems of housing, social order, and public health.

Not all the refugee traffic was away from the coast. In western New York, Pennsylvania, Virginia, and the Carolinas, frontier settlements collapsed under British and Indian assaults.

Wherever the armies went, they generated a swirl of refugees, who spread vivid tales of the war's devastation. This refugee traffic, and the constant movement of soldiers between army and civilian life, brought the war home to countless people who did not experience it firsthand. And disease followed the armies, ravaging soldiers and civilians alike.

Armies lived off the land, taking what they needed. Britain's German mercenaries raised additional fears, particularly among women. In April 1777, a committee of the Congress, taking affidavits from women who had been raped, reported that it had "authentic information of many instances of the most indecent treatment, and actual ravishment of married and single women." Such was the

In September 1776, as American troops fought unsuccessfully for control of New York, nearly a quarter of the city was destroyed by a fire apparently set by a defiant Patriot woman. Not until the war ended did reconstruction and cleanup of the ruins begin. (Library of Congress)

nature of that "most irreparable injury," however, that the persons suffering it, "though perfectly innocent, look upon it as a kind of reproach to have the facts related and their names known." Whether the report had any effect is unknown.

The Loyalists

No Americans suffered greater losses than those who remained loyal to the crown. On September 8, 1783, Thomas Danforth, formerly a prosperous lawyer from Cambridge, Massachusetts, appeared in London before the official commission that was supposed to ascertain Loyalists' losses. He began by explaining the consequences of his loyalty: having devoted his whole life to "preparing himself for future usefulness," he was now "near his fortieth year, banished under pain of death, to a distant country, where he has not the most remote family connection . . . cut off from his profession, from every hope of importance in life, and in a great degree from social enjoyments." Without assistance, he would sink to "a station much inferior to that of a menial servant . . . ."

Many of the several thousand Loyalists who appeared before the commission were reimbursed for about one-third of their losses—more than most other Loyalist refugees ever received. This was meager compensation for the loss of house and property, expulsion from a familiar community, and relocation in a distant land.

We do not know how many colonists remained loyal to England, but we do know that tens of thousands left with British troops from New York, Charleston, and Savannah. At least as many slipped away to England, Canada, or the West Indies while fighting was still under way. Additional thousands who had opposed independence remained in the new nation.

These are substantial numbers when set against the total American population, black and white, of about 2.5 million. The incidence of loyalism differed dramatically from region to region. Loyalists were fewest in New England and most numerous around New York City, where British authority was most stable.

Why did so many Americans remain loyal at the cost of personal danger and loss? Customs officers, members of the governors' councils, and Anglican clergy often remained with the crown, which had appointed them. Loyalism was common, as well, among groups especially dependent on British authority—for example, settlers on the Carolina frontier who believed themselves mistreated by the planter elite along the coast; ethnic minorities, such as Germans, who feared domination by the Anglo-American majority; or tenants on large estates along the Hudson River, who had struggled for years with their landlords over their leasehold terms. Many Loyalists simply made their choice because they were daunted by the prospect of confronting British military power, or doubted that independence could be won.

But there was also principled Loyalism, as Samuel Seabury made clear. "Every person owes obedience to the laws of the government," he insisted, "and is obliged in honour and duty to support them. Because if one has a right to disregard the laws of the society to which he belongs, all have the same right; and then government is at an end." Another Loyalist wondered what kind of society independence would bring when revolutionary crowds showed no respect for the rights of Loyalist dissenters such as he. Loyalists such as these claimed to be upholding reason and law against revolutionary disorder. Their loss to American society weakened conservatism in America and promoted revolutionary change.

Many who went into exile established new lives elsewhere in the empire, mostly Canada's Maritime Provinces. Those who, like Thomas Danforth, made it to England often found themselves on the fringes of English society, their finances troubled and their futures uncertain.

African-Americans and the Revolutionary War

Black Americans were deeply involved in the Revolution, which provoked the largest slave rebellion in American history prior to the Civil War. Once the war was under way, blacks found a variety of ways to turn events to their own advantage.

During the pre-revolutionary decade, hearing their white masters talk excitedly about liberty, increasing numbers of black Americans questioned their own oppression. In the North, some slaves petitioned legislatures for freedom. In the South, pockets of insurrection appeared. In 1765, more than 100 South Carolina slaves fled to the interior, where they tried to establish a colony of their own. The next year, slaves paraded through Charleston chanting "Liberty, liberty!"

In November 1775, Lord Dunmore issued a proclamation offering freedom to all Virginia slaves and servants, "able and willing to bear arms," who would leave their masters and join the British at Norfolk. Within weeks, 500 to 600 slaves responded. Among them was Thomas Peters, an African who had been brought to Louisiana about 1760. He had resisted enslavement so fiercely that he was sold into the English colonies, and by the 1770s he was toiling on a plantation on Cape Fear peninsula, near Wilmington, North Carolina.

Peters's plans for his own declaration of independence may have ripened as a result of the rhetoric of liberty he heard around the house of his master, William Campbell. A leading member of Wilmington's Sons of Liberty, Campbell talked excitedly about inalienable rights. By mid-1775, the Cape Fear region, like many areas from Maryland to Georgia, buzzed with rumors of slave uprisings. In July, the state's revolutionary government imposed martial law when the British commander of Fort Johnston, near Wilmington, encouraged blacks to "elope from their masters." When 20 British ships entered the Cape Fear River in March 1776 and disembarked royal troops, Peters seized the moment to redefine himself as a man, instead of William Campbell's property, and escaped. Before long, he would fight with the British-officered Black Pioneers.

How many African-Americans sought liberty behind British lines is unknown, but as many as 20 percent may have done so. Unlike their white masters, blacks saw in England the promise of freedom, not tyranny. As the war dragged on, English commanders pressed blacks into service. A regiment of black soldiers, formed from Virginia slaves who responded to Dunmore's proclamation, marched into battle, their chests covered by sashes emblazoned "Liberty to Slaves."

Most of the blacks who joined England achieved their freedom. At the war's end, several thousand were evacuated with the British to Nova Scotia. Their reception by the white inhabitants, however, was generally hostile. By 1800, most had left Canada to found the free black colony of Sierra Leone in West Africa. Thomas Peters was a leader among them.

Many of the slaves who fled behind English lines never won their freedom. Under the peace treaty, hundreds were returned to their American owners. Several thousand others, their value as field hands too great to be ignored, were transported to even harsher slavery on West Indian sugar plantations.

Other blacks took advantage of the confusion to flee. Numerous blacks went north, following rumors that slavery had been abolished there. Or they slipped into the southern interior. The Seminoles of Georgia and Florida generally welcomed black runaways and through intermarriage absorbed them into tribal society. Blacks met a more uncertain reception from the Cherokee and Creek. While some were taken in, others were returned to their white owners for bounties, and still others were held in slavelike conditions by new Indian masters.

Fewer blacks fought on the American side than on England's, in part because neither the Congress nor the states were eager to see them armed. Faced with the increasing need for troops, however, the Congress and all states except Georgia and South Carolina eventually relented and pressed blacks into service. Of those who served the Patriot cause, many received the freedom they were promised. The patriotism of countless others, however, went unrewarded.

THE FERMENT OF REVOLUTIONARY POLITICS

The Revolution altered people's lives in countless ways that reached beyond the sights and sounds of battle. No areas of American life were more powerfully changed than politics and government. Who would have a voice in revolutionary politics, and who would be excluded? How thoroughly would political equality penetrate revolutionary politics, or how tenaciously would people cling to the traditional belief that citizens should defer to their political leaders? And how would the new state governments balance the need for order and the security of property against the desire for democratic openness and accountability?

Other explosive issues complicated revolutionary politics and threatened to overwhelm both Congress and the states: controlling the Loyalist "menace," deciding whether to abolish slavery, arguing over religious freedom and the separation of church and state, apportioning taxes, regulating prices, issuing paper money, and providing debt relief to desperate citizens. Seldom has American politics been more heated, seldom has it struggled with a more daunting agenda than during the years of the nation's founding.

Mobilizing the People

Under the pressure of revolutionary events, politics attracted people's attention like a magnet and absorbed their energies as never before. The politicization of American society was evident in the flood of printed material issuing from American presses. Newspapers multiplied and pamphlets by the thousands fanned political debate.

Pulpits rocked with political exhortations as well. Religion and politics had never been sharply separated in colonial America, but the Revolution drew them more tightly together. In countless sermons, Congregational, Presbyterian, and Baptist clergy called on the American people to repent the sins that had brought English tyranny upon them and to rededicate themselves to God's law by fighting for American freedom. People nurtured in Puritan piety and the Great Awakening instinctively understood.

The belief that God sanctioned their Revolution strengthened Americans' resolve. It also encouraged them to identify national interest with divine intent, and thus offered convenient justification for whatever they believed necessary to do. This was not the last time Americans would make that dangerous equation.

By contrast, Loyalist clergy, such as Maryland's Jonathan Boucher, reminded parishioners that the king was head of the Anglican Church. During the months preceding independence, as the local Committee of Safety interrupted worship to harass him, Boucher carried a loaded pistol while he preached submission to royal authority.

Belief in the momentous importance of what they were doing increased the intensity of revolutionary politics. John Adams, writing to his wife Abigail as the Congress moved toward its fateful declaration, exalted independence as "the greatest question . . . which ever was debated in America . . . ." As independence was declared, people throughout the land raised toasts to the great event: "Liberty to those who have the spirit to preserve it," and "May Liberty expand sacred wings, and, in glorious effort, diffuse her influence o'er and o'er the globe." Inspired by the searing experience of rebellion, war, and nation building, they believed they held the future of human liberty in their hands. No wonder they took politics so seriously.

The expanding array of extralegal committees and spontaneous gatherings of the people that erupted during the 1770s and 1780s provided the most dramatic evidence of politicization. Prior to independence, crowds took to the streets to protest against measures like the Stamp Act. After 1776, direct political action accelerated as people intimidated Loyalists, enforced price and wage controls, administered roughhewn justice, and, as one individual protested, even directed "what we shall eat, drink, wear, speak, and think."

Those of more radical temperament celebrated these activities as the direct and legitimate expression of the popular will. More conservative republicans worried that such behavior threatened political stability. Direct popular action had been necessary in the struggle against England, but why such restlessness after the yoke of English tyranny had been thrown off? Even Thomas Paine expressed concern. "It is time to have done with tarring and feathering," he wrote in 1777. "I never did and never would encourage what may properly be called a mob, when any legal mode of redress can be had."

This dramatic expansion of popular politics resulted from an explosive combination of circumstances: the momentous events of revolution and war; the efforts of Patriot leaders to mobilize popular support for the desperate struggle against England; and the determination of artisans, workingmen, and farmers to apply the principles of liberty and natural rights to the conditions of their own lives.

A Republican Ideology

Throughout history, as people have moved from colonial subordination to independence, they have struggled to establish their identities as free and separate nations. It was no different with the American revolutionary generation. What did it mean to be not English but American? "Our style and manner of thinking," observed Thomas Paine in amazement, "have undergone a revolution . . . . We see with other eyes, we hear with other ears, and think with other thoughts than those we formerly used." The ideology of revolutionary republicanism, pieced together from English political thought, Enlightenment theories, and religious beliefs, constituted that revolution in thought. Many of its central tenets were broadly shared among the American people, but its larger meanings were sharply contested throughout the revolutionary era.

The rejection of monarchy was one basic component of America's new republican faith. "The word *republic*," explained Paine, "means the public good of the whole, in contradistinction to the despotic form which makes the good of the sovereign, or of one man, the only object of government." It was Paine's unsparing rejection of monarchy that made his pamphlet *Common Sense* seem so radical.

The American people also rejected the hierarchical authority on which monarchy rested. Under a republican system, public authority was established by the people contracting together for their mutual good. In that fundamental change lay much of the American Revolution's radical potential.

A basic part of republican belief was the notion that governmental power, if removed from the people's close oversight and control, threatened constantly to expand at the expense of liberty. The revolutionary generation's experience with England had burned that lesson indelibly into their consciousness. Although too much liberty could degenerate into political chaos, history seemed to demonstrate that trouble usually arose from too much government.

Given the need to limit governmental power, how could political order be maintained? The revolutionary generation offered an extraordinary answer. Order was not to be imposed from above through such traditional agencies of central control as monarchies, standing armies, and state churches. In a republic, political discipline had to flow upward from the self-regulated behavior of the citizens, especially from their willingness to put the public good ahead of their own interests. This radical principle of "public virtue" was an essential part of republican ideology.

By contrast, "faction," or politically organized self-interest, constituted the "mortal disease" to which popular governments throughout history had succumbed. Given the absence, in republican systems, of a strong central authority capable of imposing political order, factional conflict could easily spin out of control. This fear of "party faction" added to the intensity of political conflict in revolutionary America by encouraging people to attribute the worst motives to their political opponents.

The idea of placing responsibility for political order with the people and counting on them to act selflessly for the good of the whole, alarmed countless Americans. What if the people proved unworthy? If the attempt was made, warned one individual darkly, "the bands of society would be dissolved, the harmony of the world confused, and the order of nature subverted." A strong incentive toward Loyalism lurked in such concerns.

Few Patriots were so naive as to believe that the American people were altogether virtuous. During the first years of independence, when revolutionary enthusiasm ran high, however, many believed that public virtue was sufficiently widespread to support republican government, while others argued that the American people would learn public virtue by its practice. The revolutionary struggle would serve as a "furnace of affliction," refining the American character as it strengthened people's capacity for virtuous behavior. It was an extraordinarily hopeful but risk-filled undertaking.

The principle of political equality was another controversial touchstone of republicanism. It was broadly assumed that republican governments must be grounded in popular consent, that elections should be frequent, and that citizens must vigilantly defend their liberties. But there agreement often ended.

Some Americans took literally the principle of political equality by arguing that every citizen should have an equal voice and that public office should be open to all. This position was most forcefully articulated by tenants and small farmers in the interior, as well as workers and artisans in the coastal cities who had long struggled to claim their political voice. More cautious citizens emphasized the need for order as well as liberty, arguing that stable republics required leadership by men of ability and experience, an "aristocracy of talent" that could give the people direction. Merchants, planters, and large commercial farmers who were used to providing such leadership saw no need for radical changes in the existing distribution of political power.

Creating Republican Governments

All of these differences of ideology and self-interest appeared dramatically in the debates over the new state constitutions that occurred immediately following independence. Fashioning new, republican governments would not be easy. The American people had no experience with government-making on such a scale, but

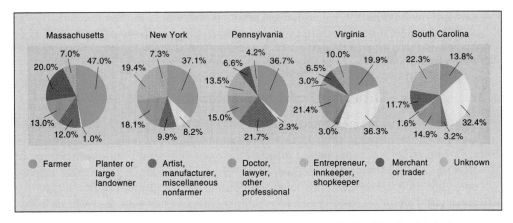

Massachusetts | New York | Pennsylvania | Virginia | South Carolina

Farmer · Planter or large landowner · Artist, manufacturer, miscellaneous nonfarmer · Doctor, lawyer, other professional · Entrepreneur, innkeeper, shopkeeper · Merchant or trader · Unknown

OCCUPATIONAL COMPOSITION OF SEVERAL STATE ASSEMBLIES IN THE 1780S Membership in the revolutionary assemblies reflected differences in the economies and societies of the various states. Those differences often generated political conflict throughout the revolutionary era. What are the major differences between Northern and Southern state assemblies, and how do you explain them? Source: Jackson T. Main, *Political Parties Before the Constitution*, 1973.

they had to attempt it in the midst of a disruptive war. And there were sharp divisions over the kinds of governments they wished to create. One person prophetically thought it the "most difficult and dangerous business" that was to be done.

The revolutionary generation began with two overriding concerns: to limit the powers of government and to make public officials closely accountable. The only certain way of accomplishing these goals was by creating a *written* constitution that could serve as a standard for regulating governmental behavior. Connecticut and Rhode Island decided that their colonial charters served this purpose, deleting all references to the British crown. The other 11 states wrote new constitutions by 1780.

In most states, the provincial congresses, extralegal successors to the defunct colonial assemblies, wrote the first constitutions. But this made people uneasy. If governmental bodies wrote the documents, they could change them, too, and what would then guarantee against the abuse of governmental power? Massachusetts first perfected the new procedures. In 1779, its citizens elected a special convention for the sole purpose of preparing a new constitution, which the people then ratified.

Through trial and argumentation, the revolutionary generation gradually worked out a clear understanding of what a constitution was and how it should be constructed. In the process it established some of the most basic doctrines of American constitutionalism, essential to the preservation of liberty: that sovereignty resides in the people; that written constitutions, produced by specially-elected conventions and then ratified by the people, embody their sovereign will; and that governments must function within clear constitutional limits.

The new constitutions redefined American government in fundamental and lasting ways. The new governments were considerably more democratic than the colonial regimes had been. Most state officials were now elected, many of them annually rather than every two or three years as before. The assemblies, moreover, were now larger and more representative than they had been prior to 1776, and many of the powers of the colonial governors (control over the budget, veto power over legislation, the right to appoint various state officials) were either abolished or reallocated to the assemblies.

Different Paths to the Republican Goal

Constitution-making generated controversy, especially over how democratic the new governments should be. In Pennsylvania, western farmers, Philadelphia artisans, and radical leaders pushed through the most democratic state constitution of all. Drafted less than three months after independence, during the most intense period of political reform, it rejected the familiar English model of two legislative houses and an independent executive. Republican governments, the radicals insisted, should be simple and easily understood. The constitution thus provided for a single, all-powerful legislative house, its members annually elected, its debates open to the public. There was no governor. A truly radical assumption underlay this unitary design: that only the "common interest of society" and not "separate and jarring private interests" should be represented in public affairs. Property-holding requirements for public office were abolished, and the franchise was opened to every taxpaying white male over 21. A bill of rights guaranteed every citizen religious freedom, trial by jury, and freedom of speech. The most radical proposal of all called for the redistribution of property. Alarmed conservatives just managed to have the offending language removed.

Debate over the constitution polarized the state. Men of wealth condemned the document's supporters as "coffee-house demagogues" seeking to introduce a "tyranny of the people." The constitution's proponents—tradesmen, farmers, and other small producers—shot back that their critics were "the rich and great men and the wise men, the lawyers and doctors," who thought they had no "common interest with the body of the people."

In 1776, the radicals had their way, and the document was approved. The Pennsylvania constitution, together with its counterparts in Vermont and Georgia, represented the most radical thrust of revolutionary republicanism. As later events would reveal, the struggle for political control in Pennsylvania was not over, for in 1790 a more conservative constitution would be approved. But for the moment, the lines of political power in Pennsylvania had been decisively redrawn.

In Massachusetts, constitution-making followed a more cautious course. There the disruptions of the war were less severe and the continuity of political leadership was greater. The constitution's main architect, John Adams, readily admitted that the new government must be firmly grounded in the people, yet he warned against reckless experimentation and regarded the Pennsylvania constitution as far too democratic. He considered a balance between two legislative houses and an independent executive essential to preserving liberty. The constitution also provided for a governor empowered to veto legislation, make appointments, command the militia, and oversee state expenditures. It did not extend the vote to men without property.

When the convention sent the document to the town meetings for approval on March 2, 1780, farmers and Boston artisans attacked it as "aristocratic." But when the convention reconvened in June 1780 it declared the constitution approved, and the document went into effect four months later.

Women and the Limits of Republican Citizenship

The revolutionary generation argued heatedly over who could be trusted with the vote and thus claim full citizenship in the new republican regimes. Most states reduced the property requirements for voting, but only Pennsylvania abolished them altogether. Because property ownership was believed necessary to ensure independent judgment that republican citizenship required, dependent sons and other males lacking sufficient property were denied the vote.

Even more significant, republican citizenship did not encompass women. Though women participated in many revolutionary crowds, they were still deprived of the franchise. Except on scattered occasions, women had neither voted nor held public office during the colonial period. Nor, with rare exceptions, did they do so in revolutionary America. Only in New Jersey did the constitution of 1776 open the franchise to "all free inhabitants" meeting property and residency requirements, and in the 1780s numerous women took advantage of that opening. Many men objected, and in 1807 the state assembly again disfranchised women.

Most women did not press for political equality, for the idea flew in the face of long-standing social convention, and its advocacy exposed a person to public ridicule. Some women did make the case, most often to each other or their husbands. "I cannot say, that I think you are very generous to the ladies," Abigail Adams chided her husband John. "For whilst you are proclaiming peace and good will to men, emancipating all nations, you insist upon retaining an absolute power over all wives." John consulted Abigail on many things but turned this admonition quickly aside. Not until the twentieth century would women fully secure the vote, that most fundamental attribute of citizenship.

Prior to independence, most women had accepted the principle that political debate fell outside their sphere. The Revolution, however, significantly altered that attitude, for women felt the urgency of the revolutionary crisis as intensely as men. With increasing frequency, women wrote and spoke to each other about public events, especially as they affected their own lives. As the war progressed, increasing numbers of women spoke out publicly. A few, such as Esther DeBerdt Reed of Philadelphia, published essays explaining women's urgent need to contribute to the Patriot cause. In her 1780 broadside "The Sentiments of an American Woman," she declared that women wanted to be "useful" and called on women to renounce "vain ornament" as they had earlier renounced English tea. The money no longer spent on clothing and hairstyles would be the "offering of the Ladies" to Washington's army. In Philadelphia, women responded by collecting $300,000 in continental currency from over 1,600 individuals. Refusing Washington's proposal that the money be mixed with general funds in the national treasury, they insisted on using it to purchase materials for shirts so that each soldier might know he had received a contribution directly from the women.

In the revolutionary context, even women's traditional roles took on new political meaning. With English imports cut off and the army badly in need of clothing, spinning and weaving assumed patriotic importance. Often coming together as Daughters of Liberty, women made shirts and other items of clothing. Charity Clarke, a New York teenager, acknowledged that she "felt Nationaly" as she knitted "stockens" for the soldiers.

The most traditional of female roles, the care and nurture of children, took on special political resonance during the revolutionary era. How could the republic be

Abigail Adams, like many women of the revolutionary generation, protested the contradiction in men's subordination of women while they extolled the principles of liberty and equality. (New York State Historical Association, Cooperstown)

sustained once independence had been won? Only by a rising generation of republican citizens schooled in the principles of public virtue and ready to assume the task. How would they be prepared? During their formative years by their "Republican Mothers," the women of the Revolution.

Women developed a variety of new connections with the public realm during the revolutionary years. Those connections, however, remained limited, for the assumption that politics and government were a male domain did not die easily. In time, further challenges to that assumption would come, and when they did, women would find guidance in the principles that the women of the Revolution had helped to define.

THE AGENDA OF REVOLUTIONARY POLITICS

Revolutionary state politics took different forms depending on the impact of the war, the extent of Loyalism, patterns of social conflict, and economic conditions. In Pennsylvania, change ran deep; elsewhere, it was more muted. Everywhere, though, citizens struggled with a bewildering and often intractable array of issues.

Separating Church and State

Among the most explosive issues was the proper relationship between church and state in a republican order. Prior to independence, only Rhode Island, New Jersey,

Pennsylvania, and Delaware had full religious liberty. The other colonies all had established churches. There, the authorities only grudgingly tolerated "dissenters" such as the Methodists and Baptists, whose numbers were growing among the lower classes and which were noisily pressing their case for religious liberty.

With independence, pressure built for severing the tie between church and state completely. Such pressure was fed by the belief that throughout history alliances between governmental and church authorities had been instruments of oppression and that voluntary choice was the only safe basis for religious association.

In Massachusetts, Connecticut, and New Hampshire, the Congregationalists fought to preserve their long-established privileges. Separating church and state, they argued, risked infidelity and disorder. Massachusetts's 1780 constitution did guarantee everyone the right to worship God "in the manner and season most agreeable to the dictates of his own conscience." But New England's most outspoken Baptist, Isaac Backus, pointed out that it also empowered the legislature to require towns to tax their residents to support "the public worship of God." Backus argued that such official support should be ended completely and that mere toleration fell far short of true religious freedom. Not until the early nineteenth century—in Massachusetts not until 1833—were laws linking church and state finally repealed.

In Virginia, the Baptists pressed their case against the Protestant Episcopal Church, successor to the Church of England. The adoption in 1786 of Thomas Jefferson's Bill for Establishing Religious Freedom, rejecting all connections between church and state and removing all religious tests for public office, decisively settled the issue. Three years later, that statute served as a model for the First Amendment to the new federal Constitution.

Religious discrimination did not end. To take a typical example, the people of Northbridge, Massachusetts, wanted to exclude "Roman Catholics, pagons, or Mahomitents" from public office. But disestablishment did firmly implant the principle of religious freedom in American law.

Loyalists and the Public Safety

Independence and the war raised troubling questions about the amount of freedom of speech and association that Loyalists could be allowed. Emotions ran high between Patriots and Loyalists, dividing both families and communities. "The son is armed against the father, the brother against the brother, family against family," lamented one individual. In the midst of the Revolutionary War, security required stern measures against Loyalist counterrevolutionaries. More than security was involved, however, for the Patriots were also determined to punish those who had rejected the revolutionary cause.

During the war, each state enacted laws depriving Loyalists of the vote, confiscating their property, and banishing them. In 1776, the Connecticut assembly passed a remarkably punitive law threatening anyone who criticized either the assembly or the Continental Congress with immediate fine and imprisonment. Probably not more than a few dozen Loyalists actually died at the hands of the revolutionary regimes, but thousands found their livelihoods destroyed, their families ostracized, and themselves subject to physical attack.

Punishing Loyalists—or people accused of Loyalism, a distinction that was often unclear—was popular. Some Patriots argued that the Loyalists had put themselves outside the protection of American law; others worried that no one's rights would be safe when the rights of Loyalists were so clearly disregarded. Republics, after all, were supposed to be "governments of law, and not of men."

When the war ended and passions cooled, most states repealed anti-Loyalist laws. But the Revolution had raised the difficult question of balancing individual liberty against public security. The issue would return to trouble the nation in future years.

Slavery Under Attack

The place of slavery in a republican society also vexed the revolutionary generation. How, asked many, could slavery be reconciled with republican ideals concerning the inalienable rights to life, liberty, and the pursuit of happiness?

While the 1760s had witnessed the largest importation of slaves in colonial history, the Revolutionary War halted the slave trade almost completely. With the end of the war, arguments were advanced for preventing a resumption of the traffic. These arguments included revolutionary principles, a reduced need for fieldhands in the depressed Chesapeake tobacco economy, the continuing natural increase among the slave population, and anxiety over black rebelliousness. By 1790, every state except South Carolina and Georgia had outlawed slave importations.

Ending the slave trade had powerful implications, for it reduced the infusion of new Africans into the black population. An ever higher proportion of blacks was now American-born, speeding the cultural transformation of Africans into African-Americans.

Slavery itself came under attack during the revolutionary era, with immense consequences for blacks and the nation's future. As the crisis with England heated up, catchwords such as *liberty* and *tyranny*, mobilized by colonists against British policies, reminded citizens that one-fifth of the colonial population was in chains. Following independence, the attacks intensified. Only in Georgia and South Carolina, where blacks outnumbered whites more than two to one and where slave labor remained essential to the prosperous rice economy, did slavery escape significant challenge. Indeed, whites tightened local slave codes, shuddering at the prospect of black freedom.

In Virginia and Maryland, by contrast, whites argued openly whether slavery was compatible with republicanism, and in these states significant change did occur. The weakened demand for slave labor posed by the depressed tobacco economy facilitated the debate. Though neither state abolished slavery, both passed laws making it easier for owners to free their slaves without continuing to be responsible for their behavior. Increasing numbers of blacks bought their own freedom or simply ran away. By 1800, more than one of every ten blacks in the Chesapeake region was free, a dramatic increase from 30 years before. For Chesapeake blacks, life slowly got better.

The most dramatic breakthrough occurred in the North. There slavery was either abolished or put on the road to gradual extinction. Abolition was possible in the North because blacks were a distinct numerical minority, and slavery had neither the economic nor social importance that it did in the South. In 1780, the

Pennsylvania assembly passed a law stipulating that all newborn blacks were to be free when they reached age 21. Other northern states adopted similar policies.

Northern blacks joined in the attacks on slavery. Following independence, they eagerly petitioned state assemblies for their freedom, and in scattered instances free blacks participated actively in revolutionary politics. In Massachusetts, Pennsylvania, and New York, African-American men occasionally cast ballots.

If civic participation by blacks was scattered and temporary in the North, it was almost totally absent in the South. With the brief exception of North Carolina, African-Americans could neither vote nor enjoy such basic rights of citizenship as protection of their persons and property under the law. In the South, blacks remained almost entirely without political voice, except in the petitions against slavery and mistreatment that they pressed upon the state regimes. Even as freemen, blacks continued to encounter pervasive discrimination.

Still, remarkable progress had been made. Prior to the Revolution, slavery had been an accepted fact of northern life. After the Revolution, it no longer was. That change made a vast difference in the lives of countless black Americans. The abolition of slavery in the North increased the sectional divergence between North and South, with enormous consequences in the nineteenth century. There now existed a coherent and publicly proclaimed antislavery argument, closely linked in Americans' minds with the nation's founding. The first antislavery organizations had been created. Although another half century would pass before antislavery became a significant force in national politics, the groundwork for slavery's final abolition had been laid.

Politics and the Economy

Together, independence and the Revolutionary War devastated the American economy. The cutoff of long-established patterns of overseas trade with England sent American commerce into a 20-year-long tailspin. While English warships prowled the coast, American ships rocked idly at empty wharves, New England's once booming shipyards grew quiet, and communities whose livelihood depended on the sea sank into depression. Virginia tobacco planters, their British markets gone and their plantations open to seaborne attack, struggled to survive. Farmers in the middle and New England states often prospered when hungry armies were nearby, but their profits plummeted when the armies moved on.

Not everyone suffered. With British goods excluded from American markets and the wearing of homespun deemed patriotic, American artisans often prospered. ("Buy American" has a long tradition.) People with the right political connections could make handsome profits from government contracts.

But even as some prospered, countless others saw their affairs fall into disarray. Intractable issues such as price and wage inflation, skyrocketing taxation, and mushrooming debt set people sharply against each other. Heated debates arose over whether the states' war debts should be funded at face value or at some reduced rate. Arguing for full value were the states' creditors—merchants and other persons of wealth who had lent the states money and had bought up large amounts of government securities at deep discounts. These people spoke earnestly of upholding the public honor and giving fair return to those who had risked

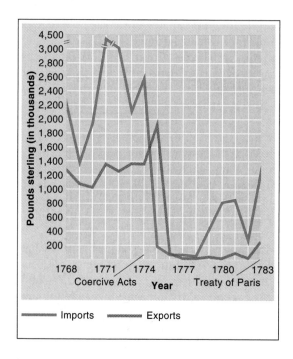

EXPORTS AND IMPORTS, 1768–1783
Nonimportation affected colonial
commerce during the late 1760s and
early 1770s, but American trade
plummeted with the Coercive Acts and
the outbreak of war. Source: U.S. Bureau of
the Census.

their own resources in the revolutionary cause. Opposed were ordinary people
angered by the speculators' large profits. No one, they argued, should reap personal advantage from public distress.

The issue of taxation, seared into Americans' consciousness by their troubles
with England, generated even more heated controversy. As the costs of the war
mounted, so did taxes. One anguished soul complained that taxes took nearly
one-third of the inhabitants' incomes. People of modest means argued that taxes
should be payable in depreciated paper money or government securities. Lacking
the hard money that the state required for paying taxes, they faced property foreclosure. Officials responded that allowing payment in depreciated paper would
deny the government critical revenue.

Controversy swirled, as well, around states' efforts to control soaring prices.
Every state experimented with price controls. Seldom were such efforts effective;
frequently, they generated political uproars. In general, the poor and those not yet
integrated into the market economy supported controls. They believed that goods
had a "just price," fair to buyer and seller alike. Merchants, shopkeepers, and
others accustomed to a commercial economy, however, believed that supply and
demand should govern transactions. "It is contrary to the nature of commerce,"
said Benjamin Franklin, "for government to interfere in the prices of commodities."
Attempts to regulate prices only created a disincentive to labor, which was "the
principal part of the wealth of every country."

Disputes over paper money divided the American people as well. Faced with
the uncontrollable escalation of wartime expenses, Congress and the states printed
money: more than $400 million in the first year of the war, and that was just the
beginning. Only the citizens' willingness to accept such paper supported its value.

That willingness was rapidly overwhelmed by the flood of paper money. Congressional bills of credit that in 1776 were pegged against gold at the ratio of 1.5 to 1 had slipped five years later to 147 to 1. State currencies depreciated even more alarmingly.

Such disastrous depreciation had ominous social consequences. James Lovell reported nervously that "sailors with clubs" paraded the streets of Boston "instead of working for paper." The upward spiral of prices was staggering. In Massachusetts, a bushel of corn that sold for less than a dollar in 1777 went for nearly $80 two years later. In Boston, a crowd of women, angered by the escalating costs of food, tossed a merchant suspected of monopolizing commodities into a cart and dragged him through the city's streets while "a large concourse of men stood amazed."

With property values in disarray, it seemed at times as if the very foundations of society were coming unhinged. "The war," wrote Thomas Paine,

> has thrown property into channels where before it never was . . . . Monies in large sums . . . enable . . . [profiteers] to roll the snow ball of monopoly and forestalling . . . [and] while these people are heaping up wealth . . . the remaining part are jogging on in their old way, with few or no advantages.

The poor suffered most severely, for they were most vulnerable to losses in the purchasing power of wages and military pay. Farmers, merchants, planters, and artisans also faced growing debt and uncertainty.

Rarely has the American economy been in such disarray. There were no ready solutions to the problems of debt, taxation, price control, and paper money, for such issues often exceeded the capacity of politics for compromise and resolution. They continued to heighten political tensions through the 1780s.

✦✦✦✦✦

CONCLUSION

The Crucible of Revolution

Independence and war redrew the contours of American life and changed the destinies of the American people. Though the Revolutionary War ended in victory, liberty had its costs. Lives were lost, property was destroyed, and local economies were deranged. The war altered relationships between Indians and whites, for it left the Iroquois and Cherokee severely weakened and opened the floodgates of western expansion. For African-Americans, the Revolution had paradoxical results. It produced an ideology that decried slavery, generated efforts to end the slave trade, and marked the first general debate over abolishing the oppressive institution. Yet slavery was eradicated only where it was least important, in the North, while in the South, where slavery had the strongest hold, its future was guaranteed. In spite of the political ferment generated by the Revolution, women reaped few clear advantages. Though they participated in many revolutionary crowds and achieved enhanced status as "Republican Mothers," they were still denied the right to vote, that critical index of full republican citizenship.

TIMELINE

1775	1776	1777	1778	1779
Lord Dunmore's proclamation to slaves and servants in Virginia; Iroquois Six Nations pledge neutrality; Continental Congress urges "states" to establish new governments	British evacuate Boston and seize New York City; Declaration of Independence; Eight states draft constitutions; Cherokee raids and American retaliation	British occupy Philadelphia; Most Iroquois join the British; Americans win victory at Saratoga; Washington's army winters at Valley Forge	War shifts to the South; Savannah falls to the British; French treaty of alliance and commerce	Massachusetts state constitutional convention; Sullivan destroys Iroquois villages in New York

1780	1780s	1781	1783	
Massachusetts constitution ratified; Charleston surrenders to the British; Pennsylvania begins gradual abolition of slavery	Virginia and Maryland debate abolition of slavery; Destruction of Iroquois Confederacy	Cornwallis surrenders at Yorktown; Articles of Confederation ratified by states	Peace treaty with England signed in Paris; Massachusetts Supreme Court abolishes slavery; King's Commission on American Loyalists begins work	

By 1783, a new nation had come into being where none had existed before, a nation based not on age-encrusted principles of monarchy and aristocratic privilege, but on the doctrines of republican liberty. That was the greatest change of all. The political transformations set in motion, however, generated angry disputes whose outcomes could be only dimly foreseen. Thomas Paine put the matter succinctly: "The answer to the question, can America be happy under a government of her own, is short and simple—as happy as she pleases; she hath a blank sheet to write upon." The years immediately ahead would determine whether America's republican experiment, launched with such hopefulness in 1776, would succeed.

Recommended Reading

The Revolutionary War

Don Higginbotham, *The War of Independence* (1983); Robert Middlekauff, *The Glorious Cause* (1982); Ronald Hoffman and Peter Albert, eds., *Arms and Independence: The Military Character of the American Revolution* (1984); Charles Neimeyer, *America Goes to War: A Social History of the Continental Army* (1996); Charles Royster, *A Revolutionary People at War* (1979).

Diplomacy

Jonathan Dull, *A Diplomatic History of the American Revolution* (1985); Reginald Horsman, *Diplomacy of the New Republic, 1776–1815* (1985); Ronald Hoffman and Peter Albert, eds., *Peace and the Peacemakers: The Treaty of 1783* (1986).

Indians and African-Americans

Anthony Wallace, *The Death and Rebirth of the Seneca* (1969); Colin Calloway, *The American Revolution in Indian Country* (1995); Isabel Kelsey, *Joseph Brant, 1743–1807: Man of Two Worlds* (1984); Tom Hatley, *The Dividing Paths: Cherokees and South Carolinians Through the Revolutionary Era* (1993); Ira Berlin and Ronald Hoffman, eds., *Slavery and Freedom in the Age of the American Revolution* (1983); Gary B. Nash, *Race and Revolution* (1990); Sylvia Frey, *Water from the Rock; Black Resistance in a Revolutionary Age* (1991).

Women and Loyalists

Linda Kerber, *Women of the Republic* (1980); Mary Beth Norton, *Liberty's Daughters* (1980); Joy Buel and Richard Buel, *The Way of Duty: A Woman and Her Family in Revolutionary America* (1984); Ronald Hoffman and Peter Albert, eds., *Women in the Age of the American Revolution* (1989); Robert Calhoon, *The Loyalists in Revolutionary America, 1760–1781* (1973); Bernard Bailyn, *The Ordeal of Thomas Hutchinson* (1974); Janice Potter, *Liberty We Seek: Loyalist Ideology in Colonial New York and Massachusetts* (1983); Mark Kann, *A Republic of Men: The American Founders, Gendered Language and Patriarchal Politics* (1998).

Revolutionary Politics

Gordon S. Wood, *The Creation of the American Republic, 1776–1787* (1969) and *The Radicalism of the American Revolution* (1992); Robert Gross, *The Minutemen and Their World* (1976); Ronald Hoffman, et al., *An Uncivil War: The Southern Backcountry During the American Revolution* (1985); Cathy Matson and Peter Onuf, *A Union of Interests: Political and Economic Thought in Revolutionary America* (1990); Alfred Young, ed., *Beyond the American Revolution: Explorations in the History of American Radicalism* (1993); Ronald Hoffman and Peter Albert, eds., *Religion in a Revolutionary Age* (1994); Jay Fliegelman, *Prodigals and Pilgrims: The American Revolution Against Patriarchal Authority, 1750–1800* (1982); Edward Countryman, *A People in Revolution: The American Revolution and Political Society in New York, 1760–1790* (1981); Mark Kruman, *Between Authority and Liberty: State Constitution Making in Revolutionary America* (1997).

Biographies

Pauline Meier, *The Old Revolutionaries: Political Lives in the Age of Samuel Adams* (1980); Eric Foner, *Tom Paine and Revolutionary America* (1976); Norman Risjord, *Representative Americans: The Revolutionary Generation* (1980); Bernard Bailyn, *Faces of Revolution* (1991); Joseph J. Ellis, *American Sphinx: The Character of Thomas Jefferson* (1996); Claude Lopez and Eugenia Herbert, *The Private Franklin: The Man and His Family* (1975); Richard Beeman, *Patrick Henry* (1974); Richard Brookhiser, *Founding Father: Rediscovering George Washington* (1996); Edith Gelles, *Portia: The World of Abigail Adams* (1992); Jeffrey Richards, *Mercy Otis Warren* (1995).

CHAPTER 7

Consolidating the Revolution

Timothy Bloodworth of New Hanover County, North Carolina, knew what the American Revolution was all about, for he had experienced it firsthand. A man of humble origins, Bloodworth had known poverty as a child. Lacking any formal education, he had worked hard and successfully during the middle decades of the eighteenth century as an innkeeper and ferry pilot, self-styled preacher and physician, blacksmith and farmer. By the mid-1770s, he owned nine slaves and 4,200 acres of land, considerably more than most of his neighbors.

His unpretentious manner and commitment to political equality earned Bloodworth the confidence of his community. In 1758, at the age of only 22, he was elected to the North Carolina colonial assembly. Over the next three decades, he remained deeply involved in the political life of his home state.

When the colonies' troubles with England drew toward a crisis, Bloodworth spoke ardently of American rights and mobilized support for independence. In 1775, he helped form the Wilmington Committee of Safety. Filled with revolutionary fervor, he urged forward the process of republican political reform and, as commissioner of confiscated property for the district of Wilmington, pressed the attack on local Loyalists.

In 1784, shortly after the war ended, the North Carolina assembly named Bloodworth one of the state's delegates to the Confederation Congress. There he learned for the first time about the problems of governing a new nation. As the Congress struggled through the middle years of the 1780s with the intractable problems of foreign trade, war debt, and control of the trans-Appalachian interior, Bloodworth shared the growing conviction that the Articles of Confederation were too weak. He supported the Congress's call for a special convention to meet in Philadelphia in May 1787 for the purpose of considering matters necessary "to render the constitution of the federal government adequate to the exigencies of the Union."

Like thousands of other Americans, Bloodworth eagerly awaited the convention's work. And like countless Americans, he was stunned by the result, for the proposed constitution described a government that seemed to him designed not to preserve republican liberty but to endanger it.

Once again sniffing political tyranny on the breeze, Bloodworth resigned his congressional seat in August 1787 and hurried back to North Carolina to help organize opposition to the proposed constitution. Over the next several years, he worked tirelessly for its defeat.

Alarmed by the prospect of such a powerful central government, Bloodworth protested that "We cannot consent to the adoption of a Constitution whose revenues lead to aristocratic tyranny, or monarchical despotism, and open a door wide as fancy can point, for the introduction of dissipation, bribery and corruption to the exclusion of public virtue." Had Americans so quickly forgotten the dangers of consolidated power? Were they already prepared to turn their backs on their brief experiment in republicanism?

A national government as strong as the one described in the proposed constitution, he feared, would remove power from the people's control, threaten political democracy, and destroy individual liberties. Alarmed by the provision that Congress "may at any time . . . make or alter" state regulations concerning elections as well as by the absence of explicit guarantees of trial by jury, Bloodworth demanded a federal bill of rights to protect individual liberties. Echoing the language of revolutionary republicanism, he warned the North Carolina ratifying convention that "Without the most express restrictions, Congress may trample on your rights. Every possible precaution should be taken when we grant powers," he continued, for "rulers are always disposed to abuse them."

Bloodworth also feared the sweeping authority Congress would have to make "all laws which shall be necessary and proper" for carrying into execution "all other powers vested . . . in the government of the United States." That language, he insisted, "would result in the abolition of the state governments. Its sovereignty absolutely annihilates them."

In North Carolina, the arguments of Bloodworth and his Anti-Federalist colleagues carried the day. By a vote of 184 to 84, the ratifying convention declared that a bill of rights "asserting and securing from encroachment the great Principles of civil and religious Liberty, and the unalienable rights of the People" must be approved before North Carolina would concur. The convention was true to its word. Not until November 1789, well after the new government had gotten under way and Congress had forwarded a national bill of rights to the states for approval, did North Carolina, with Timothy Bloodworth's cautious endorsement, finally enter the new union.

Just as Timothy Bloodworth knew the difficulties of achieving American independence, so he learned the problems of preserving American liberty once independence had been won. As a member of the Confederation Congress, Bloodworth confronted the continuing vestiges of colonialism: the patronizing attitudes of England and France, their continuing imperial ambitions in North America, and the republic's ongoing economic dependence on Europe. He also observed the Congress's inability to pay off the war debt, pry open foreign ports to American commerce, or persuade the states to join in a common tariff policy against England. As a southerner, Bloodworth was equally alarmed by the willingness of a congressional majority to forgo free navigation of the Mississippi River, deemed essential for development of the southern backcountry, in exchange for northern commercial advantages in Europe. Finally, he worried about political turmoil in the states as issues of taxation, debt, and paper money led discontented citizens openly to challenge public authority.

By 1786, Bloodworth, like countless other Americans, was caught up in an escalating debate between the Federalists, who believed that the Articles of Confederation were fatally deficient and must be replaced by a stronger national government, and the Anti-Federalists, who were committed to keeping government close to the people and were still deeply troubled by the dangers consolidated power posed to individual liberties.

That debate over the future of America's republican experiment came to a focus in the momentous Philadelphia convention of 1787, which produced not reform, but revolutionary change in the national government. With ratification of the new Constitution, the revolutionary era came to an end, and the American people opened a portentous new chapter in their history.

STRUGGLING WITH THE PEACETIME AGENDA

As the war ended, it remained unclear whether the Confederation Congress could effectively deal with the new nation's daunting problems of demobilization and adjustment to the novel conditions of independence.

Demobilizing the Army

Demobilizing the army presented the Confederation government with some difficult moments. Trouble first arose in early 1783 when officers at the continental army camp in Newburgh, New York, sent a delegation to the Congress to complain about arrears in pay and other benefits that the Congress had promised during the dark days of the war. When the Congress called for the army to disband, an anonymous address almost immediately circulated among the officers, speaking of making "a last remonstrance" and hinting darkly at more direct action if grievances were not met.

Several members of the Congress encouraged the officers' mutterings, hoping the crisis would add urgency to their own calls for a strengthened central government. Most, however, found this challenge to Congress's authority alarming. Washington moved quickly to calm the situation. Promising that the Congress would treat the officers justly, he counseled patience and urged his comrades not to tarnish the victory they had so recently won. He succeeded, for the officers reaffirmed their confidence in the Congress and agreed to disband.

Troops also took action. In June 1783, several hundred disgruntled continental soldiers and Pennsylvania militiamen gathered in front of Philadelphia's Independence Hall. When the state authorities would not guarantee the Congress's safety, it fled to Princeton, New Jersey. By November, the crisis was smoothed over, but at serious cost to congressional authority—which slid lower as the Congress shuffled between various cities in the mid-1780s. A hot-air balloon, scoffed the *Boston Evening Herald*, would "exactly accommodate the itinerant genius of Congress," because it could "when occasion requires . . . suddenly pop down into any of the states they please." Never had the Congress been mocked so bitterly.

Opening the West

Still, the Congress showed some accomplishments, most notably the two great land ordinances of 1785 and 1787. The first provided for the systematic survey and sale of the region west of Pennsylvania and north of the Ohio River. The area was to be laid out in townships six miles square, which were in turn to be subdivided into lots of 640 acres each. Thus began the rectangular grid pattern of land survey and settlement that to this day characterizes the Midwest.

Two years later, the Congress passed the Northwest Ordinance. It provided for the political organization of the same interior region, first under congressionally appointed officials, then under popularly elected territorial assemblies, and ultimately as new states to be incorporated into the Union "on an equal footing with the original states in all respects whatsoever." These two laws provided the legal mechanism for the nation's dramatic nineteenth-century territorial expansion.

Both bills enjoyed broad political support, for they opened land to settlers and profits to speculators. Income from land sales, moreover, promised to help reduce the national debt. While permitting slave owners already living north of the Ohio River to retain their chattels, the Ordinance of 1787 prohibited the importation of new slaves. This made the area more attractive to white farmers from the Northeast who worried about having to compete with slave labor or live among blacks. Southern delegates in the Congress accepted the restriction because they could extend slavery south of the Ohio. During the 1780s, the country's interior seemed large enough to accommodate everyone's needs.

The Congress, however, could neither get British troops out of the western posts nor guarantee free navigation of the Mississippi. Nor was it able to clear the tribes of the Ohio region out of white settlers' way. These failings led many Americans to question whether the Confederation government was capable of promoting westward expansion.

During the immediate postwar years, the Congress operated as if the Native Americans of the interior were "conquered" peoples—allies of England who had lost the war and come under the American government's control. This policy was fully consistent with white attitudes about Indians. Even the most sympathetic whites believed that Native Americans must become "civilized" and "Christianized" before they could coexist with white society. Most whites, including George Washington, doubted that such "improvements" could take place at all and argued that the Indians must simply be driven out of white settlers' way.

For a few years, the conquest strategy seemed to work. During the mid-1780s, the Congress imposed several important land treaties on the interior tribes, including the Iroquois, many of whom fled into Canada. Those who remained deeded away most of their land. At the Treaty of Fort Stanwix in 1784, the Six Nations ceded most of their lands to the United States and retreated to small reservations, which by the 1790s constituted only a small remnant of the once imposing Iroquois domain. There, the Iroquois struggled against disease and poverty, their traditional lifeways gone, their self-confidence broken. In January 1785, representatives of the Wyandotte, Chippewa, Delaware, and Ottawa tribes relinquished claim to most of present-day Ohio.

Many of the treaties did not hold. Exacted under the threat of force, they generated widespread Indian resentment. Two years after the Fort Stanwix negotiations, the Iroquois repudiated the treaty. By the mid-1780s, tribal groups above and below the Ohio River were directly resisting white expansion into the interior. While the Creek resumed hostilities in Georgia, Indians north of the Ohio strengthened their Western Confederacy, asserting that the river was the boundary between them and the United States. Devastating Indian raids greeted settlers moving west, setting the entire region from the Great Lakes to the Gulf of Mexico aflame with war. With the continental army disbanded, the Congress could do little. Many Americans took alarm: speculators facing the loss of their investments, farmers and revolutionary soldiers eager to start afresh in the West, and leaders such as Thomas Jefferson who believed that republican liberty depended on an expanding nation of yeoman farmers.

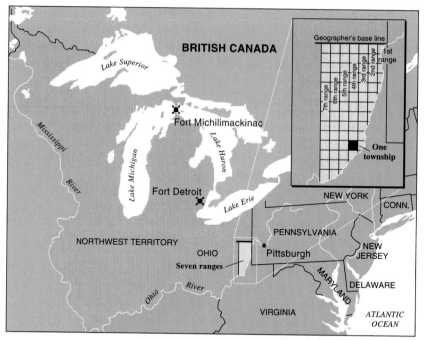

OLD NORTHWEST SURVEY PATTERNS
The Land Ordinance passed by Congress in 1785 provided for townships divided into lots of 640 acres. Its purpose was to promote the rapid and orderly settlement of the Old Northwest.

One township (6 miles square)

31	30	19	18	7	6
32	29	20	17	Section 16 income supports schools	5
33	28	21			4
34	27	22	15	10	3
35	26	23	14	11	2
36	25	24	13	12	1

The Congress also failed to resolve problems with the European nations that still laid claim to areas of the Trans-Appalachian West. In June 1784, Spain closed the mouth of the Mississippi River to American shipping, outraging settlers in the West who could only get their produce to market by floating it downstream to New Orleans, where ocean-going vessels picked it up. Rumors spread that Spanish agents were using their control of New Orleans to leverage American frontiersmen into loyalty to Spain. Washington commented uneasily that throughout the West settlers were "on a pivot." When the Congress's secretary for foreign affairs, John Jay, failed to get the Spanish to back down on the New Orleans issue, he set that demand aside in return for a new trade treaty favorable to northern merchants. While the northern states supported the bargain, southern state delegations in the Congress were outraged at this betrayal of their interests and opposed it. Thus stalemated, the Congress could take no action at all.

Wrestling with the National Debt

Further evidence of the Confederation's weakness was the Congress's inability to deal effectively with the nation's war debt, estimated at $35 million. Much of it was held by French and Dutch bankers. The Congress could not make regular payments against the loan's principal and even had to borrow abroad to pay the accumulating interest. At home, things were no better. The government could only delay and try to borrow more.

In 1781, the Congress appointed Robert Morris, a wealthy Philadelphia merchant, as superintendent of finance and gave him broad authority to deal with the nation's troubled affairs. Morris urged the states to stop issuing paper money and persuaded the Congress to demand that the states pay their requisitions in specie (gold and silver coin). In addition, he got the Congress to charter the Bank of North America and tried to make the Congress's bonds more attractive to investors.

Though Morris made considerable progress, the government's finances remained shaky. Unable to tax, the Congress continued to depend on the states' willingness to meet their financial obligations. This arrangement, however, proved unworkable. Desperate, in October 1781 the Congress requested $8 million from the states. Two and a half years later, less than $1.5 million had come in. In January 1784, Morris resigned. By 1786, federal revenue totaled $370,000 a year, not enough, one official lamented, to provide for "the bare maintenance of the federal government."

Not all Americans were alarmed. Some pointed out approvingly that several state governments, having brought their own financial obligations under control, were beginning to assume responsibility for portions of the national debt. Others, however, saw that as additional evidence of the Congress's weakening condition and wondered how long a government unable to maintain its credit could endure.

Surviving in a Hostile Atlantic World

Even after the United States had formally won independence, Britain, France, and Spain continued to threaten it. The Revolutionary War had dramatically transformed America's foreign relationships. England, once the nurturing "mother country" had become the enemy, while France was at best an uncertain friend. As an imperial power and an absolute monarchy, it feared colonial rebellions and regarded republicanism as deeply subversive. French efforts to manipulate the peace process for its own advantage, moreover, had taught the Americans a hard lesson in power politics. Before the century was over, it would regain most of the continent west of the Mississippi River. Meanwhile Great Britain's Union Jack still flew over Canada, and British troops still held strategic outposts on American soil, while Spain continued to conjure up grim memories of past New World conquests.

The reason for America's diplomatic troubles was clear: the country was new, weak, and republican in an Atlantic world dominated by strong, monarchical governments and divided into warring empires.

Nothing revealed more starkly the difficulties of national survival than the Congress's largely futile efforts to rebuild America's overseas commerce. When the war ended, familiar and highly desired British goods once again flooded American

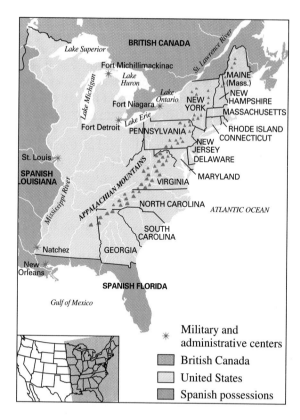

BRITISH AND SPANISH POSSESSIONS IN EASTERN NORTH AMERICA, 1783
Though victorious in its struggle for independence, the United States remained surrounded on three sides by British and Spanish possessions. North America continued to be a focus of European colonial ambitions after 1783.

Legend:
* Military and administrative centers
British Canada
United States
Spanish possessions

markets. Few American goods, however, flowed the other way. John Adams learned why. In 1785, he arrived in London as the first American minister to England. The Congress had ordered him to negotiate a commercial treaty, but after endless rebuffs he reported in frustration that England had no intention of reopening the empire's ports to American shipping. British officials testily reminded him that Americans had desired independence and must now live with its consequences.

Progress was slow as Americans searched for new commercial arrangements during the 1780s. Not only did England remain intractable, but France and Spain also gradually withdrew wartime trading privileges. The Congress failed to secure state cooperation in a program of economic recovery since each state wanted to channel its own trade for its own advantage. As a result, overseas trade languished and domestic hardship deepened. By the late 1780s, the per capita value of American exports had fallen a startling 30 percent from the 1760s. No wonder that merchants and artisans, carpenters and shopkeepers, sailors and dockworkers—all directly dependent on shipbuilding and overseas commerce—suffered. In an Atlantic world divided into exclusive, imperial trading spheres, the United States stood alone, unable to protect its interests.

POLITICAL TUMULT IN THE STATES

As the Confederation Congress struggled to chart a postwar course, controversy continued to embroil state politics. Two issues from the revolutionary agenda came together with particularly explosive force: problems of debt relief and paper money on the one hand, and continuing arguments over political equality on the other.

The Limits of Republican Experimentation

In a pattern that would frequently recur in American history, the postwar era witnessed growing social and political conservatism. In part that was because Americans, exhausted by the war's ordeal, turned their energies toward solving the many problems troubling their personal lives. And with the mobilizing crusade against England over, the initial surge of republican reform subsided.

As popular voting declined, leadership in the state governments fell increasingly to people convinced that republican experimentation had gone too far, that order had to balance liberty, and that the "better sort" should hold public office. The repeal of anti-Loyalist legislation and the occasional reappearance of Loyalists in public life provided additional evidence of the changing political climate. In 1786, the Connecticut assembly invited exiled Loyalists home, hoping that their skills and experience would spur economic recovery.

Just as dramatic was the replacement in 1790 of the radical Pennsylvania constitution of 1776 by a more conservative document. The new constitution provided for a strong governor who could veto legislation and control the militia, and for a senate balancing the more democratic assembly. Gaining control of the assembly, conservatives dismantled much of the radicals' program, stopped issuing paper money, and rechartered the Bank of North America. Pennsylvania's experiment in radical republicanism was over.

Shays's Rebellion

In Pennsylvania, the conservative political shift generated little controversy. In other states, however, popular opposition to hard money and high-tax policies provoked vigorous protest. Nowhere was the situation more volatile than in Massachusetts. The controversy that erupted there in 1786 echoed strongly of equal rights and popular consent, staples of the rhetoric of 1776.

Given the war's intense disruption of economic affairs, increasing numbers of Massachusetts citizens found by the mid-1780s that they had to borrow just to pay their taxes and support their families. The more fortunate borrowed so they could speculate in western land or government securities. Lacking commercial banks in the state, people borrowed from each other in a complicated pyramid of credit and debt that reached from wealthy merchants along the coast to shopkeepers and farmers in the interior. If creditors at any level demanded payment, trouble could quickly spiral through the entire system.

Trouble began when British goods glutted the American market, forcing down prices. In 1785, a number of British banks, heavily overcommitted in the American trade, called in their American loans. When American merchants in turn tried to collect debts due them, a credit crisis surged through the state's economy.

Hardest hit were the small farmers and laboring people in the countryside and small towns. They turned to the state government for "stay laws" suspending the collection of private debts and thus easing the threat of foreclosure. They also demanded new issues of paper money with which to pay debts and taxes.

The largest creditors, most of whom lived in commercial towns along the coast, fought these relief proposals because they wanted to collect what was owed them in hard money. They argued against new paper money out of fear that it would quickly depreciate and further confound economic affairs.

By 1786, Massachusetts farmers, desperate in the face of mounting debt and a lingering agricultural depression, were petitioning the Massachusetts assembly for relief in words that echoed the colonial protests of the 1760s. Their appeals however, fell on deaf ears, for commercial and creditor interests now controlled the government, which passed a law calling for full repayment of the state debt and levied a heavy new round of taxes that would make such payment possible. No matter that, as one town's tax collector reported, "there was not . . . the money in possession or at command among the people . . . to discharge taxes." Between 1784 and 1786, 29 towns failed to meet their tax obligations.

As frustrated Americans had done before and would do again when the law proved unresponsive, Massachusetts farmers took matters into their own hands. A Hampshire County convention of 50 towns condemned the state senate, court fees, and the tax system. It advised against violence, but mobs soon began to form. By September, armed men closed the courts at Northampton and Worcester. When farmers threatened similar actions elsewhere, the alarmed governor dispatched 600 militiamen to protect the state Supreme Court, then on circuit at Springfield.

About 500 insurgents had gathered near there under the leadership of Daniel Shays, a popular Revolutionary War captain. A "brave and good soldier," Shays had returned home in 1780, tired and frustrated, to await payment for his military service. Like thousands of others, he had a long wait. Meanwhile his farming went badly, debts accumulated, and, as he later recalled, "the spector of debtor's jail . . . hovered close by." Most of the men around Shays were also debtors and veterans.

The Continental Congress, worried about a possible raid on the federal arsenal at Springfield and encouraged by the Massachusetts delegates to take action, authorized 1,300 troops, ostensibly for service against the Indians but actually ready for use against Shays and his supporters. For a few weeks, Massachusetts seemed on the brink of civil war.

The insurrection collapsed in eastern Massachusetts in late November, but in the west it was far from over. When several insurgent groups refused Governor James Bowdoin's order to disband, he called out a force of 4,400 men, financed and led by worried eastern merchants. On January 26, 1787, Shays led 1,200 men toward the federal arsenal at Springfield. Its frightened defenders opened fire, killing four of the attackers and sending the Shaysites into retreat across the state. By the end of February, the rebellion was over. In March, the legislature pardoned all but Shays and three other leaders; in another year, they too had been forgiven.

Similar challenges to public authority, fired by personal troubles and frustration over unresponsive government, erupted in six other states. In Cecil County, Maryland, farmers circulated unsigned handbills threatening state officers if they seized people's property for unpaid taxes. The governor condemned the "riotous and tumultuous" proceedings and warned against further "violence and outrages." In South Carolina in May 1785, one Hezekiah Mayham "being served by the sheriff with a [foreclosure] writ, obliged him to eat it on the spot."

Across the states, politics were in turmoil. Although some felt betrayed by the Revolution's promise of equal rights and were angered by the "arrogant unresponsiveness" of government, others were alarmed by the "democratic excesses" that the Revolution appeared to have unleashed. What the immediate future might hold seemed exceedingly uncertain.

TOWARD A NEW NATIONAL GOVERNMENT

By 1786, belief was spreading among members of the Congress and other political leaders that the nation was in crisis and that the republican experiment was in danger. Explanations and remedies varied, but attention focused on the inadequacies of the Articles of Confederation. Within two years, following a raucous political struggle, a new and more powerful Constitution replaced the Articles, altering forever the course of American history.

The Rise of Federalism

Supporters of a stronger national government called themselves Federalists (forcing their opponents to adopt the name Anti-Federalists). Led by men such as Washington, Hamilton, Madison, and Jay, whose experiences in the continental army and Congress had strengthened their national vision, the Federalists believed that the nation's survival was at risk. Such men had never been comfortable with the more democratic impulses of the Revolution. While supporting moderate republicanism, they believed that social and political change had carried too far, that an aristocracy of talent should lead, and that property rights should be protected.

Federalist leaders feared the loss of their own social and political power, but they were concerned as well about the collapse of the orderly world they believed essential to the preservation of republican liberty. In 1776, American liberty had required protection against overweening British power. Danger now arose from excessive liberty, which threatened to degenerate into license. "We have probably had too good an opinion of human nature in forming our Constitution," concluded Washington somberly. "Experience has taught us, that men will not adopt and carry into execution measures the best calculated for their own good, without the intervention of a coercive power." What America now needed was a "strong government, ably administered."

The Federalists regarded outbursts like Shays's uprising in Massachusetts not as evidence of genuine social distress but as threats to social and political order. Although they were reassured by the speed with which the Shaysites had been dispatched, that episode persuaded them of the need for a stronger national government managed by the "better sort."

Congress's inability to handle the national debt, establish public credit, and restore overseas trade also troubled the Federalists. Sensitive to America's economic and military weakness, smarting from French and English arrogance, and aware of continuing Anglo-European designs on North America, the Federalists called for a new national government capable of extending American trade, spurring economic recovery, and protecting national interests.

Beyond that, the Federalists shared a vision of an expanding commercial republic, its people spreading across the rich lands of the interior, its merchant ships connecting America with the markets of Europe and beyond. That vision, so rich in national promise, seemed also at risk.

The Grand Convention

The first step toward governmental reform came in September 1786. Delegates of five states had gathered in Annapolis, Maryland, to discuss interstate commerce but issued an appeal for a larger, more ambitious convention. Written by the ardent nationalist Alexander Hamilton, it called for a new gathering in Philadelphia in May 1787. In February, the Confederation Congress cautiously endorsed the idea of a convention to revise the Articles of Confederation. Before long, it became clear that substantially more than a revision of the Articles was afoot.

During May, delegates representing every state except Rhode Island began assembling in Philadelphia. Eventually, 55 delegates would participate in the convention's work, though daily attendance hovered between 30 and 40. The roster read like an honor roll of the Revolution. From Virginia came the distinguished lawyer George Mason, chief author of Virginia's trailblazing bill of rights, and the already legendary George Washington. Proponents of the convention had held their breath while Washington considered whether or not to attend. His presence vastly increased the prospects of success. James Madison was there as well. No one, with perhaps the single exception of Alexander Hamilton, was more committed to nationalist reform. Certainly, no one had worked harder to prepare for the convention than he. Poring over treatises on republican government and natural law that his friend Thomas Jefferson sent from France, Madison brought to Philadelphia his own design for a new national government. That design, presented to the convention as the Virginia Plan, would serve as the basis for the new constitution. Nor did anyone rival the diminutive Madison's contributions to the convention's work. Tirelessly, he took the convention floor to argue the nationalist cause or buttonhole wavering delegates. Somehow he also found the energy to keep extensive notes—our essential record of the convention's proceedings.

Two distinguished Virginians were conspicuously absent. Thomas Jefferson was serving as U.S. minister to France, and the veteran patriot Patrick Henry, one of Madison's political foes and an ardent champion of state supremacy, wanted no part of what he feared the convention would do.

From Pennsylvania came the venerable Franklin, too old to contribute significantly to the debates, but able still, at several key moments, to call quarreling members to account and reinspire them. His colleagues from Pennsylvania included the erudite Scots lawyer James Wilson, whose nationalist sympathies had been inflamed when a democratic mob attacked his elegant Philadelphia townhouse in 1779. Robert Morris, probably the richest man in America, was there, too. Massachusetts was ably represented by Elbridge Gerry and Rufus King, while South Carolina sent John Rutledge and Charles Pinckney. Roger Sherman led Connecticut's contingent.

James Madison of Virginia, only 36 years old when the Philadelphia convention met, worked tirelessly between 1786 and 1788 to replace the Articles of Confederation with a new and more effective national constitution. (Mead Art Museum, Amherst Collection, Bequest of Herbert L. Pratt, 1895, 1945.82)

The New York assembly sent a deeply divided delegation. Governor George Clinton, long a personal enemy of Alexander Hamilton and determined to protect New York's autonomy as well as his own political power, saw to it that several Anti-Federalist skeptics made the trip to Philadelphia. They were no match for Hamilton.

Born in the Leeward Islands, the "bastard brat of a Scots-peddlar" and a strong-willed woman with a troubled marriage, Hamilton used his immense intelligence and ingratiating charm to rise rapidly in the world. Sent to New York by wealthy sponsors, he quickly established himself as a favorite of the city's mercantile community. Still in his early twenties, he became Washington's wartime aide-de-camp. That relationship served Hamilton well for the next 20 years. Returning from the war, he married the wealthy Elizabeth Schuyler, thereby securing his personal fortunes and strengthening his political connections. Together with Madison, Hamilton had promoted the abortive Annapolis convention. At Philadelphia, he was determined to drive his nationalist vision ahead.

Meeting in Independence Hall, the convention elected Washington as its presiding officer, adopted rules of procedure, and, after spirited debate, voted to close the doors and conduct its business in secret.

Debate focused first on the Virginia Plan, introduced on May 29 by Edmund Randolph. It outlined a potentially powerful national government and effectively set the convention's agenda. There would be a bicameral Congress, with the lower house elected by the people and the upper house, or senate, chosen by the lower house from nominees proposed by the state legislatures. The plan also called for a president who would be named by the Congress, a national judiciary, and a council of revision, whose task was to review the constitutionality of federal legislation.

The smaller states quickly objected to the Virginia Plan's call for proportional rather than equal representation of the states. On June 15, William Paterson introduced a counterproposal, the New Jersey Plan. It urged retention of the Articles of Confederation as the basic structure of government while conferring on the

Congress long-sought powers to tax and regulate both foreign and interstate commerce. After three days of heated debate, by a vote of seven states to three, the delegates adopted the Virginia Plan as the basis for further discussions. It was now clear that the convention would set aside the Articles for a much stronger national government. The only question was how powerful the new government would be.

At times over the next four months, it seemed that the Grand Convention would collapse under the weight of its disagreements and the oppressive summer heat. How were the sharply conflicting interests of large and small states to be reconciled? How should the balance of power between national and state governments be struck? How should an executive be fashioned, strong enough to govern but not so strong as to endanger republican liberty? And what, if anything, should the convention say about slavery, issues on which northerners and southerners, antislavery and proslavery advocates so passionately disagreed?

At one extreme was Hamilton's audaciously conservative proposal, made early in the convention's deliberations, for a Congress and president elected for life and a national government so powerful that the states would become little more than administrative agencies. His plan under attack and his influence rapidly eroding, Hamilton left the convention in late June. He would return a month later but make few additional contributions to the convention's work.

At the other extreme stood the ardent Anti-Federalist Luther Martin of Maryland. Rude and unkempt, Martin uncompromisingly opposed anything that threatened state sovereignty or smacked of aristocracy. Increasingly isolated by the convention's nationalist inclinations, Martin also returned home, in his case to spread the alarm.

By early July, with tempers frayed and frustration growing over the apparent deadlock, the delegates agreed to recess, ostensibly for Independence Day, but actually to let Franklin, Roger Sherman, and others make a final effort at compromise. Only a bold stroke could prevent collapse.

That stroke came on July 12, as part of what has become known as the Great Compromise. The reassembled delegates settled one major point of controversy by agreeing that representation in the lower house should be based on the total of each state's white population plus three-fifths of its blacks. Though African-Americans were not accorded citizenship and could not vote, the southern delegates argued that they should be fully counted for this purpose. Delegates from the northern states, where relatively few blacks lived, did not want them counted at all. So the bargain was struck. As part of this compromise, the convention agreed that direct taxes would also be apportioned on the basis of population and that blacks would be counted similarly in that calculation. On July 16, the convention accepted the principle that each state should have an equal vote in the Senate. Thus the interests of large states and small were effectively accommodated.

The convention then submitted its work to a committee of detail for drafting in proper constitutional form. That group reported on August 6, and for the next month the delegates hammered out the language of the document's seven articles. Sometimes differences seemed so great that it was uncertain whether the convention could proceed. In each instance, however, agreement was reached.

Determined to give the new government a stability that state governments lacked, the delegates created an electoral process designed to bring only persons of experience and reputation into national office. An Electoral College of wise and experienced leaders would meet to choose the president. The process functioned exactly that way during the first several presidential elections.

Selection of the Senate would be similarly indirect, for its members were to be named by the state legislatures. (Not until 1913, with ratification of the Seventeenth Amendment, would the American people directly elect their senators.) Even the House of Representatives, the only popularly elected branch of the new government, was to be filled with people of standing and wealth, for the Federalists were confident that only experienced and well-established leaders would be able to attract the necessary votes.

The delegates' final set of compromises touched the fate of black Americans, though the words *slavery* or *slave trade* were never used. At the insistence of southerners, the convention agreed that the slave trade would not formally end for another 20 years. Despite Gouverneur Morris's impassioned charge that slavery was a "nefarious institution" that would bring "the curse of Heaven on the states where it prevails," the delegates firmly rejected a proposal to abolish slavery, thereby tacitly acknowledging its legitimacy. More than that, they guaranteed slavery's protection by writing in Section 2 of Article 4 that "No person held to service or labour in one state, . . . [and] escaping into another, shall, in consequence of any law . . . therein, be discharged from such service, but shall be delivered up on claim of the party to whom such service or labour may be due." The delegates thus provided federal sanction for the capture and return of runaway slaves. This fugitive slave clause would haunt northern consciences in the years ahead. At the time, however, it seemed a small price to pay for sectional harmony and a new government. Northern accommodation to the demands of the southern delegates was eased, moreover, by knowledge that southerners in the Confederation Congress had just agreed to prohibit new slaves from entering the Northwest Territory.

Although the Constitution's unique federal system of governance called for shared responsibilities between the nation and the states, it decisively strengthened the national government. Congress would now have authority to levy and collect taxes, regulate commerce with foreign nations and between the states, devise uniform rules for naturalization, administer national patents and copyrights, and control the federal district in which it would eventually be located.

Conspicuously missing was any statement reserving to the states all powers not explicitly conferred on the central government. Such language had proved crippling in the Articles of Confederation. On the contrary, the Constitution contained a number of clauses bestowing vaguely defined grants of power on the new government. Section 8 of Article 1, for example, granted Congress the authority to "provide for the . . . general welfare of the United States" as well as to "make all laws . . . necessary and proper for carrying into execution . . . all . . . powers vested by this Constitution in the government of the United States." Later generations would call these phrases "elastic clauses" and would use them to expand the federal government's activities. A final measure of the Federalists' determination to make the new government supreme over the states was the assertion in Article 6 that the Constitution and all laws passed under it were the "supreme Law of the Land."

When the convention had finished its business, 3 of the 42 remaining delegates refused to sign the document. The other 39, however, affixed their names and forwarded it to the Confederation Congress along with the request that it be sent on to the states for approval. On September 17, the Grand Convention adjourned.

Federalists versus Anti-Federalists

Ratification presented the Federalists with a more difficult problem than they had faced at Philadelphia. The debate now shifted to the states, where sentiment was sharply divided and the political situation would be more difficult to control. Recognizing the unlikelihood of quick agreement by all 13 states, the Federalists stipulated that the Constitution should go into effect when any 9 agreed to it. Other states could then enter the Union as they were ready. Ratification was to be decided by specially elected conventions rather than by the state assemblies, because under the Constitution the assemblies would lose substantial amounts of power. Ratification by such conventions was also more constitutionally sound, because it would give the new government its own direct grounding in the people.

In the Confederation Congress, opponents of the new Constitution charged that the Philadelphia Convention had exceeded its authority. But after a few days' debate, the Congress forwarded the document to the states for consideration. Word of the dramatic changes being proposed spread rapidly. In each state, Federalists and Anti-Federalists, the latter now actively opposing the Constitution, prepared to debate the new articles of government.

Although levels of Federalist and Anti-Federalist strength differed from state to state, opposition to the Constitution was widespread and vocal. Some critics feared that a stronger central government would threaten state interests or their own political power. Others, like Timothy Bloodworth, charged the Federalists with betraying revolutionary republicanism. The new government would be corrupted by its own power. Far from the watchful eyes of the citizenry, its officials would behave as power wielders always had, and American liberty, so recently preserved at such high cost, would once again come under attack.

The Anti-Federalists were aghast at the Federalists' vision of an expanding "republican empire." "The idea of . . . [a] republic, on an average of 1,000 miles in length, and 800 in breadth, and containing 6 millions of white inhabitants all reduced to the same standards of morals, . . . habits . . . [and] laws," exclaimed one incredulous critic, "is itself an absurdity, and contrary to the whole experience of mankind." Such a huge, extended republic would quickly fall prey to factional conflict and disorder. The Anti-Federalists continued to believe that republican liberty could be preserved only in simple, homogeneous societies, where the seeds of faction were absent and public virtue guided citizens' behavior.

Nor did the Anti-Federalists believe that the proposed separation of executive, legislative, and judicial powers or the balancing of state and national governments would prevent power's abuse. Government must be kept simple, for complexity only confused the people and cloaked selfish ambition.

Not all the "Anti's" were democrats. In the South, many of them held slaves, and their appeals to local authority did not always mean support for political equality even among whites. Yet along with their warnings against wealth and power and their distrust of centralization, they often spoke fervently of democratic principles.

Certainly, they believed more firmly than their Federalist opponents that if government was to be safe, it must be tied closely to the people.

Federalist spokesmen moved quickly to counter the Anti-Federalists' attack, for many of those criticisms carried the sanction of the revolutionary past. Their most important effort was a series of essays penned by James Madison, Alexander Hamilton, and John Jay and published in New York under the pseudonym Publius. *The Federalist Papers,* as they were called, were written to promote ratification in New York but were quickly reprinted by Federalists elsewhere.

Madison, Hamilton, and Jay moved systematically through the Constitution, explaining its virtues and responding to the Anti-Federalists' attacks. They described a political vision fundamentally different from that of the Anti-Federalists.

No difference was more dramatic than the Federalists' discussion of governmental power. Power, the Federalists now argued, was not the enemy of liberty, but its guarantor. Where government was not sufficiently "energetic" and "efficient" (these were favorite Federalist words), demagogues and disorganizers would do their nefarious work. It is far better, Hamilton wrote in *Federalist No. 26,* "to hazard the abuse of . . . confidence than to embarrass the government and endanger the public safety by impolitic restrictions of . . . authority."

The authors of the *Federalist Papers* also countered the Anti-Federalists' warning that a single, extended republic encompassing the country's economic and social diversity would lead inevitably to factional conflict and destroy republican liberty. Turning the Anti-Federalists' classic republican argument on its head, they explained that factional divisions were the inevitable accompaniment of human liberty. Wrote Madison in *Federalist No. 10:* "Liberty is to faction what air is to fire, an aliment without which it instantly expires." To suppress faction would require the destruction of liberty itself.

Earlier emphasis on public virtue as the guarantor of political order, the Federalists explained, had been naive, for most people would not consistently put the public good ahead of their own interests. Politics had to heed this harsh fact and provide for peaceful compromise among conflicting groups. That could be best accomplished by expanding the nation so that it included innumerable factions. Out of the clash and accommodation of multiple social and economic interests would emerge compromise and the best possible approximation of the public good.

The Federalists' argument established the basic rationale for modern democratic politics, but it left the Anti's sputtering in frustration. Where in the Federalists' scheme was there a place for that familiar abstraction, the public good? What would become of public virtue in a system built on the notion of competing interests? In such a free market of competition, the Anti-Federalists warned, the wealthy and powerful would benefit, while ordinary folk would suffer.

As the ratification debate revealed, the Federalists and Anti-Federalists held sharply contrasting visions of the new republic. The Anti's remained much closer to the original republicanism of 1776, with its suspicion of power and wealth, its emphasis on the primacy of local government, and its fears of national development. They envisioned a decentralized republic filled with self-reliant citizens, limited in personal ambition and guided by public virtue, whose destiny was determined primarily by what happened in the states rather than the nation. Anxious for the future, they wanted to preserve their world much as it had been.

The Federalists, on the other hand, had persuaded themselves that America's situation had changed dramatically since 1776. They eagerly embraced the idea of nationhood and looked forward with anticipation to the development of a rising "republican empire" based on commercial development and led by men of wealth and talent. Both Federalists and Anti-Federalists claimed to be heirs of the Revolution, yet they differed dramatically in their understanding of that heritage.

The Struggle over Ratification

No one knows what most Americans thought of the proposed Constitution, for no national plebiscite on it was ever taken. Probably no more than several hundred thousand people participated in the elections for the state ratifying conventions, and many of the delegates carried no binding instructions from their constituents on how they should vote. A majority of the people very likely opposed the document, either out of indifference or alarm. Fortunately for the Federalists, they did not have to persuade most Americans; they needed only to gain majorities in nine of the state ratifying conventions, a much less formidable task.

They set about it with determination. As soon as the Philadelphia Convention adjourned, its members hurried home to organize the ratification movement in their states. In Delaware and Georgia, New Jersey and Connecticut, where the Federalists were confident of their strength, they pressed quickly for a vote. Where the outcome was uncertain, as in New York and Virginia, they delayed, hoping that word of ratification elsewhere would work to their benefit.

It took less than a year to secure approval by the necessary nine states. Delaware, Pennsylvania, and New Jersey ratified first, in December 1787. Approval came a month later in Georgia and Connecticut. Massachusetts ratified in February 1788, but only after considerable political maneuvering. In an effort to woo Anti-Federalist delegates and persuade the uncommitted, Federalist leaders agreed to forward a set of amendments outlining a federal "bill of rights" along with notice of ratification. The strategy worked, for it brought Samuel Adams and John Hancock into line, and with them the crucial convention votes that they controlled.

Maryland and South Carolina were the seventh and eighth states to approve. That left New Hampshire and Virginia as the most likely candidates for the honor of being ninth, putting the Constitution over the top. There was staunch opposition in both states. The New Hampshire convention met on February 13. Sensing that they lacked the votes, the Federalists adjourned until mid-June and worked feverishly to build support. When the convention reconvened, it took but three days to secure a Federalist majority. New Hampshire ratified on June 21.

Two massive gaps in the new Union remained—Virginia and New York. Clearly, the nation could not endure without them. In Virginia, Madison gathered support by promising that the new Congress would immediately consider a federal bill of rights. Other Federalists spread the rumor that Patrick Henry, most influential of the Anti-Federalist leaders, had changed sides. Henry angrily denied it, but his oratory proved no match for the careful politicking of Madison and the others. On June 25, the Virginia convention voted to ratify by the narrow margin of ten votes.

The New York convention gathered on June 17 at Poughkeepsie, with the Anti-Federalist followers of Governor Clinton firmly in command. Hamilton worked for delay, hoping that news of the results in New Hampshire and Virginia would turn

Ratification of the Constitution	*Votes of State Ratifying Conventions*		
State	**Date**	**For**	**Against**
Delaware	December 1787	30	0
Pennsylvania	December 1787	46	23
New Jersey	December 1787	38	0
Georgia	January 1788	26	0
Connecticut	January 1788	128	40
Massachusetts	February 1788	187	168
Maryland	April 1788	63	11
South Carolina	May 1788	149	73
New Hampshire	June 1788	57	47
Virginia	June 1788	89	79
New York	July 1788	30	27
North Carolina	November 1789	194	77
Rhode Island	May 1790	34	32

the tide. For several weeks, approval hung in the balance while the two sides maneuvered. On July 27, approval squeaked through, 30 to 27.

That left two states still uncommitted. North Carolina (with Timothy Bloodworth's skeptical approval) finally ratified in November 1789. Rhode Island did not enter the Union until May 1790, more than a year after the new government got under way.

The Social Geography of Ratification

A glance at the geographic pattern of Federalist and Anti-Federalist strength reveals their different sources of political support. Federalist strength was concentrated in areas along the coast and navigable rivers, and was strongest in cities and towns.

Merchants and businessmen supported the Constitution most ardently. Enthusiasm also ran high among urban laborers, artisans, and shopkeepers—surprisingly so, given the Anti-Federalists' criticism of wealth and power and their emphasis on democratic political equality. City artisans and workers, after all, had been in the vanguard of political reform during the Revolution. But in the troubled circumstances of the late 1780s, they worried primarily about their livelihoods and believed that a stronger government could better promote overseas trade and protect American artisans from foreign competition.

On July 4, 1788, a grand procession celebrating the Constitution's ratification wound through the streets of Philadelphia. Seventeen thousand strong, it graphically demonstrated working-class support for the Constitution—lawyers, merchants, and others of the elite marched at the head, but close behind came representatives of virtually every trade in the city. For the moment, declared the democratic-minded physician Benjamin Rush in amazement, "rank . . . forgot all its claims." Within a few years, political disputes would divide them once again. Now, however, people of all ranks celebrated the new Constitution.

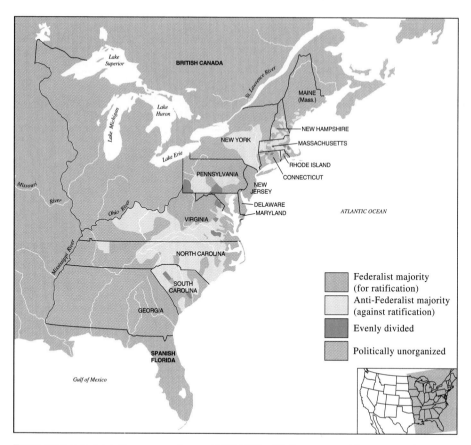

Federalist and Anti-Federalist Areas, 1787–1790   Distinct geographic patterns of Federalist and Anti-Federalist strength developed during the ratification debate. This map shows areas whose delegates to the state ratifying conventions voted for and against the Constitution.

In other settings, class and geography helped define political attitudes. The Constitution found support among commercial farmers and southern planters eager for profit and anxious about overseas markets. But in the interior, Federalist enthusiasm waned and Anti-Federalist sentiment increased. The centers of Anti-Federalism lay away from the coast in central New England, upstate New York, the Virginia Piedmont and southside, and western Carolina. Among ordinary farmers living outside the market economy, the republicanism of 1776 outweighed their interests in national affairs.

Why did the Federalists finally prevail? After all, the Anti-Federalists had only to arouse people's deep-seated fears of central government and play on local loyalties. The Federalists, by contrast, had to explain how republicanism had suddenly become compatible with a powerful national government and an expanding empire. Moreover, they faced the complicated task of coordinating ratification in the various states.

The Federalists' task was simplified by the widespread perception that the Articles needed strengthening. The obvious troubles of the Confederation made it easier for Federalists to argue that America's experiment in republican indepen-

TIMELINE

1784	1785	1786	1786–1787	1787
Treaty of Fort Stanwix with the Iroquois; Spain closes the Mississippi River to American navigation	Treaty of Hopewell with the Cherokee; Land Ordinance for the Northwest Territory; Jay-Gardoqui negotiations	Virginia adopts "Bill for Establishing Religious Freedom"; Annapolis Convention calls for revision of the Articles of Confederation	Shays's Rebellion	Northwest Ordinance Constitutional Convention; *Federalist Papers* published by Hamilton, Jay, and Madison

1788
Constitution ratified

dence was doomed unless dramatic action was taken. More than anything, however, the Federalists succeeded because of their determination and political skill. Most of the Revolution's major leaders were Federalists. Time and again these worthies spoke out for the Constitution, and time and again their support proved decisive. Their experience as army officers and as members of the Continental and Confederation Congresses caused them to identify with the nation and to imagine what it might become. They brought their vision to the ratification process and asked others to share it. It was an impressive political performance. With their success, the Federalists turned the American republic in a new and fateful direction.

✦✦✦✦✦✦

Conclusion

Completing the Revolution

Only five years had passed between England's acknowledgment of American independence in 1783 and ratification of the new national Constitution, yet to many Americans it seemed far longer. At war's end, the difficulties of sustaining American liberty were evident. The experience of the next half decade added to them. Whether struggling to survive in a hostile Atlantic environment or trying to cope with economic distress and political turmoil at home, Americans continued to argue about their experiment in republicanism, above all about how democratic it could safely be, and to wonder whether it would actually work at all.

At the same time, the American people retained an immense reservoir of optimism about the future. Had they not defeated mighty England? Was not their revolution destined to change the course of history and preserve liberty for all mankind? Did not America's wonderfully rich interior contain a limitless promise of economic and social opportunity? Most Americans, still filled with the enthusiasm of their new beginning, answered with a resounding "Yes." Much would depend, of course, on their new Constitution and the government soon to be created under it.

As the ratification debate subsided and Congress prepared for the transition, the American people looked eagerly and anxiously ahead.

Recommended Reading

The Articles of Confederation and the 1780s

Merrill Jensen, *The New Nation: A History of the United States During the Confederation, 1781–1789* (1950); Jack Rakove, *The Beginnings of National Politics: An Interpretive History of the Continental Congress* (1979); Peter Onuf, *The Origins of the Federal Republic: Jurisdictional Controversies in the United States, 1775–1787* (1983); Jackson T. Main, *Political Parties Before the Constitution* (1973); Ronald Hoffman and Peter Albert, eds., *Sovereign States in an Age of Uncertainty* (1978); Peter Onuf, *Statehood and Union: A History of the Northwest Ordinance* (1987); David Szatmary, *Shays's Rebellion: The Making of an Agrarian Rebellion* (1980); Eric Foner, *Tom Paine and Revolutionary America* (1976); Richard Buel, Jr., *In Irons: Britain's Naval Supremacy and the American Revolutionary Economy* (1998).

The Constitution

Gordon Wood, *The Creation of the American Republic, 1776–1787* (1969); Richard Morris, *Witnesses at the Creation: Hamilton, Madison, Jay and the Constitution* (1985); Gary Wills, *Explaining America: The Federalist* (1981); Frederick W. Marks, III, *Independence on Trial: Foreign Affairs and the Making of the Constitution* (1973); Richard Beeman et al., eds., *Beyond Confederation: Origins of the Constitution and American National Identity* (1987); Steven Boyd, *The Politics of Opposition: Antifederalists and the Acceptance of the Constitution* (1979); Patrick Conley and John Kaminski, eds., *The Constitution and the States* (1988); Richard K. Mathews, *If Men Were Angels: James Madison and the Heartless Empire of Reason* (1995).

Chapter 8

Creating a Nation

I n October 1789, David Brown arrived in Dedham, Massachusetts. Born about 50 years before in Bethlehem, Connecticut, Brown had served in the Revolutionary army. After the war, he shipped out on an American merchantman to see the world. His travels took him to "nineteen different . . . Kingdoms in Europe, and nearly all the United States." For two years before settling in Dedham, he visited scores of Massachusetts towns, supporting himself as a day laborer while discussing the troubled state of public affairs with local townspeople.

Initially, the people of Dedham took little notice of Brown, but he soon made his presence felt. Though he had little formal schooling, he was a man of powerful opinions and considerable natural ability. His reading and personal experience had persuaded him that government was a conspiracy of the rich to exploit farmers, artisans, and other common folk, and he was quick to make that known.

"The occupation of government," Brown declared bluntly in one of his numerous pamphlets, "is to plunder and steal." The object of his wrath was the central government recently established under the new national constitution. Though he could cite no evidence, he accused the leaders of government with engrossing the nation's western lands for themselves. "Five hundred [people] out of the union of five millions receive all the benefit of public property and live upon the ruins of the rest of the community." Brown warned that such policies would not last long, because no government could survive "after the confidence of the people was lost, for the people are the government."

In the highly charged political climate of the 1790s, Brown's radical language and exaggerated attacks on the new government's leaders brought a sharp response. In 1798, John Davis, the federal district attorney in Boston, issued a warrant for Brown's arrest on charges of sedition, while government-supported newspapers attacked him as a "rallying point of insurrection and disorder." Brown fled to Salem, where he was caught and charged with intent to defame the government and aid the country's enemies. Lacking $400 bail, he was clapped in prison.

In June 1799, Brown came before the U.S. Circuit Court, Justice Samuel Chase presiding. Chase's behavior was anything but judicious. Sure that critics of the administration were enemies of the republic, Chase was determined to make Brown an example. Brown, confused and hoping for leniency, pleaded guilty. That made no difference to Chase.

Ignoring Brown's plea, he directed the federal prosecutor to "examine the witness . . . that the degree of his guilt might be duly ascertained." Before sentencing him, Chase demanded that Brown provide the names of his accomplices and a list of subscribers to his writings. When Brown refused, protesting that he would "lose all my friends," Chase sentenced him to a fine of $480 and 18 months in jail, no matter that Brown could not pay the fine and faced the prospect of indefinite imprisonment.

In rendering judgment, Chase castigated Brown for his "disorganizing doctrines and . . . falsehoods, and the very alarming and dangerous excesses to which he attempted to incite the uninformed part of the community." Not all citizens, Chase thought, should be allowed to comment so brashly on public affairs. For nearly two years, Brown languished in prison. Not until the Federalist party was defeated in the election of 1800 and the Jeffersonian Republicans had taken office was he freed.

David Brown discovered how easy it was for critics of the government to get into trouble during the 1790s, a decade of extraordinary political controversy. Even though the Revolutionary War was long past, the debate over revolutionary principles and the struggle to define America's republican political order continued. As Benjamin Rush, Philadelphia physician and revolutionary patriot, explained: "The American War is over, but this is far from being the case with the American Revolution. On the contrary, nothing but the first act of the great drama is closed. It remains [for us] . . . to establish and perfect our new forms of government."

Efforts to perfect America's new governments proceeded differently in state and nation, for they differed markedly in leadership, public agenda, and the politics that surrounded them. In the states, government and its attendant politics remained close to the people. There the fires of political controversy, fanned to a white heat during the Revolution over economic issues, slavery, and the separation of church and state, continued to burn. Controversy swirled as well between the advocates of political democracy and defenders of a more conservative form of republican politics.

The new ingredient in American political life during the 1790s was the national government established under the new federal Constitution. There had been no popular elections under the Articles of Confederation, because members of the Confederation Congress had been appointed by the state legislatures. The Federalists had been careful at Philadelphia to buffer the new national government against the passions of democracy so that it would support a continuing system of conservative, gentry-led politics. During the 1790s, such a system, setting Federalist supporters of President Washington's administration against Jeffersonian opponents, began to form in the new Congress.

Events, however, soon began to force together this politics of national elites and the rapidly evolving democratic politics in the states. As the 1790s progressed, controversy was fanned by Federalist economic policies, the French Revolution and the outbreak of European war, the internal security legislation imposed during John Adams's administration, and the election of 1800, which brought the Federalists' defeat and Thomas Jefferson's election to the presidency.

As political controversy increased, it caught up countless people like David Brown in its toils. By decade's end, it had become apparent how fragile, and at the same time how resilient, America's new constitutional order could be.

LAUNCHING THE NATIONAL REPUBLIC

Once the Constitution had been ratified, most Anti-Federalists seemed ready to give the experiment a chance. But they would watch closely for the first signs of danger. It was not many months before they sounded the alarm.

This imaginative scene of President-elect Washington's reception in Trenton, New Jersey, during his trip from Virginia to New York City for his first inauguration depicts the popular adulation that surrounded him, as well as the sharply different political roles of men and women. (Library of Congress)

Beginning the New Government

On April 16, 1789, George Washington started north from Virginia toward New York City to be inaugurated as the first president of the United States. The Electoral College had unanimously elected him. Washington's feelings were mixed. "I bade adieu to Mount Vernon, to private life, and to domestic felicity," he confided to his diary, "and with a mind oppressed with more anxious and painful sensations than I have words to express, set out for New York . . . with the best disposition to render service to my country in obedience to its call, but with less hope of answering its expectations." He had good reason for such foreboding.

Washington's journey north resembled a royal procession, with constant adulation along the way. On April 23, accompanied by a flotilla of boats, Washington was rowed on an elegant, flower-festooned barge from the New Jersey shore to New York City, where citizens and newly-elected members of Congress greeted him. That night, bonfires illuminated the city.

Inaugural day was April 30. Shortly after noon, on a small balcony overlooking Wall Street, Washington took his oath. "It is done," exulted New York's chancellor, Robert Livingston. "Long live George Washington, President of the United States!" With the crowd roaring its approval and 13 guns booming in the harbor, the president bowed his way off the balcony. Celebrations lasted late into the night.

Though hopefulness and excitement surrounded the new government's beginning, those first weeks were not easy, for it was especially important that things begin on a proper footing. For example, when Washington addressed the first Congress, republican purists complained that it smacked too much of the English monarch's speech from the throne at the opening of Parliament. Congress had to decide how it should reply and whether it should address him with a title. Vice President Adams proposed "His Most Benign Highness," while others offered "His Highness, the President of the United States, and Protector of the Rights of the Same." Howls of outrage arose from those who thought titles had no place in a republic. Good sense finally prevailed, and Congress settled on the now-familiar "Mr. President."

Every decision under the new government seemed filled with significance, for people believed that they were setting its direction for years to come. That belief gave special intensity to politics.

The Bill of Rights

Among the new government's tasks was consideration of the constitutional amendments that several states had made conditions of their ratification. Although Madison, Hamilton, and other Federalists had argued that a national bill of rights was unnecessary, they were ready to keep their promise that such amendments would be considered. That would reassure the fearful, weaken calls for a second constitutional convention, and build support for the new regime.

Madison culled from the great variety of proposals offered by the states a set of specific propositions. After considerable debate, Congress reached agreement in September 1789 on 12 amendments and sent them on to the states for approval. By December 1791, 10 had been ratified. Those 10 became the national Bill of Rights. Among other things, they guaranteed freedom of speech, press, and religion; pledged the right of trial by jury and due process of law; forbade "unreasonable searches and seizures;" and protected individuals against self-incrimination in criminal cases. The Bill of Rights was the most important achievement of these early years, and has protected citizens' democratic rights ever since.

The People Divide

During its first months, Washington's administration enjoyed almost universal support. The honeymoon, however, did not last. By the mid-1790s, opposition groups had formed a coalition known as the Jeffersonian Republicans, and the administration's remaining supporters rallied under the name of Federalists.

Disagreement began in January 1790, when Secretary of the Treasury Alexander Hamilton submitted to Congress the first of several major policy statements, the "Report on the Public Credit." Seldom in the nation's history has a single official so dominated public affairs as did Hamilton in these first years. A man of extraordinary intelligence and ambition, Hamilton preferred to act behind the scenes. His instincts for locating and seizing the levers of political power were unerring.

Hamilton was an ardent proponent of America's economic development. Perhaps more clearly than any of the nation's founders, he foresaw the country's future strength and was determined to promote its growth by encouraging domestic manufacturing and overseas commerce. Competitive self-interest, whether of nations or of individuals, he thought the surest guide to behavior. He most admired ambitious entrepreneurs eager to tie their fortunes to America's rising empire, and regarded a close alliance between such people and government officials as essential to achieving American greatness.

If Hamilton's economic policies were liberal in looking forward to enhanced economic opportunity, his politics were profoundly conservative. He continued to be deeply impressed by the stability of the British monarchy and the confident governing style of the British upper class. Hamilton distrusted the people, doubted their wisdom, and feared their purposes.

Hamilton had thought the Constitution that had emerged from the Philadelphia convention not "high-toned" enough. But once it was ratified, he set out to give it proper direction. His opportunity came when Washington named him secretary of the treasury. Recognizing the potential importance of his office, he determined to use it to build the kind of nation he envisioned.

Alexander Hamilton used both the office of secretary of the treasury and his personal relationship with President Washington to shape national policy during the early 1790s. (White House Collection)

In his first "Report on the Public Credit," Hamilton recommended funding the remaining Revolutionary War debt by enabling the government's creditors to exchange their badly depreciated securities at face value for new interest-bearing government bonds. The foreign held debt Hamilton set at $11.7 million; domestic debt, including back interest, he fixed at $40.4 million. Second, he proposed that the federal government assume responsibility for the $21.5 million in remaining state war debts. These actions, he hoped, would stabilize the government's finances, establish its credit, build confidence in the new nation at home and abroad, and tie business and commercial interests firmly to the new administration.

The proposal to fund the foreign debt aroused little controversy, but Hamilton's plans for handling the government's domestic obligations generated immediate opposition. In the House of Representatives, James Madison, Hamilton's recent ally in the ratification process, protested the unfairness of funding depreciated securities at their face value, especially because speculators had acquired most of them at a fraction of their initial worth. In addition, Madison and many of his southern colleagues knew that northern businessmen held most of the securities and that funding would bring little benefit to the South.

Hamilton was not impressed. The speculators, he observed, "paid what the commodity was worth in the market, and took the risks." They should therefore "reap the benefit." If his plan served the interests of the wealthy, that was exactly as he intended, for it would further strengthen the ties between wealth and national power. After grumbling, Congress endorsed the funding plan.

Federal assumption of the remaining state debts, another important part of Hamilton's program, aroused even greater criticism. States with the largest remaining unpaid obligations, such as Massachusetts, thought assumption a splendid idea. But others, such as Virginia and Pennsylvania, which had already retired

Patriotic Paintings

The questions that historians ask are limited only by their imagination and the historical evidence left behind for them to study. In addition to written documents, historians also examine visual evidence such as paintings and sculpture, for these, too, can provide insight into the life and culture of the past. With the proper mixture of care and ingenuity, historians can tease surprising amounts of information out of materials that at first glance seem silent and unrewarding.

Paintings offer unique insights into the past. They can tell us about the development over time of artistic styles and techniques. They also offer a window into the past for social and cultural historians, for they reveal how people lived and looked and did their work, as well as what the landscape and home furnishings were like.

During the revolutionary era and the early national period, American artists employed painting and other visual arts to record the great events of the nation's founding. John Trumbull, for example, completed four large canvasses depicting the signing of the Declaration of Independence, the surrender of General Burgoyne at Saratoga and Lord Cornwallis at Yorktown, and Washington resigning his commission at the end of the war in 1783—paintings that now hang in the rotunda of the nation's Capitol in Washington, D.C. Explained Trumbull in a letter to Thomas Jefferson: "The greatest motive I [have] had . . . for engaging in my pursuit of painting, has been the wish of commemorating the great events of our country's revolution."

The Founders were also popular subjects of the painter's brush. As a member of the Pennsylvania militia, Charles Willson Peale carried his paint kit and canvas along with his musket as he followed George Washington during the war. Before it was over, he had completed four portraits of the general.

Although Washington left the presidency in 1797 amid a storm of controversy, his death in 1799 generated a surge of public mourning. During the following year, eulogists celebrated him as a man "first in war, first in peace, and first in the hearts of his countrymen," while people decked out in black crepe, gold mourning rings, and funeral medals joined in countless memorial processions. In New York, an enterprising bookseller named Mason Weems published a best-selling biography of the great hero, complete with invented accounts of the cherry tree episode and other mythical stories. Weems's book went through 80 highly profitable editions over the next 100 years.

The Apotheosis of Washington, painted by an anonymous artist after an 1802 engraving by John Barralet and reproduced here, shows how Washington was mythologized during the years immediately following his death. Examine the painting carefully, for it is filled with a fascinating mixture of patriotic, religious, and cultural symbolism. Why is Washington depicted with his arms extended? Who is the woman standing at the left of the picture, and why are the children included? The bottom quarter of the picture is crowded with objects and human forms, each of them carefully chosen for what it might contribute to the painting's overall effect. Identify them and explain their meaning. Visual images have also been used to commemorate more recent American heroes such as Martin Luther King, Jr., and President Kennedy. How have they differed from this depiction of Washington?

Anonymous Chinese artist, The Apotheosis of Washington, *after J. Barralet, 1802. (Peabody Essex Museum, Salem, MA, photo by Mark Sexton)*

much of their debt, were opposed. Critics also pointed out that assumption would strengthen the central government at the expense of the states, for wealthy individuals would now look to it rather than the states for a return on their investments. Moreover, with its increased need for revenue to pay off the accumulated debt, the federal government would have additional reason to exercise its newly acquired power of taxation. That was exactly what Hamilton intended.

Once again, Congress supported Hamilton's bill, in good measure because Madison and Jefferson approved it as part of a deal to move the seat of government first to Philadelphia and eventually to a special federal district on the Potomac River. Southerners hoped that moving the government away from northern commercial centers would enable them to control its development and keep it more closely aligned with their own interests.

Opposition to the funding and assumption scheme, however, did not die. In December 1790, the Virginia assembly passed a series of resolutions, framed by Patrick Henry, warning that a monied aristocracy was taking control of the government, that southern agriculture was being subordinated to northern commerce, and that government powers were expanding dangerously. In response, Hamilton wrote privately that "This is the first symptom of a spirit which must either be killed, or will kill the Constitution."

As controversy grew, Hamilton proposed the second phase of his financial program in December 1790: a national bank capable of handling the government's financial affairs and pooling private investment capital for economic development. He had the Bank of England and its ties with the royal government clearly in mind, though he did not say so publicly.

Congressional opposition to the bank came almost entirely from the South. It seemed obvious that the bank would serve the needs of northern merchants and manufacturers far better than those of southern agrarians. Still, in February 1791, Congress approved the bank bill.

Washington asked his cabinet whether he should sign the bill. Hamilton said yes. Following the constitutional doctrine of "implied powers"—the principle that the government had the authority to make any laws "necessary and proper" for exercising the powers specifically granted to it—he argued that Congress could charter such a bank under its power to collect taxes and regulate trade. Secretary of State Jefferson advised a veto. He saw in Hamilton's argument a blueprint for the indefinite expansion of federal authority and argued that the government possessed only those powers specifically itemized in the Constitution. The Constitution said nothing about chartering banks, therefore the bill was unconstitutional. Jefferson also opposed the bank because he feared the rapid development of commerce and manufacturing that the bank was intended to promote. To Jefferson's distress, Washington took Hamilton's advice and signed the bank bill.

In December 1790, in his second "Report on the Public Credit," Hamilton proposed a series of excise taxes, including one on the manufacture of distilled liquor. This so-called Whiskey Tax was intended to signal the government's intention to use its new taxing authority to increase federal revenue. The power to tax and spend, Hamilton knew, was the power to govern. The Whiskey Tax became law in March 1791.

Finally, in his "Report on Manufactures," issued in December 1791, Hamilton called for protective tariffs for American industry, bounties to encourage the expansion of commercial agriculture, and a network of federally-sponsored internal improvements such as roads and lighthouses. These were intended to stimulate commerce and bind the nation together. Neither the agrarian South nor northern seaport districts, however, wanted tariffs that might reduce trade and raise the cost of living, so Congress never endorsed this report.

Criticism of Hamilton's policies grew. In October 1791, opposition leaders in Congress established a newspaper and vigorously attacked the administration's program. Hamilton responded with a series of anonymous articles in the administration's paper, accusing Jefferson (inaccurately) of having opposed the Constitution and (also inaccurately) of fomenting opposition to the government. Alarmed, Washington pleaded for restraint.

Congressional criticism of Hamilton's policies climaxed in January 1793 when resolutions were introduced in the House calling for an inquiry into the condition of the Treasury, accusing Hamilton of using the office for his own benefit, and censuring his conduct. Hamilton vigorously defended himself, and none of the resolutions passed. The debate showed just how bitter political discourse at the seat of government had become. The debate was now spreading beyond the Congress, among ordinary Americans. In northern towns and cities, artisans and other working people generally supported Hamilton's efforts to improve credit and stimulate economic development. Though many of them would eventually move into the Jeffersonian opposition, their own circumstances were now improving, and they seemed undisturbed by the benefits his policies brought to a few.

The Whiskey Rebellion

The farmers of western Pennsylvania condemned government policies most dramatically. They had special reason to hate the Whiskey Tax, for their livelihood depended on marketing grain surpluses. Shipping it over the mountains in bulk was prohibitively expensive, so they moved it more cost-efficiently as whiskey. Hamilton's tax threatened to make this unprofitable. The farmers also objected that people charged with tax evasion were tried in federal rather than state court. (The nearest federal court was hundreds of miles away in Philadelphia.)

Westerners' frustration went deeper than that, however, for they felt control of their local affairs slipping away as they became caught up in a market economy and a system of politics dominated by populous, commercialized areas to the east. In southern states like South Carolina, coastal planters were able to extend their control more easily over farmers of the interior because of their similar agricultural interests and their shared antipathy to black slaves. In the more economically diverse and racially homogenous states to the north, however, coastal-interior conflicts were sharp.

Hamilton cared little what the farmers thought either about the Whiskey Tax or local self-reliance. The government needed revenue, and the farmers would have to bear the cost. The farmers resented the Federalists' arrogance as much as the tax and quickly made their resentment known. By the summer of 1792, angry farmers gathered in mass meetings across western Pennsylvania. In August, a convention at Pittsburgh declared that the people would prevent the tax's collection.

Like opponents of the Stamp Act in 1765, they expected that repression would follow if resistance did not soon begin.

Alarmed, Washington issued a proclamation warning against such "unlawful" gatherings and insisting that the tax be enforced. As collections began, the farmers took direct action.

In July 1794, a federal marshal and a local excise inspector attempted to serve papers on several recalcitrant farmers near Pittsburgh. An angry crowd soon cornered a dozen federal soldiers in the marshall's house, which, after an exchange of gunfire and the troops' surrender, was torched. Similar episodes involving the erection of liberty poles reminiscent of the revolution erupted across the state, while a convention of 200 delegates debated armed resistance and talked about seceding from the United States.

Alarmed that the protests might spread through the entire whiskey-producing backcountry from New York to Georgia, Washington called out troops to restore order. For more than a year, Hamilton had been urging the use of force against protesters. To him, the insurrection was not evidence of an unjust policy needing change, but a chance for the government to show its ability to govern. He eagerly volunteered to accompany the troops west.

In late August, a force of nearly 13,000 men marched into western Pennsylvania, the president and the secretary of the treasury at its head. Persuaded by aides of the danger to his safety, Washington soon returned to Philadelphia, but Hamilton pressed on. The battle for which Hamilton had hoped never materialized, for as the federal army approached, the "Whiskey Rebels" dispersed. The army took 20 prisoners. Two were convicted of high treason and sentenced to death. Later, Washington pardoned both.

As people quickly realized, the "Whiskey Rebellion" had never threatened the government. "An insurrection was . . . proclaimed," Jefferson scoffed, "but could never be found." Even such an ardent Federalist as Fisher Ames was uneasy at the sight of federal troops marching against American citizens. "Elective rulers," he warned, "can scarcely ever employ the physical force of a democracy without turning the moral force or the power of public opinion against the government."

THE REPUBLIC IN A THREATENING WORLD

Because the nation was so new and the outside world so threatening, foreign policy issues generated extraordinary excitement during the 1790s. This was especially so after the French Revolution began and an accompanying European war erupted. In their arguments over the revolution in France and its implications for the new American republic, Americans revealed once again how sharply they differed in values and beliefs.

The Promise and Peril of the French Revolution

France's revolution began in 1789 as an effort to reform an arbitrary but weakened monarchy. Pent-up demands for social justice quickly outran initial attempts at moderate reform. By January 1793, when the recently proclaimed republican regime beheaded Louis XVI, France had plunged into a profoundly radical revolution. Soon Europe was locked in a deadly struggle between revolutionary France and a counterrevolutionary coalition that included Great Britain. For more than a decade, the French Revolution dominated European affairs.

The revolution also cut like a plowshare through the surface of American politics, dividing Americans deeply against each other. Not only did it raise immediate threats to the nation's security, but it also polarized debate over the future of democratic politics.

The outbreak of European war posed thorny diplomatic problems for Washington's administration. Under international law, neutral nations could continue to trade with warring powers as long as such trade did not involve goods directly related to the war effort. American merchants eagerly took advantage of that opportunity and earned handsome profits. For the first time since the Revolutionary War, prosperity returned to the nation's coastal cities. By 1800, American exports had more than doubled, and American ships were carrying an astonishing 92 percent of all commerce between America and Europe. Though the benefits were most evident in the ports, they radiated into the surrounding countryside, where the cargoes of agricultural and forest goods and the provisions required by the ships' crews were produced.

America's expanding commerce, however, was also at risk, for both Britain and France, while seeking American goods for themselves, stopped American ships headed for the other's ports. Neither country was willing to bind itself by legal formalities when locked in such a deadly struggle.

America's relations with the British were further complicated by the Royal Navy's practice of impressing American sailors into service aboard its warships to meet a growing demand for seamen. Washington faced the difficult problem of upholding the country's neutral rights and protecting its citizens without getting drawn into the European war.

The old French alliance of 1778 compounded the government's dilemma. It seemed to require the United States to aid France, much as France had assisted the American states a decade and a half before. Those sympathetic to the French cause argued that America's commitment still held. Others, however, fearing the consequences of American involvement and the political infection that closer ties with revolutionary France might bring, insisted that the treaty had lapsed when the French king was overthrown.

The American people's intense reaction to the European drama further complicated the situation. At first the French Revolution seemed to Americans an extension of their own struggle for liberty. Even the swing toward genuine social revolution did not immediately dampen American enthusiasm.

By the mid-1790s, however, especially after France's revolutionary regime attacked organized Christianity, many Americans pulled back in alarm. What connection could there possibly be between the principles of 1776 and the chaos of revolutionary France? Insisted a staunchly Federalist newspaper, "In America no barbarities were perpetrated—no men's heads were stuck upon poles—no mangled ladies' bodies were carried thro' the streets in triumph . . . . Whatever blood was shed, flowed gallantly in the field." The writer conveniently ignored the violence meted out by the supporters of monarchy in France, and betrayed a selective memory of America's own revolution. Even so, the differences were indeed profound.

For the Federalists, revolutionary France now symbolized social anarchy and threatened the European order on which they believed America's commercial and diplomatic well-being depended. With increasing vehemence, they castigated the revolution, championed England as the defender of European civilization, and sought ways of linking England and the United States more closely together.

Many Americans, however, continued to support France. While decrying the revolution's excesses, they noted how difficult it was to uproot the forces of reaction. Moreover, they believed that political liberty would ultimately emerge from the turmoil. Though Jefferson regretted the shedding of innocent blood, he thought it was necessary if true liberty was to be achieved.

Citizen Genêt and the Democratic-Republican Societies

Popular associations known as the Democratic-Republican societies provided the most vocal American support for revolutionary France. As early as 1792, ordinary citizens began to establish "constitutional societies" dedicated to "watching over the rights of the people, and giving an early alarm in case of governmental encroachments." During the government's first years, several dozen such societies, modeled after the Sons of Liberty and complete with Committees of Correspondence (see Chapter 5), had formed in opposition to Hamilton's financial program.

The arrival in April 1793 of Citizen Edmund Genêt, the French republic's minister to the United States, sparked a blazing fire of democratic enthusiasm. Genêt landed at Charleston, South Carolina, to a tumultuous reception. His instructions were to court popular support and negotiate a commercial treaty. Immediately after his arrival, however, he began commissioning American privateers to raid British shipping in the Caribbean and to attack Spanish Florida, both clear violations of American neutrality.

As he traveled north toward Philadelphia, Genêt met enthusiastic receptions. His popularity soon led him beyond the bounds of diplomatic propriety. Despite a warning from Secretary of State Jefferson and in open defiance of diplomatic protocol, he urged Congress to reject Washington's recently issued neutrality proclamation and side with revolutionary France. That was the final straw. On August 2, the president demanded Genêt's recall.

If Genêt failed as a diplomat, he succeeded in fanning popular enthusiasm for revolutionary France. In June 1793, with his open encouragement, the largest and most influential of the new societies, the Democratic Society of Pennsylvania, was founded in Philadelphia. It called immediately for the formation of similar societies elsewhere to join in supporting France and promoting the "spirit of freedom and equality" at home. Washington and his colleagues might wonder whether that challenge was aimed at them.

Although a full network of popular societies never developed, about 40 organizations scattered from Maine to Georgia sprang up during the next several years. Working people—artisans and laborers in the cities, small farmers and tenants in the countryside—provided the bulk of membership. The societies' leaders were generally individuals of acknowledged respectability, such as doctors, lawyers, and tradesmen. All were united by a common dedication to what they called the "principles of '76" and a determination to preserve those principles against the "royalizing" tendencies of Washington's administration. They especially denounced the president's proclamation of neutrality. Several of the societies openly urged the United States to enter the war on France's behalf.

In the West, societies agitated against British occupation of the frontier posts around the Great Lakes and the Spanish closing of the Mississippi River. In the Northeast, they castigated England for its "piracy" against American shipping. In the Carolinas, they demanded greater representation for the growing backcountry in the state's assembly. Everywhere, they protested the Excise Tax, opposed the administration's overtures to England, demanded that public officials attend to popular wishes, and called for a press free from control of Federalist "aristocrats."

President Washington and his supporters were incensed by the societies' support of Genêt and their criticism of the government. Such "nurseries of sedition," thundered one Federalist, threatened to revolutionize America as the Jacobins had revolutionized France. In 1794 a Virginia Federalist called Kentucky's Democratic Society "that horrible sink of treason, that hateful synagogue of anarchy, that odious conclave of tumult, that frightful cathedral of discord, that poisonous garden of conspiracy, that hellish school of rebellion and opposition to all regular and well-balanced authority!" Such polemics illustrated how inflamed public discourse had become.

Jay's Controversial Treaty

Uproar over Jay's Treaty with England further heightened tensions at mid-decade. Alarmed by the deteriorating relations with England, Washington sent Chief Justice John Jay to London in the spring of 1794 with instructions to negotiate a wide range of troublesome issues left over from the Revolutionary War, especially the occupation of western posts, interference with American shipping, and impressment of American seamen. Jay's Treaty, which the chief justice brought home early in 1795, resolved almost none of these grievances, and when its terms were made public they triggered an explosion of protest.

The administration's pleas that the agreement headed off an open breach with England and was the best that could be obtained failed to pacify critics. In New York City, Hamilton was stoned when he defended the treaty at a mass meeting. Southern planters were angry because the agreement brought no compensation for their stolen slaves. Westerners complained that the British were not evacuating the posts, while merchants and sailors railed against Jay's failure to open the British West Indies to American trade or to stop impressment. Only by the narrowest of margins, and after a long and acrimonious debate, did the Senate ratify the treaty.

The administration made better progress on the still volatile issue of free transit at New Orleans. In Pinckney's Treaty, negotiated by Thomas Pinckney in 1795, Spain for the first time gave up all claim to U.S. territory in the West. Spain also granted Americans free navigation of the Mississippi and the right to unload goods for transshipment at New Orleans—but only for three years. What would happen then was uncertain.

By mid-decade, political harmony had disappeared as the American people divided sharply on virtually every important issue of foreign and domestic policy. Increasingly estranged from the administration, Jefferson resigned as secretary of state in July 1793. He soon joined politicians such as Madison and Albert Gallatin of Pennsylvania in open opposition.

In September 1796, in what came to be called his Farewell Address, Washington announced that he would not accept a third term. He had long been contemplating retirement, for he was now 64 and no longer immune to attack. "As to you, sir," fumed Thomas Paine in an open letter published in a newspaper, "treacherous in private friendship . . . and a hypocrite in public life, the world will be puzzled to decide, whether you are an apostate or an impostor; whether you have abandoned good principles, or whether you ever had any." Seldom has an American president been subjected to such public abuse.

THE POLITICAL CRISIS DEEPENS

By 1796, bitter controversy surrounded the national government. That controversy intensified during the last half of the 1790s until it seemed to threaten the very stability of the country.

The Election of 1796

The presidential election of 1796 reflected the political storms buffeting the nation. Four years before, Washington and Adams had been reelected without significant opposition. Now the situation was vastly different.

With Washington out of the picture, the contest quickly narrowed to Adams versus Jefferson. Both had played distinguished roles during the Revolution when they had become friends and shared in the electrifying task of drafting the Declaration of Independence. During the 1780s, they had joined forces again, when Adams served as first U.S. minister to Great Britain and Jefferson as minister to France. They came together a third time during the early 1790s, Adams as vice president and Jefferson as Washington's first secretary of state.

But they differed in many ways. Short, rotund, and fastidious, Adams contrasted sharply with the tall and frequently disheveled Jefferson. At once intensely ambitious and deeply insecure about the judgments both of his contemporaries and of history, Adams struggled self-consciously to construct his public career. Jefferson, by contrast, charted his course more quietly. Jefferson's mind was more expansive and his interests far wider. Politician and political theorist, he was also an avid naturalist, architect, and philosopher. Adams's interests were more tightly focused on legal and constitutional affairs.

By the mid-1790s, they also differed in their visions of the nation's future. Though fearing Hamilton's ambition and his infatuation with England, Adams was a committed Federalist, distrustful of democracy and of the French Revolution. Jefferson, while firmly supporting the Constitution, was alarmed by Hamilton's financial program, viewed France's revolution as a logical if chaotic extension of

As one of the elder statesmen of the early republic, Thomas Jefferson almost became the second president in the 1796 election after Washington declined to run for a third term. John Adams won that election by only three votes, and Jefferson—as Vice President, became the nominal leader of those in opposition to the Federalists.—(The Metropolitan Museum of Art, Bequest of Cornelia Cruger, 1923, 24.19.1)

America's struggle for freedom, and hoped to expand democracy. By 1796, he had become the vocal leader of an increasingly articulate political opposition.

In the 1796 election, Adams was the Federalists' candidate. Though Jefferson did not officially oppose him, his followers campaigned vigorously on Jefferson's behalf. Adams received 71 electoral votes and became president. Jefferson came in second with 68 and, as then specified in the Constitution, assumed the vice presidency. The narrowness of Adams's majority indicated the Federalists' weakness and the Jeffersonians' strength.

The War Crisis with France

Adams had no sooner taken office than he confronted a deepening crisis with France. Hoping to ease relations between the two countries, he sent three commissioners to negotiate an accord.

When the Americans arrived in Paris, three unnamed agents ("X, Y, and Z") of the French foreign minister, Talleyrand, made it clear that the success of their mission depended on a prior loan to the French government and a $240,000 gratuity for them. The two staunchly Federalist commissioners, John Marshall and Charles Pinckney, indignantly sailed home. The third commissioner, Elbridge Gerry, stayed, still hoping for an accommodation and alarmed by Talleyrand's intimation that if all three Americans left, France would declare war.

When Adams reported to Congress on the XYZ Affair, Americans were out-raged. The Federalists quickly exploited the French blunder. Secretary of State Pickering urged an immediate declaration of war, while Federalist congressmen thundered "Millions for defense, but not one cent for tribute!" Adams found him-self an unexpected hero. Caught up in the anti-French furor and emboldened by the petitions of support that flooded in from around the country, the president lashed out at "enemies" both at home and abroad. The nation, he warned ominously, had never been in greater danger. Emotions were further inflamed by the so-called Quasi War, a series of naval encounters between American and French ships.

Publicly, Republican leaders deplored the French government's behavior and pledged to uphold the nation's honor. But they were alarmed about the Federalists' intentions—with good reason, because the Federalists soon mounted a crash pro-gram not only to repel invaders but also to root out traitors at home.

The Alien and Sedition Acts

In May 1798, Congress created the Navy Department and called for the rapid development of a naval force to defend the American coast against the French. In July, Congress moved closer to an open breach with France by repealing the treaty of 1778, and called for the formation of a 10,000-man army. The army's stated mis-sion was to repel a French invasion, but this was unlikely given France's desperate struggle in Europe. The Jeffersonians feared the army would be used for a differ-ent, domestic, and more partisan purpose, remembering the speed with which the Federalists had deployed troops against the Whiskey Rebels.

As criticism of the army bill mounted, Adams had second thoughts. He was still enough of an old revolutionary to worry about the dangers of standing armies. The navy, he believed, should be America's first line of defense. He was further angered when some members of his party sought to put Hamilton at the head of the army. To the dismay of hard-line Federalists, Adams issued only a few of the officers' commissions that Congress had authorized. Without officers, the troops could not be mobilized.

Fearful of foreign subversion and aware that French immigrants were active in the Jeffersonian opposition, the Federalist-dominated Congress in the summer of 1798 curbed the flow of aliens into the country. The Naturalization Act raised from 5 to 14 years the residence requirement for citizenship, and the Alien Act autho-rized the president to expel aliens whom he judged "dangerous to the peace and safety of the United States." Imprisonment and permanent exclusion from citizen-ship awaited those who were warned to leave but refused to go. Another bill, the Alien Enemies Act, empowered the president in time of war to arrest, imprison, or banish the subjects of any hostile nation without specifying charges against them or providing opportunity for appeal. A Federalist congressman explained that there was no need "to invite hordes of Wild Irishmen, nor the turbulent and disor-derly of all parts of the world, to come here with a view to distract our tranquillity."

The implications of these acts for basic political liberties were ominous enough, but the Federalists had not yet finished. In July 1798, Congress passed the Sedition Act, aimed directly at the Jeffersonian opposition. The bill made it punishable by fine and imprisonment for anyone to conspire in opposition to "any measure or measures of the government," or to aid "any insurrection, riot, unlawful assembly, or combination." Fines and prison awaited people who "write, print, utter, or publish . . . any false, scandalous and malicious writing" bringing the government, Congress, or the president into disrepute.

The Federalist moves stunned the Jeffersonians, for they threatened to smother all political opposition. Federalists now equated their own political domination with the survival of the nation.

Under the terms of the Alien Act, Secretary of State Pickering launched investigations intended to force all foreigners to register, and soon noted approvingly that large numbers of aliens, especially people of French ancestry, were leaving the country. As Sedition Act prosecutions went forward, 25 people, among them David Brown of Dedham, were arrested. Fifteen were indicted, and ten were ultimately convicted, the majority of them Jeffersonian printers and editors. In Congress, Representative Matthew Lyon, a cantankerous, acid-tongued Jeffersonian from Vermont, got embroiled in a heated debate over the Sedition Act and spat in the face of a Federalist opponent, Roger Griswold of Connecticut. Two weeks later, Griswold caned Lyon on the House floor. Later that year, Lyon was hauled into court, fined $1,000, and sentenced to four months in prison. His crime? Referring in a personal letter to President Adams's "unbounded thirst for ridiculous pomp, foolish adulation, and selfish avarice."

Local Reverberations

The Alien and Sedition Acts generated a firestorm of protest across the country, including a direct challenge to the Federalist laws by the Virginia and Kentucky assemblies. The Kentucky Resolutions, drafted by Jefferson and passed on November 16, 1798, declared that the national government had violated the Bill of Rights. Faced with the arbitrary exercise of federal power, the resolutions continued, each state "has an equal right to judge [of infractions] by itself . . . [and] the mode and measure of redress." Nullification (declaring a federal law invalid within a state's borders) was the "rightful remedy" for unconstitutional laws. The Virginia Resolutions, written by Madison and passed the following month, asserted that when the central government threatened the people's liberties, the states "have the right and are in duty bound to interpose for arresting the progress of the evil." It would not be the last time in American history that state leaders would claim authority to set aside a federal law.

The Kentucky and Virginia resolutions received little support elsewhere, and neither state actually attempted to obstruct enforcement of the Alien and Sedition Acts. Still, the resolutions indicated the depth of popular opposition. As the Federalists pressed ahead, some Jeffersonians prepared for open conflict. The Virginia assembly called for the formation of a state arsenal at Harpers Ferry, reorganization of the militia, and a special tax to pay for these preparations. In Philadelphia, Federalist patrols walked the streets to protect government officials from angry crowds. As a precaution, President Adams smuggled arms into his residence. As 1799 began, the country seemed on the brink of upheaval.

Within a year, however, the cycle turned decisively against the Federalists. From Europe, Adams's son, John Quincy Adams, sent reassurances that Talleyrand was ready to negotiate an honorable accord. Alarmed at the political furor consuming the nation and fearful that war with France "would convulse the attachments of the country," Adams eagerly seized the opening. "The end of war is peace," he explained, "and peace was offered me." He had also concluded that his only chance of reelection lay in fashioning a peace coalition out of both parties. But Adams's cabinet was enraged, for the Federalist war program depended for its legitimacy on the continuation of the French crisis. After Secretary of State Pickering repeatedly ignored presidential orders to dispatch the new peace commissioners, Adams personally ordered them to depart and fired Pickering. By year's end, the envoys secured an agreement releasing the United States from the 1778 alliance and restoring peaceful relations.

The "Revolution of 1800"

As the election of 1800 approached, the Federalists had squandered the political advantage handed them by the XYZ Affair in 1798 and, with peace a reality, stood charged with the unconstitutional exercise of federal power, the suppression of dissent, and the intention of using the federal army against American citizens. Hamiltonians were furious at Adams's "betrayal," and when he stood for reelection, they plotted his defeat.

Emotions ran high as the election approached. Both sides believed that the republic's survival depended on their own political triumph. In Virginia, rumors of a slave insurrection briefly interrupted the feuding, but the scare quickly passed and soon Federalists and Jeffersonians were back at each others' throats.

As the results were tallied, it became clear that the Jeffersonians had decisively defeated the Federalists. The two Republican candidates for president, Jefferson, the Republicans' first choice, and Aaron Burr, their other nominee, each had 73 electoral votes, compared to Adams's 65.

Because of the tie vote, the election was thrown into the House of Representatives, where a deadlock quickly developed. After a bitter struggle in which the Federalists backed Burr, the House finally elected Jefferson, ten states to four, on the thirty-sixth ballot. (Seeking to prevent a recurrence of such a crisis, the new Congress soon passed, and the states ratified, the Twelfth Amendment, providing for separate electoral college ballots for president and vice president.) The magnitude of the Federalists' defeat was even more evident in the congressional elections, where they lost their majorities in both House and Senate.

The election's outcome revealed the strong sectional divisions increasingly evident in the country's politics. The Federalists dominated New England because of regional loyalty to Adams, the area's commercial ties with England, and fears (fed by local ministers and politicians) that the Jeffersonians intended to import social revolution. From Maryland south, Jeffersonian control was almost as complete. In the middle states, where issues of foreign and domestic policy cut across society in more complicated ways, Federalists and Jeffersonians were more evenly balanced. In the years ahead, such sectional differences would continue to shape American politics.

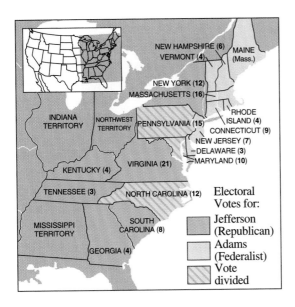

Electoral Votes for:

Jefferson (Republican)

Adams (Federalist)

Vote divided

THE PRESIDENTIAL ELECTION OF 1800
Though the federal government was little more than a decade old, the electoral vote in 1800 revealed the sectional divisions that already troubled national politics.

The Federalist-Jeffersonian conflict was deeply rooted as well in socioeconomic divisions among the American people. The Federalists were strongest among merchants, manufacturers, and commercial farmers situated within easy reach of the coast—groups that had supported the Constitution in 1787 and 1788. In both New York City and Philadelphia, the Federalists were strongest in the wards where assessments were highest, houses largest, and addresses most fashionable.

By contrast, the Jeffersonian coalition included most of the old Anti-Federalists, as well as agriculturists in both North and South. The Jeffersonians, however, marshaled significant urban support among workers and artisans, many of whom had once been staunch Federalists.

In the politically charged setting of the 1790s, when the Revolution's legacy was still in dispute, tensions between social privilege and democratic equality suffused American political life. Given the Jeffersonians' opposition to Federalist arrogance, support for revolutionary France, challenge to the Alien and Sedition Acts, and defense of religious liberty, those tensions worked steadily in the Jeffersonians' favor.

The political alignment evident in the election of 1800 resembled but did not duplicate the Federalist-Anti-Federalist division of 1787–1788. The Jeffersonian coalition was much broader than the Anti-Federalists' had been, for it included countless individuals, from urban workers to leaders such as Madison and Jefferson, who had supported the Constitution and had helped set the new government on its feet. Unlike the Anti-Federalists, the Jeffersonians were ardent supporters of the Constitution, but they insisted that it be implemented consistently with political liberty and a strong dependence on the states. Far more than the Federalists, they also believed that government should be broadly accountable to the people. Nationally, the Jeffersonians now enjoyed a clear political majority. Their coalition would dominate American politics well into the nineteenth century.

TIMELINE

1789	1790	1791	1792	1793
George Washington inaugurated as first president; Outbreak of the French Revolution	Slave trade outlawed in all states except Georgia and South Carolina; Hamilton's "Reports on the Public Credit"	Bill of Rights ratified; Whiskey Tax and national bank established; Hamilton's "Report on Manufactures"	Washington reelected	Outbreak of war in Europe; Washington's Neutrality Proclamation; Jefferson resigns from cabinet; Controversy over Citizen Genêt's visit
1794	**1795**	**1796**	**1797**	**1798**
Whiskey Rebellion in Pennsylvania	Controversy over Jay's Treaty with England	Washington's Farewell Address; John Adams elected president	XYZ Affair in France	Naturalization Act; Alien and Sedition acts; Virginia and Kentucky resolutions
1798–1800	**1799**	**1801**		
Undeclared naval war with France	Trial of David Brown	Jefferson elected president by House of Representatives		

✦✦✦✦✦✦

CONCLUSION

Toward the Nineteenth Century

The election of 1800 was a remarkable outcome to more than a decade of political crisis. It had begun in the late 1780s with the intensifying debate over the Articles of Confederation and the movement toward a stronger central government. Then had come the heated contest over ratification of the new Constitution. Scarcely had the new government gotten under way than divisions began to form, first among political leaders in Congress but increasingly among the American people.

Hamilton's domestic policies generated the first outburst of political conflict, but it was the French Revolution, the European war, Jay's Treaty, and the Federalists' war program that galvanized political energies and set the Federalists and Jeffersonians so adamantly against each other.

By 1800, the system of gentry-led politics centered in Congress and the more popular, democratic politics brewing in the states had drawn more closely together. The years immediately ahead would bring them into even more intimate political alignment, with dramatic consequences for the nation's future.

In the election of 1800, control of the federal government passed for the first time from one political party to another, not easily but peacefully and legally. "The

Revolution of 1800," the Jeffersonians called it—"as real a revolution in the principles of our government as that of 1776 was in its form." The future would show whether the Jeffersonians were correct. But for the moment the crisis had passed, the Federalists had been defeated, and the government was in the hands of the Jeffersonians.

Recommended Reading

The Bill of Rights and Civil Liberties

Robert Rutland, *The Birth of the Bill of Rights, 1776–1791* (1983); Bernard Schwartz, *The Great Rights of Mankind* (1977); Leonard Levy, *Freedom of the Press from Zenger to Jefferson* (1966); James M. Smith, *Freedom's Fetters: The Alien and Sedition Laws and American Civil Liberties* (1956).

Party Politics at the Seat of Government

John Hoadley, *Origins of American Political Parties, 1789–1803* (1986); John Nelson, Jr., *Liberty and Property: Political Economy and Policymaking in the New Nation, 1789–1812* (1987); Ralph Ketcham, *Presidents Above Party: The First American Presidency, 1789–1829* (1984); James Sharp, *American Politics in the Early Republic: The New Nation in Crisis* (1993); Gerhard Casper, *Separating Power: Essays on the Founding Period* (1997).

Politics in the States

Norman Risjord, *Chesapeake Politics, 1781–1800* (1978); Charles Steffen, *The Mechanics of Baltimore: Workers and Politics in the Age of Revolution, 1763–1812* (1984); Ronald Schultz, *The Republic of Labor: Philadelphia Artisans and the Politics of Class, 1720–1830* (1993); Thomas Slaughter, *The Whiskey Rebellion: Frontier Epilogue to the American Revolution* (1986); Alan Taylor, *Liberty Men and Great Proprietors: The Revolutionary Settlement on the Maine Frontier, 1760–1812* (1990); Richard Beeman, *Evolution of the Southern Backcountry* (1988); David Waldstreicher, *In the Midst of Perpetual Fêtes: The Making of American Nationalism, 1776–1820* (1998).

Diplomacy and the French Revolution

Daniel Lang, *Foreign Policy in the Early Republic* (1985); William Stinchcombe, *The XYZ Affair* (1981); Albert Bowman, *The Struggle for Neutrality: Franco-American Diplomacy During the Federalist Era* (1974); Jerald Combs, *The Jay Treaty* (1970).

Federalists Versus Jeffersonians

Joyce Appleby, *Capitalism and the New Social Order: The Republican Vision of the 1790s* (1984); Lance Banning, *The Jeffersonian Persuasion: The Evolution of a Party Ideology* (1978); Aleine Austin, *Matthew Lyon: "New Man" of the Democratic Revolution, 1749–1800* (1981); Merrill Peterson, *Adams and Jefferson: A Revolutionary Dialogue* (1976); John Nelson, *Liberty and Property: Political Economy and Policymaking in the New Nation, 1789–1812* (1987).

CHAPTER 9

Society and Politics in the Early Republic

In May 1809, Mary and James Harrod gathered their five children, loaded a few belongings on a wagon, fell in line with a dozen other families, and headed west from Virginia toward a new life in Kentucky. They left behind 10 acres of marginal upland, 15 years of wearying effort at trying to wring a modest living from it, and a family cemetery holding two children and Mary's parents.

Beyond the Appalachian Mountains, 450 difficult miles ahead, lay more hard work and uncertainty. Though central Kentucky where the Harrods would settle contained few Indian villages, powerful tribes from north and south of the Ohio River hunted there and fought for its control. They fought also against the growing tide of white settlers. The first years would be especially hard for John and Mary as they "opened up" the land, planted the first crops, and built a cabin. They would be lonesome as well, unlikely to see even the chimney smoke from their nearest neighbors.

James and Mary were hopeful, though, as they trudged west. The land agent who had sold them their claim had promised rich, fertile soil that in time would support a good life. They looked forward as well to escaping Virginia's slave society with its arrogant planters and oppressed slaves—no place for poor whites. Just as important, Mary and James had shared in excited talk about new opportunities beyond the mountains. There they established themselves on their own plot of land, joined with their neighbors in fashioning a new community, and took responsibility for their own lives.

In April 1795, Ben Thompson started north from Queen Anne's County, Maryland, for New York City. Ben knew little beyond farming, but he was ambitious. In New York he listened carefully to the ship captains who recruited men for their crews. Ben was lucky, for he arrived just as American overseas commerce, stimulated by renewed war in Europe, was entering a decade of unprecedented prosperity. Sailors were in demand, pay was good, and few questions were asked. For five years, Ben sailed the seas. Then he returned to New York and hired out as an apprentice to a ship's carpenter.

About the same time, Phyllis Sherman left Norwalk, Connecticut. She also headed for New York, where she took a job as a maid in the household of one of the city's wealthy merchants. As fate would have it, Phyllis and Ben met, fell in love, and in the spring of 1802 were married.

There is little remarkable in this, except that Ben and Phyllis were former slaves and were married in the African Methodist Episcopal Zion Church. Ben had cast off his slave name,

Cato, as a sign of liberation, while Phyllis kept the name her master had given her. Ben was doubly fortunate, for he had purchased his freedom just as cotton production began to expand through the Chesapeake region; a decade later, he would have faced greater difficulty securing his independence. Phyllis had been freed as a child when slavery ended in Connecticut. As she grew up, she tired of living as a servant with her former owner's family and longed to be with other blacks. She had heard that there were people of color in New York, and she was correct. In 1800, it was home to 6,300 African-Americans, more than half of them free.

Though life in New York was better than either Ben or Phyllis had known before, it was hardly easy. They shared only marginally in the city's commercial prosperity. In 1804, they watched helplessly as yellow fever carried off their daughter and many of their friends. And while they found support in newly established African-American churches and the expanding black community, they had to watch out because slave ships still moved in and out of the port and slave catchers pursued southern runaways in the city's streets.

✦✦✦✦✦✦

During the early years of the nineteenth century, thousands of people like Mary and James, like Ben and Phyllis, seized opportunities to improve their lives. Doing so, they helped strengthen the nation's commitment to social equality, individual opportunity, political democracy, and personal autonomy—doctrines that would gradually transform a nation still precariously balanced between an eighteenth-century world and the accelerating forces of social change.

This transformation—some have called it the "opening" of American society—was driven in part by the accelerating expansion of white settlement out of long-settled areas along the Atlantic coast onto new lands in the trans-Appalachian interior. This expansion disrupted families and older communities. It required, as well, the creation of countless new communities and the fashioning of new social relationships. Also at work was the expansion of an increasingly dynamic market economy, with its relentless discipline of supply and demand, its emphasis on impersonal, contractual relationships, and its focus on individual profit. The growing market economy strengthened these values and weakened earlier commitments to a "just price" and "moral economy."

Contributing as well to the erosion of long-established systems of authority and the promotion of individualism and equality was the wave of religious revivalism known as the Second Great Awakening that swept American society beginning about 1800. Its message, carried by swarms of itinerant Methodist and Baptist preachers, stressed universal salvation, the equality of all believers before God, and the individual's responsibility for her or his own soul.

The transformation of American society was also spurred by the aggressive challenge posed by local democratic forces to an older, more conservative, gentry-led form of politics centered in the national Congress, democratic forces that had been energized by the colonial struggle against England and strengthened during the political conflicts of the 1790s. America's strengthening democracy also found support among a younger generation of political leaders eager to perfect their skills in popular politics.

Not all Americans benefited equally from these changes. Doctrines of equality, opportunity, and individual autonomy resonated far more powerfully in the lives of white men than of white women, while numerous Americans were actually disadvantaged by the changes that were under way. African-Americans, for example, found their lives more harshly constrained by a revitalized slavery, while Native Americans confronted a tide of white settlement in the West.

By the mid-nineteenth century, social, economic, and political change would transform the American nation. Even during the 1820s, their effects were becoming evident.

The years of the early republic witnessed as well a diplomatic revolution of major importance as the American people broke free from their centuries-old dependence on Europe and focused on occupying North America. At the same time, the United States laid claim to a bold, new place among the emerging nations of the Western Hemisphere as Latin America also threw off the yoke of colonialism.

RESTORING AMERICAN LIBERTY

The Jeffersonians entered office in March 1801 with several objectives in mind: calming the political storms that had threatened to rend the country, consolidating their recent victory, purging the government of Federalist holdovers, and setting it on a proper republican course.

The Jeffersonians Take Control

In November 1800 the government had moved from Philadelphia to the isolated new capital in the District of Columbia. Gone were the sophisticated surroundings of New York and Philadelphia. To the amazement of arriving politicians, the new capital was little more than a swampy clearing with about 5,000 inhabitants. The Capital wing containing the House of Representatives was finished, but the Senate chamber and president's house were uncompleted.

To rid the government of Federalist pomp, Jefferson planned a simple inauguration. Shortly before noon on March 4, he walked to the Capitol from his nearby boardinghouse. Dressed as a plain citizen, the president-elect read his short inaugural address; Chief Justice John Marshall, a fellow Virginian and staunch Federalist, administered the oath of office; and a militia company fired a 16-gun salute. Despite the modesty of the occasion, the moment was filled with significance. For the first time in American history, control of the government had shifted from one party to another.

In his inaugural speech, Jefferson enumerated the "essential principles" that would guide his administration: "equal and exact justice to all," support of the states as "the surest bulwarks against anti-republican tendencies," "absolute acquiescence" in the decisions of the majority, supremacy of civil over military authority, reduction of government spending, "honest payment" of the public debt, freedom of the press, and "freedom of the person under the protection of the habeas corpus." Though Jefferson never mentioned the Federalists, his litany of principles reverberated with the dark experience of the 1790s.

Jefferson spoke also of political reconciliation, asserting that "We are all republicans—we are all federalists." Not all his followers welcomed that final flourish. Jefferson eventually agreed that a "general sweep" of Federalist officeholders was necessary. By 1808, virtually all government offices were solidly in Republican hands.

Politics and the Federal Courts

Having lost Congress and the presidency, the Federalists turned to the federal judiciary for protection against the expected Jeffersonian onslaught. In the last months of the Adams administration, the Federalist-controlled Congress had passed a new Judiciary Act increasing the number of circuit courts, complete with judges, marshals, and clerks. Before leaving office, Adams filled many of those offices with staunch Federalists. When the new Republican-dominated Congress convened, it challenged the Federalist hold on the judiciary.

Momentous issues were at stake: the independence of the judiciary from political attack, the doctrine of judicial review, and the notion that it was the federal courts' responsibility to judge the constitutionality of congressional laws and executive behavior. Gouverneur Morris, Federalist senator from New York, declared that an independent judiciary was necessary "to save the people from their most dangerous enemy, themselves." The Jeffersonians argued that each branch of the government—executive and legislative as well as judicial—must have the right to decide the validity of an act. Congressional debate over repeal of the Judiciary Act drew wide public attention, for it offered a vivid contrast between Federalist and Jeffersonian notions of republican government.

In early 1802, by a strict party vote, Congress repealed the Judiciary Act of 1801, and as Federalists wrung their hands, exultant Jeffersonians prepared to purge several highly partisan Federalist judges. In March 1803, the House of Representatives impeached District Judge John Pickering of New Hampshire. The grounds were not the "high crimes and misdemeanors" required by the Constitution but the Federalist diatribes with which Pickering regularly assaulted defendants and juries. Impeachment, claimed a Republican congressman, is nothing more than a declaration by Congress that an individual holds "dangerous opinions," which if allowed to go into effect "will work the destruction of the Union"—phrases echoing the language of repression used by Federalists only a few years earlier. The Republican-controlled Senate convicted Pickering by a straight party vote. Next, the Jeffersonians impeached Supreme Court Justice Samuel Chase, one of the most notorious Republican baiters. But when the trial revealed that Chase had committed no impeachable offense, he was acquitted and returned triumphantly to the bench.

Chase was a sorry hero, but constitutional principles are often established in the defense of less than heroic people. Had Chase's impeachment succeeded, Chief Justice Marshall would almost certainly have been next, and that would have precipitated a serious constitutional crisis. Sensing the danger, the Jeffersonians pulled back, content to allow time and attrition to cleanse the courts of Federalist control. The vital principle of judicial independence had been narrowly preserved.

Marshall's Supreme Court issued two trailblazing decisions that established some of the most fundamental doctrines of American constitutional law. The first, *Marbury v. Madison* (1803), laid down the constitutional principle of judicial review—the assertion that the Court must judge the constitutionality of congressional laws and executive behavior. In his decision, Marshall declared that "It is emphatically the province and duty of the judicial department to say what the law is." Sixteen years later, in another landmark decision, *McCulloch v. Maryland*, the Court struck down a Maryland law taxing the Baltimore branch of the Second Bank of the United States. No state, ruled Marshall, had the right to tax a nationally chartered bank, for "the power to tax involves the power to destroy." In *McCulloch*, Marshall also affirmed the constitutionality of the bank's congressional charter and established the constitutional basis for broad congressional authority. Let congressional intent "be within the scope of the Constitution," he wrote, "and all means which are appropriate . . . which are not prohibited, but consist with the letter and spirit of the Constitution, are constitutional."

Dismantling the Federalist War Program

The Jeffersonians had regarded the Federalists' war program as a threat to liberty, and quickly dismantled it. Jefferson ended Sedition Act prosecutions, freed its victims, and in 1802 let it lapse. He undercut the Alien Acts by allowing enforcement to lapse, and in 1802 Congress restored the requirement of 5 rather than 14 years of residence before a foreigner could become a citizen. While various Federalist editors did feel the government's displeasure, Jefferson never duplicated the Federalists' efforts to stifle dissent. The Federalists' provisional army was disbanded; no longer would federal troops intimidate American citizens.

The Jeffersonians' ideal was a small debt-free, government. They reduced the national debt from $83 million in 1801 to $57 million a decade later. By modern standards, the government was already tiny when the Jeffersonian's took office: in 1802 it had fewer than 3,000 civilian employees, only 300 of them (including the cabinet and Congress) in Washington. There was one federal official for every 1,914 people; today there is one for every 62. Even so, Jefferson wrote that he was "hunting out and abolishing multitudes of useless offices." The federal government, he thought, should do little more than deal with foreign policy, deliver mail, deal with Indians on federal land, and administer the public domain.

Not everything the Jeffersonians did was consistent with strict notions of a limited government. As the nation grew, so did pressures for a federal program of internal improvements, especially from new states beyond the Appalachians that sought closer ties with the East. Soon the government responded by opening several western routes, including the National Road (1811) from Cumberland, Maryland, to Wheeling (now in West Virginia) on the Ohio River. The states, however, continued to carry major responsibility for internal improvements. Though the Jeffersonians may not have "revolutionized" the government as they claimed, they reduced it and pointed it in a new direction.

BUILDING AN AGRARIAN NATION

The Jeffersonians did far more than reverse Federalist initiatives, for they worked vigorously to implement their own vision of an expanding, agrarian nation. That vision was mixed and inconsistent, for the Jeffersonian party consisted of conflicting groups: southern patricians, like Jefferson himself, determined to maintain a gentry-led, slavery-based agrarian order; lower- and middle-class southern whites committed to black servitude but ardent proponents of white political equality; northern artisans who brought to the Jeffersonian party an aversion to slavery (though rarely a commitment to racial equality) and a fierce dedication to honest toil and their own economic interests; western farmers devoted to self-sufficiency on the land; and northern intellectuals committed to political democracy. In time, this diversity would splinter the Jeffersonian coalition. For the moment, however, these groups found unity not only against their common Federalist enemies, but also in a set of broadly shared principles that guided Jeffersonian policies through the administrations of Jefferson (1801–1809), James Madison (1809–1817), and James Monroe (1817–1824).

The Jeffersonian Vision

Political liberty, the Jeffersonians believed, could survive only under conditions of broad economic and social equality. Their strategy centered on the independent, yeoman farmer—self-reliant, industrious, and concerned for the public good.

The Jeffersonian vision, however, was threatened because industriousness generated wealth, wealth bred social inequality, and inequality threatened to destroy the very foundation of a democratic society. The solution lay in rapid territorial expansion. The expansion of white settlement across the continent, by offering opportunity to a restless people and drawing them out of crowded, eastern cities, would delay, perhaps even prevent, the cyclical process of growth, maturity, and decay through which all past societies had moved. Rapid and continuing territorial expansion was thus indispensable to the Jeffersonian vision.

There were practical reasons for promoting expansion, too. Occupation of the West would secure U.S. borders against British, French, and Spanish threats. And Jeffersonians calculated that new western states, committed to more democratic forms of politics, would strengthen them and ensure the Federalists' demise.

Time would reveal that American exceptionalism—the idea that the United States could avoid Europe's woes by continental expansion—was more limited than Jefferson imagined. Yet from the perspective of the early nineteenth century, the Jeffersonians offered a compelling and hopeful vision of the nation's future.

The Windfall Louisiana Purchase

Securing agrarian democracy by territorial expansion explains Jefferson's most dramatic accomplishment, buying the Louisiana Territory in 1803. The purchase nearly doubled the nation's size.

In 1800, Spain had ceded the vast trans-Mississippi region called Louisiana to France. Jefferson was profoundly disturbed at this clear evidence that European nations still coveted North American territory. His fears were well grounded, for in October 1802 the Spanish commander at New Orleans, which Spain had retained, once again closed the Mississippi to American commerce. Spain's action raised great consternation both in Washington and the West.

In January 1803, the president sent James Monroe to Paris with instructions to purchase New Orleans and West Florida (which contained Mobile, the only good harbor on the Gulf Coast). Monroe was surprised to find the ruler of France,

Napoleon Bonaparte, ready to sell all of Louisiana (though not West Florida). Faced with a renewed threat of war against England, he also feared American designs on Louisiana, and knew he could not keep American settlers out. In April, the deal was struck. For $15 million, the United States obtained all of Louisiana's 830,000 square miles.

Federalists reacted with alarm, rightly fearing that the states carved from Louisiana would be staunchly Jeffersonian. Moreover, they worried that a rapidly expanding frontier would "decivilize" the entire nation.

National expansion did not stop with Louisiana. In 1810, American adventurers fomented a revolt in Spanish West Florida, and in May 1812, over vigorous Spanish objections, Congress annexed the region. In 1819 Spain ceded East Florida as well. As part of that agreement, the United States also extended its territorial claims to include the Pacific Northwest.

Opening the Trans-Mississippi West

In the summer of 1803, Jefferson dispatched an expedition led by his secretary, Meriwether Lewis, and army officer William Clark to explore the Far Northwest, make contact with the Native Americans there, open the fur trade, and bring back scientific information. For nearly two and a half years, the intrepid explorers, assisted by the Shoshoni woman Sacajawea, made its way across thousands of miles of hostile and unmapped terrain—up the Missouri River, through the Rockies, down the Columbia to the Pacific coast and back again, finally reemerging at St. Louis in September 1806. Lewis and Clark's journey established an American presence in the region, fanned American interest in the trans-Mississippi West, and demonstrated the feasibility of an overland route to the Pacific.

In 1805 and 1806, Lieutenant Zebulon Pike explored the sources of the Mississippi in northern Minnesota and undertook an equally bold venture into the Rockies. In the following decade, the government established a string of military posts from Minnesota to Arkansas, all intended to secure the frontier, promote the fur trade, and support white settlement.

The Jeffersonians' blueprint for an agrarian democracy also guided changes in federal land policy. Federalists had viewed federal land as something to be sold to generate government revenue; Jeffersonians wanted to speed up its settlement. The Land Act of 1801 reduced the minimum required purchase from 640 to 320 acres, established a credit system, and offered discounts for cash sales. Over the next year and a half, settlers, speculators, and land companies bought more than four times as much federal land as during the entire 1790s.

During the 1820s, squatters were allowed to secure title to land simply by occupying it, and land that did not readily sell was offered at discounts or even given away. Though Jeffersonian land policy fostered widespread speculation and contributed to the Panic of 1819, it speeded the privatization of public land.

A NATION OF REGIONS

During the early years of the republic, the vast majority of Americans drew their living from the land. In 1800, fully 83 percent of the labor force was engaged in

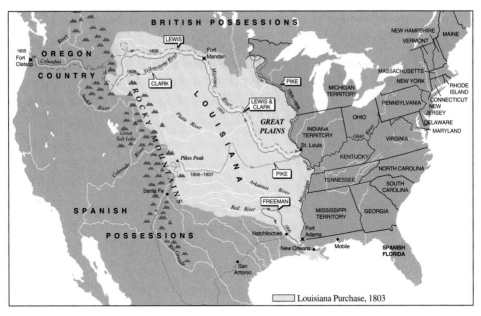

EXPLORING THE TRANS-MISSISSIPPI WEST, 1804–1807 With the nation nearly doubled in size following the Louisiana Purchase, President Jefferson sent out exploring expeditions to map the region and lay claim to it.

agriculture. That figure had hardly changed by 1825, yet people occupied the land in very different ways in different regions of the nation.

The Northeast

In the Northeast, from eastern Pennsylvania and New Jersey to New England, family farms predominated. On New England's poor land, farmers often abandoned crop raising to make greater profits from dairying and livestock. On the richer agricultural lands of New York and Pennsylvania, farmers cultivated their land intensively. Before 1776, the mid-Atlantic landscape had looked unkempt, with wide areas still covered by timber and fallow lands lapsing into brush. Fifty years later, the countryside looked increasingly clean and orderly, its carefully cultivated fields delineated by hedges or stone walls. Farmers along the Hudson River and in southeastern Pennsylvania produced an agricultural surplus, the produce left over after they met their family's needs, and exchanged it in nearby towns for commodities such as tea, sugar, window glass, and tools.

Across much of the rural Northeast, cash still played only a small part in economic exchanges. People, noted an observant Frenchman, "supply their needs in the countryside by direct reciprocal exchanges. The tailor and the bootmaker go and do the work of their calling at the home of the farmer . . . who most frequently provides the raw material for it and pays for the work in goods . . . . They write down what they give and receive on both sides, and at the end of the year they settle a large variety of exchanges with a very small quantity of coin."

Most farms were not large. By 1800, the average farm in the longer-settled areas of New England and the mid-Atlantic states was no more than 100 to 150 acres, down substantially from half a century before, primarily as a result of the continuing division of farm property from fathers to sons. Even in southeastern Pennsylvania, the most productive agricultural region in the entire Northeast, opportunity was declining. Long and continuous cropping had robbed the soil of fertility, forcing farmers to bring more marginal land under cultivation. As that happened, young men delayed marriage longer until they could establish themselves financially.

Whereas the majority of northeasterners made their living from the land, growing numbers also worked as artisans or day laborers in the cities, or toiled in the small-scale manufactories—grain and saw mills, potash works, and iron forges—that dotted the rural landscape. Not for another generation would young men leave the land to work in urban factories.

By 1830, the relentless demands of the Northeast's expanding population for new agricultural land and a wide variety of wood products had significantly transformed the region's once heavily-forested landscape. Iron furnaces dotting the countryside consumed firewood voraciously. The production of potash, turpentine, planking for wooden houses, and fencing caused further depletion. More than anything else, however, it was the demand for heating fuel during the long winter months that made the woodcutter's axe ring. Rural households burned from 20 to 30 cords of firewood annually in highly inefficient open fireplaces. As the region's coastal cities grew and nearby woodlots were exhausted, wood had to be fetched from as far away as 100 miles. As fuel prices rose, wealthier urbanites purchased more efficient Franklin stoves or switched from wood to coal, while the poor shivered.

Though much of the coastal plain had been denuded of trees by the early nineteenth century, vast areas of the northeastern interior remained densely wooded. Here and there, deserted farm lands lapsed into new growth forest, contributing a bit of ecological renewal.

The Urban Northeast

Though most Northeasterners lived on the land or in small towns, increasing numbers dwelt in coastal cities. From 1790 to 1830, the nation's population increased by nearly 230 percent, but "urban" places of more than 2,500 residents grew almost twice as fast. Most of them were in the Northeast. By 1830, New York had well over 100,000 people.

Though gaining rapidly in population, America's urban places remained small in area. In these "walking cities," residents mostly got about on foot and could easily stroll from one side of town to the other. The result was increasing crowding and congestion, and serious problems of public health and safety. Though Philadelphia led the way in street paving, dust and (in rainy seasons) mud were constant presence in urban life. As one urbanite observed, "After a little rain the cart wheels sink literally up to the axle-tree in the filth."

More than mud clogged urban streets in the early nineteenth century. Garbage was dumped there, privies often leached into open drains and, cows, goats, and sheep roamed the streets. Though one urban woman regarded as "disgusting" the packs of scavenging hogs, she acknowledged that without them the streets would soon be choked with filth. Under such conditions, typhoid and dysentery, spread by contaminated water, took a continuous toll on urban populations.

As during the colonial era, the economies of the northeastern cities continued to be dominated by overseas trade. Economic life still centered on the wharves where sailing ships from around the world tied up, and the warehouses where their cargoes were unloaded. Sailors, often speaking strange tongues, added raucous behavior and, at times, an edge of danger to urban life.

Though true industrialization would not hit the cities of the northeast until the second half of the nineteenth century, large-scale manufacturing was already transforming their economies and societies by 1830. The expansion of southern cotton production was turning Philadelphia into a textile manufacturing center, while New York and other urban centers were producing shoes, metal-based equipment, and other manufactured products. As these enterprises expanded, artisan production began to give way to factory-based wage labor.

As this happened, the gap between cities' richer and poorer inhabitants widened. Prosperous merchants, reaping the rewards of overseas trade and investing in budding manufacturing enterprises, rested securely at the top. Below them came an aspiring middle class of artisans, shopkeepers, and professional men whose families shared modestly in the general prosperity. At the bottom spread an underclass of common laborers, dock workers, and the unemployed, their lives a continuous struggle for survival. Though rich and poor had often lived close together in colonial cities, rising land values now forced the lower classes into crowded alleys and tenements, while more prosperous urban dwellers began clustering in fashionable neighborhoods. Their households were now more likely to possess table linens and china bowls, store-bought furniture, and tailor-made clothes, the artifacts of increasing prosperity.

The South

Life was very different in the South, which ran southward from Maryland along the coast and into the interior from Georgia and the Carolinas. In 1800, much of southern agriculture was in disarray. Low prices, worn-out land, war, and the extensive loss of slaves left the Chesapeake tobacco economy in shambles.

Southern planters had experimented with wheat and other grains in hopes of boosting their sagging fortunes, but recovery began in earnest only when they turned to a new staple crop—cotton. They were most successful in cultivating the long-staple variety. Its silky fibers were highly valued and could easily be separated from the cotton's seeds. But it grew only on the sea islands off the coast of Georgia and South Carolina. Though the hardier short-staple variety could be cultivated across much of the South, it clung tenaciously to the plant's sticky, green seeds. A slave could clean no more than a pound of short-staple cotton a day.

Demand for cotton was growing in Great Britain, the center of the Industrial Revolution, and also in the textile mills of New England. Demand and supply began to come together in 1793 when Eli Whitney, a Yankee schoolteacher seeking employment in the South, designed a functioning model of what he called a

Although the cotton gin, invented in 1793, simplified one step of cotton processing, much of the work on a plantation continued to be done by slaves using rudimentary tools. This Benjamin Latrobe sketch is of *An Overseer Doing His Duty.*
(Maryland Historical Society, Baltimore)

"cotton gin." It was merely a box with a roller, worked by a hand crank, that pulled the fibers through a comblike barrier, thus stripping them from the seeds. With it, a laborer could clean up to 50 pounds of short-staple cotton a day.

In 1790, the South had produced only 3,135 bales of cotton; by 1820, output had mushroomed to 334,378 bales. In 1805, cotton accounted for 30 percent of the nation's agricultural exports; by 1820, it exceeded half. Across both the old coastal South and the newly developing states of Alabama, Mississippi, and Tennessee, cotton was becoming king. The growing demand of textile mills in England and the American Northeast provided the stimulus, but a combination of other factors made possible the South's dramatic response: wonderfully productive virgin soil; a long, steamy growing season; ample slave labor; and southern planters' long experience in producing and marketing staple crops.

The swing to cotton was momentous. Not only did it raise the value of prime southern land and open economic opportunity for countless southern whites, but it also breathed new life into slavery. Some of the escalating demand for slave labor was met from overseas. In 1803 alone, Georgia and South Carolina imported 20,000 new slaves, as southern planters and northern merchant suppliers rushed in before the slave trade was scheduled to end in 1807. Much of the demand for agricultural labor, however, was met by the internal slave trade that moved African-Americans from the Chesapeake to the lush cotton fields of the Deep South.

Trans-Appalachia

West of the Appalachian Mountains, a third region was forming as the nineteenth century began. Trans-Appalachia, extending from the mountains to the Mississippi

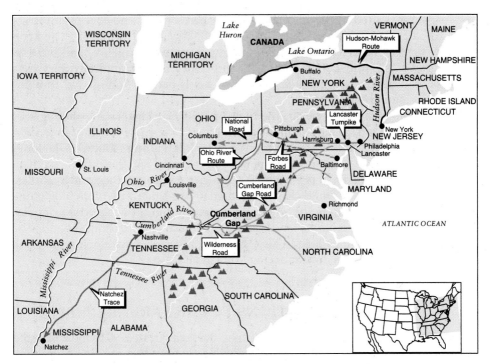

IMPORTANT ROUTES WESTWARD   Through mountain passes and down the Ohio River, white settlers streamed into Trans-Appalachia in the early republic.

River and from the Great Lakes to the Gulf of Mexico, constituted a broad and shifting zone of cultural, economic, and military interaction between Native Americans and European-Americans. In 1790, scarcely 100,000 white settlers lived there. By 1800, their number had swollen to nearly a million; by 1820, fed by people like Mary and James Harrod, over a million more had come. They came by wagon through mountain passes into Kentucky and by flatboat down the Ohio River.

The human tide seemed to grow with each year. Thousands of settlers surged into western New York. "The woods are full of new settlers," wrote an amazed observer near Batavia, New York, in 1805. "Axes are resounding, and the trees literally falling around us as we passed."

Settlers were drawn by the promotions of speculators seeking their fortunes in the sale of western land. Between 1790 and 1820, land companies hawked vast areas of New York, Ohio, and Kentucky to prospective settlers like James and Mary Harrod. Many ventures failed, but countless others proved profitable. Individual settlers shared in the speculative fever, often going deeply into debt to buy extra land to resell when population increased and land prices rose.

North of the Ohio River, settlement followed the grid pattern prescribed in the Land Ordinance of 1785. Mixed, free-labor agriculture took hold, and towns like Columbus and Cincinnati emerged quickly. South of the Ohio people distributed themselves more randomly across the land. In Kentucky and Tennessee, free-labor agriculture was soon challenged by the spread of slavery-based cotton.

As people poured in, they established churches, schools, and colleges. Even so, trans-Appalachia retained a reputation for loneliness as well as for rough and colorful ways. No characters were more famous in popular folklore than western adventurers like Daniel Boone. And nothing revealed more graphically the West's rawness than the eye-gouging, ear-biting, no-holds-barred, "rough and tumble" brawls that regularly erupted.

As settlers came, they began the long process of transforming the region's heavily forested land. In mountainous areas, hillsides were denuded of trees used to brake the wagons during the jolting ride downhill. Farmers followed the long-established practice of cutting a girdle of bark off the trees, and then setting them on fire or leaving them to die in place while planting crops around the decaying hulks. By this method, a family could clear from three to five acres a year for cultivation.

The relentless demands for wood generated by the growing white population—for log cabins and barns, fences and fuel, potash and turpentine—added to the assault on the region's forests. As expanding areas of trans-Appalachia came under the farmers' plows, forests and wildlife gave way.

INDIAN-WHITE RELATIONS IN THE EARLY REPUBLIC

Indian-white relations took a dramatic turn in the years from 1790 to the end of the 1820s. In 1790, vast areas of Trans-Appalachia were still controlled by Native American tribes. North of the Ohio, the Shawnee, Delaware, and Miami formed a western confederacy capable of mustering several thousand warriors. South of the river lived five major tribal groups: the Cherokee, Creek, Choctaw, Chickasaw, and Seminole. By 1830, the balance of power had decisively shifted as white settlers streamed in, bringing their black slaves with them south of the Ohio.

In response, tribal groups devised various strategies of resistance and survival. Many among the Cherokee sought peaceful accommodation. Others, like the Shawnee and the Creek, fought back. Neither strategy was altogether successful, for by 1830 the Indians faced a future of continued acculturation, military defeat, or forced migration west of the Mississippi River.

Less dramatic but no less important, the social and cultural separation of Indians and white Americans sharpened during these years. As late as the 1780s, Indians still walked the streets of New York and Philadelphia, while countless Indians and white Americans interacted regularly as friends or enemies, traders or workers, or marriage partners. By 1830, such contacts were much less common as Indians were confined on reservations or forced west of the Mississippi. During the years from 1790 to 1830, the federal government established policies that would govern Indian-white relations through much of the nineteenth century. Intended in part to promote the eventual assimilation of Native Americans into white society, in fact they speeded the transfer of Indian land to whites and helped set the stage for large scale removal.

The Initial Goals of Indian Policy

With the government's initial "conquest" theory rendered obsolete by the Indians' refusal to regard themselves as a conquered people (see Chapter 7), U.S. officials

INDIAN LAND CESSIONS, 1750–1830 As white settlers streamed across the nation's interior, state and federal governments wrung land cessions from the Indians. By 1830, only the southeastern tribes still controlled significant areas of their ancestral land east of the Mississippi River. *Labels in red* indicate the major Native American groups of the Old Southeast and Old Northwest.

shifted course by recognizing Indian rights to the land they inhabited and declaring that all future land transfers would come through treaty agreements.

Henry Knox, Washington's first secretary of war, laid out the government's new position in 1789. The Indians, he explained, "being the prior occupants of the soil, possess the right of the soil." It should not be taken from them "unless by their free consent, or by the right of conquest in case of just war." Though Knox helped establish a more humane Indian policy, the acquisition of Indian land for white settlement remained the overarching goal.

The new strategy proved effective. Native American leaders frequently ceded land for trade goods, yearly annuity payments, and assurances that there would be no further demands. Reluctant tribal leaders could often could be persuaded to cooperate by warnings about the inevitable spread of white settlement, or more tractable chieftains could be found. Thus vast areas of tribal land throughout Trans-Appalachia passed to white settlers.

Federal policy also attempted to regulate the fur trade, from which both Native Americans and whites benefited. The Indians, in return for their abundant furs, secured the blankets, guns, rum, and ironware that they valued highly, while white traders acquired valuable furs in exchange for inexpensive trade items.

While the fur trade brought handsome profits to private trading companies, it often worked to the Indians' disadvantage. Trade goods frequently transmitted diseases such as measles and smallpox. Indians often became dependent on the trade because it provided the only certain supplies of rum and firearms. As demand for furs and pelts increased, Native Americans frequently overtrapped their hunting grounds and competed with other tribes for new sources of furs further west.

In 1796, trying to reduce fraud and the resultant conflict, Congress created government trading posts, or "factories," where Indians could come for fair treatment. The system lasted until 1822, but it never supplanted private traders.

A third initial objective of federal Indian policy was to civilize and Christianize the Native Americans, then assimilate them. In the Trans-Appalachian West, most settlers regarded Indians as savages to be moved out of white settlement's way. In the East, however, clergymen and government officials displayed greater concern over the Native Americans' well-being. Although the assimilationists often cared deeply about the physical and spiritual fate of Native American people, they showed little sympathy for Indian culture because they insisted that Indians adopt the ways of the white society.

Education and Christianization were the major instruments of assimilationist policy. After the Revolution, Moravians, Quakers, and Baptists sent scores of missionaries to live among the Indians, preach the Gospel, and teach white ways. Among the most selfless were Quaker missionaries who labored with the Iroquois in New York, attempting to inspire conversion and improve the conditions of Iroquois life. In spite of the missionaries' best efforts, however, most Native Americans remained aloof, for the chasm between Christianity and their own religions was wide (see Chapter 1), and the missionaries' denigration of Indian culture was apparent.

Education was the other weapon of the assimilationists. In 1793, Congress appropriated $20,000 to promote literacy, agriculture, and vocational instruction. Federal officials encouraged missionaries to establish schools in which Indian children could learn Christianity, the three R's, and vocational skills. But the vast majority of Indian children never attended. They and their parents feared the alien, threatening environment of the schools.

Strategies of Survival: The Iroquois and the Cherokee

Among the Iroquois, a prophet named Handsome Lake led his people through a religious renewal and cultural revitalization. In 1799, following a series of visions, he preached a combination of Indian and white ways: temperance, peace, land retention, and a new religion combining elements of Christianity and traditional Iroquois belief. His vision offered renewed pride in the midst of the Iroquois's radically changed lives.

Far to the south, the Cherokee followed a different path of accommodation. As the nineteenth century began, the Cherokee still controlled millions of acres in Tennessee, Georgia, and the western Carolinas. Their land base, however, was shrinking. Southern state governments, responding to white demands for Indian land, undercut tribal autonomy. In 1801, Tennessee unilaterally brought Cherokee lands under the authority of state courts. The Cherokee, who had their own system of justice and distrusted the state courts as biased, rejected Tennessee's demands. A group of full-blood leaders called for armed resistance. Others,

Sequoyah, who sat for this portrait in 1838, devised the Cherokee alphabet, which formed the basis for the first written Indian language in North America. (The Newberry Library, Chicago)

including mixed-bloods like John Ross, insisted that accommodation offered the best hope for survival.

After a bitter struggle, the accommodationists won out and began bringing the tribe's scattered villages under a common government, the better to defend their freedom and prevent the further loss of land. In 1808, the Cherokee National Council adopted a written legal code combining elements of American and Indian law, and in July 1827 the Cherokee devised a written constitution patterned after those of nearby states. They also issued a bold declaration that they were an independent nation with full sovereignty over their lands. In 1829, the Cherokee government made it an offense punishable by death for any member of the tribe to transfer land to white ownership without the consent of tribal authorities.

Meanwhile, the process of social and cultural accommodation, encouraged by Cherokee leaders such as Ross and promoted by white missionaries and government agents, went forward. As the Cherokee turned from their traditional hunting, gathering, and farming economy to settled agriculture, many moved from town settlements onto individual farmsteads. Others established sawmills, country stores, and blacksmith shops. In contrast to traditional practices of communal ownership, concepts of private property took hold. The majority of Cherokee kept their crude log cabins and continued to live a hand-to-mouth. But some, especially mixed-bloods who understood how to deal with white authorities, accumulated hundreds of acres of fertile land and scores of black slaves.

Since the mid-eighteenth century, the Cherokee had held a few runaway blacks in slavelike conditions. During the early nineteenth century, Cherokee slavery expanded and became more harsh. By 1820, there were nearly 1,300 black slaves in the Cherokee nation. A Cherokee law of 1824 forbade intermarriage with blacks. The accelerating spread of cotton cultivation increased demand for slave labor among Cherokee, as among whites. As accommodation increased, slave ownership became a mark of social standing.

By 1820, peaceful accommodation had brought clear rewards. Tribal government was stronger and the sense of Cherokee identity was reasonably secure. But success would prove the Cherokee people's undoing. As their self-confidence grew, so did the hostility of whites impatient to grab their land. That hostility would soon erupt in a campaign to drive the Cherokee from their land, as we will discuss in Chapter 13.

Patterns of Armed Resistance: The Shawnee and the Creek

Not all tribes proved so accommodating to white expansion. Facing growing threats to political and cultural survival, the Shawnee and Creek rose in armed resistance. Conflict, smoldering as the century began, burst into open flame during the War of 1812.

In the late 1780s, chieftains like Little Turtle of the Miami and Blue Jacket of the Shawnee had led devastating raids across Indiana, Ohio, and western Pennsylvania, panicking white settlers and openly challenging U.S. control of the Old Northwest. After two federal efforts to quell the uprising failed, President Washington determined to smash the Indians' resistance once and for all. In 1794, a federal army led by the old Revolutionary War general Anthony Wayne won decisively over 2,000 Indians in the Battle of Fallen Timbers. Shortly after, in the Treaty of Greenville, the assembled chiefs ceded the southern two-thirds of Ohio. That action opened the heart of the Old Northwest to white control. Later treaties further reduced the Indians' land base, driving the tribes more tightly in upon each other.

By 1809, two Shawnee leaders, the brothers Tecumseh and Elskwatawa, the latter known to whites as "the Prophet," were traveling among the region's tribes warning of their common dangers and forging an alliance against the invading whites. They established headquarters at an ancient Indian town named Kithtippecanoe in northern Indiana. Soon it became a gathering point for Native Americans from all over the region responding to the messages of cultural pride, land retention, and pan-Indian resistance presented by the Shawnee brothers.

Between 1809 and 1811, Tecumseh carried his message south to the Creek and the Cherokee. His speeches rang with bitterness. "The white race is a wicked race," he said. "Since the days when the white race first came in contact with the red men, there has been a continual series of aggressions. The hunting grounds are fast disappearing, and they are driving the red men farther and farther to the west . . . . The only hope . . . is a war of extermination against the paleface." Though the southern tribes refused to join, by 1811 over 1,000 fighting men gathered at Kithtippecanoe.

Alarmed, the governor of the Indiana Territory, William Henry Harrison, surrounded the Indian stronghold with a force of 1,000 soldiers. After an all-day battle, he burned Kithtippecanoe to the ground. Whites would remember the place, and Harrison's victory there, as the Battle of Tippecanoe.

But the Indians were not yet beaten. Over the next several months, Tecumseh's followers, taking advantage of the recent outbreak of the War of 1812 with England and aided by British troops from Canada, mounted devastating raids across

Indiana and southern Michigan. With the British, they crushed American armies at Detroit and Fort Nelson and attacked Fort Wayne. The tide turned, however, at the Battle of the Thames near Detroit. There Harrison inflicted a grievous defeat on a combined British and Indian force. Among those slain was Tecumseh.

The American victory at the Thames signaled the collapse of Tecumseh's confederacy and an end to Indian resistance in the Old Northwest. Beginning in 1815, American settlers surged once more across Ohio and Indiana and on into Illinois and Michigan. The balance of power in the Old Northwest had decisively shifted.

To the south, the Creek challenged white intruders with similar militancy. As the nineteenth century began, white settlers were pushing onto Creek lands in northwestern Georgia and central Alabama. Although some Creek leaders urged accommodation, others, called Red Sticks, prepared to fight. The embers of this conflict were fanned into flame by an aggressive Tennessee militia commander, Andrew Jackson. Citing Creek atrocities, Jackson in 1808 urged Jefferson to endorse war against the Creek. He got his chance in 1813, when the Red Sticks devastated the frontier and assaulted Fort Mims on the Alabama River, killing up to 500 men, women, and children and eliciting cries for revenge. At the head of 5,000 Tennessee and Kentucky militia, augmented by warriors from other tribes eager to punish their traditional Creek enemies, Jackson attacked. As he moved south, the ferocity of the fighting grew. Davey Crockett, one of Jackson's soldiers, later reported that the militia volunteers shot down the Red Sticks "like dogs." The Indians gave like measure in return.

The climactic battle of the Creek War came in March 1814 at Horseshoe Bend in central Alabama. Over 800 Native Americans died, more than in any other Indian-white battle in history. Jackson followed up his victory with a scorched-earth sweep through the remaining Red Stick towns. With no hope left, Red Eagle, one of the few remaining Red Stick leaders, walked alone into Jackson's camp. "General Jackson," he said, "I am not afraid of you. I fear no man, for I am a Creek warrior. I have nothing to request in behalf of myself; you can kill me if you desire. But I come to beg you to send for the women and children of the war party, who are now starving in the woods . . . . I am now done fighting." Jackson allowed Red Eagle and his followers to go home, but in August 1814 exacted his final revenge by constructing Fort Jackson on the most sacred spot of the Creek nation. Over the following months, he seized 22 million acres, nearly two-thirds of the Creek domain. Before his Indian-fighting days were over, Jackson would gain for the United States, through treaty or conquest, nearly three-fourths of Alabama and Florida, a third of Tennessee, and a fifth of Georgia and Mississippi.

Tecumseh's death had signaled the end of Indian resistance in the North. Jackson's defeat of the Creek at Horseshoe Bend similarly broke the back of Indian defenses in the South.

PERFECTING A DEMOCRATIC SOCIETY

The American people have launched a variety of reform movements aimed at achieving social justice and bringing the conditions of daily life into conformity with democratic ideals. The first of those reform eras occurred in the early nineteenth century.

The Revolutionary Heritage

Reform efforts were inspired by democratic ideals fostered during the Revolution and still fresh in countless Americans' minds. Preeminent among them was the principle of social equality. In part, this meant equality of opportunity, the notion that people should have a chance to rise as far as ability and ambition would carry them. Such an idea appealed to social democrats, for it spoke of setting privilege aside and giving everyone an equal chance. Social conservatives could also embrace it, for it could be used to justify the inequalities that individual effort often produced. Social equality also had a powerful moral dimension, implying an equality of worth among individuals, no matter what their social standing. Though Americans generally accepted differences of wealth and social position, they were less willing to tolerate social pretension or the assumption that such differences made some people better than others.

The Evangelical Impulse

A surge of evangelical religion inspired the reform impulse as well. Throughout our history, religion has been a major force in American public life. This was true in the early republic, when a wave of Protestant enthusiasm known as the Second Great Awakening swept across the American nation. From its beginnings in the 1790s through much of the nineteenth century, and in settings ranging from the Cane Ridge district of backwoods Kentucky to the cities of the Northeast, Americans by the tens of thousands sought personal salvation and social belonging in the shared experience of religious enthusiasm.

Displayed most spectacularly at Methodist and Baptist camp meetings, the revivals crossed boundaries of class and race. Rough-hewn itinerant preachers, black as well as white, many of them theologically untrained but all of them afire with religious conviction, spread the Gospel message, in the process knitting networks of believers closely together.

Though preaching and the salvation of souls were the central purposes of the camp meetings, they ministered to a variety of other human needs. Wrote an observer of a camp meeting near Washington, D.C.: "The illumination of the woods, the novelty of a camp especially to the women and children, the dancing and singing, and the pleasure of a crowd, so tempting to the most fashionable," imparted a powerful sense of social belonging.

Offering a simple message that ordinary folks could readily grasp, the Awakening emphasized the equality of all believers before God, held out the promise of universal salvation, and declared each individual responsible for his or her soul. The power and inclusiveness of that message, driven home by the itinerant preachers, would be registered in the explosive growth in membership and number of Methodist and Baptist churches. By mid-century, they would surpass Presbyterians and Congregationalists as the nation's largest denominations.

The Awakening also called on believers to demonstrate their faith by going into the world to uplift the downtrodden and do good. That religious impulse would provide much of the energy for antebellum reforms such as temperance and abolition (see Chapter 12). Its influence was evident, as well, in earlier efforts at perfecting American society.

Patterns of Wealth and Poverty

In the early republic, as at other times, social ideals jarred against reality. One source of tension was the contrast between democratic equality and class distinctions.

As the nineteenth century began, women continued to hold far less property than men. For the large majority of black slaves, moreover, ownership of anything more than the smallest items was unthinkable. Though the condition of free blacks such as Ben and Phyllis was better, they, too, owned little of the country's wealth.

Among white males, property was most broadly shared in rural areas of the North, where free labor and family-farm agriculture predominated, and least so in the South, where the planters' control of slave labor and the best land gave them the lion's share of the region's wealth. As we have seen, the class structure was sharply drawn in the port cities. The most even distribution of wealth existed on the edges of white settlement in Trans-Appalachia, but there it was an equality of want. As the frontier developed, differences in wealth appeared there as well.

Though America, unlike Europe, contained no permanent, destitute under-class (at least among white citizens), poverty was real and increasing. In the South, it was most evident among poor whites of the backcountry. In the North, port cities held growing numbers of the poor. Boston artisans and shopkeepers who together had owned 20 percent of the city's wealth in 1700 held scarcely half as much in 1800.

Recurring recessions hit the urban poor with particular force, and winter added to hard times as shipping slowed and jobs disappeared. During the winter of 1805, New York's Mayor DeWitt Clinton worried publicly about the fate (and potentially disruptive behavior) of 10,000 impoverished New Yorkers, and asked the state legislature for help. During the winter of 1814–1815, relief agencies assisted nearly one-fifth of the city's population. In rural New England and southeastern Pennsylvania, propertyless men and women roamed the countryside searching for work.

Three other groups were conspicuous among the nation's poor. One consisted of old Revolutionary War veterans like Long Bill Scott, who had found poverty as well as adventure in the war. State and federal governments were peppered with petitions from grizzled veterans describing their misery and seeking relief. Women and children suffered disproportionately from poverty.

For every American who actually suffered poverty's effects, several others lived just beyond its reach. How thin their margin of safety was became clear during the depression of 1819–1822. Triggered by a financial panic created by the unsound practices of hundreds of newly chartered state banks, a deep depression began, generating bankruptcies and sending unemployment soaring. By the early 1820s, the depression was lifting, but it left behind broken fortunes and shattered dreams.

Alleviating Poverty and Distress

Alleviating poverty was one goal of the early reformers. In New York City, private and public authorities established more than 100 charitable and relief agencies to aid unfortunates, from orphans to poor seamen. Across the nation, a "charitable revolution" increased benevolent institutions from 50 in 1790 to nearly 2,000 by 1820. Most of these ventures distinguished between the "worthy poor," who merited help, and the "idle" or "vicious poor," who were deemed to lack character and deserve their fate. No matter that a New York commission in 1823 found only 43 able-bodied adults among the 851 inmates of the city's almshouses.

Municipal authorities and private charities also established orphanages, insane asylums, and hospitals. Most efforts were short-lived, but they attested to the continuing strength of revolutionary and religious ideals, and provided a foundation for the more ambitious reform efforts that would come later.

Women's Lives

Women's lives were not markedly altered during these years. But changes occurred that helped set the stage for later, more dramatic breakthroughs.

Divorce was one area where women achieved greater equality. Securing a divorce was not easy, for most states allowed it only for adultery, and South Carolina did not permit it at all. Moreover, women typically had to present an all-male court with detailed evidence of their husbands' infidelities. (Accusations of a wife's transgressions, by contrast, were more easily proven.) Still, divorce was becoming more available to women. In Massachusetts during the decade after independence, 50 percent more women than men got divorces. Part of the explanation lay in the war's disruptions, which led large numbers of men to desert and thus encouraged their wives to take action. It seems just as certain, however, that women shared the values of individualism and equality, which led them to expect more of marriage.

Changes also occurred in women's education. Given women's special role as Republican Mothers, young women would have to prepare for the responsibilities of motherhood. Judith Sargeant Murray, along with other women, demanded even more of women's education. In the 1790s, Murray criticized parents who "pointed their daughters" exclusively toward marriage and dependence. "They should be enabled to procure for themselves the necessaries of life; independence should be placed within their grasp," Murray wrote. "A woman should reverence herself."

Between 1790 and 1820, a number of female academies were established, mostly in northeastern cities. Most proposals for female education assumed that the curriculum should be less demanding than for boys. Though Benjamin Rush prescribed bookkeeping, reading, geography, singing, and history as proper elements of girls' as well as boys' education, traditionalists were decidedly more conservative. Even the most ardent supporters of female learning, like Murray, insisted that education was primarily important so that women might more effectively function within the domestic sphere.

The evangelical impulse, to which many women were drawn, actually reduced women's roles in the evangelical churches. Women had previously served as religious exhorters and participated in Baptist and Methodist church governance, but now they found themselves marginalized as those denominations strove for social acceptance and adopted older denominations' rigidly gendered rules.

Race, Slavery, and the Limits of Reform

As we saw in Chapter 7, the Revolution initiated the end of slavery in the northern states and challenged it in the Upper South. As the new century began, however,

Female academies in the early republic provided young middle- and upper-class women with the knowledge and skills necessary for their roles as Republican Mothers. (Jacob Marling, *The Crowning of Flora*, 1816/The Chrysler Museum of Art, Norfolk, VA, Gift of Edgar William and Bernice Chrysler Garbisch 80.118.20)

antislavery sentiment and private manumissions were both declining. The gradual abolition of slavery in the North had soothed many consciences, while in the South the spread of cotton cultivation increased the value of slave labor.

Equally important were two slave rebellions that generated alarm among whites. Panic-stricken whites fleeing the successful revolt of black Haitians on the French Caribbean island of Santo Domingo in 1791 spread terror through the South. Immediately southern whites tightened their Black Codes, cut the importation of new slaves from the Caribbean, and weeded out malcontents among their own chattels.

A second shock followed in the summer of 1800, when another rebellion just outside Richmond, Virginia, was nipped in the bud. Gabriel Prosser, a 24-year-old slave, had devised a plan to arm 1,000 slaves for an assault on the city. Prosser and his accomplices were native-born African-Americans who spoke English, worked at skilled jobs, and could articulate ideals of freedom and equality. No whites died in the abortive rebellion, but scores of slaves and free blacks were arrested, and 25 suspects, including Prosser, were hanged at the personal order of Governor James Monroe.

In the early nineteenth century, antislavery appeals all but disappeared from the South. Even religious groups that had once denounced slavery now grew quiet. "A large majority of the [white] people of the southern states," declared a Georgia

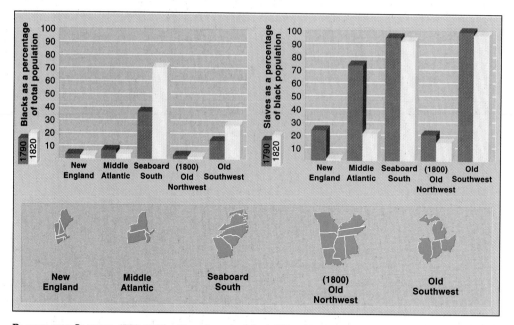

BLACKS AND SLAVERY, 1790–1820   Though regions had differed in the importance of slavery and the number of blacks in their population as the Revolutionary War ended, those differences increased significantly over the next 30 years. Source: U.S. Bureau of the Census.

Congressman in 1806, "do not consider slavery as a crime" or consider it "immoral to hold human flesh in bondage."

In the North, sentiment was increasingly conciliatory toward slave owners. Most of slavery's critics aimed at gradual, private manumission and assumed that freed blacks should be relocated to Africa. The American Colonization Society, founded in 1816, typified these attitudes. Many of its supporters, while detesting slavery, believed that the two races could not coexist together. The Colonization Society never sent many blacks abroad, but it did help allay white anxieties.

During the half century following independence, strong and growing black communities appeared in the port cities, fed by emancipation in the North and the increase of freed men and women in the Upper South. In 1776, approximately 4,000 slaves and a few hundred free blacks had called the major port cities home; 50 years later, more than 30,000 African-Americans did so.

Black men worked as laborers and dock hands, and black women as domestics. The lives of Ben Thompson and Phyllis Sherman revealed African-Americans' eagerness to seek out other people of color in urban settings, as well as their exclusion from white neighborhoods. Family formation was eased because many of the migrants were women, thus correcting a long-standing urban imbalance in the black population. Former slaves often created extended households that included relatives, friends, and boarders. As circumstances allowed, single-family units were formed. By 1820, most blacks in the northern cities lived in autonomous households.

As their numbers grew, African-Americans created organizations independent of white control. Schools educated black children excluded from white academies, mutual aid societies offered help to the down-and-out, and fraternal associations provided fellowship and mutual support.

Black churches quickly emerged as the cornerstones of black community life. Following the Revolution, growing numbers of free blacks joined integrated Methodist and Baptist congregations, drawn by their strongly biblical theology, enthusiastic worship, and antislavery stand. As the numbers of blacks in white congregations grew, however, they found themselves segregated in church galleries, excluded from leadership roles, and even denied communion. In 1794, a small group of black Methodists led by Richard Allen, a slaveborn itinerant preacher, organized the Bethel African-American Methodist Church in Philadelphia. Originally established as an integral part of American Methodism, Allen's congregation moved toward separatism. In 1815, it rejected all oversight by the white Methodist leadership, and a year later it joined a similar congregation in Baltimore to form the African Methodist Episcopal Church—the first independent black denomination in the United States. Though never as numerous as black Methodists, black Baptists established separate churches during the early nineteenth century.

Located in areas of densest black urban settlement, these churches not only nurtured distinctive African-American forms of Christian worship but also offered black people education and burial sites. Equally important, they provided secure places where the basic rituals of family and community life—marriages and birth announcements, funerals and anniversaries—could be celebrated, and where community norms could be enforced. By the 1830s a rich cultural and institutional life had taken root in the black neighborhoods of American cities.

White hostility, however, remained a reality of black urban life. Slavery's abolition might actually have increased white enmity in the North, especially during hard times when free blacks competed for jobs with white laborers. Working-class whites were unnerved as well by growing black competition for cheap housing. Overt violence against free blacks was infrequent during the early decades of the century, but even so, blacks found themselves increasingly segregated.

A FOREIGN POLICY FOR THE NEW NATION

During the early decades of the nineteenth century, the Jeffersonians struggled to fashion a foreign policy appropriate for the expanding agrarian nation. They pursued several goals: protecting American interests on the high seas, clearing the West of foreign troops, and breaking away from dependence on Europe. Those goals were not easily accomplished, yet by the 1820s the Jeffersonians had fashioned a new relationship with Europe, and in the Monroe Doctrine of 1823, they projected a momentous new role for the United States within the Americas as well.

Jeffersonian Principles

Jeffersonian foreign policy was based on the doctrine of "no entangling alliances" with Europe that Washington had articulated in his Farewell Address of 1796. In Jeffersonian minds, England was still the principal enemy, but France also became suspect. Although some Jeffersonians still harbored hopes for French liberty the French Revolution had ended in Napoleon Bonaparte's dictatorial rule, and most were sobered by that outcome.

Second, the Jeffersonians emphasized the importance of overseas commerce for the agrarian nation's well-being. Foreign trade provided both markets for America's agricultural produce and a source of manufactured goods. Federalists had nurtured domestic manufacturing by offering tariff protection against European goods, but Jeffersonians hoped to keep out European-style, large-scale manufacturing. They feared the concentrations of wealth and dependent working classes that manufacturing would bring.

Peace was the Jeffersonians' third goal. Wars to them were objectionable not just because they killed people and destroyed property; they also endangered liberty by enflaming politics, stiffling free speech, swelling public debt, and expanding government power.

While seeking peace, the Jeffersonians understood the dangers lurking throughout the Atlantic world and knew that protecting the nation's interests might require force. Between 1801 and 1805, Jefferson dispatched naval vessels to defend American commerce against the Barbary States (Algiers, Morocco, Tripoli, and Tunis) in North Africa. War, however, they regarded as a policy of last resort. The Jeffersonians' handling of the crisis leading into the War of 1812 illustrates how eagerly, and in this case futilely, they tried to avoid conflict.

Struggling for Neutral Rights

After a brief interlude of peace, European war resumed in 1803. Once again Britain and France seized American shipping. Britain's overwhelming naval superiority made its attacks especially serious. Continuing British refusal to negotiate about impressment, occupation of the Great Lakes fur-trading posts, and reopening the West Indian trade increased Anglo-American tension.

In response to increasing British seizures of American shipping, Congress in April 1806 passed the Non-Importation Act, banning British imports that could be produced domestically or acquired elsewhere. A month later, Britain blockaded the European coast. In retaliation, Napoleon forbade all commerce with the British Isles.

Tension between Britain and the United States reached the breaking point in June 1807, when the British warship *Leopard* stopped the American frigate *Chesapeake* off the Virginia coast and demanded that four crew members be handed over as British deserters. When the American commander refused, protesting that the crew members were Americans, the *Leopard* opened fire, killing 3 men and wounding 18. After the *Chesapeake* limped back into port with the story, cries of outrage rang across the land.

Knowing that the United States was not ready to confront Britain, Jefferson withdrew American ships from the Atlantic. In December 1807, Congress passed the Embargo Act, forbidding all American vessels from sailing for foreign ports. Recommending the embargo was one of Jefferson's most ill-fated decisions.

The embargo had relatively little effect. British shipping actually profited from the withdrawal of American competition, and Britain imported badly needed agricultural produce from Latin America. The embargo's domestic impact, however, was far-reaching. American exports fell 80 percent in a year, and imports dropped by more than half. New England was hardest hit, as ships lay idle and thousands of jobs were lost.

Everywhere, coastal communities openly violated the embargo as attempts to police it failed and English goods were smuggled in across the Canadian border. Throughout the Federalist Northeast, bitterness threatened to escalate into rebellion. The governor of Connecticut, echoing the Virginia and Kentucky Resolutions, warned that if Congress exceeded its authority, the states were duty-bound "to interpose their protecting shield between the rights and liberties of the people and the assumed power of the general government."

In the election of 1808, the Federalists rebounded after nearly a decade's decline. James Madison handily succeeded Jefferson in the presidency, but the Federalist candidate, C. C. Pinckney, got 47 electoral votes. The Federalists also made gains in Congress and recaptured several state legislatures.

Faced with the embargo's ineffectiveness abroad and disastrous consequences at home, Congress repealed it in 1809. Over the next several years, Congress tried more limited trade restrictions to reduce British and French attacks on American shipping. As these failed, war fever mounted.

The War of 1812

The loudest shouts for war came from the West and the South. The election of 1810 brought to Congress a new group of western and southern leaders, firmly Republican in party loyalty but impatient with the administration's bumbling policy and demanding tougher measures. These War Hawks included such future political giants as Henry Clay of Kentucky and John C. Calhoun of South Carolina.

For too long, the War Hawks cried, the United States had tolerated Britain's presence on American soil, encouragement of Indian raids, and attacks on American commerce. They talked freely of expanding north into Canada and south into Spanish Florida. Most of all, these young, nationalistic War Hawks resented British arrogance and America's humiliation. No government, they warned, could last unless it protected its people's interests and upheld the nation's honor. Nor could the Jeffersonian party survive unless it proved able to govern.

Responding to the pressure, President Madison finally asked Congress for a declaration of war on June 1, 1812. Opposition came entirely from the New England and Middle Atlantic states—ironically, the regions British policies affected most adversely—whereas the South and West voted solidly for war. Rarely had sectional alignments been more sharply drawn.

Rarely, either, had American foreign policy proven less effective. Madison decided to abandon economic for military coercion just as the British government, under domestic pressure to seek accommodation, suspended the European blockade. Three days later, unaware of Britain's action (it took weeks for news to cross the Atlantic), the United States declared war.

The war was a strange affair. Britain beat back several American forays into Canada and launched a series of attacks across the Canadian border, along the Gulf Coast, and inland from the Atlantic. The British navy blockaded American coastal waters, while British landing parties launched punishing attacks along the East Coast. On August 14, a British force occupied Washington, burned the Capitol and the president's mansion (soon to be called the White House after being repaired

THE WAR OF 1812   The War of 1812 scarcely touched the lives of most Americans, but areas around the Great Lakes, Lake Champlain, Chesapeake Bay, and the Gulf Coast witnessed significant fighting.

and whitewashed), and sent Madison, Congress, and panic-stricken American troops fleeing into Virginia. Britain, however, did not press its advantage, for it was preoccupied with Napoleon's armies in Europe.

On the American side, emotions ran high among the war's Federalist critics and Republican supporters. In June 1812, particularly bloody riots gripped Baltimore, and several people, including an old Federalist Revolutionary War general, were beaten to death in the streets. In Federalist New England, opposition to the war veered toward outright disloyalty. In December 1814, delegates from the five New England states met at Hartford, Connecticut, to debate proposals for secession. Cooler heads prevailed, but before adjourning, the Hartford Convention asserted the right of a state "to interpose its authority" against "unconstitutional" acts of the government. Now it was New England's turn to play with the nullification fire. As the war dragged on, Federalist support soared in the Northeast, while elsewhere bitterness grew over New England's disloyalty.

Before the war ended, American forces won several impressive victories, among them Commander Oliver Hazard Perry's defeat of the British fleet on Lake Erie in 1813. The most dramatic American triumph was Andrew Jackson's smashing victory in 1815 over an attacking British force at New Orleans. It had nothing to do with the war's outcome, for it occurred after preliminary terms of peace had already been signed.

Increasingly concerned about Europe, the British government offered to begin peace negotiations. Madison eagerly accepted, and on Christmas Eve in 1814, at Ghent, Belgium, the two sides reached agreement. Britain agreed to evacuate the West, but otherwise the treaty ignored all outstanding issues, including impressment, neutral rights, and American access to Canadian fisheries. It merely declared the fighting over, returned prisoners and captured territory, and called for several joint commissions to deal with lingering disputes.

Still, the war left its mark on the American nation. It made Andrew Jackson a national hero and established him as a major political leader. The American people, moreover, regarded the contest as a "Second War of American Independence" that finally secured the nation from outside interference.

Following 1815, the nation turned its energies primarily toward internal development—occupying the continent, building the economy, and reforming its society. At the same time, European nations, preoccupied with their own problems, entered what would prove to be nearly a century free of general war. In the past, European wars had drawn in the American people; in the twentieth century, they would do so again. For the rest of the nineteenth century, however, that fateful link was broken. Finally, European colonialism now shifted to Africa and Asia, and that diverted European attention from the Americas as well.

The United States and the Americas

While disengaging from Europe, the Jeffersonians fashioned new policies for Latin America that would guide the nation's hemispheric relations for years to come. Americans cheered when Spain's Western Hemisphere colonies began their struggle for independence in 1808 and held up the American Revolution as a model. After initial reluctance (primarily for fear of disrupting delicate efforts then under way to secure Florida from Spain), President Monroe sent Congress a message proposing formal recognition of the new Latin American republics. Congress quickly agreed.

Trouble, however, arose in November 1822, when the major European powers talked of helping Spain regain its American empire. Such prospects alarmed Great Britain as well as the United States, and in August 1823 the British foreign secretary broached the idea of Anglo-American cooperation.

Secretary of State John Quincy Adams opposed the idea. John Adams's son had joined the Jeffersonians some years before as part of the continuing exodus from the Federalist party. Filled with the new spirit of postwar nationalism and suspicious of British intentions, Adams urged that the United States not "come in as a cockboat in the wake of the British man-of-war." He called for independent action based on two principles: a sharp separation between the Old World and the New, and U.S. dominance in the Western Hemisphere.

Monroe agreed that the United States should issue its own policy statement. In his annual message of December 1823, he outlined a new Latin American policy. Though known as the Monroe Doctrine, Adams had devised it.

The doctrine asserted four basic principles: (1) the American continents were closed to new European colonization, (2) the political systems of the Americas were separate from those of Europe, (3) the United States would consider as dangerous to its peace and safety any attempts to extend Europe's political influence into the Western Hemisphere, and (4) the United States would neither interfere with existing colonies in the New World nor meddle in Europe's affairs.

Monroe's statement had little effect. The United States possessed neither the economic nor the military power to enforce it. By the end of the nineteenth century, when the nation's might had increased, however, it would become clear what a fateful moment in the history of the Western Hemisphere Monroe's declaration had been.

POLITICS IN TRANSITION

For two decades after Jefferson's election in 1800, Jeffersonian Republicans monopolized the presidency and dominated Congress, while the Federalists gradually collapsed, discredited by charges of wartime disloyalty and tainted by an "aristocratic" image. By the late 1820s, however, the Jeffersonian ascendancy ended, and the Federalist-Jeffersonian party system was in disarray.

As the old gentry-based politics declined, a new, democratic system centered in the states emerged. It was in the states that governments acted decisively on people's lives, claimed their attention, and lured voters to the polls in extraordinary numbers. It was there that vestiges of gentry elitism came under sharpest attack and political equality was most forcefully demanded. And it was in the states that a younger generation of political leaders, uninhibited by their elders' fear of party faction, first learned how to create sophisticated political parties capable of managing a new kind of democratic electoral politics. By the end of the 1820s, America stood on the threshold of a new political era.

Division Among the Jeffersonians

The Jeffersonians' overwhelming political success after the War of 1812 proved their undoing. No single party could contain the nation's swelling diversity of economic and social interests, its increasing sectional differences, or the personal ambitions of a new generation of political leaders.

In response to growing pressures from the West and Northeast, as well as to nationalist sentiment stimulated by the War of 1812, Madison's administration launched a Federalist-like program of national development. In March 1816, Madison signed a bill creating a second Bank of the United States (the first Bank's charter had expired in 1811), intended to stimulate economic expansion and regulate the loose currency-issuing practices of countless state-chartered banks. At Madison's urging, Congress also passed America's first protective tariff.

The administration's program of national economic development, with its perceived threat to states' rights, drew sharp criticism from so-called Old Republicans, southern politicians who regarded themselves as guardians of the Jeffersonian conscience. Over the following decade, the Old Republicans continued to sound the alarm, even as their numbers dwindled.

Madison also recommended construction of a federally subsidized network of roads and canals to speed economic development and enhance national security. He warned that a constitutional amendment should be passed authorizing such action, but Representatives John C. Calhoun and Henry Clay, unwilling to delay, pushed an internal improvements bill through Congress. True to his principles, Madison vetoed the bill. Schemes for federal programs of national development, however, would not die. By the early 1820s, Clay and others, now calling themselves National Republicans, were proposing an even more ambitious program of tariffs and internal improvements, under the name the American System.

The Specter of Sectionalism

Despite the surge of national spirit following the War of 1812, wartime Federalist talk of disunion had revealed just how fragile national unity continued to be. Though Congressional debates over the tariff, internal improvements, and the national bank echoed with sectional tensions, the Missouri crisis of 1819–1820 revealed just how deep-seated sectional rivalries had become.

Ever since 1789, politicians had labored to keep the explosive issue of slavery tucked safely beneath the surface of political life, for they recognized how quickly it could jeopardize national unity. Their fears were borne out in 1819 when Missouri's application for admission to the Union raised anew the question of slavery's expansion. The Northwest Ordinance of 1787 had limited slavery north of the Ohio River while allowing its expansion to the south. But Congress had said nothing about slavery's place in the vast Louisiana territory west of the Mississippi purchased in 1803.

Senator Rufus King of New York demanded that Missouri prohibit slavery before entering the Union. His proposal triggered a fierce debate over Congress's authority to prevent the spread of slavery in the new territories. Southerners were adamant that the trans-Mississippi West remain open to their slave property and were determined to maintain the Senate's equal balance between slave and free states. Already by 1819, the North's more rapidly growing population had given it a 105-to-81 advantage in the House of Representatives. Equality in the Senate offered the only sure protection of southern interests. Northerners, however, vowed to keep the trans-Mississippi West open to free labor, which meant closing it to slavery.

For nearly three months, Congress debated the issues. During much of the time, free blacks listening intently to northern antislavery speeches filled the House gallery. "This momentous question," worried the aged Jefferson, "like a fire-bell in the night, [has] awakened and filled me with terror." Northerners were similarly alarmed. The Missouri question, declared the editor of the New York *Daily*

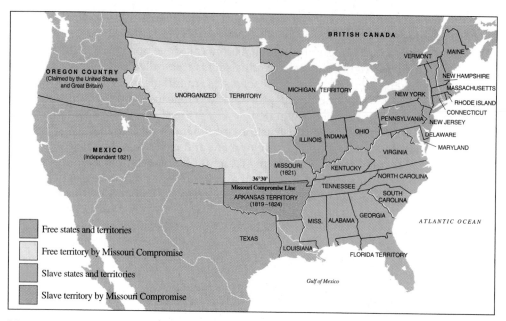

MISSOURI COMPROMISE OF 1820   In the early nineteenth century, politicians struggled to contain the explosive issue of slavery's expansion. In 1820, they did so by balancing Missouri's admission as a slave state with Maine's as a free state, and drawing the Missouri Compromise line separating free territories from slave territories.

Advertiser, "involves not only the future character of our nation, but the future weight and influence of the free states. If now lost—it is lost forever."

In the end, compromise did prevail. Missouri gained admission as a slave state, while Maine came in as a counterbalancing free state, and a line was drawn west from Missouri at latitude 36° 30´ to the Rocky Mountains, dividing the lands that would be open to slavery from those that would not. For the moment, the dangerous issue had been put to rest. It would not be long, however, before the problem of slavery's expansion would set North and South even more violently against each other.

Collapse of the Federalist-Jeffersonian Party System

The final collapse of the gentry-based Federalist-Jeffersonian party system was triggered by the presidential election of 1824. For the first time since 1800, when the "Virginia dynasty" of Jefferson, Madison, and Monroe began, there was competition for the presidency from every major wing of the Jeffersonian party. Of the five candidates, John Quincy Adams of Massachusetts and Henry Clay of Kentucky advocated strong federal programs of economic development. William Crawford of Georgia and Andrew Jackson of Tennessee clung to Jeffersonian principles of limited government, agrarianism, and states' rights. In between stood John C. Calhoun of South Carolina, just beginning his fateful passage from nationalism to sectionalism.

Attracting limited support, Calhoun withdrew to stand for vice president. When none of the presidential candidates received an electoral majority, the election, as in

TIMELINE

1789	1790s	1794	1795	1796
Knox's report on Indian affairs	Second Great Awakening begins	Battle of Fallen Timbers	Treaty of Greenville	Congress establishes Indian Factory System
1800	**1801**	**1802**	**1803**	**1803–1806**
Capital moves to Washington	Thomas Jefferson elected president; Judiciary Act; New Land Act	Judiciary Act repealed	Marbury v. Madison; Louisiana Purchase	Lewis and Clark expedition
1803–1812	**1804**	**1805–1807**	**1806**	**1807**
Napoleonic wars resume; British impress American sailors	Jefferson reelected	Pike explores the West	Non-Importation Act	Embargo Act; Chesapeake-Leopard affair; Congress prohibits slave trade
1808	**1809**	**1811**	**1812**	**1813**
James Madison elected president; Cherokee legal code established	Tecumseh's confederacy formed	Battle of Kithtippecanoe	Madison reelected; West Florida annexed; War declared against Great Britain	Battle of the Thames
1813–1814	**1814**	**1814–1815**	**1815**	**1816**
Creek War	Treaty of Ghent; Battle of Horseshoe Bend	Hartford Convention	Battle of New Orleans; U.S. establishes military posts in trans-Mississippi West	James Monroe elected president; Second Bank of the United States chartered
1819	**1819–1822**	**1820**	**1822**	**1823**
Spain cedes East Florida to United States; McCulloch v. Maryland	Bank panic and depression	Missouri Compromise	Diplomatic recognition of Latin American republics	Monroe Doctrine proclaimed
1824	**1827**			
John Quincy Adams elected president	Cherokee adopt written constitution			

1800, moved into the House of Representatives. There, an alliance of Adams and Clay supporters gave the New Englander the election, even though he had trailed

Jackson in electoral votes, 84 to 99. The Jacksonians' charges of a "corrupt bargain" gained credence when Adams appointed Clay secretary of state.

Adams's ill-fated administration revealed the disarray in American politics. His stirring calls for federal road and canal building, standardization of weights and measures, a national university, and government support for science and the arts quickly fell victim to sectional conflicts, factionalism, and his own scorn for the increasingly democratic politics of the day. For example, Adams declined an invitation to attend the Maryland Agricultural Society's annual cattle show: presidents, he thought, should stand above such efforts to court popular favor. That attitude was political suicide in the 1820s. Within a year, Adams' administration foundered. For the rest of his term, politicians jockeyed for position in the political realignment that was under way.

A New Style of Politics

At the same time, new political energies were stirring in the states, most dramatically evident in the surge of voter participation in state elections. Women, blacks, and Native Americans continued to be excluded, but white men flocked to the polls in unprecedented numbers.

The flood of voters resulted in part from the removal of long-established, property-holding franchise restrictions. The constitutions of new states such as Indiana and Alabama provided for universal white, male suffrage, and older states such as Connecticut and New York abolished property requirements as well.

Equally important were the growing strength of democratic beliefs and the continuing drive of urban artisans and rural farmers for a larger share of political power. Just as significant was the emergence of a postrevolutionary generation of political leaders ready to set aside old worries about "party faction" and eager to make their political mark by perfecting the techniques of mass, democratic politics. Even some of the younger Federalists, learning from the disastrous consequences of their elders' elitism, changed their political style. By the 1820s, successful politicians of every persuasion vied for voters' support through registration drives, party conventions, and the creation of highly partisan newspapers. The antiparty, gentry-dominated politics of a generation before was increasingly a thing of the past.

Initially, the conduct of mass, democratic politics was most evident in state elections, for it was in the states that party techniques could be easily developed. Beginning in 1828, with the first election of Andrew Jackson to the presidency, the techniques of mass politics would be applied to presidential electioneering as well. When that happened, American politics would change forever.

✦✦✦✦✦✦

CONCLUSION

The Passing of an Era

During the first quarter of the nineteenth century, Americans dramatically reshaped the social, geographic, and political dimensions of their republic. The nation's territory more than doubled in size. Safely in control of the federal government, the

Jeffersonians labored to set it on a new and more democratic course. In the process, they fashioned domestic policies designed to promote the country's agrarian expansion and foreign policies that transformed the country's relations with Europe and the Americas. They also sought, less successfully, to reconcile Native American rights with national growth.

By the end of the 1820s, American politics was no longer so clearly divided between a gentry-led politics situated at the seat of the national government and a more democratic form of politics centered in the states. As events would show, Andrew Jackson's election to the presidency in 1828 would represent the emergence of a new, unified system of democratic politics.

All these changes heralded the continued strengthening of a powerful democratic faith built around the values of equality, opportunity, and individual autonomy. Those values would continue to reverberate throughout the coming years.

During the 1820s, the American people turned from an earlier era of founding, when the national government was new and the outcome of their republican experiment seemed still uncertain, to a new era of rapid national development. That transition was dramatized on July 4, 1826, the fiftieth anniversary of American independence, when two of the last remaining revolutionary patriarchs, John Adams and Thomas Jefferson, died within a few hours of each other. "The sterling virtues of the Revolution are silently passing away," mused George McDuffie of South Carolina, "and the period is not distant when there will be no living monument to remind us of those glorious days of trial." As those anniversary celebrations died away, the American people faced the future with both confidence and concern.

Recommended Reading

Jeffersonians Versus Federalists

Drew McCoy, *The Elusive Republic* (1980); Noble Cunningham, *The Process of Government Under Jefferson* (1978); Richard Buel, *Securing the Revolution* (1972); Merrill Peterson, *Thomas Jefferson and the New Nation* (1970); Ralph Ketcham, *James Madison: A Biography* (1990); Robert Shalhope, *John Taylor of Caroline: Pastoral Republican* (1980); Francis Stites, *John Marshall, Defender of the Constitution* (1981); Richard Ellis, *The Jeffersonian Crisis: Courts and Politics in the Young Republic* (1971).

Foreign Policy

Lawrence Kaplan, *"Entangling Alliances With None:" American Foreign Policy in the Age of Jefferson* (1987); J. C. A. Stagg, *Mr. Madison's War* (1983); Ernest May, *The Making of the Monroe Doctrine* (1975); Robert Rutland, *The Presidency of James Madison* (1990); J. Leitch White, Jr., *Britain and the American Frontier, 1783–1815* (1975).

Society and Economy in the Early Republic

Robert Wiebe, *The Opening of American Society: From the Adoption of the Constitution to the Eve of Disunion* (1984); Christopher Clark, *The Roots of Rural Capitalism: Western Massachusetts, 1780–1860* (1990); Stephen Hahn and Jonathan Prude, *The Countryside in the Age of Capitalist Transformation* (1985); Howard Rock et al., *American Artisans: Crafting Social Identity* (1995); Jeanne Boydston, *Home and Work: Housework, Wages, and the Ideology of Labor in the Early Republic* (1990); Jack Larkin, *Reshaping Everyday Life, 1790–1840* (1988); Jeremy Atack and Fred Bateman, *To Their Own Soil: Agriculture in the Antebellum North* (1987); Ronald Schultz, *The Republic of Labor: Philadelphia Artisans and the Politics of Class, 1720–1830* (1989).

Trans-Appalachia and the West

Andrew Cayton, *The Frontier Republic: Ideology and Politics in the Ohio Country, 1780–1825* (1986); Donald Jackson, *Thomas Jefferson and the Stony Mountains: Exploring the West from Monticello* (1981); James Ronda, *Lewis and Clark Among the Indians* (1984); John Mack Faragher, *Daniel Boone: The Life and Legend of an American Pioneer* (1992); Wilma Dunaway, *The First American Frontier: Transition to Capitalism in Southern Appalachia, 1700–1860* (1995); Stephen Aron, *How the West Was Lost: The Transformation of Kentucky from Daniel Boone to Henry Clay* (1998); Craig Friend, ed., *The Buzzell About Kentucky: Settling the Promised Land* (1999).

Native Americans and Indian Policy

Bernard Sheehan, *Seeds of Extinction: Jeffersonian Philanthropy and the American Indian* (1973); Gregory Dowd, *Spirited Resistance: The North American Indian Struggle for Unity, 1745–1815* (1992); William McLoughlin, *Cherokee Renascence in the New Republic* (1986); R. David Edmunds, *Tecumseh and the Quest for Indian Leadership* (1984); Richard White, *The Middle Ground: Indians, Empires, and Republics in the Great Lakes Region, 1650–1815* (1991); Francis Paul Prucha, *American Indian Policy in the Formative Years* (1970).

Perfecting American Society

Paul Conkin, *Cane Ridge: America's Pentecost* (1990); Nathan Hatch, *The Democratization of American Christianity* (1989); Randolph Roth, *The Democratic Dilemma: Religion, Reform, and the Social Order in the Connecticut River Valley of Vermont, 1791–1850* (1987); Robert Cray, Jr., *Paupers and Poor Relief in New York City and Its Rural Environs, 1700–1830* (1988); Conrad Wright, *The Transformation of Charity in Post-Revolutionary New England* (1992); Michael Meranze, *Laboratories of Virtue: Punishment, Revolution, and Authority in Philadelphia, 1760–1835* (1996); Nancy Cott, *The Bonds of Womanhood: "Women's Sphere" in New England, 1780–1835* (1977); Lee Chambers-Schiller, *Liberty, A Better Husband* (1984); Joan Jensen, *Loosening the Bonds: Mid-Atlantic Farm Women, 1750–1850* (1986); Susan Juster, *Disorderly Women: Sexual Politics and Evangelicalism in Revolutionary New England* (1994); Laurel Thatcher Ulrich, *A Midwife's Tale: The Life of Martha Ballard, 1785–1812* (1990).

African-Americans and Slavery

Gary B. Nash, *Forging Freedom: The Formation of Philadelphia's Black Community, 1720–1840* (1988); Douglas Egerton, *Gabriel's Rebellion: The Virginia Slave Conspiracies of 1800 and 1802* (1993); Margaret Creel, *"A Peculiar People:" Slave Religion and Community Culture Among the Gullahs* (1988); John Lofton, *Denmark Vesey's Revolt* (1983); Michael Gomez, *Exchanging our Country Marks: The Transformation of African Identities in the Colonial and Antebellum South* (1998); Sylvia Frey and Betty Wood, *Come Shouting to Zion: African-American Protestantism in the American South and British Caribbean to 1830* (1998); T. Stephen Whitman, *The Price of Freedom: Slavery and Manumission in Baltimore and Early National Maryland* (1997); Joanne Pope Melish, *Disowning Slavery: Gradual Emancipation and "Race" in New England, 1780–1860* (1995).

Political Realignment and the 1820s

Steven Watts, *The Republic Reborn: War and the Making of Liberal America, 1790–1820* (1987); Drew McCoy, *The Last of the Fathers: James Madison and the Republican Legacy* (1989); Ronald Formisano, *The Transformation of Political Culture: Massachusetts Parties, 1790s–1840s* (1983); Robert Remini, *Andrew Jackson and the Course of American Empire, 1767–1821* (1983); Mary Hargreaves, *The Presidency of John Quincy Adams* (1985).

CHAPTER 10

Currents of Change in the Northeast and the Old Northwest

For her first 18 years, Susan Warner was little touched by the economic and social changes that were transforming the country and her own city of New York. Some New Yorkers toiled to make a living by taking in piecework; others responded to unsettling new means of producing goods by joining trade unions to agitate for wages that would enable them to "live as comfortable as others." But Susan was surrounded by luxuries. Much of the year was spent in the family's townhouse in St. Mark's Place. There Susan acquired the social graces and skills appropriate for a girl of her position: dancing, singing, Italian and French lessons, and the etiquette of receiving visitors and making calls. When hot weather made life in New York unpleasant, the Warners escaped to cooler Canaan, where they had a summer house. Like any girl of her social class, Susan realized that marriage, which she confidently expected some time in the future, would bring significant new responsibilities, but not the end of her comfortable life.

It was not marriage and motherhood that disrupted the pattern of Susan's life, but financial disaster. Sheltered as she had been from the far-reaching and unsettling economic and social changes of the early nineteenth century, Susan found that she, too, was at the mercy of forces beyond her control. Her hitherto successful father lost most of his fortune in the Panic of 1837. Like others experiencing a sharp economic reversal, the Warners had to make radical adjustments. The fashionable home in St. Mark's Place and the pleasures of New York gave way to a modest existence on an island in the Hudson River. Susan turned "housekeeper" and learned tasks once relegated to others: sewing and making butter, pudding sauces, and johnny cake.

The change of residence and Susan's attempt to master domestic skills did not halt the family's financial decline. Prized possessions went up for auction. "When at last the men and the confusion were gone," Susan's younger sister, Anna, recalled, "then we woke up to life."

Waking up to life meant facing the necessity of making money. But what could Susan do? True, some women labored as factory operatives, domestics, seamstresses, or schoolteachers, but it was doubtful Susan could even imagine herself in any of these occupations. Her Aunt Fanny, however, had a more congenial suggestion. Knowing that the steam-powered printing press had revolutionized the publishing world and created a mass readership, much of it female, Aunt Fanny told her niece, "Sue, I believe if you would try, you could write a story." "Whether she added 'that . . . would sell,' I am not sure," recalled Anna later, "but of course that was what she meant."

Taking Aunt Fanny's advice, Susan started to write a novel that would sell. She constructed her story around the trials of a young orphan girl, Ellen Montgomery. As Ellen suffered one reverse after another, she learned lessons that allowed her to survive and eventually triumph: piety, self-denial, discipline, and the power of a mother's love. Entitled *The Wide, Wide World,* the novel was accepted for publication only after the mother of the publisher, George Putnam, read it and told her son, "If you never publish another book, you must make *The Wide, Wide World* available for your fellow men." The cautious Putnam printed 750 copies. Much to his surprise, if not to his mother's, 13 editions appeared within two years. *The Wide, Wide World* became the first American novel to sell more than a million copies. It was one of the bestsellers of the century.

Long before she realized the book's success, Susan, always aware of the need to make money, was working on a new story. Drawing on her own experience, Susan described the spiritual and intellectual life of a young girl thrust into poverty after an early life of luxury in New York. It was also a great success.

Though her fame as a writer made Susan Warner unusual, her books' popularity suggested how well they spoke to the concerns and interests of a broad readership. The background of social and financial uncertainty, with its sudden changes of fortune so prominent in several of the novels, captured the reality and fears of a fluid society in the process of transformation. While one French writer was amazed that "in America a three-volume novel is devoted to the history of the moral progress of a girl of thirteen," pious heroines like Ellen Montgomery, who struggled to master their passions and urges toward independence, were shining exemplars of the new norms for middle-class women. Their successful efforts to mold themselves heartened readers who believed that the future of the nation depended on virtuous mothers and who struggled to live up to new ideals. Susan's novels validated their efforts and spoke to the importance of the domestic sphere. "I feel strongly impelled to pour out to you my most heartful thanks," wrote one woman. None of the other leading writers of the day had been able to minister "to the highest and noblest feelings of my nature *so much as yourself.*"

Susan Warner's life and her novels underscore the far-reaching changes that this chapter explores. Between 1820 and 1860, as Warner discovered, economic transformations in the Northeast and the Old Northwest reshaped economic, social, cultural, and political life. Though most Americans still lived in rural settings rather than in factory towns or cities, economic growth and the new industrial mode of production affected them through the creation of new goods, opportunities, and markets. In urban communities and factory towns, the new economic order ushered in new forms of work, new class arrangements, and new forms of social strife.

After discussing the factors that fueled antebellum growth, the chapter turns to the industrial world, where so many of the new patterns of work and life appeared. An investigation of urbanization reveals shifting class arrangements and values as well as rising social and racial tensions. Finally, an examination of rural communities in the East and on the frontier in the Old Northwest highlights the transformation of these two sections of the country. Between 1840 and 1860, industrialization and economic growth increasingly knit them together.

ECONOMIC GROWTH

Between 1820 and 1860, the American economy entered a new and more complex phase. It moved away from reliance on agriculture as the major source of growth and turned toward an industrial and technological future. Amid general national expansion, real per capita output grew an average of 2 percent annually between 1820 and 1840 and slightly less between 1840 and 1860. This doubling of per capita income over a 40-year period suggests that many Americans were enjoying a rising standard of living.

But the economy was also unstable, as the Warners discovered. Periods of boom (1822–1834, mid–1840s–1850s) alternated with periods of bust (1816–1821, 1837–1843). As never before, Americans faced dramatic and recurrent shifts in the availability of jobs and goods and in prices and wages. Particularly at risk were working-class Americans, a third of whom lost their jobs in depression years. And because regional economies were increasingly linked, problems in one area tended to affect conditions in others.

Factors Fueling Economic Development

An abundance of natural resources and an expanding population provided the indispensable raw materials, brawn, and brains for the expansion. Immigration from Europe helped sustain growth because the size of American families was gradually shrinking: In 1800, the average white woman bore seven children, but that number shrank to five by 1860. Foreigners supplied the new workers, new households, and new consumers essential to economic development. They also contributed essential capital and technological ideas.

Improved transportation played a key role. Early in the century, high freight rates had discouraged production for distant markets and the exploitation of resources, and primitive transportation had hindered western settlement. "A coal mine may exist in the United States not more than ten miles from valuable ores of iron and other materials," noted a Senate committee, "and both of them be useless . . . as the price of land carriage is too great to be borne by either." This situation was dramatically transformed during the 1820s and 1830s by canals—especially the 363-mile-long Erie Canal, the last link in a chain of waterways binding New York City to the Northwest.

But even at the height of the canal boom, railroads were also being promoted and built by entrepreneurs and politicians. Great Britain was already showing the benefits of rail transportation. Unlike canals, railroads did not freeze during the winter nor need large amounts of water. They could be built almost anywhere, an advantage that encouraged Baltimore merchants, envious of New York's water link to the Northwest, to begin the Baltimore & Ohio Railroad in 1828.

The first trains jumped their tracks and their sparks set fields ablaze, but such difficulties were quickly overcome. By 1840, there were 3,000 miles of track, mostly in the Northeast. By the end of the 1850s, total mileage soared to 30,000. Like canals, railroads strengthened links between the Old Northwest and the East.

Some historians have used the term *Transportation Revolution* in recognition of the importance of the improved transportation for economic development. Goods,

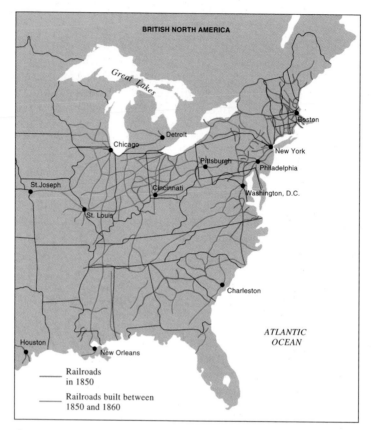

GROWTH OF THE RAILROADS, 1850–1860   This map shows the
tremendous surge of railroad building between 1850 and 1860 and the
ways in which the railroad strengthened the ties between the Northeast
and the Midwest. Notice that the railroad has crossed the Mississippi River.
Because of the transportation revolution, almost the entire area east of the
Mississippi was within a week's journey of New York City by 1860.

people, and information flowed more predictably, rapidly, and cheaply. Canals
and railroads gave farmers, merchants, and manufacturers inexpensive, reliable
access to distant markets and goods, and they encouraged Americans to settle the
frontier. They fostered technological innovations, in turn spurring production.
Eventually, the strong ties that transportation fostered between the Northwest and
the East led to shared political outlooks.

The dramatic rise in railroad construction helped to shape western settlement
and national economic growth after 1839. As the railroads followed—or led—settlers westward, their routes could determine whether a city, a town, or even a
homestead survived. The railroad turned the tiny settlement of Chicago into a
bustling commercial and transportation center.

Transportation links stimulated agricultural expansion and regional specialization. Farmers began to plant larger crops for the market, concentrating on those
most suited to their soil and climate—grain in the Old Northwest and dairy goods
or produce in New England. By 1860, American farmers were producing four to

five times as much wheat, corn, cattle, and hogs as in 1810. American workers had plentiful, cheap food, and farmers had more income to spend on new consumer goods.

Capital and Government Support

These "internal improvements" demanded capital, much of it from European investors but some brought by immigrants. Between 1790 and 1861, over $500 million flowed into the United States from Europe. Europeans financed as much as a third of all canal construction and bought about a quarter of all railroad bonds.

American mercantile capital fueled growth as well. Those merchants who prospered in the half century after the Revolution invested in schemes ranging from canals to textile factories. Many became manufacturers.

Local and state government played their part. States often helped new ventures raise capital by passing laws of incorporation, by awarding tax breaks or monopolies, by underwriting bonds for improvement projects (which increased their investment appeal), and by providing loans for internal improvements. New York, Pennsylvania, Ohio, Indiana, Illinois, and Virginia publicly financed almost 75 percent of the canal systems in their states between 1815 and 1860.

The national government also encouraged economic expansion by cooperating with states on some internal improvements, such as the National Road from Maryland to Illinois. Federal tariff policy shielded American products, and the second U.S. Bank provided the financial stability investors required. So widespread was the enthusiasm for growth that the line separating the public sector from the private often became unclear.

The law also helped to promote aggressive economic growth. Judicial decisions created a new understanding of property rights. Land was increasingly defined as a productive asset for exploitation, not merely subsistence.

Investors and business operators alike wanted to increase predictability in the conduct of business. Contracts lay at the heart of commercial relationships, but contract law hardly existed in 1800. Between 1819 and 1824, major Supreme Court decisions established the basic principle that contracts were binding. In *Dartmouth College* v. *Woodward,* the Court held that a state charter could not be modified unless both parties agreed, and in *Sturges* v. *Crowninshield* it declared unconstitutional a New York law allowing debtors to repudiate debts.

A New Mentality

Economic expansion also depended on intangible factors. When a farmer decided to specialize in apples for the New York market rather than to concentrate on raising food for his family, he was thinking in a new way. So was a merchant who invested in banks that would, in turn, finance a variety of economic enterprises. The entrepreneurial outlook—the *"universal desire,"* as one newspaper editor put it, *"to get forward"*—was shared by millions of Americans. By encouraging investment, new business and agricultural ventures, and land speculation, it played a vital role in antebellum development.

Europeans often recognized another intangible factor when they described Americans as energetic and open to change. As one Frenchman explained in 1834, "All here is circulation, motion, and boiling agitation. Experiment follows experiment; enterprise succeeds to enterprise." Others described an American mechanical "genius." "In Massachusetts and Connecticut, there is not a labourer who had not invented a machine or tool," one Frenchman insisted. He exaggerated (many American innovations drew on British precedents), but every invention did attract scores of imitators.

Mechanically-minded Americans prided themselves on developing efficient tools and machines. The McCormick harvester, the Colt revolver, Goodyear vulcanized rubber products, and the sewing machine—all were developed, refined, and developed further. Such improvements cut labor costs and increased efficiency. By 1840, the average American cotton textile mill was about 10 percent more efficient and 3 percent more profitable than its British counterpart.

Although the shortage of labor in the United States stimulated technological innovations that replaced humans with machines, the rapid spread of education after 1800 also spurred innovation and productivity. By 1840, most whites were literate, and public schools were educating 38.4 percent of white children between the ages of 5 and 19. The belief that education meant economic growth fostered enthusiasm for public education, particularly in the Northeast. The development of the Massachusetts common school illustrates the connections many saw between education and progress.

Although several states had decided to use tax monies for education by 1800, Massachusetts was the first to move toward mass education. In 1827 it mandated that taxes pay the whole cost of the state's public schools, and in 1836 it forbade factory managers to hire children who had not spent 3 of the previous 12 months in school. Still, the Massachusetts school system limped along with run-down school buildings, nonexistent curricula, and students with nothing to do.

The reform of state education for white children began in earnest in 1837, spearheaded by Horace Mann. He and others pressed for graded schools, uniform curricula, and teacher training, and fought the local control that often blocked progress. Mann's success inspired reformers everywhere. For the first time in American history, primary education became the rule for most children outside the South between ages 5 and 19. The expansion of education created a whole new career of schoolteaching, mostly attracting young women.

Mann believed that education promoted inventiveness. Businessmen often agreed. Prominent industrialists in the 1840s were convinced that education produced reliable workers who could handle complex machinery without undue supervision. Manufacturers valued education not merely because of its intellectual content, but also because it encouraged habits necessary for a disciplined and productive work force.

Ambivalence Toward Change

While supporting education as a means to economic growth, many Americans also firmly believed in its social value. They expected the public schools to mold student character and promote "virtuous habits." Rote learning taught discipline and concentration. Schoolbooks reinforced classroom goals. "It is a great sin to be idle," children read in one 1830 text.

The concern with education and character indicates that as much as Americans welcomed economic progress, they also feared its results. The much-heralded improvements in transportation that encouraged trade and emigration, for example, also created anxieties that civilization might disintegrate as people moved far from familiar institutions. Others worried that rapid change undermined the American family and turned children into barbarians. Schools, which taught students to be deferential, obedient, and punctual, could counter the worst by-products of change.

Other signs of cultural uneasiness appeared. Popularizers in the 1830s reinforced Benjamin Franklin's message of hard work. As a publishing revolution lowered costs and speeded up printing, out poured tracts, stories, and self-help manuals touting diligence, punctuality, temperance, and thrift. All these habits probably assisted economic growth. But the success of early nineteenth-century economic ventures frequently depended on the ability to take risks. The emphasis these publicists gave to the safe but stolid virtues suggests their fear of social disintegration. Their books and tracts aimed to counter unsettling effects of change and reinforce middle-class values.

The Advance of Industrialization

Significant economic growth between 1820 and 1860 resulted from a reorganization of production. Before industrialization, individual artisans fashioned goods with hand tools. As late as 1820, Americans made two-thirds of all their clothes at home.

Factory production moved away from this decentralized system of artisan or family-based manufacturing, breaking down the manufacture of an article into discrete steps. Manufacturers farmed out some steps in the manufacturing process to workers in shops and homes, paying them by the piece, and then marketed the finished product. This was the "putting-out" system. But other steps in the production process were consolidated in central shops, and eventually all the steps of production came under one roof, with hand labor gradually giving way to power-driven machinery such as "spinning jennies."

Sometimes, would-be American manufacturers sought the help of British immigrants, who had the experience and know-how that no American yet possessed. Thus in 1789 William Ashley and Moses Brown, Rhode Island merchants, hired 21-year-old Samuel Slater, a former apprentice in an English cotton textile mill, to devise a water-powered, yarn-spinning machine. Slater did that, but he also developed a machine capable of carding, or straightening, the cotton fibers. Within a year, Ashley and Brown's spinning mill had begun operations in Pawtucket, Rhode Island. Its initial work force consisted of nine children, ranging in age from 7 to 12. Ten years later, their number had grown to over 100. As factory workers replaced artisans and home manufacturers, the volume of goods rose, and prices dropped dramatically. The price of a yard of cotton cloth fell from 18 to 2 cents over the 45 years preceding the Civil War.

The transportation improvements that gave access to large markets after 1820 also encouraged the reorganization of production and the use of machinery. The

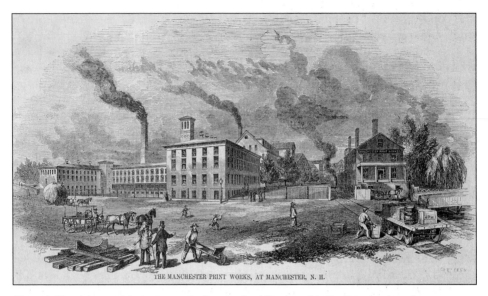

THE MANCHESTER PRINT WORKS, AT MANCHESTER, N. H.

Gleason's Pictorial, one of the many modestly priced publications that the introduction of steam-powered printing presses put within reach of the reading public, pictures the Manchester Print Works in New Hampshire in 1854. Although the smokestacks spewing forth black clouds of smoke hint at the pollution that accompanied the industrial revolution, nineteenth-century viewers most likely were impressed by the dignified mill building and the seeming spacious surroundings. Men appear in the foreground, but over half the workers in this calico factory were female. (Library of Congress)

simple tastes and rural character of the American people suggested the wisdom of manufacturing inexpensive everyday goods like cloth and shoes rather than luxuries for the rich.

Between 1820 and 1860, textile manufacturing became the country's leading industry. Textile mills sprang up across the New England and Middle Atlantic states. These regions had swift-flowing streams to power the mills, capitalists eager to finance ventures, children and women willing to tend machines, and numerous cities and towns with ready markets for cheap textiles. Early mills were small, containing only the machines for carding and spinning. The thread was then put out to home workers, who wove it into cloth. The early mechanization of cloth production supplemented, but did not replace, home manufacture.

Experiments were under way that would further transform the industry. In 1813, Boston merchant Francis Cabot Lowell and mechanic Paul Moody devised a power loom to weave cloth, based on Lowell's study of mechanical looms in England and Scotland. Eventually, they installed their loom in a mill at Waltham, Massachusetts, capitalized at $300,000 by Lowell and his Boston Associates.

The most important innovation of the Waltham operation was Lowell's decision to combine all the steps of cotton cloth production under one roof. The Waltham mill thus differed from mills in Rhode Island and Great Britain, which separated spinning and weaving. Centralizing in one factory could produce mass-market cloth more cheaply and profitably. In 1823, the Boston Associates expanded their operations to Lowell, a renamed village on the Merrimack River. The Lowell system became the prototype for most New England mills. Although most of the South's cotton went to England, an increasing share flowed to northeastern mills.

The cumulative impact of the rise of the textile industry was to supplant the home production of cloth, though some women would continue to spin and weave for their families and hand-loom weavers would survive for another generation. More and more, Americans abandoned earth-colored homespun garments for clothes made of colorful manufactured cloth.

Textile mills and other manufacturing such as shoemaking gave the Northeast an increasingly industrial character. By 1860, fully 71 percent of all manufacturing workers lived in there. Elsewhere, in communities of 200 families or more, power-driven machinery processed wheat, timber, and hides. Although a third of them were clustered in Philadelphia, paper mills were widespread. Ironworking and metalworking stretched from Albany, New York, to Maryland and Cincinnati.

Environmental Consequences

Although canals, railroads, steamboats, and the growth of industry undergirded economic growth, their impact on the environment was far-reaching and often harmful. Steamboats, early railroads, and household stoves, for example, depended on wood for fuel. The eastern forest and its wildlife rapidly disappeared. Better transportation, which encouraged western settlement, also destroyed forest cover as settlers cleared land for crops and cut wood for housing. Sawmills and milldams interfered with the spawning of fish and changed the flow of rivers.

As late as 1840, wood was the main source for the country's energy needs. But the high price of wood and the discovery of anthracite coal in Pennsylvania signaled the beginning of a shift to coal as the major power source. While the East gradually regained some of its forest cover, the heavy use of coal fouled the air. Dams and canals supporting industrial activities contributed to erosion.

Some Americans recognized the environmental consequences of rapid growth and change. "Industrial operations," declared the Vermont fish commissioner in 1857, are "destructive to fish that live or spawn in fresh water." Novelist James Fenimore Cooper had one of his characters in *The Pioneers* condemn those who destroyed nature "without remorse and without shame." Yet most Americans accepted a changing environment as the price of progress.

EARLY MANUFACTURING

Industrialization created a more efficient means of producing more goods at a much lower cost. A Philadelphian's diary reveals some of the new profusion and range of goods. "Went to town principally to see the Exhibition of American Manufactures at the Masonic Hall," he noted in 1833. "More than 700 articles have been sent. Among this great variety, I distinguished the Philadelphia porcelains, beautiful Canton cotton, made at York in this state, soft and capacious blankets, silver plate, cabinet ware, marble mantels, splendid pianos and centre tables, chymical drugs, hardware, saddlery, and the most beautiful black broadcloth I ever saw."

The Impact of Industrialization

Two examples illustrate how industrialization transformed American life in both simple and complex ways. Before the nineteenth century, local printing shops used manual labor to produce relatively expensive books and newspapers. Many literate families had little to read other than a Bible and an almanac.

Between 1830 and 1850, however, the adoption and improvement of British inventions revolutionized the American printing and publishing industries. Like other changes in production, the transformation of publishing involved not only technological innovations, but also managerial and marketing changes. A $2.5 million market in 1830, the book business quintupled by 1850.

As books and magazines dropped in cost and grew in number, far more people could afford them. Susan Warner's literary success became possible. Inexpensive reading material inspired and nourished literacy, and it encouraged a new sort of independence. No longer needing to rely solely on the "better sort" for information, people could form their own views from what they read. At the same time, however, readers everywhere were exposed repeatedly to the mainstream norms expressed in magazines and books. Even pioneer women could study inexpensive ladies' magazines or be inspired by *The Wide, Wide World*. Their husbands could follow political news, prices, and theories about scientific farming; their children learned to read from the moralistic McGuffey readers.

Meanwhile the making of inexpensive timepieces affected the pace and rhythms of American life. Before the 1830s, owning a clock was a luxury, and rigid schedules were impossible. But by mid-century inexpensive mass-produced clocks could be found everywhere, encouraging a more disciplined use of time. Timepieces were essential for the successful operation of railroads and imposed a new rhythm in many workplaces—for some Americans, clocks represented a new form of oppression.

A NEW ENGLAND TEXTILE TOWN

The process of industrialization and its impact on work and the work force are well illustrated by Lowell, the "model" Massachusetts textile town, and Cincinnati, a bustling midwestern industrial center. Though there were similarities in the industrialization of these two communities, there were also significant differences. Lowell reveals the importance of women in the early manufacturing work force. Cincinnati shows that industrialization was often uneven and complex.

Lowell was a new town, planned and built for industry in the 1820s. Planners gave most attention to the shops, mills, and workers' housing, but the bustling town had a charm that prompted visitors to see it as a model factory community. In 1836, Lowell, with 17,000 inhabitants, was the country's most important textile center.

By 1830, women composed nearly 70 percent of the Lowell textile work force. They were the first women to labor outside their homes in large numbers, and also among the first Americans to experience the full impact of the factory system.

Lowell's planners realized the difficulty of persuading men to leave farming for mill work, but saw that they might recruit unmarried women relatively cheaply for a stint. Unlike mill owners farther south, they decided not to depend on child labor. By hiring women who would work only until marriage, they hoped to avoid the depraved and depressed work force so evident in Great Britain. New England factory communities, they hoped, would become models for the world.

Working and Living in a Mill Town

At the age of 15, Mary Paul wrote to her father asking him "to consent to let me go to Lowell if you can." This young woman from Vermont was typical of those drawn to work in Lowell. In 1830, more than 63 percent of Lowell's population was female, and most were between the ages of 15 and 29.

Women workers came from New England's middling rural families and took jobs in the mills for a variety of reasons, but desperate poverty was not one of them. The decline of home manufacture deprived many women, especially daughters in farming families, of their traditional productive role. Mill work offered them a chance for economic independence, and paid better than domestic service. The lure of the "privileges" of the new environment also drew young women to Lowell. Most came to work for a few years, felt free to go home or to school for a few months, and then returned to mill work. Once married—and the majority of women did marry—they left the mill work force forever.

Mill work was regimented and exhausting. Six days a week, the workers began at dawn or even earlier and ended about seven o'clock in the evening, with a half hour for breakfast and lunch.

Within the factory, the organization of space facilitated production. In the basement was the waterwheel, the source of power. Above, successive floors were completely open, each containing the machines necessary for the different steps of cloth making. Elevators moved materials from one floor to another. The operatives' job was to ensure that their machines worked properly, and they themselves were watched by a male overseer. The rooms were noisy, poorly lit, and badly ventilated.

Mill work required that women operatives adapt to both new work and new living situations. Hoping to attract respectable female workers and to ensure their productivity, mill owners built company boardinghouses for them. Headed by female housekeepers, the boardinghouse maintained strict rules and afforded little personal privacy. These living conditions encouraged close ties and a strong sense of community. Strong group norms dictated acceptable behavior, clothing, and speech. Shared leisure activities included lectures, night classes, sewing and literary circles, and church.

Female Responses to Work

Although mill work offered better wages than other occupations open to women, female workers had limited job mobility. Even those in the best female positions could never earn as much as senior male employees. Economic and job discrimination were integral to the early American industrial system.

Job discrimination generally went unquestioned; but the sense of sisterhood, so much a part of the Lowell work experience, supported open protest against a system that workers feared was turning them into dependent wage earners. Lowell women's critique of the new industrial order drew on both the sense of female community and the revolutionary tradition.

Trouble began when hard times hit Lowell in February 1834. Falling prices, poor sales, and rising inventories prompted managers to announce a 15 percent

This anonymous drawing shows a neatly dressed young woman carefully tending her machine. Her task, the most highly skilled in the textile factory, involved pulling warp threads through the harness and weave. A close examination reveals the repetitive nature of her work, but there is no hint of the tedium, noise, or other difficulties of millwork that the young women often mentioned in their letters. (Museum of American Textile History, Lowell, Massachusetts)

wage cut. The mill workers sprang into action, threatening a strike. At one lunchtime gathering, the company agent, hoping to end the protests, fired an apparent ringleader. But, as the agent reported, "she declared that every girl in the room should leave with her," then "made a signal, and . . . they all marched out and few returned the ensuing morning." Strikers roamed the streets appealing to other workers and visited other mills. In all, about a sixth of the work force turned out.

Though this work stoppage was brief and failed to prevent the wage reduction, it demonstrated women workers' concern about the impact of industrialization on the labor force. Pointing out that they were daughters of free men, strikers sought to link their protest to their fathers' and grandfathers' efforts to throw off the bonds of British oppression during the Revolution.

During the 1830s, wage cuts, long hours, increased work loads, and production speedups mandated by owners' desires to protect profits constantly reminded Lowell women and other textile workers of the possibility of "wage slavery." In Dover, New Hampshire, 800 women formed a union in 1834 to protest wage cuts. In the 1840s, women in several New England states agitated for the ten-hour day, and petitions from Lowell prompted the Massachusetts legislature to hold the first official hearings on industrial working conditions.

The Changing Character of the Work Force

Most protest efforts had limited success. The short tenure of most women mill workers prevented permanent labor organizations, and owners could easily replace strikers. Increasingly, owners found that they could do without the Yankee women altogether. The waves of immigration that deposited so many penniless foreigners in northeastern cities in the 1840s and 1850s created a new pool of labor, desperate for jobs and willing to work for less than New England farm girls. By 1860, Irish men composed nearly half the workers.

Massive immigration had a far-reaching effect on antebellum life. Immigration, of course, had been a constant part of the country's experience from the early seventeenth century. But what had been a trickle in the 1820s—some 128,502 foreigners came to U.S. shores during that decade—became a torrent in the 1850s, with more than 2.8 million migrants to the United States. The majority of the newcomers were young European men of working age.

This vast movement of people, which continued throughout the nineteenth century, resulted from dramatic changes in European life. Between 1750 and 1845, Europe experienced a population explosion. New farming and industrial practices undermined or destroyed traditional means of livelihood, and agricultural disaster uprooted the Irish from their homeland. In 1845, a terrible blight attacked and destroyed the potato crop, on which Irish peasants depended for their basic food supply. Years of devastating famine followed. One million Irish starved to death between 1841 and 1851; another million and a half emigrated. Irish were the most numerous of all newcomers to America in the two decades preceding the Civil War, usually arriving penniless and with only their unskilled labor to sell.

German immigrants, the second-largest group of immigrants during this period (1,361,506 arrived between 1840 and 1859), were not driven to the United States by the same kind of desperate circumstances as the Irish. Some even arrived with sufficient resources to go west and buy land. Others had the training to join the urban working class as shoemakers, cabinetmakers, and tailors.

The arrival of so many non-British newcomers made American society more diverse. Because over half of the Irish and German immigrants were Roman Catholics, religious differences acerbated economic and ethnic tensions.

The Irish had a far-reaching impact on Lowell. As the ethnic makeup of the work force changed in the city, so did its gender composition. More men came to work in the mill, making Yankee women expendable.

It was easy for New England women to blame the Irish for declining pay and deteriorating conditions. Gender no longer unified women workers, not only because there were more men in the mills but also because New England women had little in common with Irish mill girls, who started working as early as age 13 to earn money to help keep their families alive. Segregated living conditions further divided the work force and undermined the likelihood of united worker actions in the 1850s. A permanent work force, once the owners' nightmare, became a reality by 1860. Lowell's reputation as a model factory town faded away.

Factories on the Frontier

Cincinnati, a small Ohio River settlement of 2,540 in 1810, grew to be the country's third-largest industrial center by 1840. With a population of 40,382, it had a variety of industries at different stages of development. Manufacturers who turned out machines, machine parts, hardware, and furniture quickly mechanized. Other trades, like carriage making and cigar making, moved far more slowly toward mechanization. Artisans still labored in small shops, using traditional hand tools. The new and the old coexisted in Cincinnati, as in most manufacturing towns.

No uniform work experience prevailed in Cincinnati. Some craftsmen continued to use a wide array of skills as they produced goods in time-honored ways. Others used their skills in new factories, focusing on more specialized tasks. Though in the long run machines threatened to replace them, skilled factory workers often had reason in the short run to praise the factory's opportunities. Less fortunate was the new class of unskilled factory laborers who performed limited operations at their jobs, with or without machinery. Having no skills to sell, they were easily replaced, and during business slowdowns were casually dismissed.

Cincinnati's working women had a different work experience. A majority of black women labored as washerwomen, cooks, or maids. Many white women earned money as "outworkers" for the city's growing ready-to-wear clothing industry. Manufacturers purchased the cloth, cut it into basic patterns, and then contracted out the finishing work to women in small workshops or at home. Like many other urban women, Cincinnati women sought such employment because they could not count on their husbands or fathers to bring in enough to support the family and because outwork allowed them to earn money at home. Middle-class domestic ideology prescribed that home, not the workplace, was the proper sphere for women. Many working men supported these views because they feared female labor would undercut their wages and destroy order in the family.

Paid by the piece, female outworkers were among the most exploited of Cincinnati's workers. Long days of sewing in darkened rooms not only often failed to bring an adequate financial reward, but also led to ruined eyes and curved spines. The introduction of sewing machines in the 1850s made stitching easier, increasing both the pool of potential workers and the volume of work expected.

Cincinnati employers claimed that the new industrial order offered great opportunities to most of the city's male citizens. Manufacturing work encouraged the "manly virtues" necessary for the "republican citizen." Not all Cincinnati workers agreed. The workingman's plight, as Cincinnati labor leaders analyzed it, stemmed from his loss of independence. A new kind of worker had emerged, having only his raw labor to sell and facing a lifetime of "wage slavery." Like workers in Lowell and other manufacturing communities, Cincinnati's laborers rose up against their bosses in the decades before the Civil War.

Workers also resented attempts to control their lives. In the new factories, owners insisted on a steady pace of work and uninterrupted production. Artisans accustomed to working in spurts, stopping for a few moments of conversation or a drink, disliked the new routines. Those who took a dram or two at work got fired. Even outside the workplace, manufacturers attacked Cincinnati's working-class culture. Middle-class crusades to abolish "nonproductive" volunteer fire companies and saloons suggested how little equality the Cincinnati worker enjoyed in an industrializing society.

The fact that workers' wages in Cincinnati, as in other cities, lagged behind food and housing costs compounded discontent. The working class sensed it was losing ground just as the city's rich were visibly growing richer. In 1817, the top tenth of the city's taxpayers owned over half the wealth, whereas the bottom half possessed 10 percent. In 1860, the share of the top tenth had increased to two-thirds and the bottom half's share had shrunk to 2.4 percent.

In 1848, an unknown photographer took this picture of Cincinnati. The prominence of steamboats in the picture suggests the role location and improvements in transportation played in the city's growth. Although the countryside is visible in the background, the rows of substantial commercial and industrial buildings make Cincinnati's status as a bustling urban center clear. (Public Library of Cincinnati and Hamilton County, Ohio)

In the decades before the Civil War, Cincinnati workers formed unions, struck for fair wages, and rallied for the ten-hour day. Like the Lowell mill girls, they cloaked their protest with the mantle of the Revolution. Because the republic depended on a free and independent citizenry, male workers warned that their bosses' policies undermined the republic itself.

Only in the early 1850s did Cincinnati workers begin to suspect that their employers formed a distinct class of parasitic "nonproducers." Although most strikes still revolved around familiar issues of better hours and wages, signs appeared of the more hostile labor relations that would emerge after the Civil War.

As elsewhere, skilled workers were in the forefront of Cincinnati's labor protest and union activities. But they won only temporary victories. Depression and bad times always hurt labor organizations and canceled employers' concessions. Furthermore, Cincinnati workers did not readily unite, for the uneven pace of industrialization meant that they, unlike the Lowell mill women, had no common working experience. Growing cultural, religious, and ethnic diversity compounded workplace differences. By 1850, almost half the people in the city were foreign-born (mostly German), whereas only 22 percent had been in 1825. Ethnic and religious tensions simmered. Immigrants faced limited job choices and cultural suspicions, which exploded in Cincinnati in the spring of 1855. Americans attacked barricades in German neighborhoods, shouting death threats. Their wrath visited the Irish as well. Ethnic, cultural, and social differences often drove workers apart, enabling businesses to maximize productivity and profits.

URBAN LIFE

Americans experienced the impact of economic growth most dramatically in the cities. In the four decades before the Civil War, urbanization in the United States rose faster than ever before or since. In 1820, about 9 percent of the American people lived in cities (defined as areas with a population of 2,500 or more). Forty years later, almost 20 percent of them did. Older cities like Philadelphia and New York mushroomed, while new cities like Cincinnati, Columbus, and Chicago sprang up "as if by enchantment." Urban growth was most dramatic in the East. By 1860, more than a third of the people living in the Northeast were urban residents, compared with only 14 percent of westerners and 7 percent of southerners.

The Process of Urbanization

Three distinct types of cities—commercial centers, mill towns, and transportation hubs—emerged during these years of rapid economic growth. Although a lack of water power limited industrial development, commercial seaports like Boston, Philadelphia, and Baltimore expanded steadily and developed diversified manufacturing to supplement the older functions of importing, exporting, and providing services and credit. New York replaced Philadelphia as the country's largest and most important city. The completion of the Erie Canal allowed New York merchants to gain control of much of the trade with the West. By 1840, they had also seized the largest share of the country's import and export trade.

Access to water power spurred the development of a second kind of city, exemplified by Lowell, Massachusetts; Trenton, New Jersey; and Wilmington, Delaware. Situated inland along the waterfalls and rapids that provided the power to run their mills, these cities burgeoned.

A third type of city arose between 1820 and 1840, west of the Appalachian Mountains, where one-quarter of the nation's urban growth occurred. Louisville, Cleveland, and St. Louis were typical of cities that had served as transportation and distribution centers from the earliest days of frontier settlement. In the 1850s, Chicago's most significant business was selling lumber to prairie farmers.

The growing number of urban dwellers generated economic growth. They created new markets for farmers and for manufacturers of shoes and clothing, furniture and carriages, cast-iron stoves and pipes.

Until 1840, the people eagerly crowding into cities came mostly from the American countryside. Then ships began to spill their human cargoes into seaboard cities. Immigrants who could afford it, many of them Germans or Scandinavians, left the crowded port cities for the interior. The penniless had to look for work in eastern cities. By 1860, fully 20 percent of the people living in the Northeast were immigrants; in some of the largest cities, they and their children comprised more than half the population. The Irish were the largest foreign group in the Northeast.

Philadelphia reveals the character, rhythms, rewards, and tensions of antebellum urban life. The city was second only to New York in population. A bustling mercantile city, Philadelphia's shops churned out textiles, metals, and a host of other products. Speculators found the grid pattern the cheapest and most efficient way to divide land for development.

Not all citizens enjoyed the benefits of urban life. Overwhelmed by rapid growth, city governments provided few of the services we consider essential today, and usually only to those who paid for them. Poor families devoted many hours to securing necessities, including water. The ability to pay for services determined not only comfort, but health.

Class Structure in the Cities

The drastic differences in the quality of urban life reflected social fluidity and the growing economic inequality that characterized Philadelphia and other American cities. The first half of the nineteenth century witnessed a dramatic rise in the concentration of wealth in the United States. The pattern was most extreme in cities.

Because Americans believed that capitalists deserved most of their profits, the well-to-do profited handsomely from this period of growth. The merchants, brokers, lawyers, bankers, and manufacturers of Philadelphia's upper class gained control of more and more of the city's wealth. By the late 1840s, the wealthiest 4 percent of the population held about two-thirds of the wealth. This widening gap between the upper class and the working class did not translate into mass suffering because more wealth was being generated. But the growing inequality hardened class lines and contributed to the labor protests of the antebellum period.

Between 1820 and 1860, a new working and middle class took shape in Philadelphia and elsewhere. As preindustrial ways of producing goods yielded to factory production and as the pace of economic activity quickened, some former artisans and skilled workers seized newly created opportunities. Perhaps 10 to 15 percent of Philadelphians in each decade before the Civil War improved their occupations and places of residence. Increasingly, membership in this middle class meant having a nonmanual occupation and a special place of work suited to activities that demanded brainpower rather than brawn. But downward occupational mobility increased. Former artisans or journeymen became part of a new class of permanent manual workers, dependent on wages. Fed by waves of immigrants, the lower class grew at an accelerating rate. The percentage of unskilled wage earners living in poverty or on its brink increased from 17 to 24 percent between 1820 and 1860, while the proportion of craftsmen, once the heart of the laboring class, shrank from 56 to 47 percent.

The Urban Working Class

As with so much else in urban life, housing patterns reflected social and economic divisions. The poorest rented quarters in crowded, flimsy shacks and two-room houses, and because they moved often, it was difficult for them to create close-knit neighborhoods and support networks. Substantial houses fronting the main streets concealed the worst urban housing, in back alleys or even in backyards.

Slums were not just abodes of poverty; they represented the transformation of working-class family life. Men could no longer be sure of supporting their wives and children; even when they were employed, they felt that they had lost much of their authority and power in the family. Some found their wives no longer subservient or seemingly careless with their hard-earned money. One woman angered her husband by failing to give a clear account of what she had done with the grocery money. "He said if she did not give him a full account . . . he would kill her or something like that," a well-meaning middle-class observer noted. This particular squabble over grocery money ended in murder. Although this was an extreme case, family violence that spilled out onto the streets was not uncommon in working-class quarters.

Middle-Class Life and Ideals

Members of the new middle class profited from the dramatic increase in wealth in antebellum America. They lived in pleasantly furnished houses, enjoying more peace, more privacy, and more comfort. Franklin stoves gave warmth in winter, and iron cookstoves made cooking easier. New lamps made it possible to read after dark. Bathing stands and bowls ensured higher standards of cleanliness. Genteel behavior, proper dress, and an elegantly furnished parlor all identified one as middle class.

New expectations about male and female roles, prompted partly by economic change, also shaped middle-class life. In the seventeenth and eighteenth centuries, the labor of men and women, adults and children, had all been necessary for the family's economic welfare. But in the nineteenth century improved transportation, new products, and the rise of factory production and large businesses changed the family economy. Falling prices for processed and manufactured goods like soap, candles, clothing, and even bread made it unnecessary for women (except those on the frontier) to continue making these items at home.

As men increasingly involved themselves in a money economy, whether through commerce or market farming, women's and children's contributions to the family welfare became relatively less significant. Even the rhythm of their lives, oriented to housework rather than the demands of the clock, separated them from their husbands' bustling commercial world. By 1820, it was generally being said that the sexes occupied separate spheres: Men's sphere was the public world, and their responsibility was to provide financial support—a responsibility that, as Susan Warner's family experience suggested, was a heavy one in a changing economy. Women's sphere was the home, where they were housekeepers.

The role of housekeeper had both pleasure and frustration built into it. Susan Warner's celebration of domestic life in her novels suggested the satisfactions of a cozy household. Yet it was sometimes impossible to achieve the new standards of cleanliness, order, and beauty, especially while they were meeting their new, more elevated responsibilities as moral and cultural guardians—not only of their own families, but also of society.

Antebellum clergymen and publicists built on arguments, first advanced in revolutionary days, that women were innately pious, virtuous, unselfish, and modest—all characteristics that men presumably lacked. By training future citizens and workers to be obedient, moral, patriotic, and hardworking, mothers ensured the welfare of the republic. Just as important, they preserved important values in a time of rapid change.

This view of women had important consequences for female life. Because women thought they had a unique nature and because their husbands spent much of their time working away from home, friendship with other women often became central. Women felt that they shared more with one another than with men, even their husbands. Similar social experiences made female friendships a source of comfort, security, and happiness.

Although the concept of domesticity seemed to confine women to the home and to emphasize the private nature of family life, it actually prompted women to take on activities in the outside world. If women were the guardians of morality, why should they not carry out their tasks in the public sphere? "WOMAN," said Sarah Hale, editor of the popular magazine *Godey's Lady's Book*, was "God's appointed agent of *morality*." Such reasoning lay behind the tremendous growth of voluntary female associations in the early nineteenth century. Initially, most involved religious and charitable activities. But in the 1830s, as we shall see in Chapter 12, women added specific moral concerns like the abolition of slavery to their missionary and benevolent efforts. As these women took on more active and controversial tasks, they often clashed with men and with social conventions about "woman's place."

Domesticity described norms, not the actual conduct of middle-class women. Obviously, not all women were pious, disinterested, selfless, virtuous, cheerful, and loving. But these ideas, expressed so movingly by novelists like Susan Warner, influenced how women thought of themselves and promoted "female" behavior by encouraging particular choices. Domestic ideals helped many women make psychological sense of their lives. The new norms, effectively spread by the publishing industry, influenced rural and urban working women. The insistence on marriage and service to family discouraged married women from entering the work force. Those who had to work often bore a burden of guilt. Many took in piecework which paid poorly so that they could stay home. Though the new feminine ideal may have seemed noble to middle-class women in cities and towns, it created difficult tensions in the lives of working-class women.

As family roles were reformulated, a new view of childhood emerged. Middle-class children were no longer expected to contribute economically to the family. Middle-class parents now came to see childhood as a special stage of life, a period of preparation for adulthood. In a child's early years, mothers were to impart important values, including the necessity of behaving in accordance with gender prescriptions. Harsh punishments lost favor. Schooling also prepared a child for the future, and urban middle-class parents supported the public school movement.

Children's fiction, which poured off the printing presses, also socialized children. Stories pictured modest youngsters happily making the correct choices of playmates and activities, obeying their parents, and being dutiful, religious, loving, and industrious.

New notions of family life supported the widespread use of contraception for the first time in American history. Because children required so much loving attention and needed careful preparation for adulthood, many parents desired smaller families. The declining birthrate was evident first in the Northeast, particularly in cities and among the middle class. Abortion, which was legal in many states until 1860, terminated perhaps as many as a third of all pregnancies. Other birth control methods included coitus interruptus and abstinence. The success of these methods for family limitation suggests that many men and women adopted the new definitions of the female sex as naturally affectionate but passionless and sexually restrained.

Mounting Urban Tensions

The social and economic changes transforming U.S. cities in the half century before the Civil War produced unprecedented urban violence. American cities were slow to establish modern police forces. Traditional constables and night watches did not try to stop crimes, discover offenses, or "prevent a tumult."

Racial tensions contributed to Philadelphia's unsavory riot in August 1834. White-against-black rioting lasted several days. At least one black was killed, and numerous others were injured. As one shocked eyewitness reported, "The mob exhibited more than fiendish brutality, beating and mutilating some of the old, confiding and unoffending blacks with a savageness surpassing anything we could have believed men capable of."

This racial explanation does not reveal the range of causes underlying the rampage of violence and destruction. The rioters were young and generally of low social standing. Many were Irish; some had criminal records. A number of those arrested, however, were from a "class of mechanics of whom better things are expected," and middle-class onlookers egged the mob on. The rioters revealed that in the event of an "attack by the city police, they confidently counted" on the assistance of these bystanders.

The mob's composition hints at some of the reasons for participation. Many of the rioters were newly-arrived Irish immigrants at the bottom of the economic ladder who competed with blacks for jobs. Subsequent violence against blacks suggested that economic rivalry was an important component of the riot.

If blacks threatened the dream of advancement of some whites, this was not quite the complaint of the skilled workers. These men were more likely to have felt themselves injured by a changing economic system that undermined the small-scale mode of production. Dreams of a better life seemed increasingly illusory as declining wages pushed them closer to unskilled workers than to the middle class. Like other rioters, they were living in one of the poorest and most crowded parts of the city. Their immediate scapegoats were blacks, but the intangible villain was the economic system itself.

Urban expansion also figured as a factor in the racial violence. Most of the rioters lived either in the riot area or nearby. Racial tensions generated by squalid surroundings and social proximity go far to explain the outbreak of violence. The same area would later become the scene of race riots and election trouble and became infamous for harboring criminals and juvenile gangs. The absence of middle- or upper-class participants did not mean that these groups were untroubled during times of growth and change, but their material circumstances cushioned them from some of the more unsettling forces.

Philadelphia, like other eastern cities, was beginning to create a police force, but only continued disorder would convince residents and city officials there (and in other large cities) to support an expanded, quasi-military, preventive, and uniformed police force. By 1855, most sizable eastern cities had such forces.

Finally, the character of the free black community itself was a factor in producing those gruesome August events. Not only was the community large and visible, but it also had created its own institutions and its own elite. The mob vented its rage against black affluence by targeting the solid brick houses of middle-class blacks and robbing them of silver and watches. Black wealth threatened the notion of the proper social order held by many white Philadelphians and seemed unspeakable when whites could not afford life's basic necessities or lacked jobs.

The Black Underclass

Despite the emergence of small African-American elites, most blacks failed to benefit from economic expansion and industrial progress. Black men, often with little or no education, held transient and frequently dangerous jobs. Black women, many of whom headed their households because men were away working or had died, held jobs before and after marriage. In Philadelphia in 1849, almost half of the black women washed clothes for a living. Others took boarders into their homes, adding to their domestic chores.

Northern whites, like southerners, believed in black inferiority and depravity and feared black competition for jobs and resources. Although northern states had passed gradual abolition acts between 1780 and 1803 and the national government had banned slaves from the Northwest Territory, nowhere did any government extend equal rights and citizenship or economic opportunities to free blacks. In the 1830s, black men in most northern states began losing the right to vote, and by 1840 fully 93 percent of the northern free black population lived in states where law or custom kept them from the polls. In five northern states, blacks could not testify against whites or serve on juries. In most states, the two races were thoroughly segregated in railway cars, steamboats, hospitals, prisons, and other asylums. In some states, they could enter public buildings only as personal servants of white men. They sat in "Negro pews" in churches and took communion only after whites had left the church.

As the Philadelphia riot revealed, whites were driving blacks from their jobs. In 1839, *The Colored American* blamed the Irish. "These impoverished and destitute beings . . . are crowding themselves into every place of business . . . and driving the poor colored American citizen out." Increasingly after 1837, these "white niggers" became coachmen, stevedores, barbers, cooks, house servants—all occupations blacks had once held.

Educational opportunities for blacks were also severely limited. Only a few school systems admitted blacks, in separate facilities. In 1833 when Prudence Crandall, a Quaker schoolmistress in Canterbury, Connecticut, tried to admit "young colored ladies and Misses" to her private school, townspeople used intimidation and violence to block her. Eventually she was arrested, and after two trials—in which free blacks were declared to have no citizenship rights—she finally gave up and moved to Illinois.

Crandall likely did not find the Old Northwest much more hospitable. The fast-growing western states were intensely committed to white supremacy and black exclusion. In 1829 in Cincinnati, where evidence of freedom papers and $500 bond were demanded of blacks who wished to live in the city, white rioters ran nearly 2,000 blacks out of town.

As an Indiana newspaper editor observed in 1854, informal customs made life dangerous for blacks. An Indiana senator proclaimed in 1850 that a black could "never live together equally" with whites because "the same power that has given him a black skin, with less weight or volume of brain, has given us a white skin with greater volume of brain and intellect." Abraham Lincoln in neighboring Illinois, soon to be a nationally prominent politician, would not have disagreed.

RURAL COMMUNITIES

Although the percentage of families involved in farming fell from 72 to 60 percent between 1820 and 1860, agriculture was still the country's most significant economic activity and the source of most of its exports. The small family farm still characterized eastern and western agriculture.

Agriculture changed in the antebellum period, however. Vast new tracts of land came under cultivation in the West. Railroads, canals, and better roads drew rural Americans into a wider world. Some crops were shipped to regional markets; others, like grain, hides, and pork, stimulated industrial processing. Manufactured goods, ranging from cloth to better tools, flowed to farm families. Like city dwellers, farmers and their families read books, magazines, and papers that exposed them to new ideas. Commercial farming encouraged different ways of thinking and acting and lessened the isolation that was so typical before 1820.

Farming in the East

Antebellum economic changes created new rural patterns in the Northeast. After 1830, farmers gradually abandoned marginal land, forest returned, and the New England hill country began a slow decline. By 1860, almost 40 percent of people who had been born in Vermont had left the state. Eastern farmers, unable to compete with western grain, sought new agricultural opportunities. The extension of railroad lines into rural areas allowed farmers as far away as Vermont to ship cooled milk to the city. Other farmers used the new railroads to get fruit and vegetables to the cities. By 1837, a Boston housewife could buy a wide variety of fresh vegetables and fruits at the central market.

As northern farmers adopted new crops, they began to consider farming as a scientific endeavor. After 1800, northern farmers started using manure as fertilizer rather than disposing of it as a smelly nuisance. By the 1820s, some farmers were rotating their crops and planting new grasses and clover to restore fertility to the soil. These techniques recovered worn-out wheat and tobacco lands in Maryland and Delaware for livestock farming.

Farmers in the Delaware River valley were leaders in adopting new methods, but interest in scientific farming was widespread. By 1860, American farmers had developed thousands of special varieties of plants for local conditions. Many improvements resulted from experimentation, but farmers also enjoyed better information. New journals informed readers of modern farming practices, and many states established agricultural agencies. Although wasteful farming practices did not disappear, they became less characteristic of the Northeast. Improved farming methods contributed to increased agricultural output and helped reverse a 200-year decline in farm productivity in some of the oldest areas of settlement. A "scientific" farmer in 1850 could often produce two to four times as much per acre as in 1820.

This 1856 print titled "Preparing for Market" shows the farm as a center of human and animal activity and suggest the shifts in eastern agriculture that took place in the East as competition from the Midwest stimulated farmers to raise new crops for the market. The rise of commercial farming also encouraged technological innovation. The McCormick reaper was patented in 1834. (Yale University Art Gallery, New Haven. CT/Mabel Brady Garvan Collection)

Attitudes also changed. Cash transactions replaced the exchange of goods. Country stores became more reluctant to accept wood, rye, corn, oats, and butter as payment for goods instead of cash. Some farmers adopted the "get-ahead" ethic. Those content with just getting along rather than becoming involved in the market economy fell behind as wealth inequality increased throughout the rural Northeast.

Frontier Families

In 1820, less than one-fifth of the American population lived west of the Appalachians. By 1860, almost half did.

After the War of 1812, Americans flooded into the Old Northwest, settling first along the Ohio River and sending corn and pork down the Ohio and Mississippi to southern buyers. By 1830, Ohio, Indiana, and southern Illinois were heavily settled, but Michigan, northern Illinois, Wisconsin, and parts of Iowa and Missouri were still frontier.

The 1830s were boom times in the Old Northwest. Changes in federal land policy, which reduced both prices and the minimum acreage a settler had to buy, helped stimulate migration. Eastern capital poured in for loans, mortgages, and speculative buying.

Internal improvement schemes contributed to new settlement patterns and tied the Old Northwest firmly to the East. These links encouraged farmers to send wheat to the eastern market rather than corn and hogs for the southern market. Between 1840 and 1860, Illinois, southern Wisconsin, and eastern Iowa became the country's fastest-growing grain regions.

Although the Old Northwest passed rapidly through the frontier stage between 1830 and 1860, its farming families faced severe challenges. Western farms were small, for there were limits to what a family with hand tools could manage. A family with two healthy men could care for about 50 acres. In wooded areas, it took several years to get even that much land under cultivation, for only a few acres could be cleared in a year.

It took capital to begin farming—a minimum initial investment of perhaps $100 for 80 acres of government land, $300 for basic farming equipment, and another $100 or $150 for livestock. To buy an already "improved" farm cost more, and free bidding at government auctions could drive the price of unimproved federal land far above the minimum price. Once farmers moved onto the prairies of Indiana and Illinois, they needed an initial investment of about $1,000, because they had to buy materials for fencing, housing, and expensive steel plows. If farmers invested in the new horse-drawn reapers, they could cultivate more land, but all their costs also increased.

Opportunities in the Old Northwest

It was possible to begin farming with less, however. Some farmers borrowed; others rented land from farmers who had bought more acres than they could manage. Tenants who furnished their own seeds and animals could expect to keep about a third of the yield, and within a few years some could buy their own farms. Those without capital could earn good wages as farm hands. Five to ten years of frugal living and steady work would bring the sum needed to get started. Probably about a quarter of the western farm population consisted of young men laboring as tenants or hired hands.

Widespread ownership of land characterized western rural communities. Unlike the cities, there was no growing class of propertyless wage earners. But there were inequalities. In Butler County, Ohio, for example, 16 percent of people leaving wills in the 1830s held half the wealth. By 1860, the wealthiest 8 percent held half the wealth. Nevertheless, the Northwest offered many American families the chance to become independent producers and to enjoy a "pleasing competence." The rigors of frontier life faded with time.

Commercial farming brought new patterns of family life. As one Illinois farmer told his wife and daughter, "Store away . . . all of your utensils for weaving cloth up in the loft. The boys and I can make enough by increasing our herds." Many farm families had money to spend on new goods. As early as 1836, the *Dubuque Visitor* was advertising the availability of ready-made clothing and "Calicoes, Ginghams, Muslins, Cambricks, Laces and Ribbands."

Agriculture and the Environment

Shifting agricultural patterns in the East and expanding settlement into the Old Northwest contributed to the changing character of the American landscape. John

TIMELINE

1816	1817	1819	1820	1824
Second U.S. Bank	New York Stock Exchange	*Dartmouth College* v. *Woodward*	Lowell founded by Boston Associates; Land Act of 1820; The expression "woman's sphere" becomes current	*Sturges* v. *Crowninshield*

1824–1850	1825–1856	1828	1830s	1833
Construction of canals in the Northeast	Construction of canals linking the Ohio, the Mississippi, and the Great Lakes	Baltimore & Ohio Railroad begins operation	Boom in the Old Northwest; Increasing discrimination against free blacks; Public education movement spreads	Philadelphia establishes small police force

1834	1837	1837–1844	1840	1840s–1850s
Philadelphia race riots; Lowell work stoppage; Cyrus McCormick patents his reaper	Horace Mann becomes secretary of Massachusetts Board of Education	Financial panic and depression	Agitation for ten-hour day	Rising tide of immigration

Audubon, the naturalist, mused in 1826 that "a century hence," the rivers, swamps, and mountains "will not be here as I see them." A French visitor remarked that Americans would never be satisfied until they had subdued nature.

More than the subjugation of nature was involved, however. When eastern farmers changed their agricultural practices as they became involved in the market economy, their decisions left an imprint on the land. Selling wood and potash stimulated clearing of forests. So did the desire for new tools, plow castings, threshing machines, or wagon boxes, which were produced in furnaces fueled by charcoal. As forests disappeared, so did their wildlife. Even using mineral manures like gypsum or lime or organic fertilizers like guano to revitalize worn-out soil and increase crop yields depleted land elsewhere.

When farmers moved into the old Northwest, they used new steel plows, like the one developed in 1837 by Illinois blacksmith John Deere. Unlike older eastern plows, the new ones could cut through the dense, tough prairie cover. Deep plowing and the intensive cultivation of large cash crops had immediate benefits. But these practices could rob the soil of necessary minerals. When farmers built new timber houses as frontier conditions receded, they speeded the destruction of the country's forests.

❖❖❖❖❖❖

Conclusion

The Character of Progress

Between 1820 and 1860, the United States experienced tremendous growth and economic development. Transportation improvements facilitated the movement of people, goods, and ideas. Larger markets stimulated both agricultural and industrial production. There were more goods and ample food for the American people. Cities and towns were established and thrived. Visitors constantly remarked on the amazing bustle and rapid pace of American life. The United States was, in the words of one Frenchman, "one gigantic workshop, over the entrance of which there is the blazing inscription 'no admission here, except on business.'"

Although the wonders of American development dazzled foreigners and Americans alike, economic growth had its costs. Expansion was cyclic, and financial panics and depression punctuated the era. Industrial profits were based partly on low wages to workers. Time-honored routes to economic independence disappeared, and a large class of unskilled, impoverished workers appeared in U.S. cities. Growing inequality characterized urban and rural life, prompting some labor activists to criticize new economic and social arrangements. But workers, still largely unorganized, did not speak with one voice. Ethnic, racial, and religious diversity divided Americans in new and troubling ways.

Yet a basic optimism and sense of pride also characterized the age. To observers, however, it frequently seemed as if the East and the Old Northwest were responsible for the country's achievements. During these decades, many noted that the paths between the East, Northwest, and South seemed to diverge. The rise of King Cotton in the South, where slave rather than free labor formed the foundation of the economy, created a new kind of tension in American life, as the next chapter will show.

Recommended Reading

Economic Change

Charles G. Sellars, *The Market Revolution: Jacksonian America, 1815–1848* (1991); Albert W. Niemi, *U.S. Economic History: A Survey of the Major Issues* (1975); Thomas C. Cochran, *Frontiers of Change: Early Industrialism in America* (1981); David J. Jeremy, *Transatlantic Industrial Revolution: The Diffusion of Textile Technology Between Britain and America, 1790–1830* (1981); David A. Hounshell, *From the American System to Mass Production, 1800–1832: The Development of Manufacturing Technology in the United States* (1984); Robert F. Dalzell, Jr., *Enterprising Elite: The Boston Associates and the World They Made* (1987); Walter Licht, *Industrializing America: The Nineteenth Century* (1995); Carol Sheriff, *The Artificial River: The Erie Canal and the Paradox of Progress, 1817–1862* (1996).

Laborers and Communities

Thomas Dublin, *Women at Work: The Transformation of Work and Community in Lowell, Massachusetts, 1826–1860* (1979); Mary H. Blewett, *Men, Women, and Work: Class, Gender, and Protest in the New England Shoe Industry, 1780–1910* (1988); Steven J. Ross, *Workers on the Edge: Work, Leisure, and Politics in Industrializing Cincinnati, 1788–1890* (1985); Richard B. Stott, *Workers in the Metropolis: Class, Ethnicity, and Youth in Antebellum New York City* (1990); Gary

B. Nash, *Forging Freedom: The Formation of Philadelphia's Black Community, 1720–1840* (1988); Bruce Laurie, *Artisans into Workers: Labor in Nineteenth-Century America* (1989).

American Society

Stuart M. Blumin, *The Emergence of the Middle Class: Social Experience in the American City, 1760–1900* (1989); John F. Kasson, *Rudeness and Civility: Manners in Nineteenth-Century America* (1990); Mary P. Ryan, *Cradle of the Middle Class: The Family in Oneida County, New York, 1790–1865* (1981); Karen Lystra, *Searching the Heart: Women, Men, and Romantic Love in Nineteenth-Century America* (1989); Christine Stansell, *City of Women: Sex and Class in New York, 1789–1860* (1986); Harvey J. Graff, *Conflicting Paths: Growing Up in America* (1995).

Agricultural Change and the Frontier

Jeremy Atack and Fred Bateman, *To Their Own Soil: Agriculture in the Antebellum North* (1987); Christopher Clark, *The Roots of Rural Capitalism: Western Massachusetts, 1780–1860* (1992); Joan M. Jensen, *Loosening the Bonds: Mid-Atlantic Farm Women, 1750–1850* (1986); John Denis Haeger, *The Investment Frontier: New York Businessmen and the Economic Development of the Old Northwest* (1981); John Mack Faragher, *Sugar Creek: Life on the Illinois Prairies* (1986); Donald H. Parkerson, *The Agricultural Transition in New York State: Markets and Migration in Mid-Nineteenth Century America* (1995); Susan E. Gray, *The Yankee West: Community Life on the Michigan Frontier* (1996).

CHAPTER 11

Slavery and the Old South

As a young slave, Frederick Douglass was sent by his master to live in Baltimore. When he first met his mistress, Sophia Auld, he was "astonished at her goodness" as she began to teach him to read. Her husband, however, ordered her to stop. Maryland law forbade teaching slaves to read. Master Auld's opposition, however, inspired Douglass "with a desire" to learn.

In the seven years he lived with the Aulds, young Frederick used "various stratagems" to teach himself to read and write. In the narrative of his early life, written after his escape to the North, Douglass acknowledged that his master's "bitter opposition" had helped him achieve his freedom as much as did Mrs. Auld's "kindly aid."

Most slaves did not, like Douglass, escape. But all were as tied to their masters as Douglass was to the Aulds. Nor could whites in antebellum America escape the influence of slavery. Otherwise decent people were often compelled by the "peculiar institution" to act inhumanely. After her husband's interference, Sophia Auld, Douglass observed, was transformed into a demon by the "fatal poison of irresponsible power." Her formerly tender heart turned to "stone" when she ceased teaching him. "Slavery proved as injurious to her," Douglass wrote, "as it did to me."

A Mr. Covey, to whom Douglass was sent in 1833 to have his will broken, also paid the cost of slavery. Covey succeeded for a time, Douglass reported, in breaking his "body, soul, and spirit" by brutal work and discipline. But one hot August day in 1833, the two men fought a long, grueling battle. Douglass won. Victory, he said, "rekindled the few expiring embers of freedom, and revived within me a sense of my own manhood." Although it would be four more years before his escape north, the young man never again felt like a slave. The key to Douglass's resistance to Covey's power was not just his strong will, or even the magical root he carried in his pocket, but rather his knowledge of how to jeopardize Covey's livelihood as a slavebreaker. The oppressed survive by knowing their oppressors.

As Mrs. Auld and Covey discovered, as long as some people were not free, no one was free. Douglass observed, "You cannot outlaw one part of the people without endangering the rights and liberties of all people. You cannot put a chain on the ankle of the bondsman without finding the other end of it about your own necks." After quarreling with a house servant, one plantation mistress complained that she "exercises dominion over me—or tries to do it. One would have thought . . . that I was the Servant, she the mistress." Many whites lived in constant fear of a slave revolt. A Louisiana planter recalled that he had "known times here when there was not a single planter who had a calm night's rest; they then never lay down to sleep without a brace of loaded pistols at their sides." In slave folktales, the clever Brer Rabbit usually outwitted the more powerful Brer Fox or Brer Wolf, thus reversing the roles of oppressed and oppressor.

Slavery was both an intricate web of human relationships and a labor system. After tracing the economic development of the Old South, in which slavery and cotton played vital roles, this chapter will emphasize the daily lives and relationships of masters and slaves who, like Douglass and the Aulds, lived, loved, learned, worked, and struggled with one another in the years before the Civil War.

❧❧❧❧❧❧

Perhaps no issue in American history has generated as many interpretations or as much emotional controversy as slavery. Three interpretive schools developed over the years, each adding to our knowledge of the peculiar institution. The first saw slavery as a relatively humane and reasonable institution in which plantation owners took care of helpless, childlike slaves. The second depicted slavery as a harsh and cruel system of exploitation. The third, and most recent, interpretation described slavery from the perspective of the slaves, who did indeed suffer brutal treatment yet nevertheless survived with integrity, self-esteem, and a sense of community and culture.

The first and second interpretive schools emphasized workaday interactions among masters and mostly passive, victimized slaves, while the third focused on the creative energies and agency of life in the slave quarters from sundown to sunup. In a unique structure, this chapter follows these masters and slaves through their day, from morning in the Big House through hot afternoon in the fields to the slave cabins at night. Although slavery was the crucial institution in defining the Old South, many other social groups and patterns contributed to the tremendous economic growth of the South from 1820 to 1860. We will look first at these diverse aspects of antebellum southern life.

BUILDING THE COTTON KINGDOM

Many myths obscure our understanding of the antebellum South. It was not a monolithic society filled only with large cotton plantations worked by hundreds of slaves. The realities were much more complex. Large-plantation agriculture was dominant, but most southern whites were not even slaveholders. Most southern farmers lived in two-room cabins. Cotton was a key cash crop in the South, but it was not the only crop grown there. Some masters were kindly, but many were not; some slaves were contented, but most were not.

There were many Souths. The older Upper South of Virginia, Maryland, North Carolina, and Kentucky grew different staple crops from those grown in the newer, Lower or "Black Belt" South, from South Carolina to eastern Texas. Within each state, moreover, the economies of flat coastal areas, inland upcountry forests, and pine barrens all differed. A still further diversity existed between these areas and the Appalachian highlands, running from northern Alabama to western Virginia. New Orleans, Savannah, Charleston, and Richmond differed dramatically from rural areas.

Although the South was diverse, agriculture dominated its industry and commerce. In 1859, a Virginia planter complained about a neighbor who was considering abandoning his farm to become a merchant. "To me it seems to be a wild idea," the planter wrote in his diary. Southerners placed a high value on agricultural labor. Slavery was primarily a labor system intended to produce wealth for landowners. Although slavery in older areas was paternalistic, with masters and slaves owing mutual obligations, increasingly it became a capitalistic enterprise intended to maximize profits.

Economic Expansion

In the 20 years preceding the Civil War, the South's economy grew slightly faster than the North's. Personal income in 1860 was 15 percent higher in the South than in the prosperous states of the Old Northwest. If the South had become an independent nation in 1860, it would have ranked as one of the wealthiest countries in the world per capita. One dramatic technological breakthrough, the cotton gin, had two momentous effects: It tied the southern economy to cotton production for a century, and it allowed slavery's expansion into vast new territories.

As we learned in Chapter 9, most cotton farmers planted "long-staple" cotton before Eli Whitney invented the cotton gin in 1793. Thereafter, the "short-staple" variety, which could grow anywhere in the South, predominated. But only large-plantation owners could afford gins and the fertile bottomlands of the Gulf states. The plantation system spread with the rise of cotton as men rushed westward to fresh, fertile lands. Large-scale farming increased, demanding ever more slave labor. As a valuable investment, slaves needed some care and protection. But despite the abolition of slavery in the North and occasional talk of emancipation in the South, slavery became seemingly a permanent part of southern life. Any thought of ending it could be dispelled by one word: cotton.

Although more acreage was planted in corn, cotton was the largest cash crop and for that reason was called "king." In 1820 the South became the world's largest producer of cotton, and from 1815 to 1860 cotton represented more than half of all American exports. Cotton spurred economic growth throughout the country. Northern merchants profitably shipped, insured, and marketed it; western farmers found in the cotton South a major market for their foodstuffs.

The supply of cotton from the South grew at an astonishing rate. Cotton production amounted to 461,000 bales in 1817 and peaked at 4.8 million bales in 1860, a more than tenfold jump. This rapid growth was stimulated by world demand, especially from British textile mills.

White and Black Migrations

Seeking profits from worldwide demand for cotton, southerners migrated south-westward in huge numbers between 1830 and 1860. They pushed the southeastern Indians and the Mexicans in Texas out of the way and were moving into Texas as the Civil War began.

Like northern grain farmers, southern farmers followed parallel migration paths westward. From the coastal states they trekked westward into the lower Midwest and down into the Lower South. By the 1830s, the center of cotton production had shifted from South Carolina and Georgia to Alabama and Mississippi. This process continued in the 1850s as southerners forged into Arkansas, Louisiana, and eastern Texas.

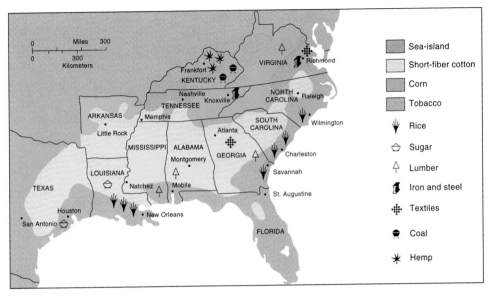

The Varied Economic Life in the South

Not only were these migrating southern families pulled by the prospect of fresh land and cheap labor, but they also were pushed westward by deteriorating economic conditions. Beginning in the 1820s, the states of the Upper South entered a long depression affecting tobacco and cotton prices. Years of constant use had exhausted their lands, and families with numerous children struggled to give each child an inheritance or financial help. In a society that valued land ownership, farm families had several choices. One was to move west; another was to stay and diversify. Therefore, the older states of the Upper South continued to shift to grains, mainly corn and wheat. Because these crops required less labor than tobacco, slave owners, especially those with pressing debts, began to sell slaves.

The internal slave trade from Virginia "down the river" to the Old Southwest thus became a multimillion-dollar "industry" in the 1830s. Between 1830 and 1860, an estimated 300,000 Virginia slaves were transported south for sale. One of the busiest routes was from Alexandria, Virginia, almost within view of the nation's capital, to a huge depot near Natchez, Mississippi. Although most southern states attempted occasionally to outlaw or control the traffic in slaves, these efforts were poorly enforced and usually short-lived. Besides, the reason for outlawing the slave trade was generally not humanitarian, but rather reflected fear of a rapid increase in the slave population. Alabama, Mississippi, and Louisiana all banned the importation of slaves after the Nat Turner revolt in Virginia in 1831 (described later in this chapter). But all three permitted the slave trade again during the profitable 1850s.

Congress formally ended slave imports on January 1, 1808, the earliest date permitted by the Constitution. Enforcement by the United States was weak, and many thousands of blacks continued to be smuggled to North America until the

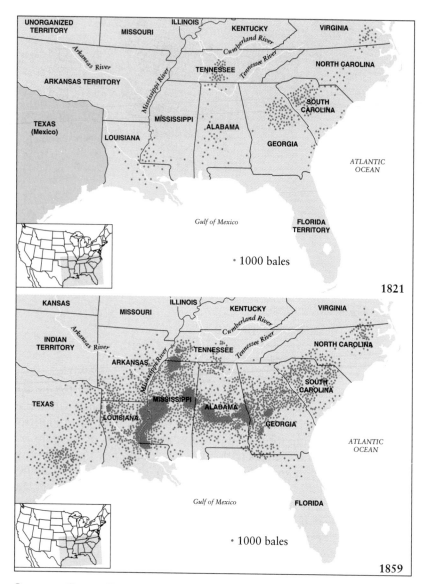

SOUTHERN COTTON PRODUCTION, 1821 AND 1859

end of the Civil War. The tremendous increase in the slave population was the result not of this illegal trade, however, but of natural reproduction, often encouraged by slave owners.

The Dependence on Slavery

The rapid increase in the number of slaves, from 1.5 million in 1820 to 4 million in 1860, paralleled southern economic growth and its dependence on slavery. Economic development and migration southwestward changed the geographic distribution of slaves, hindering abolition.

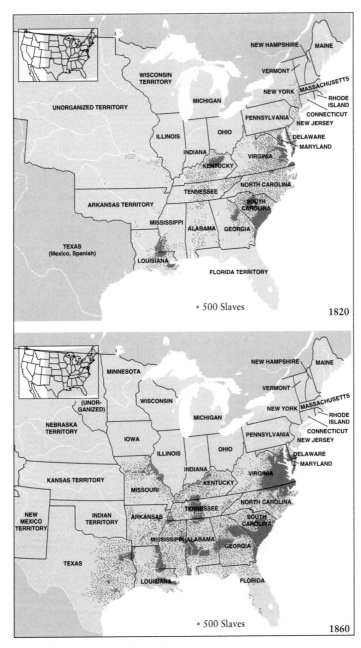

CONCENTRATION OF SLAVERY, 1820 AND 1860

Although most slaves worked on plantations and medium-size farms, they were found in all segments of the southern economy. In 1850, some 75 percent of all slaves were engaged in agricultural labor: 55 percent growing cotton, 10 percent tobacco, and 10 percent rice, sugar, and hemp. Of the remaining one-fourth, about 15 percent were domestic servants, and the remainder were in mining, lumbering, construction, and industry. A visitor to Natchez in 1835 saw slaves working as "mechanics, draymen, hostelers, labourers, hucksters, and washwomen, and the heterogeneous multitude of every other occupation, who fill the streets of a busy city—for slaves are trained to every kind of manual labour."

Masters also used slaves in industry. The Tredegar Iron Company of Richmond decided in 1847 to shift from white labor "almost exclusively" to slave labor in order to destroy the potential power of organized white workers to strike.

Whether in factories, mines, or cotton fields, slavery was profitable as a source of labor and as an investment. In 1859, the average plantation slave produced $78 in cotton earnings for his master annually while costing only about $32 to be fed, clothed, and housed. Slaves were also a good investment. In 1844, a "prime field hand" sold for $600. A cotton boom beginning in 1849 raised this price to $1800 by 1860. A slave owner could prosper by buying slaves, working them for several years, and selling them for a profit. Rising slave prices reflected planters' optimism.

The economic growth of the slaveholding South was impressive, but slavery still limited it. Generally, agricultural growth spurs the rise of cities and industry, but not in the Old South. In 1860, the South had 35 percent of the U.S. population and only 15 percent of its manufacturing. Just before the Civil War, 1 southerner in 14 was a city dweller, compared with 1 of every 3 northerners. The South would continue its economic backwardness as long as whites with capital insisted on putting all their business energies toward cotton production.

Some southerners were aware of the dangers of following a single path to wealth. De Bow's *Review*, an important journal published in New Orleans, called for greater economic independence in the South through agricultural diversification, industrialization, and an improved transportation system. De Bow thought that slave labor could fuel an industrial revolution. But the planter class disagreed. As long as money could be made through an agricultural slave system, plantation owners saw no reason to risk capital in new ventures.

Slavery and Class in the South

Slavery also served social purposes. Although the proportion of southern white families that owned slaves slowly declined from 40 to 25 percent as some families sold slaves to cotton planters, the ideal of slave ownership still permeated all classes and determined southern society's hierarchical character. At the top stood the planter aristocracy, much of it new wealth, elbowing its way among old established families. Some 10,000 rich families owned 50 or more slaves in 1860; about 3,000 of these owned over 100. A slightly larger group of small planters held from 10 to 50 slaves. But the largest group, 70 percent of all slaveholders in 1860, comprised 270,000 middle-level farm families with fewer than 10 slaves. The typical slaveholder worked a small family farm of about 100 acres with 8 or 9 slaves, perhaps members of the same family. The typical slave, however, was more likely to be in a group of 20 or more other slaves on a large farm or small plantation.

In 1841, a young white North Carolinian, John Flintoff, went to Mississippi dreaming of wealth and prestige. Beginning as an overseer managing an uncle's farm, he bought a "negro boy 7 years old" even before he owned any land. After several years of unrewarding struggle, Flintoff married and returned to North Carolina. There he finally bought 124 acres and a few more cheap, young blacks, and by 1860 he had a modest farm with several slaves growing corn, wheat, and tobacco. Although he never realized his grand dreams, his son went to college, and his wife, he reported proudly, "has lived a Lady."

Slavery was a powerful force in the lives of middle-level farmers like Flintoff, who had only a few slaves, and even for those who owned none. Economic, social, and political standing depended on owning slaves. Whites like John Flintoff hoped to purchase one slave, perhaps a female who would bear children, and then climb the socioeconomic ladder. White southerners thus supported slavery whether they owned slaves or not.

They also defended the institution because it gave them feelings of superiority over blacks and of kinship, if not quite equality, with other whites. Although there were always a few southern whites who believed in emancipation, most did not. A small Alabama farmer told a northern visitor in the 1850s that if the slaves got their freedom, "they'd all think themselves just as good as we . . . . How would you like to hev a nigger feelin' just as good as a white man?"

The Nonslaveholding South

Below Flintoff and other middling farmers lived the majority of white southerners, who owned no slaves but were equally, or even more, antiblack. The 75 percent of southern whites who owned no slaves were scattered throughout the South. Many of these "yeomen farmers" were Scots-Irish. Most lived in the foothills and worked poorer land than the large planters. They did not need to be near commercial centers because they were largely self-sufficient, raising almost all their food and trading hogs, eggs, small game, or homemade items for cash and other goods. They lived in two-room log houses separated by a "dog run." The yeoman farmer's drab, isolated life was brightened when neighbors and families gathered at corn huskings and quilting parties, logrolling and wrestling matches, and political stump and revivalist camp meetings.

In many ways, the yeoman farmers were the backbone of the South. In 1860 in North Carolina, 70 percent of the farmers held fewer than 100 acres, whereas in Mississippi and Louisiana, reputedly large plantation states, more than 60 percent of the farms were under 100 acres. Fiercely proud of their independence, the yeoman farmers had a share of political power. They voted overwhelmingly for Andrew Jackson. Although some resented the tradition of political deference to "betters," these farmers were not yet ready to challenge planters for political power. Yeoman farmers fought with the Confederacy during the Civil War; but some ended up organizing a guerrilla band of Unionists in southern Mississippi.

Another little-known group of southern whites were herdsmen raising hogs and other livestock. They supplied bacon and pork to local slaveholders (who often thought hog growing beneath their dignity) and drove herds to stockyards in Nashville, Louisville, and Savannah. The South raised two-thirds of the nation's hogs. In 1860, the value of southern livestock was $500 million, twice that of cotton. Although much of the corn crop fed the hogs, many herdsmen preferred to let their stock roam loose in the woods. However valuable the total size of the hog business, hog herdsmen did not stand very high on the southern social ladder.

Below them were the poor whites of the South, about 10 percent of the population. Often sneeringly called "crackers," they eked out a living in isolated, inhospitable areas. Some made corn whiskey, and many hired out as farmhands.

Because of poor diet and bad living conditions, these poor whites often suffered from hookworm and malaria. This, and the natural debilitation of heat and poverty, gave them a reputation as lazy, shiftless, and illiterate.

Poor whites stayed poor partly because the slave system allowed the planter class to accumulate a disproportionate amount of land and political power. High slave prices made entry into the planter class increasingly difficult, increasing class tensions.

MORNING: MASTER IN THE BIG HOUSE

It is early morning in the South. Imagine four scenes. In the first, William Waller of Virginia and a neighbor are preparing to leave with 20 choice slaves on a long trip to the slave market in Natchez, Mississippi. Waller is making this "intolerable" journey to sell some of his slaves in order to ease his heavy debts. Although he "loaths the vocation of slave trading," he must recover some money to see his family "freed from my bondage" of indebtedness. To ease his conscience, he intends to supervise the sale personally, thus securing the best possible deal not only for himself but also for his departing slaves.

On another plantation, owned by James Hammond of South Carolina, the horn blows an hour before daylight to awaken slaves for field work. Hammond rises soon after, ever aware that "to continue" as a wealthy master he must "draw the rein tighter and tighter" to hold his slaves "in complete check." "In general 15 to 20 lashes will be sufficient flogging" for most offenses, but "in extreme cases" the punishment "must not exceed 100 lashes in one day."

On an Alabama plantation, Hugh Lawson is up early, writing a sorrowful letter telling of the death of a "devotedly attached and faithful" slave, Jim. A female slave has already awakened and "walked across a frosty field in the early morning and gone to the big house to build a fire" for her mistress. As the mistress wakes up, she says to the slave, a grown woman responsible for the welfare of two families, "Well, how's my little nigger today?"

In a fourth household, this one a medium-size farm in upcountry Georgia, not far from Hammond's huge plantation, Charles Brock wakes up at dawn and joins his two sons and four slaves to work his modest acreage of grains and sweet potatoes, while Brock's wife and a female slave tend cows. On small and medium-size family farms with five or fewer slaves, blacks and whites commonly worked together, as one observer noted, with the "axe of master and man [slave] falling with alternate strokes . . . [and] ploughing side by side."

As these diverse scenes suggest, slavery thoroughly permeated the lives of southern slaveholders. For slaves, morning was a time for getting up and going to work. But for white slaveholders, morning involved contact with slaves in many ways: as burdens of figuring profit and loss, as objects to be kept obedient and orderly, as intimates and fellow workers, and as ever-present reminders of fear, hate, and uncertainty.

The Burdens of Slaveholding

Robert Francis Withers Allston (1801–1864) was a major rice planter in the Georgetown district of South Carolina, a low, swampy, mosquito-infested tidal area. It was a perfect spot for growing rice, but so unhealthy that few whites wanted to live there. The death rate among slaves was appallingly high. Robert was the fifth generation of Allstons to live in this inhospitable land. By 1860, he owned seven plantations along the Peedee River, totaling some 4,000 acres, in addition to another 9,500 acres of pasture and timberland. He held nearly 600 slaves, 236 of whom worked at the home plantation. The total value of his land and slaves in the 1850s was approximately $300,000. Rich in land and labor, he nevertheless had large mortgages and outstanding debts.

Allston was an enlightened, talented, public-spirited man. Educated at West Point but trained in the law, he did far more than practice agriculture. He served in the South Carolina state senate for 24 years and as governor from 1856 to 1858. His political creed, he wrote in 1838, was based on "the principles of Thomas Jefferson." The core of his conviction was a "plain, honest, commonsense reading of the Constitution," which for Allston meant the constitutionality of slavery and nullification and the illegitimacy of abolitionism and the United States Bank.

Allston also reflected Jefferson's humane side. He was an ardent reformer, advocating liberalization of South Carolina's poor laws; an improved system of public education open to rich and poor; humanitarian care of disabled people; and the improvement of conditions on the reservations of the Catawba Indians. He was active in the Episcopal Church and generously supported ministerial students.

In 1832, Allston married Adele Petigru, an equally enlightened and hardworking woman. She participated fully in the management of the plantation and ran it while Robert was away on political business. In a letter to her husband, written in 1850, Adele demonstrated her diverse interests by reporting on family affairs and the children's learning, sickness among the slaves, the status of spring plowing, the building of a canal and causeway, her supervision of the bottling of some wine, and current politics. After Robert's death during the Civil War, she would assume control of the Allston plantations, abandoned when Union troops arrived.

State politics lured Allston from his land for part of each year, but he was by no means an absentee owner. Except during the worst periods of mosquitoes and heat, the Allstons were fully engaged in the operation of their plantations. Managing thousands of acres of rice required not only an enormous investment in labor and equipment, but also careful supervision of both the slaves and an elaborate irrigation system. Although Allston's acreage and slave population were larger than those of most big planters and he grew rice rather than cotton, his concerns were typical.

Allston's letters frequently expressed the serious burdens of owning slaves. Although he was careful to distribute enough cloth, blankets, and shoes to his slaves and to give them sufficient rest, the sickness and death of slaves, especially young fieldworkers, headed his list of concerns. He tried to keep slave families together, but sold slaves when necessary. In a letter to his son Benjamin, he expressed concern over the bad example set by a slave driver who was "abandon'd by his hands" because he had not worked with them the previous Sunday. In the same letter, Allston urged Benjamin to keep up the "patrol duty," less to guard against runaway slaves, he said, than to restrain "vagabond whites." Clearly, the planter class felt a duty to control lower-class whites as well as black slaves.

Other planters likewise saw slavery as both a duty and a burden. Many planters insisted that they worked harder than their slaves to feed and clothe them. R. L. Dabney of Virginia exclaimed that "there could be no greater curse inflicted

Adele and Robert F. W. Allston shared the work and burdens of managing their rice plantations. (South Carolina Library, Columbia)

on us than to be compelled to manage a parcel of Negroes." Curse or not, Dabney and other planters profited from their burdens, a point they seldom admitted.

Their wives experienced other kinds of burdens. "The mistress of a plantation," wrote Susan Dabney Smedes, "was the most complete slave on it." Southern women were expected to adhere to the cult of domesticity both by improving their husbands' morals, which often meant restraining them from excessive cruelty, and by beautifying their parlors. Moreover, plantation mistresses suffered under a double standard of morality. They were expected to act as chaste ladies, whereas their husbands had virtually unrestricted sexual access to slave women. "God forgive us, but ours is a monstrous system," Mary Boykin Chesnut wrote in her diary. "Any lady is ready to tell you who is the father of all the mulatto children in everybody's household but her own. Those, she seems to think, drop from the clouds."

Chesnut called the sexual dynamics of slavery "the sorest spot." There were others. Together with female slaves, plantation mistresses had to tend to the food, clothing, health, and welfare of not just their husbands and children, but the slaves too. Adele Allston added plantation management to these duties. The plantation mistress, then, served many roles: as a potential humanizing influence on men; as a tough, resourceful, responsible manager of numerous plantation affairs; as a coercer of slaves and perpetuator of the system; and sometimes as a victim herself.

Justifying Slavery

The behavior of Douglass's mistress discussed at the beginning of this chapter suggests that as an institution slavery pressured well-intentioned people to act inhumanely. Increasingly attacked as immoral, slaveholders felt compelled to justify the institution. Until the 1830s, they explained away slavery as a "necessary evil." After abolitionists stepped up their attack in that decade, however, they shifted to justifying slavery as a "positive good."

A biblical justification was based in part on the curse that had fallen upon the son of Ham, one of Noah's children, and in part on Old and New Testament admonitions to servants to obey their masters. As a historical justification, south-erners claimed slavery had always existed and all the great ancient civilizations had depended on it.

The legal justification rested on United States Constitution's refusal to forbid slavery and on three passages clearly implying its legality (the "three-fifths" clause, the protection of the overseas slave trade for 20 years, and the mandate for return-ing fugitive slaves across state lines).

A fourth justification for slavery was scientific. Until the 1830s, most white southerners believed that blacks were degraded not by nature but by African cli-mate and their slave condition. With the rise of the "positive good" defense in the 1830s, southerners began to argue that blacks had been created separately as an inherently inferior race, and therefore the destiny of the inferior Africans was to serve the superior Caucasians in work. At best, the patriarchal slave system would domesticate uncivilized blacks. As Allston put it, "The educated master is the negro's best friend upon earth."

A sociological defense of slavery was implicit in Allston's paternalistic state-ment. George Fitzhugh, a leading advocate of this view, argued that "the Negro is but a grown child and must be governed as a child," and so needed the paternal guidance and protection of a white master. Many southerners believed that chaos and race-mixing would ensue if slaves were freed. Fitzhugh compared the treat-ment of southern slaves favorably with that of free blacks and of free laborers working in northern factories. These "wage slaves," he argued, worked as hard as slaves, yet with their paltry wages they had to feed, clothe, and shelter themselves. Southern masters took care of all these necessities. Emancipation, therefore, would be heartless and unthinkable, a burden to both blacks and whites.

Southern apologists for slavery faced the difficult intellectual task of justifying a system that ran counter to the main ideological directions of nineteenth-century American society: the expansion of individual liberty, mobility, economic oppor-tunity, and democratic political participation. Moreover, the southern defense of slavery had to take into account the 75 percent of white families who owned no slaves but envied those who did. To deflect potential for class antagonisms among whites, wealthy planters developed a justification of slavery that pictured all whites as superior to all blacks but equal to one another. Democratic equality among whites, therefore, was made consistent with racism and slaveholding.

The underlying but rarely admitted motive behind all these justifications was that slavery was profitable. As the southern defense of slavery intensified in the 1840s and 1850s, it aroused greater opposition from northerners and from slaves themselves. Perhaps slavery's worst cruelty was not physical but psychological: to be enslaved and barred from participation in a nation that put a high value on free-dom and equality of opportunity.

NOON: SLAVES IN HOUSE AND FIELDS

It is 2 o'clock on a hot July afternoon on the plantation. The midday lunch break is over, and the slaves are returning to field work. Lunch was the usual cornmeal and pork. The slaves now work listlessly, their low stamina resulting from a deficient diet and suffocating heat and humidity. Douglass remembered that "we worked all weathers . . . . It was never too hot, or too cold."

Daily Toil

The daily work schedule for most slaves, whether in the fields or the Big House, was long and demanding. Awakened before daybreak, they worked on an average day 14 hours in the summer and 10 hours in the winter; during harvest, 18 hours were not uncommon. Depending on the size of the work force and the crop, the slaves were organized either in gangs or according to tasks. Gangs, usually of 20 to 25, worked the cotton rows under the watchful eye and quick whip of a driver. Ben Simpson, a Georgia slave, remembered vividly his master's "great, long whip platted out of rawhide" that struck any slave who would "fall behind or give out."

Under the task system, each slave had a specific task to complete daily. It gave slaves incentive to work hard enough to finish early, but their work was scrutinized constantly. An overseer's weekly report to Robert Allston in 1860 noted that he had "flogged for hoeing corn bad Fanny 12 lashes, Sylvia 12, Monday 12, Phoebee 12, Susanna 12, Salina 12, Celia 12, Iris 12." Black slave drivers were no less demanding.

An average slave was expected to pick 130 to 150 pounds of cotton per day, and work on sugar and rice plantations was even harder. Sugar demanded constant cultivation and ditch-digging in snake-infested fields. At harvest time, cutting, stripping, and carrying the cane to the sugar house for boiling was exhausting, as was cutting and hauling huge quantities of firewood. Working in the low-country rice fields was worse: Slaves spent long hours standing in water up to their knees.

House slaves, mostly women, had relatively easier assignments, though they were usually called on to help with the harvest. Their usual work was in or near the Big House as maids, cooks, seamstresses, laundresses, coachmen, drivers, gardeners, and "mammies." Slaves did most of the artisanal work on the plantation; many became highly skilled. More intimacy between whites and blacks occurred near the house. House slaves ate and dressed better than those in the fields. But there were disadvantages: close supervision, duty day and night, and personality conflicts with the whites that could range from being given unpleasant jobs to insults, spontaneous angry whippings, and sexual assault. The most feared punishment, however, other than sale to the Deep South, was to be sent to the fields.

Slave Health and Punishments

Although slave owners had an interest in keeping their bondspeople healthy, slaves led sickly lives. Home was a crude one-room log cabin with a dirt floor and a fireplace; some such houses were well made, but most were not. Cracks and holes allowed mosquitoes easy entry. Typical furnishings included a table, some stools or boxes to sit on, an iron pot and wooden dishes, and perhaps a bed. Cabins were crowded, usually housing more than one family. Clothing was shabby and uncomfortable.

Studies on the adequacy of slave diet disagree. Compared with Latin American slavery, however, American slaves were well fed. Once a week, each slave got an average ration of a peck of cornmeal, 3 to 4 pounds of salt pork or bacon, some molasses, and perhaps some sweet potatoes. The mainstay was corn. While some slaves were able to grow vegetables and to fish or hunt, they rarely enjoyed fresh meat, dairy products, fruits, or vegetables. The limitations of their diet led to theft of food and the practice of eating dirt, which caused worms. Skin disorders, cracked lips, sore eyes, vitamin deficiency diseases, and even mental illness were other results of the slave diet.

Women slaves especially suffered weaknesses caused by vitamin deficiency, hard work, and disease, as well as those associated with menstruation and child-birth. Women were expected to do the same tasks in the fields as the men, in addition to cooking, sewing, child care, and traditional female jobs in the quarters when the fieldwork was finished. "Pregnant women," the usual rule stated, "should not plough or lift" and had a three-week recovery period following birth. But these guidelines were often violated. Mortality of slave children under 5 years of age was twice as high as for white children.

Life expectancy for American slaves was longer than for those in Latin America and the Caribbean, but not very high for either blacks or whites in the antebellum South (21.4 for blacks and 25.5 for whites in 1850). In part because of poor diet and the climate, slaves were highly susceptible to epidemics. Despite some resistance as a result of the sickle-cell trait, many slaves died from malaria, yellow fever, cholera, and other diseases spread by mosquitoes or bad water. Slaves everywhere suffered and died from intestinal ailments in the summer and respiratory diseases in the winter. An average of 20 percent (and sometimes 50 to 60 percent) of the slaves on a given plantation would be sick at one time, and no overseer's report was complete without recording sicknesses and days of lost labor.

The relatively frequent incidence of whippings and other physical punishments aggravated the poor physical condition of the slaves. Many slaveholders offered rewards—a garden plot, an extra holiday, hiring oneself out, or passes—as inducements for faithful labor, and withheld these privileges as punishment. But southern court records, newspapers, plantation diaries, and slave memoirs reveal that sadistic punishments were frequent. Slaveholders had many theories on the appropriate kind of lash to inflict sufficient pain and punishment without damaging a valuable laborer. Other punishments included confinement in stocks and jails during leisure hours, chains, muzzling, salting lash wounds, branding, burning, and castration.

Nothing testifies better to the physical brutality of slavery than the advertisements for runaways that slaveholders printed in antebellum newspapers. In searching for the best way to describe the physical characteristics or brands of a missing slave, slave owners unwittingly condemned their own behavior. One fugitive, Betty, was described as recently "burnt . . . with a hot iron on the left side of her face." "I tried to make the letter M," her master admitted in his diary.

Slave Law and the Family

Complicating master-slave relationships was the status of slaves as both human beings and property, a legal and psychological ambiguity the South never resolved. On the one hand, the slaves had names, personalities, families, and wills of their own, making them fellow humans. On the other hand, they were items of property, purchased to perform specific profit-making tasks.

This ambiguity led to confusion in the laws governing treatment of slaves. Until the early 1830s, some southern abolitionist activity persisted, primarily in the

Upper South, and slaves had slight hopes of being freed. But they also suffered careless, often brutal treatment. This confusion changed with the threatening convergence in 1831 of Nat Turner's revolt and William Lloyd Garrison's publication of the abolitionist newspaper, the *Liberator*. After 1831, the South tightened up the slave system. Laws prohibited manumission, and slaves' hopes of freedom other than by revolt or escape vanished. At the same time, laws protecting them from overly severe treatment were strengthened, and material conditions generally improved.

Treatment varied with individual slaveholders and depended on their mood and other circumstances. Most planters, like Robert Allston, encouraged their slaves to marry and tried to keep families intact, believing that families made black males more docile and less inclined to run away. But some masters failed to respect slave marriages or broke them up because of financial problems, which southern law permitted them to do.

Adding to the pain of forced breakup of the slave family was the sexual abuse of black women. Although the frequency of such abuse is unknown, the presence of thousands of mulattoes in the antebellum era points to the practice. White men in the South took advantage of black slave women by offering gifts for sexual "favors," by threatening those who refused sex with physical punishment or the sale of a child or loved one, by purchasing concubines, and by outright rape.

To obtain cheap additional slaves for the work force, slaveholders encouraged young slave women to bear children, whether married or not. If verbal prodding and inducements such as less work and more rations did not work, masters would force mates on slave women. Massa Hawkins, for example, selected Rufus to live with an unwilling 16-year-old Rose Williams. When Rufus persisted, Rose took a poker and "lets him have it over de head." Hawkins then threatened Rose with a "whippin' at de stake" or sale away "from my folks." This was too much for her. "What am I's to do?"

Slaves, however, usually chose their own mates on the basis of mutual attraction during an uneasy courtship complicated by the threat of white interference. As among poor whites, premarital intercourse was frequent, but promiscuous behavior was rare. Most couples maintained affectionate, lasting relationships. This, too, led to numerous sorrows. Members of slave families had to witness the flogging or physical abuse of loved ones and were powerless to intervene. William Wells Brown remembered that "cold chills ran over me and I wept aloud" when he saw his mother whipped. For this reason, some slaves preferred to marry a spouse from another plantation.

Although motherhood was the key event in a slave woman's life, bearing children and the double burden of work and family responsibilities challenged her resourcefulness. Some masters provided time off for nursing mothers, but the more common practice was for them to work in the fields with their newborn infants lying nearby. Women developed support networks, looking after one another's children; meeting to sew, quilt, cook, or do laundry; and attending births, caring for the sick and dying, and praying together.

The most traumatic problem for slaves was the separation of families, a haunting fear rarely absent from slave consciousness. Although many slaveholders had both moral and economic reasons to maintain families, inevitably they found themselves destroying them. One study of 30 years of data from the Deep South shows

Despite separation, sale, and sexual abuse by white masters, many slave families endured and provided love, support, and self-esteem to their members. This 1862 photograph shows five generations of a slave family, all born on the plantation of J. J. Smith of Beaufort, South Carolina. (Library of Congress)

that masters dissolved one-third of all slave marriages. Even then, the slaves tried to maintain contact.

There was much basis, in fact, for the abolitionists' contention that slavery was a harsh, brutal system. However, two points need to be emphasized. First, although slavery led otherwise decent human beings to commit inhumane acts, many slaveholders throughout the South were neither sadistic nor cruel; they did what they could for their slaves, out of both economic self-interest and Christian morality. Second, whether under kind or cruel masters, the slaves endured with dignity, communal sensitivity, and even some joy. If daytime in the fields describes slavery at its worst, nighttime in the quarters, as examined from the black perspective, reveals the slaves' survival powers and their capacity to mold an African-American culture even under slavery.

NIGHT: SLAVES IN THEIR QUARTERS

It is near sundown, and the workday is almost over. Some slaves begin singing the gentle spiritual "Steal Away to Jesus," and others join in. To the unwary overseer or master, the song suggests happy slaves, looking forward to heaven. To the slaves, however, the songs are a signal that, as ex-slave Wash Wilson put it, they are to "steal away to Jesus" because "dere gwine be a 'ligious meetin' dat night."

In the slave quarters, away from whites and daily work, an elaborate black community helped the slaves make sense out of their lives. In family life, religion, song, dance, the playing of musical instruments, and the telling of stories, the slaves both described their experiences and sought release from suffering.

Black Christianity

As suggested by the scene Wash Wilson described, Christian worship was indispensable to life in the slave quarters. The revivals of the early nineteenth century led to an enormous growth of Christianity among black Americans. Some independent black Baptist and Methodist churches, especially in border states and cities, served both slaves and free blacks and occasionally even whites. These separate churches had to steer a careful path to maintain their freedom and avoid white interference. But the vast majority of southern blacks were slaves, attending plantation churches set up by their masters.

Robert Allston built a prayer house for his slaves, reporting with pride that they were "attentive . . . . and greatly improved in intelligence and morals." For the slaveholders, religion often represented a form of social control. Black religious gatherings were usually forbidden unless white observers were present or white preachers led them. Whether in slave or white churches (where blacks sat in the back), the biblical text was often "Servants, obey your masters."

There were limits, however, to white control. Although some slaves accommodated themselves to the master's brand of Christianity and patiently waited for heavenly deliverance, others rebelled and sought earthly liberty. Not far from Allston's plantation, several slaves were discovered (and imprisoned) for singing "We'll soon be free / We'll fight for liberty / When de Lord will call us home." Douglass had an illegal Sabbath school on one plantation, where he and others risked being whipped while learning about Christianity and how to read.

In religious schools and meetings like these, the slaves created an "invisible" church. On Sunday morning, they dutifully sat through the master's service and waited for "real preachin'" later that night.

Long into the night, they would sing, dance, shout, and pray. "Ya' see," one slave woman explained, "niggers lack ta shout a whole lot an' wid de white fo'ks al'round 'em, dey couldn't shout jes' lack dey want to." But at night they could, taking care to deaden the sound to keep the whites away. Dance, forbidden by Methodists, was transformed into the "ecstatic shout," praising the Lord. The religious ceremony itself, with its camp meeting features, relieved the day's burdens and expressed communal religious values.

Although many of the expressive forms were African, the message was the Christian theme of suffering and deliverance from bondage. "We prayed a lot to be free," Anderson Edwards recalled, but the freedom the slaves sought was a complex blend of a peaceful soul and an earthly escape from slavery.

The Power of Song

A group of slaves gathers at night in the woods behind their quarters to sing and shout together. Two moods are expressed. After moaning of being stolen from Africa and sold in Georgia, with families "sold apart," they sing: "There's a better day a-coming. / Will you go along with me? / There's a better day a-coming. / Go sound the jubilee."

Music was a crucial form of expression in the slave quarters on both secular and religious occasions. The slaves were adept at creating a song, as one slave woman recalled, "on de spurn of de moment." Jeanette Robinson Murphy described a process of spontaneous creation that, whether in rural church music or urban jazz, describes black music to this day. "We'd all be at the 'prayer house' de Lord's day," she said, when all of a sudden, perhaps even in the midst of a white preacher's sermon, "de Lord would come a-shinin' thoo dem pages and revive dis ole nigger's heart, and I'd jump up dar and den and holler and shout and sing and pat, and dey would all cotch de words and I'd sing it to some ole shout song I'd heard 'em sing from Africa, and dey'd all take it up and keep at it, and keep a-addin' to it, and den it would be a spiritual."

Spirituals reiterated one basic Judeo-Christian theme: A chosen people, the children of God, were held in bondage but would be delivered. What they meant by deliverance often had a double meaning: freedom in heaven and freedom in the North. Where, exactly, was the desired destination of "Oh Canaan, sweet Canaan / I am bound for the land of Canaan"? Was it heaven? Freedom "anyplace else but here"? A literal reference to the terminus of the underground railroad? For different slaves, and at different times for the same person, it meant all of these.

"The songs of the slave," Douglass wrote, "represent the sorrows of his heart." But they also expressed joy, triumph, and deliverance. Each expression of sorrow usually ended in an outburst of eventual affirmation and justice.

Slave songs did not always contain hidden meanings. Sometimes slaves gathered simply for music, to play fiddles, drums, and other instruments fashioned in imitation of West African models. Some musicians were invited to perform at white ceremonies and parties. But most played for the slave community. Sacred and secular events such as weddings, funerals, holiday celebrations, family reunions, and a successful harvest were all occasions for a communal gathering, usually with music. So, too, was news of external events that affected their lives—a crisis in the master's situation, a change in the slave code, a Civil War battle, or emancipation.

The Enduring Family

The role of music in all milestones of family life suggests that the family was central to life in the slave quarters. Although sexual abuse and family separation were real or potential experiences, so was the hope for family continuity. Naming practices, for example, show that children were connected to large extended families.

The benefits of family cohesion were those of any group: love, protection, education, moral guidance, cultural transmission, status, role models, and basic support. All these existed in the slave quarters. In this way, they preserved cultural traditions, which enhanced the identity and self-esteem of parents and children alike. Parents taught their children how to survive in the world and how to cope with slavery. As the young ones neared the age for full-time field work, their parents instructed them in the best ways to pick cotton or corn, how to avoid the overseer's whip, whom to trust and learn from, and ways of fooling the master.

Opportunities existed on many plantations for parents to work extra for money to buy sugar or clothing, by hunting and fishing to add protein to the diet, or to tend a small garden to grow vegetables. In such small ways, they improved the welfare of their families.

Slaves were not always totally at the mercy of abusive masters and overseers. Occasionally, one family member could intervene to prevent the abuse of another. Harriet Jacobs fended off her master's advances partly by her cleverness and sass, and partly by a threat to use her free black grandmother's considerable influence in the community against him. That enraged but stopped him.

When family intervention, appeals for mercy, or conjurers' magic did not work, some slaves resorted to force. In 1800, a slave called Ben shot dead a white man for living with Ben's wife, and another slave killed an overseer in 1859 for raping his wife. Female slaves, too, risked serious consequences to protect themselves or family members. When Cherry Loguen was attacked by a knife-wielding rapist, she knocked him out with a large branch.

Despite numerous incidents of mutual support, the love and affection that slaves had for each other was sometimes a liability. Many slaves, women especially, were reluctant to run away because they did not want to leave their families. Those who fled were easily caught because, as an overseer near Natchez, Mississippi, told a northern visitor, they "almost always kept in the neighborhood, because they did not like to go where they could not sometimes get back and see their families."

As these episodes suggest, violence, sexual abuse, and separation constantly threatened slave families. But despite them, slave parents served as protectors, providers, comforters, transmitters of culture, and role models for their children.

RESISTANCE AND FREEDOM

Songs, folktales, and other forms of cultural expression enabled slaves to articulate their resistance to slavery. For example, Old Jim was going on a "journey" to the "kingdom," and, as he invited others to "go 'long" with him, he taunted his owner: "O blow, blow, Ole Massa, blow de cotton horn / Ole Jim'll neber wuck no mo' in de cotton an' de corn." From refusal to work, it was a short step to outright revolt. In another song, "Samson," the slaves clearly stated their determination to abolish the house of bondage: "An' if I had-'n my way / I'd tear the buildin' down! / . . . And now I got my way / And I'll tear this buildin' down." Every hostile song, story, or event, like Douglass's victory over Covey, was an act of resistance.

Forms of Black Protest

One way slaves protested the burdensome demands of continuous forced labor was in various "day-to-day" acts of resistance. These ranged from breaking tools to burning houses, from stealing food to defending fellow slaves from punishment, from self-mutilation to work slowdowns, and from poisoning masters to feigning illness.

Slave women, aware of their childbearing value, were adept at missing work on account of "disorders and irregularities." They established networks of support while winnowing and pounding rice or shucking corn, sharing miseries but also encouraging each other in private acts of subtle defiance such as ruining the master's meals and faking sickness.

Overseers also suffered from these acts of disobedience, for their job depended on productivity, which in turn depended on the goodwill of the slave workers. Slaves adeptly played on the frequent struggle between overseer and master.

Many slaveholders resorted to using black drivers rather than overseers, but this created other problems. Slave drivers were "men between," charged with the tricky job of getting the master's work done without alienating fellow slaves or compromising their own values. Although some drivers were as brutal as white overseers, many became leaders and role models for other slaves. A common practice of the drivers was to appear to punish without really doing so. Solomon Northrup reported that he "learned to handle the whip with marvellous dexterity and precision, throwing the lash within a hair's breadth of the back, the ear, the nose, without, however, touching either of them."

Another form of resistance was to run away. The typical runaway was a young male, who ran off alone and hid out in a nearby wood or swamp. He left to avoid a whipping or because he had just been whipped, to protest excessive work demands, or, as one master put it, for "no cause" at all. But there was a cause—the need to experience a period of freedom away from the restraints and discipline of the plantation. Many runaways would sneak back to the quarters for food, and after a few days, if not tracked down by hounds, they would return, perhaps to be whipped, but also perhaps with some concessions for better treatment.

Some slaves left again and again. Remus and his wife Patty ran away from their master in Alabama. They were caught and jailed three times, but each time they escaped again. Runaways hid out for months and years in communities of escaped slaves, especially in Florida, where Seminole and other Indians befriended them. In these areas, blacks and Indians, sharing a common hostility to whites, frequently intermarried, though sometimes southeastern Indians were hired to track down runaway slaves.

The means of escape were manifold: forging passes, posing as master and servant, disguising one's sex, sneaking aboard ships, and pretending loyalty until taken by the master on a trip to the North. One slave even had himself mailed to the North in a large box. The underground railroad, organized by abolitionists, was a series of safe houses and stations where runaway slaves could rest, eat, and spend the night before continuing. Harriet Tubman, who led some 300 slaves out of the South on 19 separate trips, was the railroad's most famous "conductor." It is difficult to know exactly how many slaves actually escaped to the North and Canada, but the numbers were not large. One estimate suggests that in 1850, about 1,000 slaves (out of over 3 million) attempted to run away, and most of them were returned. Nightly patrols by white militiamen reduced the chances for any slave to escape and probably deterred many slaves from even trying.

Other ways in which slaves sought their freedom included petitioning Congress and state legislatures, bringing suit against their masters that they were being held in bondage illegally, and persuading masters to provide for emancipation in their wills. Many toiled to purchase their own freedom by hiring out to do extra work at night and on holidays.

Slave Revolts

The ultimate act of resistance was rebellion. Countless slaves committed individual acts of revolt. In addition, there were hundreds of conspiracies whereby slaves met to plan a group escape and often the massacre of whites. Most of these conspiracies never led to action, either because circumstances changed or the slaves lost the will to follow through or, more often, because some fellow slave—perhaps

planted by the master—betrayed the plot. Such spies thwarted the elaborate conspiracies of Gabriel in Virginia in 1800 and Denmark Vesey in South Carolina in
1822. Both men were skilled, knowledgeable leaders who planned their revolts in
hopes that larger events would support them—a possible war with France in 1800
and the Missouri debates in 1820. Both conspiracies were thwarted before revolts
could begin, and both resulted in severe reprisals by whites, including mass exe-
cutions of leaders and the random killing of innocent blacks. The severity of these
responses indicated southern whites' enormous fear of slave revolt.

Only a few organized revolts ever actually took place. The most famous slave
revolt, led by Nat Turner, occurred in Southampton County, Virginia, in 1831. Turner
was an intelligent, skilled, unmarried, religious slave who had experienced many
visions of "white spirits and black spirits engaged in battle." He believed himself
"ordained for some great purpose in the hands of the Almighty." He and his followers intended, Turner said, "to carry terror and devastation" throughout the country. They crept into the home of Turner's master—a "kind master" with "the greatest
confidence in me"—and killed the entire family. Before the insurrection was finally
put down, 55 white men, women, and children had been murdered and twice as
many blacks killed in the aftermath. Turner hid for two weeks before he was appre-
hended and executed, but not before dictating a chilling confession to a white
lawyer. The Nat Turner revolt was a crucial moment for southern whites. A Virginia
legislator said that he suspected there was "a Nat Turner . . . in every family."

The fact that Turner was an intelligent and trusted slave and yet led such a terrible revolt suggests again how difficult it is to generalize about slavery and slave
behavior. Slaves, like masters, had diverse personalities and changeable moods,
and their behavior could not be easily predicted. Sometimes humble and deferential, at other times obstinate and rebellious, the slaves made the best of a bad situation and did what they needed to do to survive with a measure of self-worth.

Free Blacks: Becoming One's Own Master

When Frederick Douglass forged a free black's papers as a seaman and sailed from
Baltimore to become his own master in the North, he found "great insecurity and
loneliness." Apart from the immediate difficulties of finding food, shelter, and
work, he realized that he was a fugitive in a land "whose inhabitants are legalized
kidnappers" who could at any moment seize and return him to the South. Apart
from this fear, which haunted blacks in the North, what was life like for the 11 percent of the total African-American population who in 1860 were not slaves?

Between 1820 and 1860, the number of free blacks in the United States doubled, from 233,500 to 488,000. This rise resulted from natural increase, successful
escapes, "passing" as whites, purchasing of freedom, and some manumissions.

More than half the free blacks lived in the South, most (85 percent in 1860) in
the Upper South, where the total number of slaves had declined slightly. They
were found least frequently in the Deep South, scattered on impoverished rural
farmlands and in small towns and cities, and feared by whites as an inducement to
slave unrest. Even so, one-third of the southern free African-American population
lived in cities or towns.

In part because it took a long time to buy freedom, free blacks tended to be
older, more literate, and lighter-skinned than other African-Americans. In 1860,

The young Frederick Douglass, shown here in a photograph from about 1855, understood as well as any American the profound human, social, and political complexities and consequences of slavery. (New York Public Library, Schomburg Center for Research in Black Culture)

over 40 percent of free blacks were mulattoes (compared with 10 percent of the slaves). With strong leadership, Baltimore, Richmond, Charleston, New Orleans, and other southern cities developed African-American communities, their churches, schools, and benevolent societies vibrant in the midst of white hostility.

Most free African-Americans in the antebellum South were poor farmhands, day laborers, or woodcutters. In the cities, they worked in factories and lived in appalling poverty. A few skilled jobs, such as barbering, shoemaking, and plastering, were reserved for black men, but they were barred from more than 50 other trades. Women worked as cooks, laundresses, and domestics. The 15 percent of free African-Americans who lived in the Lower South were divided into two distinct castes. Most were poor. But in New Orleans, Charleston, and other southern cities, a small, mixed-blood free black elite emerged, closely connected to white society and distant from poor blacks. A handful even owned land and slaves.

Most free blacks had no such privileges. In most states, they could not vote, bear arms, buy liquor, assemble, speak in public, form societies, or testify against whites in court. Nevertheless, the African-American persistence to support each other was stronger than white efforts to impede it.

Urban whites sought to restrain free blacks from mixing with whites in working-class grogshops, gambling halls, and brothels, as well as to confine them to certain sections of the city or (increasingly by the 1850s) to compel them to leave altogether. Those who stayed had trouble finding work, were required to carry papers, and had to have their actions supervised by a white guardian. Southern whites especially feared contact between free blacks and slaves, which did occur despite all attempts to limit it.

The key institution in these developments was the African-American church. Welcoming the freedom from white control, independent urban black churches grew enormously in the two decades before the Civil War. These institutions gave spiritual solace, set community standards, and offered a host of educational, insurance, self-help, and recreational opportunities.

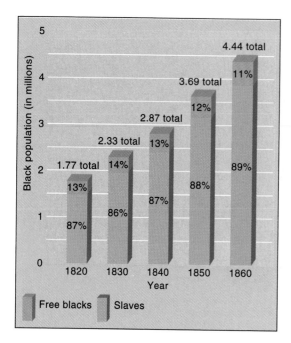

**GROWTH OF BLACK POPULATION: SLAVE
AND FREE, 1820–1860**
Although the number of free African-
Americans doubled in size between
1820 and 1860, their proportion relative
to the total black population actually
decreased. This indicates that the
institution of slavery seemed unlikely to
be ended voluntarily by southerners.

The African-American churches not only were centers of vital urban black
community activities, but also were springboards for activist black preachers seeking larger changes in American society. The Reverend J. C. Pennington, an escaped
slave, attended lectures at Yale Divinity School (though denied the right to enroll or
borrow books). Licensed to preach in 1838, he headed prominent black churches in
New Haven, Hartford, and finally New York City. Pennington started several
schools, was an abolitionist leader of the National Negro Convention movement
(described in Chapter 12), and founded the Union Missionary Society in 1841, a
black organization that focused on African missions. Such black religious leaders
prepared the way not only for Civil War, but also for an unprecedented postwar
growth of African-American churches.

In part because free blacks were becoming more of a "people," they faced a
crisis in the 1850s. Growing prosperity and the worsening conflict between North
and South over slavery in the territories caused many white southerners to be
even more concerned than usual with the presence of free blacks. Pressures
increased in the late 1850s either to deport or enslave them. Some black leaders, not
surprisingly, began to look more favorably on migration to Africa. That quest was
interrupted, however, by the outbreak of the Civil War, rekindling in Douglass the
"expiring embers of freedom."

❦❦❦❦❦❦

CONCLUSION

Douglass's Dream of Freedom

Frederick Douglass eventually won his freedom by forging a free black sailor's
pass and escaping through the Chesapeake Bay to New York. In a real sense, he

TIMELINE

1787	1793	1800	1808	1820
Constitution adopted with proslavery provisions	Eli Whitney invents cotton gin	Gabriel conspiracy in Virginia	External slave trade prohibited by Congress	South becomes world's largest cotton producer

1822	1830s	1831	1845	1850s
Denmark Vesey's conspiracy in Charleston	Southern justification of slavery changes from a necessary evil to a positive good	Nat Turner's slave revolt in Virginia	*Narrative of the Life of Frederick Douglass* published	Cotton boom

1851	1852	1860
Indiana state constitution excludes free blacks	Harriet Beecher Stowe publishes best-selling *Uncle Tom's Cabin*	Cotton production and prices peak

wrote himself into freedom. The *Narrative of the Life of Frederick Douglass*, "written by himself" in 1845, was a way both of exposing the many evils of slavery and of creating his own identity, even to the point of choosing his own name. Ironically, Douglass had learned to value reading and writing, we recall, from his Baltimore masters, the Aulds. This reminds us again of the intricate and subtle ways in which the lives of slaves and masters were tied together in the antebellum South. Our understanding of the complexities of this relationship is enhanced as we consider the variations of life in the Big House in the morning, in the fields during the afternoons, in the slave quarters at night, and in the degrees of freedom blacks achieved through resistance, revolt, and free status.

In a poignant moment in his *Narrative*, Douglass described his dreams of freedom as he looked out at the boats on the waters of Chesapeake Bay as a boy. Contrasting his own enslavement with the boats he saw as "freedom's swift-winged angels," Douglass vowed to escape: "This very bay shall yet bear me into freedom . . . . There is a better day coming." As we will see later, southern white planters also bemoaned their lack of freedom relative to the North and made their own plans to achieve independent status through secession. Meanwhile, as that struggle brewed beneath the surface of antebellum life, many other Americans were dismayed by various evil aspects in their society, slavery among them, and sought ways of shaping a better America. We turn to these other dreams in the next chapter.

Recommended Reading

Morning: Building the Cotton Kingdom: Masters, Mistresses, and the Social and Economic Life of the Old South

Charles Bolton, *Poor Whites of the Antebellum South: Tenants and Laborers in Central North Carolina and Northeast Mississippi* (1994); Victoria E. Bynum, *Unruly Women: The Politics of*

Social and Sexual Control in the Old South (1990); Catharine Clinton, *Plantation Mistress* (1983); Bruce Collins, *White Society in the Antebellum South* (1985); Charles B. Dew, *Bond of Iron: Master and Slave at Buffalo Forge* (1994); Elizabeth Fox-Genovese, *Within the Plantation Household: Black and White Women of the Old South* (1988); George Fredrickson, *The Black Image in the White Mind: The Debate on Afro-American Character and Destiny, 1817–1914* (1971); Eugene Genovese, *The Slaveholder's Dilemma: Freedom and Progress in Southern Conservative Thought, 1820–1860* (1992); Suzanne Lebsock, *The Free Women of Petersburg: Status and Culture in a Southern Town, 1784–1860* (1984); James Oakes, *The Ruling Race: A History of American Slaveholders* (1982) and *Slavery and Freedom: An Interpretation of the Old South* (1990); Frank Owsley, *Plain Folk in the Old South* (1949); William Stanton, *The Leopard's Spots: Scientific Attitudes Toward Race in America, 1815–1859* (1960); Steven Stowe, *Intimacy and Power in the Old South: Rituals in the Lives of the Planters* (1987).

Noon: The Institution of Slavery

Ira Berlin, *Many Thousands Gone: The First Two Centuries of Slavery in North America* (1998); John Blassingame, ed., *Slave Testimony* (1977); Eugene Genovese, *Roll, Jordan, Roll: The World the Slaves Made* (1974); Larry E. Hudson, Jr., *To Have and to Hold: Slave Work and Family Life in Antebellum South Carolina* (1997); Nathan I. Huggins, *Black Odyssey: The Afro-American Ordeal in Slavery* (1977); Peter Kolchin, *American Slavery, 1619–1877* (1993); Ulrich B. Phillips, *American Negro Slavery* (1919) and *Life and Labor in the Old South* (1929); Willie Lee Rose, ed., *Documentary History of Slavery in North America* (1976); Kenneth Stampp, *The Peculiar Institution: Slavery in the Ante-Bellum South* (1956); Robert Starobin, *Industrial Slavery in the Old South* (1970); Richard Wade, *Slavery in the Cities* (1964).

Night: Black Culture and Community

William L. Andrews, *To Tell a Free Story: The First Century of Afro-American Autobiography, 1760–1865* (1986); John Blassingame, *The Slave Community*, rev. ed. (1979); Jennifer Fleischner, *Mastering Slavery: Memory, Family, and Identity in Women's Slave Narratives* (1996)); Helen Bradley Foster, *"New Rainments of Self": African American Clothing in the Antebellum South* (1997); Charles Joyner, *Down by the Riverside: A South Carolina Slave Community* (1984); Herbert Gutman, *The Black Family in Slavery and Freedom, 1750–1925* (1976); James Oliver Horton, *Free People of Color: Inside the African-American Community* (1993); Lawrence Levine, *Black Culture and Black Consciousness: Afro-American Folk Thought from Slavery to Freedom* (1977); Albert Roboteau, *Slave Religion: The "Invisible Institution" in the Ante-bellum South* (1978); George Rawick, *From Sundown to Sunup: The Making of a Black Community* (1972); Sterling Stuckey, *Slave Culture: Nationalist Theory and the Foundation of Black America* (1987); Deborah Gray White, *Arn't I a Woman?* (1985).

Slave Resistance and Free Blacks

William L. Andrews, ed. *The Oxford Frederick Douglass Reader* (1996); Herbert Aptheker, *Nat Turner's Slave Rebellion* (1966); Ira Berlin, *Slaves Without Masters: The Free Negro in the Antebellum South* (1976); Merton L. Dillon, *Slavery Attacked: Southern Slaves and Their Allies, 1619–1865* (1990) Michael P. Johnson and James L. Roark, *No Chariot Down: Charleston's Free People of Color on the Eve of the Civil War* (1984); Norrece R. Jones, Jr., *Born a Child of Freedom, Yet a Slave: Mechanisms of Control and Strategies of Resistance in Antebellum South Carolina* (1990); Robert S. Levine, *Martin Delany, Frederick Douglass, and the Politics of Representative Identity* (1997); John Lofton, *Denmark Vesey's Plot: The Slave Plot That Lit a Fuse to Fort Sumter* (1983); William S. McFeely, *Frederick Douglass* (1991).

Fiction

Harriet Beecher Stowe, *Uncle Tom's Cabin* (1852).

CHAPTER 12

Shaping America in the Antebellum Age

In November 1836, as the second term of Andrew Jackson neared its end, 30-year-old Marius Robinson and Emily Rakestraw were married near Cincinnati, Ohio. Two months later, Marius went on the road to speak against slavery and organize abolitionist societies in Ohio. Emily stayed in Cincinnati to teach in a school for free blacks. During their ten-month separation, their affectionate letters told of their love and work.

Writing after midnight from Concord, Ohio, Marius complained of the "desolation of loneliness" he felt without her. Emily responded that she felt "about our separation just as you do" and confessed that her "womanish nature" did not enjoy self-denial. In their letters, each imagined the "form and features" of the other and chided the other for not writing more often. Each thought of burdens of the other's work. Each expressed comfort, doubted his or her own abilities ("a miserable comforter I am"), and agreed that in their separation "we must look alone to God."

With such love for each other, what prompted this painful early separation? Emily wrote of their duty "to labor long in this cause so near and dear to us both," together if possible, but apart if so decreed by God. Marius, who had been converted by revivalist Charles G. Finney and his abolitionist disciple Theodore Weld, described the reason for their separation: "God and humanity bleeding and suffering demand our services apart." Driven by a strong religious commitment to serve others, these two young reformers dedicated themselves to several social causes: the abolition of slavery, equal rights and education for free blacks, temperance, and women's rights.

Their commitments cost more than separation. When Emily went to Cincinnati to work with other young reformers, her parents disapproved. When she married Marius, who already had a reputation as a "rebel," her parents disowned her. Emily wrote with sadness that her sisters and friends also "love me less . . . than they did in by-gone days." Marius responded that he wished he could "dry your tears" and sought to heal the rift. Although Emily's family eventually accepted their marriage, there were other griefs. Teaching at the school in Cincinnati was demanding, and Emily could not get rid of a persistent cough. Furthermore, the white citizens of the city treated the school and the young abolitionists in their midst with contempt. Earlier in the year, Marius had escaped an angry mob by disguising himself and mingling with the crowd that came to sack the offices of a reformist journal edited by James G. Birney. Emily, meanwhile, tirelessly persisted in the work of "our school" while worrying about the health and safety of her husband.

She had good reason for concern, for Marius's letters were full of reports of mob attacks, disrupted meetings, stonings, and narrow escapes. At two lectures, he was "mobbed thrice, once most rousingly," by crowds of "the veriest savages I ever saw," armed with clubs and intense hatred for those speaking against slavery. In June, he was dragged from his Quaker host's home, beaten, and tarred and feathered. Never quite recovering his health, Marius spent six months in bed, weak and dispirited. For nearly ten years after that, the Robinsons lived on an Ohio farm, only slightly involved in abolitionist activity. Despite the joyous birth of two daughters, they felt lonely, restless, and guilt-ridden, "tired of days blank of benevolent effort and almost of benevolent desires."

✦✦✦✦✦✦

The work of Emily and Marius Robinson represents one response by the American people to the rapid social and economic changes of the antebellum era described in Chapters 10 and 11. In September 1835, a year before the Robinsons' marriage, the *Niles Register* commented on some 500 recent incidents of mob violence and social upheaval. "Society seems everywhere unhinged, and the demon of 'blood and slaughter' has been let loose upon us . . . . [The] character of our countrymen seems suddenly changed." How did Americans adapt to these changes? In a world that seemed everywhere "unhinged," in which old rules and patterns no longer provided guidance, how did people maintain some sense of control over their lives? How did they seek to shape their altered world? How could they both adopt the benefits of change and reduce the accompanying disruptions?

One way was to embrace the changes fully. Thus, some Americans became entrepreneurs in new industries; invested in banks, canals, and railroads; bought more land and slaves; and invented new machines. Others went west or to the new textile mills, enrolled in common schools, joined trade unions, specialized their labor in the workplace and the home, and celebrated modernization's practical benefits. Marius Robinson eventually went into life insurance, though he and Emily never fully gave up their reformist efforts and idealism.

But many Americans were uncomfortable with the character of the new era. Some worried about the unrestrained power and materialism symbolized by the slavemaster's control over his slaves. Others feared that institutions like the U.S. Bank represented a "monied aristocracy" capable of undermining the country's honest producers. Seeking positions of leadership and authority, these critics of the new order tried to shape a nation that retained the benefits of economic change without sacrificing humane principles of liberty, equality of opportunity, and community virtue. This chapter examines four ways in which the American people responded to change by attempting to influence their country's development: religious revivalism, party politics, utopian communitarianism, and social reform.

RELIGIOUS REVIVAL AND REFORM PHILOSOPHY

When the Frenchman Alexis de Tocqueville visited the United States in 1831 and 1832, he observed that he could find "no country in the whole world in which the Christian religion retains a greater influence over the souls of men than in America." Tocqueville was describing a new and powerful religious enthusiasm among American Protestants. Religious rebirth gave some Americans a mooring in a fast-changing world, while others were inspired to refashion their society, working through new political parties to shape an agenda for the nation or through reform associations targeting a particular social evil. Although not all evangelicals agreed about politics or even about what needed reform, religion was the lens through which they viewed events and sought change.

Finney and the Second Great Awakening

From the late 1790s until the late 1830s, a wave of religious revivals that matched the intensity of the earlier Great Awakening swept the United States. The turn-of-the-century frontier camp meeting revivals and the New England revivals sparked by Lyman Beecher took on a new emphasis and location after 1830. Led by the spellbinding Charles G. Finney, under whose influence Marius Robinson had been converted, revivalism shifted to upstate New York and the Old Northwest. Both areas had been gripped by profound economic and social changes.

Rochester, New York, was typical. By the 1830s it, like Lowell and Cincinnati, was booming. Located on the Erie Canal, it was a flour-milling center for western New York, changed by the canal from a sleepy village of 300 in 1815 to a bustling city of nearly 20,000 by 1830. As in other cities, economic growth affected relationships between masters and workers. As the gulf widened, the masters' control over laborers weakened. Saloons and unions sprang up, and workers became more transient, following opportunities westward.

In 1830, prominent Rochester citizens therefore invited Charles Finney to lead what became one of the most successful revivals of the Second Great Awakening. Finney preached nearly every night and three times on Sundays, converting first the city's business elite, often through their wives, and then many workers. For six months, Rochester experienced a citywide prayer meeting in which one conversion led to another.

The Rochester revival was part of a wave of religious enthusiasm in America that contributed to the tremendous growth of Methodists, Baptists, and other evangelical denominations in the first half of the nineteenth century. By 1844, Methodism became the country's largest denomination with over a million members. Revivalist preachers emphasized emotion over doctrine, softening such Calvinist tenets as predestination and original sin.

Unlike Jonathan Edwards, who had believed that revivals were God's miracles, Finney understood that the human "agency" of the minister was crucial in causing a revival. He even published a do-it-yourself manual for revivalists. But few could match his powerful preaching style. When he threw an imaginary brick at the Devil, people ducked. A former lawyer, Finney used logic as well as emotion to bring about conversions.

Many revivalists, especially in the South, sought individual salvation. American Catholics also caught the revival fervor in the 1830s. Scattered in small but growing numbers, urban Catholic leaders recognized that survival as a small and often despised religion depended on constant reinvigoration and evangelism. Focusing on the parish mission, energetic retreats and revivals gathered Catholics from miles around to preserve a religious heritage seriously threatened by life in Protestant America.

The Finney revivals differed from Catholic and southern revivalism because they insisted that conversion and salvation were not the end of religious experience but the beginning. Finney believed that humans were not passive objects of God's predestined plan, but moral free agents who could choose good over evil and

This 1839 painting of a camp meeting captures the religious fervor that many Americans turned to in the face of social and economic upheavals. These mass conversions led some believers to individual salvation and others to social reform. (New Bedford Whaling Museum)

thereby eradicate sin. Finney's idea of the "utility of benevolence" meant not only individual reformation, but also the commitment to do one's sacred duty in reforming society.

The Transcendentalists

No one knew this better than Ralph Waldo Emerson, a Concord, Massachusetts, essayist who was the era's foremost intellectual figure. Emerson's essays of the 1830s influenced the mid-century generation of reformist American intellectuals, artists, and writers. The small but influential group of New England intellectuals who lived near Emerson were called Transcendentalists because of their belief that truth was found beyond (transcended) experience. Casting off the European intellectual tradition, Emerson urged Americans to look inward and to nature for self-knowledge, self-reliance, and the spark of divinity within them. Such examinations would lead to social reform. "What is man born for," Emerson asked, "but to be a Reformer?"

Inspired by self-reflection, Transcendentalists asked troublesome questions. They challenged not only slavery, an obvious evil, but also the obsessive competitive pace of economic life, the overriding materialism, and the restrictive conformity of social life.

Although not Transcendentalists, Nathaniel Hawthorne and Herman Melville, two giants of mid-century American literature, wrote of these concerns in their fiction. Like Emerson, they celebrated emotion over reason. Hawthorne's great subject was the "truth of the human heart." In his greatest novel, *The Scarlet Letter*

(1850), Hawthorne sympathetically told the story of a courageous Puritan woman's adultery and her eventual loving triumph over the narrowness of both cold intellect and intolerant conformity.

Herman Melville dedicated his epic novel *Moby Dick* (1851) to Hawthorne. At one level a rousing story of whaling, *Moby Dick* was actually an immense allegory of good and evil, bravery and weakness, innocence and experience. Like Emerson, Hawthorne and Melville mirrored the tensions of the age as they explored issues of freedom and control.

When Emerson wrote "Whoso would be a man, must be a nonconformist," he described his friend Henry David Thoreau. No one thought more deeply about the virtuous natural life than Thoreau. On July 4, 1845, he went to live in a small hut by Walden Pond, near Concord, to confront the "essential facts of life"—to discover who he was and how to live well. When Thoreau left Walden two years later, he protested against slavery and the Mexican War by refusing to pay his taxes. He went to jail briefly and wrote an essay, "On Civil Disobedience" (1849), and a book, *Walden* (1854), both classic statements of what one person can do to protest unjust laws and wars and live a life of principle.

THE POLITICAL RESPONSE TO CHANGE

Although transcendentalism touched only a few elite New Englanders, perhaps 40 percent of Americans were affected by evangelical Protestantism. Evangelical values and religious loyalties colored many people's understanding of the appropriate role of government and influenced their politics. As politics became more a popular than an elite vocation, it was not surprising that religious commitments spilled over into it.

At the heart of American politics was the concern for the continued health of the republican experiment. As American society changed, so did the understanding of what was needed to maintain that health. Before the 1820s, politics was primarily for the social and economic elite. Even though many states were removing voting restrictions in the early nineteenth century, the majority of white men ignored politics. But the Panic of 1819 and the spirited presidential campaigns for Andrew Jackson helped create widespread interest in politics. For many Americans, political participation became an important way of asserting and supporting important values and promoting their vision of the republic.

Changing Political Culture

Jackson's presidency was crucial in bringing politics to the center of many Americans' lives. Styling himself the people's candidate in 1828, Jackson derided the Adams administration as corrupt and aristocratic and promised a more democratic political system. He told voters that he intended to "purify" and "reform the Government," purging all "who have been appointed from political considerations or against the will of the people." Most Americans believed campaign rhetoric. Four times more men turned out to vote in the election of 1828 than had four years earlier. They gave Jackson a resounding 56 percent of their ballots. No other president in the century would equal that percentage of popular support.

Despite campaign rhetoric and his image as a democratic hero, Jackson was not personally very democratic, nor did the era he symbolized involve any significant redistribution of wealth. Jackson owned slaves, defended slavery, and condoned mob attacks on abolitionists like Marius Robinson. He disliked Indians and ordered the forcible removal of southeastern Native Americans to west of the Mississippi River in blatant disregard of treaty rights and a Supreme Court decision. Belying promises of widening opportunity, the rich got richer during the Jacksonian era, and most farming and urban laboring families did not prosper.

But the nation's political life had changed in important ways. The old system of politics, based on elite coalitions and dependent on voters deferring to their "betters," largely disappeared. In its place emerged a competitive party system, begun early in the republic but now oriented toward heavy voter participation. The major parties grew adept at raising money, selecting and promoting candidates, and bringing voters to the polls. A new "democratic" style of political life emerged as parties sponsored conventions, rallies (much like evangelical revivals), and parades to encourage political participation and identification. Party politics became a central preoccupation for many adult white males. In the North, even women turned out for political hoopla.

Parties appealed to popular emotions, religious views, and ethnic prejudices. Party-subsidized newspapers regularly indulged in scurrilous attacks on political candidates. The language of politics became contentious and militaristic. Jackson's rhetoric exemplified the new trends. He described an opponent as an "enemy." Politicians talked of elections as battles and of their disciplined "rank and file." Strong party identification became part of the new political culture.

Jackson's Path to the White House

The early career of Andrew Jackson gave few hints of his future political importance. Orphaned at 14, young Jackson was rowdy, indecisive, and often in trouble. As a law student, he was "a most roaring, rollicking, game-cocking, horse-racing, card-playing, mischievous fellow." Despite these preoccupations, which included dueling, Jackson passed the bar and set out to seek his fortune in the West. Settling in frontier Nashville, the tall, redheaded young man built up a successful law practice and went on to become state attorney general, a substantial landowner, and a prominent citizen of Nashville.

Jackson's national reputation stemmed mainly from his military exploits, primarily against Indians. As major general of the Tennessee militia, he proved able and popular. His troops nicknamed him "Old Hickory." His savage victory over the Creeks in 1813 and 1814 brought notoriety and an appointment as major general in the U.S. Army. Then his victory at New Orleans in 1815 made him a national hero. As early as 1817, he was talked of as a presidential candidate.

Although Jackson's aggressive military forays into Spanish Florida in 1818 bothered rival politicians and added to his reputation for scandal, they increased his popularity and his interest in the presidency. Jackson recognized that his greatest appeal lay with ordinary people, whom he cultivated. But he also secured effective political backing. Careful political maneuvering in Tennessee in the early 1820s brought him election as U.S. senator and nomination for the presidency in 1824.

As depicted in the Robert Cruikshank lithograph, *All Creation Going to the White House*, the first inauguration of Andrew Jackson in 1829 was the scene of wild festivities, a harbinger of the excesses in American life and politics in the ensuing years. (Library of Congress)

Jackson won both the popular and the electoral votes in 1824, but lost in the House of Representatives to John Quincy Adams. This failure to win the presidency taught him the importance of political organization. Confident of his strength in the West, and helped by Adams's vice president, Calhoun, in the South, Jackson organized his campaign by setting up committees and newspapers in many states and by encouraging efforts to undermine Adams and Clay.

A loose coalition promoting Jackson's candidacy began to call itself the Democratic party. Politicians of diverse views from all sections of the country were drawn to it, including Martin Van Buren of New York. Jackson masterfully waffled on controversial issues. He concealed his dislike of banks and paper money and vaguely advocated a "middle and just course" on the tariff. And he promised to cleanse government of corruption and privilege.

The Jackson-Adams campaign in 1828 degenerated into a nasty but entertaining contest. The Democrats whipped up enthusiasm with barbecues, mass rallies, and parades, and gave out buttons and hats with hickory leaves attached. Few people discussed issues. Both sides made slanderous personal attacks. Supporters of Adams and Clay, who called themselves National Republicans, branded Jackson "an adulterer, a gambler, a cockfighter, a brawler, a drunkard, and a murderer." His wife Rachel was maligned as common and immoral.

The Jacksonians charged Adams with buying Clay's support in 1824. They described him as a "stingy, undemocratic" aristocrat determined to destroy the people's liberties. Worse yet, they said, Adams was an intellectual. Campaign slogans emphasized the differences between the hero of New Orleans, "a man who can fight," and wimpy Adams, "a man who can write."

Jackson's supporters in Washington worked to ensure his election by devising a tariff bill to win necessary support in key states. Under the leadership of Van Buren, who hoped to replace Calhoun as Jackson's heir apparent, the Democrats in Congress managed to pass what opponents called the "Tariff of Abominations." It arbitrarily raised rates to protect New England textiles, Pennsylvania iron, and some agricultural goods, winning voters in those states where the Democrats needed more support.

The efforts of Jackson and his party paid off as he won an astonishing 647,286 votes, about 56 percent of the total. Organization, money, effective publicity, and a popular style of campaigning had brought the 60-year-old Jackson to the presidency. His inauguration, however, horrified many. Washington was packed for the ceremonies. When Jackson appeared to take the oath of office, wild cheering broke out. Few heard him, but many hoped to shake the new president's hand, and Jackson was all but mobbed.

The White House reception got completely out of hand. A throng of people, "from the highest and most polished, down to the most vulgar and gross," Justice Joseph Story observed, poured into the White House with muddy boots to overturn furniture in a rush for food and punch. Jackson had to leave by a side door. When wine and ice cream were carried out to the lawn, many guests followed by diving through the windows. The inauguration, to Story, meant the "reign of King Mob." Another observer called it a "proud day for the people." These contrasting views on the events of the inauguration captured the essence of the Jackson era.

Old Hickory's Vigorous Presidency

Although Jackson had taken vague positions on important issues during the campaign, as president he needed to confront many of them. His decisions, often controversial, helped sharpen what it meant to be a Democrat.

A few key convictions—the principle of majority rule, the limited power of the national government, the obligation of the national government to defend the interests of the nation's average people against the "monied aristocracy"—guided Jackson's actions as president. Seeing himself as the people's most authentic representative (only the president was elected by all the people), Jackson intended to be a vigorous executive. More than any predecessor, Jackson used presidential power in the name of the people and justified his actions by appeals to the voters.

Jackson asserted his power most dramatically through the veto. His six predecessors had cast only nine vetoes, mostly against measures that they had believed unconstitutional. Jackson vetoed 12 bills during his two terms, often because they conflicted with his political agenda.

Jackson had promised to correct what he called an undemocratic and corrupt system of government officeholding. Too often "unfaithful or incompetent" men clung to government jobs for years. Jackson proposed to throw these scoundrels out and establish rotation of office. The duties of public office were so "plain and simple," he said, that ordinary men could fulfill them.

Jackson's rhetoric was more extreme than his actions. He did not replace officeholders wholesale. In the first year and a half of his presidency, he removed 919 officeholders of a total of 10,093, mostly for corruption or incompetence. Nor were the new Democratic appointees especially plain, untutored, or honest; they were much like their predecessors. Still, Jackson's rhetoric helped create a new democratic political culture for most of the nineteenth century.

His policy on internal improvements—roads, canals and other forms of transportation—was less far-seeing. Like most Americans, Jackson recognized their economic importance. But Jackson opposed infringement on states' rights. When proposals for federal support for internal improvements seemed to rob local and state authorities of their proper function, he opposed them. In 1830, he vetoed the Maysville Road bill, which proposed federal funding for a road in Henry Clay's

Kentucky. But projects of national significance, like river improvements or lighthouses, were different. During his presidency Jackson supported an annual average of $1.3 million in internal improvements.

In a period of rapid economic change, tariffs stirred heated debate. New England and the Middle Atlantic states, the center of manufacturing, favored tariffs. The South had long opposed them because they made it more expensive to buy manufactured goods from the North or abroad, and threatened to provoke retaliation against southern cotton and tobacco exports. Feelings ran particularly high in South Carolina. Some of that state's leaders mistakenly believed the tariff was the prime reason for the depression that hung over their state. In addition, some worried that the federal government might eventually interfere with slavery, a frightening prospect in a state where slaves outnumbered whites.

Vice President Calhoun, a brilliant political thinker and opponent of the tariff, provided the appropriate theory to check federal power and protect minority rights. "We are not a nation," he once remarked, "but a Union, a confederacy of equal and sovereign states." In 1828, the same year as the hateful tariff, Calhoun anonymously published *Exposition and Protest*, presenting nullification as a means by which southern states could protect themselves from harmful national action by declaring legislation null and void.

Two years later, Calhoun's doctrine was aired in a Senate debate over public land policy. South Carolina's Robert Hayne defined nullification and urged western states to adopt it. Daniel Webster responded. The federal government, he said, was no mere agent of the state legislatures. It was "made for the people, made by the people, and answerable to the people." Aware that nullification could mean a "once glorious Union . . . drenched . . . in fraternal blood," Webster cried in his powerful closing words that the appropriate motto for the nation was not "Liberty first and Union afterwards, but Liberty and Union, now and forever, one and inseparable!"

The drama was repeated a month later in the toast at a dinner, when President Jackson declared himself on the issue. Despite his support of states' rights, Jackson did not believe that any state had the right to reject the will of the majority or to destroy the Union. Jackson rose for a toast, held high his glass, and said, "Our Union—it must be preserved." Challenged, Calhoun followed: "The Union—next to our liberty most dear." The split between them widened over personal as well as ideological issues, and in 1832 Calhoun resigned as vice president. Final rupture came in a collision over the tariff and nullification.

In 1832, hewing to Jackson's "middle course," Congress modified the tariff of 1828 by retaining high duties on some goods but lowering other rates to an earlier level. A South Carolina convention later that year adopted an Ordinance of Nullification, voiding the tariffs of 1828 and 1832 in the state. The legislature funded a volunteer army and threatened secession if the federal government tried to force the state to comply.

South Carolina had attacked the principles of union and majority rule, and Jackson responded forcefully. To the "ambitious malcontents" in South Carolina, he proclaimed emphatically that "the laws of the United States must be executed . . . . Disunion by armed force is treason . . . . The Union will be preserved and treason and rebellion promptly put down."

Jackson's proclamation stimulated an outburst of patriotism all over the country. South Carolina stood alone, abandoned even by other southern states. Jackson asked Congress for legislation to enforce tariff duties (the Force Bill of 1833), and new tariff revisions, engineered by Clay and supported by Calhoun, called for reductions over a ten-year period. South Carolina quickly repealed its nullification of the tariff laws but saved face by nullifying the Force Bill, which Jackson ignored. The crisis was over, but left unresolved were the constitutional issues it raised. Was the Union permanent? Was secession a valid way to protect minority rights? Such questions would trouble Americans for three decades.

Jackson's Indian Policy

Jackson threatened force on South Carolina; he used it on southeastern Indians. His policy of forcible relocation defined white practice toward Native Americans for the rest of the century.

In the early nineteenth century, the vast lands of the five "civilized nations" of the Southeast (the Cherokee, Choctaw, Chickasaw, Seminole, and Creek) had been seriously eroded by land-hungry whites supported by military campaigns led by professional Indian fighters like Jackson. The Creek lost 22 million acres in Georgia and Alabama after Jackson defeated them in 1814. Cessions to the government and private sales accounted for even bigger losses: Cherokee holdings of more than 50 million acres in 1802 dwindled to only 9 million 20 years later.

The trend was bolstered by a Supreme Court decision in 1823 declaring that Indians could occupy but not hold title to land in the United States. Seeing that their survival was threatened, Indian nations acted. By 1825, the Creek, Cherokee, and Chickasaw restricted land sales to government agents. The Cherokee, having already assimilated such elements of white culture as agricultural practices and slaveholding (see Chapter 9), established a police force to prevent local leaders from selling off tribal lands. Indian determination to resist confronted white resolve to gain their land. Jackson's election in 1828 boosted efforts to relocate the Indians west of the Mississippi.

In 1829, Jackson recommended to Congress removal of the southeastern tribes. Appealing at first to sympathy, Jackson argued that because the Indians were "surrounded by the whites, "they were inevitably doomed to "weakness and decay." Removal was justified by "humanity and national honor." State laws, he also insisted, should prevail over the claims of either Indians or the federal government (thus contradicting his tariff policy).

The crisis came to a head that same year, when the Georgia legislature declared the Cherokee tribal council illegal and claimed jurisdiction over both the tribe and its lands. In 1830, the Cherokee were forbidden to bring suits or testify against whites in the Georgia courts. The Cherokee protested to the Supreme Court. In 1832, Chief Justice Marshall supported them in *Worcester v. Georgia.*

Legal victory could not, however, suppress white land hunger. With Jackson's blessing, Georgia defied the Court ruling. By 1835, harassment, intimidation, and bribery had persuaded a minority of chiefs to sign a removal treaty. That year, Jackson informed the Cherokee, "You cannot remain where you are. Circumstances . . . render it impossible that you can flourish in the midst of a civilized community." But most Cherokee refused to leave. So in 1837 and 1838, the U.S. Army gathered the terrified Indians in stockades before herding them west to the "Indian Territory" in present-day Oklahoma.

The removal, whose $6 million cost was deducted from the $9 million award-ed the Cherokee for its eastern lands, killed perhaps a quarter of the 15,000 who set out. The Cherokee remember this as the "Trail of Tears." Other southern and some northwestern tribes between 1821 and 1840 shared a similar fate. The Chickasaw suffered as high a death rate, while the Seminole and the Sac and Fox fought back. Most nations were, in the end, removed. Although both Jackson and the Removal Act of 1830 had promised to protect and forever guarantee the Indian lands in the West, within a generation those promises, like others before and since, would be broken. Indian removal left the eastern United States open for the enormous eco-nomic expansion described in Chapter 10.

Jackson's Bank War and "Van Ruin's" Depression

As the (white) people's advocate, Jackson could not ignore the Second Bank of the United States, which in 1816 had received a charter for 20 years. The bank gener-ated intense feelings. Jackson called it a "monster" that threatened the people's lib-erties. But it was not so irresponsible as Jacksonians imagined.

Guided since 1823 by aristocratic Nicholas Biddle, the Philadelphia bank and its 29 branches generally played a responsible economic role in an expansionary period. As the nation's largest commercial bank, "the B.U.S." could shift funds around the country as needed and could influence state banking activity. It restrained state banks from making unwise loans by insisting that they back their notes with specie (gold or silver coin) and by calling in its loans to them. The bank accepted federal deposits, made commercial loans, and bought and sold govern-ment bonds. Businessmen, state bankers needing credit, and nationalist politicians such as Webster and Clay, who were on the bank's payroll, all favored it.

Other Americans, led by the president, distrusted the bank. Businessmen and speculators in western lands resented its careful control over state banking and wanted cheap, inflated money. Some state bankers resented its power. Southern and western farmers regarded it as immoral because it dealt with paper rather than landed property. Others simply thought it was unconstitutional.

Jackson had long opposed the B.U.S. He hated banks in general because of a near financial disaster in his own past, and also because he and his advisers con-sidered the B.U.S. the chief example of a special privilege monopoly that hurt the common man—farmers, craftsmen, and debtors. Jackson called the bank a threat to the Republic. Its power and financial resources, he thought, made it a "vast elec-tioneering engine."

Aware of Jackson's hostility, Clay and Webster persuaded Biddle to ask Congress for a new charter in 1832, four years ahead of schedule. They reasoned that in an election year, Jackson would not risk a veto. The bill to recharter the bank swept through Congress. Jackson took up the challenge. "The bank . . . is trying to kill me," he told Van Buren, "but I will kill it."

Jackson determined not only to veto the bill, but also to carry his case to the public. His veto message, condemning the bank as undemocratic, un-American, and unconstitutional, was meant to stir up voters. He presented the bank as a dan-gerous monopoly that gave the rich special privileges and harmed "the humble members of society." He also pointed to the high percentage of foreign investors in the bank. Jackson's veto message turned the rechartering issue into a struggle between the people and the aristocracy. His oversimplified analysis made the bank into a symbol of everything that worried many Americans in a time of change.

The bank furor helped to clarify party differences. In 1832, the National Republicans, now calling themselves Whigs, nominated Henry Clay, and they and Biddle spent thousands of dollars trying to defeat "King Andrew." Democratic campaign rhetoric pitted Jackson, the people, and democracy against Clay, the bank, and aristocracy. The Anti-Masons, the first third party in American political life and the first to hold a nominating convention, expressed popular resentments against the elitist Masonic order (Jackson was a member) and other secret societies.

Jackson won handsomely, with 124,000 more popular votes than the combined total for Clay and the Anti-Mason candidate, William Wirt. "He may be President for life if he chooses," said Wirt of Jackson.

Jackson saw the election as a victory for his bank policy and closed in on Biddle, even though the bank's charter had four years to run. He decided to weaken the bank by transferring $10 million in government funds to state banks. Although two secretaries of the treasury balked at the request as financially unsound, Jackson persisted until he found one, Roger Taney, willing to do it. When Chief Justice Marshall died in 1835, Jackson replaced him with Taney.

Jackson's war with Biddle and the bank had serious economic consequences. A wave of speculation in western lands and ambitious new state internal-improvement schemes in the mid-1830s produced inflated land prices and a flood of paper money. Even Jackson was concerned, and he tried to curtail irresponsible economic activity. In July 1836, he issued the Specie Circular, announcing that the government would accept only gold and silver in payment for public lands. Panicky investors rushed to change paper notes into specie, and banks started calling in loans. The result was the Panic of 1837. Jackson was blamed for this rapid monetary expansion followed by sudden deflation, but international trade problems probably contributed more to the panic and to the ensuing seven years of depression.

Whatever the primary cause, Jackson left his successor, Martin Van Buren, who was elected in 1836 over a trio of Whig opponents, with an economic crisis. Van Buren had barely taken the oath of office in 1837 when banks and businesses began to collapse. "Martin Van Ruin's" presidency was dominated by a severe depression. As New York banks suspended credit and began calling in loans, some $6 million was lost on defaulted debts. By the fall of 1837, one-third of America's workers were unemployed, and thousands of others had only part-time work. Those who kept their jobs saw wages fall by 30 to 50 percent within two years. The price of necessities nearly doubled. As winter neared in 1837, a journalist estimated that 200,000 New Yorkers were "in utter hopeless distress with no means of surviving the winter but those provided by charity." They took to the streets, but as one worker said, most laborers called "not for the bread and fuel of charity, but for Work!"

The pride of workers was dampened as soup kitchens and bread lines grew faster than jobs. Laboring families found themselves defenseless, for the depression destroyed the trade union movement begun a decade earlier—a demise hastened by employers who imposed longer hours, cut wages and piece rates, and divided workers. Job competition, poverty, and ethnic animosities led to violent clashes in other eastern cities, as we saw in Chapter 10.

The Second American Party System

By the mid-1830s, a new two-party system and a lively national political culture had emerged in the United States. The parties had taken shape amid the conflicts of Jackson's presidency and the religious fervor of the Second Great Awakening. Although both parties included wealthy and influential leaders and mirrored the nation's growing diversity, Democrats had the better claim to be "the party of the common man," with strength in all sections of the country.

Whigs represented greater wealth than Democrats and were strongest in New England and in areas settled by New Englanders across the Upper Midwest. Appealing to businessmen and manufacturers, Whigs generally endorsed Clay's American System: a national bank, federally supported internal improvements, and tariff protection for industry. Many large southern cotton planters joined the Whig party because of its position on bank credit and internal improvements. Whigs ran almost evenly with Democrats in the South for a decade, and artisans and laborers belonged equally to each party. The difficulty in drawing clear regional or class distinctions between Whigs and Democrats suggests that ethnic, religious, and cultural background also influenced party choice.

In the Jeffersonian tradition, the Democrats espoused liberty and local rule. They wanted freedom from legislators of morality, from religious tyranny, from special privilege, from too much government. For them, the best society was one in which all Americans were free to follow individual interests. The Democrats appealed to members of denominations that had suffered discrimination in colonies and states where there had been an established church. Scots-Irish, German, French, and Irish Catholic immigrants, as well as free thinkers and labor organizers, tended to be Jacksonians. Democrats were less moralistic than Whigs on matters like drinking and slavery. Their religious background generally taught the inevitability of sin and evil, and Democrats sought to separate politics from moral issues.

By contrast, for many Whigs the line between reform and politics was hazy. Indeed, politics seemed an appropriate arena for cleansing society of sin. Calling themselves the party of law and order, most Whigs did not think Americans needed more freedom; rather, they had to learn to use the freedom they already had. If all men were to vote, they should learn how to use their political privileges. Old-stock Yankee Congregationalists and Presbyterians were usually Whigs. So were Quakers and evangelical Protestants, who believed that positive government action could change moral behavior and eradicate sin. Whigs supported a wide variety of reforms, such as temperance, antislavery, public education, and strict observance of the Sabbath, as well as government action to promote economic development.

Party identification played an increasingly large part in the lives of American men. Gaudy new electioneering styles were designed to recruit new voters into the political process and ensure loyalty. Politics offered excitement, entertainment, camaraderie, and a way to shape the changing world.

The election of 1840 illustrated the new political culture. Passing over Henry Clay, the Whigs nominated William Henry Harrison, the aging hero of the Battle of Tippecanoe of 1811. Virginian John Tyler was nominated as vice-president to underline the regional diversity of the party. The Democrats had no choice but to renominate Van Buren, who conducted a quiet campaign. The Whig campaign, however, used every form of popularized appeal—songs, cartoons, barbecues, and torchlight parades. Creating a potent political symbol, Harrison (who lived in a mansion) was posed in front of a log cabin with a barrel of hard cider.

The Whigs reversed conventional images by labeling Van Buren an aristocratic dandy and their man as a simple candidate. Harrison reminded voters of General Jackson, and they swept him into office, 234 electoral votes to Van Buren's 60. In one of the largest turnouts in American history, over 80 percent of eligible voters marched to the polls. A Democratic party journal acknowledged that the Whigs had out-Jacksoned the Jacksonians: "We taught them how to conquer us."

Concern over the new politics outlasted Harrison, who died only a month after taking office. One man complained during the campaign that he was tired of all the hoopla over "the Old Hero. Nothing but politics . . . mass-meetings are held in every groggery." His comment about the combination of politics and drinking was especially telling. For many Americans, usually Whigs and often women, it was precisely the excesses of Jacksonian politics, most notably intemperance and the inherent violence of slavery, that led them to seek ways other than politics to impose order and morality on American society.

PERFECTIONIST REFORM AND UTOPIANISM

"Be ye therefore perfect even as your Father in heaven is perfect," commanded the Bible. Mid-nineteenth-century reformers, inspired by the Finney revivals, took the challenge seriously. Eventually, a perfected millennial era—1,000 years of peace, harmony, and Christian brotherhood—would bring the Second Coming of Christ.

This perfectionist thrust in religion fit America's sense of itself as chosen by God to reform the world. The impulse to reform in the 1830s had deep-rooted causes: the Puritan idea of American mission; the secular examples of founding fathers like Benjamin Franklin to do good, reinforced by Republican ideology and romantic beliefs in the natural goodness of human nature; the social activist tendencies in Whig political ideology; anxiety over shifting class relationships and socioeconomic change; family influence and the desire of young people to choose careers of principled service; and the direct influence of the revivals.

The Dilemmas of Reform

Religious reformers and Whig politicians both faced timeless dilemmas about how best to effect change. Is it more effective to appeal to people's minds in order to change bad institutions, or to change institutions first, assuming that altered behavior will then change attitudes? Taking the first path, the reformer relies on education, sermons, tracts, literature, argument, and personal testimony. Following the second, the reformer acts politically and institutionally, seeking to pass laws, win elections, form unions, boycott goods, and create or abolish institutions.

Reformers must decide whether to attempt to bring about limited, piecemeal practical change on a single issue or go for perfection. Should they use or recommend force or enter into coalitions with less principled potential allies? As Thoreau asked, are their attitudes and actions thoroughly consistent with the behavior they would urge on others?

As Marius and Emily Robinson understood, promoting change has its costs. Reformers invariably disagree on appropriate ideology and tactics, and so end up quarreling with one another. Although reformers suffer pressure to conform and cease questioning things, their duty to themselves, their society, and their God sustains their commitment.

Utopian Communities: Oneida and the Shakers

Thoreau tried to lead an ideal solitary life. Others tried to redeem a flawed society that was losing the cohesion and traditional values of small community life by creating miniature utopian societies—alternatives to a world of factories, foreigners, immorality, and entrepreneurs.

In 1831, as Jackson and the nullifiers squared off, as Nat Turner planned his revolt, and as the citizens of Rochester sought ways of controlling their workers' drinking habits, a young man in Putney, Vermont, heard Charles Finney preach. John Humphrey Noyes was an instant, if unorthodox, convert.

Noyes believed that final conversion led to perfection and complete release from sin. But his earthly happiness was soon sorely tested when a woman he loved rejected both his doctrine and his marriage offer. Among those who were perfect, he argued, all men and women belonged equally to each other. Others called his doctrines "free love" and socialism. Noyes recovered from his unhappy love affair and married a loyal follower. When she bore four stillborn babies within six years, Noyes again revised his unconventional ideas about sex.

In 1848, Noyes and 51 followers founded a "perfectionist" community at Oneida, New York. Under his strong leadership, it prospered. Sexual life at the commune was subject to many regulations, including male continence except under carefully prescribed conditions. Only certain spiritually advanced males (usually Noyes) could father children. Other controversial practices included communal child rearing, sexual equality in work, the removal of the competitive spirit from both work and play, and an elaborate program of "mutual criticism" at community meetings presided over by "Father" Noyes. Wise economic decisions bound community members in mutual prosperity. Noyes opted for modern manufacturing, at first steel animal traps and later silverware.

Noyes greatly admired the Shakers, who also believed in perfectionism, communal property, and bringing on the millennial kingdom of heaven. Unlike the Oneidans, Shakers condemned sexuality and demanded absolute chastity, so that only conversions could bring in new members. Founded by an Englishwoman, Mother Ann Lee, Shaker conversions grew in the Second Great Awakening and peaked around 6,000 souls by the 1850s, with communities from Maine to Kentucky. They believed that God had a dual personality, male and female, and that Mother Ann was the female counterpart to the masculine Christ. Shaker communities, some of which survived long into the twentieth century, were known for their communal ownership of property, equality of women and men, simplicity, and beautifully crafted furniture.

Other Utopias

Over 100 utopian communities were founded. Some were religiously motivated; others were secular. Most were small and lasted only a few months or years. All eventually collapsed, though giving birth to significant social ideas.

While pietist German-speaking immigrants founded the earliest utopian communities in America to preserve their language, spirituality, and ascetic lifestyle, other antebellum utopian communities focused on the regeneration of this world, or responded more directly to the social misery and wretched working conditions accompanying industrialization. Evil, these communities assumed, came from bad environments, not individual sin.

Robert Owen was the best known of the secular communalists. A Scottish industrialist who saw the miserable lives of cotton mill workers, he envisioned a society of small towns with good schools and healthy work. In 1824, he established his first town in America at New Harmony, Indiana. But little harmony prevailed, and it failed within three years.

Brook Farm, founded by two Concord friends of Emerson, tried to integrate "intellectual and manual labor." Residents would hoe for a few hours each day and then recite poetry. Although the colony lasted less than three years, it produced some notable literature in a journal, *The Dial,* edited by Margaret Fuller. Hawthorne briefly lived at Brook Farm and wrote a novel, *The Blithedale Romance* (1852), criticizing the utopians' naive optimism.

The utopian communities all failed for similar reasons. Americans seemed unwilling to share either their property or their spouses. Nor did celibacy arouse much enthusiasm. Other recurring problems included unstable leadership, financial bickering, local hostility toward sexual experimentation and other unorthodox practices, the indiscriminate admission of members, and waning enthusiasm. As Emerson said of Brook Farm, "It met every test but life itself."

Millerites and Mormons

If utopian communities failed to bring about the peaceful millennium, an alternative hope was to leap directly to the Second Coming of Christ. William Miller, a shy farmer from upstate New York, figured out its exact time: 1843, probably in March. A sect gathered around him to prepare for Christ's return and the Day of Judgment.

Excitement and fear grew as the day came closer. Some people gave away all their belongings, put on robes, and flocked to high hills and rooftops. When 1843 passed without the end of the world, Miller recalculated. Each new disappointment diminished his followers, and he died discredited in 1848. But a small Millerite sect, the Seventh-Day Adventists, had already taken root and continues to this day.

Other groups that emerged from the same religiously active area of upstate New York were more successful. As Palmyra, New York, was being swept by Finney revivalism, young Joseph Smith, a recent convert, claimed to be visited by the angel Moroni, who led him to golden tablets buried near his home. On these were inscribed *The Book of Mormon*, which described the one true church and a "lost tribe of Israel" missing for centuries. The book also predicted the appearance of an American prophet who would establish a new and pure kingdom of Christ in America. Smith published his book in 1830 and soon founded the Church of Jesus Christ of Latter-Day Saints (the Mormons). His visionary leadership attracted thousands of ordinary people trying to escape what they viewed as social disorder, religious impurity, and commercial degradation in the 1830s.

Smith and a steadily growing band of converts migrated first to Ohio, next to Missouri, and then back to Illinois, everywhere meeting ridicule, persecution, and violence. Hostility stemmed in part from their active missionary work, in part from their beliefs and support for local Indian tribes, and in part from rumors of unorthodox sexual practices.

Despite persecution and dissension over Smith's strong leadership style, the Mormons prospered. Converts from England and northern Europe added substantially to their numbers. By the mid-1840s, Nauvoo, Illinois, with a thriving population of nearly 15,000, was the showplace of Mormonism. Smith petitioned Congress for territorial status and ran for president of the United States in 1844. Such boldness was too much for local citizens. Violence culminated in Smith's trial for treason and his lynching. Under the brilliant leadership of his successor, Brigham Young, the Mormons headed west in 1846.

REFORMING SOCIETY

The Mormons and the utopian communitarians had as their common goal, in Young's words, "the spread of righteousness upon the earth." Most people, however, preferred to focus on a specific social evil.

"We are all a little wild here," Emerson wrote in 1840, "with numberless projects of social reform." Mobilized in part by their increased participation in the political parties of Jacksonian America, the reformers created and joined all kinds of social-uplift societies. The reform ranks were swelled by thousands of women, stirred to action by the religious revivals and freed from domestic burdens by delayed marriage and smaller families. In hundreds of voluntary societies, people like Emily Rakestraw and Marius Robinson tackled such issues as alcohol, diet and health, sexuality, the institutional treatment of social outcasts, education, the rights of labor, slavery, and women's rights.

Temperance

On New Year's Eve in 1831, a Finney disciple, Theodore Dwight Weld, delivered a four-hour temperance lecture in Rochester. Graphically he described the awful fate of those who refused to stop drinking and urged his audience not only to cease their tippling, but also to stop others. Several were converted on the spot. The next day, the largest providers of whiskey in Rochester smashed their barrels as cheering Christians applauded.

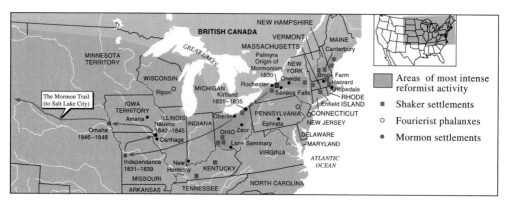

RELIGION, REFORM, AND UTOPIAN ACTIVITY, 1830–1850   Reformist activity followed both religious revival areas and the Erie Canal into the growing states of the Old Northwest.

Nineteenth-century Americans drank heavily. It was said that "a house could not be raised, a field of wheat cut down, nor could there be a log rolling, a husking, a quilting, a wedding, or a funeral without the aid of alcohol." With drinking came poverty, crime, illness, insanity, battered and broken families, and corrupt politics.

Early efforts at curbing alcohol emphasized moderation. Local societies agreed to limit what they drank. Some met in taverns to toast moderation. But influenced by the revivals, the movement achieved better organization and clearer goals. The American Temperance Society, founded in 1826, aimed at the "teetotal" pledge. Within a few years, thousands of local and state societies had formed.

Temperance advocates copied revival techniques. Fiery lecturers expounded on the evil consequences of drink and urged group pressure on the weak-willed. A deluge of graphic and sometimes gory temperance tracts poured out. One "intemperate man," it was claimed, died when his "breath caught fire by coming in contact with a lighted candle."

By 1840, disagreements split the temperance movement into many separate organizations. In depression times, when jobs and stable families were harder to find than whiskey and beer, laboring men and women moved more by practical concerns than religious fervor joined the crusade. The Washington Temperance Society, founded in a Baltimore tavern in 1840, was enormously popular with unemployed young workers and grew to an estimated 600,000 members in three years. The Washingtonians, arguing that alcoholism was a disease rather than moral failure, changed the shape of the temperance movement. They replaced revivalist techniques with those of the new party politics by organizing parades, picnics, melodramas, and festivals to encourage people to take the pledge.

Tactics in the 1840s also shifted away from moral suasion to political action. Temperance societies lobbied for local option laws, which allowed communities to prohibit the sale, manufacture, and consumption of alcohol. The first such law in the nation was passed in Maine in 1851. Fifteen other states followed with similar laws before the Civil War. Despite weak enforcement, per capita drinking fell dramatically in the 1850s. Interrupted by the Civil War, the movement reached its ultimate objective with passage of the Eighteenth Amendment in 1919.

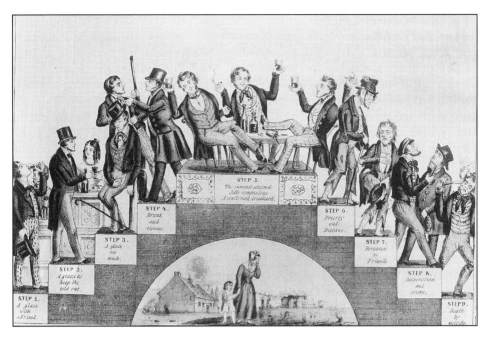

The temperance movement of the 1830s and 1840s used the tactics of religious revivalists to scare drinkers into taking the "teetotal" pledge. Who could resist this poignant 1846 portrayal of *The Drunkard's Progress*? (Library of Congress)

The temperance crusade reveals the many practical motivations for Americans to join reform societies. For some, as in Rochester, temperance provided an opportunity for the Protestant middle class to exert some control over laborers, immigrants, and Catholics. Perfectionists saw abstinence as a way of practicing self-control. For many women, the temperance effort was a respectable way to control drunken abusers. For many young men, especially after the onset of the depression of 1837, a temperance society provided entertainment, fellowship, and contacts to help their careers. In temperance societies as in political parties, Americans found jobs, purpose, support, spouses, and relief from loneliness and uncertainty.

Health and Sexuality

It was a short step from the physical and psychological ravages of drink to other potentially harmful effects on the body. Reformers were quick to attack too much eating, too many stimulants, and, above all, too much sex. Many endorsed a variety of special diets and exercise programs for maintaining good health. Some promoted panaceas, including hydropathy (bathing and water purges), hypnotism, phrenology (the study of bumps on the head), and "spiritualist" seances.

Sylvester Graham, inventor of the Graham cracker, combined all these enthusiasms. In 1834 he delivered a series of lectures on chastity, later published as an advice book. To those "troubled" by sexual desire, he recommended cold baths and open-air exercise. Women were advised to "have intercourse only for procreation." Although females learned to control sexuality for their own purposes, male "sexual purity" advocates urged restraint to protect various male interests. One doctor argued that women ought not to be educated because blood needed for the womb would be diverted to the head, thus breeding "puny men."

The authors of antebellum "health" manuals advocated abstinence from sex as vehemently as from alcohol. Semen must be saved for reproductive purposes and should not be wasted, either in masturbation or intercourse. Such waste would cause enervation, disease, insanity, and death. Some argued that the "expenditure" of sperm meant a loss of energy from the economy.

Humanizing the Asylum

Struggling to restore order to American society, some reformers preferred to work not for private influence over individuals, but toward public changes in institutions. They wanted to transform such social institutions as asylums, almshouses, prisons, schools, and even factories. Horace Mann, who led the struggle for common schools in Massachusetts (see Chapter 10), was a typical antebellum reformer. He blended dedicated idealism with a canny, practical sense of how to institutionalize educational improvements in one state: teacher training schools, higher teachers' salaries, and compulsory attendance laws.

Dealing with social outcasts presented special challenges. Colonial families or communities had looked after orphans, paupers, the insane, and even criminals. Beginning early in the nineteenth century, states built various institutions to uplift and house social victims. In some, the sane and the insane, children and hardened adult criminals, were thrown together in terrible conditions. In 1843, Dorothea Dix, horrified the Massachusetts legislature with her famous report that imprisoned insane people in the state were subject to the "extremest state of degradation and misery." They were confined in "cages, closets, stalls, pens! Chained, naked, beaten with rods, and lashed into obedience!" Dix recommended special asylums where the insane could be "humanly and properly controlled" by trained attendants.

Many perfectionist reformers like Dix believed that asylums could reform outcasts. Convinced that bad institutions corrupted basically good human beings, they reasoned that reformed institutions could rehabilitate them. In 1853, Charles Loring Brace started a Children's Aid Society in New York City that was a model of change through effective education and self-help. Reformers like Dix and Brace, as well as Samuel Gridley Howe and Thomas Gallaudet, who founded institutions for the care and education of the blind and deaf, achieved remarkable results.

But all too often, results were disappointing. Reformers believed that a proper penitentiary could bring a criminal "back to virtue." Some preferred the prison at Auburn, New York, with its tiny cells and common workrooms; others praised Pennsylvania's penitentiaries, each inmate in solitary confinement. All prison reformers assumed that "penitents" in isolated cells, studying the Bible and reflecting on their wrongdoing, would eventually decide to become good citizens. In fact, many inmates went mad or committed suicide. Institutions built by well-intentioned reformers became dumping places for society's outcasts. By mid-century, American prisons and mental asylums had become what they remain: sadly impersonal, understaffed, and overcrowded.

Working-Class Reform

Efforts to improve the institutional conditions of America life were not all top-down movements initiated and led by middle-class reformers. For working-class Americans, the institution most in need of transformation was the factory. Workers, many of them involved in other issues such as temperance, peace, and abolitionism, tried to improve their own lives.

Between 1828 and 1832, dozens of workingmen's parties arose. They advocated free, tax-supported schools, free public lands in the West, equal rights for the poor, and elimination of monopolistic privilege. Trade union activity began in Philadelphia in 1827 as skilled workers organized journeymen carpenters, plasterers, printers, weavers, tailors, and other tradesmen. That same year, 15 unions combined into a citywide federation, a process followed in other cities. The National Trades Union, founded in 1834, was the first attempt at a national labor organization.

Trade unions fared better than labor parties. Jacksonian Democrats siphoned off workers' votes. Union programs set more practical goals, including shorter hours, wages that would keep pace with rising prices, and ways (such as the closed shop) of warding off the competitive threat of cheap labor. In addition, both workers and their middle-class supporters called for the abolition of imprisonment for debt and of compulsory militia duty (both of which often cost workers their jobs) free public education, improved living conditions in workers' neighborhoods, and the right to organize. Discouraged by anti-union decisions of New York State courts, workers compared themselves to the rebels of the Boston Tea Party.

Fired by revolutionary tradition, by rising political influence, and by a union membership of near 300,000, workers struck some 168 times between 1834 and 1836. Over two-thirds of the strikes were over wages (see Chapter 10); the others were for shorter hours. The Panic of 1837 ushered in a depression that dashed the hopes and efforts of American workers. But the organizational work of the 1830s promised that the labor movement would reemerge, strengthened, later in the century.

ABOLITIONISM AND WOMEN'S RIGHTS

As American workers struggled in cities like Lowell for better wages and hours in 1834, Emily and Marius Robinson arrived in Cincinnati to fight for their causes. They and many other young idealists had been attracted by the newly founded Lane Seminary, a school to train abolitionist leaders. Financed by two wealthy New York brothers, Arthur and Lewis Tappan, Lane soon became a center of reformist activity. When nervous citizens persuaded the school's president, Lyman Beecher, to crack down, 40 "Lane rebels," led by Theodore Weld, fled to Oberlin in northern Ohio. The rebels turned Oberlin College into the first institution in the United States open to women and men, blacks and whites. The movements to abolish slavery and for equal rights to women and free blacks coalesced.

The goals of the struggle against slavery and subtle forms of racism and sexism often seemed as distant as the millennium itself. Yet antislavery and feminist advocates persisted in their efforts to abolish what they believed were visible, ingrained social wrongs. Whether seeking to eliminate coercion in the cotton fields or in the kitchen, they faced the dual challenge of pursuing elusive goals while achieving practical changes.

Tensions within the Antislavery Movement

Although the antislavery movement was smaller than temperance advocacy, it revealed more clearly the difficulties of pursuing significant social change. William Lloyd Garrison passionately desired to improve, if not to perfect, a flawed world. He was also ambitious and said that his name would "one day be known to the world." He was right. On January 1, 1831, eight months before Nat Turner's revolt, Garrison published the first issue of *The Liberator*, soon to become the leading anti-slavery journal in the United States. "I am in earnest," he wrote. "I will not equivocate—*and I will be heard.*" After organizing the New England Anti-Slavery Society with a group of blacks and whites, in 1833 Garrison and 62 others established the American Anti-Slavery Society.

Until then, most antislavery whites had advocated gradual emancipation by individual slave owners. Many joined the American Colonizationist Society, founded in 1816, which sent a few ex-slaves to Liberia. But these efforts proved inadequate and racist, the main goal being to rid the country of free blacks.

Garrison furiously opposed the colonizationists. "No! no! tell a man whose house is on fire to give a moderate alarm." There would be "no Union with slaveholders," he cried, condemning the Constitution that perpetuated slavery as "an agreement with Hell." The American Anti-Slavery Society called for immediate and total abolition. After escaping, Frederick Douglass agreed: "Power concedes nothing without a demand. It never did and it never will." But abolitionists did not always agree, splitting into colonizationists, gradualists, and immediatists.

Abolitionists also differed over tactics. Their primary method was to convince slaveholders and their supporters that slavery was a sin. Abolitionists tried to overwhelm slaveholders with moral guilt so that, repentant, they would free their slaves. But as Marius wrote to Emily Robinson, "The spirit of slavery is not confined to the South." His Ohio trip suggests that northerners were equally guilty in providing the support necessary to maintain the slave system.

The abolitionists by 1837 flooded the nation with over a million pieces of anti-slavery literature. Their writing described slave owners as "mansteelers" who gave up all claim to humanity. In 1839, Weld published *American Slavery as It Is,* which described in the goriest possible detail the inhumane treatment of slaves.

Other abolitionists preferred more direct methods. Some brought antislavery petitions before Congress and formed third parties. Boycotting goods made by slave labor was a third tactic. A fourth approach, although rare, was to call for slave rebellion, as did two northern blacks, David Walker in an 1829 pamphlet and Henry Highland Garnet in a speech at a convention of black Americans in 1843.

Abolitionists' tactical disagreements helped splinter the movement. Garrison's unyielding style and commitment to even less popular causes such as women's rights offended many abolitionists. In 1840, at its annual meeting in New York, the American Anti-Slavery Society split. Several delegates walked out when a woman, Abby Kelley, was elected to a previously all-male committee. One group, which supported multiple issues and moral suasion, stayed with Garrison; the other followed James Birney and the Tappans into the Liberty party.

Class differences and race further divided abolitionists. Northern workers, though fearful of the potential job competition with blacks implicit in emancipation, nevertheless saw their "wage slavery" as similar to chattel slavery. Strains between northern labor leaders and middle-class abolitionists (who minimized workingmen's concerns) were similar to those between white and black antislavery forces. Whites like Wendell Phillips decried slavery as a moral blot on American society; blacks like Douglass were more concerned with the effects of slavery and discrimination on African-Americans. Moreover, white abolitionists tended to see slavery and freedom as absolute opposites: A person was either slave or free. Blacks knew that there were degrees of freedom and that northern blacks had less of it, just as there were degrees of servitude in the South.

Furthermore, black abolitionists themselves experienced prejudice, not just from ordinary northern citizens, but also from white abolitionists. Many antislavery businessmen refused to hire blacks. The antislavery societies usually provided less than full membership rights for blacks, permitted them to do only menial tasks, and perpetuated black stereotypes in their literature. Conflict between Garrison and Douglass reflected these tensions. The famous runaway was one of the most effective orators in the movement. But after a while, rather than simply describing his life as a slave, Douglass began skillfully to analyze abolitionist policies. Garrison warned him that if he sounded too sophisticated audiences would never believe he had been a slave, and other whites told him to stick to the facts and let them take care of the philosophy.

Douglass gradually moved away from Garrison's views, endorsing political action and sometimes even slave rebellion. Garrison's response, particularly when Douglass came out for the Liberty party, was to denounce his independence as "ungrateful ... and malevolent in spirit." In 1847, Douglass started his own journal, the *North Star*, later called *Frederick Douglass's Paper*. In it, he expressed his appreciation for the help of that "noble band of white laborers," but declared that it was time for those who "suffered the wrong" to lead the way in advocating liberty.

Moving beyond Garrison, a few black nationalists, like fiery Martin Delany, totally rejected white society and advocated emigration to Africa. Most blacks, however, agreed with Douglass to work to end slavery and discrimination in the United States.

These black leaders were practical. David Ruggles in New York and William Still in Philadelphia led black vigilance groups that helped fugitive slaves escape to Canada or to safe northern black settlements. Ministers, writers, and orators such as Douglass, Garnet, William Wells Brown, Samuel Cornish, Lewis Hayden, and Sojourner Truth lectured and wrote journals and slave narratives on the evils of slavery. They also organized a National Negro Convention Movement, which began annual meetings in 1830. These blacks met not only to condemn slavery, but also to discuss issues of discrimination facing free blacks in the North.

Flood Tide of Abolitionism

Black and white abolitionists, however, usually worked together well. Weld and Garrison often stayed in the homes of black abolitionists when they traveled. Black and white "stations" cooperated on the underground railroad, too, passing fugitives from one hiding place to the next.

Yᵉ ABOLITIONISTS IN COUNCIL—Yᵉ ORATOR OF Yᵉ DAY DENOUNCING Yᵉ UNION, MAY, 1859.

This woodcut illustration of an abolitionist convention from *Harper's Weekly* magazine in 1859 shows the mixture of both black and women delegates in the hall. The black man on the stage could be Frederick Douglass. (The Newberry Library, Chicago)

The two races worked together fighting discrimination as well as slavery. When David Ruggles was dragged from the "white car" of a New Bedford, Massachusetts, railway in 1841, Garrison, Douglass, and 40 other protesters organized what may have been the first successful integrated "sit-in" in American history. Blacks and whites also worked harmoniously in protesting segregated public schools, and after several years of boycotts and legal challenges they forced Massachusetts in 1855 to became the first state to outlaw them. Not for 99 years would the U.S. Supreme Court begin desegregating schools throughout the country.

White and black abolitionists were united perhaps most closely by defending themselves against attacks by people who regarded them as dangerous fanatics bent on disrupting society. As abolitionists organized to rid the nation of slavery, they aroused many, northerners as well as southerners, who were eager to rid the nation of abolitionists. Mob attacks, like the one on Marius Robinson in Ohio, occurred frequently in the mid-1830s. Abolitionists were stoned, dragged through streets, driven from homes and jobs, and reviled by northern mobs, often led by leading citizens. Weld could hardly finish a speech without disruption. Douglass endured similar attacks. Garrison was saved from a Boston mob only by being put in jail. In 1837, an antislavery Illinois editor, Elijah Lovejoy, was murdered.

Antiabolitionsts were as fervid as the abolitionists. "I warn the abolitionists, ignorant and infatuated barbarians as they are," growled one South Carolinian, "that if chance shall throw any of them into our hands, they may expect a felon's death." One widely circulated book in 1836 described opponents of slavery, led by "gloomy, wild, and malignant" Garrison, as "crack-brained enthusiasts" and "female fanatics." Jackson denounced abolitionists in his annual message in 1835 as "incendiaries" who deserved to have their "unconstitutional and wicked" activities broken up by mobs, and he urged Congress to ban antislavery literature from the U.S. mails. A year later, southern Democratic congressmen, with crucial support from Van Buren, passed a "gag rule" to stop the flood of abolitionist petitions in Congress.

By the 1840s the antislavery movement had gained significant strength. Many northerners, including workers otherwise unsympathetic to ending slavery, decried mob violence, supported free speech, and denounced the South and its northern defenders as undemocratic. The gag rule, interference with the mails, and Lovejoy's killing seemed proof of the growing influence of an evil slave power. Former president John Quincy Adams, now a Massachusetts congressman, devoted himself for several years to the repeal of the gag rule, which he finally achieved in 1844, keeping the matter alive until the question of slavery in the territories became the dominant political issue of the 1850s (see Chapter 14). Meanwhile, black and white abolitionists struggled on with many different tactics.

Women's Rights

As a young teacher in Massachusetts in 1836, Abby Kelley circulated petitions for the local antislavery society. She came to reform from revivalism. In 1838 she braved a crowd in Philadelphia by delivering an abolitionist speech to a convention of antislavery women so eloquently that Weld told her that if she did not join the movement full time, "God will smite you." Before the convention was over, a mob, incensed by both abolitionists and women speaking in public, burned the hall to the ground.

After a soul-searching year, Kelley left teaching to devote all her efforts to antislavery and women's rights. When she married, she retained her own name and went on lecture tours of the West while her husband stayed home to care for their daughter. Other young women were also defining unconventional new relationships while illustrating the profound difficulty of both fulfilling traditional roles and speaking out for change. Angelina and Sarah Grimké, outspoken Quaker sisters from Philadelphia who had grown up in South Carolina, went to New England in 1837 to lecture to disapproving audiences on behalf of abolitionism and the rights of women. After the tour, Angelina married Theodore Weld and stopped her public speaking to show that she could also be a good wife and mother. But she and Sarah, who moved in with her, undertook most of the research and writing for Weld's book attacking American slavery.

Young couples like these, while pursuing reform, also experimented with equal relationships in an age that assigned distinctly unequal roles to husbands and wives. Domesticity told women that their sphere was the home, upholding piety and virtue. As one clergyman said, although women did not "step beyond the threshold" of the home, their ethical influence would be "felt around the globe." Not surprisingly, many women joined the perfectionist movement to cleanse America of its sins. Active in every reform movement, women discovered the need to improve their own condition.

To achieve greater personal autonomy, antebellum American women pursued several paths depending on their class, cultural background, and situation. In 1834, Lowell textile workers went on strike against wage reductions while looking to

Elizabeth Cady Stanton (1815–1902) and Lucretia Mott (1793–1880) were the leaders of the 1848 gathering for women's rights at Seneca Falls, New York. "The acquaintance of Lucretia Mott, who was a broad, liberal thinker on politics, religion, and all questions of reform," Stanton wrote in her autobiography, "opened to me a new world of thought." (Sophia Smith Collection, Smith College, Northampton, Massachusetts)

marriage as an escape from mill work. Catharine Beecher argued that it was by accepting marriage and the home as a woman's sphere and by mastering domestic duties there that women could best achieve power and autonomy. In another form of "domestic feminism," American wives exerted considerable control over their bodies by convincing their husbands to practice abstinence, coitus interruptus, and other forms of birth control.

Other women found an outlet for their role as moral guardians by attacking the sexual double standard. In 1834, a group of Presbyterian women formed the New York Female Moral Reform Society. Inspired by revivalism, they visited brothels, opened a refuge to convert prostitutes, and even publicly identified brothel patrons. Within five years, there were 445 auxiliaries of the society.

Lowell mill workers and New York moral reformers generally accepted the duties—and attractions—of female domesticity. Other women, usually from upper-middle-class families, did not. They sought control over their lives by working directly for more legally protected rights. Campaigns to secure married women's control of their property and custody of their children involved many of them. Others gained from abolitionism a growing awareness of similarities between the oppression of women and of slaves. Collecting antislavery signatures and speaking out publicly, they continually faced denials of their right to speak or act politically. American women "have good cause to be grateful to the slave," Kelley wrote, for in "striving to strike his iron off, we found most surely, that we were manacled *ourselves*."

The more active women became in antislavery activities, the more hostility they encountered, especially from antifeminist clergymen quoting the Bible. Sarah Grimké was criticized once too often. She struck back in 1837 with *Letters on the Condition of Women and the Equality of the Sexes,* concluding that she sought "no favors for my sex. I surrender not our claim to equality. All I ask of our brethren is, that they will take their feet from off our necks and permit us to stand upright on that ground which God designed us to occupy."

Male abolitionists were divided about women's rights. In London, at the World Anti-Slavery Convention in 1840, attended by many American abolitionists, the delegates refused to let women participate. Two of the women, Elizabeth Cady Stanton and Lucretia Mott, had to sit behind curtains and were forbidden to speak. When they returned home, they resolved to "form a society to advocate the rights of women." In 1848, in Seneca Falls, New York, their intentions, though delayed, were fulfilled in one of the most significant antebellum protest gatherings.

In preparing for the meeting, Mott and Stanton drew up a list of women's grievances. For example, even though some states had awarded married women control over their property, they still had none over their earnings. Modeling their "Declaration of Sentiments" on the Declaration of Independence, the women at Seneca Falls proclaimed it a self-evident truth that "all men and women are created equal" and that men had usurped women's freedom and dignity. The remedy was expressed in 11 resolutions calling for equal opportunities in education and work, equality before the law, and the right to appear on public platforms. The most controversial resolution called for women's "sacred right to the elective franchise." The convention approved Mott and Stanton's list of resolutions.

Throughout the 1850s, led by Stanton and Susan B. Anthony, women continued to meet in annual conventions, working by resolution, persuasion, and petition campaign to achieve equal political, legal, and property rights with men. The right to vote, however, was considered the cornerstone of the movement. It remained so for 72 years of struggle until 1920, when passage of the Nineteenth Amendment made woman's suffrage part of the Constitution. The Seneca Falls convention was crucial in beginning the campaign for equal public rights. The seeds of psychological autonomy and self-respect, still continuing, were sown in the struggles of countless women like Abby Kelley, Sarah Grimké, and Emily Robinson.

✦✦✦✦✦✦

CONCLUSION

Perfecting America

Inspired by religious revivalism, advocates for women's rights and temperance, abolitionists, and other reformers carried on very different crusades from those waged by Andrew Jackson against Indians, nullificationists, and the U.S. Bank. In fact, Jacksonian politics and antebellum reform were often at odds. Most abolitionists and temperance reformers were anti-Jackson Whigs. Jackson and most Democrats repudiated the passionate moralism of reformers.

Yet both sides shared more than either side would admit. Reformers and political parties were both organized rationally. Both mirrored new tensions in a changing,

TIMELINE

1824	1825	1826	1828	1828–1832
New Harmony established	John Quincy Adams chosen president by the House of Representatives	American Temperance Society founded	Calhoun publishes "Exposition and Protest"; Jackson defeats Adams for the presidency; Tariff of Abominations	Rise of workingmen's parties

1832–1836	1833	1834	1835–1836	1836
Removal of funds from U.S. Bank to state banks	Force Bill; Compromise tariff; Calhoun resigns as vice president; American Anti-Slavery Society founded	New York Female Moral Reform Society founded; National Trades Union founded; Whig party established	Countless incidents of mob violence	"Gag rule"; Specie circular; Van Buren elected president

1844	1846–1848	1847	1848	1850
Joseph Smith murdered in Nauvoo, Illinois	Mormon migration to the Great Basin	First issue of Frederick Douglass's *North Star*	Oneida community founded; First women's rights convention at Seneca Falls, New York	Nathaniel Hawthorne, *The Scarlet Letter*

growing society. Both had an abiding faith in change and the idea of progress yet feared that sinister forces jeopardized that progress. Whether ridding the nation of alcohol or the national bank, slavery or nullification, mob violence or political opponents, both forces saw these responsibilities in terms of patriotic duty. Whether inspired by religious revivalism or political party loyalty, both believed that by stamping out evil forces, they could shape a better America. In this effort, they turned to politics, religion, reform, and new lifestyles. Whether politicians like Jackson and Clay, religious community leaders like Noyes and Ann Lee, or reformers like Garrison and the Grimkés, these antebellum Americans sought to remake their country politically and morally as it underwent social and economic change.

As the United States neared mid-century, slavery emerged as the most divisive issue. Against much opposition, the reformers had made slavery a matter of national political debate by the 1840s. Although both major political parties tried to evade the question, westward expansion and the addition of new territories to the nation would soon make avoidance impossible. Would new states be slave or free?

1830	1830–1831	1831	1832	1832–1833
Webster-Hayne debate and Jackson-Calhoun toast; Joseph Smith, *The Book of Mormon*; Indian Removal Act	Charles Finney's religious revivals	Garrison begins publishing *The Liberator*	Jackson vetoes U.S. Bank charter; Jackson reelected; *Worcester* v. *Georgia*	Nullification crisis

1837	1837–1838	1840	1840–1841	1843
Financial panic and depression; Sarah Grimké's, *Letters on the Equality of the Sexes*; Emerson's "American Scholar" address	Cherokee "Trail of Tears"	William Henry Harrison elected president; American Anti-Slavery Society splits; World Anti-Slavery Convention; Ten-hour day for federal employees	Transcendentalists found Hopedale and Brook Farm	Dorothea Dix's report on treatment of the insane

1851	1853	1854	1855
Maine prohibition law; Herman Melville, *Moby Dick*	Children's Aid Society established in New York City	Thoreau, *Walden*	Massachusetts bans segregated public schools

The question increasingly aroused the deepest passions of the American people. For the pioneer family, who formed the driving force behind the westward movement, however, questions involving their fears and dreams seemed more important. We turn to this family and that movement in the next chapter.

Recommended Reading

Religious Revival and Reform

Robert Abzug, *Cosmos Crubmling: American Reform and the Religious Imagination* (1994); Richard J. Carwardine, *Evangelicals and Politics in Antebellum America* (1993); Richard Rabinowitz, *The Spiritual Self in Everyday Life: The Transformation of Personal Religious Experience in 19th Century New England* (1989); Mary Ryan, *Cradle of the Middle Class: The Family in Oneida County, New York, 1790–1865* (1981); Ronald Walters, *American Reformers, 1815–1860* (1978); Charles E. Hambrick-Stowe, *Charles G. Finney and the Spirit of American*

Evangelicalism (1996); Steven Mintz, *Moralists and Modernization: American Pre-Civil War Reformers* (1995).

Politics and Party in the Age of Jackson

Jean Baker, *Affairs of Party* (1983); Donald B. Cole, *The Presidency of Andrew Jackson* (1993); Richard Ellis, *The Union at Risk: Jacksonian Democracy, States Rights, and the Nullification Crisis* (1987); Ronald Formisano, *The Transformation of Political Culture* (1983); Lawrence F. Kohl, *The Politics of Individualism: Parties and the American Character in the Jackson Era* (1989); Charles Sellers, *The Market Revolution: Jacksonian America, 1815–1846* (1992); Thurman Wilkins, *Cherokee Tragedy: The Ridge Family and the Decimation of a People,* 2d ed. rev. (1986); Major L. Wilson, *The Presidency of Martin Van Buren* (1984).

Political Biography

Maurice G. Baxter, *One and Inseparable: Daniel Webster and the Union* (1984); Daniel B. Cole, *Martin Van Buren and the American Political System* (1984); John Niven, *John C. Calhoun and the Price of Union* (1988); Merrill O. Peterson, *The Great Triumvirate: Webster, Clay, and Calhoun* (1987); Robert Remini, *Life of Andrew Jackson* (1988), *Andrew Jackson and the Course of American Freedom, 1822–1832* (1981), and *Andrew Jackson and the Course of American Democracy* (1984).

Utopian Communitarianism

Priscilla Brewett, *Shaker Communities, Shaker Lives* (1986); Robert Fogarty, ed., *American Utopianism* (1972); Lawrence Foster, *Women, Family, and Utopia: Communal Experiments of the Shakers, the Oneida Community, and the Mormons* (1991); William Kephart and William Zellner, *Extraordinary Groups: An Examination of Unconventional Life Styles,* 4th ed. (1991); Carol A. Kolmerten, *Women in Utopia: The Ideology of Gender in the American Owenite Communities* (1990); Kenneth H. Winn, *Exiles in a Land of Liberty* (1989); Grant Underwood, *The Millenarian World of Early Mormonism* (1993).

Temperance and Other Reforms

Susan Cayleff, *Wash and Be Healed: The Water-Cure Movement and Women's Health* (1987); Stephen Nissenbaum, *Sex, Diet, and Debility in Jacksonian America: Sylvester Graham and Health Reform* (1980); W. J. Rorabaugh, *The Alcoholic Republic: An American Tradition* (1979); David Rothman, *The Discovery of the Asylum: Social Order and Disorder in the New Republic* (1971); Ian Tyrrell, *Sobering Up: From Temperance to Prohibition in Antebellum America, 1800–1860* (1979); Sean Wilentz, *Chants Democratic: New York City and the Rise of the American Working Class, 1788–1850* (1983).

Abolitionism and Women's Rights

Ellen DuBois, *Feminism and Suffrage: The Emergence of an Independent Women's Movement in America, 1848–1869* (1978); Lawrence Friedman, *Gregarious Saints: Self and Community in American Abolitionism, 1830–1870* (1982); Elisabeth Griffith, *In Her Own Right: The Life of Elizabeth Cady Stanton* (1984); Jane A. Pease and William H. Pease, *They Who Would Be Free: Blacks' Search for Freedom, 1830–1861* (1974); Ronald Walters, *The Antislavery Appeal: American Abolitionism After 1830* (1976); Julie Roy Jeffrey, *The Great Silent Army of Abolitionism: Ordinary Women in the Antislavery Movement* (1998).

CHAPTER 13

Moving West

By the 1840s, the frontier was retreating across the Mississippi. As Americans contemplated the lands west of the great river, they debated expansion. Some, like Michigan's senator Lewis Cass, saw the Pacific Ocean as the only limit to territorial expansion. Cass believed that the West represented not only economic opportunity for Americans, but also political stability for the nation as well. People crowded into cities and confined to limited territories endangered the Republic, he told fellow senators in a speech. But if they headed west to convert the "woods and forests into towns and villages and cultivate fields" and to extend the "dominion of civilization and improvement over the domain of nature," they would find rewarding personal opportunities that would ensure political and social harmony.

Cass's arguments supporting the righteousness and necessity of westward expansion were echoed again and again in the 1840s. Thousands of men seconded his sentiments by volunteering to join American forces in the war against Mexico in the summer of 1845. Largely untrained, dressed in fanciful uniforms, and called by names like Eagles, Avengers, and Tigers, the companies hurried south. But before long, these supporters of expansion saw the ugly side of territorial adventures: insects, bad weather, poor food, and unsanitary conditions. They discovered that such illnesses as the "black vomit" (yellow fever), dysentery, and diarrhea could kill more men than Mexican bullets. As a member of the American occupying army, Henry Judah also experienced the hostility of conquered peoples. In his diary, he reported, "It is dangerous to go out after night . . . . Four of our men were stabbed today." Not only, he wrote, was a man "by the name of Brown" stabbed in the back, but an "infernal villain cut his throat."

Like Henry Judah, Thomas Gibson, a captain of Indiana volunteers, also paid some of the costs of winning new territories. Less than a month after Cass's speech, he wrote to his wife, Mary, in Charlestown, Indiana. Although glad to report news of an American victory, he described a battlefield "still covered with [Mexican] dead" where "the stench is most horrible." Indiana friends had been killed, and Gibson himself had narrowly escaped. "The ball struck me a glancing blow on the head and knocked me down, but it did not harm me." As for the rest, the weather was foul, and so too was the food—"hard biscuit full of bitter black bugs."

Despite war's harsh realities, Gibson did not challenge the enterprise. He bragged to Mary that "our little army could go out tomorrow in a fair field of battle and whip fifty thousand of the best Mexican troops that ever were on a field of battle. One thing is certain, we would be willing to try it."

Like other wives and family members at home, Mary was less interested in heroics than in the simple truth: Was Tommy dead or alive? As she anxiously awaited news, she wrote of her great hope: "May God bless you and send you home." Yet even with all her worries and prayers for the war's rapid conclusion, she could not escape the heady propaganda for national expansion. She had heard that Indiana soldiers "shode themselves great cowards by retreating during battle," and she disapproved. "We all would rather you had stood like good soldiers," she told her husband.

✦✦✦✦✦✦

Lewis Cass, Henry Judah, Thomas and Mary Gibson, and thousands of other Americans played a part in the nation's expansion into the trans-Mississippi West. The differences and similarities in their perspectives and in their responses to territorial growth unveil the complex nature of the western experience. Lewis Cass's speech illustrates the hold the West had on people's imagination and shows how some linked expansion to the American belief in individual opportunity and national progress. His reference to its riches reminds us of the gigantic contribution western resources made to national development and wealth. Yet his assumption that the West was vacant points to the costs of white expansion for Mexican-Americans and Native Americans and the challenge non-Anglo groups would pose to the inclusiveness of American ideals. The Gibsons' letters show similar preconceptions and racial prejudices. They also portray the winning of the West on a human level: the anxieties, deprivation, enthusiasm, and optimism felt by those who fought for and settled in the West.

This chapter concerns movement into the trans-Mississippi West between 1830 and 1865. First, we will consider how and when Americans moved west, by what means the United States acquired the vast territories that in 1840 belonged to other nations, and the meaning of "Manifest Destiny," the slogan used to defend the conquest of the continent west of the Mississippi River. Then, we explore the nature of life on the western farming, mining, and urban frontiers. Finally, the chapter examines responses of Native Americans and Mexican-Americans to expansion and illuminates the ways in which different cultural traditions intersected in the West.

PROBING THE TRANS-MISSISSIPPI WEST

Until the 1840s, most Americans lived east of the Mississippi. By 1860, however, some 4.3 million Americans had moved beyond the great river into the trans-Mississippi West.

Foreign Claims and Possessions

In 1815, except for the Louisiana Territory, Spain held title to most of the trans-Mississippi region. For hundreds of years, Spaniards had marched north from Mexico to explore, settle, and convert the lands across the Rio Grande. Eventually, Spanish holdings included present-day Texas, Arizona, New Mexico, Nevada, Utah, western Colorado, California, and small parts of Wyoming, Kansas, and Oklahoma. Spain had tried to keep foreigners out of its northern frontier areas, but increasingly this policy was hard to enforce. When Mexico won its independence from Spain in 1821, it inherited this vast area with 75,000 Spanish-speaking inhabitants and numerous Native Americans living there. It also met an avid U.S. appetite for expansion.

North of California lay the Oregon country, a vaguely defined area extending up to Alaska. Both Great Britain and the United States claimed Oregon on the basis of explorations in the late eighteenth century and fur trading in the early nineteenth. Joint occupation, agreed on in 1818 and 1827, delayed settling the boundary question.

Early Interest in the West

Americans penetrated the trans-Mississippi West long before the great migrations of the 1840s and 1850s and knew some of its people and terrains. The fur business brought American trappers and traders to Oregon as early as 1811, and a decade later to the Rockies. Many of these men married Indian wives, creating a hybrid way of life with which Americans who later entered the region had little sympathy.

Religious idealism also drew some Americans west. Two Presbyterian missionary couples, Marcus and Narcissa Whitman and Henry and Eliza Spalding, were among the first to travel to the Oregon Territory with help from fur traders. Like Methodist and Roman Catholic missionaries (sent from Europe), the Presbyterians hoped to convert Oregon Indians to Christianity. Their fervor drew strength from the fires of the Second Great Awakening and their conviction that unconverted Indians were doomed to hell. Less successful initially in converting the Indians than their Catholic counterparts (who were more tolerant of Indian culture), American missionaries also tried to teach Indians how to live like whites.

In the Southwest, the collapse of the Spanish Empire in 1821 gave Americans their long-sought chance. Each year caravans from "the States" followed the Santa Fe Trail, loaded with weapons, tools, and brightly colored calicoes. New Mexico's 40,000 inhabitants proved eager buyers. Eventually, some "Anglos" settled there. Their economic activities prepared the way for conquest.

In Texas, land for cotton attracted settlers and squatters in the 1820s, just as the local Hispanic population of 2,000 was adjusting to Mexico's independence. Cheap land lured more Americans to that area than to any other—by 1835, almost 30,000 of them. As the largest group of Americans outside the nation's boundaries at that time, their numbers dwarfed the Hispanic Tejanos.

On the Pacific, a handful of New England traders carrying sea-otter skins to China anchored in the harbors of Spanish California in the early nineteenth century. By the 1830s, as the near extermination of the animals ruined this trade, a commerce in California cowhides and tallow developed, bringing in exchange clothes, boots, hardware, and furniture manufactured in the East.

Among the earliest easterners to settle in the trans-Mississippi West were tribes from the South and the Old Northwest, driven by the American government into present-day Oklahoma and Kansas. Ironically, some of these eastern tribes acted as agents of white civilization by introducing cotton, the plantation system, black slavery, and schools. Other tribes triggered conflicts that weakened the western tribes with whom they came into contact. These disruptions foreshadowed white incursions later in the century.

American economic or missionary activities were not deterred by the fact that much of the trans-Mississippi West lay outside U.S. boundaries or that the government had guaranteed Indian tribes permanent possession of some western territories. By the 1840s, a growing volume of published information fostered dreams of possession. Lansford Hastings's *Emigrants' Guide to Oregon and California* (1845) provided not only practical information that emigrants would need, but also encouragement.

Hastings minimized the importance of Mexican and British sovereignty. While Mexican California presented a problem, he conceded, Great Britain had "no right" to Oregon. Indeed, American settlers were already trickling into the Pacific Northwest, bringing progress with them.

Hastings's belief that Americans would obtain rights to foreign holdings in the West came true within a decade. During the 1840s the United States, by war and diplomacy, acquired Mexico's territories in the Southwest and on the Pacific, as well as title to the Oregon country up to the 49th parallel. Later, with the Gadsden Purchase in 1853, the country obtained another chunk of Mexican territory.

Manifest Destiny

Bursts of florid rhetoric accompanied territorial growth, and Americans used the slogan "Manifest Destiny" to justify and account for it. The phrase, coined in 1845 by a Democratic journalist, referred to the conviction that the country's superior institutions and culture constituted a God-given right, even an obligation, to spread American civilization across the entire continent. Lewis Cass, Henry Judah, the Gibsons, Lansford Hastings, and most other Americans agreed.

A sense of uniqueness and mission was a legacy of Puritan utopianism and revolutionary republicanism. By the 1840s, absorption of the Louisiana Territory, rapid population growth, and advances in transportation, communication, and industry bolstered a sense of national superiority. Publicists of Manifest Destiny proclaimed that the nation not only could but must absorb new territories.

WINNING THE TRANS-MISSISSIPPI WEST

Manifest Destiny justified expansion, but events in Texas triggered the national government's determination to move west of the Mississippi. The Texas question originated in the years when Spain held the Southwest. Although some settlements like Santa Fe, founded in 1609, were almost as old as Jamestown, the Spanish considered the sparsely populated and underdeveloped Southwest primarily a buffer zone for Mexico. The main centers of Spanish settlement were far apart and thousands of miles from Mexico City. Vulnerable as this defensive perimeter of the Spanish Empire might seem, the United States had recognized its legal status by treaty in 1819, which specifically conceded Texas to Spain.

Annexing Texas, 1845

By the time the treaty was ratified in 1821, Mexico had won its independence but scarcely could cope with the borderlands or develop powerful bonds of national identity. Mexicans soon had reason to wonder whether the American disavowal of any claim to Texas in the treaty would last. Fear about American expansionism permeated Mexican politics.

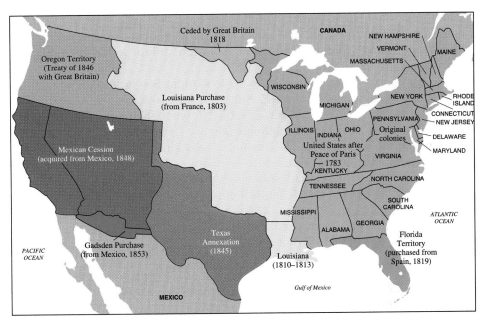

UNITED STATES TERRITORIAL EXPANSION BY 1860 This map makes the rapidity of the acquisition of the Far West clear.

In 1823, the Mexican government resolved to strengthen border areas by increasing their population. To attract settlers, it offered land in return for token payments and pledges to become Roman Catholics and Mexican citizens. Stephen F. Austin, who gained rights to bring 300 families into Texas, was among the first of the Americans to take advantage of this opportunity. Most of the American settlers came from the South, and some brought slaves. By the end of the decade, the population of Texas consisted of some 15,000 white Americans, 1,000 slaves, and just 5,000 Tejanos.

Mexican officials soon had second thoughts. While Austin converted to Roman Catholicism, most settlers remained far more American than Mexican. Some were malcontents who disliked Mexican laws and limitations on their opportunities. In late 1826, a small group of them declared the Republic of Fredonia. Although Stephen Austin assisted in putting down the brief uprising, American newspapers hailed the rebels as "apostles of democracy."

Mexican anxiety rose. Secretary of Foreign Relations Lucas Aláman branded American settlers advance agents of the United States. In 1829, the Mexican government altered its Texas policy. It abolished slavery in Texas, and the next year it forbade further emigration from the United States. Officials began to collect duties on imports. But little changed in Texas. Americans evaded the mandate to abolish slavery. Emigrants still crossed the border and continued to outnumber Mexicans.

Tensions escalated, and in October 1835 a skirmish between the colonial militia and Mexican forces opened hostilities. Sam Houston, onetime governor of Tennessee and army officer, became commander in chief of the Texas forces. Mexican dictator and general Antonio López de Santa Anna hurried north with an army of 6,000 conscripts, many of them Mayan Indian draftees who spoke no

Spanish and were exhausted by the long march. Supply lines were spread thin. Nevertheless, Santa Anna and his men won at first: The Alamo at San Antonio fell, taking Davy Crockett and Jim Bowie with it. So, too, did the fortress of Goliad, to the southeast.

As he pursued Houston and the Texans toward the San Jacinto River, carelessness proved Santa Anna's undoing. Although fully anticipating an American attack, the Mexican general and his men settled down to their usual siesta on April 21, 1836, without posting an adequate guard. As the Mexicans dozed, the Americans attacked. With cries of "Remember the Alamo! Remember Goliad!" the Texans overcame the army, captured its commander in his slippers, and won the war within 20 minutes. They had few casualties; 630 Mexicans lay dead.

Victory at San Jacinto gave Texas its independence. Threatened with lynching, Santa Anna signed a treaty setting the republic's boundary at the Rio Grande. When news of the disaster reached Mexico City, however, the Mexican Congress repudiated an "agreement carried out under the threat of death," insisting that Texas was still part of Mexico.

The new republic was financially unstable, unrecognized by its enemy, and rejected when it sought admission to the United States. Jackson, whose agent in Texas had reported that the republic was so weak that "her future security must depend more upon the weakness and imbecility of her enemy than upon her own strength," was reluctant to act quickly. With 13 free and 13 slave states, many northerners violently opposed taking in another slave state. Petitions poured into Congress in 1837 opposing annexation, and Congressman John Quincy Adams repeatedly denounced it. Soon the explosive idea was dropped.

For the next few years, the Lone Star Republic led a precarious existence. Mexico refused to recognize it, but sent only an occasional raiding party across the border. Texans suffered an ignominious defeat in an ill-conceived attempt to capture Santa Fe in 1841. Diplomatic maneuvering in European capitals for financial aid and recognition was only moderately successful. Financial ties with the United States increased.

Texas became headline news again in 1844. "It is the greatest question of the age," an Alabama expansionist declared, "and I predict will agitate the country more than all the other public questions ever have." He was right. The annexation issue exploded after President John Tyler (who assumed office upon Harrison's sudden death) reopened it, hoping to ensure his reelection. Powerful sectional, national, and political tensions sprang to life, demonstrating the divisiveness of the slavery-expansion question. Southern Democrats insisted that their region's future hinged on annexing Texas. John C. Calhoun hoped by exploiting the issue he could win the White House.

Other wings of the Democratic party capitalized more successfully on the issue, however. Lewis Cass and Stephen Douglas of Illinois, among others, vigorously supported annexation not because it would expand slavery (a topic they carefully avoided), but because it would spread American civilization. Their arguments, classic examples of Manifest Destiny, put the question into a national context of expanding American freedom. So powerfully did they link Texas to Manifest Destiny and avoid sectional issues that their candidate, James Polk of Tennessee, won the Democratic nomination in 1844. Polk called for "the reannexation of Texas at the earliest practicable period" and the occupation of the Oregon Territory.

Whigs tended to oppose annexation, fearing the addition of another slave state. They accused the Democrats of exploiting Manifest Destiny, more as a means of securing office than of bringing freedom to Texas.

The Whigs were right that the annexation issue would bring victory to the Democrats. Polk won a close election in 1844. But by the time he took the oath of office in March 1845, Tyler had resolved the question of annexation. In his last months in office, the outgoing president pushed through Congress a joint resolution admitting Texas to the Union. Unlike a treaty, which required the approval of two-thirds of the Senate and which Tyler had failed to win in 1844, a joint resolution needed only majority support. Nine years after its revolution, Texas finally joined the Union, with the right to split into five states if it chose to do so.

War with Mexico, 1846–1848

When Mexico learned of Texas's annexation, it promptly severed diplomatic ties with the United States. It was easy for Mexicans to interpret the events from the 1820s on as part of a gigantic American plot to steal Texas. During the war for Texas independence, American papers, especially those in the South, had enthusiastically hailed the rebels, while southern money and volunteers had aided the Texans. Now that the Americans had gained Texas, would they want still more?

In his inaugural address in 1845, Polk pointed out "that our system may easily be extended to the utmost bounds of our territorial limits, and that as it shall be extended the bonds of our Union, so far from being weakened will become stronger." Did those territorial limits extend deeper into Mexico?

Polk, like many other Americans, failed to appreciate how the annexation of Texas humiliated Mexico and increased pressures on its government to respond belligerently. The president anticipated that a weak Mexico would grant his grandiose demands: Texas bounded by the Rio Grande rather than the Nueces River 150 miles to its north, as well as California and New Mexico.

As a precaution, Polk ordered General Zachary Taylor to move "on or near the Rio Grande." By October 1845, Taylor and 3,500 American troops had reached the Nueces River. The positioning of an American army in Texas did not mean that Polk expected war. Rather, he hoped that a show of military force, coupled with secret diplomacy, would bring the desired concessions. In November, the president sent his secret agent, John L. Slidell, to Mexico City with instructions to secure the Rio Grande border and to buy Upper California and New Mexico. When the Mexican government refused to receive Slidell, Polk decided to force Mexico into accepting American terms. He ordered Taylor south of the Rio Grande. To the Mexicans, this was an act of war. Democratic newspapers and expansionists enthusiastically hailed Polk's provocative decision; Whigs opposed it.

In late April, the Mexican government declared a state of defensive war. Two days later, a skirmish broke out between Mexican and American troops, resulting in 16 American casualties. When Polk heard the news, he quickly drafted a war message for Congress, claiming that Mexico had "passed the boundary of the United States . . . invaded our territory and shed American blood upon American soil." "War exists," he claimed, and, he added untruthfully, "notwithstanding all our efforts to avoid it, exists by act of Mexico."

Although Congress declared war, the conflict bitterly divided Americans. Many Whigs, including Abraham Lincoln, questioned Polk's truthfulness, and

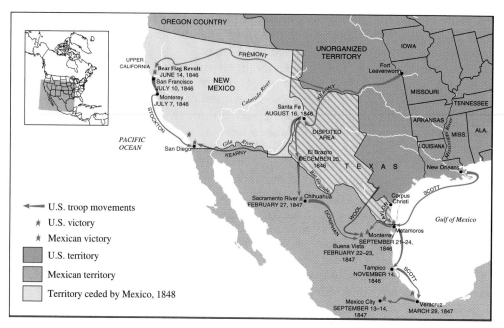

THE MEXICAN-AMERICAN WAR   This map shows not only the movements of American troops during the Mexican-American War, but also the large area that was in dispute. The vast territorial acquisitions, the fruit of victory, are clear.

their opposition grew more vocal. Lincoln called the war one "of conquest brought into existence to catch votes." The American Peace Society revealed sordid examples of army misbehavior in Mexico, and Frederick Douglass accused the country of "cupidity and love of dominion." Many workers also were critical of the war.

Debate continued as American troops swept toward Mexico City, but the Mexican government refused to admit defeat. Yet Polk enjoyed the enthusiastic support of expansionists. Thomas Gibson's men, like most other soldiers, were eager volunteers. Some expansionists even urged permanent occupation of Mexico.

Inflated rhetoric did not win the war, however. In the end, chance helped draw hostilities to a close. Mexican moderates approached Polk's diplomatic representative, Nicholas Trist, who accompanied the American army in Mexico. In Trist's baggage were detailed, though out-of-date, instructions outlining Polk's requirements: the Rio Grande boundary, Upper California, and New Mexico. Although the president lost confidence in Trist and ordered him home in chains, Trist stayed in Mexico to negotiate an end to the war. Having obtained most of Polk's objectives, Trist returned to Washington and an ungrateful president.

California and New Mexico

Although Texas and Mexico dominated the headlines, Polk made it clear from the early days of his presidency that California and New Mexico were part of any resolution of the Mexico crisis. Serious American interest in California dated only from the late 1830s. A few Americans, mostly traders, had settled there during the

1820s and 1830s, but they constituted only a small part of the Spanish-speaking Californio population that had reached 3,200 by 1821. Many Americans married into Californio families and took Mexican citizenship. But gradual recognition of California's fine harbors and favorable position for the China trade, as well as suspicions that Great Britain had designs on it, nourished the conviction that California must become part of the United States.

In 1845, Polk appointed Thomas Larkin, a successful American merchant in Monterey, as his confidential agent. "If the people [of California] should desire to unite their destiny with ours," wrote Polk's secretary of state, James Buchanan, to Larkin, "they would be received as brethren." Polk was sensitive to the fragility of American claims to the region. But Santa Anna, who bore the burden of having lost Texas, was in no position to sell. Thus, in 1846, a few American settlers rose up against Mexican "tyranny" and established the "Bear Flag Republic."

New Mexico was also on Polk's list. Ties with the United States began in the 1820s, when American traders began to bring their goods to Santa Fe. Profits stimulated American territorial appetites. As the oldest and largest Mexican community in North America, however, New Mexicans had little desire for annexation. The unsuccessful attempt by the Texans to capture Santa Fe in 1841 and border clashes in the two following years did not enhance the attractiveness of their Anglo neighbors. But standing awkwardly in the path of westward expansion and further isolated from Mexico by the annexation of Texas in 1846, New Mexico's future was uncertain.

In June 1846, shortly after the declaration of war with Mexico, American troops led by Colonel Stephen W. Kearney left Fort Leavenworth, Kansas, for New Mexico. Kearney had orders to occupy Mexico's northern provinces and to protect the lucrative Santa Fe trade. Two months later, the army took Santa Fe without a shot, although one eyewitness noticed "surly countenances." New Mexico's upper class, who had already begun to intermarry with American merchants and send some sons to colleges in the United States, readily accepted the new rulers. However, ordinary Mexicans and Pueblo Indians did not take conquest so lightly. After Kearney departed for California, resistance erupted in New Mexico. Californios also fought the American occupation force. Kearney was wounded, and the first appointed American governor of New Mexico was killed. In the end, superior American military strength won the day. By January 1847, both California and New Mexico were firmly in American hands.

The Treaty of Guadalupe Hidalgo, 1848

Negotiated by Trist and signed on February 2, 1848, the Treaty of Guadalupe Hidalgo decided the fate of most people living in the Southwest. The United States absorbed the region's 75,000 Spanish-speaking inhabitants and 150,000 Native Americans and increased its territory by 529,017 square miles, almost a third of prewar Mexico. It paid Mexico $15 million, agreed to honor all American claims against Mexico, and guaranteed the civil, political, and property rights of former Mexican citizens. These immense territorial gains came at the cost of 13,000 American lives, lost mostly to diseases. Although sporadic violence would continue for years in the Southwest as Mexicans protested the outcome, the war was over, and the Americans had won.

The Oregon Question, 1844–1846

In the Pacific Northwest, the presence of mighty Great Britain suggested reliance on diplomacy rather than war. Glossing over the uncertainty of American claims, Polk assured the inauguration day crowd that "our title to the country of Oregon is 'clear and unquestionable.'" The British did not agree.

Though the British considered the president's speech belligerent, Polk was correct in saying that Americans had not hesitated to settle the disputed territories. Between 1842 and 1845, the number of Americans in Oregon grew from 400 to more than 5,000, mostly south of the Columbia River in the Willamette valley. By 1843, these settlers had written a constitution and soon after elected a legislature. At the same time, declining British interest in the area set the stage for an eventual compromise.

Polk's flamboyant posture and the expansive American claims made mediation difficult, however. Polk's campaign slogan claimed a boundary of 54°40′. But Polk was not willing to go to war with Great Britain for Oregon. Privately, he considered reasonable a boundary at the 49th parallel, which would extend the existing Canadian-American border to the Pacific.

Soon after his inauguration, Polk offered his compromise to Great Britain, but in a tone that antagonized the British. Polk compounded his error by gracelessly withdrawing the suggestion. In his year-end address to Congress in 1845, the president created more diplomatic difficulties by again publicly claiming Oregon and giving the required one-year's notice of American intention to cancel the joint occupation.

Despite slogans, most Americans did not want to fight for Oregon. As war with Mexico loomed, the task of resolving the disagreement became more urgent. The British, too, were eager to settle, and in June 1846 they agreed to the 49th parallel boundary if Vancouver Island remained entirely theirs. Polk and the Senate assumed some of the responsibility for retreating from the slogans, accepting this compromise just a few weeks before the declaration of war with Mexico.

Manifest Destiny was an idea that supported and justified expansionist policies. It corresponded, at the most basic level, to what Americans believed: Expansion was both necessary and right. As early as 1816, American geography books pictured the nation's western boundary at the Pacific and included Texas. Popular literature typically described Indians as a dying race and Mexicans as "unjust and injurious neighbor[s]." Only whites could make the wilderness flower. Thus, as lands east of the Mississippi filled up, Americans automatically called on familiar ideas to justify expansion.

GOING WEST

Americans lost little time in moving into the new territories. By 1860, California alone had 380,000 settlers. Some took the expensive trip by sea, but most emigrants chose land routes. Between 1841 and 1867, some 350,000 traveled over the overland trails to California or to Oregon, while others trekked to intermediate points like Colorado and Utah.

The Emigrants

Most of the emigrants who headed for the Far West, where slavery was prohibited, were white and American-born. They came from the Midwest and the Upper South. A few free blacks made the trip as well. Emigrants from the Deep South usually headed for Arkansas or Texas, and many took their slaves with them. By 1840, over 11,000 slaves toiled in Texas and 20,000 in Arkansas.

Except for the Gold Rush, migration was a family experience, usually involving men and women from their late twenties to early forties. A sizable number had recently married. For most, migration to the Far West was the latest in a series of earlier moves, often as children or as newlyweds. But this time, vast distances seemed to mean a final separation from home.

Migrants' Motives

Emigrant expectations varied widely. Thousands sought gold. Others anticipated making their fortune as merchants, shopkeepers, and peddlers. Some intended to speculate in land, acquiring large blocks of public lands and reselling to later settlers at a handsome profit. Practicing law or medicine on the frontier attracted still others.

Most migrants dreamed of bettering their life by farming, and government policies made it easier to get land. During the 1830s and 1840s, preemption acts allowed "squatters" to settle public lands before the government offered them for sale and then to purchase these lands at the minimum price once they came on the market. The amount of land a family had to buy shrank to only 40 acres. (In 1862, the Homestead Act would offer 160 acres of government land free to citizens or future citizens over 21 who lived on the property, improved it, and paid a small registration fee.) Oregon's land policy was even more generous. It awarded a single man 320 acres of free land and a married man 640 acres provided he occupied his claim for four years and made improvements.

Some emigrants went west for their health. Invalids grasped at the advice offered by one doctor in 1850, who urged them to "attach themselves to the companies of emigrants bound for Oregon or Upper California."

Others pursued religious or cultural missions in the West. Missionary couples like David and Catherine Blaine, who settled in Seattle when it was a frontier outpost, were determined to bring Protestantism and education to the area. Stirred by stories of the "deplorable morals" on the frontier, they left the comforts of home to evangelize and educate westerners. Still others, like the Mormons, made the long trek to Utah to establish a society conforming to their religious beliefs.

Unlike going to earlier frontiers, the trip to the Far West involved considerable expense: $600 paid for one person for the relatively comfortable Cape Horn voyage, or for four people to go on the overland Trail. (If emigrants sold their wagons and oxen at the journey's end, the final expenses might be only $220.) Such outlays were enough to rule out the trip for the very poor. Migration to the Far West (with the exception of group migration to Utah) was a movement of middle-class Americans.

Personal Diaries

Nineteenth-century journals kept by hundreds of ordinary men and women traveling west on the overland trails constitute a rich source for exploring the nature of the westward experience. They are also an example of how private sources can be used to deepen our understanding of the past. Diaries, journals, and letters all provide us with a personal perspective on major happenings. These sources tend to focus on the concrete, so they convey the texture of daily life in the nineteenth century, daily routines and amusements, clothing, habits, and interactions with family and friends. They also provide evidence of the varied concerns, attitudes, and prejudices of the writers, thus providing a test of commonly accepted generalizations about individual and group behavior.

Like any historical source, personal documents must be used carefully. It is important to note the writer's age, sex, class, and regional identification. Although this information may not be available, some of the writer's background can be deduced from what he or she has written. It is also important to consider for what purpose and for whom the document was composed. This information will help explain the tone or character of the source and what has been included or left out. It is, of course, important to avoid generalizing too much from one or even several similar sources. Only after reading many diaries, letters, and journals is it possible to make valid generalizations about life in the past.

Here we present excerpts from two travel journals of the 1850s. Few of the writers considered their journals to be strictly private. Often, they were intended as a family record or as information for friends back home. Therefore, material of a personal nature has often been excluded. Nineteenth-century Americans referred to certain topics, such as pregnancy, only indirectly or not at all.

One excerpt comes from Mary Bailey's 1852 journal. Mary was 22 when she crossed the plains to California with her 32-year-old doctor husband. Originally a New Englander, Mary had lived in Ohio for six years before moving west. The Baileys were reasonably prosperous and were able to restock necessary supplies on the road west. The other writer, Robert Robe, was 30 when he crossed along the same route a year earlier than the Baileys, headed for Oregon. Robert was a native of Ohio and a Presbyterian minister.

As you read these brief excerpts, notice what each journal reveals about the trip west. What kinds of challenges did the emigrants face on their journey? Can you see indications of the divisions of work based on gender? How is the focus of their interests different? What sorts of interactions seem to have occurred between men and women?

Even these short excerpts suggest that men and women, as they traveled west, had different concerns and different perspectives on the journey. How are the two accounts similar and different?

Journal of Robert Robe

[May] [1851]

29. Have arrived in the region abounding in Buffalo. At noon a considerable herd came in sight. The first any of us had ever seen. Thus now for the chase—the horsemen proved too swift in pursuit and frightened them into the Bluffs without capturing any—the footmen pursued however and killed three pretty good success for the first.

30. Nothing remarkable today.

31. Game being abundant we resolved to rest our stock and hunt today—Started in the morning on foot. Saw probably 1,000 Buffalo. Shot at several and killed one. Where ever we found them wolves were prowling around as if to guard them. Their real object is however no doubt to seize the calves as their prey. Saw a town of Prairie dogs, they are nearly as large as a gray squirrel. They bark fiercely when at a little distance but on near approach flee to their holes. Wherever they are we see

numerous owls. After a very extensive ramble and having seen a variety of game we returned at sunset with most voracious appetites.

[June]

1. The Bluffs became beautifully undulating losing their precipitous aspect and the country further back is beautifully rolling prairie.
2. In the evening camped beside our old friends Miller and Dovey. They had met with a great loss this morning their 3 horses having taken fright at a drove of buffalo and ran entirely away. Some of our company killed more buffalo this evening & a company went in the night with teams to bring them in.
3. Spent the forenoon in an unsuccessful search for the above mentioned horses. In the afternoon pursued & caught our company after.
4. Crossed the south fork of the Platte at 2 p.m.

Pacific Northwest Quarterly 19 (January 1928): 52–63.

Journal of Mary Stuart Bailey

Wednesday, April 13, 1852

Left our hitherto happy home in Sylvania amid the tears of parting kisses of dear friends, many of whom were endeared to me by their kindness shown to me when I was a stranger in a strange land, when sickness and death visited our small family & removed our darling, our only child in a moment, as it were. Such kindness I can never forget. . . .

Friday, 21st [May]

Rained last night. Slept in the tent for the first time. I was Yankee enough to protect myself by pinning up blankets over my head. I am quite at home in my tent.

12:00 Have traveled in the rain all day & we are stuck in the mud. I sit in the wagon writing while the men are at work doubling the teams to draw us out . . . .

Sunday, 23rd.

Walked to the top of the hill where I could be quiet & commune with nature and nature's God. This afternoon I was annoyed by something very unpleasant & shed many tears and felt very unhappy . . . .

Sunday, 4th [July]

Started at 3 o'clock to find feed or know where it was. Had to go 4 or 5 miles off the road. Found water & good grass. Camped on the sand with sage roots for fuel. It is wintery, cold & somewhat inclined to rain, not pleasant. Rather a dreary Independence Day. We speak of our friends at home. We think they are thinking of us . . . .

Monday, 12th.

Stayed in camp another day to get our horse better. He is much improved. It is cold enough. Washed in the morning & had the sick headache in the afternoon . . . .

Saturday, 18th [September]

Very pleasant, delightful weather. Feel much better today. We are not stirring this afternoon. We have heard to a great deal of suffering, people being thrown out on the desert to die & being picked up & brought to the hospital . . . .

Tuesday, November 8th

Sacramento city has been nearly consumed. The Dr. has had all his instruments & a good deal of clothing burned, loss not exceeding $300. It really seems as though it was not right for us to come to California & lose so much. I do not think that we shall be as well off as at home.

Source: Sandra L. Myers, ed., Ho for California! Women's Overland Diaries from the Huntington Library (San Marino, CA: Henry F. Huntington Library, 1980).

The Overland Trails

The trip started in the late spring when emigrants converged on the starting points: Council Bluffs, Iowa, or Independence, Missouri. When grass was up for the stock, usually in mid-May, they set out. Emigrant trains, making only 15 miles a day, first followed the valley of the Platte River up to South Pass in the Rockies. This part of the trip seemed novel, even enjoyable. Until the 1850s, conflict with Indians was rare. The traditional division of labor persisted: Men did "outdoor" work like driving and repairing wagons, hunting, and standing guard at night; women labored at domestic chores. Young children stayed out of the way, while older brothers and sisters walked alongside and lent a hand. Many later remembered the trip as an adventure. Wagon trains might stop to observe the Sabbath, allowing for rest and laundry.

Later, difficulties multiplied. Cholera often took a heavy toll. Deserts and mountains replaced rolling prairies. Emigrants needed to cross the final mountain ranges—the Sierras and the Cascades—before the first snowfall, so they pushed on relentlessly. Animals weakened by constant travel, poor feed, and bad water sickened, collapsed, and often died. Families had to lighten wagons by throwing out possessions lovingly brought from home. Food grew scarce. The familiar division of responsibilities often broke down. Women found themselves driving wagons, loading them, even helping to drag them over rocky mountain trails. Their husbands worked frantically with the animals and the wagons as the time of the first snowfall drew closer. Tempers frayed. Finally, five or six months after setting out, emigrants arrived, exhausted and often penniless, in Oregon or California. As one wrote on a September day in 1854, her journey had ended "which for care, fatigue, tediousness, perplexities and dangers of various kinds, can not be excelled."

Strains led some groups to draw up rules and elect officers. This did not prevent dissension, however. Many companies split up because of arguments over the pace of travel or because some changed their minds about their eventual destination. Family harmony often collapsed. Mary Power, who with her husband and three children crossed in 1853, revealed exasperation and depression in her journal: "I felt my courage must fail me, for there we were in a strange land, almost without anything to eat, [with] a team that was not able to pull an empty wagon." Men, too, lost nerve as they confronted the hazards of travel.

LIVING ON THE FRONTIER

When emigrants finally reached their destinations, their feelings ranged from acute disappointment to buoyant enthusiasm. As they turned toward building a new life, they naturally drew on their experiences back East. "Pioneers though we are, and proud of it, we are not content with the wilds . . . with the idleness of the land, the rudely construct[ed] log cabin," one Oregon settler explained.

The Agricultural Frontier

Pioneer farmers faced the urgent task of establishing homesteads and beginning farming. First, they had to locate a suitable claim. Clearing land and constructing a crude shelter followed. Only then could crops be planted.

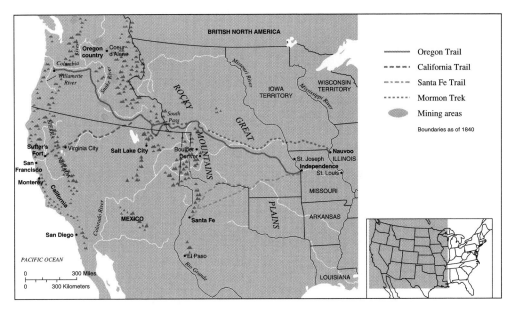

OVERLAND TRAILS TO THE WEST   The various trails over which thousands of Americans traveled during the 1840s, 1850s, and 1860s are depicted on this map.

As farmers labored "to get the land subdued and the wilde nature out of it," they repeated a process that had occurred on earlier frontiers. Felling timber, pulling out native plants that seemed to have no value, and planting familiar crops began a transformation of the landscape (see Chapter 10). Results were often unanticipated. When they planted seed brought from home, farmers unknowingly also introduced weeds that did all too well, like the Canadian thistle that gradually displaced native grass and rendered land useless for grazing.

Because emigrants brought so few of their possessions west, getting started was even more difficult than it would have been in the East. The Oregon bride who set up housekeeping in the 1840s with only a stew kettle and three knives was not unusual. After months of intense interaction with other travelers, families were now alone on their claims. Although frontier families might interact with nearby Indians, cultural biases made close friendships difficult. No wonder the pioneers often felt lonely. No wonder either that women helped men with their work and men assisted their wives in domestic chores.

One pioneer remembered that "in those days anyone residing within twenty miles was considered a neighbor." But the isolation usually ended within a few years as new emigrants arrived and old settlers sought better claims. As rural communities grew, settlers established schools, churches, and clubs. These organizations redefined acceptable forms of behavior and enforced conventional standards.

Determination to reestablish familiar institutions was most apparent in law and politics. In Oregon, pioneers set up a political system based on eastern models before territorial status was resolved. Before permanent schools or churches existed, men resumed familiar political rituals of electioneering, voting, and talking politics. They went to court to ensure law and order. Despite modern movies and

This undated photograph of two emigrant wagons and their occupants gives a good idea of the family character of emigration and the limited space that was available for family possessions and items needed at the end of the trip. Note that the children are barefoot. (Denver Public Library, Western History Collection)

novels suggesting that western everyday life was full of violence, courts, not vigilante groups, usually handled the occasional flareups in farming communities.

Setting up a common school system and churches was more difficult and less urgent than beginning political life. Few settlers initially thought education important enough to tax themselves for permanent public schools; what schools there were operated sporadically and were not free. When confirmed believers gathered in their own churches, they often discovered that the congregation was too small to survive. Nor were converts plentiful, for many settlers had lost the habit of regular churchgoing. "This is an awfully wicked country," Catherine Blaine concluded.

The chronic shortage of cash on the frontier retarded the growth of both schools and churches. Until farmers could send their goods to market, they had little cash to spare. Geographic mobility also contributed to institutional instability. Up to three-quarters of the population of a frontier county might vanish within a ten-year period. Some farmed in as many as four locations until they found a satisfactory claim. Institutions relying on continuing personal and financial support suffered accordingly.

Yet newspapers, journals, and books, which circulated early on the frontier, reinforced familiar norms and kept determination strong. As more settlers arrived, the numbers willing to support educational, religious, and cultural institutions grew. In the end, as one pioneer pointed out, "We have a telegraph line from the East, a daily rail road train, daily mail and I am beginning to feel quite civilized. And here ended my pioneer experience." Only 16 years had passed since she had crossed the Plains.

Although the belief in special economic and social opportunities on the frontier encouraged emigration, the dream was often illusory. Western society rapidly acquired a social and economic structure similar to that of the East. Frontier newspapers referred to leading settlers as the "better" sort, and workers for hire and tenant farmers appeared. Widespread geographic mobility also indicates that many found it difficult to capitalize on the benefits of homesteading. Those who moved were generally less successful than the core of stable residents, who became the community's economic and social leaders. Those on the move believed that fortune would finally smile at their next stop. Said one wife when her husband announced another move: "I seemed to have heard all this before."

The Mining Frontier

News of the discovery of gold in 1848 in California swept the country like "wildfire," according to a Missouri emigrant. Within a year, California's population ballooned from 14,000 to almost 100,000. By 1852, that figure more than doubled.

The forty-niners were mostly young. (In 1850, over half the people in California were in their twenties.) Unlike farming pioneers, gold seekers were unmarried, predominantly male, and heterogeneous. Of those pouring into California in 1849, about 80 percent came from the United States and 13 percent from Mexico and South America; the rest were Europeans and Asians. Most thought only of going home rich.

California was only the first and most dramatic of the western mining frontiers. Rumors of gold propelled 25,000 to 30,000 emigrants, many from California, to British Columbia in 1858. A year later, gold strikes in Colorado set off another frantic rush. Precious metals discovered in the Pacific Northwest, Montana, and Idaho in the 1860s kept prospectors moving. In the mid-1870s, yet another discovery of gold, this time in the Black Hills of North Dakota, attracted hordes.

Unlike isolated farming settlements, the mining frontier came to life almost overnight after a strike had been made. Mining camps, often hastily constructed, soon housed hundreds or even thousands of miners and people serving them. Merchants, saloonkeepers, cooks, druggists, gamblers, and prostitutes hurried in as fast as the prospectors. Usually about half the residents of any mining camp were there to prospect the miners.

Given the motivation, character, and ethnic diversity of those flocking to boomtowns and the feeble attempts to set up local government in what were perceived as temporary communities, it was hardly surprising that mining life was disorderly. Racial antagonisms led to ugly riots and lynchings. Miners had few qualms about eliminating Indians and others who got in the way. Fistfights, drunkenness, and murder occurred often enough to become part of the lore of the gold rush. Wrote one woman, "In the short space of twenty four days, we have had murders, fearful accidents, bloody deaths, a mob, whippings, a hanging, an attempt at suicide, and a fatal duel."

Mining life was not usually this violent, but it did tolerate behavior that would have been unacceptable farther east. Miners were trying to get rich, not to recreate eastern communities. Married men, knowing the raucous and immoral character of mining communities, hesitated to bring wives and families west.

Although the lucky few struck it rich or at least made enough money to return home with pride intact, miners' journals and letters reveal that many made only enough to keep going. Easily mined silver and gold deposits soon ran out.

Although Chinese miners proved adept at finding what early miners overlooked, the remaining rich deposits lay deeply embedded in rock or gravel. Extraction required cooperative efforts, capital, technological experience, and expensive machinery. Eventually, mining became a corporate industrial concern, with miners as wage earners. As early as 1852, the changing nature of mining in California had transformed most of the shaggy miners into wage workers.

Probably 5 percent of early gold rush emigrants to California were women and children. Many of the women also anticipated getting "rich in a hurry." Because there were so few of them, the cooking, nursing, laundry, and hotel services women provided had a high value. When Luzena Wilson arrived in Sacramento, a miner offered her $10 for a biscuit. Yet the work was tiring, and some wondered if the money compensated for the exhaustion. As Mary Ballou thought it over, she decided, "I would not advise any Lady to come out here and suffer to toil and fatigue I have suffered for the sake of a little gold." As men's profits shrank, so, too, did those of the women who served them.

Some of the first women to arrive on the mining frontier were prostitutes, hoping that the sex ratio would make their profession especially profitable. Prostitutes may have constituted as much as 20 percent of California's female population in 1850, and they probably vastly outnumbered other women in early mining camps. During boom days, they made good money and sometimes won a recognized place in society. But prostitution was a risky business in such a disorderly environment.

The Mexicans, South Americans, Chinese, and small numbers of blacks seeking their fortunes in California soon discovered that although they contributed substantially to California's growth, racial discrimination flourished vigorously. At first, American miners hoped to force foreigners out of the gold fields altogether. An attempt to declare mining illegal for all foreigners failed, but a high tax on them was more successful. Thousands of Mexicans left the mines, and the Chinese found other jobs in San Francisco and Sacramento. As business stagnated in mining towns, however, white miners reduced the levy. By 1870, when the tax was declared unconstitutional, the Chinese, paying 85 percent of it, had "contributed" $5 million to California for the right to prospect. The hostility that led to this legislation also fed widespread violence against Chinese and Mexicans.

Black Americans found that their skin color placed them in a situation akin to that of foreigners. Deprived of the vote, forbidden to testify in civil or criminal cases involving whites, excluded from the bounties of the state's homestead law, blacks led a precarious existence in Golden California.

In fact, fantasies of riches rarely came true. Western ghost towns testified to the typical pattern: boom, bust, decay, death. The landscape bore the scars of careless exploitation. Forests were devastated to provide timber for the flumes miners constructed to divert rivers from their channels in the hopes of exposing gold in dry river beds. During heavy rains, mounds of debris oozed over fields and choked waterways.

Yet for all the negative consequences, gold also had many positive effects on the West as a whole. Between 1848 and 1883, California mines supplied two-thirds of the country's gold. Gold transformed sleepy San Francisco into a bustling metropolis. It fueled the agricultural and commercial development of California and Oregon, as miners provided a market for goods and services. Gold

This 1852 photograph of miners and the constructions they built on the American River hints at some of the environmental consequences of mining activity. The formal clothing of the woman contrasts sharply with that worn by the men and suggests that she has not forgotten the standards of civilized life. (California State Library)

built harbors, railroads, and irrigation systems all over the West. Though few people made large fortunes, both the region and the nation profited from gold.

The Mormon Frontier

In the decades before 1860, many emigrants heading for the Far West stopped to rest and buy supplies in Salt Lake City, the heart of the Mormon state of Deseret. There they encountered a society that seemed familiar and orderly, yet also foreign and shocking. Visitors admired the attractively laid out town, but they also gossiped about polygamy and searched the faces of Mormon women for signs of rebellion—and were amazed that so few Mormon women seemed interested in escaping the bonds of plural marriage, which outsiders equated with slavery.

Violence had driven the Mormons to the arid Great Basin area. Joseph Smith's murder in 1844 did not end persecution of his followers, and by the fall of 1846 angry mobs had chased the last of the "Saints" out of Nauvoo, Illinois. Smith's successor, Brigham Young, realized that flight from the United States represented the best hope for survival. The Saints must create the kingdom of God anew in the West, far from the United States, that "Babylon" of corruption and injustice.

The Mexican-American war unexpectedly furthered Mormon plans. Young realized that war might provide capital for the new Mormon kingdom. By raising 500 Mormon young men for Kearney's Army of the West, Young acquired vital resources. The battalion's advance pay bought wagonloads of supplies for starving and sick Mormons strung out along the trail between Missouri and Iowa and helped finance the impending great migration.

Young selected the Great Basin area, still part of Mexico, as the best site for his future kingdom. It was arid and remote, 1,000 miles from its nearest "civilized" neighbors. But if irrigated, Mormon leaders concluded it might prove as fertile as ancient Israel. In April 1847, Young led an exploratory expedition of 143 men, 3 women, and 2 children to this promised land. In late July, after reaching Salt Lake, he exclaimed "This is the place," and announced his land policy. Settlers would receive virtually free land on the basis of a family's size and ability to cultivate it. While he returned to lead the main body, the expeditionary group dug irrigation ditches and began planting.

Young's organizational talents and his followers' cooperative abilities were fully tested. By September 1847, fully 566 wagons and 1,500 Saints made the arduous trek to Salt Lake City; more came the next year. Church leaders directed everything. By 1850, the Mormon frontier had over 11,000 settlers. Missionary efforts in the United States, Great Britain, and Scandinavia drew thousands of converts to the Great Basin, with a Church-administered loan fund facilitating the journey for many. By the end of the decade, over 30,000 Saints lived in Utah, not only in Salt Lake City but also in more than 90 village colonies. Despite hardship, the Mormons thrived.

Most Mormons were farmers from New England and the Midwest and shared many of the same customs, attitudes, and political structure. But "Gentile" outsiders perceived profound differences, for the heart of Mormon society was not the individual farmer on his own homestead, but the cooperative village.

Persecution had nourished a strong sense of group identity and acceptance of Church leadership. Organized by Church leaders, who made the essential decisions, farming became a collective enterprise. All farmers were allotted land and access to community water. Said one woman tartly, "We do not believe in having any drones in the hive."

Nothing separated Church and state in Utah. Church leaders occupied all important political posts. Young's Governing Quorum contained the high priests of the Church, who made both religious and political decisions.

When it became clear that Utah would become a territory, Mormon leaders drew up a constitution that divided religious and political power. But once in place, powers overlapped. As one Gentile pointed out, "This intimate connection of church and state seems to pervade everything that is done. The supreme power in both being lodged in the hands of the same individuals, it is difficult to separate their two official characters, and to determine whether in any one instance they act as spiritual or merely temporal officers."

The Treaty of Guadalupe Hidalgo officially incorporated Utah into the United States, but little affected political and religious arrangements. Young became territorial governor. Bishops continued to act as spiritual leaders as well as civil magistrates.

Other aspects of the Mormon frontier were distinctive. Mormon policy toward the Indian tribes was remarkably enlightened. After 1850, Mormons concentrated on converting rather than killing Native Americans. Mormon missionaries learned Indian languages and encouraged Native Americans to farm.

Although most Gentiles could tolerate some of the differences they encountered on the Mormon frontier, few could accept the seeming immorality of polygamy. Although Smith and other Church leaders had secretly practiced polygamy in the early 1840s, Young publicly revealed the doctrine only in 1852, when the Saints were safely in Utah. Smith believed that the highest or "celestial" form of marriage brought special rewards in the afterlife. Because wives and children contributed to these rewards, polygamy was a means of sanctification. From a practical standpoint, polygamy incorporated into Mormon society single female converts who had left their families to come to Utah.

Although most Mormons accepted the doctrine and its religious justification, some found it hard to follow. During the 40-year period in which Mormons practiced plural marriage, perhaps only 10 to 20 percent of Mormon families were polygamous. Few men had more than two wives. Personal strains and the expense of maintaining several families ensured that usually only the most successful and visible Mormon leaders practiced polygamy.

Polygamous family life was a far cry from outsiders' fantasies. Jealousy among wives could destroy it, so Mormon leaders minimized romantic love and sexual attraction in courtship and marriage. Instead, they encouraged marriages founded on mutual attachment, with sex primarily for procreation.

To the shock of outsiders, Mormon women considered themselves not slaves but highly regarded members of the community. Whether plural wives or not, they saw polygamy as the cutting edge of their society and defended it to outsiders. Polygamy was preferable to monogamy, which left the single woman outside family life and forced some into prostitution.

Although they faced obvious difficulties, many plural wives found rewards in polygamy. Without the constant presence of husbands, they had an unusual opportunity for independence. Many treated visiting husbands as revered friends, deriving day-to-day emotional satisfaction from their children. Occasionally, plural wives lived together and became close friends.

The Mormon frontier succeeded in terms of its numbers, its growing prosperity, and its unity. Long-term threats loomed, however, once the area became part of the United States. Attacks on Young's power as well as heated verbal denunciations of polygamy proliferated. Efforts began in Congress to outlaw polygamy. In the years before the Civil War, Mormons withstood these assaults. But as Utah became more connected to the rest of the country, the tide would turn.

The Urban Frontier

Many emigrants went west to cities like San Francisco, Denver, and Portland. There they pursued business and professional opportunities or a fortune in real estate speculation.

Cities were integral to frontier life. Some, like San Francisco and Denver, turned into cities almost overnight as the discovery of precious metals sent thousands of miners with diverse demands and desires to and through them. Once the strike ran out, many miners returned to these cities to make a new start. Other places supplied frontier farmers, only gradually acquiring urban characteristics.

Frontier commercial life offered residents a wide range of occupations and services. As a Portland emigrant remarked in 1852, "In many ways life here . . . was more primitive than it was in the early times in Illinois and Missouri. But in others it was far more advanced . . . . We could get the world's commodities here which could not be had then, or scarcely at all, in the interior of Illinois or Missouri."

Young, single men seeking their fortunes made up a disproportionate share of urban populations. Frontier Portland had more than three men for every woman. Predictably, urban life was often noisy, rowdy, and occasionally violent. Mothers worried about bad company. Some attempted to reform the atmosphere by pressing for Sunday store closings or prohibition. Other women, of course, enjoyed all the attention that came with the presence of so many young men. Eventually, the sex ratio became balanced, but as late as 1880, fully 18 of the 24 largest western cities had more men than women.

Western cities soon lost their distinctiveness. The history of Portland suggests the common pattern of development. In 1845, it was only a clearing in the forest, with lively speculation in town lots. By the early 1850s, Portland had grown into a small trading center with a few rough log structures and muddy tracks for streets. As farmers poured into Oregon, the city became a regional commercial center. More permanent structures were built, giving it an "eastern" appearance.

The belief that urban life in the West abounded with special opportunities initially drew many young men to cities like Portland. Many did not thrive, and opportunities were greatest for newcomers who brought assets. By the 1860s, when the city's population had reached 2,874, Portland's Social Club symbolized the emergence of an elite. Portland's businessmen, lawyers, and editors controlled an increasing share of the community's wealth and set its social standards, showing how far Portland had come from its raw frontier beginnings.

CULTURES IN CONFLICT

Looking at westward expansion through the eyes of white emigrants provides only one view of the frontier experience. An entry from an Oregon Trail journal suggests other perspectives. On May 7, 1864, Mary Warner, a bride of only a few months, described how a "fine-looking" Indian visited the wagon train and tried to buy her. Mary's husband, uncertain how to handle the situation, played along, agreeing to trade his wife for two ponies. The Indian generously offered three. "Then," wrote Mary, "he took hold of my shawl to make me understand to get out [of the wagon]. About this time I got frightened and really was so hysterical [that] I began to cry." Everyone laughed, she reported, though surely the Indian found the incident no more amusing than she had.

This ordinary encounter on the overland trail only begins to hint at the social and cultural differences separating white Americans moving west and the peoples they met. Confident of their values and rights, emigrants had little regard for those who had lived in the West for centuries and no compunction in seizing their lands. Many predicted that the Indians would disappear from the continent.

Confronting the Plains Tribes

During the 1840s, white Americans for the first time came into extensive contact with the powerful Plains tribes, whose culture differed from that of the more familiar eastern Woodlands peoples. Probably a quarter million Native Americans occupied the Plains. "Border" tribes along the Plains' eastern edge lived in villages and raised crops, supplemented with buffalo meat during summer months. On the Central Plains lived Brulé and Oglala Sioux, Cheyenne, Shoshone, and Arapaho, all aggressive tribes who followed the buffalo and often raided the border tribes. In the Southwest were Comanche, Ute, Navajo, and some Apache bands; northern and western Texas was hunting grounds for the Kiowa, Wichita, Apache, and

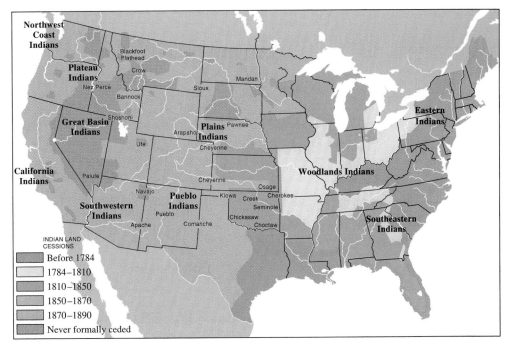

INDIAN TRIBES IN 1840 Although this map reveals the location of groups of Indian tribes in 1840, it presents too static a picture of tribal territories. Some of the Indian groups in the West had been forced across the Mississippi by events in the Midwest. What the map does make obvious, however, is the rapid pace of Indian land cessions in the nineteenth century.

southern Comanche. Many southwestern tribes had adopted aspects of Spanish culture and European domestic animals like cattle, sheep, and horses.

The Plains tribes shared certain characteristics. Most had become nomads after the introduction of Spanish horses in the sixteenth century increased their seasonal mobility from 50 to 500 miles. Horses allowed Indian men to hunt the buffalo with such success that tribes (with the exclusion of the border groups) came to depend on the beasts for food, clothing, fuel, teepee dwellings, and trading purposes. Women were responsible for processing buffalo products, and some men had more than one wife to tan skins for trading.

Mobility also increased tribal contact and conflict. War was central to the lives of the Plains tribes. No male became a fully accepted member of his tribe until he had proved himself in battle. But tribal warfare was not like the warfare of white men. Indians sought not to exterminate their enemies or to claim territory, but to steal horses and prove individual prowess. They considered it braver to touch an enemy than to kill or scalp him. This pattern of conflict on the Plains discouraged political unity. Chiefs had only limited authority, and often could not restrain young men needing to prove their prowess.

With guns, fast ponies, and skills in warfare and raiding, the Plains tribes posed a fearsome obstacle to white expansion. They had signed no treaties with the United States and had few friendly feelings toward whites. Their contact with white society had brought gains through trade in skins, but the trade had also brought alcohol and epidemics.

Alfred Jacob Miller was fascinated with the trans-Mississippi West. His 1836 depiction of a Plains Indian throwing a lasso preceded the great wave of white migration that so disrupted native life. Most artists who sketched and painted scenes like the one here anticipated that native culture would disappear with the coming of the whites. (The Beinecke Rare Book and Manuscript Library, Yale University Library)

When the first emigrants drove their wagons across the plains and prairies in the early 1840s, Indian-white relations were peaceable. But the intrusion of whites set in motion an environmental cycle that eventually made for conflict. Indians depended on the buffalo but respected this source of life. The grasses that nourished the buffalo also sustained the Indians' ponies and the animals that supported horse traders like the Cheyenne.

Whites, however, fed their oxen and horses on the grass that the Indians' ponies and the buffalo needed. And they adopted that "most exciting sport," the buffalo hunt. As the great herds began to shrink, Native American tribes began to battle one another for hunting grounds and food. The powerful Sioux swooped down into the hunting grounds of their enemies and mounted destructive raids against the Pawnee and other smaller tribes.

In 1846 the Sioux petitioned President Polk for compensation for damages to their hunting grounds caused by emigrating whites. When the president denied their request, they tried to extract taxes from emigrants, who were outraged at what they considered Indian effrontery. However, little was done to relieve the suffering of the tribes bearing the brunt of Sioux aggression, the dismay of the Sioux at the white invasion, or the fears of the emigrants themselves.

The discovery of gold in California, which lured over 20,000 across the Plains in 1849 alone, became the catalyst for federal action. The horde of gold seekers and their animals wrought such devastation in the Platte valley that it rapidly became a wasteland for the Indians. Cholera spread from whites to Indians, killing thousands.

Government officials devised a two-pronged plan. The government would construct a chain of forts to protect emigrants and, simultaneously, call the tribes to a general conference. Officials expected that in return for generous presents, Indians would end tribal warfare and limit their movements. They instructed tribes to select chiefs to speak for them at the conference.

The Fort Laramie Council, 1851

In 1851, the council convened at Fort Laramie. As many as 10,000 Indians gathered, hopeful of ending the destruction of their way of life and eager for the presents. Tribal animosities simmered, however. Skirmishes occurred on the way to the fort. Border tribes, fearful of the Sioux, refused to come; so did the Comanche, Kiowa, and Apache because their Sioux and Crow enemies would be there.

Whites told the gathered tribes that times had changed. In the past, "you had plenty of buffalo and game . . . and your Great Father well knows that war has always been your favorite amusement and pursuit. He then left the question of peace and war to yourselves. Now, since the settling of the districts West . . . by the white men, your condition has changed." There would be compensation for the destruction of their grass, timber, and buffalo and annual payments of goods and services. But the tribes had to give up their rights of free movement. The government drew tribal boundaries, and chiefs promised to stay within them. Some tribal lands were sold.

The Fort Laramie Treaty was the first agreement between the Plains tribes and the United States government. It expressed whites' conviction that Indians must stay apart in clearly defined areas.

But this system of isolation and its purported benefits were still in the future. During the conference, ominous signs of trouble appeared. The Sioux refused to be confined north of the Platte, for south of the river lay their recently conquered lands. "These lands once belonged to the Kiowas and the Crows," one Sioux explained, "but we whipped those nations out of them and in this we did what the white men do when they want the lands of the Indians." Elsewhere in the trans-Mississippi West, other tribes, like the fierce Navajo of New Mexico, also resisted white attempts to restrict them.

Overwhelming the Mexicans

In the Southwest, in Texas, and in California, Americans encountered a Spanish-speaking population and Hispanic culture. Americans regarded Mexicans as the lazy, ignorant, and cunning "dregs of society." Mexicans lacked the numbers to fend off American aggression.

Although Anglo-Mexican interaction differed from place to place, few Anglos heeded the Treaty of Guadalupe Hidalgo's assurances that Mexicans would have citizens' rights. Most Spanish-speaking people lived in New Mexico, and, of all former Mexican citizens, they probably fared the best. Most were of mixed blood, living marginally as ranch hands for rich landowners or as farmers and herdsmen in small villages dominated by a *patron*, or headman. As the century wore on, Americans produced legal titles and took over lands long occupied by peasant farmers and stock raisers. But despite economic reversals, New Mexicans survived, carrying their rural culture well into the twentieth century.

Upper-class landowners were in the best position to cope with new conditions. Even before the conquest, rich New Mexicans had protected their future by establishing contracts with American businessmen and sending their sons east to American schools. When the United States annexed New Mexico, this powerful class contracted strategic marriage and business alliances with the Anglo men who slowly trickled in. During the 1850s, they maintained their influence, prestige, and American connections. Only rarely did they worry about their poor countrymen. Class outweighed ethnic or cultural considerations.

In Texas, the Spanish-speaking residents, only 10 percent of the population in 1840, shrank to a mere 6 percent by 1860. Although the upper class also intermarried with Americans, they lost most of their power. Poor, dark-skinned Hispanics clustered in low-paying and largely unskilled jobs.

In California, the discovery of gold radically changed the situation for the Californios. In 1848, there were 7,000 Californios and about twice as many Anglos; by 1860, the Anglo population had ballooned to 360,000. Hispanic-Americans were hard pressed to cope with this influx. At first, Californios and several thousand Mexican citizens joined Anglos and others in the gold fields. But competition fed antagonism and finally open conflict. Taxes and terrorism ultimately drove most Spanish speakers from the mines and established new racial contours.

Other changes were even more disastrous. In 1851, Congress passed the Gwinn Land Law, supposedly validating Spanish and Mexican land titles. But it violated the Treaty of Guadalupe Hidalgo because it forced California landowners to defend what was already theirs and encouraged squatters to settle on land in the hopes that the Californios' titles would prove false. It took an average of 17 years to establish clear title to land. Landowners found themselves paying American lawyers large fees, often in land, and borrowing at high interest rates to cover court proceedings. A victory at court often turned into a defeat when legal expenses forced owners to sell their lands to pay debts.

Working class Hispanic-Americans became laborers for Anglo farmers or for mining and later railroad companies. Hispanic-Americans earned less money and did more unpleasant jobs than Anglo workers. For them, the coming of the Anglos presented a steadily deteriorating situation. By 1870, the average Hispanic-American worker's property was worth only about a third of its value of 20 years earlier.

Movies and novels have played a large role in forming images of the nineteenth-century West. Cowboys, sheriffs, outlaws, and bandits gallop across screens and pages. One of these outlaws, a sombrero-clad rider, points to the reality of resistance to American expansion into the Southwest. The career of Tiburcio Vásquez, a notorious *bandido* in southern California, shows that some Hispanics felt that they could protest events only through violence:

> My career grew out of the circumstances by which I was surrounded . . . . As I grew to manhood I was in the habit of attending balls and parties given by the native Californians, into which the Americans, then beginning to become numerous, would

TIMELINE

1803–1806	1818	1819	1821	1821–1840
Lewis and Clark expedition	Treaty on joint U.S.-British occupation of Oregon	Spain cedes Spanish territory in United States and sets transcontinental boundary of Louisiana Purchase, excluding Texas	Mexican independence; Opening of Santa Fe Trail; Stephen Austin leads American settlement of Texas	Indian removals
1830	**1836**	**1840s**	**1844**	**1845**
Mexico abolishes slavery in Texas	Texas declares independence; Battles of the Alamo and San Jacinto	Emigrant crossings of Overland Trail	James Polk elected president	"Manifest Destiny" coined; United States annexes Texas and sends troops to the Rio Grande; Americans attempt to buy Upper California and New Mexico
1846	**1847**	**1848**	**1849**	**1850**
Mexico declares defensive war; United States declares war and takes Santa Fe; Resolution of Oregon question	Attacks on Veracruz and Mexico City; Mormon migration to Utah begins	Treaty of Guadalupe Hidalgo	California Gold Rush begins	California admitted to the Union
1851	**1853**	**1862**		
Fort Laramie Treaty	Gadsden Purchase	Homestead Act		

force themselves and shove the native born men aside, monopolizing the dance and the women. This was about 1852. A spirit of hatred and revenge took possession of me. I had numerous fights in defense of my countrywomen. The officers were continually in pursuit of me. I believed we were unjustly and wrongfully deprived of the social rights that belonged to us.

Other Hispanics resorted to other tactics. In New Mexico, members of Las Gorras Blancas ripped up railroad ties and cut the barbed wire fences of Anglo ranchers and farmers. The religiously-oriented Penitentes tried to work through the ballot box. Ordinary men, women, and children resisted efforts to convert them to Protestantism and learned some of the skills they hoped would enable them to flourish in a changing culture while retaining many of their familiar customs and beliefs.

✦✦✦✦✦✦

CONCLUSION

Fruits of Manifest Destiny

Like Lewis Cass, many nineteenth-century Americans were convinced that the country had merely gained western territories to which it was entitled. Although the process of acquiring the western half of the continent was swift, the prospect of winning the West loomed large in the imagination of the American people for many years. A number of western settlers became folk heroes. All white Americans could be thankful for the special opportunities and the new chance for success that the West seemed to offer.

The expanding nation did gain vast natural wealth in the trans-Mississippi West. But only a small fraction of the hopeful emigrants heading for the frontier realized their dreams of success. And the move west had a dark side as Americans clashed with Mexicans and Native Americans in their drive to fulfill their "Manifest Destiny" and as the acquisition of new territories fueled the controversy over the future of slavery.

Recommended Reading

Overviews

Patricia Nelson Limerick, *The Legacy of Conquest: The Unbroken Past of the American West* (1987); David Hamer, *New Towns in the New World: Images and Perceptions of the Nineteenth-Century Frontier* (1990); William H. Troettner, *The West as America: Reinterpreting Images of the Frontier, 1820–1920* (1991); William Cronon, George Miles, and Jay Gitlin, eds., *Under An Open Sky: Rethinking America's Western Past* (1992).

Manifest Destiny and Its Fruits

Cecil Robinson, ed., *The View From Chapultepec: Mexican Writers on the Mexican-American War* (1989); David J. Weber, *The Mexican Frontier, 1821–1846* (1982); Theodore J. Karamanski, *Fur Trade and Exploration: Opening the Far Northwest, 1821–1852* (1983); David Pletcher, *The Diplomacy of Annexation: Texas, Oregon, and the Mexican War* (1973); K. Jack Bauer, *Zachary Taylor* (1985); Anders Stephanson, *Manifest Destiny: American Expansionism and the Empire of Right* (1995).

Native Americans

Sylvia Van Kirk, *Many Tender Ties: Women in the Fur Trade Society, 1670–1870* (1983); Julie Roy Jeffrey, *Converting the West: A Biography of Narcissa Whitman* (1991); Jacqueline Peters, *Sacred Encounters: Father DeSmet and the Indians of the Rocky Mountain West* (1993); Theodore Stern, *Chiefs & Chief Traders: Indian Relations at Fort Nez Perces, 1818–1855* (1993); Peter Nabakov, ed., *Native American Testimony: An Anthology of Indian and White Relations* (1978); David J. Wishart, *An Unspeakable Sadness: The Dispossession of the Nebraska Indians* (1994).

Frontier Society

Sandra Myres, ed., *Ho for California! Women's Overland Diaries from the Huntington Library* (1980); John Mack Faragher, *Women and Men on the Overland Trail* (1978); Adolf E. Schroeder and Carla Schulz-Geisberg, eds., *Hold Dear, As Always: Jette, a German Immigrant Life in Letters* (1988); Arrell Morgan Gibson, *Yankees in Paradise: The Pacific Basin Frontier* (1993);

Laurie F. Maffly-Kipp, *Religion and Society in Frontier California* (1994); Peter G. Boag, *Environment and Experience: Settlement Culture in Nineteenth-Century Oregon* (1992); Dean L. May, *Three Frontiers: Family, Land, and Society in the American West, 1850–1900* (1994); Richard L. Bushman, *Joseph Smith and the Beginnings of Mormonism* (1984); Robert J. Rosenbaum, *Mexicano Resistance in the Southwest: "The Sacred Right of Self-Preservation"* (1981); Timothy M. Marovina, *Tejano Religion and Ethnicity: San Antonio, 1821–1860* (1995); Julie Roy Jeffrey, *Frontier Women "Civilizing" the West? 1840–1880* (Second Edition, 1998).

CHAPTER 14

The Union in Peril

The autumn of 1860 was a time of ominous rumors. The election was held on November 6 in an atmosphere of crisis. In Springfield, Illinois, Abraham Lincoln, taking coffee and sandwiches prepared by the "ladies of Springfield," waited as the telegraph brought in the returns. By 1 a.m., victory was certain. "I went home, but not to get much sleep, for I then felt, as I never had before, the responsibility that was upon me." He and the American people faced the most serious crisis since the founding of the Republic.

Lincoln won a four-party election with only 39 percent of the popular vote. He appealed almost exclusively to northern voters in a blatantly sectional campaign, defeating his three opponents by carrying every free state except New Jersey. Only Illinois Senator Stephen Douglas campaigned actively in every section of the country. For his efforts, he received the second-highest number of votes. Douglas's appeal, especially in the closing days of the campaign, was "on behalf of the Union," which he feared—correctly—was in imminent danger of splitting apart.

That fall, other Americans sensed the crisis and faced their own fears and responsibilities. A month before the election, South Carolina plantation owner Robert Allston wrote his oldest son, Benjamin, that "disastrous consequences" would follow from a Lincoln victory. Although his letter mentioned the possibility of secession, he dealt mostly with plantation concerns: a new horse, the mood of the slaves, ordering supplies from the city, instructions for making trousers on a sewing machine. After Lincoln's election, Allston corresponded with a southern colleague about the need for an "effective military organization" to resist "Northern and Federal aggression." In his shift from sewing machines to military ones, Allston prepared for what he called the "impending crisis."

Frederick Douglass greeted the election of 1860 with characteristic optimism. Not only was this an opportunity to "educate . . . the people in their moral and political duties," he said, but "slaveholders know that the day of their power is over when a Republican President is elected." But no sooner had Lincoln's victory been determined than Douglass's hopes turned sour. He noted that Republican leaders, trying to keep the border states from seceding, sounded more antiabolitionist than antislavery. They vowed not to touch slavery in areas where it already existed (including the District of Columbia), to enforce the hated Fugitive Slave Act, and to put down slave rebellions. Slavery would, in fact, Douglass bitterly concluded, "be as safe, and safer" with Lincoln than with a Democrat.

Iowa farmer Michael Luark was not so sure. Born in Virginia, he was a typically mobile nineteenth-century American. Growing up in Indiana, he followed the mining booms of the 1850s to Colorado and California, then returned to the Midwest to farm. Luark sought a good living and resented the furor over slavery. He could not, however, avoid the issue.

Writing in his diary on the last day of 1860, Luark looked ahead to 1861 with a deep sense of fear. "Startling" political changes would occur, he predicted, perhaps even the "Dissolution of the Union and Civil War with all its train of horrors." He blamed abolitionist agitators, perhaps reflecting his Virginia origins. On New Year's Day, he expressed his fears that Lincoln would let the "most ultra sectional and Abolition" men disturb the "vexed Slavery question" even further, as Frederick Douglass wanted. But if this happened, Luark warned, "then farewell to our beloved Union of States."

Within four months, the guns of the Confederate States of America fired on a U.S. fort in South Carolina. The Civil War had begun. Luark's fears, Douglass's hopes, and Lincoln's and Allston's preparations for responsibility all became realities. How the Union fell apart is the theme of this chapter.

✦✦✦✦✦✦

Such a calamitous event as Civil War had numerous causes, large and small. The reactions of Allston, Douglass, and Luark to Lincoln's election suggest some of them: moral duties, sectional politics, growing apprehensions over emotional agitators, and a concern for freedom and independence on the part of blacks, white southerners, and western farmers. But as Douglass understood, by 1860 it was clear that "slavery is the real issue ... between all parties and sections. It is the one disturbing force, and explains the confused and irregular motion of our political machine."

This chapter analyzes how the momentous issue of slavery disrupted the political system and eventually the Union itself. We will look at how four major developments between 1848 and 1861 contributed to the Civil War: first, a sectional dispute over the extension of slavery into the western territories; second, the breakdown of the political party system; third, growing cultural differences in the views and lifestyles of southerners and northerners; and fourth, intensifying emotional and ideological polarization between the two regions over losing their way of life and sacred republican rights at the hands of the other. A preview of civil war, bringing all four causes together, occurred in 1855–1856 in Kansas. Eventually, emotional events, mistrust, and irreconcilable differences made conflict inevitable. Lincoln's election was the spark that touched off the conflagration of civil war, with all its "train of horrors."

SLAVERY IN THE TERRITORIES

Senator Lewis Cass had been wrong when he predicted political and social harmony as Americans moved west (see Chapter 13). White migrations threatened Native Americans and Mexicans. They also caused a collision of Yankees and slaveholders.

The North and the South had contained their differences over slavery for 60 years after the Constitutional Convention. Compromise in 1787 had resolved questions of the slave trade and how to count slaves for congressional representation. Although slavery threatened the uneasy sectional harmony in 1820, the Missouri Compromise had established a workable balance of free and slave states and defined a geographic line (36°30′) to determine future decisions. In 1833, compromise had defused South Carolina's attempt at nullification, and the gag rule in 1836 had kept the abolitionists' anti-slavery petitions off the floor of Congress.

Each apparent resolution, however, raised the level of emotional conflict between North and South and postponed ultimate settlement of the slavery question. One reason why these compromises temporarily worked was the two-party system, with Whigs and Democrats in both North and South. The parties differed over cultural and economic issues, but slavery was largely kept out of political campaigns and congressional debates. This changed in the late 1840s.

Free Soil or Constitutional Protection?

When war with Mexico broke out in 1846, Pennsylvania congressman David Wilmot added an amendment to an appropriations bill, declaring that "neither slavery nor involuntary servitude shall ever exist" in any territories acquired from Mexico. Legislators debated the Wilmot Proviso not as Whigs and Democrats, but as northerners and southerners.

A Boston newspaper prophetically observed that Wilmot's resolution "brought to a head the great question which is about to divide the American people." When the war ended, several solutions were presented to deal with slavery in the territories. First was the "free soil" idea of preventing any extensions of slavery. Two precedents suggested that Congress could do this. One was the Northwest Ordinance, which had barred slaves from the Upper Midwest; the other was the Missouri Compromise.

Free-Soilers had mixed motives. For some, slavery was an evil to be destroyed. But for many northern white farmers looking westward, the threat of economic competition with an expanding system of large-scale slave labor was even more serious. Nor did they wish to compete with free blacks. As Wilmot put it, his proviso was intended to preserve the area for the "sons of toil, of my own race and own color." Other northerners supported it as a means of restraining the growing political power and "insufferable arrogance" of the "spirit and demands of the Slave Power."

An opposing second position was the argument of Senator John C. Calhoun. Not only did Congress lack the constitutional right to exclude slavery from the territories, the South Carolinian argued, but it had a duty to protect it. The Wilmot Proviso, therefore, was unconstitutional. So was the Missouri Compromise and any other federal act that prevented slaveholders from taking their slave property into the territories.

Economic, political, and moral considerations stood behind Calhoun's position. Many southerners hungered for new cotton lands in the West and Southwest, even in Central America and the Caribbean. Southerners feared that northerners wanted to trample their right to protect their institutions against abolitionism. Southern leaders saw the Wilmot Proviso as a moral issue touching basic republican principles. Senator Robert Toombs of Georgia warned that if it passed, he would favor disunion.

Popular Sovereignty and the Election of 1848

With such divisive potential, it was natural that many Americans sought a compromise solution to exclude slavery from politics. Polk's secretary of state, James Buchanan, proposed extending the Missouri Compromise line to the Pacific Ocean, avoiding thorny questions about the morality of slavery and the constitutionality of congressional authority. So would "popular sovereignty," Senator Cass's proposal to leave decisions about permitting slavery to territorial legislatures. The idea appealed to American democratic belief in local self-government, but left many details unanswered. At what point in the progress toward statehood could a territorial legislature decide about slavery?

Democrats, liking popular sovereignty because it could mean all things to all people, nominated Cass for president in 1848. Cass denounced abolitionists and the Wilmot Proviso, but otherwise avoided the slavery issue. The Democrats, however, printed two campaign biographies of Cass, one for the South and one for the North.

The Whigs found an even better way to stick together. Rejecting Henry Clay, they nominated the Mexican-American War hero, General Zachary Taylor, a Louisiana slaveholder. Taylor compared himself to Washington as a "no party" man above politics. This was about all he stood for. Southern Whigs supported Taylor because they thought he might understand the burdens of slaveholding, and northern Whigs were pleased that he took no stand on the Wilmot Proviso.

The evasions of the two major parties disappointed Calhoun, who tried to create a new unified southern party. His "Address to the People of the Southern States" threatened secession and called for a united stand against further attempts to interfere with the southern right to extend slavery. Although only 48 of 121 southern representatives signed the address, Calhoun's argument raised the specter of secession and disunion.

Warnings also came from the North. A New York Democratic faction bolted to support Van Buren for president. At first, the split had more to do with state politics than moral principles, but it soon involved the question of slavery in the territories. Disaffected "conscience" Whigs from Massachusetts also explored a third-party alternative. These groups met in Buffalo, New York, to form the Free-Soil party and nominate Van Buren for president. The platform of the new party, an uneasy mixture of ardent abolitionists and opponents of free blacks moving into western lands, pledged to fight for "free soil, free speech, free labor and free men."

Taylor won easily, largely because defections from Cass to the Free-Soilers cost the Democrats New York and Pennsylvania. Although weakened, the two-party system survived. Purely sectional parties had failed. The Free-Soilers took only about 10 percent of the popular vote.

The Compromise of 1850

Taylor won by avoiding slavery questions. But as president he had to deal with them. As he was inaugurated in 1849, four issues faced the nation. First, the rush of some 80,000 gold miners to California qualified it for statehood. But California's entry as a free state would upset the slave-free state balance in the Senate. The unresolved status of the Mexican cession in the Southwest posed a second problem. The longer the area remained unorganized, the louder local inhabitants called for an application of either the Wilmot Proviso or the Calhoun doctrine. The Texas-New Mexico boundary was also disputed, with Texas claiming everything east of Santa Fe. Northerners feared that Texas might split into five or six slave states. A third problem, especially for abolitionists, was the existence of slavery and a huge slave market in the nation's capital. Fourth, Southerners resented the lax federal enforcement of the Fugitive Slave Act of 1793. They called for a stronger act that would end protection for runaways fleeing to Canada.

Taylor was a political novice (he had never voted in a presidential election before 1848), but he tackled these problems in a statesmanlike, if evasive, manner. Sidestepping the issue of slavery in the territories, he invited California and New Mexico to seek statehood immediately, presumably as free states. But soon he alienated both southern supporters like Calhoun and mainstream Whig leaders.

Early in 1850, the old compromiser Henry Clay sought to regain control of the Whig party by proposing solutions to the divisive issues before the nation. With Webster's support, Clay introduced a series of resolutions in an omnibus package intended to settle these issues once and for all. The stormy debates, great speeches, and political maneuvering that followed added up to a crucial and dramatic moment in American history. Yet the Senate defeated Clay's Omnibus Bill. The tired and disheartened 73-year-old Clay left Washington, dying before he could return. Into the gap stepped Senator Stephen Douglas of Illinois, who saw that Clay's resolutions had a better chance of passing if voted on individually. Under Douglas's leadership, and with the support of Millard Fillmore, who succeeded to the presidency upon Taylor's sudden death, a series of bills was finally passed.

The so-called Compromise of 1850 put Clay's resolutions, slightly altered, into law. First, California entered the Union as a free state, ending the balance of free and slave states. Second, territorial governments were organized in New Mexico and Utah, letting the people there decide whether to permit slavery. The Texas-New Mexico border was settled, denying Texas the disputed area. In return, the federal government gave Texas $10 million to pay debts owed to Mexico. Third, the slave trade, but not slavery, was abolished in the District of Columbia.

The fourth and most controversial part of the compromise was the Fugitive Slave Act, containing many provisions that offended northerners. One denied alleged fugitives a jury trial, leaving special cases for decision by commissioners (who were paid $5 for setting a fugitive free, but $10 for returning a fugitive). An especially repugnant provision compelled northern citizens to help catch runaways.

Consequences of Compromise

The Compromise of 1850 was the last attempt to keep slavery out of politics. Voting on the different bills followed sectional lines on some issues and party lines on others. Douglas felt pleased with his "final settlement" of the slavery question.

But the Compromise only delayed more serious sectional conflict, and it added two new ingredients to American politics. First, political realignment along sectional lines moved closer. Second, although repudiated by most ordinary citizens, ideas like secessionism, disunion, and a "higher law" than the Constitution entered political discussions. People wondered whether the question of slavery in the territories could be compromised away next time.

Others were immediately upset. The new fugitive slave law angered many northerners. Owners of runaway slaves hired agents (labeled "kidnappers" in the North) to hunt down fugitives. In a few dramatic episodes, notably in Boston, literary and religious intellectuals led mass protests to resist slave hunters. When Webster supported the law, New England abolitionists denounced him. Emerson said that he would not obey the "filthy law."

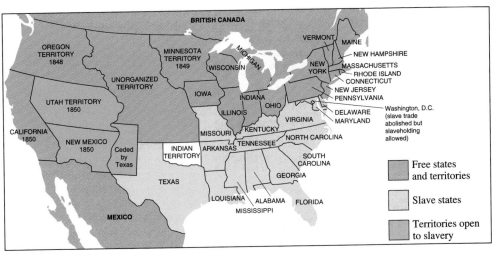

THE COMPROMISE OF 1850 "I have seen many periods of great anxiety, of peril, and of danger in this country," Henry Clay told the Congress in February of 1850, "and I have never before risen to address any assemblage so oppressed, so appalled, and so anxious." What followed were the debates that led eventually to the passage of his great compromise. Can you find three of the four major parts of the bill on the map?

Frederick Douglass would not obey it either. As a runaway slave, he faced arrest and return to the South until friends overcame his objections and purchased his freedom. Douglass still risked harm by his strong defiance of the Fugitive Slave Act. Arguing the "rightfulness of forcible resistance," he urged free blacks to arm themselves. "The only way to make the Fugitive Slave Law a dead letter," he said in Pittsburgh in 1853, "is to make a half dozen or more dead kidnappers." Douglass raised money for black fugitives, hid runaways in his home, and helped hundreds escape to Canada.

Other northerners, white and black, stepped up work for the underground railroad. Several states passed "personal liberty laws" that prohibited using state officials and institutions in the recovery of fugitive slaves. But most northerners complied. Of some 200 blacks arrested in the first six years of the law, only 15 were rescued, and only 3 of these by force. Failed rescues, in fact, had more emotional impact than did successful ones. In two cases in the early 1850s, angry mobs of abolitionists in Boston failed to prevent the forcible return of blacks to the South. These celebrated cases aroused antislavery emotions in more northerners than abolitionists had been able to do by their tracts and speeches.

But the spoken and written word also fueled emotions over slavery in the aftermath of 1850. In an Independence Day speech in 1852, Douglass wondered aloud: "What, to the American slave, is your 4th of July?" It was, he said, the day that revealed to the slave the "gross injustice and cruelty to which he is the constant victim." Douglass's speeches, like those of another ex-slave, Sojourner Truth, became increasingly strident.

At a women's rights convention in 1851 in Akron, Ohio, Truth made one of the decade's boldest statements for minority rights. The convention was attended by clergymen, who kept heckling female speakers. Up stood Sojourner Truth to speak in words still debated by historians. She pointed to her many years of childbearing

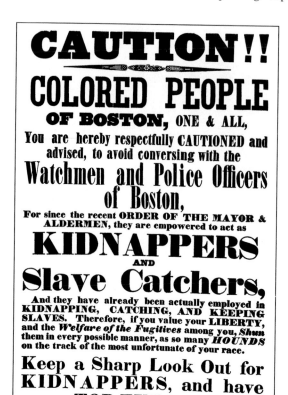

The dangers of the Fugitive Slave Act are evident in this 1851 broadside published by Boston abolitionist Theodore Parker, which alerted the city's black community to the dangers posed by the new law. (Chicago Public Library)

and hard, backbreaking work as a slave, crying out a refrain, "And ar'n't I a woman?" Where had Jesus came from? "From God and a woman: Man had nothing to do with Him." Referring to Eve, she concluded, "If the first woman God ever made was strong enough to turn the world upside down all alone, these women together ought to be able to turn it back, and get it right side up again! And now they is asking to do it, the men better let them." She silenced the hecklers.

As Truth spoke, another American woman, Harriet Beecher Stowe, was finishing a novel, *Uncle Tom's Cabin,* that would go far toward turning the world upside down. As politicians were hoping the American people would forget slavery, Stowe's novel brought it to the attention of thousands. She gave readers an absorbing indictment of the horrors of slavery and its impact on both northerners and southerners. Published initially as magazine serials, each month's chapter ended at a nail-biting moment.

Although outraging the South when published in full in 1852, *Uncle Tom's Cabin* became one of the all-time bestsellers in American history. In the first year, over 300,000 copies were printed, and Stowe's novel was eventually published in 20 languages. When President Lincoln met Stowe in 1863, he is reported to have said to her, with a twinkle in his eye, "So you're the little woman who wrote the book that made this great war!"

POLITICAL DISINTEGRATION

The response to *Uncle Tom's Cabin* and the Fugitive Slave Act indicated that politicians had congratulated themselves too soon for saving the Republic in 1850. Political developments, not all dealing with slavery, were already weakening the ability of political parties—and ultimately the nation—to withstand the passions slavery aroused.

The Apathetic Election of 1852

Political parties thrive on their ability to convince voters that they stand for moral values and economic policies crucially different from those of the opposition. Between 1850 and 1854, these differences blurred, undermining party loyalty.

First, both parties scrambled to convince voters that they had favored the Compromise of 1850. In addition, in the early 1850s several states rewrote their constitutions and remodeled their laws. These changes reduced the number of patronage jobs that politicians could dispense and regularized the process for securing banking, railroad, and other corporate charters, ending the role formerly played by the legislature. Both undermined the importance of parties in citizens' lives. In a similar manner, the return of prosperity in the early 1850s also weakened parties. For almost a quarter of a century, Whigs and Democrats had disagreed over the tariff, money and banking, and government-supported internal improvements. Now, in better times, party distinctions over economic policies seemed less important.

The election of 1852 illustrated the lessening significance of political parties. The Whigs nominated General Winfield Scott, another Mexican-American War hero, who they hoped would repeat Taylor's success four years earlier. With Clay and Webster both dead, party leadership passed to Senator William Seward of New York, who wanted a president he could influence more successfully than the prosouthern Fillmore. Still, it took 52 ballots to nominate Scott over Fillmore, alienating southern Whigs. Democrats had their own problems. After 49 ballots, the party turned to a lackluster compromise, Franklin Pierce of New Hampshire.

The two parties offered little choice and downplayed issues so as not to widen intraparty divisions. Voter interest diminished. "Genl. Apathy is the strongest candidate out here," was a typical report from Ohio. Democratic leaders resorted to bribes and drinks to buy the support of thousands of new Catholic immigrants from Ireland and Germany, who could be naturalized and were eligible to vote after only three years. Pierce won easily, 254 to 42 electoral votes.

The Kansas-Nebraska Act

The Whig party's final disintegration came on a February day in 1854 when southern Whigs supported Stephen Douglas's Nebraska bill, choosing to be more southern than Whig. The Illinois senator had many reasons for introducing a bill organizing the Nebraska Territory (which included Kansas). An ardent nationalist, he was interested in the continuing development of the West. He wanted the eastern terminus for a transcontinental railroad in Chicago rather than in rival St. Louis. This meant organizing the lands west of Iowa and Missouri.

Politics also played a role. Douglas hoped to recapture the party leadership he had held in passing the Compromise of 1850, and aspired to the presidency. Although he had replaced Cass as the great advocate of popular sovereignty, thus winning favor among northern Democrats, he needed southern Democratic support. Many southerners, especially neighboring Missouri slaveholders, opposed organizing Nebraska Territory unless it were open to slavery. But it lay north of the line where slavery had been prohibited by the Missouri Compromise.

Douglas's bill, introduced early in 1854, recommended using popular sovereignty in organizing two territories, Kansas and Nebraska. Inhabitants could vote slavery in, violating the Missouri Compromise. Douglas reasoned, however, that Kansas and Nebraska would never support slavery-based agriculture and that the people would choose to be a free state. Therefore, he could win the votes he needed for the railroad without also getting slavery. By simply stating that the state or states created out of the Nebraska Territory would enter the Union "with or without slavery, as their constitution may prescribe at the time of their admission," his bill ignored the Missouri Compromise.

Douglas miscalculated. Northerners from his own party immediately attacked him and his bill as a "criminal betrayal of precious rights" and as part of a plot promoting his own presidential ambitions by turning free Nebraska over to "slavery despotism." Whigs and abolitionists were even more outraged. Frederick Douglass branded the act the result of the "audacious villainy of the slave power."

But the more Stephen Douglas was attacked, the harder he fought. Eventually his bill passed, but it seriously damaged the party system. What began as a railroad measure ended in reopening the question of slavery in the territories, which Douglas had thought finally settled in 1850. What began as a way of avoiding conflict ended in violence over whether Kansas would enter the Union slave or free. What began as a way of strengthening party lines ended up destroying one party (Whigs), planting irreconcilable divisions in another (Democrats), and creating two new ones (Know-Nothings and Republicans).

Expansionist "Young America"

The Democratic party was weakened in the early 1850s not only by the Kansas-Nebraska Act, but also by an expansive energy that led Americans to adventures far beyond Kansas. Americans had hailed the European revolutions of 1848 as evidence that republicanism was the wave of the future. "Young America" was the label assumed by patriots eager for a continuing national mission, which ironically included the spread of slavery.

Pierce's platform in 1852 reflected this nationalism. Many Democrats took their overwhelming victory as a mandate to continue adding territory. A Philadelphia newspaper in 1853 described the United States as bound on the "East by sunrise, West by sunset, North by the Arctic Expedition, and South as far as we darn please."

Many of Pierce's diplomatic appointees were southerners interested in adding new cotton-growing lands to the Union. Pierce's ambassador to Mexico, for example, South Carolinian James Gadsden, had instructions to negotiate with Mexican president Santa Anna for the acquisition of large parts of northern Mexico. Gadsden did not get all he wanted, but he did manage to buy a strip of southwestern desert for a transcontinental railroad linking the Deep South with the Pacific Coast.

Failure to acquire more territory from Mexico legally did not discourage expansionist Americans from pursuing illegal means. During the 1850s, Texans and Californians staged dozens of raids ("filibusters") into Mexico. The most daring such adventurer was William Walker, a tiny Tennessean with a zest for danger and power. In 1853, he invaded Mexican Baja California with fewer than 300 men and declared himself president of the Republic of Sonora. Arrested and tried in the United States, he was acquitted in eight minutes. Two years later, he invaded Nicaragua, where he proclaimed himself dictator and legalized slavery. When the Nicaraguans, with British help, regained control, the U.S. Navy rescued Walker. After a triumphant tour in the South, he tried twice more to conquer Nicaragua. Walker came to a fitting end in 1860 when, invading Honduras, he was shot by a firing squad.

Undaunted, the Pierce administration looked to the acquisition of Cuba. Many Americans thought this Spanish colony was destined for U.S. annexation and would be an ideal place for expanding the slave-based economy. A decade earlier, the Polk administration had vainly offered Spain $10 million for Cuba. Unsuccessful efforts were then made to foment a revolution among Cuban sugar planters, who were expected to request annexation by the United States.

Although Pierce did not support these illegal efforts to acquire Cuba, he wanted the island. Secretary of State William Marcy instructed the minister to Spain, Pierre Soulé, to offer $130 million for Cuba. If that failed, Marcy suggested stronger measures. In 1854, the secretary arranged for Soulé and the American ministers to France and England to meet in Belgium, where they issued the Ostend Manifesto to pressure Spain to sell Cuba to the United States.

The manifesto argued that Cuba "belongs naturally" to the United States. Southern slaveholders feared that a slave rebellion would "Africanize" Cuba, like Haiti, and suggested all kinds of "horrors to the white race" in the nearby southern United States. American acquisition of Cuba was necessary, therefore, to "preserve our rectitude and self-respect." If Spain refused to sell, the ministers at Ostend threatened a revolution in Cuba with American support. If that failed, "we should be justified in wresting it from Spain."

Even Marcy was shocked, and he quickly repudiated the manifesto. Like the Kansas-Nebraska Act, the Ostend Manifesto was urged by Democrats who advocated the expansion of slavery. The outraged reaction of northerners in both cases divided and weakened the Democratic party.

Nativism, Know-Nothings, and Republicans

Increasing immigration damaged an already enfeebled Whig party and alarmed many native-born Americans. To the average hardworking Protestant American, foreigners spoke unfamiliar languages, wore funny clothes, drank alcohol freely, and bred crime and pauperism. Moreover, they seemed content with a lower standard of living and thus threatened American jobs.

Worst of all, from the Protestant perspective, Irish and German immigrants spearheaded an unprecedented growth of American Catholicism. By the 1850s, there were nearly three million Catholics in the United States, not only in eastern cities but expanding westward and—to the shocked surprise of many old-stock Americans—converting Protestants. Catholics' insistence on sending their children to Catholic schools compounded their offensiveness to Protestants.

Many Protestants charged that Catholic immigrants corrupted American politics. Indeed, most Catholics did prefer the Democratic party, which was less inclined than the Whigs to interfere with religion, schooling, drinking, and other aspects of personal behavior.

It was mostly former Whigs, therefore, who in 1854 founded the American party to oppose the new immigrants. Members wanted a longer period of naturalization to guarantee the "vital principles of Republican Government" and pledged never to vote for Irish Catholics, whose highest loyalty was supposedly to the pope. They also agreed to keep information about their order secret. If asked, they would say, "I know nothing." Hence, they were dubbed the Know-Nothing party.

The Know-Nothings appealed to the middle and lower classes—to workers worried about their jobs and to farmers and small-town Americans nervous about new forces in their lives. As one New Yorker put it in 1854, "Roman Catholicism is feared more than American slavery." It was widely believed that Catholics slavishly obeyed their priests, who represented a Church associated with European despotism. In the 1854 and 1855 elections, the Know-Nothings gave anti-Catholicism a national political focus for the first time.

To other northerners, the "slave power" seemed a more serious threat than the schemes of the pope. No sooner had debates over Nebraska ended than the nucleus of another new party appeared: the Republican party.

Drawn almost entirely from "conscience" Whigs and disaffected Democrats (including ex-Free-Soilers), the Republicans combined four main elements. Moral fervor led the first group, headed by senators William Seward, Charles Sumner (Massachusetts) and Salmon P. Chase (Ohio), to demand prohibiting slavery in the territories, freeing slaves in the District of Columbia, repealing the Fugitive Slave Act, and banning the internal slave trade.

There were, however, limits to most Republicans' idealism. A more moderate and larger group, typified by Abraham Lincoln, opposed slavery in the western territories, but would not interfere with it where it already existed. This group also rejected equal rights for northern free blacks.

Republicans were anti-Catholic as well as antislavery. A third element of the party, true to traditional Whig reformist impulses, wanted to cleanse America of intemperance, impiety, parochial schooling, and other forms of immorality—including voting for Democrats, who catered to the "grog shops, foreign vote, and Catholic brethren" and combined the "forces of Jesuitism and Slavery."

The fourth element of the Republican party, a Whig legacy from Clay's American System, included those who wanted the federal government to promote economic development and the dignity of labor. This group, like the antislavery and anti-Catholic elements, idealized free labor. At the heart of both the new party and the future of America were hardworking, middle-class, mobile, free white laborers—farmers, small businessmen, and independent craftsmen.

The strengths of the Republican and Know-Nothing (American) parties were tested in 1856. The American party nominated Fillmore, who had strong support in the Upper South and border states. The Republicans chose John C. Frémont, a Free-Soiler from Missouri with virtually no political experience. The Democrats

The American (Know-Nothing) party campaign against the immigrants is dramatically shown in this cartoon of a whiskey-drinking Irishman and beer-barreled German stealing the ballot box while native-born Americans fight at the election poll in the background. (New York Public Library, Astor, Lenox & Tilden Foundations)

nominated Pennsylvanian James Buchanan, a "northern man with southern principles." Frémont carried several free states, while Fillmore took only Maryland. Buchanan, benefiting from a divided opposition, won with only 45 percent of the popular vote.

After 1856, the Know-Nothings died out, largely because Republican leaders cleverly redirected nativist fears—and voters—to their broader program. Moreover, Know-Nothing secrecy, hatreds, and occasional violent attacks on Catholic voters damaged their image. Still, the Know-Nothings represented a powerful current in American politics that would return each time social and economic changes seemed to threaten. It became convenient to label certain people "un-American" and try to root them out. The Know-Nothing party disappeared, but nativism did not.

KANSAS AND THE TWO CULTURES

The slavery issue also would not go away. As Democrats sought to expand slavery and other American institutions westward across the Plains and south into Cuba, Republicans wanted to halt the advance of slavery. In 1854, Lincoln worried that slavery "deprives our republican example of its just influence in the world." The specific cause of his concern was the likelihood that slavery might be extended into Kansas as a result of the passage that year of Stephen Douglas's Kansas-Nebraska Act.

Competing for Kansas

During the congressional debates over the Kansas-Nebraska bill, Seward accepted the challenge of slave-state senators to "engage in competition for the virgin soil of Kansas." Passage of the Kansas-Nebraska Act in 1854 opened the way for proslavery and antislavery forces to clash over Kansas. No sooner had the bill passed Congress than the Massachusetts Emigrant Aid Society was founded to recruit free-soil settlers for Kansas. By the summer of 1855, about 1,200 New England colonists had migrated to Kansas.

One migrant was Julia Louisa Lovejoy, a Vermont minister's wife. As a riverboat carried her into a slave state for the first time in her life, she wrote of the dilapidated plantation homes on the monotonous Missouri shore as the "blighting mildew of slavery." By the time she and her husband arrived in the Kansas Territory, Julia had concluded that the "inhabitants and morals" of the slaveholding Missourians moving into Kansas were of an *undescribably repulsive* and undesirable character." To her, northerners came to bring the "energetic Yankee" virtues of morality and economic enterprise to drunken, unclean slaveholders.

Perhaps she had in mind David Atchison, Democratic senator from Missouri. Atchison believed that Congress must protect slavery in the territories, allowing Missouri slaveholders into Kansas. In 1853, he pledged "to extend the institutions of Missouri over the Territory at whatever sacrifice of blood or treasure." He recommended to fellow Missourians if need be "to kill every God-damned abolitionist in the district."

Under Atchison's inflammatory leadership, secret societies sprang up in the Missouri counties adjacent to Kansas, vowed to combat the Free-Soilers. One editor exclaimed that northerners came to Kansas "for the express purpose of stealing, running off and hiding runaway negroes from Missouri [and] taking to their own bed . . . a stinking negro wench." Not slaveholders, he said, but New Englanders were immoral, uncivilized, and hypocritical. Rumors of 20,000 such Massachusetts migrants spurred Missourians to action. Thousands poured across the border late in 1854 to vote on permitting slavery in the territory. Twice as many ballots were cast as the number of registered voters.

The proslavery forces overreacted. The permanent population of Kansas consisted primarily of migrants from Missouri and other border states who were more concerned with land titles than slavery. They opposed any blacks—slave or free—moving into their state.

In March 1855, a second election was held to select a territorial legislature. The pattern of border crossings, intimidation, and illegal voting was repeated. Atchison himself, drinking "considerable whiskey," led an armed band across the state line to vote and frighten away would-be Free-Soil voters. Not surprisingly, a small minority of eligible voters elected a proslavery territorial legislature. Free-Soilers, meanwhile, held their own convention in Lawrence and created a Free-Soil government at Topeka. It banned blacks from the state. The proslavery legislature settled in Lecompton, giving Kansas two governments.

The struggle shifted to Washington. Pierce could have nullified the illegal election, but did nothing. Congress debated and sent an investigating committee to Kansas, which further inflamed passions. Throughout 1855, the call to arms grew more strident. In South Carolina, Robert Allston wrote his son Benjamin that he was

Led by Senator David Atchison, thousands of gun-toting Missourians crossed into Kansas in 1854 and 1855 in order to vote illegally for a proslavery territorial government. The ensuing bloodshed made Kansas a preview of the Civil War. (The Newberry Library, Chicago)

"raising men and money . . . to counteract the effect of the Northern hordes . . . . We are disposed to fight the battle of our rights . . . on the field of Kansas."

Both sides saw Kansas as a holy battleground. An Alabaman sold his slaves to raise money to hire an army of 300 men to fight for slavery in Kansas, promising free land to his recruits. A Baptist minister blessed their departure from Montgomery, promised them God's favor and gave each man a Bible. Northern Christians responded in kind. At Yale University, the noted minister Henry Ward Beecher presented 25 Bibles and 25 Sharps rifles to young men who would go fight for the Lord in Kansas. "There are times," he said, "when self-defense is a religious duty." Beecher suggested that rifles would be of greater use than Bibles. Missourians dubbed them "Beecher's Bibles" and vowed, as one newspaper put it, "Blood for Blood!"

"Bleeding Kansas"

As civil war threatened in Kansas, a Brooklyn poet, Walt Whitman, heralded American democracy in his epic poem *Leaves of Grass* (1855). Whitman identified himself as the embodiment of average Americans "of every hue and caste . . . of every rank and religion." But Whitman's faith in the American masses faltered in the mid-1850s. He worried that a knife plunged into the "breast" of the Union would bring on the "red blood of civil war."

Blood indeed flowed in Kansas. In May 1856, supported by a prosouthern federal marshall, a mob entered Lawrence, smashed the offices and presses of a Free-Soil newspaper, fired several cannonballs into the Free State Hotel, and destroyed homes and shops. Three nights later, doing God's will, John Brown led a small New England band, including four of his sons, to a proslavery settlement near Pottawatomie Creek and hacked five men to death with swords.

That same week, abolitionist senator Charles Sumner delivered a tirade known as "The Crime Against Kansas." He lashed out at the "incredible atrocities of the

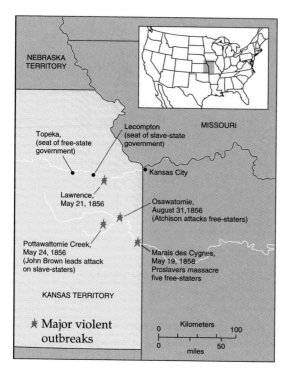

"BLEEDING KANSAS"

Assassins and . . . Thugs" from the South. Nastily, he accused proslavery Senate leaders, especially Atchison and Andrew Butler of South Carolina, of cavorting with the "harlot, Slavery." Two days later, Butler's nephew, Congressman Preston Brooks, avenged his honor by beating Sumner senseless with his cane as he sat at his Senate desk.

The sack of Lawrence, the Pottawatomie massacre, and the caning of Sumner set off a minor civil war in "Bleeding Kansas." It lasted throughout the summer. Crops were burned, homes were destroyed, fights broke out in saloons and streets, and night raiders tortured and murdered their enemies. For residents like Charles Lines, who just wanted to farm in peace, it was impossible to remain neutral. Lines hoped his neighbors near Lawrence would avoid "involving themselves in trouble." But when proslavery forces tortured to death a neighbor, Lines joined the battle. "Blood," he wrote, "must end in the triumph of the right."

Even before the bleeding of Kansas began, the New York *Tribune* warned, "We are two peoples. We are a people for Freedom and a people for Slavery. Between the two, conflict is inevitable." As the rhetoric and violence in Kansas demonstrated, competing visions of two separate cultures for the future destiny of the United States were at stake. Despite many similarities between the North and the South, the gap between the two sides widened with the hostilities of the 1850s.

Northern Views and Visions

The North saw itself, as Julia Lovejoy suggested, as a prosperous land of bustling commerce and expanding, independent agriculture. Northern farmers and workers were self-made free men who believed in individualism and democracy. The "free labor system" of the North, as both Seward and Lincoln often said, offered equality of opportunity and upward mobility. Both generated more wealth. Although the North contained many growing cities, northerners revered the values of the small towns that spread from New England across the Upper Midwest. These values included a respect for the rights of the people, tempered by the rule of law; individual enterprise, balanced by a concern for one's neighbors; and a fierce morality rooted in Calvinist Protestantism. Northerners would regulate morality—by persuasion if possible, by legislation if necessary—to purge irreligion, illiteracy, and intemperance from American society.

Northerners valued the kind of republican government that guaranteed the rights of free men, enabling them to achieve economic progress. This belief supported government action to promote free labor, industrial growth, some immigration, foreign trade (protected by tariffs), and the extension of railroads and free farm homesteads westward across the continent. Energetic mobility, both westward and upward, would dissolve state, regional, and class loyalties and increase the sense of nationhood. A strong Union could achieve national and even international greatness. These were the conditions, befitting a chosen people, that would, as Seward put it, spread American institutions around the world and "renovate the condition of mankind." These were also the principles of the Republican party.

Only free men could achieve economic progress and moral society. In northerners' eyes, therefore, the worst sin was the loss of one's freedom. Slavery was the root of all evil. It was, Seward said, "incompatible with all . . . the elements of the security, welfare, and greatness of nations." The South was the antithesis of everything that such northerners saw as good. Southerners were unfree, backward, economically stagnant, uneducated, lawless, immoral, and in conflict with the values and ideals of the nineteenth century. Julia Lovejoy's denunciation of slaveholding Missourians was mild. Other Yankee migrants saw southerners as "wild beasts" who guzzled whiskey, ate dirt, uttered oaths, raped slave women, and fought or dueled at the slightest excuse. In the slang of the day, they were "Pukes."

The Southern Perspective

Southerners were a diverse people who, like northerners, shared certain broad values, generally those of the planter class. If in the North the values of economic enterprise were most important, southerners revered social values most. They admired the English gentry and saw themselves as courteous, refined, hospitable, and chivalrous—and "Yankees" as coarse, ill-mannered, aggressive, and materialistic. In a society where one person in three was a black slave, racial distinctions and paternalistic relationships were crucial in maintaining order and white supremacy. Fear of slave revolt was ever present. The South had five times as many military schools as the North. Northerners educated the many for economic utility; southerners educated the few for character. In short, the South saw itself as an ordered society guided by the planters' genteel code.

Southerners agreed with northerners that republican sovereignty rested in the people, who created a government of laws to protect life, liberty, and property. But unlike northerners, southerners believed that the democratic principle of self-government was best preserved in local political units such as the states. They were ready to fight to resist any tyrannical encroachment on their liberty, as they had in 1776. They saw themselves as true revolutionary patriots. Like northerners, southerners cherished the Union. But they preferred the loose confederacy of the Jeffersonian past, not the centralized nationalism Seward kept invoking.

To southerners, Yankees were in too much of a hurry—to make money, to reform others' behavior, to put dreamy theories (like racial equality) into practice. Two images dominated the South's view of northerners: either they were stingy, hypocritical, moralizing Puritans, or they were grubby, slum-dwelling, Catholic immigrants.

Each side saw the other threatening its freedom and degrading proper republican society. Each saw the other imposing barriers to its vision for America's future, which included the economic systems described in Chapters 10 and 11. As hostilities rose, the views each section had of the other grew steadily more rigid and conspiratorial. Northerners saw the South as a "slave power," determined to foist the slave system on free labor throughout the land. Southerners saw the North as full of "black Republicanism," determined to destroy their own way of life.

POLARIZATION AND THE ROAD TO WAR

As long as the two major parties held their national constituencies, northern and southern cultural stereotypes and conspiratorial accusations had been largely held in check. But events in Kansas solidified the image of the Republicans as a northern party and seriously weakened the Democrats. Further events, still involving the question of slavery in the territories, soon split the Democrats irrevocably into sectional halves: the Dred Scott decision of the Supreme Court (1857), the constitutional crisis in Kansas (1857), the Lincoln-Douglas debates in Illinois (1858), John Brown's raid in Virginia (1859), and Lincoln's election (1860). These incidents further polarized the negative images each culture held of the other and pushed the nation down the road to civil war.

The Dred Scott Case

The events of 1857 reinforced the arguments of those who believed in a slave power conspiracy. Two days after James Buchanan's inauguration, the Supreme Court finally ruled in *Dred Scott v. Sandford*. The case had been before the Court for nearly three years. Back in 1846, Dred and Harriet Scott had filed suit in Missouri for their freedom. They argued that their master had taken them into territories where the Missouri Compromise prohibited slavery, and therefore they should be freed. By the time the case reached the Supreme Court, slavery in the territories was a hot political issue.

When the Court, which had a southern majority, issued its 7–2 decision, it made three rulings. First, because blacks were, as Chief Justice Roger Taney put it, "beings of an inferior order [who] had no rights which white men were bound to respect," Dred Scott was not a citizen and had no right to sue in federal court. The second ruling stated that the Missouri Compromise was unconstitutional because Congress had no power to ban slavery in a territory. Third, the Court decided that the Scotts' being taken in and out of free states did not affect their status. Despite two eloquent dissenting opinions, Dred and Harriet Scott remained slaves.

The implications of these decisions went far beyond the Scotts' personal freedom. The arguments about black citizenship infuriated many northerners. Frederick Douglass called the ruling "a most scandalous and devilish perversion of the Constitution." Many citizens worried about the few rights free blacks still held. Even more troubling, the decision hinted that slavery might be legal in the free states of the North. People who suspected a conspiracy were not calmed when Buchanan endorsed the *Dred Scott* decision as a final settlement of the right of citizens to take their "property of any kind, including slaves, into the common Territories . . . and to have it protected there under the Federal Constitution." Far from settling the issue of slavery in the territories, as Buchanan had hoped, *Dred Scott* threw it back into American politics. It opened new questions and increased sectional hostilities.

Douglas and the Democrats

The *Dred Scott* decision and Buchanan's endorsement fed northern suspicions of a slave power conspiracy to impose slavery everywhere. Events in Kansas, which still had two governments, heightened these fears. In the summer of 1857, Kansas had yet another election, with so many irregularities that only 2,000 out of a possible 24,000 voters participated. A proslavery slate of delegates was elected to a constitutional convention meeting at Lecompton as a preparation for statehood. The convention barred free blacks from the state, guaranteed the property rights of the few slaveholders in Kansas, and asked voters to decide in a referendum whether to permit more slaves.

The proslavery Lecompton constitution, clearly unrepresentative of the wishes of the majority of the people of Kansas, was sent to Congress for approval. Eager to retain southern Democratic support, Buchanan endorsed it. Stephen Douglas challenged the president's power and jeopardized his standing with southern Democrats by opposing it. Facing reelection to the Senate in 1858, Douglas needed to hold the support of the northern wing of his party. Congress sent the Lecompton constitution back to the people of Kansas for another referendum. This time they defeated it, which meant that Kansas remained a territory rather than becoming a slave state. While Kansas was left in an uncertain status, the larger political effect of the struggle was to split the Democratic party almost beyond repair.

No sooner had Douglas settled the Lecompton question than he faced reelection in Illinois. Douglas's opposition to the Lecompton constitution had restored his prestige in the North as an opponent of the slave power. This cut some ground out from under the Republican party's claim that only it could stop the spread of southern power. Republican party leaders from the West, however, had a candidate who understood the importance of distinguishing Republican moral and political views from those of the Democrats.

Lincoln and the Illinois Debates

Although relatively unknown nationally and out of elective office for several years, by 1858 Abraham Lincoln emerged in Illinois to challenge Seward for leadership of the Republican party. Lincoln's character was shaped on the midwestern frontier, where he had educated himself, developed mild abolitionist views, and dreamed of America's greatness.

Douglas was clearly the leading Democrat, so the 1858 Senate election in Illinois gave a preview of the presidential election of 1860. The other Douglass, Frederick, observed that "the slave power idea was the ideological glue of the Republican party." Lincoln's handling of this idea would be crucial in distinguishing him from Stephen Douglas. The Illinois campaign featured seven debates between Lincoln and Douglas which took place in different cities. Addressing a national as well as a local audience, the debaters confronted the heated racial issues before the nation.

Lincoln was solemn when he accepted the Republican senatorial nomination. The American nation, he said, was in a "crisis" and building toward a worse one. "A House divided against itself cannot stand. I believe this government cannot endure, permanently half *slave* and half *free*." Lincoln said he did not expect the Union "to be dissolved" or "the house to fall," but rather that "it will become *all* one thing, or *all* the other." Then he rehearsed the history of the South's growing influence over national policy since the Kansas-Nebraska Act, which he blamed on Douglas. Lincoln stated his firm opposition to the *Dred Scott* decision, which he believed part of a conspiracy involving Pierce, Buchanan, Taney, and Douglas. He and others like him opposing this conspiracy wished to place slavery on a "course of ultimate extinction."

Debating Douglas, Lincoln reiterated these controversial themes. Although far from a radical abolitionist, in these debates Lincoln also skillfully staked out a moral position not only in advance of Douglas but well ahead of his time.

Lincoln was also very much a part of his time. He believed in white superiority, opposed granting specific equal civil rights to free blacks, and said that differences between whites and blacks would "forever forbid the two races from living together on terms of social and political equality." "Separation" and colonization was the best solution.

But Lincoln differed from most contemporaries in his deep commitment to the equality and dignity of all human beings. Douglas continually made racial slurs. Lincoln said that he believed not only that blacks were "entitled to all the natural rights . . . in the Declaration of Independence," but also that they had many specific economic rights, like "the right to put into his mouth the bread that his own hands have earned." In these rights, blacks were "my equal and the equal of Judge Douglas, and the equal of every living man."

Unlike Douglas, Lincoln hated slavery. "I contemplate slavery as a moral, social, and political evil." The difference between a Republican and a Democrat was simply whether one thought slavery wrong or right. Douglas was more equivocal and dodged the issue in Freeport, pointing out that slavery would not exist if local legislation did not support it. But Douglas's moral indifference was clear: He did not care if a territorial legislature voted it "up or down." Republicans did care, Lincoln answered, warning that by stopping the expansion of slavery, the course toward "ultimate extinction" had begun. Although barred by the Constitution from interfering with slavery where it already existed, Lincoln said that Republicans believed slavery wrong, and "we propose a course of policy that shall deal with it as a wrong."

This 1860 photograph of Lincoln shows him without the look of strain and overwhelming stress commonly seen in photographs taken during the Civil War. (Corbis/Bettmann)

What Lincoln meant by "policy" was not yet clear, even to himself. However, he did succeed in affirming that the Republican party was the only moral and political force capable of stopping the slave power. It seems ironic now (though not then) that Douglas won the election. Elsewhere in 1858, however, Democrats did poorly, losing 18 congressional seats to the Republicans.

John Brown's Raid

Unlike Lincoln, John Brown was prepared to act decisively against slavery. On October 16, 1859, he and a band of 22 men attacked a federal arsenal at Harpers Ferry, Virginia (now West Virginia). He hoped to provoke a general uprising of slaves throughout the Upper South or at least provide arms for slaves to make their way to freedom. Federal troops soon overcame him. Nearly half his men died, including two sons. Brown was captured, tried, and hanged. So ended a lifetime of failures.

In death, however, Brown was not a failure. His daring if foolhardy raid and his dignified behavior during his trial and speedy execution unleashed powerful passions. The North-South gap widened. Northerners responded to his death with an outpouring of sympathy. Thoreau compared him to Christ. Abolitionist William Lloyd Garrison, a pacifist, wished "success to every slave insurrection" in the South. Ministers called slave revolt a "divine weapon" and glorified Brown's treason as "holy." Brown's raid, Frederick Douglass said, showed that slavery was a "system of brute force" that would only be ended when "met with its own weapons."

Southerners were filled with "dread and terror" over the possibility of a wave of slave revolts led by hundreds of imaginary John Browns and Nat Turners, and concluded that northerners would stop at nothing to free the slaves. This suspicion eroded freedom of thought and expression. A North Carolinian described a "spirit of terror, mobs, arrests, and violence" in his state. Twelve families in Berea, Kentucky, were evicted from the state for their mild abolitionist sentiments. A Texas minister who criticized the treatment of slaves in a sermon got 70 lashes.

With Brown's raid, southerners also became more convinced, as the governor of South Carolina put it, of a "black Republican" plot in the North "arrayed against the slaveholders," now a permanent minority. Southern Unionists lost their influence, and power passed to those favoring secession.

The Election of 1860

When the Democratic convention met in Charleston, South Carolina, a secessionist hotbed, it sat for a record ten days and went through 59 ballots without being able to name a candidate. Reconvening in Baltimore, the Democrats acknowledged their irreparable division by choosing two candidates at two separate conventions: Douglas for northern Democrats, and John C. Breckinridge, Buchanan's vice president, for the proslavery South. The Constitutional Union party, made up of former southern Whigs and border-state nativists, claimed the middle ground and nominated John Bell, a slaveholder from Tennessee favoring compromise.

With Democrats split and a new party in contention, the Republican strategy aimed at keeping the states carried by Frémont in 1856 and adding Pennsylvania, Illinois, and Indiana. Seward, the leading candidate, had been tempering his antislavery views to appear more electable. So had Lincoln, who seemed more likely than Seward to carry those key states. After shrewd maneuvers emphasizing his "availability" as a moderate, Lincoln was nominated.

The Republican platform also exuded moderation, opposing only slavery's extension. Mostly it spoke of tariff protection, subsidized internal improvements, free labor, and a homestead bill. Above all, the Republicans, like southern Democrats, defended their view of what republican values meant for America's future. It did not include the equal rights envisioned by Frederick Douglass. An English traveler in 1860 observed that in America "we see, in effect, two nations— one white and another black—growing up together within the same political circle, but never mingling on a principle of equality."

The Republican moderate strategy worked as planned. Lincoln was elected by sweeping the entire Northeast and Midwest. Although he got less than 40 percent of the popular vote nationwide, his triumph in the North was decisive. Even a united Democratic party could not have defeated him. With victory assured, Lincoln finished his sandwich and coffee on election night in Springfield and prepared for his awesome responsibilities. They came even before his inauguration.

THE DIVIDED HOUSE FALLS

The Republicans overestimated Unionist sentiment in the South. A year earlier, some southern congressmen had walked out in protest when the House chose an

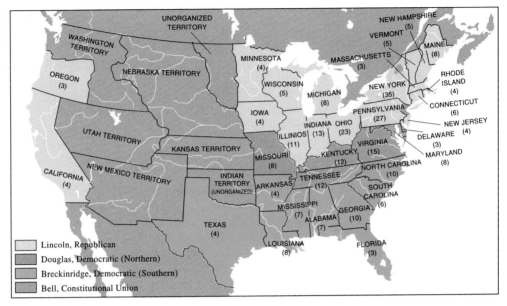

THE PRESIDENTIAL ELECTION OF 1860   Lincoln's election, the first by a Republican, was on the basis of a totally northern sectional victory, and with only 40 percent of the popular vote.

antislavery speaker. A Republican leader, Carl Schurz, recalling this, said that the southerners had taken a drink and then come back. Now, Schurz predicted, they would walk out, take two drinks, and come back again. He was wrong.

Secession and Uncertainty

On December 20, 1860, South Carolina seceded, declaring the "experiment" of putting people with "different pursuits and institutions" under one government a failure. By February 1, the other six Deep South states (Mississippi, Florida, Alabama, Georgia, Louisiana, and Texas) also left. A week later, delegates meeting in Montgomery, Alabama, created the Confederate States of America and elected Jefferson Davis, a Mississippi senator and cotton planter, its provisional president. The divided house had fallen, as Lincoln had predicted. But it was not yet certain whether the house could be put back together, or whether there would be civil war.

The government in Washington had three options. First was compromise, but the emotions of the time ruled that out. (All the compromises mentioned were pro-southern.) Second, as suggested by New York *Tribune* editor Horace Greeley, it might let the seven states "go in peace," taking care not to lose the border states. This was opposed by northern businessmen, who would lose profitable economic ties with the South, and by those who believed in an indissoluble Union. Or third, the secessionist states could be compelled to return. That probably meant war.

Republican hopes that southern Unionism would assert itself and avoid all these options seemed possible in February 1861. No more states seceded. The nation waited, wondering what Virginia and the border states would do, what outgoing President Buchanan would do, and what Congress would do.

Prosouthern and determined not to start a civil war in the last weeks of his already dismal administration, Buchanan did nothing. Congress made some feeble efforts to pass compromise legislation, waiting in vain for the support of the president-elect. And as Union supporters struggled with secessionists, Virginia and the border states, like the entire nation, waited for Lincoln.

Frederick Douglass waited, too, without much hope. He wanted the "complete and universal *abolition* of the whole slave system," as well as equal suffrage and other rights for free blacks. His momentary expectation during the presidential campaign, that Lincoln and the Republicans had the will to do this, had been thoroughly dashed. Douglass foresaw northern politicians and businessmen "granting the most demoralizing concessions to the Slave Power."

In his despair, Douglass began to explore possibilities for emigration and colonization in Haiti, an idea he had long opposed. To achieve full freedom and citizenship in the United States for all blacks, he said in January 1861, he would "welcome the hardships consequent upon a dissolution of the Union." In February, Douglass said, "Let the conflict come." He opposed all compromises, hoping that with Lincoln's inauguration in March it would "be decided, and decided forever, which of the two, Freedom or Slavery, shall give law to this Republic."

Lincoln and Fort Sumter

As Douglass penned these thoughts, Lincoln began a long, slow train ride from Springfield to Washington, writing and rewriting his inaugural address. Lincoln's quietness in the period between his election and his inauguration led many to judge him weak and indecisive. He was not. Lincoln firmly opposed secession and any compromises with the principle of stopping the extension of slavery. He would neither conciliate secessionist southern states nor force their return.

But Lincoln believed in his constitutional responsibility to uphold the laws of the land, and would not yield. The focus of his attention was a federal fort in the harbor of Charleston. Major Robert Anderson, the commander of Fort Sumter, was running out of provisions and had requested new supplies from Washington. Lincoln would enforce the laws and protect federal property at Fort Sumter.

As the new president delivered his inaugural address on March 4, he faced a tense and divided nation. Lincoln asserted his unequivocal intention to enforce the laws of the land, arguing that the Union was "perpetual" and indissoluble. He reminded the nation that the "only substantial dispute" was that "one section of our country believes slavery is *right*, and ought to be extended, while the other believes it is *wrong*, and ought not to be extended." Still appealing to Unionist strength among southern moderates, Lincoln said that he would make no attempts to interfere with existing slavery and would respect the law to return fugitive slaves. Nearing the end, Lincoln put the burden of initiating civil war on the "dissatisfied fellow-countrymen" who had seceded. As if foreseeing the horrible events that would follow, he closed his speech eloquently:

> I am loath to close. We are not enemies, but friends. We must not be enemies. Though passion may have strained, it must not break our bonds of affection. The mystic chords of memory, stretching from every battlefield, and patriot grave, to every living heart and hearthstone, all over this broad land, will yet swell the chorus of the Union, when again touched, as surely they will be, by the better angels of our nature.

Table 14.1 *The Causes of the Civil War*

Date	Issues and Events	Deeper, Underlying Causes of Civil War
1600s–1860s	Slavery in the South	Major underlying pervasive cause
1700s–1860s	Development of two distinct socioeconomic systems and cultures	Further reinforced slavery as fundamental socioeconomic, cultural moral issue
1787–1860s	States' rights, nullification doctrine	Ongoing political issue, less fundamental as cause
1820	Missouri Compromise (36°30′)	Background for conflict over slavery in territories
1828–1833	South Carolina tariff nullification crisis	Background for secession leadership in South Carolina
1831–1860s	Antislavery movements, southern justification	Thirty years of emotional preparation for conflict
1846–1848	War with Mexico (Wilmot Proviso, Calhoun, popular sovereignty)	Options for issue of slavery in territories
1850	Compromise of 1850	Temporary and unsatisfactory "settlement" of divisive issue
1851–1854	Fugitive slaves returned and rescued in North; personal liberty laws passed in North; Harriet Beecher Stowe's *Uncle Tom's Cabin*	Heightened northern emotional reactions against the South and slavery
1852–1856	Breakdown of Whig party and national Democratic party; creation of a new party system with sectional basis	Made national politics an arena where sectional and cultural differences over slavery were fought
1854	Ostend Manifesto and other expansionist efforts in Central America; formation of Republican Party	Reinforced image of Democratic party as favoring slavery; major party identified as opposing the extension of slavery
	Kansas-Nebraska Act	Reopened "settled" issue of slavery in the territories
1856	"Bleeding Kansas;" Senator Sumner physically attacked in Senate	Foretaste of Civil War (200 killed, $2 million in property lost) inflamed emotions and polarized North and South
1857	*Dred Scott* decision; proslavery Lecompton constitution in Kansas	Made North fear a "slave power conspiracy," supported by President Buchanan and the Supreme Court
1858	Lincoln-Douglas debates in Illinois; Democrats lose 18 seats in Congress	Set stage for election of 1860
1859	John Brown's raid and reactions in North and South	Made South fear a "black Republican" plot against slavery; further polarization and irrationality
1860	Democratic party splits in half; Lincoln elected president; South Carolina secedes from Union	Final breakdown of national parties and election of "northern" president; no more compromises
1861	Six more southern states secede by February 1; Confederate Constitution adopted February 4; Lincoln inaugurated March 4; Fort Sumter attacked April 12	Civil War begins

Frederick Douglass was not impressed with Lincoln's "honied phrases." Also unmoved, Robert Allston wrote his son from Charleston, where he was watching the crisis over Fort Sumter, that the Confederacy's "advantage" was in having a "much better president than they have."

On April 6, Lincoln notified the governor of South Carolina that he was sending "provisions only" to Fort Sumter. No effort would be made "to throw in men, arms, or ammunition" unless the fort were attacked. On April 10, Jefferson Davis directed General P. G. T. Beauregard to demand the surrender of Fort Sumter. Davis told Beauregard to reduce the fort if Major Anderson refused.

On April 12, as Lincoln's relief expedition neared Charleston, Beauregard's batteries began shelling Fort Sumter, and the Civil War began. Frederick Douglass was about to leave for Haiti when he heard the news. He immediately changed his plans: "This is no time . . . to leave the country." He announced his readiness to help end the war by aiding the Union to organize freed slaves "into a liberating army" to "make war upon . . . the savage barbarism of slavery." The Allstons had changed places, and it was Benjamin who described the events in Charleston harbor to his father. On April 14, Benjamin reported the "glorious, and astonishing news that Sumter has fallen." With it fell America's divided house.

↤↤↤↤↤↤

CONCLUSION

The "Irrepressible Conflict"

Lincoln had been right. The nation could no longer endure half-slave and half-free. The collision between North and South, William Seward said, was not an "accidental, unnecessary" event, but an "irrepressible conflict between opposing and enduring forces." Those forces had been at work for many decades, but developed with increasing intensity after 1848 in the conflict over the question of the extension of slavery into the territories. Although economic, cultural, political, constitutional, and emotional forces all contributed to the developing opposition between North and South, slavery was the fundamental, enduring force that underlay all others, causing what Walt Whitman called the "red blood of civil war."

Recommended Reading

Overviews of the Imperiled Union and Crises of the 1850s

Eric Foner, ed., *Politics and Ideology in the Age of the Civil War* (1980); David Potter, *The Impending Crisis, 1848–1861* (1976); Brian Holden Reid, *The Origins of the American Civil War* (1996); Richard Sewall, *A House Divided: Sectionalism and Civil War, 1848–1865* (1988); Kenneth Stampp, *The Imperilled Union: Essays on the Background of the Civil War* (1980); Mark Summers, *The Plundering Generation: Corruption and the Crisis of the Union, 1849–1861* (1987);

Compromises and Slavery in the Territories

Frederick Moore Binder, *James Buchanan and the American Empire* (1994); William W. Freehling, *The Road to Disunion: I. Secessionists at Bay, 1776–1854* (1990); Robert W. Johanssen,

TIMELINE

1832	1835–1840	1840	1846	1848
Nullification crisis	Intensification of abolitionist attacks on slavery; Violent retaliatory attacks on abolitionists	Liberty party formed	Wilmot Proviso	Free-Soil party founded; Zachary Taylor elected president
1850	**1850–1854**	**1851**	**1852**	**1854**
Compromise of 1850, including Fugitive Slave Act	"Young America" movement	Women's rights convention in Akron, Ohio	Harriet Beecher Stowe, *Uncle Tom's Cabin;* Franklin Pierce elected president	Ostend Manifesto; Kansas-Nebraska Act nullifies Missouri Compromise; Republican and Know-Nothing parties formed
1855	**1855–1856**	**1856**	**1857**	**1858**
Walt Whitman, *Leaves of Grass*	Thousands pour into Kansas, creating months of turmoil and violence	John Brown's massacre in Kansas; Sumner-Brooks incident in Senate; James Buchanan elected president	Dred Scott decision legalizes slavery in territories; Lecompton constitution in Kansas	Lincoln-Douglas debates
1859	**1860**	**1860–1861**	**1861**	
John Brown's raid at Harpers Ferry	Democratic party splits; Four-party campaign; Abraham Lincoln elected president	Seven southern states secede	Confederate States of America founded; Attack on Fort Sumter begins Civil War	

The Frontier, the Union, and Stephen A. Douglas (1989) and *Stephen Douglas* (1973); Michael A. Morrison, *Slavery and the American West: The Eclipse of Manifest Destiny and the Coming of the Civil War* (1997); E. Smith, *The Presidencies of Zachary Taylor and Millard Fillmore* (1988); Mark J. Stegmaier, *Texas, New Mexico, and the Compromise of 1850: Boundary Dispute & Sectional Crisis* (1996).

Politicians, Political Disintegration and Realignment

Irving H. Bartlett, *John C. Calhoun: A Biography* (1993);Eric Foner, *Free Soil, Free Labor, Free Men: The Ideology of the Republican Party Before the Civil War* (1970); William E. Gienapp, *The Origins of the Republican Party, 1852–1856* (1987); Anthony Gronowicz, *Race and Class Politics in New York City before the Civil War* (1997); Michael Holt, *The Political Crisis of the 1850s* (1978); Merrill Peterson, *The Great Triumvirate: Webster, Clay, and Calhoun* (1987); Robert V. Remini, *Daniel Webster: The Man and His Time* (1997).

Kansas, Two Cultures, and the Emotions of Slavery Politics

William J. Cooper, *The South and the Politics of Slavery* (1978); Donald Fehrenbacher, *Slavery, Law, and Politics: The Dred Scott Case in Historical Perspective* (1981); Thomas F. Gossett, *Uncle Tom's Cabin and American Culture* (1985); David S. Heidler, *Pulling the Temple Down: The Fire-Easters and the Destruction of the Union* (1994); Nell Irvin Painter, *Sojourner Truth: A Life, A Symbol* (1996); James Rawley, *Race and Politics: "Bleeding Kansas" and the Coming of the Civil War* (1969); Richard Sewell, *Ballots for Freedom: Antislavery Politics in the United States, 1837–1865* (1976).

Lincoln and the Divided House: The Road to Civil War

Steven Channing, *Crisis of Fear: Secession in South Carolina* (1970); David H. Donald, *Lincoln* (1995); Don Fehrenbacher, ed., *Abraham Lincoln: A Documentary Portrait Through His Speeches and Writings* (1977); Maury Klein, *Days of Defiance: Sumter, Secession, and the Coming of the Civil War* (1997); Mark E. Neely, *The Last Best Hope of Earth: Abraham Lincoln and the Promise of America* (1993); Kenneth Stampp, *America in 1857: A Nation on the Brink* (1990); David Zarefsky, *Lincoln, Douglas and Slavery in the Crucible of Public Debate* (1990).

CHAPTER 15

The Union Severed

"We cannot escape history," Abraham Lincoln reminded Congress in 1862. "We of this Congress and this administration will be remembered in spite of ourselves. No personal significance, or insignificance, can spare . . . us. The fiery trial through which we pass, will light us down, in honor or dishonor, to the latest generation." Lincoln's conviction that Americans would long remember him and other major actors of the Civil War was correct. Jefferson Davis, Robert E. Lee, Ulysses S. Grant—these men's characters, actions, and decisions have been endlessly discussed. Whether as heroes or villains, great men have dominated the story of the Civil War.

Yet from the earliest days, the war touched the lives of even the most uncelebrated Americans. From Indianapolis, 20-year-old Arthur Carpenter wrote to his parents in Massachusetts begging for permission to volunteer: "I have always longed for the time to come when I could enter the army and be a military man, and when this war broke out, I thought the time had come, but you would not permit me to enter the service . . . now I make one more appeal to you." The pleas worked, and Carpenter enlisted, spending most of the war fighting in Kentucky and Tennessee.

In that same year, in Tennessee, George and Ethie Eagleton faced anguishing decisions. Though not an abolitionist, George, a 30-year-old Presbyterian preacher, was unsympathetic to slavery and opposed to secession. But when his native state left the Union, George felt compelled to follow and enlisted in the 44th Tennessee Infantry. Ethie, his 26-year-old wife, despaired over the war, George's decision, and her own forlorn situation.

> "Mr. Eagleton's school dismissed—and what for? O my God, must I write it? He has enlisted in the service of his country—to war—the most unrighteous war that ever was brought on any nation that ever lived. Pres. Lincoln has done what no other Pres. ever dared to do—he has divided these once peaceful and happy United States. And Oh! the dreadful dark cloud that is now hanging over our country—'tis enough to sicken the heart of any one . . . . Mr. E. is gone . . . . What will become of me, left here without a home and relatives, a babe just nine months old and no George."

Both Carpenter and the Eagletons survived the war, but it transformed their lives. Carpenter had difficulty settling down. Filled with bitter memories of the war years in Tennessee, the Eagletons moved to Arkansas. Ordinary people like Carpenter and the Eagletons are historically anonymous. Yet their actions on and off the battlefield helped to shape the course of events, as their leaders realized, even if today we tend to remember only the famous and influential.

❖❖❖❖❖

For thousands of Americans, from Lincoln and Davis to Carpenter and the Eagletons, war was both a profoundly personal and a major national event. Its impact reached far beyond the four years of hostilities. The war that was fought to conserve two political, social, and economic visions ended by changing familiar ways of political, social, and economic life in both North and South. War was a transforming force, both destructive and creative in its effect on the structure and social dynamics of society and on the lives of ordinary people. This theme underlies this chapter's analysis of the war's three stages: the initial months of preparation, the years of military stalemate between 1861 and 1865, and, finally, resolution.

ORGANIZING FOR WAR

The Confederate bombardment of Fort Sumter on April 12, 1861 and the surrender of Union troops the next day ended uncertainties. The North's response to Fort Sumter was a virtual declaration of war as President Lincoln called for state militia volunteers to crush the "insurrection." His action pushed Virginia, North Carolina, Tennessee, and Arkansas into the secessionist camp. Three other slave states (Maryland, Kentucky, and Missouri) agonizingly debated which way to go. The "War Between the States" was a reality.

Many Americans were dismayed. Southerners like George Eagleton only reluctantly followed their states out of the Union. When he enlisted, Eagleton complained of the "disgraceful cowardice" of those who were "now refusing self and means for the prosecution of war." Robert E. Lee of Virginia was equally hesitant to resign his federal commission but finally decided that he could not "raise [a] hand against . . . relatives . . . children . . . home." Whites in the southern uplands (where blacks were few and slaveholders were heartily disliked), yeomen farmers in the Deep South (who owned no slaves), and many residents of border states opposed secession and war. Many would eventually join the Union forces.

In the North, large numbers supported neither the Republicans nor Lincoln. Irish immigrants fearing the competition of free black labor and southerners living in Illinois, Indiana, and Ohio opposed war. Northern Democrats at first blamed Lincoln and the Republicans almost as much as the secessionists for the crisis.

Nevertheless, the days following Fort Sumter and Lincoln's call for troops saw an outpouring of support on both sides, fueled in part by relief at decisive action, in part by patriotism and love of adventure, and in part by unemployment. Northern blacks and even some southern freedmen proclaimed themselves "ready to go forth and do battle," while whites like Carpenter flocked to enlist. In some places, workers were so eager to join up that trade unions collapsed. Women set to work making uniforms.

The war fever produced so many volunteers that officials could not handle the throng. Northern authorities turned aside offers from blacks to serve. Both sides sent thousands of white would-be soldiers home. The conviction that the conflict would rapidly come to a glorious conclusion fueled the eagerness to enlist. Lincoln's call for 75,000 state militiamen for only 90 days of service, and a similar enlistment term for Confederate soldiers, supported the notion that the war would be short.

The Balance of Resources

But the outcome was much in doubt. Although statistics of population and industrial development suggested a northern victory, Great Britain had similar advantages in 1775, yet had lost that war. Many northern assets would become effective only with time.

The North's white population greatly exceeded the South's, giving the appearance of a military advantage. Yet early in the war, the armies were more evenly matched. Almost 187,000 Union troops bore arms in July 1861, while just over 112,000 men marched under Confederate colors. Southerners believed that their army would prove to be superior fighters. Many northerners feared so, too. And slaves could carry on vital work behind the lines, freeing most adult white males to serve the Confederacy.

The Union also enjoyed impressive economic advantages. In the North, one million workers in 110,000 manufacturing concerns produced goods valued at $1.5 billion annually, while 110,000 southern workers in 18,000 manufacturing concerns produced goods valued at only $155 million a year. But northern industrial resources had to be mobilized. That would take time, especially because the government did not intend to direct production. A depleted northern treasury made the government's first task the raising of funds to pay for military necessities.

The South depended on imported northern and European manufactured goods. If Lincoln cut off that trade, the South would have to create its industry almost from scratch. Its railroad system was organized to move cotton, not armies and supplies. Yet the agricultural South did have important resources of food, draft animals, and, of course, cotton, which southerners believed would secure British and French support. By waging a defensive war, the South could tap regional loyalty and enjoy protected lines. Because much of the South raised cotton and tobacco rather than food crops, Union armies could not live off the land, and extended supply lines were always vulnerable. The Union had to conquer and occupy; the South merely had to survive until its enemy gave up.

The Border States

Uncertainty and divided loyalties produced indecision in the border states. When the seven Deep South states seceded in 1860–1861, all the border states except Unionist Delaware adopted a wait-and-see attitude. Their decisions were critically important to both North and South.

The states of the Upper South could provide natural borders for the Confederacy along the Ohio River, access to its river traffic, and vital resources, wealth, and population. The major railroad link to the West ran through Maryland and western Virginia. Virginia boasted the South's largest ironworks, and Tennessee was its principal source of grain. Missouri provided the road to the West and controlled Mississippi River traffic.

For the North, every border state that remained loyal was a psychological triumph. Nor was the North indifferent to the economic and strategic advantages of keeping the border states with the Union. However, Lincoln's call for troops precipitated the secession of Virginia, Arkansas, Tennessee, and North Carolina

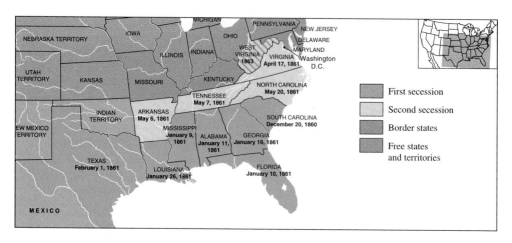

SECESSION OF THE SOUTHERN STATES   The map provides a chronology of secession and shows the geographical importance of the border states. The map also highlights the vulnerable position of Washington and explains many of Lincoln's actions in the early days of the war.

between April 17 and May 20, 1861. Maryland, precariously balanced between the pro-Confederate southern and Eastern Shore counties and Unionist western and northern areas, and with pro-Southern enthusiasts abounding in Baltimore, vividly demonstrated the significance of border state loyalty.

On April 19, the 6th Massachusetts Regiment, heading for Washington, marched through Baltimore and was attacked by a mob of some 10,000 southern sympathizers. Finally, said an eye-witness, the "patience of their commander was . . . exhausted. He cried out in a voice, which was heard even above the yells of the mob, 'Fire!' . . . A scene of bloody confusion followed." Washington was temporarily cut off from the rest of the Union.

Lincoln took stern measures to secure Maryland. The president agreed temporarily to route troops around Baltimore. In return, the governor called the state legislature into session at Frederick in Unionist western Maryland. This action and Lincoln's swift violation of civil liberties damped secessionist enthusiasm. Hundreds of southern sympathizers, including 19 state legislators and Baltimore's mayor, were imprisoned without trial. Although Chief Justice Roger B. Taney challenged the president's action and issued a writ of habeas corpus for the release of a southern supporter, Lincoln ignored him. A month later, Taney ruled that if the public's safety was endangered, only Congress could suspend habeas corpus. By then, Lincoln had secured Maryland.

Though Lincoln's quick and harsh response ensured Maryland's loyalty, he was more cautious elsewhere. Above all, he had to deal with slavery prudently, for hasty action would push border states into the Confederacy. Thus, when General John C. Frémont issued an unauthorized declaration of emancipation in Missouri in August 1861, Lincoln revoked the order and recalled him. The president expected a chain reaction if certain key states seceded. After complex maneuvering, the remaining border states stayed in the Union.

Challenges of War

The tense weeks after Fort Sumter spilled over with unexpected challenges. Both North and South faced enormous organizational problems.

Southerners had to create a nation-state and devise everything from a constitution to a flag. In February 1861, the original seceding states began work on a provisional framework and chose a provisional president and vice president. The delegates swiftly wrote a constitution, much like the federal constitution but emphasizing the "sovereign and independent character" of the states and explicitly recognizing slavery. Provisional President Davis tried to put together a balanced cabinet with a moderate face, but it turned out to be unstable.

Davis's cabinet appointees faced the formidable challenge of creating government departments from scratch. The president's office was in a hotel parlor. When an army captain came to the treasury with a warrant from Davis for blankets, he found only one clerk. After reading the warrant, the clerk offered the captain a few dollars of his own, explaining, "This, Captain, is all the money that I will certify as being in the Confederate Treasury at this moment."

Lincoln did not face quite such difficulties, but without administrative experience he, like his Confederate counterpart, faced organizational problems. Military officers and government clerks daily defected to the South. The treasury was empty. Office seekers thronged into the White House.

Lincoln did not know many of the "prominent men of the day" and so appointed important Republicans to cabinet posts whether they agreed with him or not. Several scorned him as a backwoods bumbler. Treasury Secretary Salmon P. Chase hoped to replace Lincoln as president in four years' time. Secretary of State William Seward sent Lincoln a memo condescendingly offering to oversee the formulation of presidential policy.

Lincoln and Davis

A number of Lincoln's early actions illustrated that he was no fool. As his Illinois law partner, William Herndon, pointed out, Lincoln's "mind was tough—solid—knotty—gnarly, more or less like his body." The president firmly told Seward that he would run his own administration. After Sumter, he swiftly called up the state militias, expanded the navy, suspended habeas corpus, blockaded the South, and approved spending funds for military purposes—all without congressional sanction, because Congress was not in session. As Lincoln told legislators later, "The dogmas of the quiet past are inadequate to the stormy present . . . . As our case is new, so must we think anew, and act anew . . . and then we shall save our country." This willingness to "think anew" was a valuable personal asset, even though some critics called his expansion of presidential power despotic.

By coincidence, Lincoln and his rival, Jefferson Davis, were born only 100 miles apart in Kentucky. However, the course of their lives diverged radically. Lincoln's father migrated north and eked out a simple existence as a farmer. Lincoln himself had only a rudimentary education. Davis's family moved to Mississippi to become cotton planters. Davis grew up in comfortable circumstances, went to West Point, fought in the Mexican-American War, was elected to the U.S. Senate, and served as secretary of war under Franklin Pierce.

Although Davis had not been eager to accept the presidency, he had loyally responded to the call of the provisional congress in 1861 and worked tirelessly as the chief executive of the Confederacy. As his wife observed, "the President hardly takes time to eat his meals and works late at night." Some contemporaries suggested that Davis's inability to delegate details explained this schedule. Others observed that he was sickly, reserved, humorless, and sensitive to criticism. But Davis, like Lincoln, found it necessary to "think anew." He reassured southerners in his inaugural address that his aims were conservative, "to preserve the Government of our fathers in spirit." Yet under the pressure of events, he moved toward creating a new kind of South.

CLASHING ON THE BATTLEFIELD, 1861–1862

The Civil War was the most brutal and destructive conflict in American history. Much of the bloodshed resulted from changing military technology. The range of rifles had increased from 100 to 500 yards, in part owing to the new French minié bullet, which had tremendous velocity and accuracy. It was no longer possible to move artillery close enough to enemy lines to support an infantry charge. Attacking infantry soldiers faced a 500-yard dash into deadly fire.

As it became clear that infantry charges produced horrible carnage, military leaders increasingly valued strong defensive positions. Although Confederate soldiers at first criticized General Lee as "King of Spades," the epithet evolved into one of affection as it became obvious that earthworks saved lives. Union commanders followed suit.

War in the East

The war's brutal character only gradually revealed itself. The Union's commanding general, 70-year-old Winfield Scott, at first pressed for a cautious, long-term strategy, the Anaconda Plan. Scott proposed weakening the South gradually through blockades on land and at sea until the northern army was strong enough for the kill. The public, however, hungered for quick victory. So did Lincoln: He knew that the longer the war lasted, the more embittered the South and the North would both become, making reunion ever more difficult. So 35,000 partially-trained men led by General Irwin McDowell left Washington in sweltering July weather, heading for Richmond.

On July 21, 1861, only 25 miles from the capital at Manassas Creek (also called Bull Run), inexperienced northern troops confronted 25,000 raw Confederate soldiers commanded by Brigadier General P. G. T. Beauregard, a West Point classmate of McDowell's. Although sightseers, journalists, and politicians accompanied the Union troops, expecting only a Sunday outing, Bull Run was no picnic. The battle was inconclusive until the arrival of 2,300 fresh Confederate troops, brought by trains, decided the day. Union soldiers and sightseers fled toward Washington. "Pretty well whipped" the Union forces certainly were. Yet inexperienced Confederate troops had failed to turn the rout into a quick and decisive victory. As General Joseph E. Johnston pointed out, his men were disorganized, confused by victory, and not well enough supplied with food to chase the Union army back toward Washington.

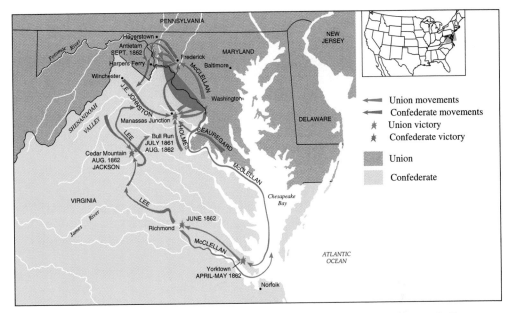

EASTERN THEATER OF THE CIVIL WAR, 1861–1862   The map reveals the military actions in the East during the early years of the war. Initially, military planners hoped to end the war quickly by capturing Richmond. They soon discovered that the Confederate army was too powerful to allow them an easy victory. Eventually, Lincoln decided to combine military pressure on Virginia with an effort in the West aimed at cutting the Confederacy in two.

   In many ways, the Battle of Bull Run was prophetic. Victory would be neither quick nor easy. Both armies were unprofessional, and bravado would not win the war. Both sides faced problems with short-term enlistments and with logistics. Hardly surprisingly, the armies floundered.

   South Carolinian Robert Allston viewed the battlefield at Bull Run and decided it had been a "glorious tho bloody" day. For the Union, the loss was sobering. Lincoln began his search for a winning commander by replacing McDowell with 34-year-old General George McClellan. Formerly an army engineer, McClellan had to transform the Army of the Potomac into a fighting force. Short-term militias went home. In the fall of 1861, McClellan became general in chief of the Union armies.

   McClellan had considerable organizational ability but no desire to be a daring battlefield leader. Convinced that the North must combine military victory with persuading the South to rejoin the Union, he sought to avoid embittering loss of life and property—to win "by maneuvering rather than fighting."

   In March 1862, pushed by an impatient Lincoln, McClellan finally led his army of 130,000 toward Richmond, now the Confederate capital. But just as it seemed that victory was within grasp, Lee drove the Union forces away.

   Other Union defeats followed in 1862 as commanders came and went. In September, the South took the offensive with a bold invasion of Maryland. But after a costly defeat at Antietam, in which more than 5,000 soldiers were slaughtered and another 17,000 wounded on the grisliest day of the war, Lee withdrew to Virginia. The war in the East was stalemated.

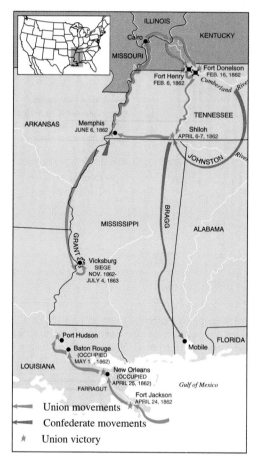

TRANS-MISSISSIPPI CAMPAIGN OF THE CIVIL WAR

The military movements in the trans-Mississippi West appear here. Union forces operating in the Mississippi Valley were attempting to separate Texas, Arkansas, and Louisiana from other southern states as part of an attempt to squeeze the Confederacy.

War in the West

The early struggle in the East focused on Richmond, the Confederacy's capital and one of the South's most important railroad, industrial, and munitions centers. But the East was only one of three theaters. Between the Appalachians and the Mississippi lay the western theater. The Mississippi River, with its vital river trade and its great port, New Orleans, was a major strategic objective. Here both George Eagleton and Arthur Carpenter served. Beyond lay the trans-Mississippi West—Louisiana, Arkansas, Missouri, Texas, and the Great Plains—where Native American tribes joined the conflict on both sides.

Union objectives in the West were twofold. The army tried to dominate Kentucky and eastern Tennessee, and it sought to win control of the Mississippi in order to split the South in two.

In the western theater Ulysses S. Grant rose to prominence. Grant had only modest military credentials. He had attended West Point and served creditably in the Mexican-American War, but his undistinguished career in the peacetime army ended in resignation. But after Fort Sumter, Grant enlisted as a colonel in an Illinois militia regiment. Within two months, he was a brigadier general.

Grant's military genius consisted of an ability to see beyond individual battles to larger goals. In 1862, he realized that the Tennessee and Cumberland rivers were the paths for the successful invasion of Tennessee. A premature Confederate invasion of Kentucky allowed Grant to bring his forces into that state without arousing sharp local opposition. Assisted by gunboats, Grant was largely responsible for the capture of Fort Henry and Fort Donelson, key points on the rivers, in February 1862. His successes there raised fears among Confederate leaders that southern mountaineers, loyal to the Union, would rush to Grant's support.

Despite Grant's grasp of strategy, his army was nearly destroyed by a surprise Confederate attack at Shiloh Church in Tennessee. The North won, but at enormous cost. In that two-day engagement, the Union suffered over 13,000 casualties, while 10,000 Confederates lay dead or wounded. More American men fell in this single battle than in the American Revolution, the War of 1812, and the Mexican-American War combined. Because neither army offered sufficient care on the battlefield, untreated wounds caused many of the deaths. A day after the battle ended, nine-tenths of the wounded still lay in the rain, many dying of exposure or drowning. Those who survived the downpour had infected wounds by the time they received medical attention.

Though more successful than efforts in the East, such devastating Union campaigns failed to bring decisive results. Western plans were never coordinated with eastern military activities. Victories there did not force the South to its knees.

The war in the trans-Mississippi West was a sporadic, far-flung struggle. California was the prize that lured both armies into the Southwest. Confederate Texan troops held Albuquerque and Santa Fe briefly in 1862, but a mixed force, including volunteer soldiers from the Colorado mining fields and Mexican-Americans, drove them out. A Union force recruited in California arrived after the Confederates were gone. It spent the remainder of the Civil War years fighting the Apache and the Navajo and with brutal competence crushed both Native American nations.

Farther east was another prize, the Missouri River, which flowed into the Mississippi River, bordered Illinois, and affected military campaigns in Kentucky and Tennessee. Initially, Confederate troops were successful here, as they had been in New Mexico. But in March 1862, at Pea Ridge in northern Arkansas, Union forces whipped a Confederate Army that included a brigade of Native Americans from the Five Civilized Nations. Missouri entered the Union camp for the first time in the war, but fierce guerrilla warfare continued.

Naval Warfare

At the beginning of the war, Lincoln decided to strangle the South with a naval blockade. But success was elusive. In 1861, the navy intercepted only about one blockade runner in ten and in 1862, one in eight.

More successful were operations to gain footholds along the southern coast. In November 1861, a Union expedition took Port Royal Sound, where it freed the first slaves, and the nearby South Carolina sea islands. By gaining these and other important coastal points, the navy increased the possibility of making the blockade effective. The Union's greatest naval triumph in the early war years was the capture

This photograph taken at a field hospital in Virginia during a battle in the summer of 1862 shows surgeons trying to attend to the crowds of wounded lying on the ground. Many deaths resulted from inadequate care for the wounded and sick of both armies. Although there was initial resistance to the idea of women becoming nurses in such hospitals, the dreadful shortage of qualified medical men and the huge workload that they faced eventually resulted in allowing women nurses into hospitals. (Library of Congress)

of the South's biggest port, New Orleans, in 1862. The success of this amphibious effort stimulated other joint attempts to cut the South in two.

The Confederates, recognizing that they could not match the Union fleet, concentrated on developing new weapons like torpedoes and ironclad vessels. The *Merrimac* was one key to southern naval strategy. Originally a U.S. warship sunk as the federal navy hurriedly abandoned the Norfolk Navy Yard early in the war, the Confederates raised the vessel and covered it with heavy iron armor. Rechristened the *Virginia,* the ship steamed out of Norfolk in March 1862, heading directly for the Union ships blocking the harbor. Using its 1,500-pound ram and guns, the *Virginia* drove a third of the ships aground and destroyed the squadron's largest ships. Victory was short-lived. The next day, the *Virginia* confronted the *Monitor,* a newly completed Union iron vessel. They dueled inconclusively, and the *Virginia* withdrew. It was burned during the evacuation of Norfolk that May. Southern attempts to buy ironclad ships abroad faded and, with them, southern hopes of escaping the northern noose.

Still, Confederate attacks on northern commerce brought some success. Southern raiders, many of them built in Britain, wreaked havoc on northern shipping. In its two-year career, the *Alabama* destroyed 69 Union merchant vessels valued at more than $6 million. But such blows did not seriously damage the North's war effort.

Thus the first two years brought victories to both sides, but the war remained deadlocked. The South was far from defeated; the North was equally far from giving up. Costs in manpower and supplies far exceeded what either side had expected.

Cotton Diplomacy

Both sides realized that attitudes in Europe could be critical. European diplomatic recognition would give the Confederacy international credibility, and European loans and assistance might bring the South victory—just as French and Dutch aid had helped the American colonies win independence. If the European nations refused to recognize the South, however, the fiction of the Union was kept alive, undermining long-term Confederate chances. European powers, of course, consulted their own interests. Neither Britain nor France wished to back a loser. Nor did they wish to upset Europe's delicate balance of power by hasty intervention in American affairs. One by one, therefore, the European states declared neutrality.

Southerners were sure that cotton would be their trump card. British and French textile mills needed cotton, and southerners believed that their owners would eventually force government recognition of the Confederacy and end the North's blockade. But a glut of cotton in 1860 and 1861 left foreign mill owners oversupplied. As stockpiles dwindled, European industrialists found cotton in India and Egypt. The conviction that cotton was "king" proved false.

Union Secretary of State Seward sought above all else to prevent diplomatic recognition of the Confederacy. The North had its own economic ties with Europe, so the Union was not as disadvantaged as southerners thought. Seward threatened Great Britain with war if it interfered. Some called his boldness reckless, but it succeeded. Although Britain allowed the construction of Confederate raiders in its ports, it did not intervene in American affairs in 1861 or 1862. Nor did the other powers. Unless the military situation changed dramatically, the Europeans would sit on the sidelines.

Common Problems, Novel Solutions

As the conflict dragged on into 1863, unanticipated problems appeared. In response, both Union and Confederate leaders devised novel solutions.

The problem of fighting a long war was partly monetary. Both treasuries had been empty initially, and the war proved extraordinarily expensive. Neither side considered imposing direct taxes, which would have alienated support, but both initiated taxation on a small scale. Ultimately, taxes financed 21 percent of the North's war expenses, but only 1 percent of southern expenses. Both treasuries also tried borrowing. Northerners purchased over $2 billion worth of bonds, but southerners proved reluctant to buy their government's securities.

As in the American Revolution, printing paper money became the unwanted solution. In August 1861, the Confederacy put into circulation $100 million in crudely engraved bills. Millions more followed the next year. Five months later, the

Union issued $150 million in paper money, soon nicknamed "greenbacks." Although financing the war with paper money was unexpected, the resulting inflation was not. Inflation was particularly bad in the Confederacy, but even a "modest" 80 percent increase in food prices brought Union city families near starvation and contributed to wartime urban misery.

Both sides confronted similar manpower problems as initial enthusiasm for the war evaporated. Soldiering was nothing like militia parades. Robert Carter of Massachusetts saw bodies tossed into trenches "with not a prayer, eulogy or tear to distinguish them from so many animals." Those in the service longed to go home. The swarm of volunteers disappeared. Rich northern communities offered bounties of $800 to $1,000 to outsiders who would join up.

Arthur Carpenter's letters give a good picture of life in the ranks and a young man's growing disillusionment with the war. As Carpenter's regiment moved into Kentucky and Tennessee in 1862, his enthusiasm evaporated. "Soldiering in Kentucky and Tennessee is not so pretty as it was in Indianapolis . . . . We have been half starved, half frozen, and half drowned. The mud in Kentucky is awful." Soldiering often meant marching with 50 or 60 pounds of equipment and insufficient food, water, or supplies. One blanket was not enough in the winter. In the summer, stifling woolen uniforms attracted lice. Poor food, bugs, inadequate sanitation, and exposure invited disease. Carpenter marched through Tennessee suffering from diarrhea and fever. His regiment left him behind in a convalescent barracks in Louisville, which he fled as soon as he could. "[Ninety-nine] Surgeons out of a hundred," he wrote his parents, "would not know whether his patient had the horse distemper, lame toe, or any other disease."

Confederate soldiers, even less well supplied than their northern foes, complained similarly. In 1862, a Virginia captain described what General Lee called the best army "the world ever saw:"

> During our forced marches and hard fights, the soldiers have been compelled to throw away their knapsacks and there is scarcely a private in the army who has a change of clothing of any kind. Hundreds of men are perfectly barefooted and there is no telling when they can be supplied with shoes.

Such circumstances often led to desertion. An estimated one of every nine Confederate soldiers and one of every seven Union troopers deserted.

As manpower problems became critical, both governments resorted to the draft. Despite sacrosanct states' rights, the Confederate Congress passed the first conscription act in American history in March 1862. Four months later, the Union Congress also approved a draft measure. Both laws encouraged men already in the army to reenlist and sought volunteers rather than men forced to serve. Ultimately, over 30 percent of the Confederate Army and 6 percent of the Union forces were draftees. The South relied more heavily on the draft because the North's manpower pool was larger and growing. During the war, 180,000 foreigners of military age poured into the northern states. Some came specifically to claim bounties and fight. Immigrants made up at least 20 percent of the Union army.

Although necessary, draft laws were very unpopular. The first Confederate conscription declared all able-bodied men between the ages of 18 and 35 eligible for military service but allowed numerous exemptions and the purchase of substitutes.

The exemption from military service granted to every planter with more than 20 slaves fed class tension and encouraged disloyalty and desertion, particularly among mountaineers. The advice one woman shouted after her husband as he was dragged off to the army was hardly unique. "You desert again, quick as you kin . . . . Desert, Jake!"

Northern legislation was neither more popular nor fairer. The 1863 draft allowed the hiring of substitutes, and $300 bought an exemption from military service. Workers, already suffering from inflation, resented the ease with which moneyed citizens could avoid army duty. In July 1863, the resentment boiled over in New York City in the largest civil disturbance of the nineteenth century, a three-day riot that erupted a month after a work stoppage on the New York waterfront. Events spun out of control as a mob (mainly Irish workmen) burned draft records and the armory, plundered the houses of the rich, and looted jewelry stores. Blacks, hated as economic competitors and the cause of the war, became special targets. Mobs beat and lynched blacks and burned the Colored Orphan Asylum. More than 100 people died. There was much truth in the accusation that the war on both sides was a rich man's war but a poor man's fight.

Political Dissension, 1862

As the war continued, rumbles of dissension grew louder. On February 24, 1862, the *Richmond Examiner* summarized many southerners' frustration. "The Confederacy has had everything that was required for success but one, and that one thing it was and is supposed to possess more than anything else, namely Talent." Criticism of Confederate leaders mounted. Vice President Alexander Stephens became one of the administration's bitterest accusers.

Because the South had no party system, dissatisfaction with Davis's handling of the war tended to be factional, petty, and personal. Detractors rarely offered alternative policies. Without a party leader's traditional weapons and rewards, Davis had no mechanism to generate support.

Although Lincoln has since become a folk hero, at the time many northerners derided his performance. Peace Democrats, called Copperheads, claimed that Lincoln betrayed the Constitution and that working-class Americans bore the brunt of his conscription policy. Immigrant workers in eastern cities and citizens in the southern Midwest had little sympathy for abolitionism or blacks, and they supported the antiwar Copperheads. Even pro-war Democrats found Lincoln arbitrary and tyrannical, and worried that extremist Republicans would push Lincoln into making the war an anti-slavery crusade. Some Republicans judged Lincoln indecisive and inept.

Republicans split gradually into two factions. The moderates favored a cautious approach toward winning the war, fearing the possible consequences of emancipating slaves, confiscating Confederate property, or arming blacks. The radicals, however, urged Lincoln to make emancipation a wartime objective. They hoped for a victory that would revolutionize southern social and racial arrangements. The reduction of the congressional Republican majority in the fall elections of 1862 made it imperative that Lincoln listen not only to both factions but also to the Democratic opposition.

THE TIDE TURNS, 1863–1865

Hard political realities and Lincoln's sense of the public's mood help explain why he delayed action on emancipation until 1863. Many northerners supported a war for the Union, not for emancipation. Most whites saw blacks as inferior and feared that emancipation would lure former slaves north to steal white jobs and political rights. Northern urban race riots dramatized white attitudes.

The Emancipation Proclamation, 1863

If the president moved too fast on emancipation, he risked losing the allegiance of northern racists, offending the border states, and increasing the Democrats' chances for political victory. Moreover, he had at first hoped that pro-Union sentiment would emerge in the South and compel its leaders to abandon their rebellion. But if Lincoln did not move at all, he would alienate abolitionists and lose the support of radical Republicans, which he could ill afford.

So Lincoln proceeded cautiously. At first, he hoped the border states would take the initiative. In the early spring of 1862, he urged Congress to pass a joint resolution offering federal compensation to states beginning a "gradual abolishment of slavery." Border state opposition killed the idea. Abolitionists and northern blacks, however, greeted Lincoln's proposal with a "thrill of joy."

That summer, Lincoln told his cabinet he intended to emancipate the slaves. Secretary of State Seward urged the president to delay any general proclamation until the North won a decisive military victory. Otherwise, Lincoln would appear to be urging racial insurrection behind the Confederate lines to compensate for northern military bungling.

Lincoln took Seward's advice, using the summer and fall to prepare the North for the shift in the war's purpose. To counteract white fears of free blacks, he promoted schemes for establishing black colonies in Haiti and Panama. In August, Horace Greeley, the influential abolitionist editor of the New York *Tribune*, printed an open letter to Lincoln attacking him for failing to act on slavery. Replying, Lincoln linked emancipation to military necessity:

> If I could save the Union without freeing any slave, I would do it; and if I could save it by freeing all the slaves, I would do it; and if I could do it by freeing some and leaving others alone, I would also do that. What I do about Slavery and the colored race, I do because I believe it helps to save this Union.

If Lincoln attacked slavery, then, it would be only because emancipation would save white lives, preserve the democratic process, and restore the Union.

In September 1862, the Union victory at Antietam gave Lincoln the opportunity to issue a preliminary emancipation proclamation. It stated that unless rebellious states (or parts of states in rebellion) returned to the Union by January 1, 1863, the president would declare their slaves "forever free." Although supposedly aimed at bringing the southern states back into the Union, Lincoln never expected the South to lay down arms after two years of bloodshed. Rather, he was preparing northerners to accept the eventuality of emancipation on the grounds of necessity. Frederick Douglass greeted the president's action with jubilation. But not all northerners shared Douglass's joy. The September proclamation probably harmed Republicans in the fall elections.

Frank Leslie's Illustrated Newspaper showed this scene of Emancipation Day at Smith's Plantation, Port Royal, South Carolina. Black soldiers, some from the southern states, were accepted for combat duty in the Union army as the war progressed. Note that the officer of the First Carolina Volunteers is white and that the white people are seated on the stage, well above the crowds of African-Americans. (January 24, 1863)

Although the elections of 1862 weakened the Republicans' grasp on the national government, they did not destroy it. Still, cautious cabinet members begged Lincoln to forget about emancipation. His refusal demonstrated his vision and humanity. So did his efforts to reduce racial fears. "Is it dreaded that the freed people will swarm forth and cover the whole land?" he asked. "Are they not already in the land? Will liberation make them any more numerous? Equally distributed among the whites of the whole country, and there would be but one colored to seven whites. Could the one, in any way, greatly disturb the other?"

Finally, on New Year's Day, 1863, Lincoln issued the final Emancipation Proclamation as he had promised. It was an "act of justice, warranted by the Constitution upon military necessity." Thus, what had started as a war to save the Union now also became a struggle that, if victorious, would free the slaves. Yet the proclamation had no immediate impact on slavery. It affected only slaves living in the unconquered portions of the Confederacy, and was silent about slaves in the border states and in parts of the South already in northern hands. These limitations led Elizabeth Cady Stanton and Susan B. Anthony to establish the woman's Loyal National League to lobby Congress to emancipate all southern slaves.

The Emancipation Proclamation had a tremendous symbolic importance. On New Year's Day, blacks gathered outside the White House to cheer the president and tell him that if he would "come out of that palace, they would hug him to death." They realized that the proclamation had changed the nature of the war. For the first time, the government had committed itself to freeing slaves. Jubilant blacks could only believe that the president's action heralded a new era for their race. More immediately, the proclamation sanctioned the policy of accepting black as soldiers. Blacks also hoped that the news would reach southern slaves, encouraging them either to flee to Union lines or subvert the southern war effort.

Diplomatic concerns also lay behind the Emancipation Proclamation. Lincoln and his advisers anticipated that the commitment to abolish slavery would favorably impress foreign powers. European statesmen did not abandon their cautious stance toward the Union. However, important segments of the British public who opposed slavery now came to regard any attempt to help the South as immoral. Foreigners could better understand and sympathize with a war to free the slaves than they could with a war to save the Union. In diplomacy, where image is so important, Lincoln had created a more attractive picture of the North. The Emancipation Proclamation became the North's symbolic call for human freedom.

Unanticipated Consequences of War

The Emancipation Proclamation was but one example of the war's surprising consequences. In the final two years of the war, both North and South experimented on the battlefields and behind the lines in desperate efforts to win.

One of the Union's experiments involved using black troops in combat. Blacks had offered themselves as soldiers in 1861 but had been turned away. They were serving as cooks, laborers, teamsters, and carpenters in the army, however, and composed as much as a quarter of the navy. As white casualties mounted, so did pressure for black service on the battlefield. The Union government allowed states to escape draft quotas if they enlisted enough volunteers, and they allowed them to count southern black enlistees on their state rosters. Northern governors grew increasingly interested in black military service.

Anticipating blacks' postwar interests, Frederick Douglass pressed for military service. "Once let the black man get upon his person the brass letter, U.S., let him get an eagle on his button, and a musket on his shoulder and bullets in his pocket," Douglass believed, "there is no power on earth that can deny that he has earned the right to citizenship." By the war's end, 186,000 blacks (10 percent of the army) had served the Union cause, 134,111 of them escapees from slave states.

But the black experience in the army highlighted some of the obstacles to racial acceptance. Black soldiers, usually led by white officers, were second-class soldiers for most of the war, receiving lower pay, poorer food, often more menial work, and fewer benefits than whites. Even whites who were working to equalize black and white pay often considered blacks inferior.

The army's racial experiment had mixed results. But the faithful and courageous service of black troops helped modify some of the most demeaning white racial stereotypes of blacks. The black soldiers, many of them former slaves, who conquered the South felt pride and dignity. Wrote one, "We march through these fine thoroughfares where once the slave was forbid being out after nine p.m. . . . Negro soldiers!—with banners floating."

As the conflict continued, basic assumptions about how it should be waged weakened. One wartime casualty was the courtly idea that war involved only armies. Early in the war, many officers tried to protect civilians and their property. Such concern for rebel property soon vanished. Southern troops, on the few occasions when they came North, also lived off the land.

Changing Military Strategies, 1863–1865

In the early war years, southern strategy combined defense with selected maneuvers. Until the summer of 1863, the strategy seemed to be succeeding, at least in the East. But an occasional victory over the invading northern army, such as at Fredericksburg in December 1862, did not change the course of the war. Realizing

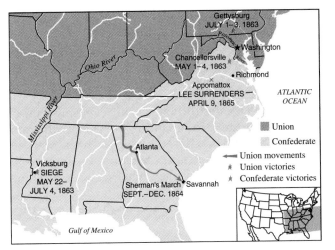

THE TIDE TURNS, 1863–1865
The map highlights important military events during the war's final two years. In the West, Union forces took Vicksburg, and in the East at the battle of Gettysburg they defeated the Confederacy's final effort to bring the war north. During the final stages of the war, Sherman and his army cut a swath through Georgia and then marched north through the Carolinas.

this, Lee concluded, "There is nothing to be gained by this army remaining quietly on the defensive." Without victories in the North, he believed, it could not prevail.

In the summer of 1863, Lee led the Confederate Army of Northern Virginia into Maryland and southern Pennsylvania. His sought a victory that would threaten Philadelphia and Washington, and maybe capture a northern city. This would surely win diplomatic recognition and might force the North to sue for peace.

At Gettysburg on a hot and humid July 1, Lee confronted a Union army led by General George Meade. During three days of fighting, the fatal obsession with the infantry charge returned as Lee ordered costly assaults that probably lost him the battle. On July 3, Lee sent about 15,000 men against the Union center. The assault, known as Pickett's Charge, was gallant but futile. At 700 yards, the Union artillery opened fire. One southern officer described the scene: "Pickett's division just seemed to melt away in the blue musketry smoke which now covered the hill. Nothing but stragglers came back."

Lee's dreams of victory died, with grave consequences for the southern cause. Fighting in the eastern theater dragged on for another year and a half, but Lee's Gettysburg losses were so heavy that he could never mount another southern offensive. Instead, the Confederacy committed itself to a desperate defensive struggle. Gettysburg marked the turn of the military tide in the East.

Despite the Gettysburg victory, Lincoln was dissatisfied with General Meade, who had failed to finish off Lee's demoralized, exhausted army. His disappointment soon faded with news of Grant's great victory on July 4 at Vicksburg, completing the Union's western campaign to gain control of the Mississippi River and divide the South. Grant's success illustrated the boldness and flexibility that Lincoln sought in a commander.

By the summer of 1863, the military situation finally looked promising for the North. The Union controlled much of Arkansas, Louisiana, Mississippi, Missouri, Kentucky, and Tennessee. In March 1864, Lincoln appointed Grant general in chief of all Union armies. Grant planned for victory within a year. "The art of war is simple enough," he reasoned. "Find out where your enemy is. Get at him as soon as you can. Strike at him as hard as you can, and keep moving on."

As an outsider to the prewar military establishment, Grant had no difficulty rejecting conventional military wisdom: "If men make war in slavish observance of rules, they will fail." He sought not one decisive engagement, but rather a grim campaign of annihilation, using the North's superior resources to grind down the South. Although Grant's plan entailed large casualties on both sides, he justified it by arguing that "now the carnage was to be limited to a single year."

A campaign of annihilation involved the destruction not only of enemy armies, but also of enemy resources. Although the idea of cutting the enemy off from needed supplies was implicit in the naval blockade, economic or "total" warfare was a relatively new and shocking idea. Grant, however, "regarded it as humane to both sides to protect the persons of those found at their homes, but to consume everything that could be used to support or supply armies." Following this policy, he set out after Lee's army in Virginia. General William Tecumseh Sherman, striking from Tennessee toward Atlanta, refined this plan.

War, Sherman believed, must also be waged on the minds of civilians, to make southerners "fear and dread" their foes. Therefore, his campaign to seize Atlanta and his march to Savannah spread destruction and terror. Ordered to forage "liberally" on the land, his army left desolation in its wake. This destruction, with its goal of total victory, showed once more how conflict produced the unexpected. The war that both North and South had hoped would be quick and relatively painless was ending after four long years with great cost to both sides. But the grimness of warfare during that final year threatened Lincoln's hopes for reconciliation.

CHANGES WROUGHT BY WAR

As bold new tactics emerged both on and off the battlefield, both governments took steps that changed their societies in surprising ways. Of the two, the South, which had left the Union to preserve a traditional way of life, experienced the more radical transformation.

A New South

The expansion of the central government's power in the South, starting with the passage of the 1862 Conscription Act, continued in the last years of the war. States' rights had inspired secession, but winning demanded centralization. Many southerners denounced Davis as a despot because he recognized the need for the central government to take the lead. Despite the accusations, the Confederate Congress cooperated with him and established important precedents, including serious interference with property rights. For example, government impressment of slaves for war work in 1863 affected the very form of private property that had originally driven the South from the Union.

The Conscription Act of 1862 did not solve the Confederate Army's manpower problems. By 1864, the southern armies were only a third the size of the Union forces. Hence, in February 1864 an expanded conscription measure made all white males between the ages of 17 and 50 subject to the draft. By 1865, the necessities of war had led to the unthinkable: arming slaves as soldiers. Black companies were recruited, but the war was over before any blacks could fight for the Confederacy.

In a message sent to Congress in November 1864, Davis speculated on some of the issues involved in arming slaves. "Should a slave who had served his country" be kept in servitude, he wondered, "or should his emancipation be held out to him as a reward for faithful service, or should it be granted at once on the promise of such service . . . ?" The South had begun the war to preserve slavery but ended it contemplating emancipation.

Southern agriculture also changed under the pressure of war. Earlier, the South had imported food from the North, concentrating on producing cotton and tobacco for market. Now, more and more land was turned over to food crops. Some farmers voluntarily shifted crops, but others responded only to state laws reducing the acreage permitted for cotton and tobacco cultivation. These measures raised enough food to feed southerners adequately. But they helped dramatically cut the production of cotton.

The South had always depended on imported manufactured goods. Although some blockade runners evaded Union ships, the noose tightened after 1862. The Confederacy could not, in any case, rely on blockade runners to equip the army. Thus, war triggered the expansion of military-related industries in the South. Here, too, the government played a crucial role. The war and navy offices directed industrial development, awarding contracts to private manufacturing firms like Richmond's Tredegar Iron Works and operating other factories themselves. The number of southerners working in industry rose dramatically. At the end of the war, rebel soldiers were better supplied with arms and munitions than with food.

Although the war did not transform the southern class structure, relations between the classes began to change. The pressures of the struggle undermined white solidarity, which was based on racism and supposed political unanimity. Draft resistance and desertion reflected growing alienation from a war perceived as serving only the interests of plantation owners. More and more yeoman families suffered grinding poverty as the men went to war and officials requisitioned resources.

The Victorious North

Although changes in the South were more noticeable, the Union's government and economy also responded to the demands of war. Like Davis, Lincoln was accused of being a dictator. Although he rarely tried to control Congress, veto its legislation, or direct government departments, Lincoln did use executive power freely. He violated the writ of habeas corpus by locking up more than 13,000 northerners without trials; he curbed press freedom by suppressing supposedly disloyal and inflammatory articles; he established conscription; he issued the Emancipation Proclamation; and he fired generals. Lincoln argued that this vast extension of presidential power was temporarily justified because, as president, he was responsible for defending and preserving the Constitution.

Many wartime changes in government proved more permanent than Lincoln had imagined. Wartime financial necessities helped revolutionize the country's banking system. Ever since Jackson's destruction of the Bank of the United States, state banks had served American financial needs. Treasury Secretary Chase found this banking system inadequate and chaotic and proposed to replace it. In 1863 and 1864, Congress passed banking acts that established a national currency issued by

Photography

The invention of photography in 1839 expanded the visual and imaginative world of nineteenth-century Americans. For the first time, Americans could visually record events in their own lives and see the images of unfamiliar people and places. Photographs also expand the boundaries of the historian's world. As photographic techniques became simpler, more and more visual information about the nineteenth century was captured. Historians can use photographs to discover many aspects of daily life: what people wore, how they celebrated events like marriages and funerals, what their families, houses, and cities looked like. Pictures of election campaigns, parades, strikes, and wars show the texture of public life. But historians also study photographs, as they do paintings, to glean information about attitudes and values. The choice of subjects, the way in which people and objects are arranged, and the relationships between people in the photographs all provide clues to the social and cultural values of the past.

Some knowledge of the early history of photography helps place the visual evidence in the proper perspective. The earliest type of photograph, the daguerreotype, was not a print, but the negative itself on a sheet of silver-plated copper. The first daguerreotypes required between 15 and 30 minutes for the proper exposure. The long exposure time explains why nineteenth-century images often seem stiff and formal. Glass ambrotypes (negatives on glass) and tintypes (negatives on gray iron bases), developed after the daguerreotypes, were easier and cheaper to produce. But both techniques produced only one picture and required what to us would seem an interminable time for exposure.

A major breakthrough came in the 1850s with the development of the wet-plate process. In this process, the photographer coated a glass negative with a sensitive solution, exposed the negative (i.e., took the picture), and then quickly developed it. The new procedure required a relatively short exposure time of about five seconds outside and one minute indoors. The resulting photographs looked more natural, but action shots were not yet possible. The entire process tied the photographer to the darkroom. Traveling photographers carried their darkrooms with them. The advantage of the wet-plate process was that it was possible to make many paper prints from one negative, opening new commercial vistas for professional photographers.

Matthew Brady, a fashionable Washington photographer, realizing that the camera was the "eye of history," asked Lincoln for permission to record the war with his camera. He and his team of photographers left about 8,000 glass negatives, currently stored in the Library of Congress and the National Archives, as their record of the Civil War. Shown here is a photograph of three Confederate soldiers captured at Gettysburg. Study and describe the soldiers. How are they posed? What kinds of clothes are they wearing? What about their equipment? Their health? Using the photograph as evidence, what might you conclude about the southern soldier's physical condition? What attitudes are conveyed through the men's facial expressions and poses? What kind of mood was the northern photographer trying to create? What might a northern viewer conclude about the southern war effort after looking at this picture?

Mathew Brady, *Confederate Captives, Gettysburg.* (National Archives)

This one photograph just begins to suggest what can be discovered through the study of images. Your local historical society and library probably have photograph collections available to you for study. Closer at hand, in family attics and cellars, there may well be photograph albums that, when examined carefully, will reveal many aspects of your own family's history.

federally chartered banks and backed by government bonds. The country once again had a federal banking system.

Northern agriculture expanded to feed soldiers and civilians, and so did investment in farm machinery. With so many men off soldiering, farmers were short of labor. Mechanical reapers performed the work of four to six men and farmers began to buy them; McCormick sold 165,000 during the war. Northern farming, especially in the Midwest, was well on the way to becoming mechanized. Farmers even accumulated a surplus for export.

The war selectively stimulated manufacturing, although overall the war retarded economic growth by consuming rather than generating wealth. Between 1860 and 1870, the annual rate of increase in real manufacturing value added was only 2.3 percent, in contrast with 7.8 percent for the years between 1840 and 1860 and 6 percent for the period 1870 to 1900. However, war industries, especially those with advantages of scale, expanded and made large profits. Each year, the Union army required 1.5 million uniforms and 3 million pairs of shoes; the woolen and leather industries grew accordingly. Meatpackers and producers of iron, steel, and pocket watches all profited from wartime opportunities.

On the Home Front, 1861–1865

In numerous, less tangible ways, the war transformed northern and southern society. The very fact of conflict established a new perspective for most civilians. They read newspapers and national weekly magazines with a new eagerness, and used the mail often. Wrote one North Carolina woman, "I never liked to write letters before, but it is a pleasure as well as a relief now." Distant events became almost as real and vivid as those at home. The war helped make Americans part of a larger world.

For some northerners like John D. Rockefeller and Andrew Carnegie, war brought unanticipated riches from army contracts. The New York *Herald* reported that New York City had never been "so gay, . . . so crowded, so prosperous," as in March 1864. Southern blockade runners made fortunes slipping in luxury goods.

For the majority of Americans, however, war meant deprivation. The war effort gobbled up a large part of each side's resources, and ultimately ordinary people suffered. To be sure, the demand for workers ended unemployment and changed employment patterns. Many women and blacks entered the work force, as they would in all future American wars. But whereas work was easy to get, real income declined. Inflation, especially destructive in the South, was largely to blame. By 1864, eggs sold in Richmond for $6 a dozen; butter brought $25 a pound. Strikes and union organizing pointed to working-class discontent.

Low wages compounded the problem of declining income and particularly harmed women workers. Often forced into the labor market because husbands could save little or nothing from small army stipends, army wives and other women took what pay they could get. As more women entered the work force, employers cut costs by slashing wages.

In the South, which bore the brunt of the fighting, wartime dislocation reduced civilian living standards most severely. Most white southerners suffered shortages in food, manufactured goods, and medicine. Farming families who had no slaves fared poorly. Urban conditions were most dismal. Food riots erupted in Richmond and other cities.

Thousands of southerners who fled as Union armies advanced suddenly found themselves homeless. "The country for miles around is filled with refugees," noted an officer in 1862. "Every house is crowded and hundreds are living in churches, in barns and tents." Caught up in the effort of mere survival, worried about what had happened to homes and possessions left behind, these southerners must have wondered if the cause was worth the sacrifices. Life was probably just as agonizing for those who chose to stay put when Union troops arrived.

White flight also disrupted slave life. Even the arrival of Union forces could prove a mixed blessing. White soldiers were unknown quantities and might be hostile to blacks whom they were supposed to be liberating. One slave described the upsetting arrival of the Yankees at his plantation in Arkansas: "Them folks stood round there all day. Killed hogs . . . killed cows . . . . Took all kinds of sugar and preserves . . . . Tore all the feathers out of the mattresses looking for money. Then they put Old Miss and her daughter in the kitchen to cooking." The next day found the Yanks gone and the Confederates back.

Throughout the South, insubordination, refusal to work, and refusal to accept punishment testified to the discontent of slaves, especially the fieldhands. Probably 20 percent of all slaves, many of them women, fled toward Union lines after the early months of the war. Their flight pointed to the changing nature of race relations and the harm slaves could do to the southern cause. Reflected one slave-owner, "The 'faithful slave' is about played out."

Women and the War

The war made it impossible for many women to live according to conventional norms, which exalted their domestic role and minimized their economic importance. With so many men in the armies, women had to find jobs and sustain farms. During the war years, southern women who had no slaves to help with the farmwork and northern farm wives who labored without the assistance of husbands or sons carried new physical and emotional burdens.

Women also participated in numerous war-related activities. North and South, they entered government service in large numbers. In the North, hundreds of women became military nurses. Under the supervision of Drs. Emily and Elizabeth Blackwell; Dorothea Dix, superintendent of army nurses; and Clara Barton, northern women nursed the wounded and dying for low or even no pay. They also fought the red tape that worsened hospital conditions.

Men largely staffed southern military hospitals, but Confederate women also played an important part in caring for the sick and wounded in their homes and in makeshift hospitals behind battle lines. Grim though the work was, many women felt that they were participating in the real world for the first time in their lives.

Women moved outside the domestic sphere in other forms of volunteer war work. Some women gained administrative experience in soldiers' aid societies and in the United States Sanitary Commission. Many others made bandages and clothes, put together packages for soldiers at the front, and helped army wives and disabled soldiers find jobs. Fund-raising activities realized substantial sums. By the end of the war, the Sanitary Commission had raised $50 million for medical supplies, nurses' salaries, and other wartime necessities.

Many of the changes women experienced during war years ended when peace returned. Jobs disappeared when men reclaimed them. Women turned over the operation of farms to returning husbands. But for women whose men came home maimed or not at all, the work had not ended. Nor had the discrimination. Trying to pick up the threads of their former lives, they found it impossible to forget what they had done in the war effort. Some of them were sure they had equaled their men in courage and commitment.

The Election of 1864

In the North, the election of 1864 brought some of the transformations of wartime into the political arena. The Democrats, capitalizing on war weariness, nominated General McClellan, branded the war a failure, and demanded an armistice. Democrats accused Lincoln of arbitrarily expanding executive power and denounced sweeping economic measures like the banking bills. Arguing that the president had transformed the war from one for Union into one for emancipation, they insinuated that a Republican victory would mean race mixing.

Although Lincoln controlled the party machinery and easily gained the Republican renomination, his party did not unite behind him. Lincoln seemed to please no one. His veto of the radical reconstruction plan for the South, the Wade-Davis bill, led to cries of "usurpation." The Emancipation Proclamation did not sit well with conservatives. In August 1864, a gloomy Lincoln told his cabinet that he expected to lose. As late as September, some Republicans hoped to reconvene the convention and select another candidate.

Sherman's capture of Atlanta in September 1864 and his march to Savannah helped swing voters to Lincoln. In the end, Lincoln won 55 percent of the popular vote and swept the Electoral College.

Why the North Won

In the months after Lincoln's reelection, the war drew to an agonizing conclusion. Sherman moved north from Georgia to North Carolina, while Grant pummeled Lee in Virginia. Grant's losses were staggering, but new recruits replaced the dead. On April 9, 1865, Grant accepted Lee's surrender at Appomattox. Southern soldiers and officers were allowed to go home with their personal equipment after promising to remain there peaceably. The war was over.

Grant's military strategy succeeded because the Union's manpower and economic resources could survive huge losses of men and equipment while the Confederacy's could not. Naval strategy eventually paid off because the North could build enough ships to make its blockade work.

The South had taken tremendous steps toward meeting war needs. But despite the impressive growth of manufacturing and the increasing acreage devoted to foodstuffs, southern troops and southern people were poorly fed and clothed. Women working alone or with disgruntled slaves could not produce enough food.

Worn-out farm equipment was not replaced. Impressments of slaves and animals cut production. So did the half-million blacks who fled to Union lines.

New industries could not meet the extraordinary demands of wartime, and advancing Union forces destroyed many of them. A Confederate officer in northern Virginia observed, "Many of our soldiers are thinly clothed and without shoes and in addition to this, very few of the infantry have tents. With this freezing weather, their sufferings are indescribable." Skimpy rations, only a third of a pound of meat for each soldier a day by 1864, weakened the Confederate force, whose trail was "traceable by the deposit of dysenteric stool." By that time, the Union armies were so well supplied that soldiers often threw away extra blankets and coats.

The South's woefully inadequate transportation system also contributed to defeat. Primitive roads deteriorated and became all but impassable without repairs. The railroad system was inefficient and inadequate. Food intended for the army rotted awaiting shipment, while soldiers went hungry and cities rioted.

Ironically, measures the Confederacy took to strengthen its ability to win the war, as one Texan later observed, "weakened and paralyzed it." Conscription, impressment, and taxes all bred resentment and sometimes open resistance. The proposal to use slaves as soldiers called into question the war's purpose. The many southern governors who refused to contribute men, money, and supplies on the scale Davis requested implicitly condoned disloyalty. The belief in states' rights and the sanctity of private property that gave birth to the Confederacy also helped kill it.

By the final months of the war, Davis had recognized how dangerous defeatism was to the Confederacy's cause. But such realization did not result in any vigorous attempts to influence public opinion or to control internal dissent.

It is tempting to compare Lincoln and Davis as war leaders. There is no doubt that Lincoln's humanity, his awareness of the terrible costs of war, his determination to save the Union, and his eloquence set him apart as one of this country's most extraordinary presidents. Yet the men's personal characteristics were probably less important than the differences between the political and social systems of the two regions. Without the support of a party behind him, Davis failed to engender enthusiasm or loyalty. Even though the Republicans rarely united behind Lincoln, they uniformly wanted to keep the Democrats from office. Despite squabbles, Republicans tended to support Lincoln's policies in Congress and back in their home districts. Commanding considerable resources of patronage, Lincoln was able to line up federal, state, and local officials behind his party and administration.

Just as the northern political system provided Lincoln with more flexibility and support, its social system also proved more able to meet the war's extraordinary demands. Although both societies innovated to secure victory, northerners were more cooperative and disciplined. In the southern states, old attitudes impeded the war effort. Wedded to states' rights, southern governors refused to cooperate with the Confederate government. When Sherman approached Atlanta, Georgia's governor would not turn over the 10,000 men in the state army to Confederate commanders. Slaveholders resisted the impressment of their slaves for war work.

In the end, the Confederacy collapsed, exhausted and bleeding. Hungry soldiers got letters revealing desperate situations at home, worried, and slipped away. By December 1864, the Confederate desertion rate exceeded 50 percent.

Replacements could not be found. Farmers hid livestock and produce from tax collectors. Many southerners resigned themselves to defeat, but some fought to the end. One Yankee described them as they surrendered at Appomattox:

> Before us in proud humiliation stood the embodiment of manhood: men whom neither toils and sufferings, nor the fact of death, nor disaster, nor hopelessness could bend from their resolve; standing before us now, thin, worn, and famished, but erect, and with eyes looking level into ours, waking memories that bound us together as no other bond.

The Costs of War

The war was over, but its memories would fester for years. About three million American men, a third of all free males between the ages of 15 and 59, had served in the army. Each would remember his personal history of the war. For George Eagleton, who had worked in army field hospitals, the history was one of "Death and destruction! Blood! Blood! Agony! Death! Gaping flesh wounds, broken bones, amputations, bullet and bomb fragment extractions." Of all American wars, none has been more deadly. The death rate was more than five times that of World War II. About 360,000 Union soldiers and another 258,000 Confederate soldiers died, about a third because their wounds were either improperly treated or not treated at all. Disease claimed more lives than combat.

Thousands upon thousands of men would be reminded of the human costs of war by the injuries they carried with them to the grave and by the missing limbs that marked them as Civil War veterans. About 275,000 on each side were maimed. Another 410,000 (195,000 northerners and 215,000 southerners) would recall their time in wretchedly overcrowded and unsanitary prison camps. The lucky ones would remember only the boredom. The worst memory was of those who rotted in prison camps, such as Andersonville in Georgia, where 31,000 Union soldiers were confined. At the war's end, over 12,000 graves were counted there.

Some Americans found it hard to readjust to peace. As Arthur Carpenter's letters suggest, he gradually grew accustomed to army life. War provided him with a sense of purpose, and afterward he felt aimless. A year after the war's end, he wrote, "Camp life agrees with me better than any other." Many others had difficulty returning to civilian routines. Even those who adjusted successfully discovered that they looked at life from a different perspective. The experience of fighting, of mixing with all sorts of people from many places, of traveling far from home had lifted former soldiers out of their familiar local world and widened their vision. Fighting the war made the concept of national union real.

Unanswered Questions

What had the war accomplished? Certainly death and destruction. Physically, the war devastated the South. Historians have estimated a 43 percent decline in southern wealth during the war years, exclusive of the value of slaves. Great cities like Atlanta, Columbia, and Richmond lay in ruins. Fields were weed-choked and uncultivated. Tools were worn out. A third or more of the South's mules, horses, and swine were gone. Two-thirds of the railroads had been destroyed. Thousands

Ruined buildings and mourning women were common sights in Richmond, Virginia, as the war came to an end. This photograph gives a vivid sense of the devastation of the South in 1865. (Library of Congress)

were hungry, homeless, and bitter about their four years of what now appeared useless sacrifice. Over three million slaves, a vast financial investment, were free.

On the other hand, the war had resolved the question of union and ended the debate over the relationship of the states to the federal government. Republicans had seized the opportunity to pass legislation that would foster national union and economic growth: the Pacific Railroad Act of 1862, which set aside huge tracts of public land to finance the transcontinental railroad; the Homestead Act of 1862, which was to provide yeoman farmers cheaper and easier access to the public domain; the Morrill Act of 1862, which established support for agricultural (land-grant) colleges; and the banking acts of 1863 and 1864.

The war had also resolved the issue of slavery that so long had plagued American life. Yet uncertainties outnumbered certainties. What would happen to ex-slaves? When blacks had fled to Union lines, commanders had not known what to do with them. Now the problem became more pressing. Should blacks have the same civil and political rights as whites? In the Union army, they had been second-class soldiers. The behavior of Union forces toward liberated blacks in the South showed how deep the stain of racism went. Would blacks now get land and economic independence? What would be their relations with their former owners?

What, indeed, would be the status of the conquered South in the nation? Should it be punished for the rebellion? Some people thought so. Should southerners keep their property? Some people thought not. There were clues to Lincoln's intentions. As early as December 1863, the president had announced a generous plan of reconciliation. He was willing to recognize the government of former Confederate states established by a group of citizens equal to 10 percent of those voting in 1860, as long as the group swore to support the Constitution and to accept the abolition of slavery. He began to restore state governments in three former Confederate states on that basis. But not all northerners agreed with his leniency, and the debate continued.

TIMELINE

1861	1862	1863	1864	1865
Lincoln calls up state militia and suspends habeas corpus; First Battle of Bull Run; Union blockades the South	Battles at Shiloh, Bull Run, and Antietam; *Monitor* and *Virginia* battle; First black regiment authorized by Union; Union issues greenbacks; South institutes military draft; Pacific Railroad Act; Homestead Act; Morrill Land-Grant College Act	Lincoln issues Emancipation Proclamation; Congress adopts military draft; Battles of Gettysburg and Vicksburg; Union Banking Act; Southern tax laws and impressment act; New York draft riots; Southern food riots	Sherman's march through Georgia; Lincoln reelected; Union Banking Act	Lee surrenders at Appomattox; Lincoln assassinated; Andrew Johnson becomes president; Congress passes Thirteenth Amendment abolishing slavery

In his 1865 inaugural address, Lincoln urged Americans to harbor "malice towards none . . . and charity for all." "Let us strive," he urged, "to finish the work we are in; to bind up the nation's wounds . . . to do all which may achieve a just and lasting peace." Privately, the president said the same thing. Generosity and goodwill would pave the way for reconciliation. On April 14, he pressed the point home to his cabinet. His wish was to avoid persecution and bloodshed. That same evening, only five days after the surrender at Appomattox, the president attended a play at Ford's Theatre. And there, said an eyewitness,

> a pistol was heard and a man . . . dressed in a black suit of clothes leaped onto the stage apparently from the President's box. He held in his right hand a dagger whose blade appeared about 10 inches long . . . . Every one leaped to his feet, and the cry of "the President is assassinated" was heard—Getting where I could see into the President's box, I saw Mrs. Lincoln . . . in apparent anguish.

John Wilkes Booth had killed the president.

❦❦❦❦❦❦

CONCLUSION

An Uncertain Future

As the war ended, many Americans grieved for the man whose decisions had so marked their lives for five years. "Strong men have wept tonight & the nation will mourn tomorrow," wrote one eyewitness to the assassination. Many more wept for friends and relations who had not survived the war, but whose actions had in one way or another contributed to its outcome. Perhaps not all Americans realized how drastically the war had altered their lives, their futures, their nation. It was only as time passed that the war's impact became clear to them. And it was only with time that they recognized how many problems the war had left unsolved. It is to these years of Reconstruction that we turn next.

Recommended Reading

Overviews

Peter J. Parrish, *The American Civil War* (1985); James McPherson, *Battle Cry of Freedom: The Civil War Era* (1988); Joseph T. Glatthatt, *Partners in Command: The Relationship between Leaders in the Civil War* (1994); Phillip S. Paludan, *"A People's Contest:" The Union and the Civil War, 1861–1865* (1989); Paul D. Escott, *Many Excellent People* (1985); Malcolm C. McMillan, *The Disintegration of a Confederate State* (1986); James M. McPherson, *Drawn to the Sword: Reflections on the American Civil War* (1996).

The Military Experience

T. Harry Williams, *The History of American Wars* (1981); Perry D. Jamieson, *Attack and Die: Civil War Tactics and the Southern Heritage* (1982); Richard E. Beringer, Herman Hattaway, Archer Jones, and William N. Still, Jr., *The Elements of Confederate Defeat: Nationalism, War Aims, and Religion* (1988); Gerald F. Linderman, *Embattled Courage: The Experience of Combat in the American Civil War* (1987); Randall C. Jimerson, *The Private Civil War* (1988); Reid Mitchell, *The Vacant Chair: The Northern Soldier Leaves Home* (1993); Laurence M. Hauptman, *The Iroquois in the Civil War: From Battlefield to Reservation* (1993); Thomas B. Buell, *The Warrior Generals: Combat Leadership in the Civil War* (1997); James M. McPherson, *For Cause and Comrades: Why Men Fought in the Civil War* (1997).

The Home Front

Eric Foner, *Politics and Ideology in the Age of Civil War* (1980); David Donald, *Lincoln* (1995); Drew Gilpin, Faust, *Mothers of Invention: Women of the Slaveholding South in the American Civil War* (1996); David E. Long, *The Jewel of Liberty: Abraham Lincoln's Re-Election and the End of Slavery* (1994); Michael Burlingame, *The Inner World of Abraham Lincoln* (1994); Glenn M. Lindend and Thomas J. Pressly, eds., *Voices From the House Divided* (1995); J. Matthew Gallman, *Mastering Wartime: A Social History of Philadelphia During the Civil War* (1990); Theodore J. Karamanski, *Rally 'Round the Flag: Chicago and the Civil War* (1993); Wayne K. Durrell, *War of Another Kind: A Southern Community in the Great Rebellion* (1990); Mary A. Decredico, *Patriotism for Profit: Georgia's Urban Entrepreneurs and the Confederate War Effort* (1990); Barbara Jeanne Fields, *Slavery and Freedom on the Middle Ground* (1985); Clarence L. Mohr, *On the Threshold of Freedom* (1986); David W. Blight, *Frederick Douglass' Civil War* (1989); Elizabeth D. Leonard, *Yankee Women: Gender Battles in the Civil War* (1994); Wendy Hamand Venet, *Neither Ballots Nor Bullets: Women Abolitionists and the Civil War* (1991); C. Vann Woodward and Elisabeth Muhlenfeld, eds., *Mary Chesnut's Civil War* (1981); Catherine Clinton, *Tara Revisited: Women, War, and the Plantation Legend* (1995); David W. Blight and Brooks D. Simpson, eds., *Union & Emancipation: Essays on Politics and Race in the Civil War Era* (1997).

Fiction

Stephen Crane, *The Red Badge of Courage* (any ed.); MacKinlay Kantor, *Andersonville* (1955).

CHAPTER 16

The Union Reconstructed

In April 1864 Robert Allston died, leaving his daughter Elizabeth and his wife Adele to manage their many rice plantations. With Yankee troops moving through coastal South Carolina in the late winter of 1864–1865, Elizabeth's sorrow turned to "terror" as Union soldiers arrived and searched for liquor, firearms, and valuables. The women fled. Later, other troops encouraged the Allston slaves to take furniture, food, and other goods from the Big House. Before they left, the Union soldiers gave the keys to the crop barns to the semifree slaves.

After the war, Adele Allston swore allegiance to the United States and secured a written order for the former slaves to relinquish those keys. She and Elizabeth returned in the summer of 1865 to reclaim the plantations and reassert white authority. She was assured that although the blacks had guns, "no outrage has been committed against the whites except in the matter of property." But property was the issue. Possession of the keys to the barns, Elizabeth wrote, would be the "test case" of whether former masters or former slaves would control land, labor and its fruits, and even the subtle aspects of interpersonal relations.

Nervously, Adele and Elizabeth Allston confronted their ex-slaves at their old home. To their surprise, a pleasant reunion took place. A trusted black foreman handed over the keys to the barns. This harmonious scene was repeated elsewhere.

But at one plantation, the Allston women met defiant and armed ex-slaves. A former black driver, Uncle Jacob, was unsure whether to yield the keys to the barns full of rice and corn, put there by black labor. Mrs. Allston insisted. As Uncle Jacob hesitated, an angry young man shouted: "Ef yu gie up de key, blood'll flow." Uncle Jacob slowly slipped the keys back into his pocket.

The African-Americans sang freedom songs and brandished hoes, pitchforks, and guns to discourage anyone from going to town for help. Two blacks, however, slipped away to find some Union officers. The Allstons spent the night safely, if restlessly, in their house. Early the next morning, they were awakened by a knock at the unlocked front door. There stood Uncle Jacob. Silently, he gave back the keys.

❦❦❦❦❦❦

The story of the keys reveals most of the essential human ingredients of the Reconstruction era. Defeated southern whites were determined to resume control of both land and labor. The law and federal enforcement generally supported property owners. The Allston women were friendly to the blacks in a maternal way and insisted on restoring prewar deference. Adele and Elizabeth, in short, both feared and cared about their former slaves.

The African-American freedmen likewise revealed mixed feelings toward their former owners: anger, loyalty, love, resentment, and pride. They paid respect to the Allstons but not to their property and crops. They wanted not revenge, but economic independence and freedom.

Northerners played a most revealing role. Union soldiers, literally and symbolically, gave the keys of freedom to the blacks, but did not stay around long enough to guarantee that freedom. Although encouraging the freedmen to plunder the master's house and seize the crops, in the crucial encounter, northern officials had disappeared. Understanding the limits of northern help, Uncle Jacob handed the keys to land and liberty back to his former owner. The blacks knew that if they wanted to ensure their freedom, they had to do it themselves.

This chapter describes what happened to the conflicting goals and dreams of three groups as they groped toward new social, economic, and political relationships during the Reconstruction era. Amid devastation and class and race divisions, Civil War survivors sought to put their lives back together. Victorious but variously motivated northern officials, defeated but defiant southern planters, and impoverished but hopeful African-American black freedmen—they could not all fulfill their conflicting goals, yet each had to try. Reconstruction would be divisive, leaving a legacy of gains and losses.

THE BITTERSWEET AFTERMATH OF WAR

"There are sad changes in store for both races," the daughter of a Georgia planter wrote in the summer of 1865. To understand the bittersweet nature of Reconstruction, we must look at the state of the nation after the assassination of President Lincoln.

The United States in 1865

The "Union" faced constitutional crisis in April 1865. What was the status of the 11 former Confederate states? The North had denied the South's constitutional right to secede but needed four years of war and over 600,000 deaths to win the point. Lincoln's official position had been that the southern states had never left the Union and were only "out of their proper relation" with the United States. The president, therefore, as commander in chief, had the authority to decide how to set relations right again. Lincoln's congressional opponents retorted that the ex-Confederate states were now "conquered provinces" and that Congress should resolve the constitutional issues and direct reconstruction.

Differences between Congress and the White House over reconstruction mirrored a wider struggle between the two branches of the national government. During war, as has usually been the case, the executive branch assumed broad powers. Many believed, however, that Lincoln had far exceeded his constitutional authority. Now Congress reasserted its authority.

In April 1865, the Republican party ruled virtually unchecked. Republicans had made immense achievements in the eyes of the northern public: winning the war, preserving the Union, and freeing the slaves. They had enacted sweeping economic programs on behalf of free labor and free enterprise. But the party remained an uneasy grouping of former Whigs, Know-Nothings, Unionist Democrats, and antislavery idealists.

The Democrats were in shambles. Republicans depicted southern Democrats as rebels, murderers, and traitors, and they blasted northern Democrats as weak-willed, disloyal, and opposed to economic growth and progress. Nevertheless, in the elections of 1864 the Republicans, needing to show that the war was a bipartisan effort, nominated a Unionist Tennessee Democrat, Andrew Johnson, as Lincoln's vice president. Now the tactless Johnson headed the government.

The United States in the spring of 1865 presented stark contrasts. Northern cities and railroads hummed; southern cities and railroads lay in ruins. Southern financial institutions were bankrupt; northern banks flourished. Mechanizing northern farms were more productive than ever; southern farms and plantations, especially those along Sherman's march, resembled a "howling waste."

Despite widespread devastation in the South, southern attitudes towards the future were mixed. As a later southern writer, Wilbur Cash, explained, "If this war had smashed the Southern world, it had left the essential Southern mind and will . . . entirely unshaken." Many white southerners braced to resist Reconstruction and restore their old world, but the minority who had remained quietly loyal to the Union dreamed of reconciliation. And nearly four million former slaves were on their own, facing the challenges of freedom. After initial joy , freedmen quickly realized their continuing dependence on former owners. Everything—and nothing—had changed.

Hopes Among Freedmen

Throughout the South in the summer of 1865, optimism surged through the old slave quarters. The slavery chain, however, broke only link by link. After Union troops swept through an area, ex-Confederate soldiers would follow, or master and overseer would return, and freedmen learned not to rejoice too quickly or openly. Former slaves became cautious about what freedom meant.

Gradually, though, freedmen began to test the reality of freedom. Typically, their first step was to leave the plantation, if only for a few hours or days. "If I stay here I'll never know I am free," said a South Carolina woman who went to work as a cook in a nearby town. Some former slaves cut their ties entirely—returning to an earlier master, or going into towns and cities to find jobs, schools, churches, and association with other blacks, safe from whippings and retaliation.

Many freedmen left the plantation in search of a spouse, parent, or child sold away years before. Advertisements detailing these sorrowful searches filled African-American newspapers. For those who found a spouse or who had been living together in slave marriages, freedom meant getting married legally, sometimes in mass ceremonies common in the first months of emancipation. Legal marriage was important morally, but it also established the legitimacy of children and meant access to land titles and other economic opportunities. Marriage brought special burdens for black women who assumed the double role of housekeeper and breadwinner. Since many newly married blacks, however, were determined to create a traditional family life, their wives left plantation field labor altogether.

Freedmen also demonstrated their new status by choosing surnames. Names connoting independence, such as Washington, were common. Revealing freedmen's mixed feelings toward their former masters, some would adopt their master's name—while others would pick "any big name 'ceptin' their master's." Emancipation changed black manners around whites as well. Masks fell, and old expressions of humility disappeared. For African-Americans, these changes were necessary expressions of selfhood, proving that things were now different, while whites saw in such behaviors "insolence."

But the primary goal for most freedmen was getting land. "All I want is to git to own fo' or five acres ob land, dat I can build me a little house on and call my home," a Mississippi black said. Only through economic independence, the traditional American goal of controlling one's own labor and land, could former slaves prove to themselves that emancipation was real.

During the war, some Union generals had put liberated slaves in charge of confiscated and abandoned lands. In the Sea Islands of South Carolina and Georgia, blacks had been working 40-acre plots of land and harvesting their own crops for several years. Farther inland, most freedmen who received land were the former slaves of Cherokees and Creeks. Some blacks held title to these lands. Northern philanthropists had organized others to grow cotton for the Treasury Department to prove the superiority of free labor. In Mississippi, thousands of ex-slaves worked 40-acre tracts on leased lands formerly owned by Jefferson Davis. In this highly successful experiment, they made profits sufficient to repay the government for initial costs, then lost the land to Davis's brother.

Many freedmen expected a new economic order as fair payment for their years of involuntary work. "Gib us our own land," said one, "and we take care ourselves; but widout land, de ole massas can hire us or starve us, as dey please." Freedmen believed that "forty acres and a mule" had been promised. Once they obtained land, family unity, and education, they looked forward to civil rights and the vote.

The White South's Fearful Response

White southerners had equally mixed goals and expectations. Yeoman farmers and poor whites stood beside rich planters in bread lines, all hoping to regain land and livelihood. White southerners responded with feelings of outrage, loss, and injustice. Said one man, "my pa paid his own money for our niggers; and that's not all they've robbed us of. They have taken our horses and cattle and sheep and everything."

A dominant emotion was fear. The entire structure of southern society was shaken, and the semblance of racial peace and order that slavery had provided was shattered. Having lost control of all that was familiar and revered, whites feared everything—from losing their cheap labor to having blacks sit next to them on trains. But southern whites' worst fears were of rape and revenge. African-American "impudence," some thought, would lead to legal intermarriage, and then would come "Africanization" and the destruction of the purity of the white race. African-American Union soldiers seemed especially ominous. But demobilization came quickly, and violence by black soldiers against whites was extremely rare.

Believing their world turned upside down, the former planter aristocracy tried to set it right again. To reestablish white dominance, southern legislatures passed "black codes" in the first year after the war. Many of the codes granted freedmen the right to marry, sue and be sued, testify in court, and hold property. But these rights were qualified. Complicated passages explained under exactly what circumstances blacks could testify against whites, own property (mostly they could not), or exercise other rights of free people. Racial intermarriage, the bearing of arms, possessing alcoholic beverages, sitting on trains (except in baggage compartments), being on city streets at night, or congregating in large groups were all forbidden. Many of the qualified rights guaranteed by the black codes were only passed to induce the federal government to withdraw its remaining troops from the South. This was a crucial issue, for in many places marauding whites were terrorizing virtually defenseless freedmen.

Key provisions of the black codes regulated freedmen's economic status. "Vagrancy" laws provided that any blacks not "lawfully employed" (which usually meant by a white employer) could be arrested, jailed, fined, or hired out to a man who would assume responsibility for their debts and behavior. The codes regulated black laborers' work contracts with white landowners, including severe penalties for leaving before the yearly contract was fulfilled. A Kentucky newspaper was blunt: "The tune . . . will not be 'forty acres and a mule,' but . . . 'work nigger or starve.'"

NATIONAL RECONSTRUCTION

The black codes directly challenged the national government in 1865. How would it use its power—to uphold the codes and reimpose racial intimidation in the South, or to defend the freedmen? Would the federal government stress human liberty, or would it emphasize property rights, order, and self-interest? Although the primary drama of Reconstruction pitted white landowners against African-American freedmen over land and labor in the South, in the background of these local struggles lurked the debate over Reconstruction policy among politicians in Washington. This dual drama would extend well into the twentieth century.

The Presidential Plan

After initially demanding that the defeated Confederates be punished for "treason," President Johnson adopted a more lenient policy. On May 29, 1865, he issued two proclamations setting forth his reconstruction program. Like Lincoln's, it rested on the claim that the southern states had never left the Union.

Johnson's first proclamation continued Lincoln's policies by offering "amnesty and pardon, with restoration of all rights of property" to most former Confederates who would swear allegiance to the Constitution and the Union. Johnson revealed his Jacksonian hostility to "aristocratic" planters by exempting ex-Confederate government leaders and rebels with taxable property valued over $20,000. They could, however, apply for individual pardons, which Johnson granted to nearly all applicants.

In his second proclamation, Johnson accepted the reconstructed government of North Carolina and prescribed the steps by which other southern states could reestablish state governments. First, the president would appoint a provisional governor, who would call a state convention representing those "who are loyal to the United States," including persons who took the oath of allegiance or were otherwise pardoned. The convention must ratify the Thirteenth Amendment, which abolished slavery; void secession; repudiate Confederate debts; and elect new state officials and members of Congress.

Under Johnson's plan, all southern states completed Reconstruction and sent representatives to Congress, which convened in December 1865. Defiant southern voters elected dozens of former officers and legislators of the Confederacy, including a few not yet pardoned. Some state conventions hedged on ratifying the Thirteenth Amendment, and some asserted former owners' right to compensation for lost slave property. No state convention provided for black suffrage, and most did nothing to guarantee civil rights, schooling, or economic protection for the freedmen. Less than eight months after Appomattox, the southern states were back in the Union, ex-slaves were working for former masters, and the new president was firmly in charge. Reconstruction seemed to be over.

Congressional Reconstruction

Late in 1865, northern leaders painfully saw that almost none of their postwar goals—moral, political, or psychological—were being fulfilled and that the Republicans were likely to lose their political power. Would Democrats and the South gain by postwar elections what they had lost by civil war?

The answer was obvious. Congressional Republicans, led by Congressman Thaddeus Stevens of Pennsylvania and Senator Charles Sumner of Massachusetts, decided to set their own policies for Reconstruction. Although labeled "radicals," the vast majority of Republicans were moderates on the issues of the economic and political rights of freedmen.

Rejecting Johnson's position that the South had already been reconstructed, Congress exercised its constitutional authority to decide on its own membership. It refused to seat the new senators and representatives from the old Confederate states. It also established the Joint Committee on Reconstruction to investigate conditions in the South. Its report documented disorder, resistance, and the appalling situation of the freedmen.

Even before the final report came out in 1866, Congress passed a civil rights bill to protect the fragile rights of African-Americans and extended for two more years the Freedmen's Bureau, an agency providing emergency assistance at the end of the war. Johnson vetoed both bills and called his congressional opponents "traitors." His actions drove moderates into the radical camp, and Congress passed both bills over his veto—both, however, watered down by weakening the power of enforcement.

In such a climate, southern racial violence erupted. In a typical outbreak, in May 1866, white mobs in Memphis, encouraged by local police, rampaged for over 40 hours of terror, killing, beating, robbing, and raping virtually helpless black residents and burning houses, schools, and churches. Forty-eight people, all but two of them black, died. The local Union army commander took his time restoring order, arguing that his troops had "hated Negroes too." A congressional inquiry concluded that Memphis blacks had "no protection from the law whatever."

A month later, Congress sent to the states for ratification the Fourteenth Amendment, the single most significant act of the Reconstruction era. The first section of the amendment promised permanent constitutional protection of the civil rights of freedmen by defining them as citizens. States were prohibited from depriving "any person of life, liberty, or property, without due process of law," and all people were guaranteed the "equal protection of the laws." Section 2 granted

A white mob burned this freedmen's school during the Memphis riot of May 1866. (Library Company of Philadelphia)

black male suffrage in the South. Other sections of the amendment barred leaders of the Confederacy from national or state offices (except by act of Congress), repudiated the Confederate debt, and denied claims of compensation to former slave owners. Johnson urged the southern states to reject the Fourteenth Amendment, and ten immediately did so.

The Fourteenth Amendment was the central issue of the 1866 midterm election. Johnson barnstormed the country asking voters to throw out the radical Republicans and trading insults with hecklers. Democrats north and south appealed openly to racial prejudice in attacking the Fourteenth Amendment. Republicans responded in kind, branding Johnson a drunken traitor. Republicans freely "waved the bloody shirt," reminding voters of Democrats' treason and draft-dodging. Voters were moved more by self-interest and local issues than by such speeches, but the result was an overwhelming Republican victory. The mandate was clear: Presidential Reconstruction had not worked, and Congress must present an alternative.

Early in 1867, Congress passed three Reconstruction acts. The southern states were divided into five military districts, whose commanders had broad powers to maintain order and protect civil and property rights. Congress also defined a new process for readmitting a state. Qualified voters—including blacks but excluding unreconstructed rebels—would elect delegates to state constitutional conventions that would write new constitutions guaranteeing black suffrage. After the new voters of the states had ratified these constitutions, elections would be held to choose governors and state legislatures. When a state ratified the Fourteenth Amendment, its representatives to Congress would be accepted, completing its readmission to the Union.

The President Impeached

Congress also restricted presidential powers and established legislative dominance over the executive branch. The Tenure of Office Act, designed to prevent Johnson from firing the outspoken Secretary of War Edwin Stanton, limited the president's appointment powers. Other measures trimmed his power as commander in chief.

Johnson responded exactly as congressional Republicans had anticipated. He vetoed the Reconstruction acts, limited the activities of military commanders in the South, and removed cabinet officers and other officials sympathetic to Congress. The House Judiciary Committee charged the president with "usurpations of power" and of acting in the "interests of the great criminals" who had led the rebellion. But moderate House Republicans defeated the impeachment resolutions.

In August 1867, Johnson dismissed Stanton and asked for Senate consent. When the Senate refused, the president ordered Stanton to surrender his office, which he refused, barricading himself inside. Now the House quickly approved impeachment resolutions, charging the president with "high crimes and misdemeanors," mostly alleged violations of the Tenure of Office Act. The three-month trial in the Senate early in 1868 featured impassioned oratory. Evidence was skimpy, however, that Johnson had committed any crime justifying his removal. With seven moderate Republicans joining Democrats against conviction, the effort to find the president guilty fell exactly one vote short of the required two-thirds majority. Not until the 1970s—and again in 1998–99—would a president face removal from office through impeachment.

Moderate Republicans may have feared the consequences of removing Johnson, for the man in line for the presidency, Senator Benjamin Wade of Ohio, was a leading radical Republican. Wade had endorsed women's suffrage, rights for labor unions, and civil rights for African-Americans in both southern and northern states. As moderate Republicans gained strength in 1868 through their support of the presidential election winner, Ulysses S. Grant, radicalism lost much of its power within Republican ranks.

Congressional Moderation

Congress's political battle against President Johnson was not matched by an idealistic resolve on behalf of the freedmen. State and local elections of 1867 showed that voters preferred moderate Reconstruction policies. It is important to look not only at what Congress did during Reconstruction, but also at what it did not do.

With the exception of Jefferson Davis, Congress did not imprison Confederate leaders, and only one person, the commander of the infamous Andersonville prison camp, was executed. Congress did not insist on a long probation before southern states could be readmitted. It did not reorganize southern local governments. It did not mandate a national program of education for the four million ex-slaves. It did not confiscate and redistribute land to the freedmen, nor did it prevent Johnson from taking land away from freedmen who had gained titles during the war. It did not, except indirectly, provide economic help to black citizens.

Congress did, reluctantly, grant citizenship and suffrage to the freedmen. Northerners were no more prepared than southerners to make African-Americans equal citizens. Proposals to give black men the vote gained support in the North only after the presidential election of 1868, when General Grant, the supposedly invincible military hero, barely won the popular vote in several states. To ensure grateful black votes, Congressional Republicans, who had twice rejected a suffrage amendment, took another look at the idea. After a bitter fight, the Fifteenth Amendment, forbidding all states to deny the vote to anyone "on account of race, color, or previous condition of servitude," became part of the Constitution in 1870.

Congress, therefore, gave blacks the vote but not land, the opposite of the freedmen's priority. Almost alone, Thaddeus Stevens argued that "forty acres . . . and a hut would be more valuable . . . than the . . . right to vote." But Congress never seriously considered his plan to confiscate the land of the "chief rebels" and give a small portion of it, divided into 40-acre plots, to the freedmen. This would have violated deeply-held beliefs of the Republican party and the American people about the sacredness of private property. Moreover, northern business interests looking to develop southern industry and invest in southern land liked the prospect of a large pool of propertyless African-Americans workers.

Congress did pass the Southern Homestead Act of 1866, making public lands available to blacks and loyal whites in five southern states. But the land was poor and inaccessible, and most black laborers were bound by contracts that prevented them from moving onto claims before the deadline. Only about 4,000 black families even applied for the Homestead Act lands, and fewer than 20 percent of them saw their claims completed. White claimants did little better.

Women and the Reconstruction Amendments

One casualty of the Fourteenth and Fifteenth amendments was the goodwill of women who had worked for suffrage for two decades. They had hoped that male legislators would recognize their wartime service in support of the Union and were shocked when the Fourteenth Amendment for the first time inserted the word male into the Constitution in referring to a citizen's right to vote. Elizabeth Stanton and Susan B. Anthony, veteran suffragists and opponents of slavery, campaigned against the Fourteenth Amendment, breaking with abolitionist allies like Frederick Douglass, who had long supported woman suffrage yet declared that this was "the Negro's hour." When the Fifteenth Amendment was proposed, suffragists wondered why the word sex could not have been added to the "conditions" no longer a basis for denial of the vote. Largely abandoned by radical reconstructionists and abolitionist activists, they had few champions in Congress and their efforts were put off for half a century.

Disappointment over the suffrage issue helped split the women's movement in 1869. Anthony and Stanton continued their fight for a national amendment for woman suffrage and a long list of other rights, while other women concentrated on securing the vote state-by-state.

LIFE AFTER SLAVERY

Union army Major George Reynolds boasted late in 1865 that in the area of Mississippi under his command he had "kept the negroes at work, and in a good state of discipline." Clinton Fisk, a well-meaning white who helped found a black college in Tennessee, told freedmen in 1866 that they could be "as free and as happy" working again for their "old master . . . as any where else in the world." Such pronouncements reminded blacks of white preachers' exhortations during slavery to work hard and obey masters. Ironically, Fisk and Reynolds were agents of the Freedmen's Bureau, the agency intended to aid former slaves' transition to freedom.

The Freedmen's Bureau

Never in American history has one small agency—underfinanced, understaffed, and undersupported—been given a harder task than was the Bureau of Freedmen, Refugees and Abandoned Lands. Its fate epitomizes Reconstruction.

The Freedmen's Bureau performed many essential services. It issued emergency food rations, clothed and sheltered homeless victims of the war, and established medical and hospital facilities. It provided funds to relocate thousands of freedmen and white refugees. It helped blacks search for relatives and get legally married, and it served as a friend in local civil courts to ensure that freedmen got fair trials. Although not initially empowered to do so, the agency also became responsible for educating the ex-slaves in schools staffed by idealistic northerners.

The Bureau's largest task was to promote African-Americans' economic well-being. This included settling them on abandoned lands and getting them started with tools, seed, and draft animals, as well as arranging work contracts with white landowners. But in this area the Freedmen's Bureau served more to "reenslave" the freedmen than to set them on their way as independent farmers.

Although some agents were self-sacrificing young New Englanders eager to help ex-slaves adjust to freedom, others were Union army officers more concerned with social order than social transformation. Working in a postwar climate of resentment and violence, Freedmen's Bureau agents were constantly accused by local whites of being partisan Republicans, corrupt, and partial to blacks. But even the best-intentioned agents would have agreed with Bureau commissioner General O. O. Howard's belief in the traditional nineteenth-century American values of self-help, minimal government interference in the marketplace, the sanctity of private property, contractual obligations, and white superiority.

On a typical day, overworked agents would visit local courts and schools, supervise the signing of work contracts, and handle numerous complaints, most involving contract violations between whites and blacks or property and domestic disputes among blacks. One agent sent a man who had complained of a severe beating back to work: "Don't be sassy [and] don't be lazy when you've got work to do." Although helpful in finding work for freedmen, often agents defended white landowners by telling blacks to obey orders, trust employers, and accept disadvantageous contracts.

Despite numerous constraints, the agents accomplished much. In little more than two years, the Freedmen's Bureau issued 20 million rations (nearly one-third to poor whites), reunited families and resettled some 30,000 displaced war refugees, treated some 450,000 people for illness and injury, built 40 hospitals and hundreds of schools, provided books, tools, and furnishings—and even some land—to the freedmen, and occasionally protected their economic and civil rights. African-American historian W. E. B. Du Bois's epitaph for the bureau might stand for the whole of Reconstruction: "In a time of perfect calm, amid willing neighbors and streaming wealth," he wrote, it "would have been a herculean task" for the bureau to fulfill its many purposes. But in the midst of hunger, sorrow, spite, suspicion, hate, and cruelty, "the work of any instrument of social regeneration was . . . foredoomed to failure."

Economic Freedom by Degrees

The economic failures of the Freedmen's Bureau forced freedmen into a new dependency on former masters. Although the planter class did not lose its economic and social power in the postwar years, southern agriculture saw major changes.

First, a land-intensive system replaced the labor intensity of slavery. Land ownership was concentrated into fewer and even larger holdings than before the war. From South Carolina to Louisiana, the wealthiest tenth of the population owned about 60 percent of the real estate in the 1870s. Second, these large planters increasingly specialized in one crop, usually cotton, and were tied into the international market. This resulted in a steady drop in postwar food production (both grain and livestock). Third, one-crop farming created a new credit system whereby most farmers, black and white, rented seed, farm implements and animals, provisions, housing, and land from local merchants. These changes affected race relations and class tensions among whites.

This new system took a few years to develop after emancipation. At first, most freedmen signed contracts with white landowners and worked very much as during slavery. All members of the family had to work to receive their rations. The freedmen resented this new semiservitude, preferring small plots of land of their own to grow vegetables and grains. They wanted to be able to send their children to school and insisted on "no more outdoor work" for women.

Many blacks therefore broke contracts, ran away, engaged in work slowdowns or strikes, burned barns, and otherwise resisted. In the Sea Islands and rice-growing regions of coastal South Carolina and Georgia, where slaves had long held a degree of autonomy, resistance was especially strong. On the Heyward plantations, near those of the Allstons, the freedmen "refuse work at any price," a Freedman's Bureau agent reported, and the women "wish to stay in the house or the garden all the time." The Allstons' former slaves also refused to sign contracts, even when offered livestock and other favors, and in 1869, Adele Allston had to sell much of her vast landholdings.

Blacks' insistence on autonomy and land of their own was the major impetus for the change from the contract system to tenancy and sharecropping. Families would hitch mules to their old slave cabin and drag it to their plot, as far from the Big House as possible. Sharecroppers received seed, fertilizer, implements, food, and clothing. In return, the landlord (or a local merchant) told them what and how much to grow, and he took a share—usually half—of the harvest. The cropper's half usually went to pay for goods bought on credit (at high interest rates) from the landlord. Thus sharecroppers remained tied to the landlord.

Tenant farmers had only slightly more independence. Before a harvest, they promised to sell their crop to a local merchant in return for renting land, tools, and

Sharecroppers and tenant farmers, though more autonomous than contract laborers, remained dependent on the landlord for their survival. (Brown Brothers)

other necessities. From the merchant's store they also had to buy goods on credit (at higher prices than whites paid) against the harvest. At "settling up" time, income from sale of the crop was compared to accumulated debts. It was possible, especially after an unusually bountiful season, to come out ahead and eventually to own one's own land. But tenants rarely did; in debt at the end of each year, they had to pledge the next year's crop. World cotton prices remained low, and whereas big landowners still generated profits through their large scale of operation, sharecroppers rarely made much money. When they were able to pay their debts, landowners frequently altered loan agreements. Thus peonage replaced slavery, ensuring a continuing cheap labor supply to grow cotton and other staples in the South. Only a very few African-Americans became independent landowners— about 2 to 5 percent by 1880, and closer to 20 percent in some states by 1900.

These changes in southern agriculture affected yeoman and poor white farmers as well, and planters worried about a coalition between poor black and pro-Unionist white farmers. As a yeoman farmer in Georgia said in 1865, "We should tuk the land, as we did the niggers, and split it, and giv part to the niggers and part to me and t'other Union fellers." But confiscation and redistribution of land was no more likely for white farmers than for the freedmen. Whites, too, had to concentrate on growing staples, pledging their crops against high-interest credit and facing perpetual indebtedness. In the upcountry piedmont area of Georgia, for example, the number of whites working their own land dropped from nine in ten before the Civil War to seven in ten by 1880, while cotton production doubled.

Reliance on cotton meant fewer food crops and greater dependence on merchants for provisions. In 1884, Jephta Dickson of Jackson County, Georgia, purchased over $50 worth of flour, meal, meat, syrup, peas, and corn from a local store; 25 years earlier, he had been almost completely self-sufficient. Fencing laws seriously curtailed the livelihood of poor whites raising pigs and hogs, and restrictions on hunting and fishing reduced the ability of poor whites and blacks alike to supplement incomes and diets.

In the worn-out flatlands and barren mountainous regions of the South, poor whites' antebellum poverty, ill health, and isolation worsened after the war. Many poor white farmers were even less productive than black sharecroppers. Some became farmhands at $6 a month (with board). Others fled to low-paying jobs in cotton mills, where they would not have to compete against blacks.

The cultural life of poor southern whites reflected their lowly position and their pride. Their emotional religion centered on camp meeting revivals. Their ballads and folktales told of debt, chain gangs, and drinking prowess. Their quilt making and house construction reflected a marginal culture in which everything was saved and reused.

In part because their lives were so hard, poor whites clung to their belief in white superiority. Many poor whites joined the Ku Klux Klan and other southern white terror groups that emerged between 1866 and 1868. But however hard life was for poor whites, things were even worse for blacks. The freedmen's high hopes slowly soured. Recalled a former Texas slave, "We soon found out that freedom could make folks proud but it didn't make 'em rich."

Black Self-Help Institutions

Many African-American leaders realized that because white institutions could not fulfill the promises of emancipation, freedmen would have to do it themselves. Traditions of black community self-help survived in the churches and schools of the antebellum free Negro communities and in the "invisible" cultural institutions of the slave quarters. Emancipation brought a rapid increase in the growth of membership in African-American churches. The Negro Baptist Church grew from 150,000 members in 1850 to 500,000 in 1870, while the membership of the African Methodist Episcopal Church exploded.

African-American ministers continued to exert community leadership. Many led efforts to oppose discrimination, some by entering politics; over one-fifth of the black officeholders in South Carolina were ministers. Most preachers, however, focused on sin and salvation. An English visitor to the South in 1867 and 1868 noted the intensity of black "devoutness." As one black woman explained: "We make noise 'bout ebery ting else . . . I want ter go ter Heaben in de good ole way."

The freedmen's desire for education was as strong as for religion. Typically, a school official in Virginia said that the freedmen were "down right crazy to learn." The first teachers of these black children were the legendary "Yankee schoolmarms." Sent by groups such as the American Missionary Association, these high-minded young women sought to convert blacks to Congregationalism and white morality. In October 1865, Esther Douglass found "120 dirty, half naked, perfectly wild black children" in her schoolroom near Savannah, Georgia. Eight months later, she reported that they could read, sing hymns, and repeat Bible verses and had learned "about right conduct which they tried to practice."

Such glowing reports changed as white teachers grew frustrated with crowded facilities, limited resources, local opposition, and absenteeism caused by fieldwork.

Along with equal civil rights and land of their own, what the freedmen wanted most was education. Despite white opposition and limited facilities for black schools, one of the most positive outcomes of the Reconstruction era was education in freedmen's schools. (Valentine Museum, Richmond, Virginia)

In Georgia, for example, only 5 percent of black children went to school for part of any one year between 1865 and 1870, as opposed to 20 percent of white children. Blacks increasingly preferred their own teachers, who could better understand them. To train African-American preachers and teachers, northern philanthropists founded Howard, Atlanta, Fisk, Morehouse, and other black universities in the South between 1865 and 1867.

Black schools, like churches, became community centers. They published newspapers, provided training in trades and farming, and promoted political participation and land ownership. These efforts made black schools objects of local white hostility. As a Virginia freedman told a congressional committee, in his county, anyone starting a school would be killed and that blacks were "afraid to be caught with a book."

White opposition to black education and land ownership stimulated African-American nationalism and separatism. In the late 1860s, Benjamin "Pap" Singleton, a former Tennessee slave, urged blacks to abandon politics and migrate westward. He organized a land company in 1869, purchased public property in Kansas, and in the early 1870s took several groups from Tennessee and Kentucky to establish separate black towns in the prairie state. In following years, thousands of "exodusters" from the Lower South bought some 10,000 infertile acres in Kansas. But natural and human obstacles to self-sufficiency often proved insurmountable. By the 1880s, despairing of ever finding economic independence in the United States, Singleton and other nationalists advocated emigration to Canada and Liberia.

Other African-American leaders, notably Frederick Douglass, continued to press for full citizenship rights within the United States.

RECONSTRUCTION IN THE STATES

Douglass's confidence in the power of the ballot seemed warranted in the enthusiastic early months under the Reconstruction Acts of 1867. With President Johnson neutralized, Republican congressional leaders finally could prevail. Local Republicans, taking advantage of the inability or refusal of many southern whites to vote, overwhelmingly elected their delegates to state constitutional conventions in the fall of 1867. Guardedly optimistic and sensing the "sacred importance" of their work, black and white Republicans began creating new state governments.

Republican Rule

Southern state governments under Republican rule were not dominated by illiterate black majorities intent on "Africanizing" the South. Nor were these governments unusually corrupt or extravagant, nor use massive numbers of federal troops to enforce their will. By 1869, only 1,100 federal soldiers remained in Virginia, and most federal troops in Texas were guarding the frontier against Mexico and hostile Indians. Lacking strong military backing, the new state governments faced economic distress and increasingly violent harassment.

Diverse coalitions made up the new governments elected under congressional Reconstruction. These "black and tan" governments (as opponents called them) were actually predominantly white, except for the lower house of the South Carolina legislature. Some new leaders came from the old Whiggish elite of bankers, industrialists, and others interested more in economic growth and sectional reconciliation than in radical social reforms. A second group consisted of northern Republican capitalists who headed south to invest in land, railroads, and new industries. Others included Union veterans seeking a warmer climate, and missionaries and teachers inspired to work in Freedmen's Bureau schools. Such people were unfairly labeled "carpetbaggers."

Moderate African-Americans made up a third group in the Republican state governments. A large percentage of black officeholders were mulattoes, many of them well-educated preachers, teachers, and soldiers from the North. Others were self-educated tradesmen or representatives of the small landed class of southern blacks. In South Carolina, for example, of some 255 African-American state and federal officials elected between 1868 and 1876, two-thirds were literate and one-third owned real estate; only 15 percent owned no property at all. This class composition meant that black leaders often supported policies that largely ignored the economic needs of the black masses. Their goals fit squarely into the American republican tradition. African-American leaders reminded whites that they were also southerners, seeking only, as an 1865 petition put it, "that the same laws which govern white men shall govern black men [and that] we be dealt with as others are—in equity and justice."

The primary accomplishment of Republican rule in the South was to eliminate undemocratic features from prewar state constitutions. All states provided universal male suffrage and loosened requirements for holding office. Underrepresented counties got more legislative seats. Automatic imprisonment for debt was ended, and laws were enacted to relieve poverty and care for the handicapped. Many southern states received their first divorce laws and provisions granting property rights to married women. Lists of crimes punishable by death were shortened.

Republican governments financially and physically reconstructed the South by overhauling tax systems and approving generous railroad and other capital investment bonds. Harbors, roads, and bridges were rebuilt; hospitals and asylums were established. Most important, the Republican governments created the South's first public school systems. As in the North, these schools were largely segregated, but for the first time rich and poor, black and white alike had access to education. By the 1880s, black school attendance increased from 5 to over 40 percent, and white from 20 to over 60 percent. All this cost money, and so the Republicans also greatly increased tax rates and state debts.

These considerable accomplishments came in the face of opposition like that expressed at a convention of Louisiana planters, which labeled the Republican leaders the "lowest and most corrupt body of men ever assembled in the South." There was some corruption, mostly in land sales, railway bonds, and construction contracts. Such graft had become a way of life in postwar American politics, South and North. Given their lack of experience with politics, the black role was remarkable. As Du Bois put it, "There was one thing that the White South feared more than negro dishonesty, ignorance, and incompetence, and that was negro honesty, knowledge, and efficiency."

The Republican coalition did not survive. As the map indicates, Republican rule lasted for different periods in different states. It lasted the longest in the black belt states of the Deep South, where the black population was equal to or greater than the white. In Virginia, Republicans ruled hardly at all. Conservative Virginia Democrats professed agreement with Congress's Reconstruction guidelines while doing as they pleased and encouraging northern investors to rebuild shattered cities and develop industry. In South Carolina, African-American leaders' unwillingness to use their power to help black laborers contributed to their loss of political control to the Democrats. Class tensions and divisions among blacks in Louisiana helped to weaken that Republican regime as well.

Violence and "Redemption"

Democrats used violence to regain power. The Ku Klux Klan was only one of several secret organizations that forcibly drove black and white Republicans from office. The cases of North Carolina and Mississippi are representative.

After losing a close election in North Carolina in 1868, conservatives waged a concentrated terror campaign in several piedmont counties. If the Democrats could win these counties in 1870, they would most likely win statewide. In the year before the election, several prominent Republicans were killed, including a white state senator and a leading black Union League organizer, who was hanged in the

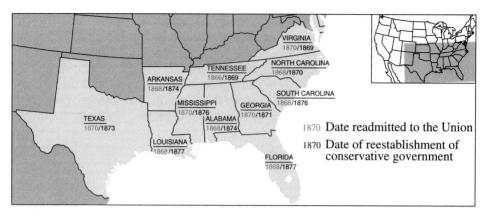

VIRGINIA
1870/1869

NORTH CAROLINA
1868/1870

TENNESSEE
1866/1869

ARKANSAS
1868/1874

SOUTH CAROLINA
1868/1876

MISSISSIPPI
1870/1876

GEORGIA
1870/1871

ALABAMA
1868/1874

TEXAS
1870/1873

LOUISIANA
1868/1877

FLORIDA
1868/1877

1870 Date readmitted to the Union

1870 Date of reestablishment of
       conservative government

THE RETURN OF CONSERVATIVE DEMOCRATIC CONTROL IN SOUTHERN STATES DURING REDEMPTION Note that the length of time Republican governments were in power to implement even moderate Reconstruction programs varied from state to state. In North Carolina and Georgia, for example, Republican rule was very brief while in Virginia it never took place at all. "Redemption," the return of conservative control, took longest in the three deep South states where electoral votes were hotly contested in the election of 1876.

courthouse square with a sign pinned to him: "Bewar, ye guilty, both white and black." Scores of citizens were fired, flogged, tortured, or driven in the middle of the night from burning homes and barns. The courts consistently refused to prosecute anyone for these crimes, which local papers blamed on "disgusting negroes and white Radicals." The conservative campaign worked. In the election of 1870, some 12,000 fewer Republicans voted in the two crucial counties than had voted two years earlier, and the Democrats swept back into power.

In Mississippi's state election in 1875, Democrats used similar tactics. Local Democratic clubs formed armed militias, marching defiantly through black areas, breaking up Republican meetings, and provoking riots to justify killing hundreds of blacks. Armed men posted during voter registration intimidated Republicans. At the election itself, voters were either "helped" by gun-toting whites to cast a Democratic ballot or chased away. Counties that had given Republican candidates majorities in the thousands managed a total of less than a dozen votes in 1875!

Democrats called their victory "redemption." As conservative Democrats resumed control of each state government, Reconstruction ended. Redemption succeeded with a combination of persistent white southern resistance, including violence and coercion, and a failure of northern persistence.

Congress and President Grant did not totally ignore southern violence. Three Force acts, passed in 1870 and 1871, gave the president strong powers to use federal supervisors to ensure that citizens were not prevented from voting by force or fraud. The third act, also known as the Ku Klux Klan Act, declared illegal secret organizations that used disguise and coercion to deprive others of equal protection of the laws. Congress created a joint committee to investigate Klan violence, and in 1872 its report filled 13 huge volumes with horrifying testimony. Grant, who had supported these measures, sent messages to Congress proclaiming the importance of the right to vote, issued proclamations condemning lawlessness, and dispatched additional troops to South Carolina. However, reform Republicans lost interest in defending blacks when they saw these voters supporting Grant, whom they opposed, and regular Republicans decided that they could do without black votes. Both groups were much more concerned with northern issues. In 1875, Grant's advisers told him that Republicans might lose important Ohio elections if he continued protecting African-Americans, so he rejected appeals by Mississippi blacks for troops to guarantee free elections. He and the nation "had tired of these annual autumnal outbreaks," the president said.

Mississippi Democrats' success in 1875, repeated a year later in South Carolina and Louisiana, indicated that congressional reports, presidential proclamations, and the Force acts did little to stop the reign of terror against black and white Republicans throughout the South. Despite hundreds of arrests, all-white juries refused to find whites guilty of crimes against blacks. The U.S. Supreme Court backed them, in two 1874 decisions throwing out cases against whites convicted of preventing blacks from voting and declaring key parts of the Force acts unconstitutional. Officially the Klan's power ended, but the attitudes (and tactics) of Klansmen would continue long into the next century.

Reconstruction, Northern Style

The American people, like their leaders, were tired of battles over the freedmen. The easiest course was to give citizenship and the vote to African-Americans, and move on. Americans of increasing ethnic diversity were primarily interested in starting families, finding work, and making money.

At both the individual and national levels, Reconstruction, northern style, meant the continuation of the enormous economic revolution of the nineteenth century. Although failing to effect a smooth transition from slavery to freedom for ex-slaves, Republican northerners did accelerate and solidify their program of economic growth and industrial and territorial expansion.

Thus as North Carolina Klansmen convened in dark forests in 1869, the Central Pacific and Union Pacific railroads met in Utah, linking the Atlantic and the Pacific. As southern cotton production revived, northern iron and steel manufacturing and western settlement of the mining, cattle, and agricultural frontiers also surged. As black farmers were "haggling" over work contracts with white landowners in Georgia, white workers were organizing the National Labor Union in Baltimore. As Elizabeth and Adele Allston demanded the keys to their barns in the summer of 1865, the Boston Labor Reform Association was demanding that "our . . . education, morals, dwellings, and the whole Social System" needed to be "reconstructed." If the South would not be reconstructed, labor relations might be.

The years between 1865 and 1875 featured not only the rise (and fall) of Republican governments in the South, but also a spectacular surge of working-class organization. Stimulated by the Civil War to improve working conditions in northern factories, trade unions, labor reform associations, and labor parties flourished, culminating in the founding of the National Labor Union in 1866. Before the depression of 1873, an estimated 300,000 to 500,000 American workers enrolled in some 1,500 trade unions, the largest such increase in the nineteenth century. This growth inevitably stirred class tensions. In 1876, hundreds of freedmen in the rice region along the Combahee River in South Carolina went on strike to protest a 40-cent-per-day wage cut, clashing with local sheriffs and white Democratic rifle clubs.

A year later, also fighting wage cuts, thousands of northern railroad workers went out in a nationwide wave of strikes, clashing with police and the National Guard.

As economic relations changed, so did the Republican party. Heralded by the moderate tone of the state elections of 1867 and Grant's election in 1868, the Republicans changed from a party of moral reform to one of material interest. In the continuing struggle in American politics between "virtue and commerce," self-interest was again winning. Abandoning the Freedmen's Bureau, Republican politicians had no difficulty handing out huge grants of money and land to the railroads. As blacks were told to help themselves, the Union Pacific was getting subsidies of between $16,000 and $48,000 for each mile of track it laid. As Susan B. Anthony and others tramped through the snows of Upstate New York with petitions for rights of suffrage and citizenship, Boss Tweed and other machine politicians defrauded New York taxpayers of millions of dollars. As Native Americans in the Great Plains struggled to preserve their sacred Black Hills from greedy gold prospectors protected by U.S. soldiers, corrupt government officials in the East "mined" public treasuries.

By 1869, the year financier Jay Gould almost cornered the gold market, the nation was increasingly defined by its sordid, materialistic "go-getters." Henry Adams, descendant of two presidents, was living in Washington, D.C., during this era. As he explained in his 1907 autobiography, *The Education of Henry Adams,* he had had high expectations in 1869 that Grant, like George Washington, would restore moral order and peace. But when Grant announced his cabinet, a group of army cronies and rich friends to whom he owed favors, Adams felt betrayed.

Honest himself, Grant showed poor judgment of others. The scandals of his administration touched his relatives, his cabinet, and his two vice-presidents. Outright graft, loose prosecution, and generally negligent administration flourished in a half dozen departments. The Whiskey Ring affair, for example, cost the public millions of dollars in tax revenues siphoned off to government officials. Gould's gold scam received the unwitting aid of Grant's Treasury Department and the knowing help of the president's brother-in-law.

Nor was Congress pure. Crédit Mobilier, a dummy corporation supposedly building the transcontinental railroads, received generous bonds and contracts in exchange for giving congressmen money, stock, and railroad lands. An Ohio congressmen described the House of Representatives in 1873 as an "auction room where more valuable considerations were disposed of under the speaker's hammer than any place on earth."

The election of 1872 showed the public uninterested in moral issues. "Liberal" Republicans, disgusted with Grant, formed a third party calling for lower tariffs and fewer grants to railroads, civil service reform, and the removal of federal troops from the South. Their candidate, Horace Greeley, editor of the New York *Tribune,* was also nominated by the Democrats, whom he had spent much of his career condemning. But despite his wretched record, Grant easily won a second term.

The End of Reconstruction

Soon after Grant's second inauguration, a financial panic, caused by railroad mismanagement and the collapse of some eastern banks, started a terrible depression that lasted throughout the mid-1870s. In these hard times, economic issues

Under a caption quoting a Democratic party newspaper, "This is a white man's government," this Thomas Nast cartoon from 1868 shows three white groups, stereotyped as apelike northern Irish workers, unrepentant ex-Confederates, and rich northern capitalists, joining hands to bring Republican Reconstruction to an end almost before it began. The immigrant's vote, the Kluxer's knife, and the capitalist's dollars would restore a "white man's government" on the back of the freedman, a Union soldier still clutching the Union flag and reaching in vain for the ballot box. No single image better captures the story of the end of Reconstruction. (*Harper's Weekly*, September 5, 1868)

dominated politics, further diverting attention from the freedmen. As Democrats took control of the House of Representatives in 1874 and looked toward winning the White House in 1876, politicians talked about new Grant scandals, unemployment and public works, the currency, and tariffs. No one said much about the freedmen. In 1875, a guilt-ridden Congress did pass Senator Charles Sumner's civil rights bill to put teeth into the Fourteenth Amendment. But the act was not enforced, and eight years later the Supreme Court declared it unconstitutional. Congressional Reconstruction, long dormant, had ended. The election of 1876 sealed the conclusion.

As their presidential candidate in 1876, the Republicans chose a former governor of Ohio, Rutherford B. Hayes, partly because of his reputation for honesty, partly because he had been a Union officer (a necessity for post-Civil War candidates), and partly because, as Henry Adams put it, he was "obnoxious to no one." The Democrats nominated Governor Samuel J. Tilden of New York, a famous civil service reformer who had broken the Tweed ring.

Tilden won a popular-vote majority and appeared to have enough electoral votes for victory—except for 20 disputed electoral votes, all but one in Louisiana, South Carolina, and Florida, where some federal troops remained and where Republicans still controlled the voting apparatus despite Democratic intimidation. To settle the dispute, Congress created a commission of eight Republicans and seven Democrats who voted along party lines to give Hayes all 20 votes and an electoral-college victory, 185 to 184.

Novels

We usually read novels, short stories, and other forms of fiction for pleasure, for the enjoyment of plot, style, symbolism, and character development. "Classic" novels such as *Moby Dick*, *Huckleberry Finn*, *The Great Gatsby*, *The Invisible Man*, and *Beloved*, for example, are not only written well, but also explore timeless questions of good and evil, of innocence and knowledge, or of noble dreams fulfilled and shattered. We enjoy novels because we often find ourselves identifying with one of the major characters. Through that person's problems, joys, relationships, and search for identity, we gain insights about our own.

We can also read novels as historical sources, for they reveal much about the attitudes, dreams, fears and ordinary everyday experiences of human beings in a particular historical period. In addition, they show how people responded to the major events of that era. The novelist, like the historian, is a product of time and place and has an interpretive point of view. Consider the two novels about Reconstruction quoted here. Neither is reputed for great literary merit, yet both reveal much about the various interpretations and impassioned attitudes of the post-Civil War era. *A Fool's Errand* was written by Albion Tourgée, a northerner; *The Clansman*, by Thomas Dixon, Jr., a southerner.

Tourgée was a young northern teacher and lawyer who fought with the Union army and moved to North Carolina after the war to begin a legal career. He became a judge and was an active Republican, supporting black suffrage and helping to shape the new state constitution. Because he boldly criticized the Ku Klux Klan, his life was threatened many times. When he left North Carolina in 1879, he published an autobiographical novel about his experiences as a judge challenging the Klan's campaign of violence and intimidation against the newly freed blacks.

The "fool's errand" in the novel is that of the northern veteran, Comfort Servosse, who like Tourgée seeks to fulfill human goals on behalf of both blacks and whites in post-Civil War North Carolina. His efforts are thwarted, however, by threats, intimidation, a campaign of violent "outrages" against republican leaders in the county, and a lack of support from Congress. Historians have verified the accuracy of the events in Tourgée's novel. While exposing the brutality of the Klan, Tourgée features loyal southern Unionists, respectable planters ashamed of Klan violence, and even guilt-ridden poor white Klansmen who try to protect or warn intended victims.

In the year of Tourgée's death, 1905, another North Carolinian published a novel with a very different analysis of Reconstruction and its fate. Thomas Dixon, Jr., was a lawyer, state legislator, Baptist minister, pro-Klan lecturer, and novelist. *The Clansman*, subtitled *A Historical Romance of the Ku Klux Klan*, reflects turn-of-the-century attitudes most white southerners still had about Republican rule during Reconstruction. According to Dixon, once the "Great Heart" Lincoln was gone, a power-crazed, vindictive radical Congress, led by scheming Austin Stoneman (Thaddeus Stevens), sought to impose corrupt carpetbagger and brutal black rule on a helpless South. Only through the inspired leadership of the Ku Klux Klan was the South saved from the horrors of rape and revenge.

Dixon dedicated *The Clansman* to his uncle, a Grand Titan of the Klan in North Carolina during the time when two crucial counties were being transformed from Republican to Democratic through intimidation and terror. No such violence shows up in Dixon's novel. When the novel was made the basis of D. W. Griffith's film classic, *Birth of a Nation*, in 1915, the novel's attitudes were firmly implanted on the twentieth-century American mind.

Both novels convey the events and issues of Reconstruction, especially attitudes toward the freedmen. Both create clearly defined heroes and villains. Both include exciting chase scenes, narrow escapes, daring rescues, and tragic deaths. Both include romantic subplots. Examining these brief excerpts is a poor substitute for reading the novels in their entirety, but notice the obvious differences of style and attitude in the depictions of Uncle Jerry and Old Aleck. How many differences can you find in these two short passages?

A Fool's Errand   Albion Tourgée (1879)

When the second Christmas came, Metta wrote again to her sister:

"The feeling is terribly bitter against Comfort on account of his course towards the colored people. There is quite a village of them on the lower end of the plantation. They have a church, a sabbath school, and are to have next year a school. You can not imagine how kind they have been to us, and how much they are attached to Comfort. . . . I got Comfort to go with me to one of their prayer-meetings a few nights ago. I had heard a great deal about them, but had never attended one before. It was strangely weird. There were, perhaps, fifty present, mostly middle-aged men and women. They were singing in soft, low monotone, interspersed with prolonged exclamatory notes, a sort of rude hymn, which I was surprised to know was one of their old songs in slave times. How the chorus came to be endured in those days I can not imagine. It was—

'Free! free! free, my Lord, free!
An' we walks de hebben-ly way!

"A few looked around as we came in and seated ourselves; and Uncle Jerry, the saint of the settlement, came forward on his staves, and said, in his soft voice,

"'Ev'nin', Kunnel! Sarvant, Missuss! Will you walk up, an' hev seats in front?'

"We told him we had just looked in, and might go in a short time; so we would stay in the back part of the audience.

"Uncle Jerry can not read nor write; but he is a man of strange intelligence and power. Unable to do work of any account, he is the faithful friend, monitor, and director of others. He has a house and piece of land, all paid for, a good horse and cow, and, with the aid of his wife and two boys, made a fine crop this season. He is one of the most promising colored men in the settlement: so Comfort says, at least. Everybody seems to have great respect for his character. I don't know how many people I have heard speak of his religion. Mr. Savage used to say he had rather hear him pray than any other man on earth. He was much prized by his master, even after he was disabled, on account of his faithfulness and character."

The Clansman   Thomas Dixon, Jr. (1905)

At noon Ben and Phil strolled to the polling-place to watch the progress of the first election under Negro rule. The Square was jammed with shouting, jostling, perspiring negroes, men, women, and children. The day was warm, and the African odour was supreme even in the open air . . . .

The negroes, under the drill of the League and the Freedman's Bureau, protected by the bayonet, were voting to enfranchise themselves, disfranchise their former masters, ratify a new constitution, and elect a legislature to do their will. Old Aleck was a candidate for the House, chief poll-holder, and seemed to be in charge of the movements of the voters outside the booth as well as inside. He appeared to be omnipresent, and his self-importance was a sight Phil had never dreamed. He could not keep his eyes off him . . . .

[Aleck] was a born African orator, undoubtedly descended from a long line of savage spell-binders, whose eloquence in the palaver houses of the jungle had made them native leaders. His thin spindle-shanks supported an oblong, protruding stomach, resembling an elderly monkey's, which seemed so heavy it swayed his back to carry it.

The animal vivacity of his small eyes and the flexibility of his eyebrows, which he worked up and down rapidly with every change of countenance, expressed his eager desires.

He was already mellow with liquor, and was dressed in an old army uniform and cap, with two horse-pistols buckled around his waist. On a strap hanging from his shoulder were strung a half-dozen tin canteens filled with whiskey.

Outraged Democrats threatened to stop the Senate from officially counting the electoral votes, thus preventing Hayes's inauguration. There was talk of a new civil war. But unlike the 1850s, a North-South compromise emerged. Northern investors wanted the government to subsidize a New Orleans-to-California railroad. Southerners wanted northern dollars but not northern political influence—no social agencies, no federal enforcement of the Fourteenth and Fifteenth amendments, and no military occupation, not even the symbolic presence left in 1876.

As the March 4 inauguration date approached, the forces of mutual self-interest concluded the "compromise of 1877." On March 2, Hayes was declared president-elect. After his inauguration, he ordered the last federal troops out of the South, appointed a former Confederate general to his cabinet, supported federal aid for economic and railroad development in the South, and promised to let southerners handle race relations themselves. On a goodwill trip to the South, he told blacks that "your rights and interests would be safer if this great mass of intelligent white men were let alone by the general government." The message was clear: Hayes would not enforce the Fourteenth and Fifteenth amendments, initiating a pattern of executive inaction not broken until the 1960s. But the immediate crisis was averted, officially ending Reconstruction.

❖❖❖❖❖❖

CONCLUSION

A Mixed Legacy

In the 12 years between Appomattox and Hayes's inauguration, victorious northern Republicans, defeated white southerners, and hopeful black freedmen each wanted more than the others would give. But each got something. The compromise of 1877 cemented reunion, providing new opportunities for economic development in both regions. The Republican party achieved its economic goals and generally held the White House, though not always Congress, until 1932. The ex-Confederate states came back into the Union, and southerners retained their grip on southern lands and black labor, though not without struggle and some changes.

And the freedmen? In 1880, Frederick Douglass wrote: "Our Reconstruction measures were radically defective . . . . To the freedmen was given the machinery of liberty, but there was denied to them the steam to put it in motion. . . . The old master class . . . retained the power to starve them to death, and wherever this power is held there is the power of slavery." The wonder, Douglass said, was "not that freedmen . . . have been standing still, but that they have been able to stand at all."

Freedmen had made strong gains in education and in economic and family survival. Despite sharecropping and tenancy, black laborers organized themselves to achieve a measure of autonomy and opportunity in their lives that could never be diminished. The three great Reconstruction amendments, despite flagrant violation over the next 100 years, held out the promise that equal citizenship and political participation would yet be realized.

TIMELINE

1865	**1865–1866**	**1866**	**1867**	**1868**
Civil War ends; Lincoln assassinated; Andrew Johnson becomes president; Johnson proposes general amnesty and reconstruction plan; Racial confusion, widespread hunger, and demobilization; Thirteenth Amendment ratified; Freedmen's Bureau established	Black codes; Repossession of land by whites and freedmen's contracts	Freedmen's Bureau renewed and Civil Rights Act passed over Johnson's veto; Southern Homestead Act; Ku Klux Klan formed; Tennessee readmitted to Union	Reconstruction acts passed over Johnson's veto; Impeachment controversy; Freedmen's Bureau ends	Fourteenth Amendment ratified; Impeachment proceedings against Johnson fail; Ulysses Grant elected president

1868–1870	**1869**	**1870**	**1870s–1880s**	**1870–1871**
Ten states readmitted under congressional plan	Georgia and Virginia reestablish Democratic party control	Fifteenth Amendment ratified	Black "exodusters" migrate to Kansas	Force acts; North Carolina and Georgia reestablish Democratic control

1872	**1873**	**1874**	**1875**	**1876**
General Amnesty Act; Grant reelected president	Crédit Mobilier scandal; Panic causes depression	Alabama and Arkansas reestablish Democratic control	Civil Rights Act; Mississippi reestablishes Democratic control	Hayes-Tilden election

1876–1877	**1877**	**1880s**		
South Carolina, Louisiana, and Florida reestablish Democratic control	Compromise of 1877; Rutherford B. Hayes assumes presidency and ends Reconstruction	Tenancy and sharecropping prevail in the South; Disfranchisement and segregation of southern blacks begins		

Recommended Reading

Overviews of Reconstruction

Laura Edwards, *Gendered Strife & Confusion: The Political Culture of Reconstruction* (1997); W. E. B. Du Bois, *Black Reconstruction* (1935); Eric Foner, *Reconstruction: America's Unfinished Revolution, 1863–1877* (1988); John Hope Franklin, *Reconstruction After the Civil War* (1961).

The Freedmen's Transition: Freedom by Degrees

James E. Bond, *No Easy Walk to Freedom: Reconstruction and the Ratification of the Fourteenth Amendment* (1997); Paul Cimbala, *Under the Guardianship of the Nation: The Freedmen's Bureau and the Reconstruction of Georgia, 1865–1870* (1997); Barbara J. Fields, *Slavery and Freedom on the Middle Ground* (1985); Eric Foner, *Nothing but Freedom: Emancipation and Its Legacy* (1983); Reginald F. Hildebrand, *The Times Were Strange and Stirring: Methodist Preachers and the Crisis of Emancipation* (1995); Jacqueline Jones, *Soldiers of Light and Love: Northern Teachers and Georgia Blacks, 1865–1873* (1980); Leon Litwack, *Been in the Storm So Long: The Aftermath of Slavery* (1980); William E. Montgomery, *Under Their Own Vine and Fig Tree: The African-American Church in the South, 1865–1900* (1993); Claude Oubré, *Forty Acres and a Mule: The Freedmen's Bureau and Black Land Ownership* (1978); Nell I. Painter, *Exodusters: Black Migration to Kansas After Reconstruction* (1977); Roger Ransom and Richard Sutch, *One Kind of Freedom: The Economic Consequences of Emancipation* (1977); Edward Royce, *The Origins of Southern Sharecropping* (1993); Julie Saville, *The Work of Reconstruction: From Slave to Wage Laborer in South Carolina, 1860–1870* (1994).

Reconstruction Politics: South and North

Richard H. Abbott, *The Republican Party and the South, 1855–1877* (1986); Michael Les Benedict, *A Compromise of Principle: Congressional Republicans and Reconstruction, 1863–1869* (1974); Dan T. Carter, *When the War Was Over: The Failure of Self-Reconstruction in the South* (1985); Richard N. Current, *Those Terrible Carpetbaggers* (1988); David Donald, *The Politics of Reconstruction* (1965); William Gillette, *Retreat from Reconstruction, 1869–1879* (1979); Thomas Holt, *Black over White: Negro Political Leadership in South Carolina During Reconstruction* (1977); William McFeeley, *Grant: A Biography* (1981); Edward A. Miller, *Gullah Statesman: Robert Smalls from Slavery to Congress, 1839–1915* (1995); George C. Rable, *But There Was No Peace: The Role of Violence in the Politics of Reconstruction* (1984); Brooks D. Simpson, *Let Us Have Peace: Ulysses S. Grant and the Politics of War and Reconstruction, 1861–1868* (1991); Hans L. Trefousse, *Thaddeus Stevens: Nineteenth-Century Egalitarian* (1997); Allen Trelease, *Andrew Johnson: A Biography* (1989); Richard Zuczek, *State of Rebellion: Reconstruction in South Carolina* 1996).

Race Relations and the Literature of Reconstruction

W. Fitzhugh Brundage, *Lynching in the New South: Georgia and Virginia, 1880–1930* (1993); Thomas Dixon, *The Clansman* (1905); W. E. B. Du Bois, *The Quest of the Silver Fleece* (1911); Howard Fast, *Freedom Road* (1944); Albion Tourgée, *A Fool's Errand* (1879); Joel Williamson, *The Crucible of Race* (1984) and *A Rage for Order: Black/White Relations in the American South Since Emancipation* (1986); C. Vann Woodward, *The Strange Career of Jim Crow*, 3d rev. ed. (1974).

Appendix

The Declaration of Independence In Congress, July 4, 1776

THE UNANIMOUS DECLARATION OF THE THIRTEEN UNITED STATES OF AMERICA

When, in the course of human events, it becomes necessary for one people to dissolve the political bonds which have connected them with another, and to assume, among the powers of the earth, the separate and equal station to which the laws of nature and of nature's God entitle them, a decent respect to the opinions of mankind requires that they should declare the causes which impel them to the separation.

We hold these truths to be self-evident: That all men are created equal; that they are endowed by their Creator with certain unalienable rights; that among these are life, liberty, and the pursuit of happiness; that, to secure these rights, governments are instituted among men, deriving their just powers from the consent of the governed; that whenever any form of government becomes destructive of these ends, it is the right of the people to alter or to abolish it, and to institute new government, laying its foundation on such principles, and organizing its powers in such form, as to them shall seem most likely to effect their safety and happiness. Prudence, indeed, will dictate that governments long established should not be changed for light and transient causes; and accordingly all experience hath shown that mankind are more disposed to suffer, while evils are sufferable, than to right themselves by abolishing the forms to which they are accustomed. But when a long train of abuses and usurpations, pursuing invariably the same object, evinces a design to reduce them under absolute depotism, it is their right, it is their duty, to throw off such government, and to provide new guards for their future security. Such has been the patient sufferance of these colonies; and such is now the necessity which constrains them to alter their former systems of government. The history of the present King of Great Britain is a history of repeated injuries and usurpations, all having in direct object the establishment of an absolute tyranny over these states. To prove this, let facts be submitted to a candid world.

He has refused his assent to laws, the most wholesome and necessary for the public good.

He has forbidden his governors to pass laws of immediate and pressing importance, unless suspended in their operation till his assent should be obtained; and, when so suspended, he has utterly neglected to attend to them.

He has refused to pass other laws for the accommodation of large districts of people, unless those people would relinquish the right of representation in the legislature, a right inestimable to them, and formidable to tyrants only.

He has called together legislative bodies at places unusual, uncomfortable, and distant from the depository of their public records, for the sole purpose of fatiguing them into compliance with his measures.

He has dissolved representative houses repeatedly, for opposing, with manly firmness, his invasions on the rights of the people.

He has refused for a long time, after such dissolutions, to cause others to be elected; whereby the legislative powers, incapable of annihilation, have returned to the people at large for their exercise; the state remaining, in the mean time, exposed to all the dangers of invasions from without and convulsions within.

He has endeavored to prevent the population of these states; for that purpose obstructing the laws for naturalization of foreigners; refusing to pass others to encourage their migration hither, and raising the conditions of new appropriations of lands.

He has obstructed the administration of justice, by refusing his assent to laws for establishing judiciary powers.

He has made judges dependent on his will alone, for the tenure of their offices, and the amount and payment of their salaries.

He has erected a multitude of new offices, and sent hither swarms of officers to harass our people and eat out their substance.

He has kept among us, in times of peace, standing armies, without the consent of our legislatures.

He has affected to render the military independent of, and superior to, the civil power.

He has combined with others to subject us to a jurisdiction foreign to our constitution, and unacknowledged by our laws, giving his assent to their acts of pretended legislation:

For quartering large bodies of armed troops among us;

For protecting them, by a mock trial, from punishment for any murder which they should commit on the inhabitants of these states;

For cutting off our trade with all parts of the world;

For imposing taxes on us without our consent;

For depriving us, in many cases, of the benefits of trial by jury;

For transporting us beyond seas, to be tried for pretended offenses;

For abolishing the free system of English laws in a neighboring province, establishing therein an arbitrary government, and enlarging its boundaries, so as to render it at once an example and fit instrument for introducing the same absolute rule into these colonies;

For taking away our charters abolishing our most valuable laws, and altering fundamentally the forms of our governments;

For suspending our own legislatures, and declaring themselves invested with power to legislate for us in all cases whatsoever.

He has abdicated government here, by declaring us out of his protection and waging war against us.

He has plundered our seas, ravaged our coasts, burned our towns, and destroyed the lives of our people.

He is at this time transporting large armies of foreign mercenaries to complete the works of death, desolation, and tyranny already begun with circumstances of cruelty and perfidy scarcely paralleled in the most barbarous ages, and totally unworthy the head of a civilized nation.

He has constrained our fellow-citizens, taken captive on the high seas, to bear arms against their country, to become the executioners of their friends and brethren, or to fall themselves by their hands.

He has excited domestic insurrection among us, and has endeavored to bring on the inhabitants of our frontiers the merciless Indian savages, whose known rule of warfare is an undistinguished destruction of all ages, sexes, and conditions.

In every stage of these oppressions we have petitioned for redress in the most humble terms; our repeated petitions have been answered only by repeated injury. A prince, whose character is thus marked by every act which may define a tyrant, is unfit to be the ruler of a free people.

Nor have we been wanting in our attentions to our British brethren. We have warned them, from time to time, of attempts by their legislature to extend an unwarrantable jurisdiction over us. We have reminded them of the circumstances of our emigration and settlement here. We have appealed to their native justice and magnanimity; and we have conjured them, by the ties of our common kindred, to disavow these usurpations, which would inevitably interrupt our connections and correspondence. They, too, have been deaf to the voice of justice and of consanguinity. We must, therefore, acquiesce in the necessity which denounces our separation, and hold them, as we hold the rest of mankind, enemies in war, in peace friends.

We, therefore, the representatives of the United States of America, in General Congress assembled, appealing to the Supreme Judge of the world for the rectitude of our intentions, do, in the name and by the authority of the good people of these colonies, solemnly publish and declare, that these United Colonies are, and of right, ought to be, FREE AND INDEPENDENT STATES; that they are absolved from all allegiance to the British crown, and that all political connection between them and the state of Great Britain is, and ought to be, totally dissolved; and that, as free and independent states, they have full power to levy war, conclude peace, contract alliances, establish commerce, and do all other acts and things which independent states may of right do. And for the support of this declaration, with a firm reliance on the protection of Devine Providence, we mutually pledge to each other our lives, our fortunes, and our sacred honor.

JOHN HANCOCK

BUTTON GWENNETT	THS. NELSON, JR.	RICHD. STOCKTON
LYMAN HALL	FRANCIS LIGHTFOOT LEE	JNO. WITHERSPOON
GEO. WALTON	CARTER BRAXTON	FRAS. HOPKINSON
WM. HOOPER	ROBT. MORRIS	JOHN HART
JOSEPH HEWES	BENJAMIN RUSH	ABRA. CLARK
JOHN PENN	BENJA. FRANKLIN	JOSIAH BARTLETT
EDWARD RUTLEDGE	JOHN MORTON	WM. WHIPPLE
THOS. HEYWARD, JUNR.	GEO. CLYMER	SAML. ADAMS
THOMAS LYNCH, JUNR.	JAS. SMITH	JOHN ADAMS
ARTHUR MIDDLETON	GEO. TAYLOR	ROBT. TREAT PAINE
SAMUEL CHASE	JAMES WILSON	ELBRIDGE GERRY
WM. PACA	GEO. ROSS	STEP. HOPKINS
THOS. STONE	CAESAR RODNEY	WILLIAM ELLERY
CHARLES CARROLL OF CARROLLTON	GEO. READ	ROGER SHERMAN
GEORGE WYTHE	THO. MiKEAN	SAMiEL. HUNTINGTON
RICHARD HENRY LEE	WM. FLOYD	WM. WILLIAMS
TH. JEFFERSON	PHIL. LIVINGSTON	OLIVER WOLCOTT
BENJA. HARRISON	FRANS. LEWIS	MATHEW THORNTON
	LEWIS MORRIS	

The Constitution of the United States of America

PREAMBLE

We the People of the United States, in Order to form a more perfect Union, establish Justice, insure domestic Tranquility, provide for the common defence, promote the general Welfare, and secure the Blessings of Liberty to ourselves and our Posterity, do ordain and establish this Constitution for the United States of America.

ARTICLE I.

Section 1 All legislative Powers herein granted shall be vested in a Congress of the United States, which shall consist of a Senate and House of Representatives.

Section 2 The House of Representatives shall be composed of Members chosen every second Year by the People of the several States, and the Electors in each State shall have the Qualifications requisite for Electors of the most numerous Branch of the State Legislature.

No Person shall be a Representative who shall not have attained to the Age of twenty five Years, and been seven Years a Citizen of the United States, and who shall not, when elected, be an Inhabitant of that State in which he shall be chosen.

Representatives and direct Taxes shall be apportioned among the several States which may be included within this Union, according to their respective Numbers, *which shall be determined by adding to the whole Number of free Persons, including those bound to Service for a Term of Years, and excluding Indians not taxed, three fifths of all other Persons.* The actual Enumeration shall be made within three Years after the first Meeting of the Congress of the United States, and within every subsequent Term of ten Years, in such Manner as they shall by Law direct. The Number of Representatives shall not exceed one for every thirty Thousand, but each State shall have at Least one Representative; *and until such enumeration shall be made, the State of New Hampshire shall be entitled to chuse three, Massachusetts eight, Rhode-Island and Providence Plantations one, Connecticut five, New-York six, New Jersey four, Pennsylvania eight, Delaware one, Maryland six, Virginia ten, North Carolina five, South Carolina five, and Georgia three.*

When vacancies happen in the Representation from any State, the Executive Authority thereof shall issue Writs of Election to fill such Vacancies.

The House of Representatives shall chuse their Speaker and other Officers; and shall have the sole Power of Impeachment.

Section 3 The Senate of the United States shall be composed of two Senators from each State, chosen by the Legislature thereof, for six Years; and each Senator shall have one Vote.

Immediately after they shall be assembled in Consequence of the first Election, they shall be divided as equally as may be into three Classes. The Seats of the Senators of the first Class shall be vacated at the Expiration of the second Year, of the second Class at the Expiration of the fourth Year, and of the third Class at the Expiration of the sixth Year, so that one third may be chosen every second Year; and if Vacancies happen by Resignation, or otherwise, during the Recess of the Legislature of any State, the Executive thereof may make temporary Appointments until the next Meeting of the Legislature, which shall then fill such Vacancies.

No Person shall be a Senator who shall not have attained to the Age of thirty Years, and been nine Years a Citizen of the United States, and who shall not, when elected, be an Inhabitant of that State for which he shall be chosen.

The Vice President of the United States shall be President of the Senate, but shall have no Vote, unless they be equally divided.

The Senate shall choose their other Officers, and also a President *pro tempore*, in the Absence of the Vice President, or when he shall exercise the Office of President of the United States.

The Senate shall have the sole Power to try all Impeachments. When sitting for that Purpose, they shall be on Oath or Affirmation. When the President of the United States is tried the Chief Justice shall preside: And no Person shall be convicted without the Concurrence of two thirds of the Members present.

Judgment in Cases of Impeachment shall not extend further than to removal from Office, and disqualification to hold and enjoy any Office of honor, Trust or Profit under the United States: but the Party convicted shall nevertheless be liable and subject to Indictment, Trial, Judgment and Punishment, according to Law.

Section 4 The Times, Places and Manner of holding Elections for Senators and Representatives, shall be prescribed in each State by the Legislature thereof; but the Congress may at any time by Law make or alter such Regulations, except as to the Places of chusing Senators.

The Congress shall assemble at least once in every Year, and such Meeting *shall be on the first Monday in December, unless they shall by Law appoint a different Day.*

Section 5 Each House shall be the Judge of the Elections, Returns and Qualifications of its own Members, and a Majority of each shall constitute a Quorum to do Business; but a smaller Number may adjourn from day to day, and may be authorized to compel the Attendance of absent Members, in such Manner, and under such Penalties as each House may provide.

Each House may determine the Rules of its Proceedings, punish its Members for disorderly Behaviour, and, with the Concurrence of two thirds, expel a Member.

Each House shall keep a Journal of its Proceedings, and from time to time publish the same, excepting such Parts as may in their Judgment require Secrecy; and the Yeas and Nays of the Members of either House on any question shall, at the Desire of one fifth of those Present, be entered on the Journal.

Neither House, during the Session of Congress, shall, without the Consent of the other, adjourn for more than three days, nor to any other Place than that in which the two Houses shall be sitting.

Section 6 The Senators and Representatives shall receive a Compensation for their Services, to be ascertained by Law, and paid out of the Treasury of the United States. They shall in all Cases, except Treason, Felony and Breach of the Peace, be privileged from Arrest during their Attendance at the Session of their respective Houses, and in going to and returning from the same; and for any Speech or Debate in either House, they shall not be questioned in any other Place.

No Senator or Representative shall, during the Time for which he was elected, be appointed to any civil Office under the Authority of the United States, which shall have been created, or the Emoluments whereof shall have been encreased during such time; and no Person holding any Office under the United States, shall be a Member of either House during his Continuance in Office.

Section 7   All Bills for raising Revenue shall originate in the House of Representatives; but the Senate may propose or concur with Amendments as on other Bills.

Every Bill which shall have passed the House of Representatives and the Senate, shall, before it become a Law, be presented to the President of the United States; If he approve he shall sign it, but if not he shall return it, with his Objections to that House in which it shall have originated, who shall enter the Objections at large on their Journal, and proceed to reconsider it. If after such Reconsideration two thirds of that House shall agree to pass the Bill, it shall be sent, together with the Objections, to the other House, by which it shall likewise be reconsidered, and if approved by two thirds of that House, it shall become a Law. But in all such Cases the Votes of both Houses shall be determined by yeas and Nays, and the Names of the Persons voting for and against the Bill shall be entered on the Journal of each House respectively. If any Bill shall not be returned by the President within ten Days (Sundays excepted) after it shall have been presented to him, the Same shall be a Law, in like Manner as if he had signed it, unless the Congress by their Adjournment prevent its Return, in which Case it shall not be a Law.

Every Order, Resolution, or Vote to which the Concurrence of the Senate and House of Representatives may be necessary (except on a question of Adjournment) shall be presented to the President of the United States; and before the Same shall take Effect, shall be approved by him, or being disapproved by him, shall be repassed by two thirds of the Senate and House of Representatives, according to the Rules and Limitations prescribed in the Case of a Bill.

Section 8   The Congress shall have Power:

To lay and collect Taxes, Duties, Imposts and Excises, to pay the Debts and provide for the common Defence and general Welfare of the United States; but all Duties, Imposts and Excises shall be uniform throughout the United States;

To borrow Money on the credit of the United States;

To regulate Commerce with foreign Nations, and among the several States, and with the Indian Tribes;

To establish an uniform Rule of Naturalization, and uniform Laws on the subject of Bankruptcies throughout the United States;

To coin Money, regulate the Value thereof, and of foreign Coin, and fix the Standard of Weights and Measures;

To provide for the Punishment of counterfeiting the Securities and current Coin of the United States;

To establish Post Offices and post Roads;

To promote the Progress of Science and useful Arts, by securing for limited Times to Authors and Inventors the exclusive Right to their respective Writings and Discoveries;

To constitute Tribunals inferior to the supreme Court;

To define and punish Piracies and Felonies committed on the high Seas, and Offences against the Law of Nations;

To declare War, grant Letters of Marque and Reprisal, and make Rules concerning Captures on Land and Water;

To raise and support Armies, but no Appropriation of Money to that Use shall be for a longer Term than two Years;

To provide and maintain a Navy;

To make Rules for the Government and Regulation of the land and naval Forces;

To provide for calling forth the Militia to execute the Laws of the Union, suppress Insurrections and repel Invasions;

To provide for organizing, arming, and disciplining, the Militia, and for governing such Part of them as may be employed in the Service of the United States, reserving to the States respectively, the Appointment of the Officers, and the Authority of training the Militia according to the discipline prescribed by Congress;

To exercise exclusive Legislation in all Cases whatsoever, over such District (not exceeding ten Miles square) as may, by Cession of particular States, and the Acceptance of Congress, become the Seat of the Government of the United States, and to exercise like Authority over all Places purchased by the Consent of the Legislature of the State in which the Same shall be, for the Erection of Forts, Magazines, Arsenals, dock-Yards, and other needful Buildings;—And

To make all Laws which shall be necessary and proper for carrying into Execution the foregoing Powers, and all other Powers vested by this Constitution in the Government of the United States, or in any Department or Officer thereof.

Section 9 *The Migration or Importation of such Persons as any of the States now existing shall think proper to admit, shall not be prohibited by the Congress prior to the Year one thousand eight hundred and eight, but a Tax or duty may be imposed on such Importation, not exceeding ten dollars for each Person.*

The Privilege of the Writ of Habeas Corpus shall not be suspended, unless when in Cases of Rebellion or Invasion the public Safety may require it.

No Bill of Attainder or ex post facto Law shall be passed.

No Capitation, or other direct, Tax shall be laid, unless in Proportion to the Census or Enumeration herein before directed to be taken.

No Tax or Duty shall be laid on Articles exported from any State.

No Preference shall be given by any Regulation of Commerce or Revenue to the Ports of one State over those of another: nor shall Vessels bound to, or from, one State, be obliged to enter, clear, or pay Duties in another.

No Money shall be drawn from the Treasury, but in Consequence of Appropriations made by Law; and a regular Statement and Account of the Receipts and Expenditures of all public Money shall be published from time to time.

No Title of Nobility shall be granted by the United States: And no Person holding any Office of Profit or Trust under them, shall, without the Consent of the Congress, accept of any present, Emolument, Office, or Title, of any kind whatever, from any King, Prince, or foreign State.

Section 10 No State shall enter into any Treaty, Alliance, or Confederation; grant Letters of Marque and Reprisal; coin Money; emit Bills of Credit; make any Thing but gold and silver Coin a Tender in Payment of Debts; pass any Bill of Attainder, ex post facto Law, or Law impairing the Obligation of Contracts, or grant any Title of Nobility.

No State shall, without the Consent of the Congress, lay any Imposts or Duties on Imports or Exports, except what may be absolutely necessary for executing it's inspection Laws: and the net Produce of all Duties and Imposts, laid by any State on Imports or Exports, shall be for the Use of the Treasury of the United States; and all such Laws shall be subject to the Revision and Controul of the Congress.

No State shall, without the Consent of Congress, lay any Duty of Tonnage, keep Troops, or Ships of War in time of Peace, enter into any Agreement or Compact with another State, or with a foreign Power, or engage in War, unless actually invaded, or in such imminent Danger as will not admit of delay.

ARTICLE II.

Section 1   The executive Power shall be vested in a President of the United States of America. He shall hold his Office during the Term of four Years, and, together with the Vice President, chosen for the same Term, be elected, as follows

Each State shall appoint, in such Manner as the Legislature thereof may direct, a Number of Electors, equal to the whole Number of Senators and Representatives to which the State may be entitled in the Congress: but no Senator or Representative, or Person holding an Office of Trust or Profit under the United States, shall be appointed an Elector.

The Electors shall meet in their respective States, and vote by Ballot for two Persons, of whom one at least shall not be an Inhabitant of the same State with themselves. And they shall make a List of all the Persons voted for, and of the Number of Votes for each; which List they shall sign and certify, and transmit sealed to the Seat of Government of the United States, directed to the President of the Senate. The President of the Senate shall, in the Presence of the Senate and House of Representatives, open all the Certificates, and the Votes shall then be counted. The Person having the greatest Number of Votes shall be the President, if such Number be a Majority of the whole Number of Electors appointed; and if there be more than one who have such Majority, and have an equal Number of Votes, then the House of Representatives shall immediately chuse by Ballot one of them for President; and if no Person have a Majority, then from the five highest on the List the said House shall in like Manner chuse the President. But in chusing the President, the Votes shall be taken by States, the Representation from each State having one Vote; A quorum for this Purpose shall consist of a Member or Members from two thirds of the States, and a Majority of all the States shall be necessary to a Choice. In every Case, after the Choice of the President, the Person having the greatest Number of Votes of the Electors shall be the Vice President. But if there should remain two or more who have equal Votes, the Senate shall chuse from them by Ballot the Vice President.

The Congress may determine the Time of chusing the Electors, and the Day on which they shall give their Votes; which Day shall be the same throughout the United States.

No Person except a natural born Citizen, *or a Citizen of the United States, at the time of the Adoption of this Constitution,* shall be eligible to the Office of President; neither shall any Person be eligible to that Office who shall not have attained to the Age of thirty five Years, and been fourteen Years a Resident within the United States.

In Case of the Removal of the President from Office, or of his Death, Resignation, or Inability to discharge the Powers and Duties of the said Office, the Same shall devolve on the Vice President, and the Congress may by Law provide for the Case of Removal, Death, Resignation or Inability, both of the President and Vice President declaring what Officer shall then act as President, and such Officer shall act accordingly, until the Disability be removed, or a President shall be elected.

The President shall, at stated Times, receive for his Services, a Compensation, which shall neither be encreased nor diminished during the Period for which he shall have been elected, and he shall not receive within that Period any other Emolument from the United States, or any of them.

Before he enter on the Execution of his Office, he shall take the following Oath or Affirmation: "I do solemnly swear (or affirm) that I will faithfully execute the Office of President of the United States, and will to the best of my Ability, preserve, protect and defend the Constitution of the United States."

Section 2   The President shall be Commander in Chief of the Army and Navy of the United States, and of the Militia of the several States, when called into the actual Service of the United States; he may require the Opinion, in writing, of the principal Officer in each of the executive Departments, upon any Subject relating to the Duties of their respective Offices, and he shall have Power to grant Reprieves and Pardons for Offences against the United States, except in Cases of Impeachment.

He shall have Power, by and with the Advice and Consent of the Senate, to make Treaties, provided two thirds of the Senators present concur; and he shall nominate, and by and with the Advice and Consent of the Senate, shall appoint Ambassadors, other public Ministers and Consuls, Judges of the supreme Court, and all other Officers of the United States, whose Appointments are not herein otherwise provided for, and which shall be established by Law: but the Congress may by Law vest the Appointment of such inferior Officers, as they think proper, in the President alone, in the Courts of Law, or in the Heads of Departments.

The President shall have Power to fill up all Vacancies that may happen during the Recess of the Senate, by granting Commissions which shall expire at the End of their next Session.

Section 3   He shall from time to time give to the Congress Information of the State of the Union, and recommend to their Consideration such Measures as he shall judge necessary and expedient; he may, on extraordinary Occasions, convene both Houses, or either of them, and in Case of Disagreement between them, with Respect to the Time of Adjournment, he may adjourn them to such Time as he shall think proper; he shall receive Ambassadors and other public Ministers; he shall take Care that the Laws be faithfully executed, and shall Commission all the Officers of the United States.

Section 4   The President, Vice President and all civil Officers of the United States, shall be removed from Office on Impeachment for, and Conviction of, Treason, Bribery, or other high Crimes and Misdemeanors.

ARTICLE III.

Section 1   The judicial Power of the United States, shall be vested in one supreme Court, and in such inferior Courts as the Congress may from time to time ordain and establish. The Judges, both of the supreme and inferior Courts, shall hold their Offices during good Behaviour, and shall, at stated Times, receive for their Services, a Compensation which shall not be diminished during their Continuance in Office.

Section 2 The judicial Power shall extend to all Cases, in Law and Equity, arising under this Constitution, the Laws of the United States, and Treaties made, or which shall be made, under their Authority;—to all Cases affecting Ambassadors, other public Ministers and Consuls;— to all Cases of admiralty and maritime Jurisdiction;—to Controversies to which the United States shall be a Party;—to Controversies between two or more States;—*between a State and Citizens of another State;*—between Citizens of different States;—between Citizens of the same State claiming Lands under Grants of different States, and between a State, or the Citizens thereof, and foreign States, Citizens or Subjects.

In all Cases affecting Ambassadors, other public Ministers and Consuls, and those in which a State shall be Party, the supreme Court shall have original Jurisdiction. In all the other Cases before mentioned, the supreme Court shall have appellate Jurisdiction, both as to Law and Fact, with such Exceptions, and under such Regulations as the Congress shall make.

The Trial of all Crimes, except in Cases of Impeachment, shall be by Jury; and such Trial shall be held in the State where the said Crimes shall have been committed; but when not committed within any State, the Trial shall be at such Place or Places as the Congress may by Law have directed.

Section 3 Treason against the United States, shall consist only in levying War against them, or in adhering to their Enemies, giving them Aid and Comfort. No Person shall be convicted of Treason unless on the Testimony of two Witnesses to the same overt Act, or on Confession in open Court.

The Congress shall have Power to declare the Punishment of Treason, but no Attainder of Treason shall work Corruption of Blood, or Forfeiture except during the Life of the Person attainted.

ARTICLE IV

Section 1 Full Faith and Credit shall be given in each State to the public Acts, Records, and judicial Proceedings of every other State. And the Congress may by general Laws prescribe the Manner in which such Acts, Records and Proceedings shall be proved, and the Effect thereof.

Section 2 The Citizens of each State shall be entitled to all Privileges and Immunities of Citizens in the several States.

A Person charged in any State with Treason, Felony, or other Crime, who shall flee from Justice, and be found in another State, shall on Demand of the executive Authority of the State from which he fled, be delivered up, to be removed to the State having Jurisdiction of the Crime.

No Person held to Service or Labour in one State, under the Laws thereof, escaping into another, shall, in Consequence of any Law or Regulation therein, be discharged from such Service or Labour, but shall be delivered up on Claim of the Party to whom such Service or Labour may be due.

Section 3 New States may be admitted by the Congress into this Union; but no new State shall be formed or erected within the Jurisdiction of any other State; nor any State be formed by the Junction of two or more States, or Parts of States, without the Consent of the Legislatures of the States concerned as well as of the Congress.

The Congress shall have Power to dispose of and make all needful Rules and Regulations respecting the Territory or other Property belonging to the United States; and nothing in this Constitution shall be so construed as to Prejudice any Claims of the United States, or of any particular State.

Section 4 The United States shall guarantee to every State in this Union a Republican Form of Government, and shall protect each of them against Invasion; and on Application of the Legislature, or of the Executive (when the Legislature cannot be convened) against domestic Violence.

ARTICLE V

The Congress, whenever two thirds of both Houses shall deem it necessary, shall propose Amendments to this Constitution, or, on the Application of the Legislatures of two thirds of the several States, shall call a Convention for proposing Amendments, which, in either Case, shall be valid to all Intents and Purposes, as Part of this Constitution, when ratified by the Legislatures of three fourths of the several States, or by Conventions in three fourths thereof, as the one or the other Mode of Ratification may be proposed by the Congress; Provided *that no Amendment which may be made prior to the Year One thousand eight hundred and eight shall in any Manner affect the first and fourth Clauses in the Ninth Section of the first Article; and* that no State, without its Consent, shall be deprived of its equal Suffrage in the Senate.

ARTICLE VI

All Debts contracted and Engagements entered into, before the Adoption of this Constitution, shall be as valid against the United States under this Constitution, as under the Confederation.

This Constitution, and the Laws of the United States which shall be made in Pursuance thereof; and all Treaties made or which shall be made, under the Authority of the United States, shall be the supreme Law of the Land; and the Judges in every State shall be bound thereby, any Thing in the Constitution or Laws of any State to the Contrary notwithstanding.

The Senators and Representatives before mentioned, and the Members of the several State Legislatures, and all executive and judicial Officers, both of the United States and of the several States, shall be bound by Oath or Affirmation, to support this Constitution; but no religious Test shall ever be required as a Qualification to any Office or public Trust under the United States.

ARTICLE VII

The Ratification of the Conventions of nine States, shall be sufficient for the Establishment of this Constitution between the States so ratifying the Same.

Done in Convention by the Unanimous Consent of the States present the Seventeenth Day of September in the Year of our Lord one thousand seven hundred and Eighty seven and of the Independence of the United States of America the Twelfth. IN WITNESS whereof We have hereunto subscribed our Names,

GEORGE WASHINGTON,
President and Deputy from Virginia

North Carolina WILLIAM BLOUNT RICHARD DOBBS SPRAIGHT HU WILLIAMSON	*Delaware* GEORGE READ GUNNING BEDFORD, JR. JOHN DICKINSON RICHARD BASSETT JACOB BROOM	*New Jersey* WILLIAM LIVINGSTON DAVID BREARLEY WILLIAM PATERSON JONATHAN DAYTON	*Connecticut* WILLIAM S. JOHNSON ROGER SHERMAN
Pennsylvania BENJAMIN FRANKLIN THOMAS MIFFLIN ROVERT MORRIS GEORGE CLYMER THOMAS FITZSIMONS JARED INGERSOLL JAMES WILSON GOUVERNEUR MORRIS	*South Carolina* J. RUTLEDGE CHARLES C. PINCKNEY PIERCE BUTLER *Virginia* JOHN BLAIR JAMES MADISON, JR.	*Maryland* JAMES MCHENRY DANIEL OF ST. THOMAS JENIFER DANIEL CARROLL *Massachusetts* NATHANIEL GORHAM RUFUS KING	*New York* ALEXANDER HAMILTON *New Hampshire* JOHN LANGDON NICHOLAS GILMAN *Georgia* WILLIAM FEW ABRAHAM BALDWIN

AMENDMENTS TO THE CONSTITUTION*

*The first ten amendments (the Bill of Rights) were adopted in 1791.

Amendment I
Congress shall make no law respecting an establishment of religion, or prohibiting the free exercise thereof; or abridging the freedom of speech, or of the press; or the right of the people peaceably to assemble, and to petition the Government for a redress of grievances.

Amendment II
A well regulated Militia, being necessary to the security of a free State, the right of the people to keep and bear Arms, shall not be infringed.

Amendment III
No Soldier shall, in time of peace be quartered in any house, without the consent of the Owner, nor in time of war, but in a manner to be prescribed by law.

Amendment IV
The right of the people to be secure in their persons, houses, papers, and effects, against unreasonable searches and seizures, shall not be violated, and no Warrants shall issue, but upon probable cause, supported by Oath or affirmation, and particularly describing the place to be searched, and the persons or things to be seized.

Amendment V
No person shall be held to answer for a capital, or otherwise infamous crime, unless on a presentment or indictment of a Grand Jury, except in cases arising in the land or naval forces, or in the Militia, when in actual service in time of War or public danger; nor shall any person be subject for the same offence to be twice put in jeopardy of life or limb; nor shall be compelled in any criminal case to be a witness against himself, nor be deprived of life, liberty, or property, without due process of law; nor shall private property be taken for public use, without just compensation.

Amendment VI

In all criminal prosecutions, the accused shall enjoy the right to a speedy and public trial, by an impartial jury of the State and district wherein the crime shall have been committed, which district shall have been previously ascertained by law, and to be informed of the nature and cause of the accusation; to be confronted with the witnesses against him; to have compulsory process for obtaining witnesses in his favor, and to have the Assistance of Counsel for his defence.

Amendment VII

In Suits at common law, where the value in controversy shall exceed twenty dollars, the right of trial by jury shall be preserved, and no fact tried by a jury, shall be otherwise re-examined in any Court of the United States, than according to the rules of the common law.

Amendment VIII

Excessive bail shall not be required, nor excessive fines imposed, nor cruel and unusual punishments inflicted.

Amendment IX

The enumeration in the Constitution, of certain rights, shall not be construed to deny or disparage others retained by the people.

Amendment X

The powers not delegated to the United States by the Constitution, nor prohibited by it to the States, are reserved to the States respectively, or to the people.

Amendment XI [Adopted 1798]

The Judicial power of the United States shall not be construed to extend to any suit in law or equity, commenced or prosecuted against one of the United States by Citizens of another State, or by Citizens or Subjects of any Foreign State.

Amendment XII [Adopted 1804]

The Electors shall meet in their respective states, and vote by ballot for President and Vice-President, one of whom, at least, shall not be an inhabitant of the same state with themselves; they shall name in their ballots the person voted for as President, and in distinct ballots the person voted for as Vice-President, and they shall make distinct lists of all persons voted for as President, and of all persons voted for as Vice-President, and of the number of votes for each, which list they shall sign and certify, and transmit sealed to the seat of the government of the United States, directed to the President of the Senate;—The President of the Senate shall, in the presence of the Senate and House of Representatives, open all the certificates and the votes shall then be counted;—The person having the greatest number of votes for President, shall be the President, if such number be a majority of the whole number of Electors appointed; and if no person have such majority, then from the persons having the highest numbers not exceeding three on the list of those voted for as President, the House of Representatives shall choose immediately, by ballot, the President. But in choosing the President, the votes shall be taken by states, the representation from each state having one vote; a quorum for this purpose shall consist of a member or members from two thirds of the states, and a majority of all the states shall be necessary to a choice. And if the House of Representatives shall not choose a President whenever the right of choice shall devolve upon them, before *the fourth day of March* next following, then the Vice-President shall act as President, as in the case of the death or other constitutional disability of the President.

The person having the greatest number of votes as Vice-President, shall be the Vice-President, if such number be a majority of the whole number of Electors appointed, and if no person have a majority, then from the two highest numbers on the list, the Senate shall choose the Vice-President; a quorum for the purpose shall consist of two thirds of the whole number of Senators, and a majority of the whole number shall be necessary to a choice. But no person constitutionally ineligible to the office of President shall be eligible to that of Vice-President of the United States.

Amendment XIII [Adopted 1865]

Section 1   Neither slavery nor involuntary servitude, except as a punishment for crime whereof the party shall have been duly convicted, shall exist within the United States, or any place subject to their jurisdiction.

Section 2   Congress shall have power to enforce this article by appropriate legislation.

Amendment XIV [Adopted 1868]

Section 1   All persons born or naturalized in the United States, and subject to the jurisdiction thereof, are citizens of the United States and of the State wherein they reside. No State shall make or enforce any law which shall abridge the privileges or immunities of citizens of the United States; nor shall any State deprive any person of life, liberty, or property, without due process of law; nor deny to any person within its jurisdiction the equal protection of the laws.

Section 2   Representatives shall be apportioned among the several States according to their respective numbers, counting the whole number of persons in each State, excluding Indians not taxed. But when the right to vote at any election for the choice of electors for President and Vice-President of the United States, Representatives in Congress, the Executive and Judicial officers of a State, or the members of the Legislature thereof, is denied to any of the male inhabitants of such State, being twenty-one years of age, and citizens of the United States, or in any way abridged, except for participation in rebellion, or other crime, the basis of representation therein shall be reduced in the proportion which the number of such male citizens shall bear to the whole number of male citizens twenty-one years of age in such State.

Section 3   No person shall be a Senator or Representative in Congress, or elector of President and Vice-President, or hold any office, civil or military, under the United States, or under any State, who, having previously taken an oath, as a member of Congress, or as an officer of the United States, or as a member of any State legislature, or as an executive or judicial officer of any State, to support the Constitution of the United States, shall have engaged in insurrection or rebellion against the same, or given aid or comfort to the enemies thereof. But Congress may by a vote of two thirds of each House, remove such disability.

Section 4   The validity of the public debt of the United States, authorized by law, including debts incurred for payment of pensions and bounties for services in suppressing insurrection or rebellion, shall not be questioned. But neither the

United States nor any State shall assume or pay any debt or obligation incurred in aid of insurrection or rebellion against the United States, or any claim for the loss or emancipation of any slave; but all such debts, obligations and claims shall be held illegal and void.

Section 5 The Congress shall have power to enforce, by appropriate legislation, the provisions of this article.

Amendment XV [Adopted 1870]

Section 1 The right of citizens of the United States to vote shall not be denied or abridged by the United States or by any State on account of race, color, or previous condition of servitude.

Section 2 The Congress shall have power to enforce this article by appropriate legislation.

Amendment XVI [Adopted 1913]

The Congress shall have power to lay and collect taxes on incomes, from whatever source derived, without apportionment among the several States, and without regard to any census or enumeration.

Amendment XVII [Adopted 1913]

The Senate of the United States shall be composed of two Senators from each State, elected by the people thereof, for six years; and each Senator shall have one vote. The electors in each State shall have the qualifications requisite for electors of the most numerous branch of the State legislatures.

When vacancies happen in the representation of any State in the Senate, the executive authority of such State shall issue writs of election to fill such vacancies: *Provided,* That the legislature of any State may empower the executive thereof to make temporary appointments until the people fill the vacancies by election as the legislature may direct.

This amendment shall not be so construed as to affect the election or term of any Senator chosen before it becomes valid as part of the Constitution.

Amendment XVIII [Adopted 1919; Repealed 1933]

Section 1 After one year from the ratification of this article the manufacture, sale, or transportation of intoxicating liquors within, the importation thereof into, or the exportation thereof from the United States and all territory subject to the jurisdiction thereof for beverage purposes is hereby prohibited.

Section 2 The Congress and the several States shall have concurrent power to enforce this article by appropriate legislation.

Section 3 This article shall be inoperative unless it shall have been ratified as an amendment to the Constitution by the legislatures of the several States, as provided in the Constitution, within seven years from the date of the submission hereof to the States by the Congress.

Amendment XIX [Adopted 1920]

Section 1 The right of citizens of the United States to vote shall not be denied or abridged by the United States or by any State on account of sex.

Section 2 Congress shall have power to enforce this article by appropriate legislation.

Amendment XX [Adopted 1933]

Section 1 The terms of the President and Vice-President shall end at noon on the 20th day of January, and the terms of Senators and Representatives at noon on the third day of January, of the years in which such terms would have ended if this article had not been ratified; and the terms of their successors shall then begin.

Section 2 The Congress shall assemble at least once in every year, and such meeting shall begin at noon on the third day of January, unless they shall by law appoint a different day.

Section 3 If, at the time fixed for the beginning of the term of the President, the President elect shall have died, the Vice-President elect shall become President. If a President shall not have been chosen before the time fixed for the beginning of his term, or if the President elect shall have failed to qualify, then the Vice-President elect shall act as President until a President shall have qualified; and the Congress may by law provide for the case wherein neither a President elect nor a Vice-President elect shall have qualified, declaring who shall then act as President, or the manner in which one who is to act shall be selected, and such person shall act accordingly until a President or Vice-President shall have qualified.

Section 4 The Congress may by law provide for the case of the death of any of the persons from whom the House of Representatives may choose a President whenever the right of choice shall have devolved upon them, and for the case of the death of any of the persons from whom the Senate may choose a Vice-President whenever the right of choice shall have devolved upon them.

Section 5 Sections 1 and 2 shall take effect on the 15th day of October following the ratification of this article.

Section 6 This article shall be inoperative unless it shall have been ratified as an amendment to the Constitution by the legislatures of three fourths of the several States within seven years from the date of its submission.

Amendment XXI [Adopted 1933]

Section 1 The eighteenth article of amendment to the Constitution of the United States is hereby repealed.

Section 2 The transportation or importation into any State, Territory, or possession of the United States for delivery or use therein of intoxicating liquors, in violation of the laws thereof, is hereby prohibited.

Section 3 This article shall be inoperative unless it shall have been ratified as an amendment to the Constitution by conventions in the several States, as provided in the Constitution, within seven years from the date of the submission hereof to the States by the Congress.

Amendment XXII [Adopted 1951]

Section 1 No person shall be elected to the office of the President more than twice, and no person who has held the office of President, or acted as President, for more than two years of a term to which some other person was elected President shall be elected to the office of the President more than once. But this Article shall not apply to any person holding the office of President when this Article was proposed by the Congress, and shall not prevent any person who may be holding the office of President, or acting as President, during the term within which this Article becomes operative from holding the office of President or acting as President during the remainder of such term.

Section 2 This article shall be inoperative unless it shall have been ratified as an amendment to the Constitution by the legislatures of three fourths of the several States within seven years from the date of its submission to the States by the Congress.

Amendment XXIII [Adopted 1961]
Section 1 The District constituting the seat of Government of the United States shall appoint in such manner as the Congress may direct:

A number of electors of President and Vice-President equal to the whole number of Senators and Representatives in Congress to which the District would be entitled if it were a State, but in no event more than the least populous State; they shall be in addition to those appointed by the States, but they shall be considered, for the purposes of the election of President and Vice-President, to be electors appointed by a State; and they shall meet in the District and perform such duties as provided by the twelfth article of amendment.

Section 2 The Congress shall have power to enforce this article by appropriate legislation.

Amendment XXIV [Adopted 1964]
Section 1 The right of citizens of the United States to vote in any primary or other election for President or Vice-President, for electors for President or Vice-President, or for Senator or Representative in Congress, shall not be denied or abridged by the United States or any State by reason of failure to pay any poll tax or other tax.

Section 2 The Congress shall have power to enforce this article by appropriate legislation.

Amendment XXV [Adopted 1967]
Section 1 In case of the removal of the President from office or his death or resignation, the Vice-President shall become President.

Section 2 Whenever there is a vacancy in the office of the Vice-President, the President shall nominate a Vice-President who shall take the office upon confirmation by a majority vote of both houses of Congress.

Section 3 Whenever the President transmits to the President pro tempore of the Senate and the Speaker of the House of Representatives his written declaration that he is unable to discharge the powers and duties of his office, and until he transmits to them a written declaration to the contrary, such powers and duties shall be discharged by the Vice-President as Acting President.

Section 4 Whenever the Vice-President and a majority of either the principal officers of the executive departments, or of such other body as Congress may by law provide, transmit to the President pro tempore of the Senate and the Speaker of the House of Representatives their written declaration that the President is unable to discharge the powers and duties of his office, the Vice-President shall immediately assume the powers and duties of the office as Acting President.

Thereafter, when the President transmits to the President pro tempore of the Senate and the Speaker of the House of Representatives his written declaration that no inability exists, he shall resume the powers and duties of his office unless the Vice-President and a majority of either the principal officers of the executive department, or of such other body as Congress may by law provide, transmit within four days to the President pro tempore of the Senate and the Speaker of the House of Representatives their written declaration that the President is unable to discharge the powers and duties of his office. Thereupon Congress shall decide the issue, assembling within 48 hours for that purpose if not in session. If the Congress, within 21 days after receipt of the latter written declaration, or, if Congress is not in session, within 21 days after Congress is required to assemble, determines by two-thirds vote of both houses that the President is unable to discharge the powers and duties of his office, the Vice-President shall continue to discharge the same as Acting President; otherwise, the President shall resume the powers and duties of his office.

Amendment XXVI [Adopted 1971]
Section 1 The right of citizens of the United States, who are eighteen years of age or older, to vote shall not be denied or abridged by the United States or any state on account of age.

Section 2 The Congress shall have power to enforce this article by appropriate legislation.

Amendment XXVII [Adopted 1992]
No law, varying the compensation for the services of Senators and Representatives, shall take effect until an election of Representatives have intervened.

PRESIDENTIAL ELECTIONS

Year	Candidates	Parties	Popular Vote	Electoral Vote	Voter Participation
1789	GEORGE WASHINGTON		*	69	
	John Adams			34	
	Others			35	
1792	GEORGE WASHINGTON		*	132	
	John Adams			77	
	George Clinton			50	
	Others			5	
1796	JOHN ADAMS	Federalist	*	71	
	Thomas Jefferson	Democratic-Republican		68	
	Thomas Pinckney	Federalist		59	
	Aaron Burr	Dem.-Rep.		30	
	Others			48	

Year	Candidates	Parties	Popular Vote	Electoral Vote	Voter Participation
1800	THOMAS JEFFERSON	Dem.-Rep.	*	73	
	Aaron Burr	Dem.-Rep.		73	
	C. C. Pinckney	Federalist		64	
	John Jay	Federalist		1	
1804	THOMAS JEFFERSON	Dem.-Rep.	*	162	
	C. C. Pinckney	Federalist		14	
1808	JAMES MADISON	Dem.-Rep.	*	122	
	C. C. Pinckney	Federalist		47	
	George Clinton	Dem.-Rep.		6	
1812	JAMES MADISON	Dem.-Rep.	*	128	
	De Witt Clinton	Federalist		89	
1816	JAMES MONROE	Dem.-Rep.	*	183	
	Rufus King	Federalist		34	
1820	JAMES MONROE	Dem.-Rep.	*	231	
	John Quincy Adams	Dem.-Rep.		1	
1824	JOHN Q. ADAMS	Dem.-Rep.	108,740 (10.5%)	84	26.9%
	Andrew Jackson	Dem.-Rep.	153,544 (43.1%)	99	
	William H. Crawford	Dem.-Rep.	46,618 (13.1%)	41	
	Henry Clay	Dem.-Rep.	47,136 (13.2%)	37	
1828	ANDREW JACKSON	Democratic	647,286 (56.0%)	178	57.6%
	John Quincy Adams	National Republican	508,064 (44.0%)	83	
1832	ANDREW JACKSON	Democratic	687,502 (55.0%)	219	55.4%
	Henry Clay	National Republican	530,189 (42.4%)	49	
	John Floyd	Independent		11	
	William Wirt	Anti-Mason	33,108 (2.6%)	7	
1836	MARTIN VAN BUREN	Democratic	765,483 (50.9%)	170	57.8%
	W. H. Harrison	Whig		73	
	Hugh L. White	Whig	739,795 (49.1%)	26	
	Daniel Webster	Whig		14	
	W. P. Magnum	Independent		11	
1840	WILLIAM H. HARRISON	Whig	1,274,624 (53.1%)	234	80.2%
	Martin Van Buren	Democratic	1,127,781 (46.9%)	60	
	J. G. Birney	Liberty	7069	—	
1844	JAMES K. POLK	Democratic	1,338,464 (49.6%)	170	78.9%
	Henry Clay	Whig	1,300,097 (48.1%)	105	
	J. G. Birney	Liberty	62,300 (2.3%)	—	
1848	ZACHARY TAYLOR	Whig	1,360,967 (47.4%)	163	72.7%
	Lewis Cass	Democratic	1,222,342 (42.5%)	127	
	Martin Van Buren	Free-Soil	291,263 (10.1%)	—	
1852	FRANKLIN PIERCE	Democratic	1,601,117 (50.9%)	254	69.6%
	Winfield Scott	Whig	1,385,453 (44.1%)	42	
	John P. Hale	Free-Soil	155,825 (5.0%)	—	
1856	JAMES BUCHANAN	Democratic	1,832,955 (45.3%)	174	78.9%
	John C. Fremont	Republican	1,339,932 (33.1%)	114	
	Millard Fillmore	American	871,731 (21.6%)	8	
1860	ABRAHAM LINCOLN	Republican	1,865,593 (39.8%)	180	81.2%
	Stephen A. Douglas	Democratic	1,382,713 (29.5%)	12	
	John C. Breckinridge	Democratic	848,356 (18.1%)	72	
	John Bell	Union	592,906 (12.6%)	39	

Year	Candidates	Parties	Popular Vote	Electoral Vote	Voter Participation
1864	ABRAHAM LINCOLN	Republican	2,213,655 (55.0%)	212	73.8%
	George B. McClellan	Democratic	1,805,237 (45.0%)	21	
1868	ULYSSES S. GRANT	Republican	3,012,833 (52.7%)	214	78.1%
	Horatio Seymour	Democratic	2,703,249 (47.3%)	80	
1872	ULYSSES S. GRANT	Republican	3,597,132 (55.6%)	286	71.3%
	Horace Greeley	Democratic; Liberal Republican	2,834,125 (43.9%)	66	
1876	RUTHERFORD B. HAYES	Republican	4,036,298 (48.0%)	185	81.8%
	Samuel J. Tilden	Democratic	4,300,590 (51.0%)	184	
1880	JAMES A. GARFIELD	Republican	4,454,416 (48.5%)	214	79.4%
	Winfield S. Hancock	Democratic	4,444,952 (48.1%)	155	
1884	GROVER CLEVELAND	Democratic	4,874,986 (48.5%)	219	77.5%
	James G. Blaine	Republican	4,851,981 (48.2%)	182	
1888	BENJAMIN HARRISON	Republican	5,439,853 (47.9%)	233	79.3%
	Grover Cleveland	Democratic	5,540,309 (48.6%)	168	
1892	GROVER CLEVELAND	Democratic	5,556,918 (46.1%)	277	74.7%
	Benjamin Harrison	Republican	5,176,108 (43.0%)	145	
	James B. Weaver	Peopleís	1,041,028 (8.5%)	22	
1896	WILLIAM McKINLEY	Republican	7,104,779 (51.1%)	271	79.3%
	William J. Bryan	democratic Peopleís	6,502,925 (47.7%)	176	
1900	WILLIAM McKINLEY	Republican	7,207,923 (51.7%)	292	73.2%
	William J. Bryan	Dem.-Populist	6,358,133 (45.5%)	155	
1904	THEODORE ROOSEVELT	Republican	7,623,486 (57.9%)	336	65.2%
	Alton B. Parker	Democratic	5,077,911 (37.6%)	140	
	Eugene V. Debs	Socialist	402,283 (3.0%)	—	
1908	WILLIAM H. TAFT	Republican	7,678,908 (51.6%)	321	65.4%
	William J. Bryan	democratic	6,409,104 (43.1%)	162	
	Eugene V. Debs	Socialist	420,793 (2.8%)	—	
1912	WOODROW WILSON	Democratic	6,293,454 (41.9%)	435	58.8%
	Theodore Roosevelt	Progressive	4,119,538 (27.4%)	88	
	William H. Taft	Republican	3,484,980 (23.2%)	8	
	Eugene V. Debs	Socialist	900,672 (6.0%)	—	
1916	WOODROW WILSON	Democratic	9,129,606 (49.4%)	277	61.6%
	Charles E. Hughes	Republican	8,538,221 (46.2%)	254	
	A. L. Benson	Socialist	585,113 (3.2%)	—	
1920	WARREN G. HARDING	Republican	16,152,200 (60.4%)	404	49.2%
	James M. Cox	Democratic	9,147,353 (34.2%)	127	
	Eugene V. Debs	Socialist	919,799 (3.4%)	—	
1924	CALVIN COOLIDGE	Republican	15,725,016 (54.0%)	382	48.9%
	John W. Davis	Democratic	8,386,503 (28.8%)	136	
	Robert M. La Follette	Progressive	4,822,856 (16.6%)	13	
1928	HERBERT HOOVER	Republican	21,391,381 (58.2%)	444	56.9%
	Alfred E. Smith	Democratic	15,016,443 (40.9%)	87	
	Normal Thomas	Socialist	267,835 (0.7%)	—	
1932	FRANKLIN D. ROOSEVELT	Democratic	22,821,857 (57.4%)	472	56.9%
	Herbert Hoover	republican	15,761,841 (39.7%)	59	
	Norman Thomas	Socialist	881,951 (2.2%)	—	

Year	Candidates	Parties	Popular Vote	Electoral Vote	Voter Participation
1936	FRANKLIN D. ROOSEVELT	Democratic	27,751,597 (60.8%)	523	61.0%
	Alfred M. Landon	Republican	16,679,583 (36.5%)	8	
	William Lemke	Union	882,479 (1.9%)	—	
1940	FRANKLIN D. ROOSEVELT	Democratic	27,244,160 (54.8%)	449	62.5%
	Wendell L. Willkie	Republican	22,305,198 (44.8%)	82	
1944	FRANKLIN D. ROOSEVELT	Democrat	25,602,504 (53.5%)	432	55.9%
	Thomas E. Dewey	Republican	22,006,285 (46.0%)	99	
1948	HARRY S TRUMAN	Democratic	24,105,695 (49.5%)	303	53.0%
	Thomas E. Dewey	Republican	21,969,170 (45.1%)	189	
	J. Strom Thurmond	State-Rights Democratic	1,169,021 (2.4%)	39	
	Henry A. Wallace	Progressive	1,156,103 (2.4%)	—	
1952	DWIGHT D. EISENHOWER	Republican	33,936,252 (55.1%)	442	63.3%
	Adlai E. Stevenson	Democratic	27,314,992 (44.4%)	89	
1956	DWIGHT D. EISENHOWER	Republican	35,575,420 (57.6%)	457	60.5%
	Adlai E. Stevenson	Democratic	26,033,066 (42.1%)	73	
	Other	—	—	1	
1960	JOHN F. KENNEDY	Democratic	34,227,096 (49.9%)	303	62.8%
	Richard M. Nixon	Republican	34,108,546 (49.6%)	219	
	Other	—	—	15	
1964	LYNDON B. JOHNSON	Democratic	43,126,506 (61.1%)	486	61.7%
	Barry M. Goldwater	Republican	27,176,799 (38.5%)	52	
1968	RICHARD M. NIXON	Republican	31,770,237 (43.4.%)	301	60.6%
	Hurbert H. Humphrey	Democratic	31,270,633 (42.7%)	191	
	George Wallace	American Indep.	9,906,141 (13.5%)	46	
1972	RICHARD M. NIXON	Republican	47,169,911 (60.7%)	520	55.2%
	George S. McGovern	Democratic	29,170,383 (37.5%)	17	
	Other	—	—	1	
1976	JIMMY CARTER	Democratic	40,828,587 (50.0%)	297	53.5%
	Gerald R. Ford	Republican	39,147,613 (47.9%)	240	
	Other	—	1,575,459 92.1%)	—	
1980	RONALD REAGAN	Republican	43,901,812 (50.7%)	489	52.6%
	Jimmy Carter	Democratic	35,483,820 (41.0%)	49	
	John B. Anderson	Independent	5,719,722 (6.6%)	—	
	Ed Clark	Libertarian	921,188 (1.1%)	—	
1984	RONALD REAGAN	Republican	54,455,075 (59.0%)	525	53.3%
	Walter Mondale	Democratic	37,577,185 (41.0%)	13	
1988	GEORGE H. W. BUSH	Republican	48,886,000 (45.6%)	426	57.4%
	Michael S. Dukakis	Democratic	41,809,000 (45.6%)	112	
1992	William J. CLINTON	Democratic	43,728,375 (43%)	370	55.0%
	George H. W. Bush	Republican	38,167,416 (38%)	168	
	Ross Perot	—	19,237,247 (19%)	—	
1996	William J. CLINTON	Democratic	45,590,703 (50%)	379	48.8%
	Robert Dole	Republican	37,816,307 (41%)	159	
	Ross Perot	Independent	7,866,284 (9%)	—	

CREDITS

Chapter 1
p. 5, William R. Iseminger/ Cahokia Mounds State Historical Site
p. 7, The Granger Collection
p. 10 (left), Museé de l'Homme, Paris
p. 20, Firenze, Biblioteca Medicea Laurenziana, Ms. Laur. Med. Palat. 220, c. 460v, Su concessione del Ministero per i beni e le attività culturali, E' vietata ogni ulteriore riproduzione con qualsiasi mezzo.

Chapter 2
p. 31, The British Museum
p. 37, Julie Roy Jeffrey
p. 40 and 46, American Antiquarian Society
p. 50, © Gibbes Museum of Art/ Carolina Art Association

Chapter 3
p. 65, Founders Society Purchase, Gibbs-Williams Fund, Photograph © 1986 The Detroit Institute of Arts
p. 77, Alexander De Batz, Desseins de Sauvages de Plusierus Natims, 1735/Peabody Museum, Harvard University.

Chapter 4
p. 87 (left) and (right), The Moravian Historical Society, Nazareth, PA
p. 93, Anonymous, The Cheney Family, c. 1795. National Gallery of Art, Washington, D. C., Gift of Edgar William and Bernice Chrysler Garbisch
p. 103, National Portrait Gallery, London

Chapter 5
p. 121, Virginia Historical Society, Richmond, VA
p. 126, Courtesy, Massachusetts Historical Society, Boston.

p. 130 (left), Library of Congress, (right), National Portrait Gallery, London
p. 132, Library of Congress

Chapter 6
p. 140, William Mercer, Battle of Princeton, c. 1786-1790, Historical Society of Pennsylvania
p. 147, National Gallery of Canada, Ottawa, Transfer from the Canadian War Memorials, 1921.
p. 153 and 155, Library of Congress
p. 164, New York State Historical Association, Cooperstown

Chapter 7
p. 183, Mead Art Museum

Chapter 8
p. 195, Library of Congress
p. 197, The White House Collection, courtesy White House Historical Association
p. 199, Peabody Essex Museum
p. 207, The Metropolitan Museum of Art, Bequest of Cornelia Cruger, 1923. (24.19.1)

Chapter 9
p. 224, Maryland Historical Society, Baltimore, Maryland.
p. 229, Newberry Library, Chicago
p. 235, © Chrysler Museum of Art, Norfolk, VA, Gift of Edgar William and Bernice Chrysler Garbish, 80.181.20. Photo by Scott Wolff, Chrysler Museum of Art

Chapter 10
p. 256, Library of Congress
p. 260, American Textile History Museum, Lowell, Mass.
p. 263, From the Collection of the Public Library of Cincinnati and Hamilton County. Photo by Charles Fontayne and William S. Porter

p. 271, Yale University Art Gallery

Chapter 11
p. 286 (left) and (right), South Carolina Library, University of South Carolina
p. 291, Library of Congress
p. 297, New York Public Library, Schomberg Center for Research in Black Culture

Chapter 12
p. 304, Old Dartmouth Historical Society-New Bedford Whaling Museum
p. 307 and 319, Library of Congress
p. 324, Newberry Library, Chicago
p. 326 (left) and (right), Smith College, Northampton, MA

Chapter 13
p. 346, The Denver Public Library, Western History Collection
p. 349, California State Library
p. 354, Beinecke Rare Book Library, Yale University

Chapter 14
p. 366, Chicago Public Library
p. 371, New York Public Library, Astor, Lenox & Tilden
p. 373, Newberry Library, Chicago
p. 379, Corbis/Bettmann

Chapter 15
p. 396, Library of Congress
p. 407, National Archives
p. 413, Library of Congress

Chapter 16
p. 422, The Library Company of Philadelphia
p. 427, Brown Brothers
p. 429, Valentine Museum, Richmond, VA
p. 435, Harper's Weekly, September 5, 1868

INDEX

The World

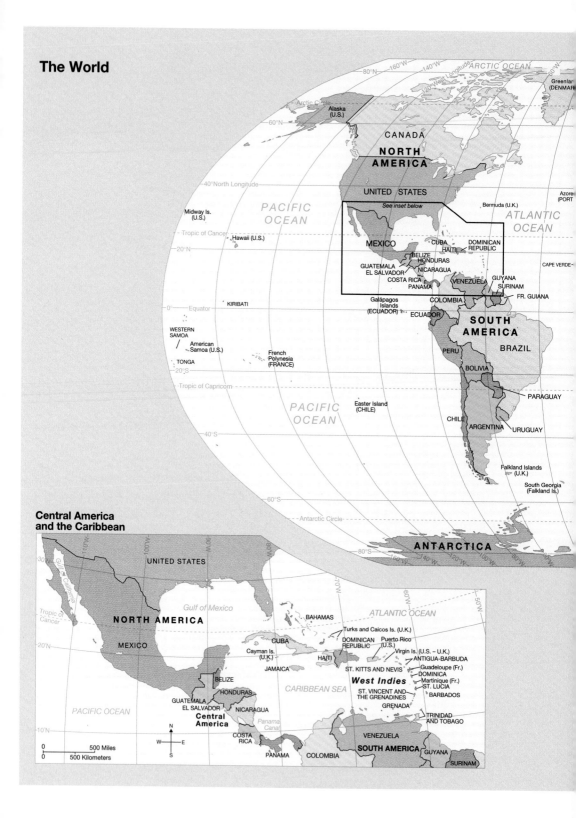

Greenlar
(DENMAR

ARCTIC OCEAN

80°N
160°W
140°W
West Longitude
120°W
60°W

Alaska
(U.S.)

60°N

CANADA

NORTH
AMERICA

UNITED STATES

Azore
(PORT

40°North Longitude

See inset below

Bermuda (U.K.)

ATLANTIC
OCEAN

PACIFIC
OCEAN

Midway Is.
(U.S.)

Tropic of Cancer

Hawaii (U.S.)

MEXICO

CUBA

HAITI

DOMINICAN
REPUBLIC

20°N

BELIZE
HONDURAS

GUATEMALA   NICARAGUA
EL SALVADOR
COSTA RICA
PANAMA

CAPE VERDE

VENEZUELA   GUYANA
SURINAM

FR. GUIANA

0°   Equator

KIRIBATI

Galápagos
Islands
(ECUADOR)

ECUADOR

COLOMBIA

SOUTH
AMERICA

WESTERN
SAMOA

American
Samoa (U.S.)

TONGA

French
Polynesia
(FRANCE)

20°S

PERU

BOLIVIA

BRAZIL

PARAGUAY

Tropic of Capricorn

PACIFIC
OCEAN

Easter Island
(CHILE)

CHILE

ARGENTINA   URUGUAY

40°S

Falkland Islands
(U.K.)

South Georgia
(Falkland Is.)

60°S

Antarctic Circle

ANTARCTICA

80°S
160°W
140°W
120°W
100°W
80°W
60°W

Central America and the Caribbean

30°W
110°W
90°W

UNITED STATES

Gulf of California

Tropic of
Cancer

80°W

Gulf of Mexico

ATLANTIC OCEAN

BAHAMAS

NORTH AMERICA

70°W

60°W

50°W

20°N

MEXICO

CUBA

Cayman Is.
(U.K.)

JAMAICA

HAITI

DOMINICAN
REPUBLIC

Turks and Caicos Is. (U.K.)

Puerto Rico
(U.S.)

Virgin Is. (U.S. – U.K.)
ANTIGUA-BARBUDA
Guadeloupe (Fr.)
DOMINICA
Martinique (Fr.)
ST. LUCIA
BARBADOS

ST. KITTS AND NEVIS

West Indies

CARIBBEAN SEA

BELIZE

HONDURAS

GUATEMALA
EL SALVADOR

NICARAGUA

Central
America

PACIFIC OCEAN

Panama
Canal

ST. VINCENT AND
THE GRENADINES

GRENADA

TRINIDAD
AND TOBAGO

10°N

COSTA
RICA

PANAMA

COLOMBIA

VENEZUELA

SOUTH AMERICA

GUYANA

SURINAM

N
W   E
S

0   500 Miles
0   500 Kilometers

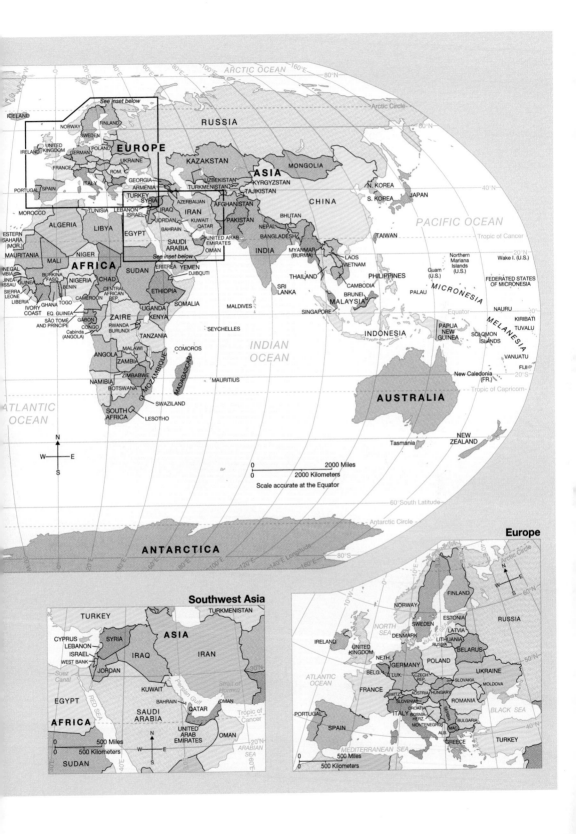